Major Problems in American History
Volume I
To 1877

Documents and Essays

EDITED BY

ELIZABETH COBBS HOFFMAN
SAN DIEGO STATE UNIVERSITY

EDWARD J. BLUM
SAN DIEGO STATE UNIVERSITY

JON GJERDE
UNIVERSITY OF CALIFORNIA, BERKELEY

GENERAL EDITOR

THOMAS G. PATERSON

WADSWORTH
CENGAGE Learning

Australia • Brazil • Japan • Korea • Mexico • Singapore • Spain • United Kingdom • United States

WADSWORTH
CENGAGE Learning™

Major Problems in American History, Volume I: To 1877, Documents and Essays, Third Edition

Elizabeth Cobbs Hoffman, Edward J. Blum, Jon Gjerde

Senior Publisher: Suzanne Jeans

Senior Sponsoring Editor: Ann West

Development Editor: Larry Goldberg

Assistant Editor: Megan Chrisman

Editorial Assistant: Patrick Roach

Media Editor: Robert St. Laurent

Senior Marketing Manager: Katherine Bates

Marketing Coordinator: Lorreen Pelletier

Marketing Communications Manager: Caitlin Green

Content Project Management: PreMediaGlobal

Senior Art Director: Cate Rickard Barr

Print Buyer: Karen Hunt

Rights Acquisition Specialist, Text: Jennifer Meyer Dare

Rights Acquisition Specialist, Image: Katie Huha

Production Service: PreMediaGlobal

Cover Designer: Gary Ragaglia

Cover Image: The Granger Collection

Compositor: PreMediaGlobal

For product information and technology assistance, contact us at **Cengage Learning Customer & Sales Support, 1-800-354-9706**

For permission to use material from this text or product, submit all requests online at **www.cengage.com/permissions**. Further permissions questions can be emailed to **permissionrequest@cengage.com**.

Library of Congress Control Number: 2010939469

ISBN-13: 978-0-495-91513-3

ISBN-10: 0-495-91513-0

Wadsworth
20 Channel Center Street
Boston, MA 02210
USA

Cengage Learning is a leading provider of customized learning solutions with office locations around the globe, including Singapore, the United Kingdom, Australia, Mexico, Brazil and Japan. Locate your local office at **international.cengage.com/region**

Cengage Learning products are represented in Canada by Nelson Education, Ltd.

For your course and learning solutions, visit **www.cengage.com**.

Purchase any of our products at your local college store or at our preferred online store **www.cengagebrain.com**.

Instructors: Please visit **login.cengage.com** and log in to access instructor-specific resources.

Printed in the United States of America
3 4 5 6 15 14 13 12

For Jon Gjerde
Fine historian, fine editor,
fine friend—gone too soon

Contents

Preface

History is a matter of interpretation. Individual scholars rescue particular stories from the flurry of human experience, organize them into patterns, and offer arguments to suggest how these phenomena reflected or reshaped human society at given moments. This means that other historians might select different stories, organize them into different patterns, and arrive at contrasting interpretations of the same period of time or even the same event. All scholars use evidence, but the choice and interpretation of evidence is to some extent inevitably an expression of personal judgment. History is not separate from historians.

The goal of *Major Problems in American History* is to place meat on this bare bones description of how the study of the past "works." Like most instructors, we want students to learn and remember the "important" facts, yet at the same time we want to make clear that historians often disagree on what is important. And, even when historians agree on what is worthy of commentary, they often disagree on what a certain piece of evidence signifies. For example, scholars agree fifty-six men signed the Declaration of Independence in 1776, but they debate why these colonists felt compelled to take this dramatic step.

The two volumes that comprise this book bring together primary documents and secondary sources on the major debates in American history. The primary sources give students evidence to work with. They represent a mix of the familiar and unfamiliar. Certain documents are a "must" in any compilation for a survey course because they had a powerful, widely noted impact on American history, such as Tom Paine's *Common Sense* (1776) or *Brown v. the Board of Education* (1954). We have also selected pieces that evoke the personal experiences of individuals who reflected their times. Included are letters, sermons, speeches, political cartoons, poems, and government reports. There are accounts from European explorers, pioneer women on the frontier, immigrant workers, soldiers, eyewitnesses to the terrors of World War I, and children in rebellion against their parents during the 1960s. These documents often show conflicting points of view, from the "bottom up," the "top down," and the various middles.

The secondary sources in these volumes fulfill a different goal. They expose students to the elemental historical debates for each broad period. We have chosen, therefore, to focus on classic debates, often combining very recent essays with more seasoned pieces by eminent historians who set the terms of discussion for an entire generation or more. Our purpose is to make the interpretive contrasts as clear as possible for students who are just learning to distinguish interpretation from fact, and to discern argument within description. In addition, the essays often make direct reference to the primary documents. This allows students to engage the historian on how she or he is using the primary documents. The students, therefore, can debate the use of the source and the differing historical arguments presented by the historians.

Volume I, prepared by Edward J. Blum in collaboration with Elizabeth Cobbs Hoffman, and based upon the original editing of Jon Gjerde, encompasses American history from its beginnings through Reconstruction. The volume grapples with momentous events that occurred in specific chronological periods, such as the encounter between indigenous people and European empires beginning in the fifteenth century, the Revolution of 1776, the market and transportation revolutions, and the Civil War. Yet this volume also considers economic developments over a long period of time in the North, South, and West that created distinctive regions and ultimately led to their collision in the mid-nineteenth century. Volume I also addresses religious change and the transformation of gender relations in the nineteenth century.

This book follows the same general format as other volumes in the *Major Problems in American History* series. Each chapter begins with a short introduction that orients the student to the topic. Following this, we include a section called "Questions to Think About" to help students focus their reading of the subsequent material. Next come eight to eleven primary documents, followed by two essays that highlight contrasting interpretations. Headnotes at the start of the document and essay sections help readers identify key themes and debates. These headnotes also show how the documents relate to each other, and how the essays differ in perspective. Each chapter concludes with a brief "Further Reading" section to tempt readers into further research. In addition, at the start of the volume, we give suggestions on how to read sources and critically analyze their content, point of view, and inferences. This introduction encourages students to draw their own conclusions and use evidence to back up their reasoning.

New to the Third Edition

This new, third edition makes several changes to previous editions. First, there is a new focus on the visual and cultural. In several chapters there are now various images from the time periods and a variety of songs and poems. Whether European settlers sketching Native American land use or northern and southern whites depicting slave emancipation during the Civil War, visual images allow students to consider various representations of people, places, and events. Poetry and music, moreover, may allow students to have a better "feeling" for an age or era. In addition, several of the scholarly essays have been added to provide new contrasts. Chapter 3 on colonial New England now contrasts the spiritual "world of wonder" described by David D. Hall with the physical "world of goods" described by T. H. Breen. Chapter 4 on the American Revolution pits the work of Gordon Wood against that of Gary Nash. Whereas Wood finds the radicalism of the American Revolution trickling down from elites, Nash locates the origins of that radicalism in society's disadvantaged. The eighth chapter now has a selection from Daniel Walker Howe on the revolutions in cotton and communication in the antebellum era, while Chapter 10 has the work of Nell Irvin Painter on Sojourner Truth where Painter focuses on the liberating and confining roles of religion in Truth's life. In Chapter 12, the work of Anthony Kaye on slave neighborhoods provides new insights into the spatial worlds of slaves, and in Chapter 13, Bruce Levine draws attention to the economic background of the Civil War.

Acknowledgments

Many friends and colleagues have contributed to these volumes. In the third edition we particularly wish to thank John Putman and Andrew Wiese from San Diego State University; Brian Balogh of the University of Virginia; Drew Cayton at Miami University of Ohio; Rebecca Goetz of Rice University; Paul Harvey of the University of Colorado, Colorado Springs; Eric Hinderaker at University of Utah; Anthony Kaye of Penn State University; Bruce Levine of the University of Illinois, Urbana-Champaign; Phil Morgan of Johns Hopkins; Daniel Rodgers of Princeton; Bruce Schulman of Boston University; Jason Scott Smith of the University of New Mexico; James Stewart of Macalaster College; and Matthew Avery Sutton of Washington State University.

For this edition, we also received detailed and extremely helpful reviews from Marc Abrams, Penn State University; Robert Bionaz, Chicago State University; David Brodnax, Trinity Christian College; Cara Converse, Moorpark College; Todd Estes, Oakland University; Peter Kuryla, Belmont University; Bernard Maegi, Normandale Community College; Todd Michney, Tulane University; Stephen Rockenbach, Virginia State University; and Robert Schultz, Illinois Wesleyan University. Thomas G. Paterson, the editor of the *Major Problems* series, provided sound advice. We are obliged to our editors at Cengage Learning/Wadsworth, Ann West and Larry Goldberg, for their kind encouragement and insightful recommendations.

The life of the mind is exceptionally fulfilling, but it is happiest when set within the life of the family. We wish to express our deep gratitude to our families, especially Jennifer Cherry Blum and Daniel Hoffman. We dedicate the book to Jon Gjerde, co-editor of the first two editions of *Major Problems in American History*. We miss him.

E. C. H.
E. J. B.

Introduction: How to Read Primary and Secondary Sources

College study encompasses a number of subjects. Some disciplines, such as mathematics, are aimed at problems and proofs. Students learn methods to discover the path to a correct answer. History is different. Unlike math, it is focused much more on interpretation and imagination. Historians study and analyze sources to construct arguments about the past. They generally understand that there is no "right" answer, even if there are some arguments that are more convincing than others. They search less for a proof than an interpretation, less for absolute truth than for understanding. A historical imagination is useful in creating these interpretations. People in the past thought and acted differently than we do today. Their views of science, of religion, of the place of women and men—to cite only a few examples—were not the same as our views. When we as historians create an argument about the past, we must imagine a world unlike the one we now inhabit. We must use empathy and suspend judgment to develop understanding.

The "problems" in U.S. history on which this text focuses, then, are different from math "problems." They are a series of issues in the American past that might be addressed, discussed, and debated, but not necessarily solved. This text provides readers with two types of tools to grapple with these problems. The first is the *primary source*, which is a piece of evidence that has survived from the period we are analyzing. Primary sources come in a variety of forms, including pictures, artifacts, and written texts. And they may have survived in a number of ways. Archaeologists uncover pieces of evidence when they undertake digs of lost civilizations; ethnologists transcribe stories told by people; economists take bits of evidence to create numerical measures of past behavior; and historians scrutinize surviving written sources. This volume by and large presents written texts, varying from political tracts to private letters. Some of the texts, however, are transcriptions, that is, texts written by someone who noted what another person said. Sometimes the texts are memoirs, in which a person recounts an event they personally experienced long before. On these occasions, you will see two dates: one that tells the year of the events, and a second in parentheses that tells the year in which the memoir was written.

As historians, we must be critical of primary sources for a number of reasons. First of all, we must consider whether a source is really from the historical period we are studying. You might have occasionally read stories in the newspaper about paintings that had been attributed to famous artists but were discovered to be frauds painted by an unknown copyist. When the fraud is discovered, the painting's value plummets. The same can be said for a primary source. If it is not valid, it is not as valuable. A letter alleged to have been written by George Washington clearly is not of much use for revealing his innermost thoughts if we discover the document was written in 1910. But we should also be aware of the opposite: not all pieces of evidence have survived to the present. We might ask if there is a bias in the likelihood of one point of view surviving and another being lost. The experiences of slaveholders, for example, were more commonly written and published than those of slaves. Because they were rarely given the opportunity to publish their thoughts, slaves—(and others, such as Native Americans)—have bequeathed us some sources that have survived as transcriptions. As essential as these sources are in reconstructing the past, as historians we must be critical of them as well. Did the people writing down the spoken words accurately set them to paper or did they inject their own thoughts? In the case of memoirs, how much might current events have affected memories of the past?

Once we consider the validity of sources and understand that some sources were more likely to survive than others, another reason to critique the sources is that they are not "objective" portrayals of the past. By nature, they are points of view. Like anyone, the writer of each primary source provides us with his or her viewpoint and thus gives us a window through which to view his or her world, complete with its biases. When we read about the American Revolution, for example, we will see many different perspectives on the events leading up to the Declaration of Independence by the American colonies. Those who opposed independence saw the events in a very different light from those who supported the movement. We have often read about the advocates of independence who saw the British as threats to American freedom. They thought that the thirteen colonies would be better off as one independent nation. Americans for generations have viewed this as a truly heroic episode. But many contemporaries were not as sure that independence was the correct course of action. A substantial minority opposed independence because they felt they were more secure if they remained in the British empire. Countless members of Indian nations were suspicious of the intentions of the American "patriots" and remained loyal to the king. African American slaves were often leery of the aims of their patriot owners. The fact that people had different viewpoints allows us to grapple with the multiple perspectives of the past.

When you are reading the documents in this volume, we urge you to look at each one critically. We are certain that these are valid sources, and so you should be especially mindful of the point of view contained in each document. Consider both the document and its author. Who wrote or spoke the words in the document? What was his or her reason for expressing the thoughts? Given the background and motivations of the authors, what were their perspectives and potential biases? How did they see the world differently from the way others did? And why do *you* think these different perspectives existed? Whose viewpoint do you agree with most? Why? It is not too much to say that the student of history is similar to a detective who seeks out sources and clues that illuminate the lives and events of the past.

In addition to primary sources, each chapter in this volume contains two essays that represent what we call a *secondary source*. Secondary sources are the written work of historians who have conducted painstaking research in primary sources. Historians work with an array of primary sources that they uncover and use as evidence to construct an argument that addresses one of the major problems in American history. A secondary source is so named because it is one step removed from the primary source. As you will notice, the writers of the essays in each chapter do not necessarily reach similar conclusions. On the contrary, they illustrate differing opinions about why events occurred and what they mean for us today.

Hence secondary sources, like primary sources, do not provide us with the "truth," even to the extent that they are based on verifiable facts. Rather, historians' conclusions vary just as your ideas about the documents might differ from those of someone else in your class. And they differ for a number of reasons. First, interpretations are influenced by the sources on which they depend. Occasionally, a historian might uncover a cache of primary sources heretofore unknown to other scholars, and these new sources might shed new light on a topic. Here again historians are like detectives.

Second and more important, however, historians carry their own perspectives to the research. As they read secondary sources, analyze primary texts, and imagine the past, historians usually develop arguments that differ in emphasis from those developed by others. As they combine their analyses with their own perspectives, they create an argument to explain the past. Historians' individual points of view and even society's dominant point of view influence their thinking. If analyzing sources resembles working as a detective, writing history is similar to being a judge who attempts to construct the most consistent argument from the sources and information at hand. And historians can be sure that those who oppose their viewpoints will analyze their use of sources and the logic of their argument. Those who might disagree with them—and that might include you—will criticize them if they make errors of fact or logic.

The essays were selected for this text in part because they reflect differing conclusions with which you may or may not agree. For example, what caused the Civil War? For decades, historians have given us a number of answers. Some have said the war could have been prevented if politicians had been more careful to avoid sectional divisions or if the U.S. political system had been suitable for compromise. Others have observed that the divisions that developed between the North and South over time became so acute that they could not be compromised away. A civil war in their view was well nigh inevitable. Or what are we to make of the "Age of Jackson"? Some historians have celebrated this period as a flowering of American democracy. The increased voting rights for men fostered raucous political parades that celebrated the American freedoms. Others have noted that these rights were given only to white men and that the "freedoms" were in name only.

An important question left unanswered in all of these chapters is what do *you* think is the correct interpretation? In the end, maybe you don't agree completely with any of the essayists. In fact, you might wish to create your own argument that uses primary sources found here and elsewhere and that accepts parts of one essay and parts of another. When you do this, you have become a historian, a person who attempts to analyze texts critically, someone who is actively engaged in the topic. If that occurs, this volume is a success.

When we discuss the discipline of history with people, we typically get one of two responses. One group of people says something like "I hated history in school." The other group says something like "history was my favorite subject when I went to school." Invariably the people who hated history cite all the boring facts that they had to memorize. In contrast, those who loved history remember a teacher or professor who brought the subject alive by invoking the worlds of people in the past.

As we have tried to indicate in this short overview, history is not about memorizing boring facts but rather an active enterprise of thought and interpretation. Historians are not rote learners; studying history does not entail simply memorization. Instead, historians are detectives and judges, people who interpret and imagine what happened in history and why, individuals who study the past in order to understand the world in which they live in the present. Facts are important, but they are only building blocks in a larger enterprise of interpretation. In sum, our intent with this text is to show how primary and secondary sources can be utilized to aid you in understanding and interpreting major problems in the American past. It is also aimed at keeping that group of people who hates studying history as small as possible and enlarging that second group who considers history their passion. Frankly, it's more fun to talk to the latter.

CHAPTER 1

Conquest and Colliding Worlds

Tisquantum, a member of the Patuxet nation, lived a life that exemplifies the intricate connections between his native people and the European invaders. In 1605, he was kidnapped by an Englishman who was exploring the coasts of Canada and New England and was carried off to England. There, he learned the English language. He eventually returned to America on another voyage of exploration in 1614 and was kidnapped again and taken to southern Spain. His abductors intended to sell him into slavery, but he was rescued by Catholic friars, with whom he lived until 1618. He returned once again to the New England coast, only to discover that his entire nation had been destroyed by disease some years before. Shortly after his return, he met a group of English colonists who called themselves Pilgrims; they were astounded when he spoke to them in English. He befriended the Pilgrims and taught them how to survive in the American wilderness—he was a participant in the first "thanksgiving"—and he became their trading partner. In late 1622, Tisquantum, whom we know today as Squanto, contracted what the English called "Indian fever" and died. Tisquantum's life, as remarkable as it was, illustrates many of the experiences of native people following contact with Europeans: slavery, travel, disease, war, cultural exchange, and trade.

While Tisquantum lived in a changing world, American Indian society had not been static before it came into contact—and conflict—with Europeans. To the contrary, the process of change had begun centuries before Squanto stumbled upon the Pilgrims. Native peoples had lived for millennia in what eventually was known as the Americas. Complex civilizations developed and evolved. The Aztec empire, located in what is today Mexico, was characterized by its military power. It was at the peak of its strength when its people first encountered Europeans. Other complex societies, such as the Anasazi culture in the regions now called Arizona and New Mexico and the Hopewell culture in present-day Illinois, ascended in power and then mysteriously declined. Native people hunted, gathered, and grew an array of foods, including potatoes, squash, beans, and maize, that nourished millions of people in what would become the United States. In short, the Americas were not an empty land when the Europeans arrived.

Yet the Indians' world changed even more dramatically beginning with the landfall of Christopher Columbus and his crew in 1492. Over the course of the centuries that followed, people from Europe, the Americas, and Africa together would create a *"new world."* The trade for West African slaves by Portuguese explorers predated Columbus's voyages, but Africans would play a dynamic role in this new world. This creation involved both an interaction between peoples of striking differences and a brutality of remarkable proportions. Perhaps at no other time did people with such different worldviews and social practices meet. Indians, West Africans, and Europeans differed not only in appearance but also in such matters as work roles between women and men, notions of private property, religious belief, and governmental structures. Some of the new arrivals simply observed these differences, whereas others used them to justify conflict and savagery.

The earliest European explorers were interested in gaining riches in the Americas and from Africa. Once they realized the abundance of wealth that the Americas offered, they sought to amass it. Spanish conquistadors, for example, conquered the Aztec empire in 1519 and gained untold riches from it. Soon, native people found themselves enslaved to provide labor for burgeoning mines. Between 1545 and 1660, over seven million pounds of silver were extracted from American lands by slaves for the Spanish empire. As other European states recognized the economic possibilities, they too searched for land, slaves, and riches. France, the Netherlands, Sweden, and England all attempted to build empires. These empires came into conflict with one another and in contact with indigenous peoples. This contact between Americans, Africans, and Europeans often resulted in conflict and war. Perhaps even more important than overt conflict was a mysterious and hidden exchange of disease. As native people were exposed to an array of diseases, ranging from smallpox to influenza with which they had had little prior contact, they suffered epidemics that weakened their societies and therefore their ability to contest additional European incursions. Like Squanto, the native people became traders, but they also became slaves and victims of strange new diseases. Their home, in effect, had become a new world for them as well as for the Europeans.

QUESTIONS TO THINK ABOUT

How would the story of Indian-European contact have differed if Indians had been better able to resist disease? In what ways did Europeans of different nationalities treat Indians? What differences did Europeans focus upon between themselves and Indians? What role did violence play in creating the new world? Was this period defined by conquest of one group over another or by contact among many groups?

DOCUMENTS

The initial interactions among Indians, Africans, and Europeans involved a strange combination of terror and wonder, as these documents indicate. Document 1 is the Iroquois creation story. Pay attention to how this narrative is similar to and varies from other creation stories with which you are familiar. Decades before Columbus sailed, a Portuguese writer (Document 2) chronicles one of the first expeditions to obtain slaves from West Africa. Christopher Columbus, in Document 3, recounts his first meeting with the people in the Caribbean and his sense of the economic possibility of the Indies. In its description of the Indians, his letter betrays an odd blending of tenderness and a brutal assessment of their potential uses. In Document 4, a Spanish priest, Fray Bernardino de Sahagun, describes the conquest of the Aztecs by Spanish conquistadors in 1519. Document 5 is a drawing of Nahua Indians from the sixteenth century infected with smallpox. Although Europeans wrote most of the documents in this chapter, Document 7 is an exception. It is a transcription of an oral tradition that describes the arrival of the Dutch on Manhattan Island. Document 6 is an engraving based on a drawing from the 1580s. It shows a Secotan village on the outer banks of North Carolina. Notice how the Secotan organized space for housing, agriculture, and religious ceremonies. Document 8 is an English description of native people in what is now New England in 1634, shortly before the bloody Pequot War. Note how author William Wood, an early settler in Massachusetts Bay, pays particular attention to the varying conditions of women in the Indian and British worlds.

1. The Iroquois Describe the Beginning of the World, n.d.

In the beginning there was no world, no land, no creatures of the kind that are around us now, and there were no men. But there was a great ocean which occupied space as far as anyone could see. Above the ocean was a great void of air. And in the air there lived the birds of the sea; in the ocean lived the fish and the creatures of the deep. Far above this unpeopled world, there was a Sky-World. Here lived gods who were like people—like Iroquois.

In the Sky-World there was a man who had a wife, and the wife was expecting a child. The woman became hungry for all kinds of strange delicacies, as women do when they are with child. She kept her husband busy almost to distraction finding delicious things for her to eat....

The woman decided that she wanted some bark from one of the roots of the Great Tree—perhaps as a food or as a medicine, we don't know. She told her husband this. He didn't like the idea. He knew it was wrong. But she insisted, and he gave in. So he dug a hole among the roots of this great sky tree, and he bared some of its roots. But the floor of the Sky-World wasn't very thick, and he broke a hole through it. He was terrified, for he had never expected to find empty space underneath the world.

But his wife was filled with curiosity. He wouldn't get any of the roots for her, so she set out to do it herself. She bent over and she looked down, and she saw the ocean far below. She leaned down and stuck her head through the hole and looked all around. No one knows just what happened next. Some say she slipped. Some say that her husband, fed up with all the demands she had made on him, pushed her.

So she fell through the hole. As she fell, she frantically grabbed at its edges, but her hands slipped. However, between her fingers there clung bits of things

---

From "The World on the Turtle's Back," as seen in *The Great Tree and the Longhouse: The Culture of the Iroquois* by Hazel W. Hertzberg.

that were growing on the floor of the Sky-World and bits of the root tips of the Great Tree. And so she began to fall toward the great ocean far below....

The great sea turtle came and agreed to receive her on his back. The birds placed her gently on the shell of the turtle, and now the turtle floated about on the huge ocean with the woman safely on his back....

When the woman recovered from her shock and terror, she looked around her. All that she could see were the birds and the sea creatures and the sky and the ocean.

And the woman said to herself that she would die. But the creatures of the sea came to her and said that they would try to help her and asked her what they could do. She told them that if they could get some soil, she could plant the roots stuck between her fingers, and from them plants would grow....

The woman took the tiny clod of dirt and placed it on the middle of the great sea turtle's back. Then the woman began to walk in a circle around it, moving in the direction that the sun goes. The earth began to grow. When the earth was big enough, she planted the roots she had clutched between her fingers when she fell from the Sky-World. Thus the plants grew on the earth.

To keep the earth growing, the woman walked as the sun goes, moving in the direction that the people still move in the dance rituals. She gathered roots and plants to eat and built herself a little hut. After a while, the woman's time came, and she was delivered of a daughter. The woman and her daughter kept walking in a circle around the earth, so that the earth and plants would continue to grow. They lived on the plants and roots they gathered. The girl grew up with her mother, cut off forever from the Sky-World above, knowing only the birds and the creatures of the sea, seeing no other beings like herself.

One day, when the girl had grown to womanhood, a man appeared. No one knows for sure who this man was. He had something to do with the gods above. Perhaps he was the West Wind. As the girl looked at him, she was filled with terror, and amazement, and warmth, and she fainted dead away. As she lay on the ground, the man reached into his quiver, and he took out two arrows, one sharp and one blunt, and he laid them across the body of the girl, and quietly went away.

When the girl awoke from her faint, she and her mother continued to walk around the earth. After a while, they knew that the girl was to bear a child. They did not know it, but the girl was to bear twins.

Within the girl's body, the twins began to argue and quarrel with one another. There could be no peace between them. As the time approached for them to be born, the twins fought about their birth. The right-handed twin wanted to be born in the normal way, as all children are born. But the left-handed twin said no. He said he saw light in another direction, and said he would be born that way. The right-handed twin beseeched him not to, saying that he would kill their mother. But the left-handed twin was stubborn. He went in the direction where he saw light. But he could not be born through his mother's mouth or her nose. He was born through her left armpit, and killed her. And meanwhile, the right-handed twin was born in the normal way, as all children are born....

These two brothers, as they grew up, represented two ways of the world which are in all people. The Indians did not call these the right and the wrong.

They called them the straight mind and the crooked mind, the upright man and the devious man, the right and the left.

The twins had creative powers. They took clay and modeled it into animals, and they gave these animals life. And in this they contended with one another. The right-handed twin made the deer, and the left-handed twin made the mountain lion which kills the deer. But the right-handed twin knew there would always be more deer than mountain lions. And he made another animal. He made the ground squirrel. The left-handed twin saw that the mountain lion could not get to the ground squirrel, who digs a hole, so he made the weasel. And although the weasel can go into the ground squirrel's hole and kill him, there are lots of ground squirrels and not so many weasels. Next the right-handed twin decided he would make an animal that the weasel could not kill, so he made the porcupine. But the left-handed twin made the bear, who flips the porcupine over on his back and tears out his belly.

And the right-handed twin made berries and fruits of other kinds for his creatures to live on. The left-handed twin made briars and poison ivy, and the poisonous plants like the baneberry and the dogberry, and the suicide root with which people kill themselves when they go out of their minds. And the left-handed twin made medicines, for good and for evil, for doctoring and for witchcraft.

And finally, the right-handed twin made man....

As the twins became men full grown, they still contested with one another. No one had won, and no one had lost. And they knew that the conflict was becoming sharper and sharper and one of them would have to vanquish the other....

2. The Portuguese Describe Battles with West Africans, 1448

... And when the ship had been provisioned, they made their voyage straight to Cape Verde, whereat in the past year they had captured the two Guineas of whom we have spoken in another place, and thence they passed on to the Cape of Masts....

And so journeying along the sea coast, in a few days they went on shore again, and came upon a village, and its inhabitants issued forth like men who showed they had a will to defend their houses, and among them came one armed with a good buckler and an assegai [spear] in his hand. And Alvaro Fernandez seeing him, and judging him to be the leader of the band, went stoutly at him, and gave him such a great wound with his lance that he fell down dead, and then he took from him his shield and assegai; and these he brought home to the Infant along with some other things, as will be related further on.

Now the Guineas, perceiving that man to be dead, paused from their fighting, and it appeared to our men to be neither the time nor the place to withdraw them from that fear. But rather they returned to their ship and on the next day landed a little way distant from there, where they espied some of the wives of those Guineas walking. And it seemeth that they were going nigh to a creek

"Of how Alvaro Fernandez returned again to the land of the Negroes...," in *Documents Illustrative of the History of the Slave Trade to America*, ed., Elizabeth Donnan (New York: Octagon Books, 1969), 1: 39–41.

collecting shell-fish, and they captured one of them, who would be as much as thirty years of age, with a son of hers who would be of about two, and also a young girl of fourteen years, who had well-formed limbs and also a favorable presence for a Guinea; but the strength of the woman was much to be marvelled at, for not one of the three men who came upon her but would have had a great labour in attempting to get her to the boat. And so one of our men, seeing the delay they were making, during which it might be that some of the dwellers of the land would come upon them, conceived it well to take her son from her and to carry him to the boat; and love of the child compelled the mother to follow after it, without great pressure on the part of the two who were bringing her. From this place they went on further for a certain distance until they lighted upon a river, into which they entered with the boat, and in some houses that they found they captured a woman, and after they had brought her to the caravel, they returned once more to the river, intending to journey higher up in order to try and make some good booty. And as they were pursuing their voyage thus, there came upon them four or five boats of Guineas prepared like men who would defend their land, and our men in the boat were not desirous to try a combat with them, seeing the great advantage their enemies had, and especially because they feared the great peril that lay in the poison with which they shot … their boat came so near that one of those Guineas made a shot at it and happened to hit Alvaro Fernandez with an arrow in the leg. But since he had already been warned of its poison, he drew out that arrow very quickly and had the wound washed with urine and olive oil, and then anointed it very well … and it pleased God that it availed him, although his health was in very troublous case, for during certain days he was in the very act of passing away from life. The others on the caravel, although they saw their captain thus wounded, desisted not from voyaging forward along that coast until they arrived at a narrow strip of sand stretching in front of a great bay, and here they put out their boat and went inside to see what kind of land they would find; and when they were in sight of the beach they saw coming toward them full 120 Guineas, some with shields and assegais, others with bows. And as soon as they came near the water these began to play and dance like men far removed from any sorrow; but our men in the boat, wishful to escape from the invitation to that festival, returned to their ship.

3. Christopher Columbus Recounts His First Encounters with Native People, 1493

Sir,

As I know that you will have pleasure of the great victory which our Lord hath given me in my voyage, I write you this, by which you shall know that in

Spanish Letter of Columbus to Luis de Sant' Angel, Escribano de Racion of the Kingdom of Aragon, Dated 15 February 1493, Reprinted in Facsimile, Translated and Edited from the Unique Copy of the Original Edition (London: 1891), 22–27. (Translator unknown; reprinted in 1891 from a copy in the possession of Bernard Quaritch.) This document can also be found in *America Firsthand*, ed. Robert Marcus and David Burner (New York: St. Martin's Press/Bedford Books, 1989), 3–8.

[thirty-three] days I passed over to the Indies with the fleet which the most illustrious King and Queen, our Lords, gave me: where I found very many islands peopled with inhabitants beyond number. And, of them all, I have taken possession for their Highnesses.... Spañola is a marvel; the mountains and hills, and plains, and fields, and land, so beautiful and rich for planting and sowing, for breeding cattle of all sorts, for building of towns and villages. There could be no believing, without seeing, such harbours as are here, as well as the many and great rivers, and excellent waters, most of which contain gold. In the trees and fruits and plants, there are great differences from those of Juana [Cuba]. In [La Spañola], there are many spiceries, and great mines of gold and other metals. The people of this island, and of all the others that I have found and seen, or not seen, all go naked, men and women, just as their mothers bring them forth; although some women cover a single place with the leaf of a plant, or a cotton something which they make for that purpose. They have no iron or steel, nor any weapons; nor are they fit thereunto; not because they be not a well-formed people and of fair stature, but that they are most wondrously timorous. They have no other weapons than the stems of reeds in their seeding state, on the end of which they fix little sharpened stakes. Even these, they dare not use.... It is true that since they have become more as-sured, and are losing that terror, they are artless and generous with what they have, to such a degree as no one would believe but him who had seen it. Of anything they have, if it be asked for, they never say no, but do rather invite the person to accept it, and show as much lovingness as though they would give their hearts. And whether it be a thing of value, or one of little worth, they are straightways content with whatsoever trifle of whatsoever kind may be given them in return for it.... I gave gratuitously a thousand useful things that I carried, in order that they may conceive affection, and furthermore may be made Christians; for they are inclined to the love and service of their High-nesses and of all the Castilian nation, and they strive to combine in giving us things which they have in abundance, and of which we are in need. And they knew no sect, nor idolatry; save that they all believe that power and goodness are in the sky, and they believed very firmly that I, with these ships and crew, came from the sky; and in such opinion they received me at every place where I landed.... They are men of very subtle wit, who navigate all those seas, and who give a marvellously good account of everything.... As I have already said, they are the most timorous creatures there are in the world, so that the men who remain there are alone sufficient to destroy all that land, and the island is without personal danger for them if they know how to behave themselves. It seems to me that in all those islands, the men are all content with a single wife; and to their chief or king they give as many as twenty. The women, it appears to me, do more work than the men. Nor have I been able to learn whether they held personal property, for it seemed to me that whatever one had, they all took share of, especially of eatable things. Down to the present, I have not found in those islands any monstrous men, as many expected, but on the con-trary all the people are very comely; nor are they black like those in Guinea, but have flowing hair; and they are not begotten where there is an excessive violence of the rays of the sun.... Since thus our Redeemer has given to our most illustrious King and Queen, and to their famous kingdoms, this victory in so high a matter, Christendom should take gladness therein and make great festivals, and give solemn thanks to the Holy Trinity for the great exaltation they shall have by the conversion of so many peoples to our holy faith; and next for the temporal benefit which will bring hither refreshment and profit, not only to Spain, but to all Christians. This briefly, in accordance with the facts. Dated, on the caravel, off the Canary Islands, the 15 February of the year 1493.

At your command,
THE ADMIRAL.

4. Fray Bernardino de Sahagun Relates an Aztec Chronicler's Account of the Spanish Conquest of the Aztecs, 1519

[In 1519, at the town of Cholula,] there arose from the Spaniards a cry summoning all the noblemen, lords, war leaders, warriors, and common folk; and when they had crowded into the temple courtyard, then the Spaniards and their allies blocked the entrances and every exit. There followed a butchery of stabbing, beating, killing of the unsuspecting Cholulans armed with no bows and arrows, protected by no shields ... with no warning, they were treacherously, deceitfully slain....

[As Cortés and his army approached Tenochtitlán, the people of the city] rose in tumult, alarmed as if by an earthquake, as if there were a constant reeling of the face of the earth.

Shocked, terrified, Moctezuma himself wept in the distress he felt for his city. Everyone was in terror; everyone was astounded, afflicted. Many huddled in groups, wept in foreboding for their own fates and those of their friends. Others, dejected, hung their heads. Some groups exchanged tearful greetings; others tried mutual encouragement. Fathers would run their hands over their small boys' hair and, smoothing it, say, "Woe, my beloved sons! How can what we fear be happening in your time?" Mothers, too: "My beloved sons, how can you live through what is in store for you?" ...

The iron of [the Spaniards'] lances ... glistened from afar; the shimmer of their swords was as of a sinuous water course. Their iron breast and back pieces, their helmets clanked. Some came completely encased in iron—as if turned to iron.... And ahead of them ... ran their dogs, panting, with foam continually dripping from their muzzles....

From an anonymous Aztec chronicler in Fray Bernardino de Sahagun, *General History of Things in New Spain* (1582).

Moctezuma's own property was then brought out ... precious things like necklaces with pendants, arm bands tufted with quetzal feathers, golden arm bands, bracelets, golden anklets with shells, rulers' turquoise diadems, turquoise nose rods; no end of treasure. They took all, seized everything for themselves ... as if it were theirs....

[In 1520, the Spanish occupied Tenochtitlán, took Moctezuma hostage, and finally strangled him. Then] they charged the crowd with their iron lances and hacked us with their iron swords. They slashed the backs of some.... They hacked at the shoulders of others, splitting their bodies open.... The blood of the young warriors ran like water; it gathered in pools.... And the Spaniards began to hunt them out of the administrative buildings, dragging out and killing anyone they could find ... even starting to take those buildings to pieces as they searched.

[The Aztecs, led by Moctezuma's brother, Cuitlehuac, counterattacked, and trapped the Spanish in Moctezuma's palace. One night two months later, Cortés and his army tried to escape. But they were so burdened with loot that two-thirds of them died trying to cross the aqueducts leading out of the city.]

That night, at midnight, the enemy came out, crowded together, the Spaniards in the lead, the Tlaxcallans following.... Screened by a fine drizzle, a fine sprinkle of rain, they were able undetected to cross the canals ... just as they were crossing, a woman drawing water saw them. "Mexicans! Come, all of you.... They are already leaving! They are already secretly getting out!" Then a watcher at the top of the temple ... also shouted, and his cries pervaded the entire city....

The canal was filled, crammed with them. Those who came along behind walked over ... on corpses.... It was as if a mountain of men had been laid down: they had pressed against one another, smothered one another....

[Then] at about the time that the Spaniards had fled from Mexico ... there came a great sickness, a pestilence, the smallpox. It ... spread over the people with great destruction of men. It caused great misery.... The brave Mexican warriors were indeed weakened by it. It was after all this had happened that the Spaniards came back.

[By the time the Spanish returned in 1521, Cuitlehuac had died of smallpox. He was succeeded by Cuauhtémoc. Tenochtitlán held out against the Spanish siege for 75 days. Finally the Spanish took the city, destroying it and killing hundreds of thousands of Aztec citizens. Many of them were already sick and starving. Cuauhtémoc was forced to surrender, and later executed.] Fighting continued, both sides took captives, on both sides there were deaths ... great became the suffering of the common folk. There was hunger. Many died of famine.... The people ate anything—lizards, barn swallows, corn leaves, saltgrass.... Never had such suffering been seen.... The enemy pressed about us like a wall ... they herded us.... The brave warriors were still hopelessly resisting....

Finally the battle just quietly ended. Silence reigned. Nothing happened. The enemy left. All was quiet, and nothing more took place. Night fell, and the next day nothing happened, either. No one spoke aloud; the people were crushed.... So ended the war.

5. A European Artist Illustrates a Smallpox Outbreak among Nahua Indians, 1585

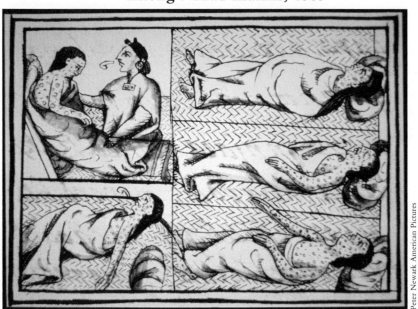

Native American Aztec people of Mexico dying of Small Pox introduced by the Spaniards, copied from the Codex

6. English Artist John White Depicts Indian Land Use, 1619

Algonquian village on the Pamlico River estuary showing Native structures, agriculture, and spiritual life.

7. Reverend John Heckewelder Records a Native Oral Tradition of the First Arrival of Europeans on Manhattan Island (1610), 1818

A great many years ago, when men with a white skin had never yet been seen in this land, some Indians who were out a fishing, at a place where the sea widens, espied at a great distance something remarkably large floating on the water, and such as they had never seen before.... At length the spectators concluded that this wonderful object was moving towards the land, and that it must be an animal or something else that had life in it; it would therefore be proper to inform all the Indians on the inhabited islands of what they had seen, and put them on their guard. Accordingly they sent off a number of runners and watermen to carry the news to their scattered chiefs, that they might send off in every direction for the warriors, with a message that they should come on immediately. These arriving in numbers, and having themselves viewed the strange appearance, and observing that it was actually moving towards the entrance of the river or bay; concluded it to be a remarkably large house in which the Mannitto (the Great or Supreme Being) himself was present, and that he probably was coming to visit them. By this time the chiefs were assembled at York island, and deliberating in what manner in which they should receive their Mannitto on his arrival. Every measure was taken to be well provided with plenty of meat for a sacrifice. The women were desired to prepare the best victuals. All the idols or images were examined and put in order, and a grand dance was supposed not only to be an agreeable entertainment for the Great Being, but it was believed that it might, with the addition of a sacrifice, contribute to appease him if he was angry with them. The conjurers were also set to work, to determine what this phenomenon portended, and what the possible result of it might be. To these and to the chiefs and wise men of the nations, men, women, and children were looking up for advice and protection. Distracted between hope and fear, they were at a loss what to do; a dance, however, commenced in great confusion. While in this situation, fresh runners arrive declaring it to be a large house of various colours, and crowded with living creatures. It appears now to be certain, that it is the great Mannitto, bringing them some kind of game, such as he had not given them before, but other runners soon after arriving declare that it is positively a house full of human beings, of quite a different colour from that of the Indians, and dressed differently from them; that in particular one of them was dressed entirely in red, who must be the Mannitto himself. They are hailed from the vessel in a language they do not understand, yet they shout or yell in return by way of answer, according to the custom of their country; many are for running off to the woods, but are pressed by others to stay, in order not to give offence to their visitor, who might find them out and destroy them. The house, some say, large canoe, at last stops, and a canoe of a smaller size comes on shore with the red man, and some others in it; some stay with his canoe to guard it.

John Heckewelder, "Indian Tradition of the First Arrival of the Dutch on Manhattan Island," *Collections of the New-York Historical Society*, I (1841), 69–74.

The chiefs and wise men, assembled in council, form themselves into a large circle, towards which the man in red clothes approaches with two others. He salutes them with a friendly countenance, and they return the salute after their manner. They are lost in admiration; the dress, the manners, the whole appearance of the unknown strangers is to them a subject of wonder; but they are particularly struck with him who wore the red coat all glittering with gold lace, which they could in no manner account for. He, surely, must be the great Mannitto, but why should he have a white skin? Meanwhile, a large *Hackhack* is brought by one of his servants, from which an unknown substance is poured out into a small cup or glass, and handed to the supposed Mannitto. He drinks— has the glass filled again, and hands it to the chief standing next to him. The chief receives it, but only smells the contents and passes it on to the next chief, who does the same. The glass or cup thus passes through the circle, without the liquor being tasted by any one, and is upon the point of being returned to the red clothed Mannitto, when one of the Indians, a brave men and a great warrior, suddenly jumps up and harangues the assembly on the impropriety of returning the cup with its contents. It was handed to them, says he, by the Mannitto, that they should drink out of it, as he himself had done. To follow his example would be pleasing to him; but to return what he had given them might provoke his wrath, and bring destruction on them. And since the orator believed it for the good of the nation that the contents offered them should be drunk, and as no one else would do it, he would drink it himself, let the consequence be what it might; it was better for one man to die, than that a whole nation should be destroyed. He then took the glass, and bidding the assembly a solemn farewell, at once drank up its whole contents. Every eye was fixed on the resolute chief, to see what effect the unknown liquor would produce. He soon began to stagger, and at last fell prostrate on the ground. His companions now bemoan his fate, he falls into a sound sleep, and they think he has expired. He wakes again, jumps up and declares, that he has enjoyed the most delicious sensations, and that he never before felt himself so happy as after he had drunk the cup. He asks for more, his wish is granted; the whole assembly then imitate him, and all become intoxicated.

After this general intoxication had ceased, for they say that while it lasted the whites had confined themselves to their vessel, the man with the red clothes returned again, and distributed presents among them, consisting of beads, axes, hoes, and stockings such as the white people wear. They soon became familiar with each other, and began to converse by signs. The Dutch made them under-stand that they would not stay here, that they would return home again, but would pay them another visit the next year, when they would bring them more presents, and stay with them awhile: but as they could not live without eating, they should want a little land of them to sow seeds, in order to raise herbs and vegetables to put into their broth. They went away as they had said, and returned in the following season, when both parties were much rejoiced to see each other…. As the whites became daily more familiar with the Indians, they at last proposed to stay with them, and asked only for so much ground for a garden spot as, they said, the hide of a bullock would cover or encompass, which hide was spread before them. The Indians readily granted this apparently reasonable request; but the whites then took a knife, and beginning at one end of the hide, cut it up to a long rope, not thicker than a child's finger, so that by the time the whole was cut up, it made a great heap; they then took the rope at one end, and drew it gently along, carefully avoiding its breaking. It was drawn out into a circular form, and being closed at its ends, encompassed a large piece of ground. The Indians were surprised at the superior wit of the whites but did not wish to contend with them about the little land, as they had still enough themselves. The white and red men lived contentedly together for a long time, though the former from time to time asked for more land, which was readily obtained, and thus they gradually proceeded higher up the Mahicannittuck, until the Indians began to believe that they would soon want all their country, which in the end proved true.

8. William Wood Describes Indian Responses to the English, 1634

Of Their Wondering at the First View of Any Strange Invention

These Indians being strangers to arts and Sciences, and being unacquainted with the inventions that are common to a civilized people, are ravisht with admiration at the first view of any such sight: They tooke the first Ship they saw for a walking Iland, the Mast to be a Tree, the Saile white Clouds, and the discharging of Ordinance for Lightning and thunder, which did much trouble them, but this thunder being over, and this moving Iland stedied with an Anchor, they manned out their cannowes to goe and picke strawberries there, but being saluted by the way with a broad side, they cried out, what much hoggery, so bigge walke, and so bigge speake, and by and by kill; which caused them to turne back, not daring to approach till they were sent for. They doe much extoll and wonder at the English for their strange Inventions, especially for a Wind-mill, which in their esteeme was little lesse than the worlds wonder, for the strangenesse of his whisking motion, and the sharpe teeth biting the corne (as they terme it) into such small peeces.... [T]he Indian seeing the plow teare up more ground in a day, than their Clamme shels could scrape up in a month, desire to see the workemanship of it, and viewing well the coulter and share, perceiving it to be iron, told the plow-man, hee was almost Abamocho, almost as cunning as the Devill....

Of Their Women, Their Dispositions, Employment, Usage by Their Husbands, Their Apparell, and Modesty

To satisfy the curious eye of women readers, who otherwise might think their sex forgotten or not worthy a record, let them peruse these few lines wherein

William Wood, *New England's Prospect* (London: 1634), 61–62, 77–78, 94–97.

they may see their own happiness, if weighed in the woman's balance of these ruder Indians who scorn the tutorings of their wives or to admit them as their equals—though their qualities and industrious deservings may justly claim the preeminence and command better usage and more conjugal esteem, their persons and features being every way correspondent, their qualifications more excellent, being more loving, pitiful, and modest, mild, provident, and laborious than their lazy husbands.

Their employments be many: first their building of houses, whose frames are formed like our garden arbors, something more round, very strong and handsome, covered with close-wrought mats of their own weaving which deny entrance to any drop of rain, though it come both fierce and long, neither can the piercing north wind find a cranny through which he can convey his cooling breath. They be warmer than our English houses.... And as is their husbands' occasion, these poor tectonists [builders or carpenters] are often troubled like snails to carry their houses on their backs, sometimes to fishing places, other times to hunting places, after that to a planting place where it abides the longest.

Another work is their planting of corn, wherein they exceed our English husbandmen, keeping it so clear with their clamshell hoes as if it were a garden rather than a corn field, not suffering a choking weed to advance his audacious head above their infant corn or an undermining worm to spoil his spurns. Their corn being ripe they gather it, and drying it hard in the sun convey it to their barns, which be great holes digged in the ground in form of a brass pot, sealed with rinds of trees, wherein they put their corn, covering it from the inquisitive search of their gourmandizing husbands who would eat up both their allowed portion and reserved seed if they knew where to find it....

Another of their employments is their summer processions to get lobsters for their husbands, wherewith they bait their hooks when they go afishing for bass or codfish. This is an everyday's walk, be the weather cold or hot, the waters rough or calm. They must dive sometimes over head and ears for a lobster, which often shakes them by their hands with a churlish nip and bids them adieu. The tide being spent, they trudge home two or three miles with a hundred weight of lobsters at their backs, and if none, a hundred scowls meet them at home and a hungry belly for two days after. Their husbands having caught any fish, they bring it in their boats as far as they can by water and there leave it: as it was their care to catch it, so it much be their wives' pains to fetch it home, or fast. Which done, they must dress it and cook it, dish it, and present it, see it eaten over their shoulders; and their loggerships having filled their paunches, their sweet lullabies scramble for their scraps. In the summer these Indian women, when lobsters be in their plenty and prime, they dry them to keep for winter, erecting scaffolds in the hot sunshine, making fires likewise underneath them (by whose smoke the flies are expelled) till the substance remain hard and dry. In this manner they dry bass and other fishes without salt, cutting them very thin to dry suddenly before the flies spoil them or the rain moist them, having a special care to hang them in their smoky houses in the night and dankish weather.

In summer they gather flags [probably cattail], of which they make mats for houses, and hemp and rushes, with dyeing stuff of which they make curious baskets with intermixed colors and protractures [drawings or designs] of antic imagery…. In winter they are their husbands' caterers, trudging to the clam banks for their belly timber, and their porters to lug home their venison which their laziness exposes to the wolves till they impose it upon their wives' shoulders. They likewise sew their husbands' shoes and weave coats of turkey feathers, besides all their ordinary house-hold drudgery which daily lies upon them, so that a big belly hinders no business, nor a childbirth takes much time….

For their carriage it is very civil, smiles being the greatest grace of their mirth; their music is lullabies to quiet their children, who generally are as quiet as if they had neither spleen or lungs….

Since the English arrival, comparison hath made them miserable, for seeing the kind usage of the English to their wives, they do as much condemn their husbands for unkindness and commend the English for their love, as their husbands— commending themselves for their wit in keeping their wives industrious—do condemn the English for their folly in spoiling good working creatures….

In a word, to conclude this woman's history, their love to the English hath deserved no small esteem, ever presenting them something that is either rare or desired, as strawberries, hurtleberries, raspberries, gooseberries, cherries, plums, fish, and other such gifts as their poor treasury yield them…. I have often heard men cast upon the English there, as if they should learn of the Indians to use their wives in the like manner and to bring them to the same subjection—as to sit on the lower hand and to carry water and the like drudgery. But if my own experience may out-balance an ill-grounded scandalous rumor, I do assure you, upon my credit and reputation, that there is no such matter, but the women find there as much love, respect, and ease as here in old England.

ESSAYS

Although the effects of the European invasion of the Americas on Indian society were profound, indigenous peoples had resided in what would become the United States for millennia. Their societies and cultures had undergone constant change. Scholars thus have puzzled over the best way of understanding the American Indian world prior to, during, and after its first contact with Europeans. James H. Merrell, who teaches history at Vassar College, argues that a "new world" was created for Indians when they encountered Europeans and Africans in the Carolinas and Virginia. Merrell stresses that the vast changes that contact brought about created a new order not unlike that encountered by the Europeans and Africans who crossed the ocean. In contrast, Neal Salisbury, a historian at Smith College, emphasizes the flux that had characterized the societies of indigenous peoples prior to contact with Europeans and Africans. Indian society, he argues, had been in transition prior to contact, as it would be afterward.

The Indians' New World

JAMES H. MERRELL

In August 1608 John Smith and his band of explorers captured an Indian named Amoroleck during a skirmish along the Rappahannock River. Asked why his men—a hunting party from towns upstream—had attacked the English, Amoroleck replied that they had heard the strangers "were a people come from under the world, to take their world from them." Smith's prisoner grasped a simple yet important truth that students of colonial America have overlooked: after 1492 native Americans lived in a world every bit as new as that confronting transplanted Africans or Europeans.

The failure to explore the Indians' new world helps explain why, despite many excellent studies of the native American past, colonial history often remains "a history of those men and women—English, European, and African—who transformed America from a geographical expression into a new nation." One reason Indians generally are left out may be the apparent inability to fit them into the new world theme, a theme that exerts a powerful hold on our historical imagination and runs throughout our efforts to interpret American development.... [S]cholars have analyzed encounters between peoples from the Old World and conditions in the New, studying the complex interplay between European or African cultural patterns and the American environment. Indians crossed no ocean, peopled no faraway land. It might seem logical to exclude them.

The natives' segregation persists, in no small degree, because historians still tend to think only of the new world as the New World, a geographic entity bounded by the Atlantic Ocean on the one side and the Pacific on the other. Recent research suggests that process was as important as place. Many settlers in New England recreated familiar forms with such success that they did not really face an alien environment until long after their arrival. Africans, on the other hand, were struck by the shock of the new at the moment of their enslavement, well before they stepped on board ship or set foot on American soil. If the Atlantic was not a barrier between one world and another, if what happened to people was more a matter of subtle cultural processes than mere physical displacements, perhaps we should set aside the maps and think instead of a "world" as the physical and cultural milieu demanding basic changes in ways of life. Considered in these terms, the experience of natives was more closely akin to that of immigrants and slaves, and the idea of an encounter between worlds can—indeed, must—include the aboriginal inhabitants of America.

For American Indians a new order arrived in three distinct yet overlapping stages. First, alien microbes killed vast numbers of natives, sometimes before the victims had seen a white or black face. Next came traders who exchanged

James H. Merrell, "The Indians' New World: The Catawba Experience," *William and Mary Quarterly*, 3rd Series, Vol. 41, No. 4 (October 1984). Reprinted by permission of William and Mary Quarterly.

European technology for Indian products and brought natives into the developing world market. In time traders gave way to settlers eager to develop the land according to their own lights. These three intrusions combined to transform native existence, disrupting established cultural habits and requiring creative responses to drastically altered conditions. Like their new neighbors, then, Indians were forced to blend old and new in ways that would permit them to survive in the present without forsaking their past. By the close of the colonial era, native Americans as well as whites and blacks had created new societies, each similar to, yet very different from, its parent culture.

The range of native societies produced by this mingling of ingredients probably exceeded the variety of social forms Europeans and Africans developed. Rather than survey the broad spectrum of Indian adaptations, this [essay] considers in some depth the response of natives in one area, the southern piedmont.... Avoiding extinction and eschewing retreat, the Indians of the piedmont have been in continuous contact with the invaders from across the sea almost since the beginning of the colonial period....

... [T]hese groups [the piedmont peoples] shared a single history once Europeans and Africans arrived on the scene. Drawn together by their cultural affinities and their common plight, after 1700 they migrated to the Catawba Nation, a cluster of villages along the border between the Carolinas that became the focus of native life in the region. Tracing the experience of these upland communities both before and after they joined the Catawbas can illustrate the consequences of contact and illuminate the process by which natives learned to survive in their own new world.

For centuries, ancestors of the Catawbas had lived astride important aboriginal trade routes and straddled the boundary between two cultural traditions, a position that involved them in a far-flung network of contacts and affected everything from potting techniques to burial practices. Nonetheless, Africans and Europeans were utterly unlike any earlier foreign visitors to the piedmont. Their arrival meant more than merely another encounter with outsiders; it marked an important turning point in Indian history. Once these newcomers disembarked and began to feel their way across the continent, they forever altered the course and pace of native development.

Bacteria brought the most profound disturbances to upcountry villages. When Hernando de Soto led the first Europeans into the area in 1540, he found large towns already "grown up in grass" because "there had been a pest in the land" two years before, a malady probably brought inland by natives who had visited distant Spanish posts. The sources are silent about other "pests" over the next century, but soon after the English began colonizing Carolina in 1670 the disease pattern became all too clear. Major epidemics struck the region at least once every generation—in 1698, 1718, 1738, and 1759—and a variety of less virulent illnesses almost never left native settlements.

Indians were not the only inhabitants of colonial America living—and dying—in a new disease environment. The swamps and lowlands of the Chesapeake were a deathtrap for Europeans, and sickness obliged colonists to discard or rearrange many of the social forms brought from England. Among native peoples long isolated from the rest of the world and therefore lacking immunity to pathogens introduced by the intruders, the devastation was even more severe....

Survivors of these horrors were thrust into a situation no less alien than what European immigrants and African slaves found. The collected wisdom of generations could vanish in a matter of days if sickness struck older members of a community who kept sacred traditions and taught special skills. When many of the elders succumbed at once, the deep pools of collective memory grew shallow, and some dried up altogether. In 1710, Indians near Charleston told a settler that "they have forgot most of their traditions since the Establishment of this Colony, they keep their Festivals and can tell but little of the reasons: their Old Men are dead." Impoverishment of a rich cultural heritage followed the spread of disease. Nearly a century later, a South Carolinian exaggerated but captured the general trend when he noted that Catawbas "have forgotten their ancient rites, ceremonies, and manufactures."

The same diseases that robbed a piedmont town of some of its most precious resources also stripped it of the population necessary to maintain an independent existence. In order to survive, groups were compelled to construct new societies from the splintered remnants of the old. The result was a kaleidoscopic array of migrations from ancient territories and mergers with nearby peoples. While such behavior was not unheard of in aboriginal times, population levels fell so precipitously after contact that survivors endured disruptions unlike anything previously known....

No mere catalog of migrations and mergers can begin to convey how profoundly unsettling this experience was for those swept up in it. While upcountry Indians did not sail away to some distant land, they, too, were among the uprooted, leaving their ancestral homes to try to make a new life elsewhere. A village and its surrounding territory were important elements of personal and collective identity, physical links in a chain binding a group to its past and making a locality sacred....

The toll could be physical as well as spiritual, for even the most uneventful of moves interrupted the established cycle of subsistence. Belongings had to be packed and unpacked, dwellings constructed, palisades raised. Once migrants had completed the business of settling in, the still more arduous task of exploiting new terrain awaited them. Living in one place year after year endowed a people with intimate knowledge of the area. The richest soils, the best hunting grounds, the choicest sites for gathering nuts or berries—none could be learned without years of experience, tested by time and passed down from one generation to the next. Small wonder that Carolina Indians worried about being "driven to some unknown Country, to live, hunt, and get our Bread in."

Some displaced groups tried to leave "unknown Country" behind and make their way back home. In 1716 Enos asked Virginia's permission to settle at "Enoe Town" on the North Carolina frontier, their location in Lawson's day. Seventeen years later William Byrd II came upon an abandoned Cheraw village on a tributary of the upper Roanoke River and remarked how "it must have been a great misfortune to them to be obliged to abandon so beautiful a dwelling." The Indians apparently agreed: in 1717 the Virginia Council received "Divers applications" from the Cheraws (now living along the Pee Dee River) "for Liberty to Seat themselves on the head of Roanoke River." Few natives managed to return permanently to their homelands. But their efforts to retrace their steps hint at a profound sense of loss and testify to the powerful hold of ancient sites.

Compounding the trauma of leaving familiar territories was the necessity of abandoning customary relationships. Casting their lot with others traditionally considered foreign compelled Indians to rearrange basic ways of ordering their existence. Despite frequent contacts among peoples, native life had always centered in kin and town. The consequences of this deep-seated localism were evident even to a newcomer like John Lawson, who in 1701 found striking differences in language, dress, and physical appearance among Carolina Indians living only a few miles apart. Rules governing behavior also drew sharp distinctions between outsiders and one's own "Country-Folks." Indians were "very kind, and charitable to one another," Lawson reported, "but more especially to those of their own Nation." A visitor desiring a liaison with a local woman was required to approach her relatives and the village headman. On the other hand, "if it be an *Indian* of their own Town or Neighbourhood, that wants a Mistress, he comes to none but the Girl." Lawson seemed unperturbed by this barrier until he discovered that a "Thief [is] held in Disgrace, that steals from any of his Country-Folks," "but to steal from the *English* [or any other foreigners] they reckon no Harm."

Communities unable to continue on their own had to revise these rules and reweave the social fabric into new designs. What language would be spoken? How would fields be laid out, hunting territories divided, houses built? How would decisions be reached, offenders punished, ceremonies performed? When Lawson remarked that "now adays" the Indians must seek mates "amongst Strangers," he unwittingly characterized life in native Carolina. Those who managed to withstand the ravages of disease had to redefine the meaning of the term *stranger* and transform outsiders into insiders....

Muskets and kettles came to the piedmont more slowly than smallpox and measles. Spanish explorers distributed a few gifts to local headmen, but inhabitants of the interior did not enjoy their first real taste of the fruits of European technology until Englishmen began venturing inland after 1650. Indians these traders met in upcountry towns were glad to barter for the more efficient tools, more lethal weapons, and more durable clothing that colonists offered. Spurred on by eager natives, men from Virginia and Carolina quickly flooded the region with the material trappings of European culture. In 1701 John Lawson considered the Wateree Chickanees "very poor in *English* Effects" because a few of them lacked muskets.

Slower to arrive, trade goods were also less obvious agents of change. The Indians' ability to absorb foreign artifacts into established modes of existence hid the revolutionary consequences of trade for some time. Natives leaped the technological gulf with ease in part because they were discriminating shoppers. If hoes were too small, beads too large, or cloth the wrong color, Indian traders refused them. Items they did select fit smoothly into existing ways. Waxhaws tied horse bells around their ankles at ceremonial dances, and some of the traditional stone pipes passed among the spectators at these dances had been shaped by metal files. Those who could not afford a European weapon fashioned arrows from broken glass. Those who could went to great lengths to "set [a new musket] streight, sometimes shooting away above 100 Loads of Ammunition, before they bring the Gun to shoot according to their Mind."

Not every piece of merchandise hauled into the upcountry on a trader's packhorse could be "set streight" so easily. Liquor, for example, proved both impossible to resist and extraordinarily destructive. Indians "have no Power to refrain this Enemy," Lawson observed, "though sensible how many of them (are by it) hurry'd into the other World before their Time." And yet even here, natives aware of the risks sought to control alcohol by incorporating it into their ceremonial life as a device for achieving a different level of consciousness. Consumption was usually restricted to men, who "go as solemnly about it, as if it were part of their Religion," preferring to drink only at night and only in quantities sufficient to stupefy them. When ritual could not confine liquor to safe channels, Indians went still further and excused the excesses of overindulgence by refusing to hold an intoxicated person responsible for his actions. "They never call any Man to account for what he did, when he was drunk," wrote Lawson, "but say, it was the Drink that caused his Misbehaviour, therefore he ought to be forgiven."

Working to absorb even the most dangerous commodities acquired from their new neighbors, aboriginal inhabitants of the uplands, like African slaves in the lowlands, made themselves at home in a different technological environment. Indians became convinced that "Guns, and Ammunition, besides a great many other Necessaries, … are helpful to Man" and eagerly searched for the key that would unlock the secret of their production. At first many were confident that the "*Quera*, or good spirit," would teach them to make these commodities "when that good Spirit sees fit." Later they decided to help their deity along by approaching the colonists. In 1757, Catawbas asked Gov. Arthur Dobbs of North Carolina "to send us Smiths and other Tradesmen to teach our Children."

It was not the new products themselves but the Indians' failure to learn the mysteries of manufacture from either Dobbs or the *Quera* that marked the real revolution wrought by trade. During the seventeenth and eighteenth centuries, everyone in eastern North America—masters and slaves, farmers near the coast and Indians near the mountains—became producers of raw materials for foreign markets and found themselves caught up in an international economic network….

By forcing Indians to look beyond their own territories for certain indispensable products, Anglo-American traders inserted new variables into the aboriginal equation of exchange. Colonists sought two commodities from Indians—human beings and deerskins—and both undermined established relationships among native groups. While the demand for slaves encouraged piedmont peoples to expand their traditional warfare, the demand for peltry may have fostered conflicts over hunting territories. Those who did not fight each other for slaves or deerskins fought each other for the European products these could bring. As fire-arms, cloth, and other items became increasingly important to native existence, competition replaced comity at the foundation of trade encounters as villages scrambled for the cargoes of merchandise....

... The mask [of the natives' control of their own destiny] came off when, in 1715, the traders—and the trade goods—suddenly disappeared during the Yamassee War.

The conflict's origins lay in a growing colonial awareness of the Indians' need for regular supplies of European merchandise. In 1701 Lawson pronounced the Santees "very tractable" because of their close connections with South Carolina. Eight years later he was convinced that the colonial officials in Charleston "are absolute Masters over the *Indians* ... within the Circle of their Trade." Carolina traders who shared this conviction quite naturally felt less and less constrained to obey native rules governing proper behavior. Abuses against Indians mounted until some men were literally getting away with murder. When repeated appeals to colonial officials failed, natives throughout Carolina began to consider war. Persuaded by Yamassee ambassadors that the conspiracy was widespread and con-vinced by years of ruthless commercial competition between Virginia and Carolina that an attack on one colony would not affect relations with the other, in the spring of 1715 Catawbas and their neighbors joined the invasion of South Carolina.

The decision to fight was disastrous. Colonists everywhere shut off the flow of goods to the interior, and after some initial successes Carolina's native enemies soon plumed the depths of their dependence. In a matter of months, refugees holed up in Charleston noticed that "the Indians want ammunition and are not able to mend their Arms." The peace negotiations that ensued revealed a desperate thirst for fresh supplies of European wares. Ambassadors from piedmont towns in-variably spoke in a single breath of restoring "a Peace and a free Trade," and one delegation even admitted that its people "cannot live without the assistance of the English." ...

By the end of the colonial period delicate negotiations across cultural boundaries were as familiar to Catawbas as the strouds they wore and the mus-kets they carried. But no matter how shrewdly the headmen loosened provincial purse strings to extract vital merchandise, they could not escape the simple fact that they no longer held the purse containing everything needed for their daily existence. In the space of a century the Indians had become thoroughly embed-ded in an alien economy, denizens of a new material world. The ancient self-sufficiency was only a dim memory in the minds of the Nation's elders.

The Catawba peoples were veterans of countless campaigns against disease and masters of the arts of trade long before the third major element of their new world, white planters, became an integral part of their life. Settlement of the Carolina uplands did not begin until the 1730s, but once underway it spread with frightening speed. In November 1752, concerned Catawbas reminded South Carolina governor James Glen how they had "complained already ... that the White People were settled too near us." Two years later five hundred families lived within thirty miles of the Nation and surveyors were running their lines into the middle of native towns. "[T]hose Indians are now in a fair way to be surrounded by White People," one observer concluded.

Settlers' attitudes were as alarming as their numbers. Unlike traders who profited from them or colonial officials who deployed them as allies, ordinary colonists had little use for Indians. Natives made poor servants and worse slaves; they obstructed settlement; they attracted enemy warriors to the area. Even men who respected Indians and earned a living by trading with them admitted that they made unpleasant neighbors. "We may observe of them as of the fire," wrote the South Carolina trader James Adair after considering the Catawbas' situation on the eve of the American Revolution, " 'it is safe and useful, cherished at proper distance; but if too near us, it becomes dangerous, and will scorch if not consume us.' "

A common fondness for alcohol increased the likelihood of intercultural hostilities. Catawba leaders acknowledged that the Indians "get very Drunk with [liquor] this is the Very Cause that they oftentimes Commit those Crimes that is offencive to You and us." Colonists were equally prone to bouts of drunkenness. In the 1760s the itinerant Anglican minister, Charles Woodmason, was shocked to find the citizens of one South Carolina upcountry community "continually drunk." ...

Even when sober, natives and newcomers found many reasons to quarrel. Catawbas were outraged if colonists built farms on the Indians' doorstep or tramped across ancient burial grounds. Planters, ignorant of (or indifferent to) native rules of hospitality, considered Indians who requested food nothing more than beggars and angrily drove them away. Other disputes arose when the Nation's young men went looking for trouble. As hunting, warfare, and other traditional avenues for achieving status narrowed, Catawba youths transferred older patterns of behavior into a new arena by raiding nearby farms and hunting cattle or horses.

Contrasting images of the piedmont landscape quite unintentionally generated still more friction. Colonists determined to tame what they considered a wilderness were in fact erasing a native signature on the land and scrawling their own. Bridges, buildings, fences, roads, crops, and other "improvements" made the area comfortable and familiar to colonists but uncomfortable and unfamiliar to Indians. "The Country side wear[s] a New face," proclaimed Woodmason proudly; to the original inhabitants, it was a grim face indeed. "His Land was spoiled," one Catawba headman told British officials in 1763. "They have spoiled him 100 Miles every way." Under these circumstances, even a settler with no wish to fight Indians met opposition to his fences, his outbuildings, his very presence. Similarly, a Catawba on a routine foray into traditional hunting territories had his weapon destroyed, his goods confiscated, his life threatened by men with different notions of the proper use of the land.

To make matters worse, the importance both cultures attached to personal independence hampered efforts by authorities on either side to resolve conflicts. Piedmont settlers along the border between the Carolinas were "people of desperate fortune," a frightened North Carolina official reported after visiting the area. "[N]o officer of Justice from either Province dare meddle with them." Woodmason, who spent even more time in the region, came to the same conclusion. "We are without any Law, or Order," he complained; the inhabitants' "Impudence is so very high, as to be past bearing." Catawba leaders could have sympathized. Headmen informed colonists that the Nation's people "are oftentimes Cautioned from ... ill Doings altho' to no purpose for we Cannot be present at all times to Look after them." "What they have done I could not prevent," one chief explained....

The Indians would have to find some way to get along with these unpleasant neighbors if the Nation was to survive. As Catawba population fell below five hundred after the smallpox epidemic of 1759 and the number of colonists continued to climb, natives gradually came to recognize the futility of violent resistance. During the last decades of the eighteenth century they drew on years of experience in dealing with Europeans at a distance and sought to overturn the common conviction that Indian neighbors were frightening and useless....

Catawbas took one of the first steps along the road to accommodation in the early 1760s, when they used their influence with colonial officials to acquire a reservation encompassing the heart of their ancient territories. This grant gave the Indians a land base, grounded in Anglo-American law, that prevented farmers from shouldering them aside. Equally important, Catawbas now had a commodity to exchange with nearby settlers. These men wanted land, the natives had plenty, and shortly before the Revolution the Nation was renting tracts to planters for cash, livestock, and manufactured goods.

Important as it was, land was not the only item Catawbas began trading to their neighbors. Some Indians put their skills as hunters and woodsmen to a different use, picking up stray horses and escaped slaves for a reward. Others bartered their pottery, baskets, and table mats. Still others traveled through the upcountry, demonstrating their prowess with the bow and arrow before appreciative audiences. The exchange of these goods and services for European merchandise marked an important adjustment to the settlers' arrival. In the past, natives had acquired essential items by trading peltry and slaves or requesting gifts from representatives of the Crown. But piedmont planters frowned on hunting and warfare, while provincial authorities—finding Catawbas less useful as the Nation's population declined and the French threat disappeared—discouraged formal visits and handed out fewer presents. Hence the Indians had to develop new avenues of exchange that would enable them to obtain goods in ways less objectionable to their neighbors. Pots, baskets, and acres proved harmless substitutes for earlier methods of earning an income.

Quite apart from its economic benefits, trade had a profound impact on the character of Catawba-settler relations. Through countless repetitions of the same simple procedure at homesteads scattered across the Carolinas, a new form of intercourse arose, based not on suspicion and an expectation of conflict but on trust and a measure of friendship. When a farmer looked out his window and saw Indians approaching, his reaction more commonly became to pick up money or a jug of whiskey rather than a musket or an axe. The natives now appeared, the settler knew, not to plunder or kill but to peddle their wares or collect their rents....

On that August day in 1608 when Amoroleck feared the loss of his world, John Smith assured him that the English "came to them in peace, and to seeke their loves." Event soon proved Amoroleck right and his captor wrong. Over the course of the next three centuries not only Amoroleck and other piedmont Indians but natives throughout North America had their world stolen and another put in its place. Though this occurred at different times and in different ways, no Indians escaped the explosive mixture of deadly bacteria, material riches, and alien peoples that was the invasion of America. Those in the southern piedmont who survived the onslaught were ensconced in their new world by the end of the eighteenth century. Population levels stabilized as the Catawba peoples developed immunities to once lethal diseases. Rents, sales of pottery, and other economic activities proved adequate to support the Nation at a stable (if low) level of material life. Finally, the Indians' image as "inoffensive" neighbors gave them a place in South Carolina society and continues to sustain them today.

Vast differences separated Catawbas and other natives from their colonial contemporaries. Europeans were the colonizers, Africans the enslaved, Indians the dispossessed; from these distinct positions came distinct histories. Yet once we acknowledge the differences, instructive similarities remain that help to integrate natives more thoroughly into the story of early America. By carving a niche for themselves in response to drastically different conditions, the people who composed the Catawba Nation shared in the most fundamental of American experiences. Like Afro-Americans, these Indians were compelled to accept a subordinate position in American life yet did not altogether lose their cultural integrity. Like settlers of the Chesapeake, aboriginal inhabitants of the uplands adjusted to appalling mortality rates and wrestled with the difficult task of "living with death." Like inhabitants of the Middle Colonies, piedmont groups learned to cope with unprecedented ethnic diversity by balancing the pull of traditional loyalties with the demands of a new social order. Like Puritans in New England, Catawbas found that a new world did not arrive all at once and that localism, self-sufficiency, and the power of old ways were only gradually eroded by conditions in colonial America.

The Indians' Old World

NEAL SALISBURY

Scholars in history, anthropology, archaeology, and other disciplines have turned increasingly over the past two decades to the study of native peoples during the colonial period of North American history. The new work in Indian history has

Neal Salisbury, "The Indians' Old World: Native Americans and the Coming of Europeans," *William and Mary Quarterly*, 3rd Series, Vol. 53, No. 3. Reprinted by permission of William and Mary Quarterly.

altered the way we think about the beginning of American history and about the era of European colonization. Historians now recognize that Europeans arrived, not in a virgin land, but in one that was teeming with several million people. Beyond filling in some of the vast blanks left by previous generations' overlooking of Indians, much of this scholarship makes clear that Indians are integral to the history of colonial North America. In short, surveys of recent textbooks and of scholarly titles suggest that Native Americans are well on their way to being "mainstreamed" by colonial historians.

Substantive as this reorientation is, it remains limited. Beyond the problems inherent in representing Indian/non-Indian interactions during the colonial era lies the challenge of contextualizing the era itself. Despite opening chapters and lectures that survey the continent's native peoples and cultures, most historians continue to represent American history as having been set in motion by the arrival of European explorers and colonizers. They have yet to recognize the existence of a North American—as opposed to English or European—background for colonial history, much less to consider the implications of such a background for understanding the three centuries following Columbus's landfall. Yet a growing body of scholarship by archaeologists, linguists, and students of Native American expressive traditions recognizes 1492 not as a beginning but as a single moment in a long history utterly detached from that of Europe....

... [I]ndigenous North Americans exhibited a remarkable range of languages, economies, political systems, beliefs, and material cultures. But this range was less the result of their isolation from one another than of the widely varying natural and social environments with which Indians had interacted over millennia. What recent scholars of pre-colonial North America have found even more striking, given this diversity, is the extent to which native peoples' histories intersected one another.

At the heart of these intersections was exchange. By exchange is meant not only the trading of material goods but also exchanges across community lines of marriage partners, resources, labor, ideas, techniques, and religious practices. Longer-distance exchanges frequently crossed cultural and linguistic boundaries as well and ranged from casual encounters to widespread alliances and networks that were economic, political, and religious. For both individuals and communities, exchanges sealed social and political relationships. Rather than accumulate material wealth endlessly, those who acquired it gave it away, thereby earning prestige and placing obligations on others to reciprocate appropriately. And as we shall see, many goods were not given away to others in this world but were buried with individuals to accompany them to another....

By the twelfth century, agricultural production had spread over much of the Eastern Woodlands as well as to more of the Southwest. In both regions, ... more complex societies were emerging to dominate widespread exchange networks. In the Mississippi Valley and the Southeast, the sudden primacy of maize horticulture is marked archaeologically in a variety of ways—food remains, pollen profiles, studies of human bone (showing that maize accounted for 50 percent of people's diets), and in material culture by a proliferation of chert hoes, shell-tempered pottery for storing and cooking, and pits for storing surplus crops. These developments were accompanied by the rise of what archaeologists term "Mississippian" societies, consisting of fortified political and ceremonial centers and outlying villages. The centers were built around open plazas featuring platform burial mounds, temples, and elaborate residences for elite families. Evidence from burials makes clear the wide social gulf that separated commoners from elites. Whereas the former were buried in simple graves with a few personal possessions, the latter were interred in the temples or plazas along with many more, and more elaborate, goods such as copper ornaments, massive sheets of shell, and ceremonial weapons. Skeletal evidence indicates that elites ate more meat, were taller, performed less strenuous physical activity, and were less prone to illness and accident than commoners....

The largest, most complex Mississippian center was Cahokia, located not far from the confluence of the Mississippi and Missouri rivers, near modern East St. Louis, Illinois, in the rich floodplain known as American Bottoms. By the twelfth century, Cahokia probably numbered 20,000 people and contained over 120 mounds within a five-square-mile area.... One key to Cahokia's rise was its combination of rich soil and nearby wooded uplands, enabling inhabitants to produce surplus crops while providing an abundance and diversity of wild food sources along with ample supplies of wood for fuel and construction. A second key was its location, affording access to the great river systems of the North American interior.

Cahokia had the most elaborate social structure yet seen in North America. Laborers used stone and wooden spades to dig soil from "borrow pits" (at least nineteen have been identified by archaeologists), which they carried in wooden buckets to mounds and palisades often more than half a mile away. The volume and concentration of craft activity in shell, copper, clay, and other materials, both local and imported, suggests that specialized artisans provided the material foundation for Cahokia's exchange ties with other peoples. Although most Cahokians were buried in mass graves outside the palisades, their rulers were given special treatment. At a prominent location in Mound 72, the largest of Cahokia's platform mounds, a man had been buried atop a platform of shell beads. Accompanying him were several group burials: fifty young women, aged 18 to 23, four men, and three men and three women, all encased in uncommonly large amounts of exotic materials. As with the Natchez Indians observed by the French in Louisiana, Cahokians appear to have sacrificed individuals to accompany their leaders in the afterlife. Cahokia was surrounded by nine smaller mound centers and several dozen villages from which it obtained much of its food and through which it conducted its waterborne commerce with other Mississippian centers in the Midwest and Southeast....

At the outset of the twelfth century, the center of production and exchange in the Southwest was in the basin of the San Juan River at Chaco Canyon in New Mexico, where Anasazi culture achieved its most elaborate expression. A twelve-mile stretch of the canyon and its rim held twelve large planned towns on the north side and 200 to 350 apparently unplanned villages on the south. The total population was probably about 15,000. The towns consisted of 200 or more contiguous, multistoried rooms, along with numerous kivas (underground ceremonial areas), constructed of veneered masonry walls and log beams imported from upland areas nearly fifty miles distant. The rooms surrounded a central plaza with a great kiva. Villages typically had ten to twenty rooms that were decidedly smaller than those in the towns. Nearly all of Chaco Canyon's turquoise, shell, and other ornaments and virtually everything imported from Mesoamerica are found in the towns rather than the villages. Whether the goods were considered communal property or were the possessions of elites is uncertain, but either way the towns clearly had primacy. Villages buried their dead near their residences, whereas town burial grounds were apparently located at greater distances, although only a very few of what must have been thousands of town burials have been located by archaeologists. Finally, and of particular importance in the arid environment of the region, the towns were located at the mouths of side canyons where they controlled the collection and distribution of water run-off....

The canyon was the core of an extensive network of at least seventy towns or "outliers," as they are termed in the archaeological literature, and 5,300 villages located as far as sixty miles from the canyon.... Facilitating the movement of people and goods through this network was a system of roads radiating outward from the canyon in perfectly straight lines, turning into stairways or footholds rather than circumventing cliffs and other obstacles....

When Europeans reached North America ... the continent's demographic and political map was in a state of profound flux. A major factor was the collapse of the great centers at Cahokia and Chaco Canyon and elsewhere in the Midwest and Southwest. Although there were significant differences between these highly centralized societies, each ran up against the capacity of the land or other resources to sustain it....

Such combinations of continuity and change, persistence and adaptability, arose from concrete historical experiences rather than a timeless tradition. The remainder of this [essay] indicates some of the ways that both the deeply rooted imperatives of reciprocity and exchange and the recent legacies of competition and upheaval informed North American history as Europeans began to make their presence felt.

Discussion of the transition from pre- to postcontact times must begin with the sixteenth century, when Indians and Europeans met and interacted in a variety of settings. When not slighting the era altogether, historians have viewed it as one of discovery or exploration, citing the achievements of notable Europeans in either anticipating or failing to anticipate the successful colonial enterprises of the seventeenth century. Recently, however, a number of scholars have been integrating information from European accounts with the findings of archaeologists to produce a much fuller picture of this critical period in North American history.

The Southeast was the scene of the most formidable attempts at colonization during the sixteenth century, primarily by Spain. Yet in spite of several expeditions to the interior and the undertaking of an ambitious colonizing and missionary effort, extending from St. Augustine over much of the Florida peninsula and north to Chesapeake Bay, the Spanish retained no permanent settlements beyond St. Augustine itself at the end of the century. Nevertheless, their explorers and missionaries opened the way for the spread of smallpox and other epidemic diseases over much of the area south of the Chesapeake and east of the Mississippi....

As in the Southeast, Spanish colonizers in the sixteenth-century Southwest launched several ambitious military and missionary efforts, hoping to extend New Spain's domain northward and to discover additional sources of wealth. The best-documented encounters of Spanish with Pueblos—most notably those of Coronado's expedition (1540–1542)—ended in violence and failure for the Spanish who, despite vows to proceed peacefully, violated Pueblo norms of reciprocity by insisting on excessive tribute or outright submission. In addition, the Spanish had acquired notoriety among the Pueblos as purveyors of epidemic diseases, religious missions, and slaving expeditions inflicted on Indians to the south, in what is now northern Mexico.

The Spanish also affected patterns of exchange throughout the Southwest. Indians resisting the spread of Spanish rule to northern Mexico stole horses and other livestock, some of which they traded to neighbors. By the end of the sixteenth century, a few Indians on the periphery of the Southwest were riding horses, anticipating the combination of theft and exchange that would spread horses to native peoples throughout the region and, still later, the Plains and the Southeast. In the meantime, some Navajos and Apaches moved near the Rio Grande Valley, strengthening ties with certain pueblos that were reinforced when inhabitants of those pueblos sought refuge among them in the face or wake of Spanish *entradas*.

Yet another variation on the theme of Indian-European contacts in the sixteenth century was played out in the Northeast, where Iroquoian-speaking villagers on the Mississippian periphery and Archaic hunter-gatherers still further removed from developments in the interior met Europeans of several nationalities. At the outset of the century, Spanish and Portuguese explorers enslaved several dozen Micmacs and other Indians from the Nova Scotia–Gulf of St. Lawrence area. Three French expeditions to the St. Lawrence itself in the 1530s and 1540s followed the Spanish pattern by alienating most Indians encountered and ending in futility. Even as these hostile contacts were taking place, fishermen, whalers, and other Europeans who visited the area regularly had begun trading with natives....

What induced Indians to go out of their way to trap beaver and trade the skins for glass beads, mirrors, copper kettles, and other goods? Throughout North America since Paleo-Indian times, exchange in the Northeast was the means by which people maintained and extended their social, cultural, and spiritual horizons as well as acquired items considered supernaturally powerful. Members of some coastal Indian groups later recalled how the first Europeans they saw, with their facial hair and strange clothes and traveling in their strange boats, seemed like supernatural figures. Although soon disabused of such notions, these Indians and many more inland placed special value on the glass beads and other trinkets offered by the newcomers. Recent scholarship on Indians' motives in this earliest stage of the trade indicates that they regarded such objects as the equivalents of the quartz, mica, shell, and other sacred substances that had formed the heart of long-distance exchange in North America for millennia and that they regarded as sources of physical and spiritual well-being, on earth and in the afterlife. Indians initially altered and wore many of the utilitarian goods they received, such as iron axe heads and copper pots, rather than use them for their intended purposes. Moreover, even though the new objects might pass through many hands, they more often than not ended up in graves, presumably for their possessors to use in the afterlife. Finally, the archaeological findings make clear that shell and native copper predominated over the new objects in sixteenth-century exchanges, indicating that European trade did not suddenly trigger a massive craving for the objects themselves. While northeastern Indians recognized Europeans as different from themselves, they interacted with them and their materials in ways that were consistent with their own customs and beliefs.

By the late sixteenth century, the effects of European trade began to overlap with the effects of earlier upheavals in the northeastern interior. Sometime between Jacques Cartier's final departure in 1543 and Samuel de Champlain's arrival in 1603, the Iroquoian-speaking inhabitants of Hochelaga and Stadacona (modern Montreal and Quebec City) abandoned their communities. The communities were crushed militarily, and the survivors dispersed among both Iroquois and Hurons. Whether the perpetrators of these dispersals were Iroquois and Huron is a point of controversy, but either way the St. Lawrence communities appear to have been casualties of the rivalry, at least a century old, between the two confederations as each sought to position itself vis-à-vis the French. The effect, if not the cause, of the dispersals was the Iroquois practice of attacking antagonists who denied them direct access to trade goods; this is consistent with Iroquois actions during the preceding two centuries and the century that followed.

The sudden availability of many more European goods, the absorption of many refugees from the St. Lawrence, and the heightening of tensions with the Iroquois help to explain the movement of most outlying Huron communities to what is now Simcoe County area of Ontario during the 1580s. This geographic concentration strengthened their confederacy and gave it the form it had when allied with New France during the first half of the seventeenth century. Having formerly existed at the outer margins of an arena of exchange centered in Cahokia, the Hurons and Iroquois now faced a new source of goods and power to the east.

The diverse native societies encountered by Europeans as they began to settle North America permanently during the seventeenth century were not static isolates lying outside the ebb and flow of human history. Rather, they were products of a complex set of historical forces, both local and wide ranging, both deeply rooted and of recent origin. Although their lives and worldviews were shaped by long-standing traditions of reciprocity and spiritual power, the people in these communities were also accustomed—contrary to popular myths about inflexible Indians—to economic and political flux and to absorbing new peoples (both allies and antagonists), objects, and ideas, including those originating in Europe. Such combinations of tradition and innovation continued to shape Indians' relations with Europeans, even as the latter's visits became permanent.

The establishment of lasting European colonies, beginning with New Mexico in 1598, began a phase in the continent's history that eventually resulted in the displacement of Indians to the economic, political, and cultural margins of a new order. But during the interim natives and colonizers entered into numerous relationships in which they exchanged material goods and often supported one another diplomatically or militarily against common enemies. These relations combined native and European modes of exchange. While much of the scholarly literature emphasizes the subordination and dependence of Indians in these circumstances, Indians as much as Europeans dictated the form and content of their early exchanges and alliances. Much of the protocol and ritual surrounding such intercultural contacts was rooted in indigenous kinship obligations and gift exchanges, and Indian consumers exhibited decided preferences for European commodities that satisfied social, spiritual, and aesthetic values. Similarly, Indians' long-range motives and strategies in their alliances with Europeans were frequently rooted in older patterns of alliance and rivalry with regional neighbors. Such continuities can be glimpsed through a brief consideration of the early colonial-era histories of the Five Nations Iroquois in the Northeast, ... and the Rio Grande Pueblos in the Southwest.

Post-Mississippian and sixteenth-century patterns of antagonism between the Iroquois and their neighbors to the north and west persisted, albeit under altered circumstances, during the seventeenth century when France established its colony on the St. Lawrence and allied itself with Hurons and other Indians. France aimed to extract maximum profits from the fur trade, and it immediately recognized the Iroquois as the major threat to that goal. In response, the Iroquois turned to the Dutch in New Netherland for guns and other trade goods while raiding New France's Indian allies for the thicker northern pelts that brought higher prices than those in their own country (which they exhausted by midcentury) and for captives to replace those from their own ranks who had died from epidemics or in wars. During the 1640s, the Iroquois replaced raids with full-scale military assaults (the so-called Beaver Wars) on Iroquoian-speaking communities in the lower Great Lakes, absorbing most of the survivors as refugees or captives. All the while, the Iroquois elaborated a vision of their confederation, which had brought harmony within their own ranks, as bringing peace to all peoples of the region. For the remainder of the century, the Five Nations fought a grueling and costly series of wars against the French and their Indian allies in order to gain access to the pelts and French goods circulating in lands to the north and west.

Meanwhile, the Iroquois were also adapting to the growing presence of English colonists along the Atlantic seaboard.... After the English supplanted the Dutch in New York in 1664, Iroquois diplomats established relations with the proprietary governor, Sir Edmund Andros, in a treaty known as the Covenant Chain. The Covenant Chain was an elaboration of the Iroquois' earlier treaty arrangements with the Dutch, but, whereas the Iroquois had termed the Dutch relationship a chain of iron, they referred to the one with the English as a chain of silver. The shift in metaphors was appropriate, for what had been strictly an economic connection was now a political one in which the Iroquois acquired power over other New York Indians. After 1677, the Covenant Chain was expanded to include several English colonies, most notably Massachusetts and Maryland, along with those colonies' subject Indians. The upshot of these arrangements was that the Iroquois cooperated with their colonial partners in subduing and removing subject Indians who impeded settler expansion. The Mohawks in particular played a vital role in the New England colonies' suppression of the Indian uprising known as King Philip's War and in moving the Susquehannocks away from the expanding frontier of settlement in the Chesapeake after Bacon's Rebellion.

For the Iroquois, such a policy helped expand their "Tree of peace" among Indians while providing them with buffers against settler encroachment around their homelands. The major drawback in the arrangement proved to be the weakness of English military assistance against the French. This inadequacy, and the consequent suffering experienced by the Iroquois during two decades of war after 1680, finally drove the Five Nations to make peace with the French and their Indian allies in the Grand settlement of 1701. Together, the Grand Settlement and Covenant Chain provided the Iroquois with the peace and security, the access to trade goods, and the dominant role among northeastern Indians they had long sought. That these arrangements in the long run served to reinforce rather than deter English encroachment on Iroquois lands and autonomy should not obscure their pre-European roots and their importance in shaping colonial history in the Northeast....

In the Southwest, the institution of Spanish colonial rule on the Rio Grande after 1598 further affected exchange relations between Pueblo Indians and nearby Apaches and Navajos. By imposing heavy demands for tribute in the form of corn, the Spanish prevented Pueblo peoples from trading surplus produce with their non-farming neighbors. In order to obtain the produce on which they had come to depend, Apaches and Navajos staged deadly raids on some pueblos, leaving the inhabitants dependent on the Spanish for protection. In retaliation, Spanish soldiers captured Apaches and Navajos whom they sold as slaves to their countrymen to the south. From the beginning, the trading pueblos of Pecos, Picuris, and Taos most resented Spanish control and strongly resisted the proselytizing of Franciscan missionaries. From the late 1660s, drought and disease, intensified Apache and Navajo raids, and the severity of Spanish rule led more and more Indians from all pueblos to question the advantages of Christianity and to renew their ties to their indigenous religious traditions. Spanish persecution of native religious leaders and their backsliding followers precipitated the Pueblo Revolt of 1680, in which the trading Pueblos played a leading role and which was actively supported by some Navajos and Apaches.

When the Spanish reimposed their rule during the 1690s, they tolerated traditional Indian religion rather than trying to extirpate it, and they participated in interregional trade fairs at Taos and other villages. The successful incorporation of Pueblo Indians as loyal subjects proved vital to New Mexico's survival as a colony and, more generally, to Spain's imperial presence in the Southwest during the eighteenth and early nineteenth centuries.

As significant as is the divide separating pre- and post-Columbian North American history, it is not the stark gap suggested by the distinction between prehistory and history. For varying periods of time after their arrival in North America, Europeans adapted to the social and political environments they found, including the fluctuating ties of reciprocity and interdependence as well as rivalry, that characterized those environments. They had little choice but to enter in and participate if they wished to sustain their presence. Eventually, one route to success proved to be their ability to insert themselves as regional powers in new networks of exchange and alliance that arose to supplant those of the Mississippians, Anasazis, and others.

To assert such continuities does not minimize the radical transformations entailed in Europeans' colonization of the continent and its indigenous peoples. Arising in Cahokia's wake, new centers at Montreal, Fort Orange/Albany, Charleston, and elsewhere permanently altered the primary patterns of exchange in eastern North America. The riverine system that channeled exchange in the interior of the continent gave way to one in which growing quantities of goods arrived from, and were directed to, coastal peripheries and ultimately Europe. In the Southwest, the Spanish revived Anasazi links with Mesoamerica at some cost to newer ties between the Rio Grande Pueblos and recently arrived, nonfarming Athapaskan speakers. More generally, European colonizers brought a complex of demographic and ecological advantages, most notably epidemic diseases and their own immunity to them, that utterly devastated Indian communities; ideologies and beliefs in their cultural and spiritual superiority to native peoples and their entitlement to natives' lands; and economic, political, and military systems organized for the engrossment of Indian lands and the subordination or suppression of Indian peoples.

Europeans were anything but uniformly successful in realizing their goals, but the combination of demographic and ecological advantages and imperial intentions, along with the Anglo-Iroquois Covenant Chain, enabled land-hungry colonists from New England to the Chesapeake to break entirely free of ties of dependence on Indians before the end of the seventeenth century. Their successes proved to be only the beginning of a new phase of Indian-European relations. By the mid-eighteenth century, the rapid expansion of land-based settlement in the English colonies had sundered older ties of exchange and alliance linking natives and colonizers nearly everywhere east of the Appalachians, driving many Indians west and reducing those who remained to a scattering of politically powerless enclaves in which Indian identities were nurtured in isolation. Meanwhile, the colonizers threatened to extend this new mode of Indian relations across the Appalachians. An old world, rooted in indigenous exchange, was giving way to one in which Native Americans had no certain place.

FURTHER READING

James Axtell, *The Invasion Within: The Contest of Cultures in Colonial North America* (1986).

Alfred W. Crosby, *The Columbian Exchange: Biological and Cultural Consequences of 1492* (1972).

Francis Jennings, *The Founders of America: From the Earliest Migrations to the Present* (1993).

Alvin M. Josephy, Jr., *America in 1492: The World of Indian Peoples Before the Arrival of Columbus* (1992).

Karen O. Kupperman, *Settling with the Indians: The Meeting of English and Indian Cultures in America, 1580–1640* (1980).

Charles C. Mann, *1491: New Revelations of the Americas before Columbus* (2005).

Calvin Martin, *Keepers of the Game: Indian-Animal Relationships and the Fur Trade* (1985).

James H. Merrill, *Into the American Woods: Negotiations on the Pennsylvania Frontier* (2000).

Anthony Pagden, *Lords of All the World: Ideologies of Empire in Spain, Britain, and France, c. 1500–c. 1800* (1995).

William and Carla Phillips, *The Worlds of Christopher Columbus* (1992).

Daniel K. Richter, *The Ordeal of the Longhouse: The Peoples of the Iroquois League in the Era of European Colonization* (1992).

Daniel K. Richter, *Facing East from Indian Country: A Native History of Early America* (2003).

David J. Weber, *The Spanish Frontier in North America* (1993).

Richard White, *The Middle Ground: Indians, Empires, and Republics in the Great Lakes Region, 1650–1815* (1991).

CHAPTER 2

The Southern Colonies
in British America

On April 26, 1607, a group of ships bearing 128 men sailed into Chesapeake Bay and began the settlement of Jamestown, the first successful English plantation in the Americas. The English had attempted to form colonies beginning in the sixteenth century in locations as varied as present-day Maine and Virginia, but all had failed. Jamestown probably would have failed as well but for some fortunate circumstances. The colony's early years were horrific. The colonists were more interested in finding precious metals than in feeding themselves. Equally dangerous, they encountered a variety of new diseases in the swampland on which Jamestown was located. Many were gentlemen who felt it below their station to clear fields or build stockades. Nine months after their arrival, only thirty-eight of the English adventurers remained alive.

A series of developments, however, led the Jamestown colony out of its privation. After several more years of starvation and disease, the colonists began planting West Indian tobacco in 1611. Within two decades, tobacco exports grew to 1.5 million pounds. Tobacco was a demanding crop. It rapidly depleted the soil, which increased the demand for land, and it required intensive labor, which led to the importation of unfree workers. Colonists, including former indentured servants, increasingly looked to the land controlled by Indians, leading to conflict between the two groups. This was the basis of the demands in Bacon's Rebellion in 1676. Although the bound laborers tended to be European indentured servants in the early years, African slaves later began to replace them. Legal distinctions between servants and slaves at first were imprecise, but over time the status of African slaves in relation to English servants deteriorated. This decline in status coincided with an increase in the slave population. By 1690, the Chesapeake area contained more African slaves than European servants.

A series of other colonies that followed the Virginia pattern were subsequently formed. Maryland (founded in 1634), the Carolinas (1669), and Georgia (1732) joined profitable British colonies in the Caribbean and were based in large part on staple crops, increasingly tended by African slaves. Unlike the Chesapeake area, which continued to grow tobacco, South Carolina and Georgia relied on indigo, a purple dye, and on rice, whereas the Caribbean colonies produced sugar. Which crops were grown profoundly influenced the workers' lives. Sugar production was particularly toilsome, and rice demanded different rhythms of labor. In all of these colonies, however, the slave population grew until the Caribbean colonies and South Carolina had an African majority. In most regions of the South, colonies with slaves ultimately became slave colonies.

By the eighteenth century, race, status, and degree of freeness profoundly divided the inhabitants of the southern colonies. As wealthy planters profited from the labor of a slave population, they began to cultivate an ideal of paternalism that rested on the notion that planters and slaves alike were knit into a world based on reciprocity and obligation. In the growing slave quarters, a slave community was forged. Families were formed, children were socialized, and the community attempted to temper the horrors of slavery. To be sure, only a minority of white people owned slaves, but the nonslaveholding class too was influenced by the institution. If their "white" race gave them privilege, they were nonetheless expected to defer to the colony's slaveholding elite.

QUESTIONS TO THINK ABOUT

Historians have been deeply divided over the reasons why Africans became slaves and Europeans were servants. One school of thought focuses on an inherent racism within English society that differentiated Africans from Europeans and justified the enslavement of the former. Another school argues that decisions were made according to the price and availability of unfree laborers. Which makes the most sense? How did the increasing complexity of the colonial South change the relationships between rich and poor; black, red, and white; free and unfree?

DOCUMENTS

Document 1 reports on an Indian attack on English colonists in 1622 and argues that the English now have a right to destroy their Indian adversaries. The life of an English indentured servant could be difficult, as Document 2 indicates. In this letter to his parents, Richard Frethorne recounts the trials of living in seventeenth-century Virginia and pleads to return to England. In contrast, in Document 3, George Alsop contends that the indentured servants enjoy good fortune. You might wish to consider why these two accounts differ so much. Document 4 is the "declaration in the name of the people" issued by Nathaniel Bacon in 1676 that documents the misdeeds of Governor William Berkeley. Note how Bacon condemns Berkeley for favoring the Indians over the English. Document 5 is a selection of Virginia laws from 1660 to 1705 that illustrate the ways in which the position of African slaves hardened when compared with that of English servants. Document 6, the secret diary of William Byrd, a wealthy slaveholder in Virginia, illustrates a strange blend of devotion to God and learning with cruelty to slaves. "Slaves Stringing and Rolling Tobacco" is illustrated in Document 7. It shows African men, women, and children working hard in the southern colonies. Document 8 is a 1757 narrative written by Olaudah Equiano that describes the terror of enslavement in Africa, the journey to the West Indies, and the bewilderment and cruelties faced by slaves.

1. Edward Waterhouse, a British Official, Recounts an Indian Attack on Early Virginia Settlement, 1622

The houses generally set open to the Savages, who were always friendly entertained at the tables of the English, and commonly lodged in their bed-chambers....

Yea, such was the treacherous dissimulation of that people who then had contrived our destruction, that even two days before the massacre, some of our men were guided through the woods by them in safety.... Yea, they borrowed our own boats to convey themselves across the river (on the banks of both sides whereof all our plantations were) to consult of the devilish murder that ensued, and of our utter extirpation, which God of his mercy (by the means of some of themselves converted to Christianity) prevented.... On Friday morning (the fatal day) the 22 of March, as also in the evening, as in other days before, they came unarmed into our houses, without bows or arrows, or other weapons, with deer, turkey, fish, furs, and other provisions, to sell, and truck with us, for glass, beads, and other trifles: yea in some places, sat down at breakfast with our people at their tables.... And by this means that fatal Friday morning, there fell under the bloody and barbarous hands of that perfidious and inhumane people, contrary to all laws of God and men, of nature and nations, 347 men, women, and children, most by their own weapons; and not being content with taking away life alone, they fell after again upon the dead, making as well as they could, a fresh murder, defacing, dragging, and mangling the dead carkasses into many pieces, carrying some parts away in derision....

Our hands which before were tied with gentleness and fair usage, are now set at library by the treacherous violence of the savages ... that we, who hitherto have had possession of no more ground then their waste, and our purchase at a valuable consideration to their own contentment, gained; may now by right of war, and law of nations, invade the country, and destroy them who sought to destroy us: whereby wee shall enjoy their cultivated places.... Now their cleared grounds in all their villages (which are situate in the fruitfullest places of the land) shall be inhabited by us, whereas heretofore the grubbing of woods was the greatest labor.

2. Indentured Servant Richard Frethorne Laments His Condition in Virginia, 1623

Loving and kind father and mother, my most humble duty remembered to you hoping in God of your good health, as I my self am at the making hereof, this is to let you understand that I your Child am in a most heavy Case by reason of the nature of the Country is such that it Causeth much sickness, as the scurvy and the bloody flux [dysentery], and divers other diseases, which maketh the body very poor, and Weak, and when we are sick there is nothing to Comfort

Susan Myra Kingsbury, ed., *The Records of the Virginia Company of London*, III (Washington, D.C.: U.S. Government Printing Office, 1933), 550–551, 556–557.

Richard Frethorne to his mother and father, March–April, 1623, in *The Records of the Virginia Company*, ed. Susan M. Kingsbury, IV (Washington, D.C.: U.S. Government Printing Office, 1935), 58–62.

us; for since I came out of the ship, I never ate any thing but peas and loblollie (that is water gruel) as for deer or venison I never saw any since I came into this land, there is indeed some fowl, but We are not allowed to go and get it, but must Work hard both early and late for a mess of water gruel, and a mouthful of bread, and beef, a mouthful of bread for a penny loaf must serve for 4 men which is most pitiful if you did know as much as I, when people cry out day, and night, Oh that they were in England without their limbs and would not care to lose any limb to be in England again, yea though they beg from door to door, for we live in fear of the Enemy every hour, yet we have had a Combat with them on the Sunday before Shrovetide, and we took two alive, and make slaves of them.... [W]e are fain to get other men to plant with us, and yet we are but 32 to fight against 3000 if they should Come, and the nighest help that We have is ten miles of us, and when the rogues overcame this place last, they slew 80 persons. How then shall we doe for we lie even in their teeth, they may easily take us but that God is merciful, and can save with few as well as with many; as he showed to Gilead and like Gilead's soldiers if they lapped water, we drink water which is but Weak, and I have nothing to Comfort me, nor there is nothing to be gotten here but sickness, and death, except that one had money to lay out in some things for profit; But I have nothing at all, no not a shirt to my backe, but two Rags nor no Clothes, but one poor suit, nor but one pair of shoes, but one pair of stockings, but one Cap, but two bands, my Cloak is stolen by one of my own fellows.... I am not half a quarter so strong as I was in England, and all is for want of victuals, for I do protest unto you, that I have eaten more in a day at home than I have allowed me here for a Week. You have given more than my day's allowance to a beggar at the door.... [I]f you love me you will redeem me suddenly, for which I do entreat and beg, and if you cannot get the merchants to redeem me for some little money then for God's sake get a gathering or entreat some good folks to lay out some little sum of money, in meal, and Cheese and butter, and beef, any eating meat will yield great profit, ... and look whatsoever you send me be it never so much, look what I make of it. I will deal truly with you. I will send it over, and beg the profit to redeem me, and if I die before it Come I have entreated Goodman Jackson to send you the worth of it, who hath promised he will. If you send you must direct your letter to Goodman Jackson, at James Town, a Gunsmith.... Good Father do not forget me, but have mercy and pity my miserable Case. I know if you did but see me you would weep to see me, for I have but one suit, but it is a strange one, it is very well guarded, wherefore for God's sake pity me. I pray you to remember my love to all my friends, and kindred, I hope all my Brothers and sisters are in good health, and as for my part I have set down my resolution that certainly Will be, that is, that the Answer of this letter will be life or death to me, there good Father send as soon as you can, and if you send me any thing let this be the mark.

Richard Frethorne
Martin's Hundred

3. George Alsop, a Resident of Maryland, Argues That Servants in Maryland Profit from Life in the Colonies, 1666

The necessariness of Servitude proved, with the common usage of Servants in Mary-Land, together with their Priviledges.

... There is no truer Emblem of Confusion either in Monarchy or Domestick Governments, then when either the Subject, or the Servant, strives for the upper hand of his Prince, or Master, and to be equal with him, from whom he receives his present subsistance: Why then, if Servitude be so necessary that no place can be governed in order, nor people live without it, this may serve to tell those which prick up their ears and bray against it, That they are none but Asses, and deserve the Bridle of a strict commanding power to rein them in: For I'me certainly confident, that there are several Thousands in most Kingdoms of Christendom, that could not at all live and subsist, unless they had served some prefixed time, to learn either some Trade, Art, or Science, and by either of them to extract their present livelihood.

Then methinks this may stop the mouths of those that will undiscreetly compassionate them that dwell under necessary Servitudes....

... [L]et such, where Providence hath ordained to life as Servants, either in England or beyond Sea, endure the pre-fixed yoak of their limited time with patience, and then in a small computation of years, by an industrious endeavour, they may become Masters and Mistresses of Families themselves. And let this be spoke to the deserved praise of Mary-Land. That the four years I served there were not to me so slavish, as a two years Servitude of a Handicraft Apprenticeship was here in London....

They whose abilities cannot extend to purchase their own transportation over into Mary-Land, (and surely he that cannot command so small a sum for so great a matter, his life must needs be mighty low and dejected) I say they may for the debarment of a four years sordid liberty, go over into this Province and there live plentiously well. And what's a four years Servitude to advantage a man all the remainder of his dayes, making his predecessors happy in his sufficient abilities, which he attained to partly by the restrainment of so small a time? ...

The Merchant commonly before they go aboard the Ship, or set themselves in any forwardness for their Voyage, has Conditions of Agreements drawn between him and those that by a voluntary consent become his Servants, to serve him, his Heirs or Assigns, according as they in their primitive acquaintance have made their bargain, some two, some three, some four years; and whatever the Master or Servant tyes himself up to here in England by Condition, the Laws of the Province will force a performance of when they come there: Yet here is this Priviledge in it when they arrive. If they dwell

George Alsop, "A Character of the Province of Maryland, 1666," in *Narratives of Early Maryland*, ed. C. C. Hall (New York: Charles Scribner's Sons, 1910; copyright renewed Barnes and Noble, 1946), 354–360.

not with the Merchant they made their first agreement withall, they may choose whom they will serve their prefixed time with; and after their curiosity has pitcht on one whom they think fit for their turn, and that they may live well withall, the Merchant makes an Assignment of the Indenture over to him whom they of their free will have chosen to be their Master, in the same nature as we here in England (and no otherwise) turn over Covenant Servants or Apprentices from one Master to another. Then let those whose chaps are always breathing forth those filthy dregs of abusive exclamations, ... against this Country of Mary-Land, saying, That those which are transported over thither, are sold in open Market for Slaves, and draw in Carts like Horses; which is so damnable as untruth, that if they should search to the very Center of Hell, and enquire for a Lye of the most antient and damned stamp, I confidently believe they could not find one to parallel this: For know, That the Servants here in Mary-Land of all Colonies, distant or remote Plantations, have the least cause to complain, either for strictness of Servitude, want of Provisions, or need of Apparel: Five dayes and a half in the Summer weeks is the alotted time that they work in; and for two months, when the Sun predominates in the highest pitch of his heat, they claim an antient and customary Priviledge, to repose themselves three hours in the day within the house, and this is undeniably granted to them that work in the Fields....

... He that lives in the nature of a Servant in this Province, must serve but four years by the Custom of the Country; and when the expiration of his time speaks him a Freeman, there's a Law in the Province, that enjoyns his Master whom he hath served to give him Fifty Acres of Land, Corn to serve him a whole year, three Sutes of Apparel, with things necessary to them, and Tools to work withall; so that they are no sooner free, but they are ready to set up for themselves, and when once entered, they live passingly well.

The Women that go over into this Province as Servants, have the best luck here as in any place of the world besides; for they are no sooner on shoar, but they are courted into a Copulative Matrimony, which some of them (for aught I know) had they not come to such a Market with their Virginity might have kept it by them until it had been mouldy....

In short, touching the Servants of this Province, they live well in the time of their Service, and by their restrainment in that time, they are made capable of living much better when they come to be free; which in several other parts of the world I have observed, That after some servants have brought their indented and limited time to a just and legal period by Servitude, they have been much more incapable of supporting themselves from sinking into the Gulf of a slavish, poor, fettered, and intangled life, then all the fastness of their pre-fixed time did involve them in before.

4. Nathaniel Bacon, Leader of a Rebellion, Recounts the Misdeeds of the Virginia Governor, 1676

Declaration of Nathaniel Bacon in the Name of the People of Virginia, July 30, 1676

1. For having, upon spacious pretences of public works, raised great unjust taxes upon the commonalty for the advancement of private favorites and other sinister ends, but no visible effects in any measure adequate; for not having, during this long time of his government, in any measure advanced this hopeful colony either by fortifications, towns, or trade.

2. For having abused and rendered contemptible the magistrates of justice by advancing to places of judicature scandalous and ignorant favorites.

3. For having wronged his Majesty's prerogative and interest by assuming monopoly of the beaver trade and for having in it unjust gain betrayed and sold his Majesty's country and the lives of his loyal subjects to the barbarous heathen.

4. For having protected, favored, and emboldened the Indians against his Majesty's loyal subjects, never contriving, requiring, or appointing any due or proper means of satisfaction for their many invasions, robberies, and murders committed upon us.

5. For having, when the army of English was just upon the track of those Indians who now in all places burn, spoil, murder and when we might with ease have destroyed them who then were in open hostility, for then having expressly countermanded and sent back our army by passing his word for the peaceable demeanor of the said Indians, who immediately prosecuted their evil intentions, committing horrid murders and robberies in all places, being protected by the said engagement and word past of him the said Sir William Berkeley, having ruined and laid desolate a great part of his majesty's country, and have now drawn themselves into such obscure and remote places and are by their success so emboldened and confirmed by their confederacy so strengthened that the cries of blood are in all places, and the terror and consternation of the people so great, are now become not only a difficult but a very formidable enemy who might at first with ease have been destroyed.

6. And lately, when, upon the loud outcries of blood, the assembly had, with all care, raised and framed an army for the preventing of further mischief and safeguard of this his Majesty's colony.

7. For having, with only the privacy of some few favorites without acquainting the people, only by the alteration of a figure, forged a commission, by we know not what hand, not only without but even against the consent of the people, for the raising and affecting civil war and destruction, which being happily and without bloodshed prevented;

"Nathaniel Bacon Esq'r, His Manifesto Concerning the Present Troubles in Virginia, 1676," *Virginia Magazine of History and Biography,* 1 (1894): 55–61.

for having the second time attempted the same, thereby calling down our forces from the defense of the frontiers and most weakly exposed places.

8. For the prevention of civil mischief and ruin amongst ourselves while the barbarous enemy in all places did invade, murder, and spoil us, his Majesty's most faithful subjects.

Of this and the aforesaid articles we accuse Sir William Berkeley as guilty of each and every one of the same, and as one who has traitorously attempted, violated, and injured his Majesty's interest here by a loss of a great part of this his colony and many of his faithful loyal subjects by him betrayed and in a barbarous and shameful manner exposed to the incursions and murder of the heathen. And we do further declare these the ensuing persons in this list to have been his wicked and pernicious councillors, confederates, aiders, and assisters against the commonalty in these our civil commotions. [A list of names is given.]

And we do further demand that the said Sir William Berkeley with all the persons in this list be forthwith delivered up or surrender themselves within four days after the notice hereof, or otherwise we declare as follows.

That in whatsoever place, house, or ship, any of the said persons shall reside, be hid, or protected, we declare the owners, masters, or inhabitants of the said places to be confederates and traitors to the people and the estates of them is also of all the aforesaid persons to be confiscated. And this we, the commons of Virginia, do declare, desiring a firm union amongst ourselves that we may jointly and with one accord defend ourselves against the common enemy. And let not the faults of the guilty be the reproach of the innocent, or the faults or crimes of the oppressors divide and separate us who have suffered by their oppressions.

These are, therefore, in his Majesty's name, to command you forthwith to seize the persons abovementioned as traitors to the King and country and them to bring to Middle Plantation and there to secure them until further order, and, in case of opposition, if you want any further assistance you are forthwith to demand it in the name of the people in all the countries of Virginia.

Nathaniel Bacon
General by consent of the people.

5. Virginia's Statutes Illustrate the Declining Status of African American Slaves, 1660–1705

1660–1661, Act XXII.

English running away with negroes.

BEE *itt enacted* That in case any English servant shall run away in company with any negroes who are incapable of makeing satisfaction by addition of time,

---

William Waller Hening, ed., The Statutes at Large: Being a Collection of all the Laws of Virginia, from the First Session of the Legislature, in the Year 1619, I, II, III, © 1823.

Bee itt enacted that the English so running away in company with them shall serve for the time of the said negroes absence as they are to do for their owne by a former act.

1662, Act XII.

Negro womens children to serve according to the condition of the mother.
WHEREAS some doubts have arrisen whether children got by any Englishman upon a negro woman should be slave or ffree, *Be it therefore enacted and declared by this present grand assembly,* that all children borne in this country shalbe held bond or free only according to the condition of the mother, *And* that if any christian shall commit ffornication with a negro man or woman, hee or shee soe offending shall pay double the ffines imposed by the former act.

1705, Chap. XLIX.

IV. *And also be it enacted, by the authority aforesaid, and it is hereby enacted,* That all servants imported and brought into this country, by sea or land, who were not christians in their native country, (expect Turks and Moors in amity with her majesty, and others that can make due proof of their being free in England, or any other christian country, before they were shipped, in order to transportation hither) shall be accounted and be slaves, and as such be here bought and sold notwithstanding a conversion to christianity afterwards....

VII. *And also be it enacted, by the authority aforesaid, and it is hereby enacted,* That all masters and owners of servants, shall find and provide for their servants, wholesome and competent diet, clothing, and lodging, by the discretion of the county courts and shall not, at any time, give immoderate corrections neither shall, at any time, whip a christian white naked, without an order from a justice of the peace....

X. *And be it also enacted,* That all servants, whether, by importation, indenture, or hire here, as well feme coverts, as others, shall, in like manner, as is provided, upon complaints of misusage, have their petitions received in court, for their wages and freedom....

XI. And for a further christian care and usage of all christian servants, *Be it also enacted, by the authority aforesaid, and it is hereby enacted,* That no negroes, mulattos, or Indians, although christians, or Jews, Moors, Mahometans, or other infidels, shall, at any time, purchase any christian servant, nor any other, except of their own complexion, or such as are declared slaves by this act....

XV. *And also be it enacted, by the authority aforesaid, and it is hereby enacted,* That no person whatsoever shall buy, sell, or receive of, to, or from, any servant, or slave, any coin or commodity whatsoever, without the leave, licence, or consent of the master or owner of the said servant, or slave....

XVII. *And also be it enacted, by the authority aforesaid, and it is hereby enacted, and declared,* That in all cases of penal laws, whereby persons free are punishable by fine, servants shall be punished by whipping, after the rate of twenty lashes for every five hundred pounds of tobacco, or fifty shillings current money, unless the servant so culpable, can and will procure some person or persons to pay the fine....

XVIII. And if any women servant shall be delivered of a bastard child within the time of her service aforesaid, *Be it enacted, by the authority aforesaid, and it is hereby enacted,* That in recompense of the loss and trouble occasioned her master or mistress thereby, she shall for every such offence, serve her said master or owner one whole year after her time by indenture, custom, and former order of court, shall be expired; or pay her said master or owner, one thousand pounds of tobacco; and the reputed father, if free, shall give security to the church-wardens of the parish where that child shall be, to maintain the child, and keep the parish indemnified; or be compelled thereto by order of the county court, upon the said church-wardens complaint....

And if any woman servant shall be got with child by her master, neither the said master, nor his executors administrators, nor assigns, shall have any claim of service against her, for or by reason of such child; but she shall, when her time due to her said master, by indenture, custom or order of court, shall be expired, be sold by the church-wardens, for the time being, of the parish wherein such child shall be born, for one year, or pay one thousand pounds of tobacco; and the said one thousand pounds of tobacco, or whatever she shall be sold for, shall be emploied, by the vestry, to the use of the said parish. And if any woman servant shall have a bastard child by a negro, or mulatto, over and above the years service due to her master or owner, she shall immediately, upon the expiration of her time to her then present master or owner, pay down to the church-wardens of the parish wherein such child shall be born, for the use of the said parish, fifteen pounds current money of Virginia, or be by them sold for five years, to the use aforesaid: And if a free christian white woman shall have such bastard child, by a negro, or mulatto, for every such offence, she shall, within one month after her delivery of such bastard child, pay to the church-wardens for the time being, of the parish wherein such child shall be born, for the use of the said parish fifteen pounds current money of Virginia, or be by them sold for five years to the use aforesaid: And in both the said cases, the church-wardens shall bind the said child to be a servant, until it shall be of thirty one years of age.

XIX. And for a further prevention of that abominable mixture and spurious issue, which hereafter may increase in this her majesty's colony and dominion, as well by English, and other white men and women intermarrying with negros or mulattos, as by their unlawful coition with them, *Be it enacted, by the authority aforesaid, and it is hereby enacted,* That whatsoever English, or other white man or woman, being free, shall intermarry with a negro or mulatto man or woman, bond or free, shall, by judgment of the county court, be committed to prison, and there remain, during the space of six months, without bail or mainprize, and shall forfeit and pay ten pounds current money of Virginia, to the use of the parish, as aforesaid.

XX. *And be it further enacted,* That no minister of the church of England, or other minister, or person whatsoever, within this colony and dominion, shall hereafter wittingly presume to marry a white man with a negro or mulatto woman; or to marry a white woman with a negro or mulatto man, upon pain of forfeiting and paying, for every such marriage the sum of ten thousand pounds of tobacco.

6. Southern Planter William Byrd Describes His Views Toward Learning and His Slaves, 1709–1710

[February 22, 1709] I rose at 7 o'clock and read a chapter in Hebrew and 200 verses in Homer's Odyssey. I said my prayers and ate milk for breakfast. I threatened Anaka with a whipping if she did not confess the intrigues between Daniel and Nurse, but she prevented by a confession. I chided Nurse severely about it, but she denied, with an impudent face, protesting that Daniel only lay on the bed for the sake of the child. I ate nothing but beef for dinner....

[June 10, 1709] I rose at 5 o'clock this morning but could not read anything because of Captain Keeling, but I played at billiards with him and won half a crown of him and the Doctor. George B-th brought home my boy Eugene.... In the evening I took a walk about the plantation. Eugene was whipped for running away and had the [bit] put on him. I said my prayers and had good health, good thought, and good humor, thanks be to God Almighty....

[September 6, 1709] ... About one o'clock this morning my wife was happily delivered of a son, thanks be to God Almighty. I was awake in a blink and rose and my cousin Harrison met me on the stairs and told me it was a boy. We drank some French wine and went to bed again and rose at 7 o'clock. I read a chapter in Hebrew and then drank chocolate with the women for breakfast. I returned God humble thanks for so great a blessing and recommended my young son to His Divine protection.

[October 6, 1709] I rose at 6 o'clock and said my prayers and ate milk for breakfast. Then I proceeded to Williamsburg, where I found all well. I went to the capitol where I sent for the wench to clean my room and when I came I kissed her and felt her, for which God forgive me. Then I went to see the President, whom I found indisposed in his ears. I dined with ... on beef. Then we went to his house and played at piquet where Mr. Clayton came to us. We had much to do to get a bottle of French wine. About 10 o'clock I went to my lodgings. I had good health but wicked thoughts, God forgive me....

[December 1, 1709] I rose at 4 o'clock and read two chapters in Hebrew and some Greek in Cassius. I said my prayers and ate milk for breakfast. I danced my dance. Eugene was whipped again for pissing in bed and Jenny for concealing it....

[December 3, 1709] I rose at 5 o'clock and read two chapters in Hebrew and some Greek in Cassius. I said my prayers and ate milk for breakfast. I danced my dance. Eugene pissed abed again for which I made him drink a pint of piss. I settled some accounts and read some news....

[March 31, 1710] I rose at 7 o'clock and read some Greek in bed. I said my prayers and ate milk for breakfast. Then about 8 o'clock we got a–horseback and rode to Mr. Harrison's and found him very ill but sensible.... In the morning

Louis B. Wright and Marion Tinling, eds., *The Secret Diary of William Byrd of Westover, 1709–1712* (Richmond, Va.: Dietz Press, 1941), 7, 46, 79–80, 90–91, 113, 159, 192.

early I returned home and went to bed. It is remarkable that Mrs. Burwell dreamed this night that she saw a person that with money scales weighed time and declared that there was no more than 18 pennies worth of time to come, which seems to be a dream with some significance either concerning the world or a sick person. In my letters from England I learned that the Bishop of Worcester was of opinion that in the year 1715 the city of Rome would be burned to the ground, that before the year 1745 the popish religion would be routed out of the world, that before the year 1790 the Jews and Gentiles would be converted to the Christianity and then would begin the millennium.

[June 17, 1710] ... I set my closet right. I ate tongue and chicken for dinner. In the afternoon I caused L–s–n to be whipped for beating his wife and Jenny was whipped for being his whore. In the evening the sloop came from Appomattox with tobacco. I took a walk about the plantation. I said my prayers and drank some new milk from the cow....

7. Illustration of Slaves Cultivating Tobacco, 1738

Scene on an American tobacco plantation From A. Pomet, *A Compleat History of Drugs* (London, 1725).

8. African Olaudah Equiano Recounts the Horrors
of Enslavement, 1757

One day, when all our people were gone to their works as usual, and only I and my dear sister were left to mind the house, two men and a woman got over our walls, and seized us both, and they stopped our mouths, and ran off with us into the nearest wood. Here they tied our hands, and continued to carry us as far as they could, till night came on, when we reached a small house, where the robbers halted for refreshment, and spent the night. We were then unbound, but were unable to take any food; and, being quite overpowered by fatigue and grief, our only relief was some sleep, which allayed our misfortune for a short time. The next morning we left the house, and continued travelling all the day....

The first object which saluted my eyes when I arrived on the coast was the sea, and a slave ship, which was then riding at anchor, and waiting for its cargo. These filled me with astonishment, which was soon converted into terror when I was carried on board.... I was now persuaded that I had gotten into a world of bad spirits, and that they were going to kill me. Their complexions too differing so much from ours, their long hair, and the language they spoke, (which was very different from any I had ever heard) united to confirm me in this belief.... When I looked round the ship too and saw a large furnace of copper boiling, and a multitude of black people of every description chained together, every one of their countenances expressing dejection and sorrow, I no longer doubted of my fate; and, quite overpowered with horror and anguish, I fell motionless on the deck and fainted. When I recovered a little I found some black people about me, who I believed were some of those who brought me on board, and had been receiving their pay; they talked to me in order to cheer me, but all in vain. I asked them if we were not to be eaten by those white men with horrible looks, red faces, and loose hair. They told me I was not; ... Soon after this the blacks who brought me on board went off, and left me abandoned to despair. I now saw myself deprived of all chance of returning to my native country, or even the least glimpse of hope of gaining the shore, which I now considered as friendly; and I even wished for my former slavery in preference to my present situation, which was filled with horrors of every kind, still heightened by my ignorance of what I was to undergo. I was not long suffered to indulge my grief; I was soon put down under the decks, and there I received such a salutation in my nostrils as I had never experienced in my life: so that, with the loathsomeness of the stench, and crying together, I became so sick and low that I was not able to eat, nor had I the least desire to taste any thing. I now wished for the last friend, death, to relieve me; but soon, to my grief, two of the white men offered me eatables; and, on my refusing to eat, one of them held me fast by the hands, and laid me across I think the windlass, and tied my feet, while the other flogged me severely. I had never experienced any thing of this kind before; and although, not being used to the water, I naturally feared that element the first time I saw it,

---

From Olaudah Equiano, *The Life of Olaudah Equiano* (1789).

yet nevertheless, could I have got over the nettings, I would have jumped over the side, but I could not; and, besides, the crew used to watch us very closely who were not chained down to the decks, lest we should leap into the water: and I have seen some of these poor African prisoners most severely cut for attempting to do so, and hourly whipped for not eating. This indeed was often the case with myself. In a little time after, amongst the poor chained men, I found some of my own nation, which in a small degree gave ease to my mind. I inquired of these what was to be done with us; they gave me to understand we were to be carried to these white people's country to work for them. I then was a little revived, and thought, if it were no worse than working, my situation was not so desperate: but still I feared I should be put to death, the white people looked and acted, as I thought, in so savage a manner; for I had never seen among any people such instances of brutal cruelty; and this not only shewn towards us blacks, but also to some of the whites themselves. One white man in particular I saw, when we were permitted to be on deck, flogged so unmercifully with a large rope near the foremast that he died in consequence of it; and they tossed him over the side as they would have done a brute. This made me fear these people the more; and I expected nothing less than to be treated in the same manner. I could not help expressing my fears and apprehensions to some of my countrymen: I asked them if these people had no country, but lived in this hollow place (the ship): they told me they did not, but came from a distant one. "Then," said I, "how comes it in all our country we never heard of them?" They told me because they lived so very far off. I then asked where were their women? had they any like themselves? I was told they had "and why," said I, "do we not see them?" they answered, because they were left behind. I asked how the vessel could go? they told me they could not tell; but that there were cloths put upon the masts by the help of the ropes I saw, and then the vessel went on and the white men had some spell or magic they put in the water when they liked in order to stop the vessel. I was exceedingly amazed at this account, and really thought they were spirits. I therefore wished much to be from amongst them, for I expected they would sacrifice me: but my wishes were vain....

... At last we came in sight of the island of Barbadoes, at which the whites on board gave a great shout, and made many signs of joy to us. We did not know what to think of this; but as the vessel drew nearer we plainly saw the harbour, and other ships of different kinds and sizes; and we soon anchored amongst them off Bridge Town. Many merchants and planters now came on board, though it was in the evening. They put us in separate parcels, and examined us attentively. They also made us jump, and pointed to the land, signifying we were to go there. We thought by this we should be eaten by these ugly men as they appeared to us; and, when soon after we were all put down under the deck again, there was much dread and trembling among us, and nothing but bitter cries to be heard all the night from these apprehensions, insomuch that at last the white people got some old slaves from the land to pacify us. They told us we were not to be eaten, but to work, and were soon to go on land, where we should see many of our country people. This report eased us much; and sure enough, soon after we were landed, there came to us Africans of all languages. We were conducted immediately to the merchant's yard, where we were all pent up together like so many sheep in a fold, without regard to sex or age. As every object was new to me everything I saw filled me with surprise. What struck me first was that the houses were built with stories, and in every other respect different from those in Africa: but I was still more astonished on seeing people on horseback. I did not know what this could mean; and indeed I thought these people were full of nothing but magical arts.... We were not many days in the merchant's custody before we were sold after their usual manner, which is this:—On a signal given (as the beat of a drum), the buyers rush at once into the yard where the slaves are confined, and make choice of that parcel they like best. The noise and clamour with which this is attended, and the eagerness visible in the countenances of the buyers, serve not a little to increase the apprehensions of the terrified Africans, who may well be supposed to consider them as the ministers of that destruction to which they think themselves devoted. In this manner, without scruple, are relations and friends separated, most of them never to see each other again. I remember in the vessel in which I was brought over, in the men's apartment, there were several brothers, who, in the sale, were sold in different lots; and it was very moving on this occasion to see and hear their cries at parting....

While I was thus employed by my master I was often a witness to cruelties of every kind, which were exercised on my unhappy fellow slaves. I used frequently to have different cargoes of new negroes in my care for sale; and it was almost a constant practice with our clerks, and other whites, to commit violent depredations on the chastity of the female slaves; and these I was, though with reluctance, obliged to submit to at all times, being unable to help them. When we have had some of these slaves on board my master's vessels to carry them to other islands, or to America, I have known our mates to commit these acts most shamefully, to the disgrace, not of Christians only, but of men. I have even known them gratify their brutal passion with females not ten years old; ... And yet in Montserrat I have seen a negro man staked to the ground, and cut most shockingly, and then his ears cut off bit by bit, because he had been connected with a white woman who was a common prostitute: as if it were no crime in the whites to rob an innocent African girl of her virtue; but most heinous in a black man only to gratify a passion of nature, where the temptation was offered by one of a different colour, though the most abandoned woman of her species. Another negro man was half hanged, and then burnt, for attempting to poison a cruel overseer. Thus by repeated cruelties are the wretched first urged to despair, and then murdered, because they still retain so much of human nature about them as to wish to put an end to their misery, and retaliate on their tyrants!

ESSAYS

Although the system of unfree labor colored all aspects of the colonial South, it was not a static institution. One issue that has concerned historians for some time is the different paths taken by African slaves and European servants. Both entered the colonies as unfree laborers, but only the Africans ultimately endured perpetual servitude. These two essays grapple with another issue: the changing relationships between slave and slaveholder over the course of the colonial era. Both argue that the ethos of patriarchalism that dominated in the seventeenth- and early-eighteenth-century colonial South gave way in the eighteenth century to a paternalist ethos, yet they differ on causes and outcomes of this shift. Kathleen M. Brown, professor of history at the University of Pennsylvania, concentrates on the anxiety of the planter class and the ways in which enslaved people used the paternalism that resulted to their own advantage. Philip D. Morgan, who teaches history at Johns Hopkins University, also considers the transition from patriarchalism to paternalism and the many-sided relationships between free and nonfree, black and white. He argues that paternalism was less austere and was based on a reciprocal relationship of obligation between slave and slaveholder. Yet he also notes that the transition to paternalism changed the relationships between poor whites and enslaved blacks, a change that would have critical implications for the future.

The Anxious World of the Slaveowning Patriarch

KATHLEEN M. BROWN

In 1711, Lucy Parke Byrd argued with her husband, William Byrd II, about her plan to pluck her eyebrows before their journey to the colonial capital in Williamsburg. Threatening not to accompany her husband, she attempted to override his objections to her beauty regimen. That she failed we can glean from William Byrd's entry in his secret journal for that day. "I refused, however, and got the better of her, and maintained my authority," he noted smugly. The couple departed from their Westover home later that morning with Lucy Byrd's eyebrows unplucked and William Byrd's position as head of household and master over his wife confirmed. Not only had Byrd's taste in female fashion held the day, but his desire to have his wife accompany him during his round of social, political, and business dealings in Williamsburg prevailed.

For colonial gentlemen like Byrd, authority was a delicate project, much like a house built upon an unstable foundation. To keep such a structure standing, the owner had to be extremely sensitive to fine cracks and imperfections, shoring up the edifice to prevent the entire house from tumbling down. Conscious of being colonials whose dependent and marginal relationship to London diminished their status, Byrd and his peers could never achieve enough success to reassure themselves that the foundation of their identity would not collapse. Maintaining authority thus required constant vigilance against even small usurpations of power such as the forbidden plucking of eyebrows, for tiny fissures not only indicated larger weaknesses in the construction but constituted a nagging remainder of contradictions inherent in colonial masculinity.

Marriage, parenthood, slaveownership, and electoral politics all tested a man, requiring him to behave with equanimity in a variety of social contexts. A man who was simultaneously a husband, father, slaveowner, and Council member needed to respond appropriately to the different challenges inherent in each relationship. Ultimately, each tried the same quality: his ability to communicate power over others by appearing to have power over himself. Authority derived not simply from a man's power over his wife, children, slaves, and lesser men but also from his ability to subdue within himself those qualities he attributed to subordinates: passion, weakness, and dependence.

By the mid-eighteenth century, elite male identity in Virginia had a complex historical, political, and emotional architecture. From the outset, the project of establishing colonies emerged from a gendered context of imperial rivalry, debates about woman's nature, and desires for far-off lands. English explorers became English men through encounters with Indians in which differences between English and Indian gender performances provided a language of self-definition and a means of expressing struggles for power. When English settlers began importing Africans to produce tobacco, gender figured prominently in the legal and political language used to distinguish slaves from free people, reflecting the importance of relationships between enslaved women and their masters to definitions of slavery. It was not until Bacon's challenge to Berkeley in 1676, however, that questions about what it meant to be a Virginian and to constitute political authority in a colonial society came to a head. The reaction against white women and the repudiation of black masculinity provided the basis for a fragile alliance of white men and the assertion of an authentic colonial identity. In this sense, Bacon's Rebellion was the crucible for colonial masculinity.

Eighteenth-century planters gentrified Bacon's legacy of masculinity, incorporating it into their mimicry of the material and emotional world of the English gentry. Domestic tranquillity became the ideal of planters who dreamed of hegemonic authority over compliant wives, children, and slaves and of unquestioned political leadership over less privileged men. An appropriate emotional lexicon for men aspiring to self-mastery, domestic tranquillity also promised to detach power from coercion, delivering authority on a silver platter to men who need never raise their voices in anger or lift the lash to inflict punishment. Self-mastery and harmonious, if not affectionate, familial relations thus went hand in hand, swathing the violent history of planter power in an insulating layer of emotional serenity.

Virginia planters, however, were perhaps more successful politically than they were domestically. Compared to the political leadership of other British colonies, the Old Dominion's elite enjoyed a relatively stable tenure throughout most of the eighteenth century. Both the political legacy of Nathaniel Bacon and the state's implication in slavery provided the colony's gentry with a firm foundation for political dominance that was not easily challenged.

At the root of planter domestic authority and political success lay slavery, the most difficult relationship for planters to translate into an English idiom. Slaves intermittently threatened to disturb gentry equanimity, forcing planters to respond as either a "fool or a fury," as Byrd once observed. Coercion thus permeated master-slave relations to a much greater degree than it did other social relations, offering a graphically violent showcase for planter authority and state power. Dismemberments, hangings, and burnings of slaves provided planters with a foundation for authority rooted in the infliction of pain. As long as planters could exercise power over slave bodies, other domestic and political relationships need not be regularly disrupted by violence.

Historians usually discuss the authority exercised by elite white men over their wives, children, slaves, and social and economic inferiors as if each relationship existed in isolation from the others. The terms describing authority are frequently defined imprecisely, if at all, and often assume completely different meanings for scholars investigating the history of different social relations. To those explicating political theory, "patriarchy" connotes state power under the rule of an absolute monarchy, whereas "paternalism" signifies reciprocal yet still deferential social relations under a weaker crown. To historians of the family, "patriarchy" means the rule of the father over his wife, children, and dependent household members but is often used interchangeably with "paternalism," by which is meant a softer, more affectionate familial system. For feminist scholars, however, "patriarchy" and "paternalism" both describe a male-dominated political and economic order, with the latter appearing, at least on the surface, to be characterized by greater mutuality and reciprocity in domestic relationships between men and women. Studies of slavery have provided perhaps the most sophisticated explanation for paternalism, yet scholars still disagree about the specific connotations of each term.

Despite different usage, most analysts share the assumption the paternalism represents a qualitative improvement in human relationships over patriarchy, gradually displacing more coercive social relations sometime during the late eighteenth century. Historians use the words "warm," "soft," "mellow," "affectionate," "companionate," and "face-to-face" to describe a paternalistic world of heightened intimacy and emotion in which the crasser, sharper edges of patriarchy have been smoothed or "domesticated," and the "impersonal" relations of a class society have not yet taken hold. The unstated assumption behind this use of language is that paternalistic social relations accompany a flowering of domestic life and emotional intimacy characterized by face-to-face contact. This view both celebrates "modern" family relations and is nostalgic for the lost intimacy of pre-industrial society. It is also based upon generalizations inappropriate for female slaves, for whom paternalism's face-to-face style presented graver dangers than less intimate relations with masters.

An eighteenth-century planter's authority cannot be easily described using either of these terms exclusively. Before 1750, it would not be unusual for the same individual to court a woman with tender words, threaten to disinherit his child, whip a slave, and offer rum to social subordinates at a militia muster. Was such a man a patriarch or a paternalist? If we were to examine only his relationship with his wife-to-be, we might conclude that harmonious domestic relations had supplanted crude patriarchal authority. Similarly, if we noted only the whipping or the disinheritance, we might come to a very different conclusion. In the instance of our fictional planter, the coexistence of paternalistic language and patriarchal tactics suggests a more complicated relationship between styles of authority often taken to be distinct.

The overlapping of different kinds of authoritative relations within the life of a single individual complicates matters further. Within the plantation house, for example, a man frequently shifted his primary identity from father to husband, master to gentry patron, host to plantation manager. Ideally, he strove to move from role to role effortlessly, conducting himself so that each identity complemented the others and augmented his authority. Although elite men enjoyed some separation of roles—the long ride to Williamsburg undoubtedly provided some men with the opportunity to don their political faces—their authority sprang from the accumulated clout of being husband and father, landowner and slaveholder, planter and politician. It is tempting to conclude that Virginia's elite planters wore many different hats, but it is perhaps more accurate to say that they wore one, appropriate for many different occasions.

By the beginning of the eighteenth century ..., Virginia's planter class had reason to consider themselves patriarchs. Planter power coalesced in 1705 with the reorganization of the colony's law codes. In that year, legislators rewrote Virginia's statutes to create a comprehensive body of slave laws that reiterated and extended the master's powers over his slaves. Within five years, lawmakers reinforced a statute forbidding infanticide by threatening severe punishments to those who concealed the death of a bastard child. The consolidation of the power of the father with that of political patron and slaveholder launched Virginia's elite planters on a nearly fifty-year reign of social and economic supremacy.

During this high-water mark of planter authority, elite men derived their power from five main sources: landownership, control over sexual access to women, rights to the labor of slaves and servants, formal access to political life, and the ability to create and manipulate symbols signifying these other sources of power. Planters such as William Byrd and Landon Carter, who kept extensive diaries, depicted their daily exertions of authority in graphic physical terms. Slaves could be whipped, shackled, or medicated; wives and enslaved women could be compelled to engage in sexual intercourse; children's diets and bodily functions required careful monitoring. Although men like Byrd and Carter tended to write self-consciously about their authority as being public and political, their management of the bodies in their households was perhaps the most vivid expression of their power.

If ever Virginia gentlemen were patriarchs, it was between 1700 and 1750. Yet, even at the peak of their power, planters compared themselves unfavourably to their English counterparts and worried that their domestic authority was being usurped. Some of their anxiety was a consequence of unrealistic expectations for hegemonic power, the tortured perfectionism of colonials who could never achieve enough of an English inflection. They were, after all, more successful as a ruling class than almost any other colonial elite, although they seemed to take little comfort in this achievement. Perhaps the collective disappointments of daily life proved too great for such ambitious, anxious men. Much to the frustration of would-be patriarchs, dependents did not passively await the planter's imprimatur on their bodies. Rather, enslaved people ran away, wives disobeyed, and children ignored their father's words of advice. Even voters, over whom planters had the least physical power but the steadiest symbolic authority, might turn a man out of office.

The ethos of self-mastery and domestic tranquillity that began to appear in eighteenth-century planter journals and letters reflected the limits of coercive power exercised on bodies, but it did not signify an end to that power. Planters continued to practice regimes of corporal punishment on recalcitrant slaves and, less frequently, disobedient servants and children even as quiet displays of sacrosanct authority, rooted in the planter's appearance of self-governance, gradually crept into elite discussions of power. Such a style represented domestic authority as unimpeachable by denying the existence of challenges that might undermine it. The quieter ideal also signaled the rise of a new technology of elite male power in which planters portrayed themselves as the guardians of reason and tranquillity, whereas white women, slaves of both sexes, children, and disorderly common folk were described as being unable to control their passions. Paternalistic styles of authority may have partially masked the cruder side of planter power, but they never fully displaced it.

By the eighteenth century, elite planters believed habitual self-control, rooted in rural plantation life, was the key to exercising power over others. Male planters diligently applied this maxim to their emotional lives early in the century and, with increasing difficulty as the century progressed, to their drinking, eating, spending, and gambling habits. With authority resting in the ability to control one's emotions, many planters placed great value on keeping anger and grief in check.

Gentlemen on both sides of the Atlantic associated emotional restraint with class position, race, and gender identity. Elite men interpreted control over emotions such as anger, sadness, and lust as the triumph of reason over passion. White women of all classes, lower-class white men, and enslaved men and women, many writers believed, were less capable of governing their appetites than elite men. Through control over self, gentlemen reminded themselves, they would have control over others. White women also made use of this discourse of reason and passion, as seen in the poem by Elizabeth Pratt. Maria Byrd, second wife of William II, articulated a similar association between slaves and passion in a letter to her son William III in which she reprimanded him for his neglect of his children's education and upbringing. His daughter's "chief time is spent with servants and Negro children her play fellows," complained Mrs. Byrd, "from whom she had learnt a dreadfull collection of words, and is intolerably passionate."

Beliefs in the efficacy of self-restraint and attempts to weave it into a technology of power contained special benefits for colonial men. Most were already battling feelings of vulnerability to elite patrons and merchants in London and worried about losing touch with London political networks. It may have been reassuring to efface within oneself all vestiges of the qualities one associated with other vulnerable individuals—wives, children, and slaves—and to insist, emphatically, that these others were repositories of unreasonable passions. Already prone to try too hard to be like English gentlemen, men like William Byrd II made a science of emotional and physical self-containment; Byrd recorded his emotional fluctuations in the same detail he did his diet, his daily physical exercise, his bowel movements, and his sexual encounters. If self-control was a quality to be admired in gentlemen, Byrd seemed to believe, he would perform the part flawlessly, striving toward the artful effortlessness expressed by Alexander Pope in an epigram on graceful writing: "True ease in writing comes from Art, not Chance/As one moves easily who has learned to dance." As we have already noted, many of Virginia's elite planters claimed that their rural estates presented the ideal environment for achieving this elusive goal.

Byrd recorded his daily battles for emotional self-restraint in the cryptic code of his secret diary. After the death of his nine-month-old son, Byrd tersely compared his own and his wife's reactions:

> I rose at 6 o'clock and as soon as I came out news was brought that the child was very ill. We went out and found him just ready to die and he died about 8 o'clock in the morning. God gives and God takes away; blessed be the name of God.... My wife was much afflicted but I submitted to His judgement better, notwithstanding I was very sensible of my loss, but God's will be done.

In the days to come, Byrd expressed concern over the intensity of his wife's grief and noted differences in their ability to submit to God's will. On the day after the boy's death, Byrd noted, "My wife had several fits of tears for our dear son but kept within the bounds of submission." Although Byrd claimed to have "submitted to His judgement better," his restraint seems to have exacted a toll; during the boy's last day of illness, Byrd developed "gripes" in his stomach, which tormented him for nearly two weeks after his son's death. This was the same illness, moreover, that afflicted him when worry, regret, grief, or anger threatened to overwhelm his efforts to control his emotions.

Despite his efforts at self-control, Byrd's life did not even come close to the domestic ideal of tranquility to which many elite Virginians aspired. Lucy and William fought frequently and bitterly. Byrd recorded one such exchange in which he barely retained control of himself: "My wife flew into such a passion that she hoped she would be revenged of me. I was moved very much at this but only thanked her for the present lest I should say things foolish in my passion." Several days later, although they had patched up their differences, Byrd wrote angrily, "I was out of humor with my wife for her foolish passions, of which she is often guilty, for which God forgive her and make her repent and amend." After intervening in his wife's violent corrections of his slave Jenny, Byrd recorded a similarly upsetting outburst: "She lifted up her hands to strike me but forebore to do it. She gave me abundance of bad words and endeavored to strangle herself, but I believe in jest only. However after acting a mad woman a long time she was passive again." Byrd's diary is littered with similar references to quarrels he claimed were started by his wife's passion and descriptions of her fits of tears and hysteria. In his view, passions unchecked, which he usually attributed to women, were nearly always the source of domestic discord....

Although master-slave relationships more frequently featured coercion than did other social relations involving elite planters, slaves successfully moved their masters toward a paternalistic style of authority by midcentury. Planters also had their reasons for preferring persuasion and personal ties to physical punishment, but the paternalism they envisioned was quite different from that of their slaves. Whereas enslaved people advanced a moral economy in which reasonable work conditions, adequate provisions, and respect for family ties all became part of a concept of just treatment within slavery, planters sought docile, respectful, and efficient obedience that confirmed their sense of righteous mastery....

White planters' attitudes about race, honor, and sexuality found expression in myriad ways that were annoying and humiliating for enslaved people. Byrd reported with amusement that, while staying at a friend's house, he threw a pan of water out his window, drenching a slave woman. High society parties in Williamsburg occasionally included raffles of slaves; at one such event, a black woman described as "fit for house business" was raffled off along with her child. Elite women described their black female servants as dirty and ugly and associated skill and tractability with light skin. Infusing an age-old epigram with new racial and social significance, one white woman communicated what she saw as an enslaved woman's limited potential for obedient and efficient domestic service by referring to the permanence of her color: "Julitt will never be washt white."

Most important to this matrix of dishonor, however, was the intertwining of race and sexuality in white male planters' attitudes toward their slaves. Although it is possible only to conjecture about the frequency with which white men visited slave quarters for the specific purpose of sexually exploiting enslaved women, there is evidence that this did indeed happen—and that its occurrence was enmeshed in attitudes about sexual domination, slave promiscuity, and sexual dishonor. As a married man approaching the age of seventy, Byrd frequently engaged in sexual activity with enslaved women, perhaps as many as nine times during a period of eighteen months. These were the only incidents of sexual activity he recorded during this time. Byrd was not alone. His brother-in-law, John Custis, allegedly maintained a long-term relationship with an enslaved woman named Alice by whom he fathered a son. The boy, Christoforo John, received special mention in his father's will.

Many historians have interpreted the sexual interests of white planters in their dependent female slaves as evidence of intimacy or racial fluidity, indicative of white people's willingness to relate to their slaves as human beings. These analyses fail to account for the skewed gender pattern of interracial sexuality among the Virginia gentry—white men and enslaved women—and for the way it reinforced the power relations encoded in legally sanctioned gender and racial hierarchies. Although it would be wrong to assume that all such relationships were a product of coercion, it is important to note that all occurred in a context where coercion was never far beneath the surface. Female slaves stood relatively disempowered compared to their masters both as black women and as unfree people. Their patterns of sexual interaction with white masters were thus part of a larger field of power relations in which masters expressed power sexually and viewed sexual activity as an expression of male power.

Confronted with the considerable power of planters, enslaved people repackaged and redirected patriarchal authority, making absolute dominance impossible. As a young planter, William Byrd frequently found himself foiled by his slaves' collaboration, despite his attempts to reinforce his authority with harsh punishments. Byrd's slave Jenny, for example, tried twice to save the slave Eugene from further punishment for bed-wetting by concealing the soiled linens; a whipping from Byrd, moreover, did not discourage her from making the second attempt. Byrd's maid Anaka, who had herself stolen rum from the liquor cellar, collaborated with the white woman "Nurse" to give the black maid Prue access to the cellar....

Planters' desires for domestic harmony offered enslaved people an opportunity to extract concessions conducive to family life, but the same ideal also provided masters with an overarching rationale for intervening in slaves' disputes. Articulated hopes for a serene domestic environment, moreover, were not incompatible with other tactics, including the denial of family privileges and outright coercion. Planters like Byrd occasionally involved themselves in the conflicts of enslaved people at the request of one of the parties in an effort to restore peace. Byrd injected himself into the troubled relations of married slaves, imposing a monogamous standard to which even he did not adhere. He recorded in his secret diary for 1710 that he "caused L——s——n to be whipped for beating his wife and Jenny was whipped for being his whore." Byrd also intervened in relationships that threatened to breed more serious conflicts. He reported that he ordered "Johnny to be whipped for threatening to strike Jimmy and caused Moll also to be whipped and made them renounce one the other." Occasionally, Byrd's deeper motive for enforcing tranquil relations—the maintenance of his own authority—surfaced in his dealings with enslaved people. "At night I talked with my people and refused to let P——p——l go to see his wife," he wrote in an entry for August 1720. Although, in this instance, Byrd denied a family privilege to a slave, his actions were not inconsistent with his previous efforts to foster domestic harmony. In both situations, he attempted to impose his will upon slaves he referred to as "my people," curbing their rights to vent anger against each other and forbidding them to leave the premises of Westover to visit spouses.

Byrd's interventions in enslaved peoples' relationships were part of a larger effort to protect his own use of "discipline" from being confused with mere violence. Like gifts of liquor and evening visits to the quarters, such interventions blunted the sharpest edges of patriarchal authority and may have prevented the escalation of master-slave conflicts into episodes of violent resistance or running away. On several occasions, as already noted, challenges to Byrd's exclusive right to use violence came not just from enslaved people but from his own wife. Byrd correctly perceived that physical contests between Lucy Byrd and the female slaves in his household did nothing to enhance white authority and much to diminish it, threatening to turn the exercise of discipline into a brawl. The subjection of enslaved people to Lucy Byrd's intensely corporal exercise of authority also disrupted his own attempts to achieve peaceful order in the household. Although Byrd himself had sometimes resorted to cruel punishments of enslaved people, he had done so as an expression of will, a flexing of patriarchal muscle that underscored more genteel manifestations of power. Uncontrolled outbursts of violence—which to Byrd meant all violent acts initiated by others—undermined his attempts to rule effortlessly over household members, disturbing his calculus of persuasion, warning, and inflicted pain.

Of all the social relations constituting and trying planters' authority, master-slave relationships were the least distanced from outright coercion. Planter efforts to achieve a genteel, restrained authority over their households somewhat mitigated the physical cruelty inherent in slavery, cushioning it with reciprocity and rhetorical, if not actual, gestures toward recognizing the existence of slave families. Planters' efforts to cultivate intimate personal relationships with enslaved people, however, supplemented rather than precluded the use of cruel punishments. Paternalism only represented an improvement of conditions for slaves if enslaved people themselves made it so. Evening walks around the plantation grounds to talk with laborers, gifts of liquor, and intervention in slave relationships allowed masters intimate access to enslaved peoples' lives, increasing the dangers of unwanted sexual contact for enslaved women. Eighteenth-century paternalism thus left an ambiguous legacy, offering a tissue-thin layer of protection from harsh corporal punishment and leaving enslaved women more vulnerable to the sexual desires of their masters....

Virginia's elite planters were at the height of their powers as a class during the first half of the eighteenth century. Compared to their seventeenth-century counterparts, they enjoyed longer lives, more stable families, larger estates, and greater security. Compared to gentlemen in other parts of the British Empire, they were a political success story, a stable regime whose most serious challenge at mid-century came from the crown rather than from below.

Despite these considerable achievements and their very real control over most of their society's resources, Virginia's elite planters were never able to allay self-doubts about the security and legitimacy of their positions. Even the most powerful of planters occasionally lost an election, fell victim to fluctuating tobacco prices, or failed to make a suitable impression on a metropolitan contact. Domestic authority, moreover, also proved elusive. In the relationships most fundamental to their patriarchal identities, men like William Byrd, Landon Carter, and Joseph Ball met with disobedience and recalcitrance. Wives refused to obey their husbands, children flouted their father's will, and slaves ran away. These acts of defiance troubled Virginia's gentlemen as much as, if not more than, their public failures because they occurred in a context in which planters' legal, economic, and coercive power was virtually untrammeled. If they were not patriarchs in their own households, many men seem to have wondered, could they hope to be gentlemen in the eyes of the colony's voters, their gentry peers, or London society?...

Relationships between masters and slaves proved to be the most difficult to recast according to the ethic of domestic tranquillity. Although the ideal of slave family integrity had begun to enter planter discourse by the 1730s, allowing slaves to press claims to remain near family members, violence and brutality continued to punctuate the relationship. Planters were more likely to inflict corporal punishment on enslaved people than they were on wives and white children. They were also more likely to experiment on their bound laborers with harsh medicines. Rhetoric about domestic harmony rarely protected enslaved people from the violence inherent in slavery.

Although the master-slave relationship was distinctive because of the violent technologies of power that lay at its core, it remained connected to other relationships of power in slaveowning households. The sexual exploitation of enslaved women, for example, was closely akin to planter conceptualizations of sex and power more generally. Planters who viewed sexual intercourse as a natural outgrowth of male dominance and female appetite easily transformed such an expression of power into domination over slave women. Perhaps most important, slavery allowed planters to showcase their coercive power without disturbing ideals for harmonious relationships with white family members. Far from proving incompatible with the ethos of domestic tranquillity, the coercion of slaves may have made such ideals possible, providing planters with a suitable foil for the serene authority they hoped to wield over wives and children.

In the absence of any significant erosion of the economic and political foundations of planters' power between 1700 and 1750, it would be mistaken to conclude that paternalistic styles represented a lesser authority than patriarchal ones. An examination of the full complement of planters' social relations reveals paternalism—in the guise of the ideals of domestic tranquillity—to be one face of patriarchy, not a softer replacement of it. Rooted in coercion, slavery remained a perpetual reminder of the limits of domestic harmony and gentility, compelling planters to confront the fact that much of their authority depended upon their ability to inflict pain.

The Effects of Paternalism Among Whites and Blacks

PHILIP D. MORGAN

The free and the unfree engaged in endless and varied encounters. To comprehend these kaleidoscopic contacts between masters and slaves, whites and blacks requires complex formulations. However cruelly whites exploited blacks, their fates were intricately intertwined. However much masters treated their slaves as chattels, the humanity of their property could not be ignored or evaded. However total the masters' exercise of power, negotiation, and compromise were necessary to make slavery function. However sincerely planter patriarchs stressed mutuality and reciprocity, their authority ultimately rested on force. However sentimentally and benevolently some late-eighteenth-century masters viewed slaves, their relentless denial of rights to bondmen increasingly placed slaves

From *Slave Counterpoint: Black Culture in the Eighteenth-Century Chesapeake and Lowcountry* by Philip D. Morgan. Published for the Omohundro Institute of Early American History and Culture. Copyright © 1998 by the University of North Carolina Press. Used by permission of the publisher.

outside society. However unequivocally daily existence brought blacks and whites together, growing race consciousness and class distinctions thrust them apart. However deep a chasm opened between whites and blacks, channels of communication arose to bridge it. However fundamentally slavery was the result of interaction between master and slave, nonslaveholders intruded to shape the institution's character. The intricacy of eighteenth-century white-black relations defies easy definition....

The dominant social ethos and cultural metaphor of seventeenth- and early-eighteenth-century Anglo-America, patriarchalism, embodied the ideal of an organic social hierarchy. Invoking the Great Chain of Being, one Virginia lawyer argued in 1772: "Societies of men could not subsist unless there were a subordination of one to another.... That in this subordination the department of slaves must be filled by some, or there would be a defect in the scale of order." Deeply ingrained assumptions about the workings not only of society but also of politics elevated the role of father to mythic heights. From this perspective, patriarchs anchored a social system based on the protection that the powerful offered the weak, just as monarchs defined a political system where royal power defended the people in return for their obedience and loyalty. Indeed, masters might draw a precise parallel, as Henry Laurens once did when he reflected, "Never was an absolute Monarch more happy in his Subjects than at the Present time I am." Suffusing the thought of the age, the patriarchal outlook was an austere code, emphasizing control, obedience, discipline, and severity. Yet patriarchalism also involved protection, guardianship, and reciprocal obligations. It defined the gentleman planter's self-image and constituted the ideals and standards by which slaveholding behavior was judged....

... Patriarchalism was reformulated over the course of the eighteenth century. Masters began to speak less of duties and obligations, more of individual rights, particularly property rights. Slaves were more and more defined as people without rights; and, because they were viewed increasingly as property, they were said to enhance their owners' independence. Whereas the patriarchal ethos held that even the lowliest person was part of an organic society, the denial of rights could place the slave completely outside society. In part because slaves were being seen as perpetual outsiders, masters could emphasize solicitude rather than authority, sentiments rather than severity, in their governance. This shift in emphasis was partly a response to political events but also resulted from the development of a more affectionate family life, the rise of evangelicalism, the growth of romanticism, and the increase of humanitarianism. It was a reflection in the realm of ideas of broad-gauged changes affecting Revolutionary America. Austere patriarchalism slowly gave way to mellow paternalism....

The duality of growing separation and common bonds applied as much to the relationship of plain white folk and blacks as it did to large planters and their slaves. Because in the late seventeenth century poor whites associated closely and openly with slaves, the growing gap between them was notable. Relations between poor whites and blacks were also part of a larger tangled web that enmeshed patriarchs, plain folks, and slaves. The existence of a large group of plain white folks, for example, encouraged planters to seek their support and recognition. To the degree that nonslaveholders honored slave-holders, they enhanced the large planters' social legitimacy. Slaves in turn saw proud, free white men defer to powerful masters, reinforcing in their eyes the authority of large planters. Paradoxically, the ties established between patriarchs and plain folks could strengthen those between grandees and slaves....

One of the reasons why slavery with all its attendant ambiguities could be readily assimilated into the early modern Anglo-American world was a long-standing patriarchal tradition that had clearly defined the relationship between master and servant. Manuals of household government in sixteenth- and seventeenth-century England spoke of servants as they did of wives and children. All were subservient members of the family, living under the authority of the paterfamilias. Gentlemen were not to let their care stop at their own children. "Let it reach to your menial servants," they were instructed, for "though you are their master, you are also their father." The relationship between master and servant received the highest ideological sanction in the concept of patriarch-alism. Patriarchal doctrines can be found, as one historian has argued, in all strata of thought in seventeenth-century England, "from well-ordered and self-conscious theories ... to the unstated prejudices of the inarticulate masses." A deep respect for rank and hierarchy infused the very marrow of the early modern British American world, and at its core lay the authority of the father-figure in his household.

Many eighteenth-century masters of slaves conspicuously defined themselves in light of this venerable tradition. None more so perhaps than William Byrd II, who in a famous passage took a quasi-spiritual view of his role, likening himself to a biblical patriarch amid his bondmen and bondwomen. Similarly, it required little imagination for a South Carolina planter to "fancy [him]self one of the Patriarchs of old ... being surrounded with near 200 Negroes who are guided by my absolute Command." As the most dependent members of the patriarchal family, slaves were, according to the Reverend Thomas Bacon of Maryland, "an immediate and necessary part of our household." He emphasized that "next to our children and brethren by blood, our servants, and especially our slaves, are certainly in the nearest relation to us." A Jesuit priest echoed his Anglican coun-terpart when he stated, "Charity to Negroes is due from all[,] particularly their Masters." As members of Christ, he continued, black slaves were "to be dealt with in a charitable, Christian, paternal manner."

Plantation owners in the eighteenth-century South were especially prone to think of themselves as all-powerful father figures. Plantation America was a remarkably underinstitutionalized world. An attenuated social and economic in-frastructure enhanced the authority of the household head. Moreover, household authority expanded rather than contracted over the colonial period in the South. Even though early modern Britain and Western Europe are generally thought to have had a more hierarchical social structure than colonial America, Carole Shammas rightly notes that "a notably higher proportion of people in the Americas," particularly in plantation America "fell into the category of legal dependents." Not accidentally, "the first thing" Robinson Crusoe did in the ad-vancement of his New World plantation was to purchase "a negro slave, and an

European servant"; he soon had prospects of becoming "a rich and thriving man" in his "new Plantation." Crusoe was later shipwrecked en route to Africa to acquire more slaves. Marooned, Crusoe establishes "two plantations." Crusoe is generally good to Friday, but, as Christopher Hill points out, the first word he taught him was "Master." Eventually, Crusoe acquires both native and foreign labor and begins to envisage himself in monarchical terms. Since the "whole country" was his property, Crusoe mused, he had "undoubted right of dominion," and since "my people," as he significantly termed them, were "perfectly subjected," he was "absolute lord and lawgiver." The family was the foundation of the plantation social order, and its head was lord, master, a monarch in miniature. In a sequel, Crusoe returns bearing goods, to be told he "was a father" to this people. He himself was "pleased" with "being the patron of those people I placed there, and doing for them in a kind of haughty majestic way, like an old patriarchal monarch; providing for them, as if I had been father of the whole family, as well as of the plantation." Defoe had shrewdly caught the tenor of idealized plantation life.

Patriarchalism cannot be dismissed as mere propaganda or apologetics—although, like all ideological rationalizations, it contained its share of self-serving cant; rather, it was an authentic, if deeply flawed, worldview. Its familial rhetoric was not just a smokescreen for exploitation, because patriarchalism offered no guarantee of benevolence. It was no sentimental self-image, but rather a harsh creed. Patriarchs in ancient Rome exercised the right to dispatch wives, children, and slaves. In Virginia, a law of 1669 allowed masters the Roman "power of the father" over the life and death of a slave, but later legislation balanced the interests of the state, masters, and white nonslaveholders with minimal protections for slaves. Although the despotic powers of masters were moderated, the cruel and authoritarian core of patriarchalism helps explain why patriarchs could ignore the enormity of what they did to their slave families. Fathers, after all, do not normally sell their children. But when patriarchs spoke of their family, both white and black, their protective domination contained little of the warmth or tenderness associated with modern familial relations....

... [A] more enlightened patriarchalism [emerged] in the second half of the eighteenth century.... Patriarchal doctrines and strategies were transformed more generally in at least three major directions. First, although late-eighteenth-century masters continued to stress order and authority, they were more inclined to emphasize their solicitude toward and generous treatment of their dependents. Second, no self-respecting patriarch would speak cloyingly of his kindness toward his slaves, but gradually masters began to express such sentiments and came in return to expect gratitude, even love, from their bondpeople. Their outlook became far more sentimental. Third, patriarchs rarely boasted of the submissiveness or docility of their bondpeople, but gradually masters began to create the fiction of the contented and happy slave. This shift in patriarchal strategies—greater softness, more reciprocity, less authoritarianism—had complex origins. In part it was a response to political and military events, but it owed far more to broader developments—a more affectionate family environment, the rise of evangelicalism, romanticism, and humanitarianism, and a growing emphasis on private property rights. Gradually it blossomed in the nineteenth century into full-blown paternalism.

Late-eighteenth-century masters sometimes appealed to rather than threatened their slaves. This change of emphasis may be attributed in part to the temporary disruption of the masters' power caused by the Revolutionary crisis. During wartime and in the early postwar years, in particular, master often had little control over their slaves. Threats were useless; exhortations became commonplace. Thus, there was the spectacle of a South Carolina slave, resident in Saint Augustine in 1784, telling his master's envoy that he was prepared to return home "willingly ... but not at present." The master's spokesman was reduced to hoping that he "might be able to persuade him" to return earlier than the slave intended. Or there was Maria Byrd's Wat, a Virginia slave who had aided the British during the war and resided in New York in the spring of 1783. Byrd assured Wat that he could "come home with Safety." She had heard that he "wishes much to return, and his wife and Children are very anxious to see him"; these were her "inducements for wishing him to come back." She was prepared to overlook past actions; indeed, she was even prepared to engage Wat's services in recovering her other lost slaves. For these "good offices," Wat would receive a "handsome" reward. She did not expect that any of her absent slaves would "return willingly whatever they may pretend to." But "to make them more happy if they are sent me," she wanted them to know that no slaves, to her knowledge, had been punished on their return and that her slaves "may rely on the best usage."

The seeming loyalty of many other slaves who did not flee their masters during the Revolutionary war, however, contributed to the growing myth that slaves might be content in their condition. In the summer of 1776, Henry Laurens proudly recorded that his slaves "to a Man are strongly attached to me ... hitherto not one of them has attempted to desert." These claims of loyalty may be more important for what they say of the owners' perceptions than what they record of the slaves' behavior. But, after the war had ended, Laurens contrasted the "faithless" behavior of his white servants with the "fidelity" of his slaves, "a very few instances excepted." As a result, he noted, "we are endeavouring to reward those and make the whole happy." Making them happy was a prescient remark. Late in life, Laurens took great pride in his various labor-saving experiments that reduced the arduousness of his slaves' labor. These "improvements," he maintained, "are the pleasure of my life, more particularly as they contribute to bring my poor blacks to a level with the happiest peasants to be found in Europe"—a refrain that would echo down the corridors of Sothern history.

A more caring attitude toward slaves also arose as the strength of their family ties became recognizable to masters and as family life in general became more egalitarian and affectionate. In 1764, James Habersham was "affected" by the death of one of his slave women, not just because she had been a favorite of his late wife or because she had nursed two of his daughters, but because she had left behind an "inconsolable" husband. Eight years later, he recalled that he had buried almost eighty slaves during his lifetime and in each case had "acquiessed in the Dispensation of divine Providence." However, he found it impossible to "divest myself of Humanity," as he put it, at the events surrounding a recent slave death. It concerned a slave boy bitten by a rabid dog.

"The Cries and Intreaties of the Mother begging her Child to be put to Death," wrote the shaken master, "the dreadfull shreiks of the Boy, and his more than pretty Behaviour in his taking leave of all around him, has rung such a Peal in my Ears, that I never can forget." Late-eighteenth-century masters seemed much more respectful of slave family ties than their predecessors. Gangs were often sold "in families" rather than individually, and many a prospective purchaser stated a preference for family units. When a South Carolina slave patron became "dissatisfied and desirous of being sold," his master was quick to assure prospective buyers that the man's wife has also to be sold "for a principle of humanity *alone,*" because "they were very unwilling to be separated." ...

Enlightened patriarchalism had limits. Where it collided with self-interest and commercial advantage, the slave invariably lost. According to one early-nineteenth-century observer, Georgia slaves were "considered nothing more than perishable property, and interest not principle clothes and feeds them." Similarly, in the early nineteenth century, a South Carolina master was willing to speak cynically of the conflict between his slaves' desire for freedom and his property rights. He described the motivations of his runaways and his own response in this way: "Liberty is sweet and in that they are right—property is comfortable and if I can stop them, I will also be right."

A sense of the flexibility and ultimate rigidity of enlightened patriarchalism is unwittingly captured in the self-justifying remarks of a loyalist slaveholder. "In this land of Nominal freedom and actual Slavery," he had been able, he admitted, to "justify the keeping my fellow beings in bondage" by alleviating the "too common weight of the[ir] chains." He explained that he "scarce used the rod except for theft and other crimes" and, for his slaves' "encouragement," provided ample supplies of corn, meat two or three times a week, and a regular and adequate clothing allowance. Not that his "slaves are used better than any others," he acknowledged, for "some Masters I know, and I hope there are many, treat theirs with the utmost humanity." At the same time, however, he was proud of how he had secured his slaves' respect. "By selling a few, who proved obstinately bad," he had "brought the others to consider their being sold" as the "greatest punishment I can inflict." He had found that the "greatest incitement to their duty" lay in their "hopes of living and dying on my property without being separated from their families, connexions, and friends." It hardly became this generous-spirited master—and, presumably, by the lights of eighteenth-century Anglo-American masterdom, he was exactly that—to rail at the possibility that his slaves might be confiscated and be "subject to the most humiliating circumstance of human nature—that of being sold like the *Brutes that perish.*"

As this master implies, humane treatment did not have to conflict with economic benefit, nor did modes of control have to be crudely coercive. Masters employed a variety of positive incentives to achieve their aims. In fact, compassion could maximum profits and enhance the masters' investment in their slaves. The threat of sale was perhaps even more effective than the whip in keeping slaves in line. When the duc de La Rochefoucauld-Liancourt visited the Lowcountry in the late eighteenth century, he encountered planters willing to laud the advantages of their new approach. One "excellent master to his negroes" claimed, "against the opinion of many others, that the plantations of mild and indulgent masters thrive most, and that the negroes are more faithful and laborious" than those who belonged to severe masters.

Paradoxically, masters felt that they could show more indulgence toward their slaves as they increasingly placed them outside civil society. As North Americans affirmed the absolute value of individual liberty, the only effective way to justify slavery was to exclude its victim from the community of man. When all free inhabitants were seen as enjoying certain unalienable rights, slaves had to be defined as lacking all rights. Moreover, as liberty was predicated on the acquisition and maintenance of private property, so slaveowners' rights to their slaves became inviolable. Slaves enhanced the independence of their owners. Arbitrarily deprive someone of his or her possessions, and that person become a slave. Whereas the partriarchal ethos held that even the lowliest person was part of an organic society, the denial of rights to slaves and the conception of private property as a basic natural right placed slaves outside society altogether. Ironically, as slavery became more firmly entrenched, masters could show more benevolence toward their dependents.

In thoroughgoing patriarchal households, the subjection of slaves was absolute and unquestioned. The master was first cause, prime mover, almost a demigod. Restraint, order, and authority were constant watchwords. Gradually, however, new values infiltrated his patriarchal citadel. Masters began to view themselves less as harsh taskmasters grandly presiding over their estates and more as benefactors providing for their dependents. They preferred to see their relationship with their slaves grounded less in the tradition of divine right than in voluntary, consensual terms. Austere, rigid patriarichalism gave way to warm, mellow paternalism. By the early nineteenth century, William Moultrie reflected on the changes that had occurred. "I am very much pleased to see the treatment of the slaves in the country is altered so much," he observed, particularly noting the "tenderness and humanity" now extended to slaves. Slavery would soon be viewed as a benign institution; slaves would, in George Fitzhugh's exaggerated words, be enveloped in "domestic affection"; before long, it would be the master for whom pity would be invoked as "the greatest slave" of all....

Plain Folk and Slaves

In general, the distance between plain white folk and black slaves grew progressively wider throughout the course of the eighteenth century. In the middle to late seventeenth century, black slaves and the poorer sections of the white community, particularly servants, associated closely and openly. By the turn of the eighteenth century, however, cooperation and alliances between white servants and black slaves began to dissolve, in part because of actions taken by the planter class, in part because servant numbers declined, and in part because the black population became more numerous and alien. Most of these processes remained at work well into the eighteenth century. Yet, the ruling class was never completely successful in wooing lower-class whites to their cause; the importation of twenty thousand convicts into the Chesapeake during the eighteenth century meant that servant ranks were never negligible—at least in that region; and, as the black population creolized, so it again became possible for lower-class whites and blacks to identify with one another. The gap between lower-class whites and blacks widened in the second half of the eighteenth century, but more slowly than before.

The growing divide that separated lower-class whites from blacks had its limits. However much the ruling class attempted to separate the races, plain white folk and slaves still shared their lives in ways impermissible for a planter-patriarch and his bondpeople. Slaves and plain white folk not only lived nearer to one another but were more likely to work alongside one another, speak the same dialect, have their children play together, commit crimes jointly, and run away together. Contacts between plain white folk and slaves were also more regular and frequent in some places than others. They were more evident in the Cheasapeake than in the Lowcountry; in both regions, they were more evident on the periphery and in towns than in plantation heartlands. Contact between plain white folk and slaves also fluctuated over time. Even though gap between the two gradually widened over the eighteenth century, the Revolutionary crisis proved that some poor whites and slaves could still cooperate....

From cradle to grave, plain white folk and black slaves lived near one another. Thus, although a patriarch's child might occasionally play with slaves of the same age, such contact was almost inevitable for the children of plain white folk. Charles Drayton became aware of such activity when his slave boy Jack, waiting on an overseer at an outlying plantation, came to Drayton Hall with a broken arm and dislocated shoulder, the product of his "idly riding about the fields with the ov[erseer's] son." Growing up in a poor white home might mean sharing living space with blacks, certainly living close to them, sharing much the same diet and clothes. Death, too, might bring lowly white and slave together, as in the scene described by a visitor to Maryland's Eastern Shore: "Last evening at dark the corps [of overseer Nathan Cullins] was put in a plain coffin, and conveyed to the grave, by four negroes, and one carrying a spade and shovel—No other person attended." A white overseer went to his grave unrecognized, except by the blacks with whom he labored....

Although white solidarity could never be assumed in eighteenth-century Virginia or South Carolina, and although a surprising level of cooperation between lower-class whites and blacks persisted through the century, the trend was in the opposite direction. Proximity of estate induced some plain white folk to throw their lot with slaves, but more often it spurred most to put as much distance as possible between themselves and bondpeople. The eighteenth century was a crucible in which the deep and increasingly reciprocal contempt felt between lower-class whites and blacks was forged. That contempt had not emerged in fully polished form by 1800, but the essentials were in place.

The gentry helped foster lower-class contempt for slaves by aligning plain folk on their side. At the end of the seventeenth century, gentlemen busily created a legal framework that gave advantages to lower-class whites at the expense of blacks. Throughout the eighteenth century, ... the status of plain white folk rose. In part, this improvement was inadvertent, a consequence of a broadly based, rising prosperity; but ruling class efforts to reduce taxes and to involve plain folk in the political process worked to the same end. More directly relevant to their interests as slaveholders, the gentry held out inducements to lower-class whites in order that they might support and police their respective slave societies. The gentry was not uniformly successful where patrolling was concerned, but the capture of runaways seems to have been a particularly rewarding activity. Eighteenth-century Virginia county court records list several thousand claims for the capture of runaways. The vast majority of claimants were individuals outside the gentry, whereas almost two-thirds of the captured blacks belonged to members of the gentry. The ruling class had recruited plain white folk to support its interests....

The resentments of poor whites toward slaves were spontaneously generated, not just encouraged from above. After all, many poor whites accurately perceived that slaves posed a threat to their livelihoods. In the Lowcountry this menace was most acute in Charleston, where a variety of white artisans expressed indignation at competition from black workers. Over the course of the eighteenth century, ship-wrights, chimney sweeps, house carpenters, brick-layers, cordwainers, master coopers, and master tailors banded together in turn to complain that blacks were taking their jobs. Their inability to halt this process was hardly designed to make them look kindly on their black counterparts. In the countryside, skilled and semi-skilled white labor increasingly felt the pressure of black competition as native-born slaves assumed positions ranging from boatman to blacksmith, wheelwright to wagoner. The nature of rural life, however, made it difficult for white laborers to organize and protest. One exception was a group of South Carolina patroons who in 1744 complained of "several Planters and others in this Province, who did order, permit and appoint their Negro Slaves to be constantly employed to go as Masters or Patroons of their Pettiaugers or small vessels without my White man on board to take any charge or care of such vessels, which hindered the Petitioners from being constantly employed there."

If plain white folk could befriend slaves and yet just as easily persecute them viciously, this ambivalence was not solely a white prerogative. Slaves sometimes turned against their erstwhile allies. They might, for example, be instrumental in the arrest of poor whites. In 1723, two York County planters claimed expenses for the capture of a runaway white servant through the combined efforts of their slaves. Sixteen years later, a witness in a Virginia county court case reported that at four o'clock in the morning he had heard "an uproar without amongst the People" and had found that his slaves had apprehended a white man who was robbing their meat house. In 1790, two whites visited the Nomini Hall estate in Lancaster County and asked directions of Robert Carter's overseer. Because it was night, the overseer was suspicious, but he let them pass. They made their way to the granary, where Carter's slave Solomon "got up and took his axe in his hand, went out and called them to, and asked them to go into his House, and warm themselves.... [T]hey accepted of his invitation—Solomon gave them some Bread, made them a good Fire, they laid down on some boards and fell asleep—Solomon suspecting they were the men that lately escaped from Northumberland Jail" went to the overseer and rounded up a number of slaves sufficient to arrest his two unsuspecting visitors. Friendly, trusting slaves were not always what they seemed.

Slaves adopted even subtler methods to provoke hostility from plain white folk. An overseer employed by Landon Carter complained that Carter's waiting man, Nassau, had "refused to bleed him." When Carter confronted the slave, Nassau denied the story, saying the overseer had "only asked a vomit of him and he gave him one." Nassau was then sent to the sick man on his "honor not to touch a drop of Spirits" and with instructions to use both blister and lancet if necessary. Apparently, Nassau broke his promise and got drunk; perhaps that helps explain why the overseers died two days later. Slaves persecuted by word as well as by action. Morgan Godwyn observed that slaves contemptuously taunted the Irish with the claim "that if the Irishman's country had first lighted in the Englishman's way, he might have gone no further to look for Negro's." As Eugene Genovese has remarked, it was probably slaves who coined the term "po'r white trash." ...

Relations between plain white folk and slaves are instructive in two important ways. The rift that progressively opened between the two was portentous for North America's future. Throughout the eighteenth century, whites gradually moved toward a sense of communal solidarity and purpose through their debasement of blacks. White unity was never fully achieved, but Chesapeake and Lowcountry slave societies moved steadily to a position where, functionally, they rested on a rationale of racial superiority. At the same time, lower-class whites had an ameliorative effect on the character of the two emerging slave systems. Where a large group of plain folk existed, as preeminently in Virginia, but to a lesser degree also in South Carolina, masters courted their support and generally received their recognition. The master class thus gained in legitimacy and respect, and the society as a whole could afford to have pretensions to culture and civilization. By contrast, the absence of a substantial class of nonslaveholding whites, as in many slave societies of the Caribbean and Dutch East Indies, helps explain why slavery in these places became so brutal and degrading to slaves and masters. Lower-class whites played a vital role in determining the nature of any slave society.

Encounters between whites and blacks in the eighteenth-century South were never simple or straightforward. As much as masters treated slaves as chattels, they were unable to ignore their inescapable humanity. As much as they devised barbarous laws to hamstring their slaves, they also sought ways to mitigate the impact of legislation. As much as they subjected slaves to personal domination, they also offered them personal protection. As much as they inflicted unspeakable cruelties on slaves, they also established warm and caring relationships with them. As much as they viewed slaves as animals, they never doubted slaves' desire for liberty and capacity to rebel. As much as they spoke the language of commercial capitalism, they also talked of reciprocal obligations and mutuality. As much as plain white folk and slaves became implacable foes, they also continued to share much and to cooperate. White-black relations in the eighteenth century were riven with ambiguities.

These paired polarities were not immutable. For most of the eighteenth century, control and discipline were the masters' watchwords. To be sure, masters acknowledged their obligations to provide and protect, but they were also quick to judge and punish. They were often brutal, whipping and dismembering their slaves almost at will. Yet, at least these severe taskmasters viewed slaves as integral parts of society, as members of their households. But new ways of thinking gradually emerged. By the late eighteenth century, masters began to augment their threats with appeals, temper their severity with solicitude, expect not just obedience but gratitude, and manumit not just for faithful service but out of respect and regard for their slaves. At the same time, masters who saw themselves less as taskmasters than as benefactors increasingly viewed slaves, not as organic members of society, but as outside civil society altogether. Just as the masters' worldview became more exclusive, so the everyday world of whites and blacks became more fissured. The distance between plain white folk and black slaves, for example, grew wider through the eighteenth century.

FURTHER READING

Ira Berlin, *Many Thousands Gone: The First Two Centuries of Slavery in North America* (1998).

Trevor Burnard, *Mastery, Tyranny, and Desire: Thomas Thistlewood and His Slaves in the Anglo-Jamaican World* (2004).

Kirsten Fischer, *Suspect Relations: Sex, Race, and Resistance in Colonial New England* (2002).

David Galenson, *White Servitude in Colonial America* (1981).

Alison Games, *Migration and the Origins of the English Atlantic World* (1999).

Rhys Isaac, *London Carter's Uneasy Kingdom: Revolution and Rebellion on a Virginia Plantation* (2004).

Rhys Isaac, *The Transformation of Virginia, 1740–1790* (1982).

Winthrop D. Jordan, *White over Black: American Attitudes Toward the Negro* (1986).

Allan Kulikoff, *Tobacco and Slaves: The Development of Southern Cultures in the Chesapeake, 1680–1800* (1986).

Daniel C. Littlefield, *Rice and Slaves: Ethnicity and the Slave Trade in Colonial South Carolina* (1981).

Sidney Mintz, *Sweetness and Power: The Place of Sugar in Modern History* (1985).

Edmund S. Morgan, *American Slavery, American Freedom: The Ordeal of Colonial Virginia* (1975).

Anthony S. Parent, Jr., *Foul Means: The Formation of a Slave Society in Virginia, 1660–1740* (2003).

Peter H. Wood, *Black Majority: Negroes in Colonial South Carolina from 1670 Through the Stono Rebellion* (1974).

CHAPTER 3

Colonial New England and the Middle Colonies in British America

In September of 1620, some one hundred English people boarded the Mayflower *and set sail for Virginia. Most of those aboard ship were dissenters from the Church of England who called themselves Pilgrims. After nine long weeks at sea, battling sickness and Atlantic storms, they lay anchor near Cape Cod, hundreds of miles away from their intended destination. Shortly thereafter, they met Squanto, described in Chapter 1. A few years after the* Mayflower's *arrival, another wave of English settlers, known as Puritans, arrived in Massachusetts. Meanwhile, small colonies of Dutch and Swedish settlers, who were particularly interested in trading with the Indians, gained toeholds to the south. Although England eventually seized both New Netherlands and New Sweden, the ethnic diversity brought by these early colonization efforts would endure. In 1681, King Charles II granted William Penn a huge tract of land, which became known as Pennsylvania, or "Penn's woods." Pennsylvania too would become a site of religious and ethnic diversity. From these modest beginnings, the colonial regions of New England (the colonies of Massachusetts, Connecticut, Rhode Island, and New Hampshire) and the Middle Colonies (New York, Pennsylvania, Delaware, and New Jersey) would grow to power and influence.*

From very early on, colonial New England and the Middle Colonies had several prominent features. First, religious belief deeply colored the aspirations and daily life of many colonists. Ironically, the Puritans' quest to create "holy communities" in Massachusetts led to religious conflict and encouraged some to flee westward and form their own colonies in Rhode Island and Connecticut. A variety of religious groups made use of Penn's promise of religious tolerance in the Middle Colonies and created additional communities into the eighteenth century. In the mid-eighteenth century, many colonists would be stirred to religious rebirth by a movement known as the Great Awakening. Second, ethnic diversity characterized the Middle Colonies, and this did not diminish over time; if anything, it increased. In the eighteenth century, immigrants from Ireland, Scotland, and Germany joined English colonists in settling the rich farmland of Pennsylvania. As the century progressed, they participated in a westward migration that brought them into contact— and often into conflict—with Indians. A third characteristic was an interest in trade; even though the Dutch traders were conquered by the British, their economic aspirations for a trading empire endured. By the eighteenth century, merchants from the Middle Colonies and New England dominated colonial trade. Fleets of ships, owned and operated by American colonists, plied their trade throughout the Atlantic world.

The endurance of these features led the economies of New England and the Middle Colonies to develop in ways that differed from those of the southern colonies. Slavery existed in all the British American colonies, but plantation agriculture never took root in the soils of the North. Rather, people in these colonies either farmed or joined a growing mercantile and artisanal class that provided services or made goods for the whole colonial economy. These activities changed the society and culture of the northern colonies as well as their economy. Religious goals tended to give way to economic ones; as some historians have pointed out, "puritans" became "yankees." Americans also began to focus on the economic opportunity that their society offered to Europe's poor. More than one American observed that their colony was "the best poor man's country" in the world.

⬛ QUESTIONS TO THINK ABOUT

Historians have been fascinated by the transformation of religious colonies into secular societies. What psychological anxieties might have resulted from this transition? In what ways might these anxieties have been manifested in society? How did the population of the northern colonies differ from that of the South in terms of occupation and ethnic background? How did this contribute to a colonial world different from that of the plantation South?

⬛ DOCUMENTS

These documents show the interplay of religious and economic forces in colonial society. The first documents illustrate the early hopes of and tensions within creating a colonial society in the first century of settlement, whereas the final documents display the growing importance of material acquisition and difficulties of everyday life. Whereas the Pilgrims wrote a contract called the Mayflower Compact in 1620, Puritan leaders also put down their beliefs about the proper organization of their society, as evidenced in document 1. Written by Governor John Winthrop in 1630, *A Model of Christian Charity* asks the people to work together to create a godly society. Unfortunately, the hopes of fostering such a society were often challenged. Document 2 is a poem written in 1656 by Anne Bradstreet, one of the original Puritan settlers. In it she discusses her feelings for her children and their activities. We see within it the mobility and instability of colonial society. Document 3 describes both the conflict between Indians and New England whites and the aspirations to set this conflict in religious terms.

Mary Rowlandson, taken captive in 1675 during King Philip's War, depicts her capture and hopes to make sense of it through her faith. When Pennsylvania was founded, William Penn wrote an account of the colony, which is document 4, that described its attributes and, more importantly, encouraged people to move there. Document 5 is an account of another challenge to New England society: the Salem witchcraft outbreak in 1692. In it, an unfree Indian woman discusses the enticements of the devil and witches. In the mid-eighteenth century, a religious revival known as the Great Awakening burst forth, again in part as a result of tensions in society. Document 6 is a eulogy by Phillis Wheatley, an African American slave, to revival minister George Whitefield. For his dramatic preaching and his numerous tours throughout the colonies, Whitefield became the most famous man in the English colonies. He inspired a wide variety of Americans, and Wheatley speaks to the radical direction of his preaching. Document 7 is from a diary by a Scottish traveler named Alexander Hamilton, who noted in 1744 that northerners were increasingly buying material goods and displaying these goods in their homes. In document 8, a German immigrant named Gottlieb Mittelberger tells how Germans coming to America often faced a frightful journey and then had to serve terms as unfree laborers to pay off the costs of their passage.

1. Puritan Leader John Winthrop Provides a Model of Christian Charity, 1630

1. For the persons, we are a Company professing ourselves fellow members of Christ....
2. For the work we have in hand, it is by a mutual consent through a special overruling providence, and a more than an ordinary approbation of the Churches of Christ to seek out a place of Cohabitation and Consortship under a due form of Government both civil and ecclesiastical....
3. The end is to improve our lives to do more service to the Lord the comfort and increase of the body of christ whereof we are members that ourselves and posterity may be the better preserved from the Common corruptions of this evil world....
4. For the means whereby this must be effected, they are 2fold, a Conformity with the work and end we aim at, these we see are extraordinary, therefore we must not content ourselves with usual ordinary means whatsoever we did or ought to have done when we lived in England, the same must we do and more also where we go: That which the most in their Churches maintain as a truth in profession only, we must bring into familiar and constant practice, as in this duty of love we must love brotherly without dissimulation, we must love one another with a pure heart fervently we must bear one another's burdens, we must not look only on

John Winthrop, *A Model of Christian Charity* (1630), in *Collections*, Massachusetts Historical Society, 3d ser., VII (1838), 3–48; reprinted in *Winthrop Papers*, Massachusetts Historical Society, II (Boston: Massachusetts Historical Society, 1931), 282–295.

our own things, but also on the things of our brethren, neither must we think that the lord will bear with such failings at our hands as he doth from those among whom we have lived....

... [F]or we must Consider that we shall be as a City upon a Hill, the eyes of all people are upon us; so that if we shall deal falsely with out god in this work we have undertaken and so cause him to withdraw his present help from us, we shall be made a story and a by-word through the world, we shall open the mouths of enemies to speak evil of the ways of god and all professors for God's sake; we shall shame the faces of many of gods worthy servants, and cause their prayers to be turned into Curses upon us till we be consumed out of the good land whether we are going.

2. Anne Bradstreet Discusses Her Children in the Colonies, 1656

I had eight birds hatcht in one nest,
Four Cocks were there, and Hens the rest.
I nurst them up with pain and care,
No cost nor labour did I spare
Till at the last they felt their wing,
Mounted the Trees and learned to sing.
Chief of the Brood then took his flight
To Regions far and left me quite.
My mournful chirps I after send
Till he return, or I do end....
My second bird did take her flight
And with her mate flew out of sight.
Southward they both their course did bend,
And Seasons twain they there did spend,
Till after blown by Southern gales
They Norward steer'd with filled sails....
One to the Academy flew
To chat among that learned crew.
Ambition moves still in his breast
That he might chant above the rest,
Striving for more than to do well,

Anne Bradstreet, "In Reference to Her Children," (1656) in *The Poems of Mrs. Anne Bradstreet (1612–1672)* (1897), 275–279.

That nightingales he might excel....

If birds could weep, then would my tears

Let others know what are my fears

Lest this my brood some harm should catch

And be surpris'd for want of watch

Whilst pecking corn and void of care

They fall un'wares in Fowler's snare; ...

3. Mary Rowlandson, a New England Woman, Recounts Her Experience of Captivity and Escape from the Wampanoag During King Philip's War, 1675

On the tenth of February 1675, came the Indians with great numbers upon Lancaster: their first coming was about sunrising; hearing the noise of some guns, we looked out; several houses were burning, and the smoke ascending to heaven....

At length they came and beset our own house, and quickly it was the dolefulest day that ever mine eyes saw. The house stood upon the edge of a hill; some of the Indians got behind the hill, others into the barn, and others behind anything that could shelter them; from all which places they shot against the house, so that the bullets seemed to fly like hail; and quickly they wounded one man among us, then another, and then a third....

Some in our house were fighting for their lives, others wallowing in their blood, the house on fire over our heads, and the bloody heathen ready to knock us on the head, if we stirred out. Now might me hear mothers and children crying out for themselves, and one another, "Lord, what shall we do?" Then I took my children (and one of my sisters', hers) to go forth and leave the house: but as soon as we came to the door and appeared, the Indians shot so thick that the bullets rattled against the house, as if one had taken an handful of stones and threw them, so that we were fain to give back....

I had often before this said that if the Indians should come, I should choose rather to be killed by them than taken alive, but when it came to the trial my mind changed; their glittering weapons so daunted my spirit, that I choose rather to go along with those (as I may say) ravenous beasts, than that moment to end my days; ...

Now away we must go with those barbarous creatures, with our bodies wounded and bleeding, and our hearts no less than our bodies....

I must turn my back upon the town, and travel with them into the vast and desolate wilderness, I knew not whither. It is not my tongue, or pen, can express

Mary Rowlandson, *The Narrative of the Captivity and the Restoration of Mrs. Mary Rowlandson* (1682). Obtained from www.library.csi.cuny.edu/dept/history/lavender/rownarr.html.

the sorrows of my heart, and bitterness of my spirit that I had at this departure: but God was with me in a wonderful manner, carrying me along, and bearing up my spirit, that it did not quite fail....

This day in the afternoon, about an hour by sun, we came to the place where they intended, viz. an Indian town, called Wenimesset, northward of Quabaug. When we were come, Oh the number of pagans (now merciless enemies) that there came about me, that I may say as David, "I had fainted, unless I had believed, etc." (Psalm 27:13). The next day was the Sabbath. I then remembered how careless I had been of God's holy time; how many Sabbaths I had lost and misspent, and how evilly I had walked in God's sight; which lay so close unto my spirit, that it was easy for me to see how righteous it was with God to cut off the thread of my life and cast me out of His presence forever. Yet the Lord still showed mercy to me, and upheld me; and as He wounded me with one hand, so he healed me with the other....

O the wonderful power of God that I have seen, and the experience that I have had. I have been in the midst of those roaring lions, and savage bears, that feared neither God, nor man, nor the devil, by night and day, alone and in company, sleeping all sorts together, and yet not one of them ever offered me the least abuse of unchastity to me, in word or action. Though some are ready to say I speak it for my own credit; but I speak it in the presence of God, and to His Glory....

Yet I see, when God calls a person to anything, and through never so many difficulties, yet He is fully able to carry them through and make them see, and say they have been gainers thereby. And I hope I can say in some measures, as David did, "It is good for me that I have been afflicted." The Lord hath showed me the vanity of these outward things. That they are the vanity of vanities, and vexation of spirit, that they are but a shadow, a blast, a bubble, and things of no continuance. That we must rely on God Himself, and our whole dependance must be upon Him. If trouble from smaller matters begin to arise to me, I have something at hand to check myself with, and say, why am I troubled? It was but the other day that if I had had the world, I would have given it for my freedom, or to have been a servant to a Christian. I have learned to look beyond present and smaller troubles, and to be quieted under them.

4. Proprietor William Penn Promotes His Colony, 1681

Since (by the good providence of God) a country in *America* is fallen to my lot, I thought it not less my duty than my honest interest to give some public notice of it to the world, that those of our own, or other nations, that are inclined to transport themselves or families beyond the seas, may find another country added to their choice.... But before I come to treat of my particular concernment, I shall take leave to say something of the benefit of *plantations* or *colonies* in general, to obviate a common objection.

Jean R. Soderlund, ed., *William Penn and the Founding of Pennsylvania, 1680–1684: A Documentary History* (Philadelphia: University of Pennsylvania Press, 1983), 58–60, 62–65.

Colonies, then, are the seeds of nations begun and nourished by the care of wise and populous countries, as conceiving them best for the increase of human stock, and beneficial for commerce.

Some of the wisest men in history have justly taken their fame from this design and service....

Nor did any of these ever dream it was the way of decreasing their people or wealth. For the cause of the decay of any of those states or empires was not their *plantations*, but their *luxury and corruption of manner*.... I deny the vulgar opinion against *plantations, that they weaken* England. They have manifestly enriched and so strengthened her, which I briefly evidence thus:

1st. Those that go into a foreign *plantation*, their industry there is worth more than if they stayed at home, the product of their labor being in commodities of a superior nature to those of this *country*....

2dly. More being produced and imported than we can spend here, we export it to other countries in *Europe*, which brings in money or the growth of those countries, which is the same thing. And this is [to] the advantage of the *English* merchants and seamen.

3dly. Such as could not only not *marry* here, but hardly live and allow themselves clothes, do marry there, and bestow thrice more in all necessaries and conveniencies (and not a little in ornamental things, too) for themselves, their wives, and children, both as to apparel and household stuff....

4thly. But let it be considered *that the plantations employ many hundreds of shipping and many thousands of seamen,* which must be in diverse respects an advantage to *England*, being an island, and by nature fitted for navigation above any country in *Europe*. This is followed by other depending trades, as *shipwrights, carpenters, sawyers, hewers*....

The place lies 600 miles nearer the sun than *England*; for *England* begins at the 50th degree and ten minutes of north latitude, and this place begins at forty, which is about the latitude of *Naples* in *Italy*, or *Montpellier* in *France*. I shall say little in its praise to excite desires in any, whatever I could truly write as to the soil, air, and water. This shall satisfy me, that by the *blessing* of God and the honesty and industry of man, it may be a good and fruitful land.

For *navigation* it is said to have two conveniencies: the one by lying nine score miles upon *Delaware* River.... The other convenience is through *Chesapeake Bay*.

For timber and other wood, there is variety for the use of man.

For *fowl, fish,* and *wild deer*, they are reported to be plentiful in those parts. Our *English* provision is likewise now to be had there at reasonable rates. The commodities that the country is thought to be *capable* of, are *silk, flax, hemp, wine, cider, wood, madder, licorice, tobacco, potashes,* and *iron,* and it does actually produce *hides, tallow, pipe-staves*, beef, pork, sheep, wool, corn, as *wheat, barley, rye,* and also *furs,* as your *peltry, minks, raccoons, martens,* and such like; store of *furs* which is to be found among the *Indians,* that are profitable commodities in *Europe*.

The way of trading in those countries is thus: they send to the southern plantations *corn, beef, pork, fish,* and *pipe-staves,* and take their growth and bring for *England,* and return with *English* goods to their own country. Their *furs* they bring for *England,* and either sell them here, or carry them out again to other parts of *Europe,* where they will yield a better price. And for those that will follow *merchandise* and *navigation,* there is conveniency, and *timber sufficient for shipping....*

These persons that Providence seems to have most fitted for plantations are,

1st. Industrious *husbandmen* and *day laborers,* that are hardly able (with extreme labor) to maintain their families and portion their children.

2dly. Laborious *handicrafts,* especially *carpenters, masons, smiths, weavers, tailors, tanners, shoemakers, shipwrights,* etc....

3dly. A plantation seems a fit place for those *ingenious spirits* that being low in the world, are much clogged and oppressed about a livelihood....

4thly. A fourth sort of men to whom a *plantation* would be proper, takes in those that are *younger brothers* of small inheritances....

Lastly, there are another sort of persons, not only fit for, but necessary in *plantations,* and that is, *men of universal spirits* that have an eye to the good of posterity, and that both understand and delight to promote good discipline and just government among a plain and well intending people. Such persons may find *room in colonies for their good counsel and contrivance,* who are shut out from being of much use or service to great nations under settled customs. These men deserve much esteem, and would be hearkened to....

To conclude, I desire all my dear country folks, who may be inclined to go into those parts, to consider seriously the premises, *as well the present inconveniences as future ease and plenty,* that so none may move rashly or from a fickle but solid mind, *having above all things, as eye to the providence of God, in the disposal of themselves.* And I would further advise all such at least, to have the permission, if not the good liking of their near relations, for that is both natural, and a duty incumbent upon all; and by this means will natural affection be preserved, and a friendly and profitable correspondence be maintained between them. In all which *I beseech Almighty God to direct us, that His blessing may attend our honest endeavor, and then the consequence of all our undertaking will turn to the glory of His great name, and the true happiness of us and our posterity.* Amen.

5. Examination and Testimony of Tituba, a Servant-Slave in Salem, Massachusetts, 1692

Salem Village, March 1, 1692

Tituba an Indian woman brought before us by Constable Joseph Herrick of Salem upon suspicion of witchcraft by her committed according to the complaint of Joseph Hutcheson and Thomas Putnam, etc. of Salem Village as appears per warrant granted Salem 29 February 1691/2. Tituba upon examination and after some denial acknowledged the matter of fact according to her examination given in more fully will appear and who also charged Sarah Good and Sarah Osborne with the same....

Salem Witchcraft Papers: Verbatim Transcripts of the Legal Documents, ed. Paul Boyer and Stephen Nissenbaum (New York: Da Capo, 1977), 3:1747–49.

John Hathorne and Jonathan Corwin, Assistants

(HATHORNE:) Titibe what evil spirit have you familiarity with?

(TITUBA:) None.

(H:) Why do you hurt these children?

(T:) I do not hurt them.

(H:) Who is it then?

(T:) The devil for ought I know.

(H:) Did you never see the devil?

(T:) The devil came to me and bid me serve him....

(H:) Who have you seen?

(T:) Four women sometimes hurt the children.

(H:) Who were they?

(T:) Goody Osborne and Sarah Good and I do not know who the other were. Sarah Good and Osborne would have me hurt the children but I would not....

(H:) When did you see them?

(T:) Last night at Boston.

(H:) What did they say to you?

(T:) They said hurt the children,...

(H:) What is this appearance you see?

(T:) Sometimes it is like a hog and sometimes like a great dog.

(H.) What did it say to you?

(T:) The black dog said serve me but I said I am afraid. He said if I did not he would do worse to me.

(H:) What did you say to it?

(T:) I will serve you no longer. Then he said he would hurt me and then he looks like a man and threatens to hurt me.... and he told me he had more pretty things that he would give me if I would serve him.

(H:) What were these pretty things?

(T:) He did not show me them.

(H:) What else have you seen?

(T:) Two rats, a red rat and a black rat....

(H:) Do you see who it is that torments these children now?

(T:) Yes, it is Goody Good. She hurts them in her own shape.

(H:) And who is it that hurts them now?

(T:) I am blind now, I cannot see....

6. A Slave, Phillis Wheatley, Laments the Death of Revivalist George Whitefield, 1770

HAIL, happy saint, on thine immortal throne,
Possest of glory, life, and bliss unknown;
We hear no more the music of thy tongue,
Thy wonted auditories cease to throng.
Thy sermons in unequall'd accents flow'd,
And ev'ry bosom with devotion glow'd;
Thou didst in strains of eloquence refin'd
Inflame the heart, and captivate the mind....
Thou moon hast seen, and all the stars of light,
How he has wrestled with his God by night.
He pray'd that grace in ev'ry heart might dwell,
He long'd to see America excell;
He charg'd its youth that ev'ry grace divine
Should with full lustre in their conduct shine;
That Saviour, which his soul did first receive,
The greatest gift that ev'n a God can give,
He freely offer'd to the num'rous throng,
That on his lips with list'ning pleasure hung.
"Take him, ye wretched, for your only good,
"Take him, ye starving sinners, for your food;
"Ye thirsty, come to this life-giving stream,
"Ye preachers, take him for your joyful theme;
"Take him my dear Americans, he said,
"Be your complaints on his kind bosom laid:
"Take him, ye Africans, he longs for you,
"Impartial Saviour is his title due:
"Wash'd in the fountain of redeeming blood,
"You shall be sons, and kings, and priests to God."...

Phillis Wheatley, "On the Death of Rev. Mr. George Whitefield" (1770).

7. Dr. Alexander Hamilton Depicts the Material Acquisitions of Northern Colonists, 1744

New York

Saturday, June 16th....

I found the city less in extent, but by the stir and frequency upon the streets, more populous than Philadelphia. I saw more shipping in the harbour. The houses are more compact and regular, and in general higher built, most of them after the Dutch model, with their gavell ends fronting the street. There are a few built of stone; more of wood, but the greatest number of brick, and a great many covered with pantile and glazed tile with the year of God when built figured out with plates of iron, upon the fronts of several of them. The streets in general are but narrow, and not regularly disposed. The best of them run parallel to the river, for the city is built all along the water, in general.

This city has more of an urban appearance than Philadelphia. Their wharfs are mostly built with logs of wood piled upon a stone foundation. In the city are several large public buildings. There is a spacious church, belonging to the English congregation, with a pretty high, but heavy, clumsy steeple, built of freestone....

Schenectady

... In the city are about 4,000 inhabitants, mostly Dutch or of Dutch extract.

The Dutch here keep their houses very neat and clean, both without and within. Their chamber floors are generally laid with rough plank, which in time, by constant rubbing and scrubbing, becomes as smooth as if it had been planed. Their chambers and rooms are large and handsome. They have their beds generally in alcoves, so that you may go thro' all the rooms of a great house and see never a bed. They affect pictures much, particularly scripture history, with which they adorn their rooms. They set out their cabinets and *buffets* much with china. Their kitchens are likewise very clean, and there they hang earthen or delft plates and dishes all round the walls, in manner of pictures, having a hole drilled thro' the edge of the plate or dish, and a loop of ribbon put into it to hang it by; but notwithstanding all this nicety and cleanliness in their houses they are in their persons slovenly and dirty. They live here very frugally and plain, for the chief merit among them seems to be riches, which they spare no pains or trouble to acquire, but are a civil and hospitable people in their way, but at best rustic and unpolished....

Nantucket Fall...

While I waited for the chocolate which I had ordered for breakfast, Angell gave me an account of his religion and opinions, which I found were as much out of

Dr. Alexander Hamilton, *Hamilton's Itinerarium; Being a Narrative of a journey... from May to September, 1744,* ed. Albert Bushnell Hart (St. Louis, Mo.: The DE Vinne Press, 1907), 51, 87–88, 182–183, 197.

the common road as the man himself. I observed a paper pasted upon the wall, which was a rabble of dull controversy betwixt two learned divines, of as great consequence to the publick as *The Story of the King and the Cobbler* or *The Cele-brated History of the Wise Men of Gotham.* This controversy was intituled *Cannons to batter the Tower of Babel.* Among the rest of the chamber furniture were several elegant pictures, finely illuminated and coloured, being the famous piece of *The Battle for the Breeches, The Twelve Golden Rules,* taken from King Charles I's study, of blessed memory (as he is very judiciously styled), *The Christian Coat of Arms,* &c., &c., &c., in which pieces are set forth divine attitudes and elegant passions all sold by Overton, that inimitable ale-house designer at the White Horse without Newgate....

New London...

I went home at six o'clock, and Deacon Green's son came to see me. He entertained me with the history of the behaviour of one Davenport, a fanatick preacher there, who told his flock in one of his enthusiastic rhapsodies, that in order to be saved they ought to burn all their idols. They began this conflagra-tion with a pile of books in the publick street, among which were Tillotson's *Sermons,* Beveridge's *Thoughts,* Drillincourt on *Death,* Sherlock, and many other excellent authors, and sang psalms and hymns over the pile while it was a-burning. They did not stop here, but the women made up a lofty pile of hoop petticoats, silk gowns, short cloaks, cambrick caps, red-heeled shoes, fans, neck-laces, gloves, and other such apparel, and, what was merry enough, Davenport's own idol, with which he topped the pile, was a pair of old wore-out plush breeches.

8. Gottlieb Mittelberger, a German Immigrant, Portrays the Difficulties of Immigration, 1750

When the ships have weighed anchor for the last time, usually off Cowes in Old England, then both the long sea voyage and misery begin in earnest. For from there the ships often take eight, nine, ten, or twelve weeks sailing to Philadelphia, if the wind is unfavorable. But even given the most favorable winds, the voyage takes seven weeks.

During the journey the ship is full of pitiful signs of distress—smells, fumes, horrors, vomiting, various kinds of sea sickness, fever, dysentery, headaches, heat, constipation, boils, scurvy, cancer, mouth-rot, and similar afflictions, all of them caused by the age and the highly-salted state of the food, especially of the meat, as well as by the very bad and filthy water, which brings about the miserable destruction and death of many. Add to all that shortage of food, hunger, thirst, frost, heat, dampness, fear, misery, vexation, and lamentation as well as other troubles. Thus, for example, there are so many lice, especially on the sick people,

Gottlieb Mittelberger, *Reise nach Pennsylvania* (*Journey to Pennsylvania*) (1756).

that they have to be scraped off the bodies. All this misery reaches its climax when in addition to everything else one must also suffer through two to three days and nights of storm, with everyone convinced that the ship with all aboard is bound to sink. In such misery all the people on board pray and cry pitifully together....

Among those who are in good health impatience sometimes grows so great and bitter that one person begins to curse the other, or himself and the day of his birth, and people sometimes come close to murdering one another. Misery and malice are readily associated, so that people begin to cheat and steal from one another. And then one always blames the other for having undertaken the voyage. Often the children cry out against their parents, husbands against wives and wives against husbands, brothers against sisters, friends and acquaintances against one another.

But most of all they cry out against the thieves of human beings! Many groan and exclaim: "Oh! If only I were back at home, even lying in my pigsty!" Or they call out: "Ah, dear God, if I only once again had a piece of good bread or a good fresh drop of water." Many people whimper, sigh, and cry out pitifully for home....

When at last after the long and difficult voyage the ships finally approach land, when one gets to see the headlands for the sight of which the people on board had longed so passionately, then everyone crawls from below to the deck, in order to look at the land from afar. And people cry for joy, pray, and sing praises and thanks to God. The glimpse of land revives the passengers, especially those who are half-dead of illness. Their spirits, however weak they had become, leap up, triumph, and rejoice within them....

When the ships finally arrive in Philadelphia after the long voyage only those are let off who can pay their sea freight or can give good security. The others, who lack the money to pay, have to remain on board until they are purchased and until their purchasers can thus pry them loose from the ship. In this whole process the sick are the worst off, for the healthy are preferred and are more readily paid for. The miserable people who are ill must often still remain at sea and in sight of the city for another two or three weeks—which in many cases means death. Yet many of them, were they able to pay their debts and to leave the ships at once, might escape with their lives....

This is how the commerce in human beings on board ship takes place. Every day Englishmen, Dutchmen, and High Germans come from Philadelphia and other places, some of them very far away, sometime twenty or thirty or forty hours' journey, and go on board the newly arrived vessel that has brought people from Europe and offers them for sale. From among the healthy they pick those suitable for the purposes for which they require them. Then they negotiate with them as to the length of the period for which they will go into service in order to pay off their passage, the whole amount of which they generally still owe. When an agreement has been reached, adult persons by written contract bind themselves to serve for three, four, five, or six years, according to their health and age. The very young, between the ages of ten and fifteen, have to serve until they are twenty-one, however.

Many parents in order to pay their fares in this way and get off the ship must barter and sell their children as if they were cattle. Since the fathers and mothers often do not know where or to what masters their children are to be sent, it frequently happens that after leaving the vessel, parents and children do not see each other for years on end, or even for the rest of their lives.

ESSAYS

Historians debate the relationship between religion and economic interests in colonial America. These two essays show distinct angles of the era. The first, by Harvard historian David D. Hall, focuses upon the religious views of the settlers in the seventeenth century. Their worlds, Hall contends, were defined by wonder and sacred judgment, and they sought to make spiritual sense of their confusing world. In contrast, T. H. Breen, a historian at Northwestern University, observes that colonial Americans were increasingly concerned with becoming part of an "empire of goods" in the eighteenth century. Americans were consumers, and in order to consume, they needed to accumulate wealth. Breen argues that Americans' patterns of consumption fostered identities that not only tied them to the British empire, but enabled them to perceive common bonds with other colonists. Both Hall and Breen focus on the ways colonists linked themselves to broader worlds spiritually and materially.

Worlds of Wonder in the Northern Colonies

DAVID D. HALL

The People of seventeenth-century New England lived in an enchanted universe. Theirs was a world of wonders. Ghosts came to people in the night, and trumpets blared, though no one saw the trumpeters. Nor could people see the lines of force that made a "long staff dance up and down in the chimney" of William Morse's house in Newbury. In this enchanted world, the sky on a "clear day" could fill with "many companies of armed men in the air, clothed in light-colored garments, and the commander in sad [somber]." The townsfolk of New Haven saw a phantom ship sail regally into the harbor. An old man in Lynn espied

> a strange black cloud in which after some space he saw a man in arms complete standing with his legs straddling and having a pike in his hands which he held across his breast.... After a while the man vanished in whose room appeared a spacious ship seeming under sail though she kept the same station.

Voices spoke from heaven and children from their cradles.

From David D. Hall, *Worlds of Wonder, Days of Judgment: Popular Religious Belief in Early America* (New York: Alfred A. Knopf, 1989), 71–72, 76–78, 90–92, 122–127, 189–193. Reprinted by permission of Alfred A Knopf, a division of Random House, Inc.

All of these events were "wonders" to the colonists, events betokening the presence of the supernatural. Some wonders were like miracles in being demonstrations of God's power to suspend or interrupt the laws of nature. The providence of God was "wonder-working" in making manifest the reach of his sovereignty; such acts of "special providence" represented God's clearer and more explicit than usual intervention into the affairs of man. But he was not alone in having supernatural power. The events that Cotton Mather described in *Wonders of the Invisible World* were the handiwork of Satan and his minions. A wonder was also any event people perceived as disrupting the normal order of things—a deformity of nature such as a "monster" birth, a storm or devastating fire. Always, wonders evidenced the will of God.

Many of the colonists experienced such wonders. Many also read about or were told stories of them. There was nothing odd about this practice. Everywhere in Europe people were observing the same kinds of portents and telling the same kinds of stories. Everywhere these stories drew upon a lore of wonders rooted in the Bible and antiquity. Chaucer used this lore in *The Canterbury Tales,* as did the fourteenth-century author of *The Golden Legend,* a collection of saints' lives. Whenever the colonists spoke or wrote of wonders, they relied on an old tradition; theirs was a borrowed language.

The transmitters of this language were the London printers and booksellers, who churned out tales of wonders in abundance. Portents and prodigies were the stuff of scores of English printed broadsides. "Strange news from Brotherton," announced a broadside ballad of 1648 that told of wheat that rained down from the sky. "A wonder of wonders" of 1663 concerned an invisible drummer boy who banged his drum about the streets of Tidworth. In "Strange and true news from Westmoreland," a tale of murder ended with the Devil pointing out the guilty person. Newssheets, which began appearing with some regularity in the 1620s, carried tales of other marvels. Pamphlets contained reports of children speaking preternaturally and offered *Strange and wonderful News… of certain dreadful Apparitions.* The yearly almanacs weighed in with their accounts of mystic forces emanating from the stars and planets.

The same events occur repeatedly. Tales of witchcraft and the Devil, of comets, hailstorms, monster births, and apparitions—these were some of the most commonplace. "Murder will out," as supernatural forces intervened to indicate the guilty. The earth could open up and swallow persons who told lies. "Many are the wonders which have lately happened," declared the man who compiled *A Miracle, of Miracles,*

> as of sodaine and strange death upon perjured persons, strange sights in the Ayre, strange births on the Earth, Earthquakes, Commets, and fierie Impressions, with the execution of God himselfe from his holy fire in heaven, on the wretched man and his wife, at Holnhurst….

A single ballad spoke of blazing stars, monstrous births, a rainstorm of blood, lightning, rainbows, and the sound of great guns. Others told of dreams and prophecies that bore upon the future of kings and countries. Almanacs and other astrological compendia reported similar events: comets, eclipses, joined fetuses, infants speaking….

Much of this great mass of materials was compounded out of four main systems of ideas—apocalypticism, astrology, natural history, and the meteorology of the Greeks. Each of these systems was in decay or disrepute by the middle of the seventeenth century, under challenge either from an alternative, more up-to-date science or from a growing disenchantment with prophetic visionaries. But even in decay these systems continued to give meaning to the wonder tales....

The meaning of the wonder owed much to these four structures of ideas. But the most crucial framework was the doctrine of God's providence. That doctrine antedated Luther and Calvin. Chaucer's Knight had spoken of "Destiny, that Minister-General/Who executed on earth and over all/That Providence which God has long foreseen," and the Psalmist sang of a God who stretched out his protection to the ends of the earth. Nonetheless, the doctrine gained fresh importance in the sixteenth century. Calvin gave providence a position of prominence in the *Institutes,* contrasting it with Stoic fatalism and mere chance. In the wake of Calvin, Thomas Beard assured his readers that God was immediately and actively present in the world, the ultimate force behind everything that happened: "Is there any substance in this world that hath no cause of his subsisting?... Doth not every thunderclap constraine you to tremble at the blast of his voyce?" Nothing in the world occurred according to contingency or "blind chance." The "all-surpassing power of God's will" was manifested in a regularity that Beard thought of as "marvellous," though never to be counted on completely since God retained the power to interrupt the laws of nature. The providence of God was as manifest in the unexpected or surprising as in the "constant" order of the world.

And Providence revealed an angry God. Portents and prodigies arose within a world besmirched with sin, a world of men and women who failed to heed his laws. The murderer, the mocking cavalier, the liar, the sabbath-breaker—all these and many others could expect that someday, somehow, their violation of the moral order would provoke awful warnings or more awful judgments. Behind the logic of this theory lay a long tradition, far older than the Reformation, of foreseeing order collapse into chaos or peace give way to violence. Strife and violence abound in the wonder tales, whether caused by man, the Devil, or an avenging God....

This attentiveness to prodigies and portents bespoke deep feelings about communal danger and security. The men who interlaced the Dorchester and Roxbury church records with providential events were consciously performing a public function. So were Winthrop and Bradford in their journal histories, and Edward Johnson in *The Wonder-Working Providence of Sions Saviour.* To chronicle the wonder was to chart the zones of danger through which a community must pass. In early modern Europe, every community had its good times and its bad. The good times were when rain came at the right moment and the harvest was abundant, when neighbors lived in peace and landlords were not greedy, when servants obeyed their masters. The hard times were when food ran low and famine threatened, when disease was epidemic, or when peace gave way to conflict. In many European villages, a craving for protection was satisfied by "miracles" or extraordinary events that promised the return of peace, health, and prosperity. Thus, when epidemics threatened, villagers in late-medieval Spain—young girls, shepherds, old men—had visions of the Virgin Mary in which she demanded that the village build a chapel or renew its vows of faith. In thirteenth-century Burgundy, women washed newborn or ailing infants in water from a well associated with a miracle.

Women were still bringing infants to the well of St. Guinefort in Burgundy when the colonists departed for New England. In the towns from which these people came, many of the customs that once addressed the dangers of everyday life had lapsed into disuse. Once past their own "starving time," these people found themselves becoming prosperous—owners of their land, blessed with healthy children, reaping ample harvests. Yet all of the first generation had risked the dangers of the sea in coming to New England. Then as well as later, the wilderness that lay around them contained hostile Indians and their Catholic allies from French Canada. Back in England, the government (except when Puritans had reigned) regarded them with disfavor. And, as they discovered, there were enemies within—those who lied, cursed, or profaned the Sabbath, old women who allied themselves with Satan, children who grew up rebellious, neighbors who disputed each stray pig and cow, and, increasingly, merchants who lived ostentatiously. Danger pressed as much upon the godly in their new home as in England.

Responding to these dangers, the colonists employed an old language of interpretation in which the key words were "sin" and "judgment." That language reached them via Beard and the ballad writers, and also via poems like *Pestilence* (1625), a narrative of epidemic illness that painted it as God's response to man's indifference. What enriched and made this language relevant was the colonists' assumption that they lived in covenant with God. For them the covenant transformed the body social into a moral order, a "Theocratie" erected on the basis of the laws of God. It was the wonder that made visible this fusion of the social and the moral, at once manifesting God's protection and—more frequently—warning of God's anger at their carelessness.

John Winthrop kept his journal not out of private curiosity but in order to record the flow of "providences" betokening the situation of a covenanted people. "It is useful to observe, as we go along," Winthrop wrote in 1635, "such especial providences of God as were manifested for the good of these plantations." What he meant by "good" was the safety of the whole, and the general welfare. Anyone who put self-interest ahead of the welfare of the whole was likely to become an example of God's judgments—to drown in a shipwreck, die in an explosion ("wherein the judgment of God appeared, for the master and company were many of them profane scoffers at us"), lose some of his property. Perhaps because he sacrificed so much of his own estate, Winthrop was especially attracted to cases of the rich and covetous becoming poor. "Divers homes were burnt this year," he noted in 1642, "by drying flax. Among others, one Briscoe, of Watertown, a rich man, a tanner, who had refused to let his neighbor have leather for corn, saying he had corn enough...." Servants and sea captains who were suddenly enriched at the expense of others often suffered bad dreams or psychological distress, or simply lost their money as rapidly as it had been acquired. Winthrop's conception of the general good extended to those standbys of the Puritan program, Sabbatarianism and temperance. He told of drunkards who drowned and of people who died after having worked on the Sabbath— in one case, after carting dung. He was much relieved when murderers and thieves were detected by special acts of providence; reporting two examples, he summed up their meaning as "show[ing] the presence and power of God in his ordinances, and his blessing upon his people, while they endeavor to walk before him with uprightness." Always portents reaffirmed the rightness of a moral order.

Meanwhile there were constant "plots" spawned by the Devil to "disturb our peace, and to raise up instruments one after another." The "old serpent" tried his hand at "sowing jealousies and differences between us and our friends at Connecticut." But God sent tokens to reveal that he stood by the colonists. Perhaps the most impressive of these tokens for the men and women who came in the 1630s was their safe passage of the ocean. A folklore emerged from the fact that every ship but one (the *Angel Gabriel*) had reached New England safely: "wherein" (as William Hibbins told the Boston congregation in 1642) "it was very observable what care the Lord had of them." Citing Hibbins in the journal, Winthrop added that "indeed such preservations and deliverances have been so frequent, to such ships as have carried those of the Lord's family between the two Englands, as would fill a perfect volume to report them all." A more confusing token was the snake that crawled into Cambridge meetinghouse while a synod of the ministers was listening to a sermon. There was panic before "Mr. Thomson, one of the elders of Braintree, (a man of much faith) trode upon the head of it." Interpretation followed, the ministers agreeing that the snake was Satan attempting "their disturbance and dissolution": "This being so remarkable, and nothing falling out but by divine providence, it is out of doubt, the Lord discovered somewhat of his mind in it." Mixed in with events Winthrop knew how to interpret were others that remained mysterious. It was not clear why "one James Everell... saw a great light in the night at Muddy River," or why "a voice was heard upon the water between Boston and Dorchester, calling out in a most dreadful manner, boy, boy, come away, come away," or why at Ipswich in 1646 "there was a calf brought forth with one head, and three mouths, three noses, and six eyes": "What these prodigies portended the Lord only knows, which in his due time he will manifest."...

Thus it was that men and women in New England learned to analyze the inward workings of the Holy Spirit and to recognize the larger structure of God's providence. For some, this recognition was confined to a diary. John Hull thus undertook to write down "Some Passages of God's Providence about myself and in relation to myself; penned down that I may be the more mindful of, and thankful for, all God's dispensations Towards men." Michael Metcalfe of Dedham, a weaver back in England but a farmer here, left but a single page of private text in which he commemorated the mercy of God that enabled him to escape the "ceremonies" of the English church. Recalling how he suffered "many times much affliction, for the sake of religion" in old England, Metcalfe remembered vividly the "many dangers, troubles, vexations and sore afflictions" that complicated his first attempt to transport all his family to New England. Succeeding on a second try, he asked that "Glory be given to God, for all his mercies to me." Edward Johnson expanded on these themes in a published book, *The Wonder-Working Providence of Sions Saviour*. Selectman, town clerk, church member, and captain of the citizens' militia in Woburn, Johnson employed several of the metaphors that pervade Foxe's *Book of Martyrs*: the colonists as "Soldiers" in Christ's "Army," the "wilderness" as the place where the colonists would "re-build the most glorious Edifice of Mount Sion." Like the writers of wonder lore, Johnson relished the surprising inversion that Christ performed in bringing "sudden, and unexpected destruction" on opponents of the Puritans. For him the overriding theme, as indicated by his running title, was the providence of God.

Mary Rowlandson, wife of the minister in Lancaster, drew on the providence tradition in describing the weeks she passed as captive of the Indians in 1676. Her tale was rich in pathos, as in her account of the moaning of the "wounded babe" she carried in her arms, and his death some ten days into their captivity. She told of being famished, and of faltering from exhaustion as she struggled through rough country with her captors. There came easily to her a sense that her "doleful" suffering had its parallel in the lives of Jacob and Lot's wife. Thus, too, she compared herself to the Prodigal Son confessing, "Father, I have sinned against heaven, and in thy sight" (Luke 15:21). There came easily to her also a way of writing that conflated her "wilderness" experience with events in Scripture. The smoke that rose above the burning houses of Lancaster was "ascending to heaven," like the smoke that rose above embattled cities in the Old Testament (see Joshua 8:20–21; Judges 20:38) or that which "ascendeth up for ever and ever" from those who suffer in hell (Revelation 14:10–11). When she was restored to the English settlements and had "bread again," the real food she craved was the "honey" that comes "out of the rock," or God's blessing. Like the martyrs she had surely read about, she praised a God who worked the most amazing inversions—turning victory into defeat or defeat into victory, and delivering the weak and helpless from the proud and mighty: "and though they had made a pit, in their own imaginations, as deep as hell for the Christians that summer, yet the Lord hurled themselves into it." "Victory and deliverance"—these were the work of a "wonderful power" that sustained the faithful.

In such narratives, pattern emerged out of the relationship between individual experience and the providential history of God's people over time. When other men and women wrote or talked about their lives, as in testifying of the "work of grace" before a body of church members, the frame of reference was the "strait and narrow way" that few would find—the way that led to Christ, the moment of "election" to salvation. Hence the questions Roger Clap remembered people asking of each other in the 1630s: "How shall we go to Heaven? Have I true Grace wrought in my Heart? Have I Christ or no?" Hundreds gave their answers to these questions as part of the process of becoming a church member. Early on, the procedure was established in most congregations that those who wished to become members must "make their faith & holynes visible" by something more emphatic than taking part in the rite of baptism. That extra something included evidence of "a civille restrained life and some religious duties performed," as the founders of the church in Dedham put it. But the more significant task was to make visible the "inward worke of faith and grace." Thus it happened that some decades before Bunyan wrote his tale *Pilgrim's Progress,* the colonists were standing up in church to describe how God worked on their hearts.

The starting point for most of those who testified was how they learned to see themselves as sinners worthy of damnation. William Manning told the Cambridge church of feeling "loathe and ashamed to make my condition… known" because he realized he was a "gross" sinner. William Andrews and Jane Winship were convinced of their "guilt" as sinners. John Fessenden acknowledged having "lived in sin." The people testifying in John Fiske's congregation spoke similarly of "unworthiness." The wife of Phineas Fiske thought of herself as in a "worse condition than any toad" by reason of the sins she had committed. She named specific failures, as did Mary Goldsmith, who recalled "the discovery of her sin of disobedience to them over her and her unfaithfulness in her particular calling." The first sentence of Francis Moore's confession in Cambridge sums up what all these people said about themselves: "The Lord revealed his estate to him that he was miserable."

Some people generalized about their sinfulness, as Mary Goldsmith did in reporting the "discovery of her accursed condition in the state of nature." Thereby she voiced a fundamental doctrine of Christianity, that everyone participated in the fall of Adam. "In Adam's Fall/We sinn'd all," ran a couplet in the *New England Primer,* and New England catechisms taught the same fundamental principle. Few people in their testimonies referred specifically to Adam or to the doctrine by name, though Brother Jackson's maid "saw my original corruption." Edward Kemp of Wenham was "convinced of his evil condition by nature," Joan White had "heard of original sin," and Sister Batchelor, perhaps responding to a question about "the doctrine of original sin," spoke of being convinced of it "from Isaiah 44:22."…

When the house of Brother Crackbone and his wife caught fire and burned down, she prayed that the "fire" of the Holy Spirit would burn her as well: "And as my spirit was fiery so to burn all I had, and hence prayed Lord would send fire of word, baptize me with fire."

Another woman who watched as her house burned to the ground turned the experience into poetry. Anne Bradstreet was more gifted as a writer than Brother Crackbone's wife, but her technique was the same, as was the moral that it taught. Sorrowing, Bradstreet shifted from complaint to recognizing it "was just" that God deprived her of so much:

> Then streight I gin my heart to chide,
> And did thy wealth on earth abide?
> Didst fix thy hope on mouldring dust,
> The arm of flesh didst make thy trust?
> Raise up thy thoughts above the skye
> That dunghill mists away may flie.

Bradstreet saw her poems as exercises in the disciplining of the self. In one poem she dramatized the tension between "The Flesh and the Spirit." In another, she fused her emotions about death with the figure of the pilgrim:

> A pilgrim I, on earth, perplext
> with sinns with cares and sorrows vext
> By age and paines brought to decay
> and my Clay house mouldring away
> Oh how I long to be at rest
> and soare on high among the blest.

The struggle to subdue the self and remain conscious of God's presence infused the prose "meditations" she wrote out and willed to her children. In them she taught how to see God's purpose even in the humble act of keeping a house clean: "That house which is not often swept, makes the cleanly inhabitant soone loath it, and that heart which is not continually purifieing itself, is no fit temple for the spirit of god to dwell in." Meditation was recurrent and unending if the "pilgrim" was to remain steadfast on his journey.

The technique of turning pain into a blessing was at the heart of the prose masterpiece in which Mary Rowlandson described her captivity during King Philip's War. One evening, as she sensed herself about to faint, she found "sweet cordial" in a verse (Jeremiah 31:16) to which she returned "many and many a time" in the classic manner of devotional practice. This facility enabled Rowlandson to perceive her captivity as a time of spiritual self-searching and renewal. The outward history of "removes"—her name for changes of location—became a tale of deepening humiliation as she realized her dependence on God's mercy.

> I then remembered how careless I had been of God's holy time, how
> many Sabbaths I had lost and misspent, and how evilly I had walked
> in God's sight; which lay so close unto my spirit, that it was easy for me
> to see how righteous it was with God to cut off the thread of my life,
> and cast me out of his presence forever.

She remembered too that living "in prosperity, having the comforts of the world about me, my relations by me, my heart cheerful," she took "little care for anything." Knowing she had sinned, Mary Rowlandson acknowledged God was justified in causing her to suffer. Quoting Psalms 119:71 on the blessing of affliction—"It is good for me that I have been afflicted"—she affirmed the lesson of the *vanitas* tradition:

> The Lord hath showed me the vanity of these outward things. That
> they are the vanity of vanities, and vexation of spirit; that they are but
> a shadow, a blast, a bubble, and our whole dependence must be upon
> Him....

A more consequential event was the collapse of witch-hunting in the aftermath of the witch craze of 1692. Witch-hunting, or the process of identifying witches and imposing proper punishment, involved fasting, execution, and confession.

One of its motifs was heresy, for like Baptists and the Quakers, witches were accused of joining with the Devil to subvert Christ's kingdom. Another was the theme of murder, for people often blamed a "witch" for unexpected deaths of children. Men and women testified of seeing apparitions of dead people who demanded that their murder be revenged. There was even more to witchcraft and witch-hunting. As a "hidden Work of Darkness," witchcraft was something that godly men must struggle to make visible. Witchcraft was a mighty "Judgment," a sign from God of sins that must be purged. These sins included the longstanding, much-lamented problem of anger between people; witches seemed especially discontented and disruptive of the Christian ethic. In using witch-hunts to purge witches, the colonists were resorting to familiar instruments, the fast day and the public execution, to cleanse their land of sin. But what if those who died as witches were innocent, not guilty?

In telling whether someone was a witch, the colonists counted on confession as the surest of the several kinds of evidence. Confession had a singular importance for two reasons: it made visible the hidden (no one actually saw the occult lines of force that witches were supposed to use), and it confirmed that the root of witchcraft was a compact with the Devil. Hence it happened that, interrogating men and women charged by neighbors with the crime of witchcraft, magistrates and ministers inquired of them if they had entered into such a compact. Some said yes. Mary Johnson, a servant girl in Wethersfield, Connecticut, admitted to "Familiarity with the Devil"; furthermore, she confessed that "she was guilty of the Murder of a Child, and that she had been guilty of Uncleanness with Men and Devils." A Springfield woman told a Massachusetts court in 1651 that she had "entred into covenant with Satan and became a witch." As though she could not resist the unfolding of the ritual, she went on (apparently) to confess the crime of infanticide. A Hartford woman, Rebecca Greensmith, confessed in 1662 that "she... had had familiarity with the Devil. Being asked whether she had made an express covenant with him, she answered, she had not, only as she promised to go with him when he called...."

Where confession blossomed was in hearings and court trials arising out of presumed witchcraft in a farming village attached to the town of Salem. Tituba, a servant in the household of the Salem Village minister, confessed to entering into compact with the Devil; as one eyewitness reported afterward, she added a description of "the times when & places where they met, with many other circumstances to be seen at large." William Barker confessed that he signed a "design" to "destroy the Church of God, and to set up Satans Kingdom, and then all will be well." In all, some fifty persons, most of them from Andover, confessed in 1692 to covenanting with the Devil, and to taking part in counter-rituals deep within the woods. Almost simultaneously, a man in Fairfield, Connecticut, acknowledged having "made a Contract with the devell five years senc with his heart and signed... the devells book and then seald it with his bloud...."

The crime to which these people confessed was making Satan master of their souls in place of God. But in several of these cases, and especially in the testimony neighbors offered of their suffering from suspected witches, it was said that witches used occult powers to cause death or sickness. The minister of

Springfield blamed Mary Parsons for the sickness of his children, she in turn accused her husband of bewitching a young child to death, and neighbors testified of other children's deaths that seemed connected to her threats. When a Newbury woman "was ill, she would often cry out and complaine" that Elizabeth Morse "had bewitched her." A daughter testified that once when Goodwife Morse came to the house, "my Mother Cryed out, that wicked Woman would kill her, be the Death of her, she could not beare it, and fell into a grievous Fitt...." Another neighbor declared that after Morse had "stroakt Goodwife Ordway['s] child over the Head, when it was sick... the Child dyed."

The evidence assembled in the Salem trials included apparitions of the dead returning to seek vengeance; thus, Ann Putnam saw "a man in a Winding Sheet; who told her that Giles Corey had Murdered him, by pressing him to Death with his Feet." Her tale had credibility because it prompted people to remember that a man who lived with Corey many years before had died inexplicably. The same Ann Putnam had seen apparitions of two former wives of George Burroughs, who came to her and declared "that their blood did crie for vengeance against him." The murderer himself had told her he had killed several persons! Susannah Sheldon testified that she had seen the apparition of Bridget Bishop, another accused witch, and "immediately" thereafter "t[w]o little children" who "said that they ware Thomas Greens two twins and tould Bridget Bishop to hir face that she had murthered them in setting them into fits wher of they dyed." On the stories flowed, stories mainly rooted in the suffering of bewildered people who watched children or their spouses die or suffer agonizing fits—thus William Brown of Salisbury, who blamed the "miserabl[e]" condition of his wife (her "strang kind of distemper & frensy uncapible of any reasional action") on Susannah Martin, and the man who traced the "grevious fitts" of his child ("who promised as much health & understanding both by Countenance and actions as any other Children of his years") to Bridget Bishop. It was the illness of his wife that moved Joseph Ballard to ride from Andover to Salem Village, a step that rapidly engulfed his town in witchcraft accusations and confessions.

How else did witches violate the order of God's people? Neighbors described those accused of witchcraft as contentious, angry people, or else (as Martha Corey said) as "idle sloathfull persons [who] minded nothing that was good." Many were the stories of a quarrel over animals that strayed into another person's garden or over work and how it was not fully performed, of requests for help that went unanswered, of bargains gone astray. Apparently because the Morses complained of an uncompleted task, their next-door neighbor described Elizabeth Morse as having "Malice and Envy [in her] Heart." Several persons described the "threatninge" manner of Hugh Parsons when they protested about the quality of his brickmaking of some business matters. A man linked the death of a calf to "a bargaine about" cattle he was engaged in with Thomas Disbrough; "they not agreeing... sd Disbroughs wife was very angry and many hard words pased..." A New Haven woman, not accused of witchcraft though "suspitious" on that poynt," was described in court as someone who made, "discord among neighbors," and who uttered "filthy & uncleane speeches." Someone's speech was often used against him: curses, in particular, betokened antisocial anger that was felt as threatening by townspeople. Rebecca Eames, accused in 1692 of witchcraft and of promising her son Daniel to Satan, acknowledged that she feared Daniel was a witch "becaus he used dredfull bad words when he was angry: and bad wishes…." Often, accused witches had been refused loans or gifts by neighbors who subsequently suffered illness or an accident. Summing up these kinds of social interaction, John Hale noted in his retrospective history of New England witchcraft that "in many of these cases there had been antecedent personal quarrels, and so occasions of revenge…."

Revenge! Associated with the wonder, a motif of the ritual of martyrdom, a favored curse of apparitions representing murdered souls, revenge was central to witchcraft and witch-hunting as these people understood them. What were witches but malicious people bent on harming Christians, in imitation of their wicked master? Rebecca Eames, confessing she had covenanted with the Devil, explained that he had "promised her… [the] powr to avenge her selfe on them that offended her." What was witch-hunting but a process of returning blow for blow, of defeating Satan's "plot" against New England? Hugh Parsons, soon to die because of his wife's testimony, came home one day and told her that he hoped "that God will find out all such wicked Persons and purge New England of all Witches…." Such cleansing of the land from witches was acted out in public executions….

A third ritual intruded in witch-hunting, the practice of confession. Not only were confessions the best evidence of witchcraft; they also were a means of reconciling with the covenanted community, of reenacting (or restoring) someone's passage out of bondage into grace. The men and women who confessed to being witches were acknowledging the power of a rite that promised them redemption if they brought all hidden sins to light. Mary Parsons had not really killed anyone, but she fell into confession because other sins (or guilt) weighed upon her. Elizabeth Knapp, a possessed girl who nearly was accused of witchcraft, had likewise to confess her "many sins, disobedience to parents, neglect of attendance upon ordinances, attempts to murder herself and others." At Salem, people had what seem like modest sins to admit; for most, it was a matter of acknowledging indifference to the ordinances or their wish to have more property. Yet upon listening to a minister insist that only by confessing could they save their souls, some fantasized of covenanting with the Devil. Poor Martha Tyler did so after being told by her minister, "Well I see you will not confess! Well, I will now leave you, and then you are undone, body and soul, for ever."

Most striking, in the records, is the exchange between Ann Foster, her daughter Mary Lacey, and her granddaughter, Mary Lacey (Jr.), and four of the magistrates:

> Q. [By the magistrates] Are you willing your daughter should make
> a full and free confession? A. Yes. Q. Are you willing to do so too?
> A. Yes. Q. you cannot expect peace of conscience without a free
> confession. A. If I knew any thing more, I would speak it to the
> utmost.—

The next voice is that of Mary Lacey, Sr.:

> Oh! mother! how do you do? We have left Christ, and the devil hath gat hold of us. How shall I get rid of this evil one? I desire God to break my rocky heart that I may get the victory this time.

Worlds of Goods in the Northern Colonies

T. H. BREEN

Just before Christmas 1721 William Moore, described in court records as "a Pedler or Petty Chapman," arrived in the frontier community of Berwick, Maine. Had Moore bothered to purchase a peddler's license, we would probably know nothing of his visit. He was undone by success. His illicit sales drew the attention of local authorities, and they confiscated Moore's "bagg or pack of goods." From various witnesses the magistrates learned that the man came to Berwick with "sundry goods and Merchandizes for Saile & that he has Travelled from town to town Exposeing said Goods to Sale and has Sold to Sundry persons."

The people of Berwick welcomed Moore to their isolated community. One can almost imagine the villagers, most of them humble farmers, rushing to Phillip Hubbard's house to examine the manufactured goods that the peddler had transported from Boston. Daniel Goodwin, for example, purchased "a yard and halfe of Stuff for handcarchiefs." Sarah Gooding could not forgo the opportunity to buy some muslin, fine thread, and black silk. She also bought "a yard and Quarter of Lase for a Cap." Patience Hubbard saw many things that she wanted, but in the end she settled for a "pare of garters." Her neighbor, Sarah Stone, took home a bundle of "smole trifles." None of the purchases amounted to more than a few pennies.

Colonial American historians have understandably overlooked such trifling transactions. They have concentrated instead on the structure of specific communities, and though they have taught us much about the people who lived in villages such as Berwick, they have generally ignored the social and economic ties that connected colonists to men and women who happened to dwell in other places. But Moore's visit reminds us that Berwick was part of an empire—an empire of goods. This unfortunate peddler brought the settlers into contact with a vast market economy that linked them to the merchants of Boston and London, to the manufacturers of England, to an exploding Atlantic economy that was changing the material culture not only of the well-to-do but also of average folk like Sarah Stone and Patience Hubbard....

... [A] major obstacle to fresh analysis of the Anglo-American empire of the eighteenth century is the almost unshakable conviction that the colonists were economically self-sufficient. Modern historians who do not agree on other points of interpretation have found themselves defending this hardy perennial. Before World War II, it was common to encounter in the scholarly literature the

From T. H. Breen, "An Empire of Goods: The Anglicization of Colonial America, 1690-1776," *The Journal of British Studies,* Vol. 25, No. 4. (1986), pp. 467-499. Reprinted by permission of The University of Chicago Press.

resourceful yeoman, an independent, Jeffersonian figure who carved a farm out of the wilderness and managed by the sweat of his brow to feed and clothe his family. This is the theme of patriotic mythology. These were men and women who possessed the "right stuff."

In recent years this self-sufficient yeoman has recruited some enthusiastic new support. James A. Henretta, in an influential essay entitled "Families and Farms," offered perhaps the most coherent argument for this position. These colonial farmers, he insisted, were not agrarian entrepreneurs who focused their energies on maximizing profit. To the contrary, they represented a "precapitalist" way of life. They saw themselves not so much as individuals as members of lineal families or of little communities. Since their primary goals were to provide for the welfare of dependents, to pass productive land on to future generations, and to achieve economic security, these colonial farmers studiously avoided the risks associated with the market economy. They rejected innovation in favor of tradition. They were deaf to market incentives. Within their households they attempted to satisfy as many of their material needs as possible, and when they required something they could not produce, they preferred to deal with neighbors rather than outside merchants. In other words, from this perspective, subsistence was not the result of personal failure or physical isolation. It was a positive expression of precapitalist values, a *mentalité*, that was slowly and painfully being eroded by the advance of commercial capitalism. If this is correct, we might as well forget about the consumer society. It hardly seems likely that a few imported English baubles would have turned the heads of such militantly self-sufficient farmers.

This thesis struck a responsive chord among some American historians. They saw the essay as an important statement in a much larger critique of capitalism in the United States, and they claim to have discovered this precapitalist mentality throughout American history, in urban as well as rural situations, in the South as well as the North. For them, colonial yeoman become "cultural heroes," warriors in what James T. Lemon has ironically termed "a desperate rear-guard action" against the encroachment of capitalism....

Though these embattled precapitalist farmers flourish in the pages of learned journals, they have proved remarkably difficult to find in the historical record. Colonial historians who have gone in search of precapitalist colonial America have discovered instead entrepreneurial types, men and women shamelessly thrusting themselves into the market economy. Joyce Appleby reviewed this literature and announced that "evidence mounts that prerevolutionary America witnessed a steady commercialization of economic life: trades of all kinds increased; frontier communities quickly integrated themselves into market networks; large and small farmers changed crops in response to commercial incentives; new consuming tastes and borrowing practices proliferated." James T. Lemon experienced no better luck than did Appleby in discovering a precapitalist mentality. This careful student of Pennsylvania agriculture stated that, "far from being opposed to the market, 'independent' farmers eagerly sought English manufactured goods and in other ways acted as agents of capitalism."...

The argument for self-sufficiency encounters other problems as well. Henretta originally posed his interpretation as a dichotomous proposition: either colonial Americans toiled to preserve the "lineal family," or they strove to participate fully in the market economy. But, surely, there is some middle ground. No one seriously maintains that the people who settled New England and the Middle Colonies were unconcerned about the well-being of family members. They knew how difficult it was to survive a hard winter. They planned ahead as best they could. They also worried about their children's futures, about providing education, about dowries for daughters and land for sons. Such human concerns would hardly seem to be the monopoly of precapitalists. Love of family certainly did not cool the enthusiasm of Pennsylvania farmers for commercial agriculture, nor for that matter did the sale of wheat on the world market unloose an outpouring of corrosive economic individualism....

Having liberated ourselves from the myth of self-sufficiency, we can return with fresh appreciation to the world of consumption. Between 1700 and 1770, the population of the mainland colonies rose approximately eightfold, from roughly 275,000 to 2,210,000. During the decade of the 1760s, it jumped almost 40 percent. Such extraordinarily rapid growth must have strained economic and political institutions. At any given time the majority of this population consisted of young people, boys and girls who were consumers but not yet full producers in this agricultural economy. And yet, contrary to Malthusian expectations, the eighteenth-century colonists were remarkably prosperous. They managed to raise the value of their exports to the mother country by some 500 percent during this period. The importation of British goods rose at an even faster rate. In 1700 the average American annually purchased British imports valued at just under a pound sterling. By 1700 the per capita figure had jumped to £1.20, a rise made all the more impressive when set against the population explosion. What this meant is each succeeding generation of colonial American farmers possessed more British imports than their fathers had. Gloria L. Main discovered that even in New England, the poorest region of the continent, "parents of each generation succeeded in raising their children in material circumstances no worse and possibly a little better than that enjoyed by themselves."

These numbers alone reveal why British merchants and manufacturers were increasingly drawn to this robust American market. Over the course of the eighteenth century, the center of Britain's commercial gravity shifted west, away from traditional linkages to the Continent to new ports such as Liverpool and Glasgow that catered to the colonial consumer demand. In other words, as the American buyers became more dependent on British suppliers, the British business community became more dependent on the colonial market. "It was thus hard facts," explains Jacob M. Price, "and not imagination that made British manufacturers so sensitive to the opening and closing of the North American market at the time of the nonimportation agreements of the 1760's and 1770's."

The Americans were only slowly integrated into the British consumer economy. The key decade in this commercial process appears to be the 1740s. Before that time, colonial demand for imports rose, but not very rapidly....

During the 1740s, the American market suddenly took off. British goods flooded the colonies, and though war occasionally disrupted trade, business always rebounded. Journals carried more and more advertisements for consumer goods. Stores popped up in little New England country villages and along the rivers of the Chesapeake. Carolinians demanded consumer goods; so too did the wheat farmers and the Indian traders of the Middle Colonies. Everywhere the pace of business picked up. By 1772 the Americans were importing British manufactures in record volume. As in the mother country, this market was driven largely by demand. To pay for these goods the colonists produced more and more tobacco, rice, indigo, wheat, fish, tar—indeed, anything that would supply the income necessary to purchase additional imports. The Staple Colonies maintained direct trade links with England and Scotland, but in New England and the Middle Colonies the consumer challenge forced merchants to peddle local products wherever there was a market. Pennsylvania merchants carried ever larger amounts of wheat and flour to southern Europe. New Englanders relied on the West Indian trade to help pay the bill for British manufactures. As one New Yorker explained in 1762, "Our importation of dry goods from England is so vastly great, that we are obliged to betake ourselves to all possible arts to make remittances to the British merchants. It is for this purpose we import cotton from St. Thomas's and Surinam; lime-juice and Nicaragua wood from Curacoa [sic]; and logwood from the bay, &c. and yet it drains us of all the silver and gold we can collect."

This consumer revolution affected the lives of all Americans. To be sure, the social effect was uneven, and the British imports initially flowed into the households of the well-to-do. These are the goods that catch our eyes in modern museums and restored colonial homes. Not surprisingly, we know a good deal about the buying habits of the gentry. Their lives were often well documented, and the fine pieces of china and silver that came into their possession are more apt to have survived to the present than were the more ordinary items that found their way into modest households. The general pattern of cultural diffusion seems clear enough. Poorer colonists aped their social betters, just as wealthy Americans mimicked English gentlemen. However slowly these new tastes may have been communicated, they eventually reached even the lowest levels of society. In her study of colonial Maryland, for example, Lorena Walsh discovered that, "by the 1750s, even the poorer sorts were finding a wide variety of non–essentials increasingly desirable. At the lowest levels of wealth this meant acquiring more of the ordinary amenities families had so long foregone—tables, chairs, bed steads, individual knives and forks, bed and table linens, and now-inexpensive ceramic tableware." A similar transformation of material culture was occurring in other regions.

Perhaps the central item in this rapidly changing consumer society was tea. In the early decades of the eighteenth century, tea began to appear in the homes of wealthier Americans. It may have replaced stronger drinks such as the popular rum punch, and by the 1740s proper ladies and gentlemen regularly socialized over tea. Taking tea became a recognized ritual requiring the correct cups and saucers, sugar bowls, and a collection of pots. By mid-century lesser sorts insisted on drinking tea, and though their tea services may not have been as costly as those of the local gentry, they performed the ritual as best they could. Even the poor wanted tea. One historian found that, during a confrontation with city officials that occurred in 1766, the residents of the Philadelphia poor house demanded Bohea tea. For all these Americans, drinking tea required cups that could hold extremely hot liquids and that, in turn, forced them to import the technically advanced ceramics that originated in Staffordshire. Not until well after the Revolution were American potters able to produce cups of such high quality at competitive prices. What catches our attention is how colonial Americans were increasingly drawn into the marketplace. A decision to buy tea led to other purchases. English glasses held imported wines. English cloth fashioned into dresses and coats looked better with imported metal buttons. One had to serve imported sugar in the appropriate imported pewter or silver bowl.

The consumer revolution also introduced choice into the lives of many Americans. With each passing generation the number of imported goods available to the colonists expanded almost exponentially. In the 1720s, for example, the newspapers carried advertisements for at most a score of British manufactures. Usually, these were listed in general categories, such as dry goods, and one has the impression that even urban merchants carried a basic and familiar stock. But after the 1740s American shoppers came to expect a much larger selection, and merchants had to maintain ever larger inventories. When Gottlieb Mittelberger, a German minister, traveled through Pennsylvania in the early 1750s, he could not believe how many imported items he saw for sale: wine, spices, sugar, tea, coffee, rice, rum, fine china, Dutch and English cloth, leather, linen cloth, fabrics, silks, damask, and velvet. "Already," Mittelberger declared, "it is really possible to obtain all the things one can get in Europe in Pennsylvania, since so many merchant ships arrive there every year." Individual merchants placed journal advertisements during the 1760s announcing the arrival from the mother country of hundreds of items. During some busy months, more than 4,000 separate goods appeared in the newspaper columns. Advertisers now broke down general merchandise groups by color and design. The consumer revolution exposed the colonists not only to a proliferation of goods but also to an ever escalating descriptive language. No doubt, as time passed, colonial buyers became more discerning, demanding increasingly better quality and wider variety.

For many consumers—particularly for women—the exercise of choice in the marketplace may have been a liberating experience, for with choice went a measure of economic power. One could literally take one's business elsewhere. We have come to think of consumerism as a negative term, as a kind of mindless mass behavior, but for the colonists of the mid-eighteenth century, shopping must have heightened their sense of self-importance. It was an arena in which they could ask questions, express individuality, and make demands. One could plausibly argue that, by exposing colonists to this world of consumer choice, the British reinforced the Americans' already strong conviction of their own personal independence....

These colonial stores, wherever they appeared, provided an important link between the common people of America and the mother country. Unfortunately, we do not know much about these scattered places of business. Most were probably small, no larger than a garage in a home today. Such certainly was the store operated by Jonathan Trumbull in rural Connecticut. But despite their modest size, these buildings—sometimes a room in the merchant's home— held an amazing variety of goods. As Glenn Weaver, Trumbull's biographer, explains, a sampling of the merchant's ledger books during the 1730s and 1740s reveals an amazingly full stock of imports: "Pepper, lace, gloves, gunpowder, flints, molasses, rum, *Watts' Psalms,* mohair, drugs, tiles, paper, garlix (a kind of cloth), pots, pans, 'manna,' cord, pails, needles, knives, indigo, logwood, earthenware, raisins, thimbles, buckles, allspice, tea, buttons, mace, combs, butter, spectacles, soap, brimstone, nails, shot, sewing silk, sugar, wire, looking glasses, tape, 'Italian crape,' 'allam,' pewter dishes, etc." One wonders what items were hidden in Weaver's "etc." He seems already to have listed just about everything that a Connecticut farm family might have desired....

Along the roads of mid-eighteenth-century America also traveled the peddlers, the chapmen, and the hawkers, figures celebrated in folklore but ignored almost completely by serious historians. The failure to explore the world of these itinerant salesmen is unfortunate, for they seem to have accounted for a considerable volume of trade. The peddlers made up a sizable percentage of James Beckman's customers, and he was one of the most successful import merchants in New York City. In Boston Thomas Hancock took good care of his "country chaps," making certain British merchants and manufacturers supplied them with the items that the colonists actually wanted to buy. These travelers seem to have hawked their goods along city streets as well as country highways. Men as well as women peddled their wares. A New York law setting conditions for this sort of business specifically mentioned "he" and "she," indicating that in this colony at least people of both sexes carried consumer goods from town to town.

But whatever their gender, itinerants sometimes traveled far, popping up everywhere, ubiquitous denizens of village taverns. When Alexander Hamilton journeyed through the northern colonies in 1744, for example, he regularly encountered peddlers. "I dined att William's att Stonington[, Connecticut] with a Boston merchant name Gardiner and one Boyd, a Scotch Irish pedlar," Hamilton scribbled. "The pedlar seemed to understand his business to a hair. He sold some dear bargains to Mrs. Williams, and while he smoothed her up with palaber, the Bostoner amused her with religious cant. This pedlar told me he had been some time agoe att Annapolis[, Maryland]." In Bristol, Rhode Island, Hamilton and his black servant were taken for peddlers because they carried large "portmanteaux," and the local residents rushed out into the street to inspect their goods. The number of peddlers on the road appears to have been a function of the general prosperity of the colonial economy. In other words, they do not seem to have represented a crude or transitional form of merchandising. As the number of stores increased, so too did the number of peddlers. In fact, the two groups often came into conflict, for the peddlers operating with little overhead could easily undercut the established merchant's price. Shopkeepers petitioned the various colonial legislatures about this allegedly unfair competition. In turn, the lawmakers warned the peddlers to purchase licenses, some at substantial fees, but judging from the repetition of these regulations in the statutes, one concludes that the peddlers more than held their own against the rural merchants....

One can only speculate about the motivation of the colonial buyer. The psychology of eighteenth-century consumption was complex, and each person entered the market for slightly different reasons. Some men and women wanted to save money and time. After all, producing one's own garments—a linen shirt, for example—was a lengthy, tedious process, and the purchase of imported cloth may have been more cost effective than was turning out homespun. Beauty also figured into the calculus of consumption. An imported Staffordshire plate or a piece of ribbon brought color into an otherwise drab environment. Contemporary merchants certainly understood that aesthetics played a major role in winning customers. In 1756, for example, one frustrated English supplier wrote to the Philadelphia merchant John Reynall, "There is no way to send goods with any certainty of sale but by sending Patterns of the several colours in vogue with you." No doubt, some Americans realized that ceramic plates and serving dishes were more sanitary to use than were the older wooden trenchers. In addition, consumer goods provided socially mobile Americans with boundary markers, an increasingly recognized way to distinguish betters from their inferiors, for though the rural farmer may have owned a tea cup, he could not often afford real china. In whatever group one traveled, however, one knew that consumer goods mediated social status. Their possession gave off messages full of meanings that modern historians have been slow to comprehend. Finally, just as it is today, shopping in colonial times was entertaining. Consumer goods became topics of conversation, the source of a new vocabulary, the spark of a new kind of social discourse.

...British imports provided white Americans with a common framework of experience. Consumption drew the colonists together even when they themselves were unaware of what was happening. Men and women living in different parts of the continent purchased a similar range of goods. The items that appeared in New England households also turned up in the Carolinas. The rice planters of Charleston probably did not know that northern farmers demanded the same kinds of imports. They may not have even cared. But however tenuous communication between mid-eighteenth-century colonists may have been, there could be no denying that British manufacturers were standardizing the material culture of the American colonies. Without too much exaggeration, Staffordshire pottery might be seen as the Coca-Cola of the eighteenth century. It was a product of the metropolitan economy that touched the lives of people living on the frontier of settlement, eroding seventeenth-century folkways and bringing scattered planters and farmers into dependence on a vast world market that they did not yet quite comprehend.

Herein lies a paradox[:] ... The road to Americanization ran through Anglicization. In other words, before these widely dispersed colonists could develop a sense of their own common cultural identity, they had first to be integrated fully into the British empire. Royal government in colonial America was never large enough to effect Anglicization. Nor could force of arms have brought about this cultural redefinition. Such a vast shift in how Americans viewed the mother country and each other required a flood of consumer goods, little manufactured items that found their way into gentry homes as well as frontier cabins....

The extent of this imperialism of goods amazed even contemporaries. In 1771, William Eddis, an Englishman living in Maryland, wrote home that "the quick importation of fashions from the mother country is really astonishing. I am almost inclined to believe that a new fashion is adopted earlier by the polished and affluent American than by many opulent persons in the great metropolis.... In short, very little difference is, in reality, observable in the manners of the wealthy colonist and the wealthy Briton." Eddis may have exaggerated, but probably not much. Students of the book trade, for example, have discovered that the colonists demanded volumes printed in England. Indeed, so deep was the Anglicization of American readers that "a false London imprint could seem an effective way to sell a local publication." Newspaper advertisements announced that merchants carried the "latest English goods." By the mid-eighteenth century, these imported items had clearly taken on symbolic value. Put simply, pride of ownership translated into pride of being part of the empire, a sentiment that was reinforced but not created by the victory of the British army over the French in the Seven Years' War.

So long as the king of England ruled over an empire of goods, his task was relatively easy. The spread of the consumer society, at least before the Stamp Act Crisis, tied the colonists ever closer to the mother country. This is what Benjamin Franklin tried to communicate to the House of Commons. He observed that before 1763 the Americans had "submitted willingly to the government of the Crown, and paid, in all their courts, obedience to acts of parliament." It cost Parliament almost nothing, Franklin explained, to maintain the loyalty of this rapidly growing population across the Atlantic. The colonists "were governed by this country at the expense only of a little pen, ink, and paper. They were led by a thread. They had not only a respect, but an affection, for Great Britain, for its laws, its customs and manners, and even a fondness for its fashions, that greatly increased the commerce." No American, of course, had a greater fondness for cosmopolitan fashion than did Franklin. And in 1763 he could not comprehend why anyone would want to upset a system that seemed to operate so well.

FURTHER READING

Bernard Bailyn, *Voyagers to the West* (1986).

Paul Boyer and Stephen Nissenbaum, *Salem Possessed: The Social Origins of Witchcraft* (1994).

T. H. Breen and Timothy D. Hall, *Colonial America in an Atlantic World* (2003).

Elaine G. Breslaw, *Tituba, Reluctant Witch of Salem: Devilish Indians and Puritan Fantasies* (1997).

Richard Bushman, *The Refinement of America: Persons, Houses, Cities* (1992).

Jon Butler, *Becoming American: The Revolution Before 1776* (2001).

Joyce Goodfriend, *Before the Melting Pot: Society and Culture in Colonial New York City, 1664–1730* (1992).

David D. Hall, *Worlds of Wonder, Days of Judgment: Popular Religious Belief in Early England* (1990).

Jane Kamensky, *Governing the Tongue: The Politics of Speech in Early New England* (1997).

Jill Lepore, *The Name of War: King Philip's War and the Origins of American Identity* (1999).

Edmund S. Morgan, *The Puritan Dilemma: The Story of John Winthrop* (1958).

Gary B. Nash, *The Urban Crucible: Social Change, Political Consciousness, and the Origins of the American Revolution* (1979).

Sharon V. Salinger, *"To Serve Well and Faithfully": Labor and Indentured Servitude in Pennsylvania, 1682–1800* (1987).

Laurel Thatcher Ulrich, *A Midwife's Tale: The Life of Martha Ballard, Based on Her Diary, 1785–1812* (1991).

CHAPTER 4

The American Revolution

When the French and Indian War concluded with the Treaty of Paris in 1763, the map of North America was radically redrawn. Because France lost the war, it was forced to relinquish vast territories in Canada to Britain. France's Indian allies faced defeat as well. For years, Indian nations had successfully played off the English and the French. When the French were removed, this strategy was no longer feasible. Pontiac, an Ottawa chief, realized this fact shortly after the war's conclusion. He forged an alliance with neighboring Indian nations and laid siege to Fort Detroit. When Pontiac was defeated, his people's situation became, if anything, worse than before.

The winners seemingly were the British empire and its American subjects. The empire had expanded, and white Americans thirsted after the opportunities for trade, farming, and land speculation promised by the new acquisitions of land. As one Bostonian put it, the "garden of the world [with] all things necessary for the conveniency and delight of life" awaited. Thirteen years after the Treaty of Paris, however, the people of thirteen of the colonies in North America were so disgusted with their position in the empire that they declared their independence. How this could have happened is one of the most important questions in American history.

The first step in the journey to separation was the British response following the end of the French and Indian War. The war had been expensive—the national debt had doubled during the war—and British officials were determined to recoup some of their losses through a reorganization of the empire. Accordingly, they enacted a series of measures that attempted to regulate settlement and trade and to increase the tax burden of the colonists. The Proclamation of 1763, for example, forbade colonists to live west of a line drawn at the crest of the Appalachian Mountains. The Sugar Act of 1764 was the first in a series of acts that attempted to enforce more rigorously the rules of trade within the British empire. And the Stamp Act of 1765 levied direct taxes on a variety of items ranging from newspapers to legal documents.

If British officials felt that these were just actions made necessary by the costs of empire, many Americans perceived this reorganization in a very different light. They saw the Proclamation of 1763 as an effort to restrict economic growth and the Stamp Act as the first step in imposing direct taxation on the colonies. The response of many was to protest in the streets and to speak out in political assemblies. As early as 1765, a secret organization

called the Sons of Liberty was formed to resist British initiatives. Though the British ultimately repealed the Stamp Act, they still felt the need to increase revenue from and control
over their American colonies. A series of additional acts, including the Townshend Acts
(1767), the Tea Act (1773), and the "Intolerable Acts" (1774), were passed, and the
colonial response continued to bewilder British officials. Legislation was followed by protest,
which often resulted in more legislation. Colonial rhetoric grew more shrill, and events like
the Boston Massacre in 1770, which followed the quartering of troops in Boston, and the
Boston Tea Party in 1773, which followed the Tea Act, only served to ratchet up the
tension between the mother country and its unruly colonies. By 1774, King George III
had concluded that "blows must decide." When independence was declared in 1776, the
colonists had already engaged in battles with the British.

American leaders differed in their views of the reorganization of the empire. Many
focused on the ways their rights as English people were being ignored. If they had no direct
representation in Parliament, were not these efforts at direct taxation intolerable? If they
had no say in the levels of taxation, was not this patently unjust? Even more serious
was the argument that imperial policy was only part of a larger plot to deny the liberties
not only of colonists, but of all English people. From this perspective, their protests were
attempts to restore the constitution of English society before this conspiracy was put in
place. Although colonists looked backward to a time when the empire was operating properly,
they increasingly looked forward to the possibilities of an independent America. Many
Americans were taken with the idea that they could best control the "garden of the world"
that lay to the west.

QUESTIONS TO THINK ABOUT

The Revolution affected virtually everyone in American society. How did it alter the lives of various groups—men and women; Indians and slaves; loyalists and
patriots—in different ways? Do the British measures leading up to the Revolution in retrospect look reasonable? If so, how can one explain the American response to them? Would you characterize the Revolution as a conflict that looked
forward or backward?

DOCUMENTS

These documents illustrate how the American colonists moved toward independence and offer questions about how radical the revolution was. Document 1 is
the Resolutions of the Stamp Act Congress, which was convened in 1765 and
which argued that no taxes could be imposed on the colonists without their consent. A speech by Patrick Henry in 1775, document 2, provides an example of
the fiery rhetoric that flourished as the colonies neared their declaration of independence. Document 3 is a selection from Thomas Paine's powerful pamphlet
Common Sense. Published in 1776, it was among the most popular tracts advocating American independence and a republican system of government. The power

and limits of revolution are shown in documents 4 and 7, which provide insights from a woman and enslaved African Americans. In document 4, Abigail Adams reminds her husband, John Adams, to "remember the ladies," and John responds by mocking her. Joseph Brant, in document 5, depicts the loyalty of many Indians to the king of England. This loyalty, as Brant points out, hurt his Mohawk nation because it brought them into further opposition with the rebelling colonists. Document 6 is a poem from the war, encouraging the people to "[t]ake up our arms and go with speed." African Americans use revolutionary ideology and biblical ideals to petition for liberty in document 7, and document 8 shows George Washington's concern about the state of his army and the need for its adequate funding.

1. The Stamp Act Congress Condemns the Stamp Act, 1765

The members of this Congress, sincerely devoted with the warmest sentiments of affection and duty to His Majesty's person and Government, inviolably attached to the present happy establishment of the Protestant succession, and with minds deeply impressed by a sense of the present and impending misfortunes of the British colonies on this continent: having considered as maturely as time will permit the circumstances of the said colonies esteem it our indispensable duty to make the following declarations of our humble opinion respecting the most essential rights and liberties of the colonists, and of the grievances under which they labour, by reason of several late Acts of Parliament.

    I.   That His Majesty's subjects in these colonies owe the same aliegiance to the Crown of Great Britain that is owing from his subjects born within the realm, and all due subordination to that august body the Parliament of Great Britain.

    II.   That His Majesty's liege subjects in these colonies are intitled to all the inherent rights and liberties of his natural born subjects within the kingdom of Great Britain.

    III.   That it is inseparably essential to the freedom of a people and the undoubted right of Englishmen, that no taxes be imposed on them but with their own consent, given personally or by their representatives.

    IV.   That the people of these colonies are not, and from their local circumstances cannot be, represented in the House of Commons in Great Britain.

    V.   That the only representatives of the people of these colonies are persons chosen therein by themselves and that no taxes ever have been, or can be constitutionally imposed on them, but by their legislatures.

    VI.   That all supplies to the Crown being free gifts of the people it is unreasonable and inconsistent with the principles and spirit of the British

"Resolutions," October 19, 1765, in *Collection of Interesting, Authentic Papers Relative to the Dispute Between Great Britain and North America*, ed. John Almon (London: 1777), 27.

Constitution, for the people of Great Britain to grant to His Majesty the property of the colonists.

VII. That trial by jury is the inherent and invaluable right of every British subject in these colonies.

VIII. That the late Act of Parliament, entitled *An Act for granting and applying certain stamp duties, and other duties, in the British colonies and plantations in America, etc.*, by imposing taxes on the inhabitants of these colonies; and the said Act, and several other Acts, by extending the jurisdiction of the courts of Admiralty beyond its ancient limits, have a manifest tendency to subvert the rights and liberties of the colonists.

IX. That the duties imposed by several late Acts of Parliament, from the peculiar circumstances of these colonies, will be extremely burthensome and grievous; and from the scarcity of specie, the payment of them absolutely impracticable.

X. That as the profits of the trade of these colonies ultimately center in Great Britain, to pay for the manufactures which they are obliged to take from thence, they eventually contribute very largely to all supplies granted there to the Crown.

XI. That the restrictions imposed by several late Acts of Parliament on the trade of these colonies will render them unable to purchase the manufactures of Great Britain.

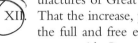XII. That the increase, prosperity, and happiness of these colonies depend on the full and free enjoyments of their rights and liberties, and an intercourse with Great Britain mutually affectionate and advantageous.

XIII. That it is the right of the British subjects in these colonies to petition the King or either House of Parliament.

Lastly, That it is the indispensable duty of these colonies to the best of sovereigns, to the mother country, and to themselves, to endeavour by a loyal and dutiful address to His Majesty, and humble applications to both Houses of Parliament, to procure the repeal of the Act for granting and applying certain stamp duties ... and of the other late Acts for the restriction of American commerce.

2. Virginian Patrick Henry Warns the British to Maintain American Liberties, 1775

Sir, we have done everything that could be done to avert the storm which is now coming on. We have petitioned; we have remonstrated, we have supplicated; we have prostrated ourselves before the throne, and have implored its interposition to arrest the tyrannical hands of the ministry and Parliament. Our petitions have been slighted; our remonstrances have produced additional violence and insult; our supplications have been disregarded; and we have been spurned, with contempt, from the foot of the throne. In vain, after these things, may we indulge the fond hope of peace and reconciliation? There is no longer

---

Patrick Henry, "Give Me Liberty, or Give Me Death" speech (1775).

any room for hope. If we wish to be free—if we mean to preserve inviolate those inestimable privileges for which we have been so long contending—if we mean not basely to abandon the noble struggle in which we have been so long engaged, and which we have pledged ourselves never to abandon until the glorious object of our contest shall be obtained, we must fight! I repeat sir, we must fight! An appeal to arms and to the God of Hosts is all that is left us! ...

It is in vain, sir, to extenuate the matter. Gentlemen may cry, "Peace, Peace!"—but there is no peace. The war is actually begun! The next gale that sweeps from the north will bring to our ears the clash of resounding arms! Our brethren are already in the field! Why stand we here idle? What is it that gentlemen wish? What would they have? Is life so dear, or peace so sweet, as to be purchased at the price of chains and slavery? Forbid it, Almighty God! I know not what course others may take; but as for me, give me liberty, or give me death!

3. Pamphleteer Thomas Paine Advocates the "Common Sense" of Independence, 1776

In the following pages I offer nothing more than simple facts, plain arguments, and common sense; and have no other preliminaries to settle with the reader, than that he will divest himself of prejudice and prepossession, and suffer his reason and his feelings to determine for themselves; that he will put *on*, or rather that he will not put *off* the true character of a man, and generously enlarge his views beyond the present day....

... Now is the seed-time of continental union, faith and honor. The least fracture now will be like a name engraved with the point of a pin on the tender rind of a young oak; the wound will enlarge with the tree, and posterity read it in full grown characters....

As much hath been said of the advantages of reconciliation, which, like an agreeable dream, hath passed away and left us as we were, it is but right, that we should examine the contrary side of the argument, and inquire into some of the many material injuries which these colonies sustain, and always will sustain, by being connected with, and dependant on Great-Britain....

I have heard it asserted by some, that as America hath flourished under her former connexion with Great-Britain, that the same connexion is necessary towards her future happiness, and will always have the same effect. Nothing can be more fallacious than this kind of argument. We may as well assert that because a child has thrived upon milk, that it is never to have meat, or that the fires twenty years of our lives is to become a precedent for the next twenty. But even this is admitting more than is true, for I answer roundly, that America would have flourished as much, and probably much more, had no European power had any thing to do with her. The commerce, by which she hath enriched herself, are the necessaries of life, and will always have a market while eating is the custom of Europe....

Thomas Paine, *The Essential Thomas Paine* (London: Penguin Books, 1986), 36–40, 43–45, 48–49, 54–57, 59.

It has lately been asserted in parliament, that the colonies have no relation to each other but through the parent country, i.e. that Pennsylvania and the Jerseys, and so on for the rest, are sister colonies by the way of England; this is certainly a very round-about way of proving relationship, but it is the nearest and only true way of proving enemyship, if I may so call it. France and Spain never were, nor perhaps ever will be our enemies as *Americans*, but as our being the *subjects of Great-Britain*.

But Britain is the parent country, say some. Then the more shame upon her conduct. Even brutes do not devour their young, nor savages make war upon their families; wherefore the assertion, if true, turns to her reproach; but it happens not to be true, or only partly so, and the phrase *parent* or *mother country* hath been jesuitically adopted by the king and his parasites, with a low papistical design of gaining an unfair bias on the credulous weakness of our minds. Europe, and not England, is the parent country of America. This new world hath been the asylum for the persecuted lovers of civil and religious liberty from *every part* of Europe. Hither have they fled, not from the tender embraces of the mother, but from the cruelty of monster; and it is so far true of England, that the same tyranny which drove the first emigrants from home, pursues their descendants still....

... Not one third of the inhabitants, even of this province, are of English descent. Wherefore I reprobate the phrase of parent or mother country applied to England only, as being false, selfish, narrow and ungenerous....

... Our plan is commerce, and that, well attended to, will secure us the peace and friendship of all Europe; because, it is the interest of all Europe to have America a *free port*. Her trade will always be a protection, and her barrenness of gold and silver secure her from invaders....

... It is the true interest of America to steer clear of European contentions, which she never can do, while by her dependance on Britain, she is made the make-weight in the scale of British politics....

As to government matters, it is not in the power of Britain to do this continent justice: The business of it will soon be too weighty, and intricate, to be managed with any tolerable degree of convenience, by a power so distant from us, and so very ignorant of us; for if they cannot conquer us, they cannot govern us....

Small islands not capable of protecting themselves, are the proper objects for kingdoms to take under their care; but there is something very absurd, in supposing a continent to be perpetually governed by an island. In no instance hath nature made the satellite larger than its primary planet, and as England and America, with respect to each other, reverses the common order of nature, it is evident they belong to different systems; England to Europe, America to itself....

... No man was a warmer wisher for reconciliation than myself, before the fatal nineteenth of April 1775, but the moment the event of that day was made known, I rejected the hardened, sullen tempered Pharaoh of England for ever; and disdain the wretch, that with the pretended title of FATHER OF HIS PEOPLE can unfeelingly hear of their slaughter, and composely sleep with their blood upon his soul.

But admitting that matters were now made up, what would be the event? I answer, the ruin of the continent. And that for several reasons.

First, The powers of governing still remaining in the hands of the king, he will have a negative over the whole legislation of this continent. And as he hath shewn himself such an inveterate enemy to liberty, and discovered such a thirst for arbitrary power, is he, or is he not, a proper man to say to these colonies, *"You shall make no laws but what I please."* And is there any inhabitant in America so ignorant, as not to know, that according to what is called the *present constitution*, that this continent can make no laws but what the king gives leave to; and is there any man so unwise, as not to see, that (considering what has happened) he will suffer no law to be made here, but such as suit *his* purpose. We may be as effectually enslaved by the want of laws in America as by submitting to laws made for us in England....

But where, says some, is the King of America? I'll tell you. Friend, he reigns above, and doth not make havoc of mankind like the Royal Brute of Britain. Yet that we may not appear to be defective even in earthly honors, let a day be solemnly set apart for proclaiming the charter; let it be brought forth placed on the divine law, the word of God; let a crown be placed thereon, by which the world may know, that so far we approve of monarchy, that in America THE LAW IS KING....

Some, perhaps, will say, that after we have made it up with Britain, she will protect us. Can we be so unwise as to mean, that she shall keep a navy in our harbours for that purpose? Common sense will tell us, that the power which hath endeavoured to subdue us, is of all others the most improper to defend us....

Another reason why the present time is preferable to all others, is, that the fewer our numbers are, the more land there is yet unoccupied, which instead of being lavished by the king on his worthless dependants, may be hereafter applied, not only to the discharge of the present debt, but to the constant support of government. No nation under heaven hath such an advantage at this....

As to religion, I hold it to be the indispensable duty of all government, to protect all conscientious professors thereof, and I know of no other business which government hath to do therewith, Let a man throw aside that narrowness of soul, that selfishness of principle, which the niggards of all professions are so unwilling to part with, and he will be at once delivered of his fears on that head. Suspicion is the companion of mean souls, and the bane of all good society. For myself, I fully and conscientiously believe, that it is the will of the Almighty, that there should be diversity of religious opinions among us: It affords a large field for our Christian kindness. Were we all of one way of thinking, our religious dispositions would want matter for probation; and on this liberal principle, I look on the various denominations among us, to be like children of the same family, differing only, in what is called, their Christian names....

These proceedings may at first appear strange and difficult; but, like all other steps which we have already passed over, will in a little time become familiar and agreeable; and, until an independence is declared, the Continent will feel itself like a man who continues putting off some unpleasant business from day to day, yet knows it must be done, hates to set about it, wishes it over, and is continually haunted with the thoughts of its necessity.

4. Abigail and John Adams Debate Women's Rights, 1776

Braintree March 31 1776

I wish you would ever write me a Letter half as long as I write you; and tell me if you may where your Fleet are gone? What sort of Defence Virginia can make against our common Enemy? Whether it is so situated as to make an able Defence? Are not the Gentery Lords and the common people vassals, are they not like the uncivilized Natives Brittain represents us to be? I hope their Riffel Men who have shewen themselves very savage and even Blood thirsty; are not a specimen of the Generality of the people....

I have sometimes been ready to think that the passion for Liberty cannot be Eaquelly Strong in the Breasts of those who have been accustomed to deprive their fellow Creatures of theirs. Of this I am certain that it is not founded upon that generous and christian principal of doing to others as we would that others should do unto us....

The Town in General is left in a better state than we expected, more oweing to a precipitate flight than any Regard to the inhabitants, tho some individuals discovered a sense of honour and justice and have left the rent of the Houses in which they were, for the owners and the furniture unhurt, or if damaged sufficent to make it good.

Others have committed abominable Ravages. The Mansion House of your President is safe and the furniture unhurt whilst both the House and Furniture of the Solisiter General have fallen a prey to their own merciless party....

I feel very differently at the approach of spring to what I did a month ago. We knew not then whether we could plant or sow with safety, whether when we had toild we could reap the fruits of our own industery, whether we could rest in our own Cottages, or whether we should not be driven from the sea coasts to seek shelter in the wilderness, but now we feel as if we might sit under our own vine and eat the good of the land....

... I long to hear that you have declared in independancy—and by the way in the new Code of Laws which I suppose it will be necessary for you to make I desire you would Remember the Ladies, and be more generous and favourable to them than your ancestors. Do not put such unlimited power into the hands of the Husbands. Remember all Men would be tyrants if they could. If perticuliar care and attention is not paid to the Laidies we are determined to foment a Rebelion, and will not hold ourselves bound by any Laws in which we have no voice, or Representation.

Source: Charles Frances Adams, ed., Familiar *Letters of John Adams and His Wife Abigail Adams* (1875).

Adams Family Correspondence, I (Cambridge, Mass.: Harvard University Press, 1963), 369–370.

That your Sex are Naturally Tyrannical is a Truth so thoroughly established as to admit of no dispute, but such of you as wish to be happy willingly give up the harsh title of Master for the more tender and endearing one of Friend. Why then, not put it out of the power of the vicious and the Lawless to use us with cruelty and indignity with impunity. Men of Sense in all Ages abhor those customs which treat us only as the vassals of your Sex. Regard us then as Beings placed by providence under your protection and in immitation of the Supreem Being make use of that power only for our happiness.

John Adams Responds

As to your extraordinary code of laws, I cannot but laugh. We have been told that our struggle has loosened the bonds of government everywhere; that children and apprentices were disobedient; that schools and colleges were grown turbulent; that Indians slighted their guardians, and negroes grew insolent to their masters. But your letter was the first intimation that another tribe, more numerous and powerful than all the rest, were grown discontented. This is rather too coarse a Compliment but you are so saucy, I won't blot it out.

Depend upon it, we know better than to repeal our masculine systems. Although they are in full force, you know they are little more than theory. We dare not exert our power in its full latitude. We are obliged to go fair and softly, and, in practice, you know we are the subjects. We have only the name of masters, and rather than give up this, which would completely subject us to the despotism of the petticoat, I hope General Washington and all our brave heroes would fight; I am sure every good politician would plot, as long as he would against despotism, empire, monarchy, aristocracy, oligarchy, or ochlocracy.

5. A Song to Inspire Revolution, 1776

WAR SONG.

HARK, hark the sound of war is heard,
And we must all attend;
Take up our arms and go with speed,
Our country to defend.

Our parent state has turned our foe,
Which fills our land with pain;
Her gallant ships, manned out for war,
Come thundering o'er the main.

There's Carleton, Howe, and Clinton too.
And many thousands more,

Songs and Ballads of the American Revolution (1905), 94–96.

May cross the sea, but all in vain,
Our rights we'll ne'er give o'er.
Our pleasant homes they do invade,
Our property devour;
And all because we won't submit
To their despotic power.

Then let us go against our foe,
We'd better die than yield;
We and our sons are all undone,
If Britain wins the field.

Tories may dream of future joys,
But I am bold to say,
They'll find themselves bound fast in chains,
If Britain wins the day.

Husbands must leave their loving wives,
And sprightly youths attend,
Leave their sweethearts and risk their lives,
Their country to defend.

May they be heroes in the field,
Have heroes' fame in store;
We pray the Lord to be their shield,
Where thundering cannons roar.

6. Mohawk Leader Joseph Brant Commits the Loyalty of His People to Britain, 1776

Brother Gorah [British Secretary of State Lord Germain]:
We have cross'd the great Lake and come to this kingdom with our Superintendant Col. Johnson from our Confederacy the Six Nations and their Allies, that we might see our Father the Great King, and joyn in informing him, his Councillors and wise men, of the good intentions of the Indians our bretheren, and of their attachment to His Majesty and his Government.

Brother: The Disturbances in America give great trouble to all our Nations, as many strange stories have been told to us by the people in that country. The Six Nations who always loved the King, sent a number of their Chiefs and Warriors with their Superintendant to Canada last summer, where they engaged

E. B. O'Callaghan, ed., *Documents Relative to the Colonial History of the State of New York*, VIII (Albany, N.Y.: Weed, Parsons, 1853–1887), 670–671.

their allies to joyn with them in the defence of that country, and when it was invaded by the New England people, they alone defeated them.

Brother: In that engagement we had several of our best Warriors killed and wounded, and the Indians think it very hard they should have been so deceived by the White people in that country, the enemy returning in great numbers, and no White people supporting the Indians, they were oblidged to retire to their vilages and sit still. We now Brother hope to see these bad children chastised, and that we may be enabled to tell the Indians, who have always been faithfull and ready to assist the King, what His Majesty intends.

Brother: The Mohocks our particular Nation, have on all occasions shewn their zeal and loyalty to the Great King; yet they have been very badly treated by his people in that country, the City of Albany laying an unjust claim to the lands on which our Lower Castle is built.... We have been often assured by our late great friend Sr William Johnson who never deceived us, and we know he was told so that the King and wise men here would do us justice; but this notwithstanding all our applications has never been done, and it makes us very uneasie.... We have only therefore to request that his Majesty will attend to this matter: it troubles our Nation & they cannot sleep easie in their beds. Indeed it is very hard when we have let the Kings subjects have so much of our lands for so little value, they should want to cheat us in this manner of the small spots we have left for our women and children to live on. We are tired out in making complaints & getting no redress. We therefore hope that the Assurances now given us by the Superintendant may take place, and that he may have it in his power to procure us justice.

Brother: We shall truly report all that we hear from you, to the Six Nations at our return. We are well informed there has been many Indians in this Country who came without any authority, from their own, and gave much trouble. We desire Brother to tell you this is not our case. We are warriors known to all the Nations, and are now here by approbation of many of them, whose sentiments we speak.

Brother: We hope these things will be considered and that the King or his great men will give us such an answer as will make our hearts light and glad before we go, and strengthen our hands, so that we may joyn our Superintendant Col. Johnson in giving satisfaction to all our Nations, when we report to them, on our return; for which purpose we hope soon to be accomodated with a passage.

Dictated by the Indians and taken down by

Jo: CHEW, Secy

7. African Americans Petition for Freedom, 1777

To the Honorable Counsel & House of [Representa]tives for the State of Massachusitte Bay in General Court assembled, Jan. 13, 1777.

The petition of A Great Number of Blackes detained in a State of slavery in the Bowels of a free & Christian Country Humbly shuwith that your Petitioners

Donald McQuade et al., eds., *The Harper American Literature*, 2nd ed. (New York: HarperCollins, 1990).

apprehend that thay have in Common with all other men a Natural and Unali-
able Right to that freedom which the Grat Parent of the Unavers hath Bestowed
equalley on all menkind and which they have Never forfuted by any Compact
or agreement whatever—but thay wher Unjustly Dragged by the hand of cruel
Power from their Derest friends and sum of them Even torn from the Embraces
of their tender Parents—from A populous Pleasant and plentiful contry and in
violation of Laws of Nature and off Nations and in defiance of all the tender
feelings of humanity Brough[t] hear Either to Be sold Like Beast of Burthen &
Like them Condemnd to Slavery for Life—Among A People Profesing the mild
Religion of Jesus A people Not Insensible of the Secrets of Rationable Being
Nor without spirit to Resent the unjust endeavours of others to Reduce them
to a state of Bondage and Subjection your honouer Need not to be informed
that A Life of Slavery Like that of your petitioners Deprived of Every social privilege of Every thing Requiset to Render Life Tolable is far worse then
Nonexistance.

[In imitat]ion of the Lawdable Example of the Good People of these States
your petiononers have Long and Patiently waited the Evnt of petition after petition By them presented to the Legislative Body of this state and cannot but with
Grief Reflect that their Success hath ben but too similar they Cannot but express
their Astonishment that It has Never Bin Considred that Every Principle from
which Amarica has Acted in the Cours of their unhappy Deficultes with Great
Briton Pleads Stronger than A thousand arguments in favowrs of your petioners
they therfor humble Beseech your honours to give this peti[ti]on its due weight
& consideration and cause an act of the Legislatur to be past Wherby they may
Be Restored to the Enjoyments of that which is the Naturel Right of all men—
and their Children who wher Born in this Land of Liberty may not be heald as
Slaves after they arive at the age of Twenty one years so may the Inhabitance of
thes Stats No longer chargeable with the inconsistancey of acting themselves the
part which they condem and oppose in others Be prospered in their present Glorious struggle for Liberty and have those Blessing to them, &c.

8. General Washington Argues for Greater Military Funding by Portraying the Plight of Soldiers at Valley Forge, 1778

I am pleased to find, that you expect the proposed establishment of the Army
will succeed; though it is a painful consideration, that matters of such pressing
importance and obvious necessity meet with so much difficulty and delay. Be
assured the success of the measure is a matter of the most serious moment, and
that it ought to be brought to a conclusion, as speedily as possible. The spirit of
resigning Commissions has been long at an alarming height, and increases
daily....

The necessity of putting the Army upon a respectable footing, both as to
numbers and constitution, is now become more essential than ever. The Enemy

The George Washington Papers at the Library of Congress, 1741–1799.

are beginning to play a Game more dangerous than their efforts by Arms, tho' these will not be remitted in the smallest degree, and which threatens a fatal blow to American Independence, and to her liberties of course: They are endeavouring to ensnare the people by specious allurements of Peace. It is not improbable they have had such abundant cause to be tired of the War, that they may be sincere, in the terms they offer, which, though far short of our pretensions, will be extremely flattering to Minds that do not penetrate far into political consequences: But, whether they are sincere or not, they may be equally destructive; for, to discerning Men, nothing can be more evident, than that a Peace on the principles of dependance, however limited, after what has happened, would be to the last degree dishonourable and ruinous. It is, however, much to be apprehended, that the Idea of such an event will have a very powerful effect upon the Country, and, if not combated with the greatest address, will serve, at least, to produce supineness and dis-union. Men are naturally fond of Peace, and there are Symptoms which may authorize an Opinion, that the people of America are pretty generally weary of the present War....

Among Individuals, the most certain way to make a Man your Enemy, is to tell him, you esteem him such; so with public bodies, and the very jealousy, which the narrow politics of some may affect to entertain of the Army, in order to a due subordination to the supreme Civil Authority, is a likely mean to produce a contrary effect; to incline it to the pursuit of those measures which that may wish it to avoid. It is unjust, because no Order of Men in the thirteen States have paid a more sanctimonious regard to their proceedings than the Army; and, indeed, it may be questioned, whether there has been that scrupulous adherence had to them by any other, [for without arrogance, or the smallest deviation from truth it may be said, that no history, now extant, can furnish an instance of an Army's suffering such uncommon hardships as ours have done, and bearing them with the same patience and Fortitude. To see Men without Cloathes to cover their nakedness, without Blankets to lay on, without Shoes, by which their Marches might be traced by the Blood from their feet, and almost as often without provisions as with; Marching through frost and Snow, and at Christmas taking up their Winter Quarters within a day's March of the enemy, without a House or Hurt to cover them till they could be built and submitting to it without a murmur, is a mark of patience and obedience which in my opinion can scarce be a parallel'd.]

ESSAYS

Historians have for decades debated the origins and meaning of the Revolution for American society. They have argued over the reasons for rebellion and the outcomes. Was it a fight for "home rule" (whether the colonies should be independent of Britain) or over "who should rule at home" (who should direct and control life in English America)? Scholars have also disputed the degree to which the Revolution altered life in the Americas. Was it a conservative affair that left little unchanged for most people or was it a radical departure from the past? The two essays here stand in direct conflict regarding the "radicalism" of the revolution. In the first essay, Gordon S. Wood, professor at Brown University, claims that white, male American patriots assaulted the bonds of traditional monarchical society. As a result, the Revolution set in motion processes of change that would transform the arrangements of state and society. The Revolution, he declares, propelled the new country in radical new directions. Gary B. Nash, professor at UCLA, finds the emphasis for liberty coming from the efforts of society's oppressed: women, African Americans, and the poor. White, male leaders, Nash asserts, took the revolutionary emphasis from the oppressed and also looked to contain just how radical the revolution would be.

Radical Possibilities of the American Revolution

GORDON S. WOOD

By the late 1760s and early 1770s a potentially revolutionary situation existed in many of the colonies. There was little evidence of those social conditions we often associate with revolution (and some historians have desperately sought to find): no mass poverty, no seething social discontent, no grinding oppression. For most white Americans there was greater prosperity than anywhere else in the world; in fact, the experience of that growing prosperity contributed to the unprecedented eighteenth-century sense that people here and now were capable of ordering their own reality. Consequently, there was a great deal of jealousy and touchiness everywhere, for what could be made could be unmade; the people were acutely nervous about their prosperity and the liberty that seemed to make it possible. With the erosion of much of what remained of traditional social relationships, more and more individuals had broken away from their families, communities, and patrons and were experiencing the anxiety of freedom and independence. Social changes, particularly since the 1740s, multiplied rapidly, and many Americans struggled to make sense of what was happening. These social changes were complicated, and they are easily misinterpreted. Luxury and conspicuous consumption by very ordinary people were increasing. So, too, was religious dissent of all sorts. The rich became richer, and aristocratic gentry everywhere became more conspicuous and self-conscious; and the numbers of poor in some cities and the numbers of landless in some areas increased. But social classes based on occupation or wealth did not set themselves against one another, for no classes in this modern sense yet existed. The society was becoming more unequal, but its inequalities were not the source of the instability and anxiety. Indeed, it was the pervasive equality of American society that was causing the problems....

... [B]ecause such equality and prosperity were so unusual in the Western world, they could not be taken for granted. The idea of labor, of hard work, leading to increased productivity was so novel, so radical, in the overall span of Western history that most ordinary people, most of those who labored, could scarcely believe what was happening to them. Labor had been so long thought to be the natural and inevitable consequence of necessity and poverty that most people still associated it with slavery and servitude. Therefore any possibility of oppression, any threat to the colonists' hard-earned prosperity, any hint of reducing them to the poverty of other nations, was especially frightening; for it seemed likely to slide them back into the traditional status of servants or slaves, into the older world where labor was merely a painful necessity and not a source of prosperity. "The very apprehension thereof, cannot but cause extreme uneasiness." "No wonder," said Gadsden, "that throughout *America*, we find these men extremely anxious and attentive, to the cause of liberty." These hard-working farmers and mechanics were extraordinarily free and well off and had much to lose, and "this, therefore, naturally accounts for these people, in particular, being so united and steady, everywhere," in support of their liberties against British oppression....

America was no doubt "the best poor Man's Country in the World." But the general well-being and equality of the society set against the gross inequality and flagrant harshness of both white servitude and especially black slavery made many people unusually sensitive to all the various dependencies and subordinations that still lurked everywhere in their lives. Thus in 1765 at the outset of the imperial crisis John Adams's fearful and seemingly anachronistic invocation of an older feudal world of "servants and vassals" holding "their lands, by a variety of duties and services ... in a state of servile dependence on their lords," could at once arouse the colonists' anxieties over the potentialities, however inchoate and remote, of a dependent world in their midst. They repeatedly put into words their wide-spread sense that very little stood between their prosperous freedom and out-and-out oppression. Indeed, they told themselves over and over that if ever they should agree to a parliamentary tax or allow their colonial assemblies to be silenced, "nothing will remain to us but a dredful expectation of certain slavery." The tenants of one of the New York landlords may have seemed to the landlord's agent to be "silly people" by their resisting a simple extension of the services required of them out of "fear [of] drawing their Posterity into Bondage," but they knew the reality of the eighteenth-century world. They knew the lot of ordinary people elsewhere, and they knew especially the lot of white and black dependents in their own society, and thus they could readily respond to images of being driven "like draft oxen," of being "made to serve as bond servants," or of foolishly sitting "quietly in expectation of a m[aste]r's promise for the recovery of [their] liberty." The immense changes occurring everywhere in their personal and social relationships—the loosening and severing of the hierarchical ties of kinship and patronage that were carrying them into modernity—only increased their suspicions and apprehensions. For they could not know then what direction the future was taking.

By the middle of the century these social changes were being expressed in politics. Americans everywhere complained of "a Scramble for Wealth and Power" by men of "worldly Spirits." Indeed, there were by the early 1760s "so many jarring and opposite Interests and Systems" that no one in authority could relax, no magistrate, no ruler, could long remain unchallenged. More and more ordinary people were participating in electoral politics, and in many of the colonies the number of contested elections for assembly seats markedly increased. This expansion of popular politics originated not because the mass of people pressed upward from below with new demands but because competing gentry, for their own parochial and tactical purposes, courted the people and bid for their support by invoking popular whig rhetoric. Opposition factions in the colonial assemblies made repeated appeals to the people as counterweights to the use of royal authority by the governors, especially as the older personal avenues of appeal over the heads of the governors to interests in England became clogged and unusable. But popular principles and popular participation in politics, once aroused, could not be easily put down; and by the eve of the Revolution, without anyone's intending or even being clearly aware of what was happening, traditional monarchical ways of governing through kin and patronage were transformed under the impact of the imperial crises. "Family Interests," like the Livingstons and De Lanceys in New York, or the Pinckneys and Leighs of South Carolina, observed one prescient British official in 1776, "have been long in a gradual Decay; and perhaps a new arrangement of political affairs may leave them wholly extinct." Those who were used to seeing politics as essentially a squabble among gentlemen were bewildered by the "strange metamorphosis or other" that was taking place.

With the weakening of family connections and the further fragmentation of colonial interests, crown officials and other conservatives made strenuous efforts to lessen popular participation in politics and to control the "democratic" part of the colonists' mixed constitutions. Some royal governors attempted to restrict the expansion of popular representation in the assemblies, to limit the meetings of the assemblies, and to veto the laws passed by the assemblies. Other officials toyed with plans for remodeling the colonial governments, for making the salaries of royal officials independent of the colonial legislatures, and for the strengthening the royal councils or upper houses in the legislatures. Some even suggested introducing a titled nobility into America in order to stabilize colonial society. But most royal officials relied on whatever traditional monarchical instruments of political patronage and influence they had available to them to curb popular disorder and popular pressure—using intricate maneuvering and personal manipulation of important men in place of whig and republican appeals to the people.

After 1763 all these efforts became hopelessly entangled in the British government's attempts to reform its awkwardly structured empire and to extract revenue from the colonists. All parts of British policy came together to threaten each colonist's expanding republican expectations of liberty and independence. In the emotionally charged atmosphere of the 1760s and 1770s, all the imperial efforts at reform seemed to be an evil extension of what was destroying liberty in England itself. Through the manipulation of puppets or placement in the House of Commons, the crown—since 1760 in the hands of a new young king, George III—was sapping the strength of popular representation in Parliament and unbalancing the English constitution. Events seemed to show that the crown, with the aid of a pliant Parliament, was trying to reach across the Atlantic to corrupt Americans in the same way.

Americans steeped in the radical whig and republican ideology of opposition to the court regarded these monarchical techniques of personal influence and patronage as "corruption," as attempts by great men and their power-hungry minions to promote their private interests at the expense of the public good and to destroy the colonists' balanced constitutions and their popular liberty....

By adopting the language of the radical whig opposition and by attacking the monarchical abuse of family influence and patronage, however, the American revolutionaries were not simply expressing their resentment of corrupt political practices that had denied some of them the highest offices of colonial government. They actually were tearing at the bonds holding the traditional monarchical society together. Their assault necessarily was as much social as it was political.

But this social assault was not the sort we are used to today in describing revolutions. The great social antagonists of the American Revolution were not poor vs. rich, workers vs. employers, or even democrats vs. aristocrats. They were patriots vs. courtiers—categories appropriate to the monarchical world in which the colonists had been reared. Courtiers were persons whose position or rank came artificially from above—from hereditary or personal connections that ultimately flowed from the crown or court. Courtiers, said John Adams, were those who applied themselves "to the Passions and Prejudices, the Follies and Vices of Great Men in order to obtain their Smiles, Esteem, and Patronage and consequently their favors and Preferments." Patriots, on the other hand, were those who not only loved their country but were free of dependent connections and influence; their position or rank came naturally from their talent and from below, from recognition by the people. "A real patriot," declared one American in 1776, was "the most illustrious character in human life. Is not the interest and happiness of his fellow creatures his care?"

Only by understanding the hierarchical structure of monarchical society and taking the patriots' assault on courtiers seriously can we begin to appreciate the significance of the displacement of the loyalists—that is, of those who maintained their allegiance to the British crown. The loyalists may have numbered close to half a million, or 20 percent of white Americans. As many as 80,000 of them are estimated to have left the thirteen colonies during the American Revolution, over six times as many émigrés per 1,000 of population as fled France during the French Revolution. Although many of these American émigrés, unlike the French émigrés, did not have to abandon their nation and could remain as much British subjects in Canada or the West Indies or Britain itself as they had been in one of the thirteen colonies, nevertheless, the emigration of the loyalists had significant effects on American society.

It was not how many loyalists who were displaced that was important; it was who they were. A disproportionate number of them were well-to-do gentry operating at the pinnacles of power and patronage—royal or proprietary officeholders, big overseas dry-goods merchants, and rich landowners. Because they commanded important chains of influence, their removal disrupted colonial society to a degree far in excess of their numbers....

To eliminate those clusters of personal and familial influence and transform the society became the idealistic goal of the revolutionaries. Any position that came from any source but talent and the will of the people now seemed undeserved and dependent. Patrimonialism, plural officeholding, and patronage of all sorts—practices that had usually been taken for granted in a monarchical society—came under attack....

It is in this context that we can best understand the revolutionaries' appeal to independence, not just the independence of the country from Great Britain, but, more important, the independence of individuals from personal influence and "warm and private friendship." The purpose of the Virginia constitution of 1776, one Virginian recalled, was "to prevent the undue and overwhelming influence of great landholders in elections." This was to be done by disfranchising the landless "tenants and retainers" who depended "on the breath and varying will" of these great men and by ensuring that only men who owned their own land could vote.

A republic presumed, as the Virginia declaration of rights put it, that men in the new republic would be "equally free and independent," and property would make them so. Property in a republic was still conceived of traditionally—in proprietary terms—not as a means of personal profit or aggrandizement but rather as a source of personal authority or independence. It was regarded not merely as a material possession but also as an attribute of a man's personality that defined him and protected him from outside pressure. A carpenter's skill, for example, was his property. Jefferson feared the rabble of the cities precisely because they were without property and were thus dependent.

All dependents without property, such as women and young men, could be denied the vote because, as a convention of Essex County, Massachusetts, declared in 1778, they were "so situated as to have no wills of their own." Jefferson was so keen on this equation of property with citizenship that he proposed in 1776 that the new state of Virginia grant fifty acres of land to every man that did not have that many. Without having property and a will of his own—without having independence—a man could have no public spirit; and there could be no republic. For, as Jefferson put it, "dependence begets subservience and venality, suffocates the germ of virtue, and prepares fit tools for the designs of ambition."

In a monarchical world of numerous patron-client relations and multiple degrees of dependency, nothing could be more radical than this attempt to make every man independent. What was an ideal in the English-speaking world now became for Americans an ideological imperative. Suddenly, in the eyes of the revolutionaries, all the fine calibrations of rank and degrees of unfreedom of the traditional monarchical society became absurd and degrading. The Revolution became a full-scale assault on dependency....

Of course, the revolutionary leaders did not expect poor, humble men—farmers, artisans, or tradesmen—themselves to gain high political office. Rather, they expected that the sons of such humble or ungenteel men, if they had abilities, would, as they had, acquire liberal and genteel republican attributes, perhaps by attending Harvard or the College of New Jersey at Princeton, and would thereby rise into the ranks of gentlemen and become eligible for high political office. The sparks of genius that they hoped republicanism would fan and kindle into flame belonged to men like themselves—men "drawn from obscurity" by the new opportunities of republican competition and emulation into becoming "illustrious characters, which will dazzle the world with the splendor of their names." Honor, interest, and patriotism together called them to qualify themselves and posterity "for the bench, the army, the navy, the learned professions, and all the departments of civil government." They would become what Jefferson called the "natural aristocracy"—liberally educated, enlightened gentlemen of character. For many of revolutionary leaders this was the emotional significance of republicanism—a vindication of frustrated talent at the expense of birth and blood. For too long, they felt, merit had been denied. In a monarchical world only the arts and sciences had recognized talent as the sole criterion of leadership. Which is why even the eighteenth-century *ancien régime* called the world of the arts and sciences "the republic of letters." Who, it was asked, remembered the fathers or sons of Homer and Euclid? Such a question was a republican dagger driven into the heart of the old hereditary order. "Virtue," said Thomas Paine simply, "is not hereditary."

Because the revolutionaries are so different from us, so seemingly aristocratic themselves, it is hard for us today to appreciate the anger and resentment they felt toward hereditary aristocracy. We tend to ignore or forget the degree to which family and monarchical values dominated colonial America. But the revolutionaries knew only too well what kin and patrimonial officeholding had meant in their lives. Up and down the continent colonial gentry like Charles Carroll of Maryland had voiced their fears that "all power might center in *one family*" and that offices of government "like a precious jewel will be handed down from *father* to *son*." Everywhere men expressed their anger over the exclusive and unresponsive governments that had distributed offices, land, and privileges to favorites....

The Revolution's assault on patriarchy inevitably affected relationships within the family, as decisions concerning women's and daughters' rights were made that conservatives later regarded as "tending to loosen the bands of society." Changes in the family begun earlier found new republican justifications and were accelerated—showing up even in paintings. In earlier-eighteenth-century family portraits fathers had stood dominantly above their wives and children; now they were portrayed on the same plane with them—a symbolic leveling. With the Revolution men lost some of their earlier patriarchal control over their wives and property. Although wives continued to remain dependent on their husbands, they did gain greater autonomy and some legal recognition of their rights to hold property separately, to divorce, and to make contracts and do business in the absence of their husbands. In the colonial period only New Englanders had recognized the absolute right to divorce, but after the Revolution all the states except South Carolina developed new liberal laws on divorce.

Women and children no doubt remained largely dependent on their husbands and fathers, but the revolutionary attack on patriarchal monarchy made all other dependencies in the society suspect. Indeed, once the revolutionaries collapsed all the different distinctions and dependencies of a monarchical society into either freemen or slaves, white males found it increasingly impossible to accept any dependent status whatsoever. Servitude of any sort suddenly became anomalous and anachronistic. In 1784 in New York, a group believing that indentured servitude was "contrary to ... the idea of liberty this country has so happily established" released a shipload of immigrant servants and arranged for public subscriptions to pay for their passage. As early as 1775 in Philadelphia the proportion of the workforce that was unfree—composed of servants and slaves—had already declined to 13 percent from the 40 to 50 percent that it had been at mid-century. By 1800 less than 2 percent of the city's labor force remained unfree. Before long indentured servitude virtually disappeared.

With the post-revolutionary republican culture talking of nothing but liberty, equality, and independence, even hired servants eventually became hard to come by or to control. White servants refused to call their employers "master" or "mistress"; for many the term "boss," derived from the Dutch word for master, became a euphemistic substitute. The servants themselves would not be called anything but "help," or "waiter," which was the term the character Jonathan, in Royall Tyler's 1787 play *The Contrast*, preferred in place of "servant."...

By the early nineteenth century what remained of patriarchy was in disarray. No longer were apprentices dependents within a family; they became trainees within a business that was more and more conducted outside the household. Artisans did less "bespoke" or "order" work for patrons; instead they increasingly produced for impersonal markets. This in turn meant that the master craftsmen had to hire labor and organize the sale of the products of their shops. Masters became less patriarchs and more employers, retail merchants, or businessmen. Cash payments of wages increasingly replaced the older paternalistic relationship between masters and journeymen. These free wage earners now came and went with astonishing frequency, moving not only from job to job but from city to city. This "fluctuating" mobility of workers bewildered some employers: "while you were taking an inventory of their property," sighed one Rhode Islander, "they would sling their packs and be off."

Although both masters and journeymen often tried to maintain the traditional fiction that they were bound together for the "good of the trade," increasingly they saw themselves as employers and employees with different interests. Although observers applauded the fact that apprentices, journeymen, and masters of each craft marched together in the federal procession in Philadelphia on July 4, 1788, the tensions and divergence of interests were already visible. Before long journeymen in various crafts organized themselves against their masters' organizations, banned their employers from their meetings, and declared that "the interests of the journeymen are separate and in some respects opposite of those of their employers." Between 1786 and 1816 at least twelve major strikes by various journeymen craftsmen occurred—the first major strikes by employees against employers in American history.

One obvious dependency the revolutionaries did not completely abolish was that of nearly a half million Afro-American slaves, and their failure to do so, amidst all their high-blown talk of liberty, makes them seem inconsistent and hypocritical in our eyes. Yet it is important to realize that the Revolution suddenly and effectively ended the cultural climate that had allowed black slavery, as well as other forms of bondage and unfreedom, to exist throughout the colonial period without serious challenge. With the revolutionary movement, black slavery became excruciatingly conspicuous in a way that it had not been in the older monarchical society with its many calibrations and degrees of unfreedom; and Americans in 1775-76 began attacking it with a vehemence that was inconceivable earlier.

For a century or more the colonists had taken slavery more or less for granted as the most base and dependent status in a hierarchy of dependencies and a world of laborers. Rarely had they felt the need either to criticize black slavery or to defend it. Now, however, the republican attack on dependency compelled Americans to see the deviant character of slavery and to confront the institution as they never had to before. It was no accident that Americans in Philadelphia in 1775 formed the first antislavery society in the world. As long as most people had to work merely out of poverty and the need to provide for a living, slavery and other forms of enforced labor did not seem all that different from free labor. But the growing recognition that labor was not simply a common necessity of the poor but was in fact a source of increased wealth and prosperity for ordinary workers made slavery seem more and more anomalous. Americans now recognized that slavery in a republic of workers was an aberration, "a peculiar institution," and that if any Americans were to retain it, as southern Americans eventually did, they would have to explain and justify it in new racial and anthropological ways that their former monarchical society had never needed. The Revolution in effect set in motion ideological and social forces that doomed the institution of slavery in the North and led inexorably to the Civil War.

With all men now considered to be equally free citizens, the way was prepared as well for a radical change in the conception of state power. Almost at a stroke the Revolution destroyed all the earlier talk of paternal or maternal government, filial allegiance, and mutual contractual obligations between rulers and ruled. The familial image of government now lost all its previous relevance, and the state in America emerged as something very different from what it had been.

The Radical Revolution from the "Bottom Up"

GARY B. NASH

"WHO SHALL WRITE THE HISTORY OF THE AMERICAN REVOLUTION? Who can write it? Who will ever be able to write it?" Thus wrote John Adams in 1815 to Thomas Jefferson, his old enemy but by this time his septuagenarian friend. "Nobody," Jefferson replied from Monticello, "except merely its external facts … The life and soul of history must be forever unknown."

Not so. For more than two centuries historians have written about the American Revolution, striving to capture the "life and soul" of which Jefferson

From Gary B. Nash, *The Unknown Revolution: The Unruly Birth of Democracy and the Struggle to Create America*, p. xv–xvii, 59–61, 91–92, 157–160, 202–206, 435–437, 454. Reprinted by permission of Penguin Group (USA) Inc.

spoke. We now possess a rich and multistranded tapestry of the Revolution, filled with engaging biographies, local narratives, weighty explorations of America's greatest explosion of political thinking, annals of military tactics and strategies, discussions of religious, economic, and diplomatic aspects of what was then called the "glorious cause," and more. Indeed we now have possession of far more that the "external facts."

Yet the great men—the founding fathers—of the revolutionary era dominate the reigning master narrative. Notwithstanding generations of prodigious scholarship, we have not appreciated the lives and labors, the sacrifices and struggles, the glorious messiness, the hopes and fears of divers groups that fought in the longest and most disruptive war in our history with visions of launching a new age filling their heads. Little is known, for example, of Thomas Peters, an African-born slave who made his personal declaration of independence in early 1776, fought for the freedom of African Americans, led former slaves to Nova Scotia after the war, and completed a pilgrimage for unalienable rights by shepherding them back to Africa to participate in the founding of Sierra Leone. Why are the history books virtually silent on Dragging Canoe, the Cherokee warrior who made the American Revolution into a two-decade life-sapping fight for his people's life, liberty, and pursuit of happiness? We cannot capture the "life and soul" of the Revolution without paying close attention to the wartime experiences and agendas for change that engrossed backcountry farmers, urban craftsmen, deep-blue mariners, female camp followers and food rioters—those ordinary people who did most of the protesting, most of the fighting, most of the dying, and most of the dreaming about how a victorious America might satisfy the yearnings of all its peoples....

[T]he true radicalism of the American Revolution ... was indispensable to the origins, conduct, character, and outcome of the world-shaking event.

By "radicalism" I mean advocating wholesale change and sharp transformation rooted in a kind of dream life of a better future imagined by those who felt most dissatisfied with the conditions they experienced as the quarrel with Great Britain unfolded. For a reformed America they looked toward a redistribution of political, social, and religious power; the discarding of old institutions and the creation of new ones; the overthrowing of ingrained patterns of conservative, elitist thought; the leveling of society so that top and bottom were not widely separated; the end of the nightmare of slavery and the genocidal intentions of land-crazed frontiersmen; the hope of women of achieving a public voice. This radicalism directed itself at destabilizing a society where the white male elite prized stability because it upheld their close grip on political, economic, religious, sexual, and social power. This radicalism, therefore, was usually connected to a multifaceted campaign to democratize society, to recast the social system, to achieve dreams with deep biblical and historical roots, to put "power in the people," as the first articles of government in Quaker New Jersey expressed it a century before the American Revolution....

Both loyal supporters of English authority and well-established colonial protest leaders underestimated the self-activating capacity of ordinary colonists. By the end of 1765, an extraordinary year in the history of the English colonies, people in the streets had astounded, dismayed, and frightened their social superiors. Resistance to English policies had emboldened people who previously counted for little in the political arena to find a mind of their own. Colonial leaders, warned the perceptive General Gage, "began to be terrified at the spirit they had raised to perceive that popular fury was not to be guided, and each individual feared he might be the next victim to their rapacity."

While crowds took to the streets up and down the Atlantic seaboard shouting "liberty and no stamps," it entered the minds of many colonists that the constant talk about liberty—and its opposite, slavery—might become highly contagious, and applied to an issue far more fundamental than a modest tax imposed by England. In every colony, white leaders began to wonder about how restive slaves might react to the rhetoric fueling the disturbances related to the Stamp Act. While seeking freedom from parliamentary taxes, while deploring English tyranny and supposed attempts to "enslave" colonists, the Americans unexpectedly faced a profound contradiction as they scrambled to suppress enslaved Africans with their own urges to be free.

George Mason, Virginia planter-politician and neighbor of Thomas Jefferson, was one of the many Virginia leaders worried over the huge increase in Africans brought across the Atlantic after the end of the Seven Years' War. "Perhaps the primary cause of the destruction of the most flourishing government that ever existed was the introduction of great numbers of slaves," he wrote in 1765 in a bill he introduced in the House of Burgesses, just after the Stamp Act riots surged through the seaboard cities. Mason was soon joined by other Virginians who had been edgy about slave unrest since the beginning of the Seven Years' War. Many white militiamen were fighting on the frontier, and this raised fear that slaves, who represented 40 percent of the population, would capitalize on their absence as slave patrollers to stage a bid for freedom. "The villainy of the Negroes on any emergency of government is what I always feared," Governor Robert Dinwiddie told Charles Carter, a tidewater planter with scores of slaves, in 1755. Pontiac's Rebellion in 1763 further increased fears of black rebellion. One militia officer told Governor Dinwiddie that the Indians raiding on Virginia's frontier "are saving and caressing all the Negroes they take," and this might "be productive of an insurrection … attended with the most serious consequences."

The Indian-African alliance never occurred, but nervousness over the possibility spread as the furor over the Stamp Act filled the air with heated talk about American liberty and British tyranny. In 1766, some of George Mason's slaves joined a plot to mount an insurrection. Other slave rebellions, including ones in Loudoun and Fairfax Counties occurred in 1767, and this convinced the House of Burgesses to double the import duty on slaves in order to limit the number of new Africans entering the colony. In the meantime, white authorities hanged seven slaves, and the heads of four "were cut off and fixed on the chimnies of the courthouse," as a Boston newspaper reported….

Charleston, South Carolina, the slave importation center of North America, suffered even greater fears of slave conspiracy after white protesters bandied about assaults on *their* freedom. Black Charlestonians heard and read the word "liberty" repeatedly in the waning months of 1765, and saw the slogan "Liberty and no Stamp Act" emblazoned on a placard hanging from the neck of the stamp distributor's effigy, strung up on October 19, 1765. A few days later, the Sons of Liberty, marching on the elegant house of merchant Henry Laurens to seize bundles of stamps they believed had been stored there, shouted "Liberty, Liberty and Stamp'd Paper." When a huge procession celebrated the resignation of Charleston's stamp distributor, they held aloft a British flag that read LIBERTY.

The repeated use of the word "liberty" was not lost on some five thousand slaves in Charleston. In 1765, the city's grand jury was already apprehensive "that slaves in Charles-Town are not under a good regulation, and that they at all times in the night go about streets rioting," undeterred by the city's handful of watchmen. Within weeks, restive slaves were gathering in knots. More ominous, in mid-December the wife of a wealthy merchant overheard two slaves conversing about a colonywide insurrection planned for Christmas Eve. "This place has been in an uproar for twelve days past," wrote one townsman. "Every company in town mount guard day and night, and the severest orders given which has prevented it hitherto."

Put on close guard, white Carolinians got through the Christmas season unscathed. But in mid-January "a peculiar incident, revealing in what dread the citizens lived among the black savages with whom they were surrounding themselves," reported Henry Laurens, "was furnished by some negroes who apparently in thoughtless imitation, began to cry 'Liberty.'" Laurens was surely mistaken that this action was "thoughtless imitations," but he was accurate that "the city was thrown under arms for a week and for 10 or 14 days messengers were sent posting through the province in the most bitterly cold weather in 19 years." Almost simultaneously, 107 slaves fled their plantations outside Charleston and "joined a large number of runaways in Colleton County, which increase[d] to a formidable Body." Concerned about their liberty with regard to stamped paper, South Carolinians were even more concerned about the liberty of Africans. More than seven thousand Africans had stumbled off slave ships in Charleston Harbor in the year 1765—a huge increase from previous years that made the colony more than 60 percent African. Quaking over real and imagined black insurrections, legislators passed a three-year stoppage of slave imports to take effect on January 1, 1766. But the black revolution in South Carolina had already begun....

The years between 1766 and 1774 were ones of intense debate and confrontation at every level of society. Thousands of well-meaning people on both sides of the Atlantic were engaged in the yeasty business of defining sound political principles, finding stable constitutional ground upon which to stand, and hammering out ideological positions that made sense within their communities. Only in a time of crisis does such hard thinking usually occur. Complicating matters, the crucial decade after 1765 produced violent economic fluctuations and difficult circumstances for people of all ranks. These difficulties cannot be sensibly separated from the course of politics and political thinking, for all politics takes place within social and economic contexts.

By 1766, most sectors of the colonies had recovered from the depression that followed the end of the Seven Years' War, but nettlesome problems remained. The growing domination of colonial wheels of commerce by English decision makers and English capital was of especial concern. The colonial economy had always been the servant of the metropolitan master; that was what it meant to be a colony, to be "underdeveloped," to be a producer and exporter of foodstuffs and raw products and an importer and consumer of finished goods. But as the colonial economies matured, restrictions on local development began to grate. The Currency Act of 1764, which strictly limited the authority of Pennsylvania and New York to issue paper currency, had a constricting effect because locally issued paper money had provided the circulating medium of local trade. When it was disallowed, internal trade shriveled up, hurting merchants and artisans alike and obliging traders to concoct ingenious schemes for issuing fiat money. The years from 1767 to 1769 were especially difficult in this regard. A number of Boston merchants, including John Hancock's younger brother, closed their doors; and Philadelphians were stunned by the collapse of Baynton, Wharton, and Morgan, one of the city's largest merchant houses that specialized in the Indian trade, with liabilities of £94,000—something akin to the collapse of Enron in 2001.

Even more punishing was the credit crisis of 1772. Touched off by the collapse of a major London banking house, it spread like a summer brushfire. English and Scottish merchants had extended credit liberally to American importers in order to spur the consumption of British goods. American merchants willingly increased their orders and passed their indebtedness on to retailers and consumers as book credit. Accepting credit in order to expand had obvious advantages, but it made borrowers far more vulnerable to cyclical swings in the British credit structure. Responding to a major bankruptcy in 1772, English merchants began to demand payment on colonial debts. When colonial merchants could not meet the demands of their overseas creditors, they declared bankruptcy; or, by calling for retailers to pay off their indebtedness, they forced shopkeepers into bankruptcy. The ripple effect was felt up and down the seaboard colonies. "Daily accounts of heavy failures among the shopkeepers" were reported in Philadelphia in late 1773, and this occurred in other seaport towns as well. The scramble for liquidity hit southern planters and small farmers as well as northern merchants and shopkeepers, for tobacco, rice, and indigo growers had deeply indebted themselves to purchase more slaves and open up more land. When English and Scottish creditors called on them to pay their debts, thousands of southern planters suffered court judgment that took away their "land, Negroes, horses, cows, hogs, and feather beds or old pots or pans," as one Fredericksburg trader explained. The early 1770s thus became a time when punishing economic fluctuations made parliamentary legislation all the more intolerable....

John Adams, especially in his public pronouncements, had nervous fits about the leveling spirit breaking out in all the colonies. It was one thing to bring the high and mighty down a rung or two, but quite another to allow those on the bottom rungs to spring upward. Like his cousin Sam, he believed that in a republic the distance between rich and poor should not be too great. But if this leveling of income and wealth shaded into indiscipline or challenges to the authority of the well-born and educated, he saw the beast of anarchy beckoning.

Writing from Philadelphia to Abigail, who was tending the farm and raising their four children in Braintree, Massachusetts, three hundred miles to the north, Adams complained that "our struggle has loosened the bands of government everywhere. That children and apprentices were disobedient—that schools and colleges were grown turbulent—that Indians slighted their guardians and Negroes grew insolent to their masters." This casting off of deference disturbed Adams. Released from the bottle, could the genie ever be recaptured?

That the genie was not always masculine also troubled Adams. His wife Abigail tasked him on just this issue. Her husband's long absences from home and the strain of running their farm by herself just outside British-occupied Boston, along with the death of her mother in the fall of 1775, all seemed to bring her to a new state of consciousness about what the looming revolution might hold for the women who were playing such an important role in the nonimportation and homespun movements. "In the Code of Laws which I suppose it will be necessary for you to make," she wrote John on March 31, 1776, "I desire you would remember the ladies, and be more generous and favourable to them than your ancestors." In this much quoted passage, Abigail went from desire to demand. "Do not put such unlimited power into the hand of the husbands. Remember all men would be tyrants if they could. If particular care and attention is not paid to the ladies, we are determined to foment a rebellion, and will not hold ourselves bound by any laws in which we have no voice or representation." A few paragraphs earlier Abigail had wondered about just how real the "passion for liberty" was among those who still kept fellow humans enslaved. Now she pushed the point home about men enslaving women. "That your sex are naturally tyrannical is a truth so thoroughly established as to admit of no dispute, but such of you as wish to be happy willingly give up the harsh title of master for the more tender and endearing one of friend. Why then, not put it out of the power of the vicious and lawless to use us with cruelty and indignity with impunity? Men of sense in all ages abhor those customs which treat us only as the vassals of your sex."

In this letter we see clearly how women of Abigail Adams's intellectual mettle nimbly made the connection between civil and domestic government. The more male leaders railed against England's intentions to 'enslave" its colonial "subjects," to rule arbitrarily, to act tyrannically, the more American women began to rethink their own marital situations. The language of protest against England reminded many American women that they too were badly treated "subjects"—the subjects of husbands who often dealt with them cruelly and exercised power over them arbitrarily. Most American women, still bound by the social conventions of the day, were not yet ready to organize in behalf of greater rights. But the protests against England stirred up new thoughts about what seemed arbitrary or despotic in their own society, and many women began to think that what had been endured in the past was no longer acceptable. This paved the way for change. Abigail's reference to the cruelty men used against their wives probably refers to the "rule of thumb" that the law upheld. Deeply imbedded in England's common law, and encoded in Blackstone's *Commentaries on the Laws of England*, the rule of thumb made it permissible for husbands to beat their wives so long as the stick or club did not exceed the thickness of a male thumb. The reference to using women with indignity probably referred to the emotional and psychological domination of wives by husbands. For all his love of Abigail, John's reply to her letter of March 31, 1776, confirmed the point. "As to your extraordinary code of laws," he wrote, "I cannot but laugh." Then referring to the growing insubordination of children, apprentices, Indians, slaves, and college students, he sniffed that "your letter was the first intimation that another tribe more numerous and powerful than all the rest were grown discontented. This is rather too coarse a compliment but you are so saucy, I won't blot it out."...

Abigail was not amused. She knew that it was not the British ministry that stirred up women and others grating against their subordination. Instead of writing John after receiving his dismissive letter. She unburdened herself to her friend Mercy Otis Warren, the sister of John Otis and wife of James Warren, a Massachusetts legislator. "He is very saucy to me in return for a list of female grievances which I transmitted to him," she wrote Mercy. "I think I will get you to join me in a petition to Congress." Why, she wondered, was her husband so insensitive to what seemed an opportunity to enact a more "generous plan," "some laws in our favor upon just and liberal principles" by which the law would curb "the power of the arbitrary and tyrannic to injure us with impunity?" Under revised law, women could gain court protection against abusive husbands and not lose their property and wages to men once they married. For raising just and liberal principles, she bitterly told Mercy, he scoffed at her and called her saucy. "So I have helped the sex abundantly," she closed, "but I will tell him I have only been making trial of the disinterestedness of his virtue, and when weighed in the balance have found in wanting." Mercy Otis Warren, who had already crossed the boundaries of correct female behavior by writing two patriot plays that pilloried Thomas Hutchinson and other Loyalists, sympathized with Abigail and told other women that the criticism of females who interested themselves in politics should be resisted.

Abigail stewed about John's dismissiveness and waited far longer than was her habit before answering his letter of April 14. "I believe tis near ten days since I wrote you a line," she wrote on May 7. "I have not felt in a humor to entertain you. If I had taken up my pen perhaps some unbecoming invective might have fallen from it." Then she let out the steam building in her on the matter of women's rights. "I can not say that I think you very generous to the ladies, for... you insist upon retaining an absolute power over wives." Again, she was using the same catchwords and phrases so familiar from the years of protesting British arrogance and insensitivity——"absolute power," "tyranny," "unlimited power." "You must remember," she continued, "that arbitrary power is like most other things which are very hard, very liable to be broken——and notwithstanding all your wise laws maxims we have it in our power not only to free ourselves but to subdue our masters, and without violence throw both your natural and legal authority at our feet." In this reference to Lysistrata, who rallied the Grecian women to withhold their sexual favors from husbands who would not listen to their pleas for peace, Abigail played her last card——at least for now. When John received her latest parry on the question of arbitrary and tyrannical men, he chose to withhold further comment. It was not that he put the matter out of mind. Rather he chose to express his dismay and horror to James Sullivan, superior court judge in Massachusetts and member of the legislature, who had offered his view that propertyless adult men should be allowed the vote. "Depend upon it, Sir," Adams wrote Sullivan: "There will be no end of it" if propertyless men were given the vote. "Women will demand a vote." Young lads would be next. "It tends to confound and destroy all distinctions and prostrate all ranks to one common level.".…

Many slaves could not wait for benevolent masters and mistresses to set them free. From northern New England to the Georgia-Florida border, previous strategies to obtain freedom——petitioning legislatures for a general emancipation, bringing individual freedom suits before local courts, and taking flight in the hope of successfully posing as free men and women——now expanded to a fourth highly risky but less complicated option: offering the British their services in exchange for freedom and inducing the British to issue a general proclamation that would provide an opportunity for masses of slaves to burst their shackles.

In Boston, after he had been appointed the military governor of Masschusetts in April 1774, General Thomas Gage was determined to ram the new British policy down the throats of truculent Bostonians. Five months later, he received offers of help in this difficult matter from an unlikely source. Knowing that Governor Gage had dissolved the Massachusetts legislature, thereby foreclosing that avenue of ending slavery, Boston's slaves now offered to take up the sword against their masters. In late September 1774, fourteen months before Virginia's royal governor issued his famous proclamation offering freedom to any salve or indentured servant reaching the British forces, enslaved Bostonians tried to turn rumors of British intentions into concrete policy. "There has been in town a conspiracy of the Negroes," Abigail Adams wrote her husband, now in Philadelphia as a delegate to the First Continental Congress. "At present it is kept pretty private and was discovered by one who endeavored to dissuade them from it; he being threatened with his life, applied … for protection." Abigail continued that "They conducted in this way … to draw up a petition to the Governor, telling him they would fight for him provided he would arm them and engage to liberate them if he conquered." For white Bostonians, who prided themselves as a different breed from Virginia and Carolina slave masters, this came as a shock. Benjamin Franklin's judgment nearly twenty years before that "every slave may be reckoned a domestic enemy" was being chillingly confirmed."

In reporting the determination of Boston slaves to seize their freedom, Abigail reiterated her hatred of slavery. "I wish most sincerely there was not a slave in the province. It always appeared a most iniquitous scheme to me—fight ourselves for what we are daily robbing and plundering from those who have as good a right to freedom as we have." All over Massachusetts, slaves agreed. In late March 1775, slaves in Bristol and Worcester counties petitioned the local committees of correspondence for assistance "in obtaining their freedom." In mid-April, just before the "shot heard round the world," slaves in Bristol County, Rhode Island, slipped away to join "Col. Gilbert's banditti," a group of thirty-five Loyalists who had obtained arms from a British man-of-war in Newport.

Then, in the aftermath of the firefight at Lexington and Concord, Worcester County's convention, sitting outside the law, resolved that "we abhor the enslaving of any of the human race, and particularly of the NEGROES, in this country," and promised to do anything possible "toward the emancipating the NEGROES...."

Not far behind Massachusetts slaves were African Americans in the southern colonies. In November 1774, apparently aware that the English might give them their freedom, a group of Virginia slaves met to choose a leader "who was to conduct them when the English troops should arrive," as the young James Madison revealed to Philadelphia's printer William Bradford. Madison recounted how the slaves "foolishly thought ... that by revolting to them [the British] they should be rewarded with their freedom." He soon learned that the slaves were not foolish at all but were anticipating what would soon become policy. Madison begged Bradford not to print anything about his plot in the *Pennsylvania Journal* for fear that the news would inspire other uprisings. Two weeks later, the dreaded insurgency surfaced in coastal Georgia when six male and four female slaves murdered their plantation overseer and his wife and then marched to neighboring plantations, where they killed several whites and wounded others. When a patrol captured the rampaging slaves, they were burned alive at the stake, not only to avenge the deaths of white planters but to terrify other slaves with rebellion on their minds."

Word leaking back from England gave southern slaves further reason to believe that their calculations about evolving British policy were not foolish. In early January 1775, the news reached southerners that a member of Parliament had proposed a general emancipation of slaves as a way of "humbling the high aristocratic spirit of Virginia and the southern colonies." The House of Commons did not pass the measure, which would have rocked overseas English slavery to the roots; but in Massachusetts Governor Gage soon expressed interest in such a policy. In a letter to John Stuart, southern superintendent of Indian affairs, Gage noted that if white South Carolinians continued their reckless opposition to British policies, "it may happen that your rice and indigo will be brought to market by negroes instead of white people."

Slaves in tidewater Virginia did their part to shape English policy on the emancipation issue through a rash of uprisings in early 1775. On April 21, only two days after the minutemen riddled Gage's troops, who were sent to capture the colonial arsenals at Lexington and Concord, determined slaves made their move. John Murray, earl of Dunmore, had already moved from the governor's mansion in Williamsburg, Virginia's capital to the *Fowey*, a British warship anchored in the lower York River. From here he dispatched a detachment to seize barrels of gunpowder in Williamsburg and bring them to the British warships. Edmund Randolph, Jefferson's son-in-law, later claimed that the governor's intention was to disarm the Virginians and "weaken the means of opposing an insurrection of the slaves ... for a protection against whom in part the magazine was at first built." Seeing their chance, a number of slaves in Williamsburg offered to join Dunmore and "take up arms." To cow white patriot Virginians, Dunmore now warned that he "would declare freedom to the slaves and reduce the City of Williamsburg to ashes" if the hastily raised militia units threatened him.

Ten days later, on May 1, 1775, Dunmore made an earthshaking decision in favor of what one white Virginian called "the most diabolical" scheme to "offer freedom to our slaves and turn them against their masters." Writing to the secretary of state in London, Dunmore set out his plan "to arm all my own Negroes and receive all others that will come to me whom I shall declare free." It was a policy, remembered South Carolina's William Drayton, that "was already known" by slaves, who "entertain ideas that the present contest was for obliging us to give them their liberty." Near panic engulfed the South. "The newspapers were full of publications calculated to excite the fears of the people—massacres and instigated insurrections were the words in the mouth of every child," remembered Indian superintendent John Stuart. Stuart himself was part of the potential insurrection. Charlestonians drove him from the city after he was suspected of plotting to draw Creek Indians into the conflict on the British side. Stuart fled to Saint Augustine, Florida, to await the British occupation of South Carolina....

Native Americans suffered disastrous losses in the war of the American Revolution. Facing a white society that was heavily armed and determined to seize the western lands that the Proclamation Act of 1763 denied white settlers, nations such as the Iroquois, Delaware, Shawnee, Wyandot, Cherokee, and Creek were forced by American commissioners to cede most of their land at gunpoint. While population buildup that had caused straitened economic conditions in seaboard settlements found a safety valve in western lands. Pouring across the Appalachians even before Benjamin Franklin, John Adams, and John Jay affixed their signatures to the peace treaty with England, thousands of settlers ignored treaty boundary lines and thumbed their noses at their elected state governments and the continental Congress. Looking east, Native Americans had to make hard choices while confronting this human torrent.

Joseph Brant, the Mohawk leader ... appeared on the scene once more to play a crucial role in attempts to forge a pan-Indian alliance that could stem the white tide in the Old Northwest. Having cowed the tribes closest to the settlers' frontier—the Iroquois, Delaware, Wyandot, Chippewa, and Ottawa—congressional commissioners in 1786 planned to humble the westernmost tribes, the Shawnee, Miami, Potawatomi, Kickapoo, and others. But meanwhile, Brant worked his own woodland diplomacy, trying to gather many tribal leaders together for a grand parley at Detroit late in 1786. He had just returned from his second voyage to England, where he did not receive what he most hoped for—promises of military support. But England promised Brant a generous compensation for Iroquois losses in the war and gave him enough encouragement to return home determined to rally England's wartime Indian allies for further resistance to the overweening Americans. Brant knew that for his own people, the Mohawks and other Iroquois, the future lay in moving north of Lake Erie and Lake Ontario where the British had granted them land in the Grand River region of Lower Canada. Yet he felt compelled to play out his years on a larger stage, working to rally the Ohio River valley tribes in defense of their homelands.

Trekking into Ohio country in September 1786 with fifty-seven Iroquois delegates to parley with the Shawnee at their main town of Wapakoneta (in today's west central Ohio), Brant narrowly escaped a punitive expedition of two thousand militiamen led by George Rogers Clark and Benjamin Logan that burned seven Shawnee towns, killed many warriors, and captured women and children. In another incident of violating the rules of civilized warfare, the Americans slaughtered Old Melanthy, a friendly Shawnee headman, under a flag of truce. "Melanthy would not fly, but displayed the thirteen stripes and held out the articles of the Miami treaty," Colonel Josiah Harmar wrote, "but all in vain; he was shot down, … although he was their prisoner." Yet Clark withdrew, still not strong enough to attack the towns farther west of the Wabash River.

Moving on to Detroit, Brant awaited the gathering of headmen from all the western tribes. In December, a moving speech was made, probably by Brant, reviewing the entire course of history since Europeans had invaded North America. "It is certain that before Christian Nations visited this continent we were the sole lords of the soil…. The Great Spirit placed us there! And what is the reason why we are not still in possession of our forefathers' birth rights?" The answer was all too obvious: that intertribal rivalry and ancient animosities had allowed the Europeans to pursue the age-old policy of divide and conquer. "The interests of any one nation should be the interests of us all," the orator counseled; "the welfare of the one should be the welfare of all the others."

The speech carried the day. Ten nations of the Ohio country spoke as one in an address to Congress calling for a reconsideration of the shotgun treaties of Fort Stanwix and Fort McIntosh. They had not been conquered, they insisted, and they had not lost their land except by intimidation and fraud. Until new negotiations took place, the surveyors laying off lands in the ceded parts of Indian country should lay down their instruments. If the United States rejected these requests, the Indian confederacy would fight.

Congress paid little heed to the address. By mid-1787, with the Constitutional Convention drawing up a new plan of government, Congress was near the end of its life. Nor were the western tribes able to maintain a united front, beset as in the past by intertribal and intertribal disputes. Once reorganized after ratification of the Constitution, the United States would do exactly what Pennsylvania's president John Dickinson promised in addressing the western tribes: Unless they quit resistance to the American treaties forced on them "we will instantly turn upon them our armies that have conquered the king of Great Britain … and extirpate them from the land where they were born and now live." …

Promoting and prosecuting the Revolution instilled in ordinary and subjected people a new sense of themselves, a certitude that they had been instrumental in one of the most mold-shattering, mass action movements of recorded history, and in a comradeship born of fighting against formidable odds. Such awareness of their political importance and their certainty about the justness of their causes insured that the ideas of ardent radicals would not be driven underground. Very seldom in history do a people imagine a new world, see it within their grasp, and then given it up. Every unfulfilled element of the Revolution—abolition of slavery; full citizenship for all free people; greater women's rights; the integrity of Native American land and political sovereignty; the entitlements of laboring people on farms and in cities; more equitable taxes; public education; religious toleration—reemerged in the late eighteenth and early nineteenth centuries. Some of these planks in the radical platform, such as strict limits for legislators or gender equality, are still agenda items today....

FURTHER READING

Fred Anderson, *Crucible of War: The Seven Years' War and the Fate of Empire in British North America, 1754–1766* (2001).

T. H. Breen, *The Marketplace of Revolution: How Consumer Politics Shaped American Independence* (2004).

Edward Countryman, *The American Revolution* (1985).

Marc Egnal, *A Mighty Empire: The Origins of the American Revolution* (1988).

David Hackett Fischer, *Paul Revere's Ride* (1995).

Sylvia Frey, *Water from the Rock: Black Resistance in a Revolutionary Age* (1991).

Linda K. Kerber, *Women of the Republic: Intellect and Ideology in Revolutionary America* (1997).

Pauline Maier, *American Scripture: Making the Declaration of Independence* (1998).

Robert Middlekauff, *The Glorious Cause: The American Revolution, 1763–1789* (1982).

Gary B. Nash, *The Unknown American Revolution: The Unruly Birth of Democracy and the Struggle to Create America* (2006).

Mary Beth Norton, *Liberty's Daughters: The Revolutionary Experience of American Women, 1750–1800* (1980).

Charles Royster, *A Revolutionary People at War: The Continental Army and American Character, 1775–1783* (1996).

Gordon S. Wood, *The Radicalism of the American Revolution* (1993).

Alfred F. Young, *Masquerade: The Life and Times of Deborah Sampson, Continental Soldier* (2004).

CHAPTER 5

The Making of the Constitution

In late May 1787, George Washington called to order a convention of fifty-five delegates in Philadelphia. Throughout a hot, steamy summer, this group deliberated and argued until it arrived at a plan to restructure the government of the United States. The Constitution, as it was called, was a controversial reform, and it was not ratified by the nine states necessary for it to take effect until the summer of 1788. Yet the Constitution continues to be the framework of the United States, one of the oldest frameworks of government still in place in the twenty-first century. Many Americans at the time, however, were not convinced of the wisdom of the Constitution or optimistic about its meaning for the future of the United States.

The Constitution was not the first framework of government for the country; the Articles of Confederation, which offered a less centralized government than the Constitution proposed, had been ratified in 1781. The central government under the Articles had limited powers: it had no power to tax, it could not compel the states to contribute to financing its operations, and it could not enforce a uniform commercial policy. Its structure was weak as well. It had no executive branch and no separate judiciary; instead, it relied on a legislature in which each state had equal representation. Given the United States's recent experiences with a monarchy, many Americans were satisfied with a decentralized government. And the Articles period was not without its successes. Perhaps its most notable achievement was the Northwest Ordinance, which laid the groundwork for the method by which new states would enter the Union. Still many Americans soon concluded that the government was inadequate to meet the country's needs.

The shortcomings of the Articles were exacerbated by the crises that the new nation encountered. An economic depression wracked the nation shortly after the conclusion of war in 1781, and this was accompanied by a monetary crisis as the value of paper money declined. The phrase "not worth a Continental" came into usage, indicating the declining value of the new nation's currency. These difficulties were compounded by diplomatic and commercial failures. The British continued to occupy western forts on American territory, and Congress could not establish a national commercial policy because federal tariffs could be passed only if all the states agreed to them. As the postwar depression worsened, Americans began to pressure their government for relief. In western Massachusetts, farmers pleaded for lower taxes and a larger supply of money. When the state government rejected all of their requests in 1786, a group of farmers began forcibly closing down the courts in which debtors were tried. Under the leadership of Daniel Shays, this rebellion spread throughout western Massachusetts, and it was ended only by calling out the state militia. Once Shays's Rebellion was put down, John Adams, who years before had led his own revolution, called these rebels "ignorant, restless, desperadoes, without conscience or principles." Many Americans concluded that the limited government under the Articles was a failure.

Given these concerns, the members of the Constitutional Convention sought to restructure the national government. Their deliberations resulted in a government with three branches, including an executive and a judiciary, as well as a legislature. The legislative branch was bicameral, with one house providing equal representation to all states and the other providing proportional representation based on population. The president was elected by the electoral college, in which the number of electors from each state was equal to the number of that state's senators and representatives. Perhaps most controversial was the three-fifths compromise, which included three-fifths of the slave population in a state's headcount; this increased the power of the states in which slavery existed.

The framers provided that the Constitution had to be ratified by nine of thirteen state conventions before it would become the law of the land. The national debate quickly divided the Federalists, who favored ratification, from the Antifederalists, who did not. The latter group argued that the Constitution was an exercise in elitism that would lead to rule by a wealthy, unrepresentative minority. They lauded the Revolution that had just been won and warned that the Constitution might lead to a return to "despotism" and "tyranny," pointing to the absence of a Bill of Rights to support their claim. In contrast, the Federalists, most brilliantly represented by Alexander Hamilton, James Madison, and John Jay in The Federalist Papers, *argued that the United States was in crisis and that the Constitution would preserve the republic and promote economic prosperity. When Jay and Hamilton pledged to support a Bill of Rights should the Constitution be ratified, they undercut much of the Antifederalist argument. By 1788, ratification was complete and the course of the United States changed yet again.*

QUESTIONS TO THINK ABOUT

Would the United States have survived as a nation if the Articles of Confederation had remained the framework of government? How would government and society have differed if the Articles had not been replaced by the Constitution? Was the framing and ratification of the Constitution "counterrevolutionary"? Compare and contrast the focus upon religious freedom and physical enslavement. How did the United States justify slavery, but accept freedom of religion? How important was slavery in this chaotic time?

DOCUMENTS

Document 1, an abridgement of the Articles of Confederation, illustrates the power of states and the weakness of the national government. Pivotal questions, ranging from the place of religion in the republic to the status of slavery, had to be decided by the new nation, as the next four documents illustrate. Document 2 is a petition from Cato, "a poor negro," to the Pennsylvania Assembly, urging it to reject conservative attempts to repeal a law that set in motion an end to slavery. Slaveholders in Virginia sought to protect slavery in document 3. With petitions, they urged the retention of slavery. Document 4 is a proposal authored by Thomas Jefferson that provides for the formal protection of religious freedom in Virginia. Documents 5 and 6 describe Shays's Rebellion in 1787 when the militia was called out to put down an uprising of farmers. The next two documents explore the debates surrounding the Constitution. Document 7 includes excerpts from *The Federalist Papers,* a series of eighty-five essays written by James Madison, Alexander Hamilton, and John Jay in 1787 and 1788 to explain and defend the Constitution. In contrast, Patrick Henry, in document 8, condemns the Constitution as creating a government that is too centralized. Finally, George Washington, in document 9, commits his nation to religious freedom in his letter to a Jewish congregation in Rhode Island. This is the first public declaration that Jews in the United States would be guaranteed religious freedom.

1. The Articles of Confederation Stress the Rights of States, 1781

Preamble

To all to whom these Presents shall come, we the undersigned Delegates of the States affixed to our Names send greeting.

Articles of Confederation and perpetual Union between the States of New Hampshire, Massachusetts bay, Rhode Island and Providence Plantations, Connecticut, New York, New Jersey, Pennsylvania, Delaware, Maryland, Virginia, North Carolina, South Carolina, and Georgia.

Article I. The Stile of this Confederacy shall be "The United States of America."

Article II. Each state retains its sovereignty, freedom, and independence, and every power, jurisdiction, and right, which is not by this Confederation expressly delegated to the United States, in Congress assembled.

Article III. The said States hereby severally enter into a firm league of friendship with each other, for their common defense, the security of their liberties, and their mutual and general welfare, binding themselves to assist each other, against all force offered to, or attacks made upon them, or any of them, on account of religion, sovereignty, trade, or any other pretense whatever.

Article V. For the most convenient management of the general interests of the United States, delegates shall be annually appointed in such manner as the legislatures of each State shall direct, to meet in Congress on the first Monday

The Articles of Confederation (1777, ratified and in force 1781).

in November, in every year, with a power reserved to each State to recall its delegates, or any of them, at any time within the year, and to send others in their stead for the remainder of the year....

In determining questions in the United States in Congress assembled, each State shall have one vote....

Article VIII. All charges of war, and all other expenses that shall be incurred for the common defense or general welfare, and allowed by the United States in Congress assembled, shall be defrayed out of a common treasury, which shall be supplied by the several States in proportion to the value of all land within each State, granted or surveyed for any person, as such land and the buildings and improvements thereon shall be estimated according to such mode as the United States in Congress assembled, shall from time to time direct and appoint.

The taxes for paying that proportion shall be laid and levied by the authority and direction of the legislatures of the several States within the time agreed upon by the United States in Congress assembled.

Article IX....The United States in Congress assembled shall never engage in a war, nor grant letters of marque or reprisal in time of peace, nor enter into any treaties or alliances, nor coin money, nor regulate the value thereof, nor ascertain the sums and expenses necessary for the defense and welfare of the United States, or any of them, nor emit bills, nor borrow money on the credit of the United States, nor appropriate money, nor agree upon the number of vessels of war, to be built or purchased, or the number of land or sea forces to be raised, nor appoint a commander in chief of the army or navy, unless nine States assent to the same: nor shall a question on any other point, except for adjourning from day to day be determined, unless by the votes of the majority of the United States in Congress assembled.

2. Cato, an African American, Pleads for the Abolition of Slavery in Pennsylvania, 1781

Mr. PRINTER.

I AM a poor negro, who with myself and children have had the good fortune to get my freedom, by means of an act of assembly passed on the first of March 1780, and should now with my family be as happy a set of people as any on the face of the earth; but I am told the assembly are going to pass a law to send us all back to our masters. Why dear Mr. Printer, this would be the cruellest act that ever a sett of worthy good gentlemen could be guilty of. To make a law to hang us all, would be *merciful,* when compared with this law.... I have read the act which made me free, and I always read it with joy—and I always dwell with particular pleasure on the following words, spoken by the assembly in the top of the said law. "We esteem it a particular blessing granted to us, that we are enabled this day to add one more step to universal civilization, by removing as much as possible the sorrows of those, who have lived in

From collections of the Historical Society of Pennsylvania. Obtained from http://www.pbs.org/wgbh/aia/part2/2h73t.html.

undeserved bondage, and from which, by the assumed authority of the kings of Great Britain, no effectual legal relief could be obtained." See it was the king of Great Britain that kept us in slavery before.—Now surely, after saying so, it cannot be possible for them to make slaves of us again—nobody, but the king of England can do it—and I sincerely pray, that he may never have it in his power.... [W]hat is most serious than all, what will our great father think of such doings? But I pray that he may be pleased to tern the hearts of the honourable assembly from this cruel law; and that he will be pleased to make us poor blacks deserving of his mercies.

CATO.

3. Slaveholders in Virginia Argue Against the Abolition of Slavery, 1784–1785

Gentlemen,

When the British parliament usurped a Right to dispose of our Property without our consent we dissolved the Union with our parent country and established a ... government of our own. We risked our Lives and Fortunes, and waded through Seas of Blood ... we understand a very subtle and daring attempt is made to dispossess us of a very important Part of our Property ... TO WREST US FROM OUR SLAVES, by an act of Legislature for general emancipation.

It is unsupported by Scripture. For we find in the Old Testament... slavery was permitted by the Deity himself....It is also exceedingly impolitic. For it involves in it, and is productive of Want, Poverty, Distress, and Ruin to FREE citizens, Neglect, Famine and Death to the black Infant.... The Horrors of all Rapes, Murders, and Outrages which a vast multitude of unprincipled unpropertied, revengeful and remorseless Banditti are capable of perpetrating ... sure and final Ruin to this now flourishing free and happy Country.

We solemnly adjure and humbly pray that you will discountenance and utterly reject every motion and proposal for emancipating our slaves....

Some men of considerable weight to wrestle from us, by an Act of the legislature, the most valuable and indispensable Article of our Property, our SLAVES by general emancipation of them.... Such a scheme indeed consists very well with the principles and designs of the North, whose Finger is sufficiently visible in it.... No language can express our indignation, Contempt and Detestation of the apostate wretches....It therefore cannot be admitted that any man had a right ... to divest us of our known rights to property which are so clearly defined.... To an unequivocal Construction therefore of this Bill of rights we now appeal and claim the utmost benefits of... in whatever may tend... to preserve our rights ... secure to us the Blessings of the free....

And we shall ever Pray....

Petitions submitted in several Virginia counties in 1784 with almost 300 signatures and in Lundenburg County in 1785 with 161 signatures, from collections of the Library of Virginia. Obtained from http://www.pbs.org/wgbh/aia/part2/2h65.html.

4. Thomas Jefferson Proposes the Protection of Religious Freedom in Virginia, 1786

Whereas, Almighty God has created the mind free; that all attempts to influence it by temporal punishment, or burthens, or by civil incapacitations, tend only to beget habits of hypocrisy and meanness, and are a departure from the plan of the Holy Author of our religion, who, being Lord both of body and mind, yet chose not to propagate it by coercions on either, as was in his Almighty power to do; that the impious presumption of legislators and rulers, civil as well as ecclesiastical, who, being themselves but fallible and uninspired men, have assumed dominion over the faith of others, setting up their own opinions and modes of thinking as the only true and infallible and as such endeavoring to impose them on others, have established and maintained false religions over the greatest part of the world, and through all time; that to compel a man to furnish contributions of money for the propagation of opinions which he disbelieves, is sinful and tyrannical, and even the forcing him to support this or that teacher of his own religious persuasion, is depriving him of the comfortable liberty of giving his contributions to the particular pastor whose morals he would make his pattern, and whose powers he feels most persuasive to righteousness, and is withdrawing from the ministry those temporary rewards which, proceeding from an approbation of their personal conduct, are an additional incitement to earnest and unremitting labors, for the instruction of mankind; that our civil rights have no dependence on our religious opinions any more than our opinions in physics or geometry; that therefore the proscribing any citizen as unworthy of the public confidence by laying upon him an incapacity of being called to offices of trust and emolument, unless he profess or renounce this or that religious opinion, is depriving him injuriously of those privileges and advantages to which, in common with his fellow citizens, he has a natural right; that it tends only to corrupt the principles of that religion it is meant to encourage, by bribing, with a monopoly of worldly honors and emoluments, those who will externally profess and conform to it; that though indeed, those are criminal who do not withstand such temptation, yet, neither are those innocent who lay the bait in their way; that to suffer the civil magistrate to intrude his powers into the field of opinion, and to restrain the profession or propagation of principles on supposition of their ill tendency, is a dangerous fallacy, which at once destroys all religious liberty, because he, being of course judge of that tendency, will make his opinions the rules of judgment, and approve or condemn the sentiments of others only as they shall square with or differ from his own; that it is time enough for the rightful purposes of civil government, for its officers to interfere, when principles break out into overt acts against peace and good order; and finally, that truth is great and will prevail, if left to herself; that she is the proper and sufficient antagonist to error, and has nothing to fear from the conflict, unless by human interposition

Thomas Jefferson, *The Virginia Statute for Religious Freedom* (1786).

disarmed of her natural weapons, free argument and debate; errors ceasing to be dangerous when it is permitted freely to contradict them:

Be it enacted by the General Assembly, that no man shall be compelled to frequent or support any religious worship, place or ministry whatsoever, nor shall he otherwise suffer on account of his religious opinions or belief; but that all men shall be free to profess, and by argument to maintain, their opinions in matters of religion, and that the same shall in no wise diminish, enlarge or affect their civil capacities.

And though we well know that this Assembly, elected by the people for the ordinary purposes of legislation only, have no power to restrain the acts of succeeding assemblies constituted with powers equal to our own, and that, therefore, to declare this act to be irrevocable would be of no effect in law; yet we are free to declare, and do declare, that the rights hereby asserted are of the natural rights of mankind; and that if any act shall be hereafter passed to repeal the present, or to narrow its operation, such act will be an infringement of natural right.

5. Daniel Shays and Followers Declare Their Intent to Protect Themselves Against "Tyranny," 1787

Pelham, January 15th, 1787.

Sir,

According to undoubted intelligence received from various parts of this Commonwealth, it is determined by the Governour and his adherents, not only to support the Court of Common Please and General Sessions of the Peace, to be holden at Worcester next week, by point of sword, but to crush the power of the people at one bold stroke, and render them incapable of ever opposing the cruel power, Tyranny, hereafter, by bringing those who have stepped forth to ward off the evil that threatens the people with immediate ruin, to an unconditional submission, and their leaders with an infamous punishment. Notwithstanding it is thought prudent, by a number of officers and others, convened at Pelham on the 15th Jan.... to consult on the exigencies of the present times, that the people of the country of Hampshire immediately assemble in arms, to support and maintain, not only the rights and liberties of the people, since our opponents, by their hasty movement, refuse to give opportunity to wait the effect of their prayers and petitions. This is therefore to desire you to assemble the company under your command, well armed and equipped, with ten days provision, and march there in season, to be at or near Dr. Hind's in Pelham, by Friday the 19th instant, there to receive further orders.

(Signed)

D. Shays
J. Powers
R. Dickinson
J. Bordwell
J. Billings

The Worchester Magazine (1787)

http://www.nps.gov/spar/historyculture/shays-reb-regulator-and-mil-docs.htm

6. Generals William Shepard and Benjamin Lincoln Regret the Disorder That Characterized Shays's Rebellion, 1787

General Shepard to Governor Bowdoin

Springfield
January 26, 1787

The unhappy time is come in which we have been obliged to shed blood. Shays, who was at the head of about twelve hundred men, marched yesterday afternoon about four o'clock, towards the public buildings in battle array. He marched his men in an open column by platoons. I sent several times by one of my aides, and two other gentlemen, Captains Buffington and Woodbridge, to him to know what he was after, or what he wanted. His reply was, he wanted barracks, and barracks he would have and stores. The answer returned was he must purchase them dear, if he had them.

He still proceeded on his march until he approached within two hundred and fifty yards of the arsenal. He then made a halt. I immediately sent Major Lyman, one of my aides, and Capt. Buffington to inform him not to march his troops any nearer the arsenal on his peril, as I was stationed here by order of your Excellency and the Secretary at War, for the defence of the public property; in case he did I should surely fire on him and his men. A Mr. Wheeler, who appeared to be one of Shays' aides, met Mr. Lyman, after he had delivered my orders in the most peremptory manner, and made answer, that was all he wanted. Mr. Lyman returned with his answer.

Shays immediately put his troops in motion, and marched on rapidly near one hundred yards. I then ordered Major Stephens, who commanded the artillery, to fire upon them. He accordingly did. The two first shots he endeavored to overshoot them, in hopes they would have taken warning without firing among them, but it had no effect on them. Major Stephens then directed his shot through the center of his column. The fourth or fifth shot put their whole column into the utmost confusion....

Had I been disposed to destroy them, I might have charged upon their rear and flanks with my infantry and the two field pieces, and could have killed the greater part of his whole army within twenty-five minutes....

I have received no reinforcement yet, and expect to be attacked this day by their whole force combined.

General Lincoln to Governor Bowdoin

Head Quarters, Springfield
January 28th, 1787

... On my arrival, I found that Shays had taken a post at a little village six miles north of this, with the whole force under his immediate command, and

Letter 1 *Collections of the Worcester Society of Antiquity*, Volume 5 (1883): 93–94.
Letter 2 "Documents," in *The American Historical Review*, Volume 2 (1897): 695.

that Day had taken post in West Springfield, and that he had fixed a guard at the ferry house on the west side of the river, and that he had a guard at the bridge over Agawam river. By this disposition all communication from the north and west in the usual paths was cut off.

From a consideration of this insult on Government, that by an early move we should instantly convince the insurgents of its ability and determination speedily to disperse them; that we wanted the houses occupied by these men to cover our own troops; that General Patterson was on his march to join us, which to obstruct was an object with them; that a successful movement would give spirits to the troops; that it would be so was reduced to as great a certainty, as can be had in operations of this kind; from these considerations, Sir, with many others, I was induced to order the troops under arms at three o'clock in the afternoon, although the most of them had been so from one in the morning.

We moved about half after three.... They made a little show of force for a minute or two near the meeting house, and then retired in the utmost confusion and disorder. Our horse met them at the west end of the village, but the insurgents found means by crossing the fields and taking to the woods to escape them; some were taken who are aggravatedly guilty, but not the most so.

7. *The Federalist Papers* Illustrate the Advantages of Ratification of the Constitution, 1787–1788

Factions and Their Remedy (James Madison, No.10)

To the People of the State of New York:

Among the numerous advantages promised by a well constructed Union, none deserves to be more accurately developed than its tendency to break and control the violence of faction. The friend of popular governments, never finds himself so much alarmed for their character and fate, as when he contemplates their propensity to this dangerous vice....

By a faction I understand a number of citizens, whether amounting to a majority or minority of the whole, who are united and actuated by some common impulse of passion, or of interest, adverse to the rights of other citizens, or to the permanent and aggregate interests of the community....

The latent causes of faction are thus sown in the nature of man, and we see them every where brought into different degrees of activity, according to the different circumstances of civil society. A zeal for different opinions concerning religion, concerning Government and many other points, as well of speculation as of practice; an attachment to different leaders ambitiously contending for pre-eminence and power; or to persons of other descriptions whose fortunes have been interesting to the human passions, have in turn divided mankind

Alexander Hamilton, John Jay, and James Madison, *The Federalist Papers* (New York: Random House, 1961), Nos. 10, 51, and 69.

into parties, inflamed them with mutual animosity, and rendered them much more disposed to vex and oppress each other, than to co-operate for their common good. So strong is this propensity of mankind to fall into mutual animosities, that where no substantial occasion presents itself, the most frivolous and fanciful distinctions have been sufficient to kindle their unfriendly passions, and excite their most violent conflicts. But the most common and durable source of factions, has been the various and unequal distribution of property.... The regulation of these various and interfering interests forms the principal task of modern Legislation, and involves the spirit of party and faction in the necessary and ordinary operations of Government....

... [A] pure Democracy, by which I mean, a Society, consisting of a small number of citizens, who assemble and administer the Government in person, can admit of no cure for the mischiefs of faction. A common passion or interest will, in almost every case, be felt by a majority of the whole; a communication and concert results from the form of Government itself; and there is nothing to check the inducements to sacrifice the weaker party, or an obnoxious individual....

A Republic, by which I mean a Government in which the scheme of representation takes place, opens a different prospect, and promises the cure for which we are seeking....

The two great points of difference between a Democracy and a Republic are, first, the delegation of the Government, in the latter, to a small number of citizens elected by the rest: secondly, the greater number of citizens, and greater sphere of country, over which the latter may be extended.

The effect of the first difference is, on the one hand to refine and enlarge the public views, by passing them through the medium of a chosen body of citizens, whose wisdom may best discern the true interest of their country, and whose patriotism and love of justice, will be least likely to sacrifice it to temporary or partial considerations....

... [T]he same advantage, which a Republic has over a Democracy, in controling the effects of faction, is enjoyed by a large over a small Republic—is enjoyed by the Union over the States composing it. Does this advantage consist in the substitution of Representatives, whose enlightened views and virtuous sentiments render them superior to local prejudices, and to schemes of injustice? It will not be denied, that the Representation of the Union will be most likely to possess these requisite endowments. Does it consist in the greater security afforded by a greater variety of parties, against the event of any one party being able to outnumber and oppress the rest? In an equal degree does the encreased variety of parties, comprised within the Union, encrease this security. Does it, in fine, consist in the greater obstacles opposed to the concert and accomplishment of the secret wishes of an unjust and interested majority? Here, again, the extent of the Union gives it the most palpable advantage....

In the extent and proper structure of the Union, therefore, we behold a Republican remedy for the diseases most incident to Republican Government.

The System of Checks and Balances (Alexander Hamilton or James Madison, No. 51)

To the People of the State of New York:

To what expedient, then, shall we finally resort, for maintaining in practice the necessary partition of power among the several departments, as laid down in the Constitution? The only answer that can be given is, that as all these exterior provisions are found to be inadequate, the defect must be supplied, by so contriving the interior structure of the government as that its several constituent parts may, by their mutual relations, be the means of keeping each other in their proper places....

... [T]he great security against a gradual concentration of the several powers in the same department, consists in giving to those who administer each department the necessary constitutional means and personal motives to resist encroachments of the others. The provision for defence must in this, as in all other cases, be made commensurate to the danger of attack. Ambition must be made to counteract ambition. The interest of the man must be connected with the constitutional rights of the place. It may be a reflection on human nature, that such devices should be necessary to control the abuses of government. But what is government itself, but the greatest of all reflections on human nature? If men were angels, no government would be necessary. If angels were to govern men, neither external nor internal controls on government would be necessary....

But it is not possible to give to each department an equal power of self-defence. In republican government, the legislative authority necessarily predominates. The remedy for this inconveniency is to divide the legislature into different branches.... As the weight of the legislative authority requires that it should be thus divided, the weakness of the executive may require, on the other hand, that it should be fortified....

A Defense of the Presidency (Alexander Hamilton, No. 69)

To the People of the State of New York:

I proceed now to trace the real characters of the proposed executive as they are marked out in the plan of the Convention. This will serve to place in a strong light the unfairness of the representations which have been made in regard to it....

The President of the United States would be an officer elected by the people for *four* years. The King of Great-Britain is a perpetual and *hereditary* prince. The one would be amenable to personal punishment and disgrace: The person of the other is sacred and inviolable. The one would have a *qualified* negative upon the acts of the legislative body: The other has an *absolute* negative. The one would have a right to command the military and naval forces of the nation: The other in addition to this right, possesses that of *declaring* war, and of *raising* and *regulating* fleets and armies by his own authority. The one would have a concurrent power with a branch of the Legislature in the formation of treaties: The other is the *sole possessor* of the power of making treaties. The one would have a like concurrent authority in appointing to offices: The other is the sole author of all appointments. The one can infer no privileges whatever: The other can make denizens of aliens, noblemen of commoners, can erect corporations with all the rights incident to corporate bodies. The one can prescribe no rules concerning the commerce or currency of the nation: The other is in several respects the arbiter of commerce, and in this capacity can establish markets and fairs, can regulate weights and measures, can lay embargoes for a limited time, can coin money, can authorise or prohibit the circulation of foreign coin. The one has no particle of spiritual jurisdiction: The other is the supreme head and Governor of the national church!—What answer shall we give to those who would persuade us that things so unlike resemble each other?—The same that ought to be given to those who tell us, that a government, the whole power of which would be in the hands of the elective and periodical servants of the people, is an aristocracy, a monarchy, and a despotism.

8. Patrick Henry Condemns the Centralization of Government If the Constitution Is Ratified, 1788

... I need not take much pains to show, that the principles of this system, are extremely pernicious, impolitic, and dangerous. Is this a Monarchy, like England—a compact between Prince and people; with checks on the former, to secure the liberty of the latter? Is this a Confederacy, like Holland—an association of a number of independent States, each of which retain its individual sovereignty? It is not a democracy, wherein the people retain all their rights securely. Had these principles been adhered to, we should not have been brought to this alarming transition, from a Confederacy to a consolidated Government. We have no detail of those great considerations which, in my opinion, ought to have abounded before we should recur to a government of this kind. Here is a revolution as radical as that which separated us from Great Britain. It is as radical, if in this transition our rights and privileges are endangered, and the sovereignty of the States be relinquished: And cannot we plainly see, that this is actually the case? The rights of conscience, trial by jury, liberty of the press, all your immunities and franchises, all pretensions to human rights and privileges, are rendered insecure, if not lost, by this change so loudly talked of by some, and inconsiderately by others. Is this same relinquishment of rights worthy of freemen?...

Gentlemen have told us within these walls, that the Union is gone—or, that the Union will be gone: Is not this trifling with the judgment of their fellow-citizens? Till they tell us the ground of their fears, I will consider them as imaginary: I rose to make inquiry where those dangers were; they could make no answer: I believe I never shall have that answer: Is there a disposition in the people of this country to revolt against the dominion of laws? Has there been a single tumult in Virginia? Have not the people of Virginia, when laboring under the severest pressure of accumulated distresses, manifested the most cordial

Patrick Henry, Speech to Virginia Ratifying Convention (1788).

acquiescence in the execution of the laws? What could be more awful than their unanimous acquiescence under general distresses? Is there any revolution in Virginia? Whither is the spirit of America gone? Whither is the genius of America fled? It was but yesterday, when our enemies marched in triumph through our country: Yet the people of this country could not be appalled by their pompous armaments: They stopped their career, and victoriously captured them: Where is the peril now compared to that? Some minds are agitated by foreign alarms: Happily for us, there is no real danger from Europe: that country is engaged in more arduous business; from that quarter there is no cause of fear; You may sleep in safety forever for them. Where is the danger? If, Sir, there was any, I would recur to the American spirit to defend us;—that spirit which has enabled us to surmount the greatest difficulties: To that illustrious spirit I address my most fervent prayer, to prevent our adopting a system destructive to liberty ....

This Constitution is said to have beautiful features; but when I come to examine these features. Sir, they appear to me horridly frightful: Among other deformities, it has an awful squinting; it squints towards monarchy: And does not this raise indignation in the breast of every American? Your President may easily become King: Your Senate is so imperfectly constructed that your dearest rights may be sacrificed by what may be a small minority; and a very small minority may continue forever unchangeably this Government, although horridly defective: Where are your checks in the Government? Your strong holds will be in the hands of your enemies: It is on a supposition that our American Governors shall be honest, that all the good qualities of this Government are founded: But its defective, and imperfect construction, puts it in their power to perpetuate the worst of mischiefs, should they be bad men: And, Sir, would not all the world, from the Eastern to the Western hemisphere, blame our distracted folly in resting our rights upon the contingency of our rulers being good or bad.

9. George Washington Promises Freedom of Religion for Jewish People, 1790

Gentlemen.

While I receive, with much satisfaction, your Address replete with expressions of esteem; I rejoice in the opportunity of assuring you, that I shall always retain grateful remembrance of the cordial welcome I experienced on my visit to Newport, from all classes of citizens....

The Citizens of the United States of America have a right to applaud Themselves for having given to mankind examples of an enlarged and liberal policy: a policy worthy of imitation. All possess alike liberty of conscience and immunities of citizenship. It is now no more that toleration is spoken of, as if it was by the indulgence of one class of people, that another enjoyed the exercise of their inherent natural rights. For happily the Government of the United States, which

George Washington, *Letter to Moses Seixas* (1790), in *The Papers of George Washington*, VI, ed. Mark A. Mastromarino (Charlottesville: University of Virginia Press, 1996).

gives to bigotry no sanction, to persecution no assistance requires only that they who live under its protection should demean themselves as good citizens in giving it on all occasions their effectual support....

May the Children of the Stock of Abraham, who dwell in this land, continue to merit and enjoy the good will of the other Inhabitants; while every one shall sit in safety under his own vine and figtree; and there shall be none to make him afraid. May the father of all mercies scatter light and not darkness in our paths, and make us all in our several vocations useful here, and in his own due time and way everlastingly happy.

ESSAYS

In 1913, Charles Beard argued that the framers of the Constitution were motivated first and foremost by a desire to protect their own economic interests. Beard's thesis initiated a debate that continues to the present over whether the Constitution was a necessary adjustment to the inadequate governmental structure provided by the Articles of Confederation or an overreaction—some might say counterrevolution—by the elite to popular government. The following two essays illustrate this argument. Alfred F. Young, professor emeritus at Northern Illinois University, takes a more critical stance toward the Constitutional Convention. He acknowledges that accommodations were made by the framers, but only because they were haunted by "ghosts," that is, by popular movements that were not represented at the Convention but surely figured in the framers' thinking. In contrast, Jack Rakove, professor of history at Stanford University, argues that the framers were actually led away from the notion that the Constitution ought to restrict entrance into public life. Rather than closing off opportunities for holding political office, they actually sought to enlarge political participation. Rakove contends that this path, in turn, created the problems of recruiting politicians who would remain in public office.

The Pressure of the People
on the Framers of the Constitution

ALFRED F. YOUNG

On June 18, 1787, about three weeks into the Constitutional Convention at Philadelphia, Alexander Hamilton delivered a six-hour address that was easily the longest and most conservative the Convention would hear. Gouverneur Morris, a delegate from Pennsylvania, thought it was "the most able and impressive he had ever heard."

Beginning with the premise that "all communities divide themselves into the few and the many," "the wealthy well born" and "the people," Hamilton added

Alfred F. Young, "Framers of the Constitution and the 'Genius' of the Pepole." *In These Times*, September 9–15, 1987. Reprinted by permission of In These Times.

the corollary that the "people are turbulent and changing; they seldom judge or determine right." Moving through history, the delegate from New York developed his ideal for a national government that would protect the few from "the imprudence of democracy" and guarantee "stability and permanence": a president and senate indirectly elected for life ("to serve during good behavior") to balance a house directly elected by a popular vote every three years. This "elective monarch" would have an absolute veto over laws passed by Congress. And the national government would appoint the governors of the states, who in turn would have the power to veto any laws by the state legislatures.

If others quickly saw a resemblance in all of this to the King, House of Lords and House of Commons of Great Britain, with the states reduced to colonies ruled by royal governors, they were not mistaken. The British constitution, in Hamilton's view, remained "the best model the world has ever produced."

Three days later a delegate reported that Hamilton's proposals "had been praised by everybody," but "he has been supported by none." Acknowledging that his plan "went beyond the ideas of most members," Hamilton said he had brought it forward not "as a thing attainable by us, but as a model which we ought to approach as near as possible." When he signed the Constitution the framers finally agreed to on September 17, 1787, Hamilton could accurately say, "no plan was more remote from his own."

Why did the framers reject a plan so many admired? To ask this question is to go down a dark path into the heart of the Constitution few of its celebrants care to take. We have heard so much in our elementary and high school civics books about the "great compromises" within the Convention—between the large states and the small states, between the slaveholders and non-slaveholders, between North and South—that we have missed the much larger accommodation that was taking place between the delegates as a whole at the Convention and what they called "the people out of doors."

The Convention was unmistakably an elite body. The official exhibit for the bicentennial, "Miracle at Philadelphia," opens appropriately enough with a large oil portrait of Robert Morris, a delegate from Philadelphia, one of the richest merchants in America, and points out elsewhere that 11 out of 55 delegates were business associates of Morris'. The 55 were weighted with merchants, slaveholding planters and "monied men" who loaned money at interest. Among them were numerous lawyers and college graduates in a country where most men and only a few women had the rudiments of a formal education. They were far from a cross section of the four million or so Americans of that day, most of whom were farmers or artisans, fishermen or seamen, indentured servants or laborers, half of whom were women and about 600,000 of whom were African-American slaves.

I. The First Accommodation

Why did this elite reject Hamilton's plan that many of them praised? James Madison, the Constitution's chief architect, had the nub of the matter. The Constitution was "intended for the ages." To last it had to conform to the "genius" of the American people. "Genius" was a word eighteenth-century political thinkers used to mean spirit: we might say character or underlying values.

James Wilson, second only to Madison in his influence at Philadelphia, elaborated on the idea. "The British government cannot be our model. We have no materials for a similar one. Our manners, our law, the abolition of entail and primogeniture," which made for a more equal distribution of property among sons, "the whole genius of the people, are opposed to it."

This was long-range political philosophy. There was a short-range political problem that moved other realistic delegates in the same direction. Called together to revise the old Articles of Confederation, the delegates instead decided to scrap it and frame an entirely new constitution. It would have to be submitted to the people for ratification, most likely to conventions elected especially for the purpose. Repeatedly, conservatives recoiled from extreme proposals for which they knew they could not win popular support.

In response to a proposal to extend the federal judiciary into the states, Pierce Butler, a South Carolina planter, argued, "the people will not bear such innovations. The states will revolt at such encroachments." His assumption was "we must follow the example of Solomon, who gave the Athenians not the best government he could devise but the best they would receive."

The suffrage debate epitomized this line of thinking. Gouverneur Morris, Hamilton's admirer, proposed that the national government limit voting for the House to men who owned a freehold, i.e. a substantial farm, or its equivalent. "Give the vote to people who have no property and they will sell them to the rich who will be able to buy them," he said with some prescience. George Mason, author of Virginia's Bill of Rights, was aghast. "Eight or nine states have extended the right of suffrage beyond the freeholders. What will people there say if they should be disfranchised?"

Benjamin Franklin, the patriarch, speaking for one of the few times in the convention, paid tribute to "the lower class of freemen" who should not be disfranchised. James Wilson explained, "it would be very hard and disagreeable for the same person" who could vote for representatives for the state legislatures "to be excluded from a vote for this in the national legislature." Nathaniel Gorham, a Boston merchant, returned to the guiding principle: "the people will never allow" existing rights to suffrage to be abridged. "We must consult their rooted prejudices if we expect their concurrence in our propositions."

The result? Morris' proposal was defeated and the convention decided that whoever each state allowed to vote for its own assembly could vote for the House. It was a compromise that left the door open and in a matter of decades allowed states to introduce universal white male suffrage.

II. Ghosts of Years Past

Clearly there was a process of accommodation at work here. The popular movements of the Revolutionary Era were a presence at the Philadelphia Convention even if they were not present. The delegates, one might say, were haunted by ghosts, symbols of the broadly based movements elites had confronted in the making of the Revolution from 1765 to 1775, in waging the war from 1775 to 1781 and in the years since 1781 within their own states.

The first was the ghost of Thomas Paine, the most influential radical democrat of the Revolutionary Era. In 1776 Paine's pamphlet *Common Sense* (which sold at least 150,000 copies), in arguing for independence, rejected not only King George III but the principle of monarchy and the so-called checks and balances of the unwritten English constitution. In its place he offered a vision of a democratic government in which a single legislature would be supreme, the executive minimal, and representatives would be elected from small districts by a broad electorate for short terms so they could "return and mix again with the voters." John Adams considered *Common Sense* too "democratical," without even an attempt at "mixed government" that would balance "democracy" with "aristocracy."

The second ghost was that of Abraham Yates, a member of the state senate of New York typical of the new men who had risen to power in the 1780s in the state legislatures. We have forgotten him; Hamilton, who was very conscious of him, called him "an old Booby." He had begun as a shoemaker and was a self-taught lawyer and warm foe of the landlord aristocracy of the Hudson Valley which Hamilton had married into. As James Madison identified the "vices of the political system of the United States" in a memorandum in 1787, the Abraham Yateses were the number-one problem. The state legislatures had "an itch for paper money" laws, laws that prevented foreclosure on farm mortgages, and tax laws that soaked the rich. As Madison saw it, this meant that "debtors defrauded their creditors" and "the landed interest has borne hard on the mercantile interest." This, too, is what Hamilton had in mind when he spoke of the "depredations which the democratic spirit is apt to make on property" and what others meant by the "excess of democracy" in the states.

The third ghost was a very fresh one—Daniel Shays. In 1786 Shays, a captain in the Revolution, led a rebellion of debtor farmers in western Massachusetts which the state quelled with its own somewhat unreliable militia. There were "combustibles in every state," as George Washington put it, raising the specter of "Shaysism." This Madison enumerated among the "vices" of the system as "a want of guaranty to the states against internal violence." Worse still, Shaysites in many slates were turning to the political system to elect their own kind. If they succeeded they would produce legal Shaysism, a danger for which the elites had no remedy.

The fourth ghost we can name [is] the ghost of Thomas Peters, although he had a thousand other names. In 1775, Peters, a Virginia slave, responded to a plea by the British to fight in their army and win their freedom. He served in an "Ethiopian Regiment," some of whose members bore the emblem "Liberty to Slaves" on their uniforms. After the war the British transported Peters and several thousand escaped slaves to Nova Scotia from whence Peters eventually led a group to return to Africa and the colony of Sierra Leone, a long odyssey to freedom. Eighteenth-century slaveholders, with no illusions about happy or contented slaves, were haunted by the specter of slaves in arms.

III. Elite Divisions

During the Revolutionary Era elites divided in response to these varied threats from below. One group, out of fear of "the mob" and then "the rabble in arms," embraced the British and became active Loyalists. After the war most of them went into exile. Another group who became patriots never lost their obsession with coercing popular movements.

"The mob begins to think and reason," Gouverneur Morris observed in 1774. "Poor reptiles, they bask in the sunshine and ere long they will bite." A snake had to be scotched. Other thought of the people as a horse that had to be whipped. This was coercion.

Far more important, however, were those patriot leaders who adopted a strategy of "swimming with a stream which it is impossible to stem." This was the metaphor of Robert R. Livingston, Jr., like Morris, a gentleman with a large tenanted estate in New York. Men of his class had to learn to "yield to the torrent if they hoped to direct its course."

Livingston and his group were able to shape New York's constitution, which some called a perfect blend of "aristocracy" and "democracy." John Hancock, the richest merchant in New England, had mastered this kind of politics and emerged as the most popular politician in Massachusetts. In Maryland Charles Carroll, a wealthy planter, instructed his anxious father about the need to "submit to partial losses" because "no great revolution can happen in a state without revolutions or mutations of private property. If we can save a third of our personal estate and all of our lands and Negroes, I shall think ourselves well off."

The major leaders at the Constitutional Convention in 1787 were heirs to both traditions: coercion and accommodation—Hamilton and Gouverneur Morris to the former, James Madison and James Wilson much more to the latter.

They all agreed on coercion to slay the ghosts of Daniel Shays and Thomas Peters. The Constitution gave the national government the power to "suppress insurrections" and protect the states from "domestic violence." There would be a national army under the command of the president, and authority to nationalize the state militias and suspend the right of habeas corpus in "cases of rebellion or invasion." In 1794 Hamilton, as secretary of the treasury, would exercise such powers fully (and needlessly) to suppress the Whiskey Rebellion in western Pennsylvania.

Southern slaveholders correctly interpreted the same powers as available to shackle the ghost of Thomas Peters. As it turned out, Virginia would not need a federal army to deal with Gabriel Prosser's insurrection in 1800 or Nat Turner's rebellion in 1830, but a federal army would capture John Brown after his raid at Harpers Ferry in 1859.

But how to deal with the ghosts of Thomas Paine and Abraham Yates? Here Madison and Wilson blended coercion with accommodation. They had three solutions to the threat of democratic majorities in the states.

Their first was clearly coercive. Like Hamilton, Madison wanted some kind of national veto over the state legislatures. He got several very specific curbs on the states written into fundamental law: no state could "emit" paper money or pass "laws impairing the obligation of contracts." Wilson was so overjoyed with these two clauses that he argued that if they alone "were inserted in the Constitution I think they would be worth our adoption."

But Madison considered the overall mechanism adopted to curb the states "short of the mark." The Constitution, laws and treaties were the "supreme law of the land" and ultimately a federal court could declare state laws unconstitutional. But this, Madison lamented, would only catch "mischiefs" after the fact. Thus they had clipped the wings of Abraham Yates but he could still fly.

The second solution to the problem of the states was decidedly democratic. They wanted to do an end-run around the state legislatures. The Articles of Confederation, said Madison, rested on "the pillars" of the state legislatures who elected delegates to Congress. The "great fabric to be raised would be more stable and durable if it should rest on the solid grounds of the people themselves"; hence, there would be popular elections to the House.

Wilson altered only the metaphor. He was for "raising the federal pyramid to a considerable altitude and for that reason wanted to give it as broad a base as possible." They would slay the ghost of Abraham Yates with the ghost of Thomas Paine.

This was risky business. They would reduce the risk by keeping the House of Representatives small. Under a ratio of one representative for every 30,000 people, the first house would have only 65 members; in 1776 Thomas Paine had suggested 390. But still, the House would be elected every two years, and with each state allowed to determine its own qualifications for voting, there was no telling who might end up in Congress.

There was also a risk in Madison's third solution to the problem of protecting propertied interests from democratic majorities: "extending the sphere" of government. Prevailing wisdom held that a republic could only succeed in a small geographic area; to rule an "extensive" country, some kind of despotism was considered inevitable.

Madison turned this idea on its head in his since famous *Federalist* essay No. 10. In a small republic, he argued, it was relatively easy for a majority to gang up on a particular "interest." "Extend the sphere," he wrote, and "you take in a greater variety of parties and interests." Then it would be more difficult for a majority "to discover their own strength and to act in unison with each other."

This was a prescription for a non-colonial empire that would expand across the continent, taking in new states as it dispossessed the Indians. The risk was there was no telling how far the "democratic" or "leveling" spirit might go in such likely would-be states as frontier Vermont, Kentucky and Tennessee.

IV. Democratic Divisions

In the spectrum of state constitutions adopted in the Revolutionary era, the federal Constitution of 1787 was, like New York's, somewhere between "aristocracy" and "democracy." It therefore should not surprise us—although it has eluded many modern critics of the Constitution—that in the contest over ratification in 1787–88, the democratic minded were divided.

Among agrarian democrats there was a gut feeling that the Constitution was the work of an old class enemy. "These lawyers and men of learning and monied men," argued Amos Singletary, a working farmer at the Massachusetts ratifying convention, "expect to be managers of this Constitution and get all the power and all the money into their own hands and then will swallow up all of us little folks … just as the whale swallowed up Jonah."

Democratic leaders like Melancton Smith of New York focused on the small size of the proposed House. Arguing from Paine's premise that the members of the legislature should "resemble those they represent," Smith feared that "a substantial yeoman of sense and discernment will hardly ever be chosen" and the government "will fall into the hands of the few and the great." Urban democrats, on the other hand, including a majority of the mechanics and tradesmen of the major cities who in the Revolution had been a bulwark of Paineite radicalism, were generally enthusiastic about the Constitution. They were impelled by their urgent stake in a stronger national government that would advance ocean-going commerce and protect American manufacturers from competition. But they would not have been as ardent about the new frame of government without its saving graces. It clearly preserved their rights to suffrage. And the process of ratification, like the Constitution itself, guaranteed them a voice. As early as 1776 the New York Committee of Mechanics held it as "a right which God has given them in common with all men to judge whether it be consistent with their interest to accept or reject a constitution."

Mechanics turned out en masse in the parades celebrating ratification, marching trade by trade. The slogans and symbols they carried expressed their political ideals. In New York the upholsterers had a float with an elegant "Federal Chair of State" flanked by the symbols of Liberty and Justice that they identified with the Constitution. In Philadelphia the bricklayers put on their banner "Both buildings and rulers are the work of our hands."

Democrats who were skeptical found it easier to come over because of the Constitution's redeeming features. Thomas Paine, off in Paris, considered the Constitution "a copy, though not quite as base as the original, of the form of the British government." He had always opposed a single executive and he objected to the "long duration of the Senate." But he was so convinced of "the absolute necessity" of a stronger federal government that "I would have voted for it myself had I been in America or even for a worse, rather than have none." It was crucial to Paine that there was an amending process, the means of "remedying its defects by the same appeal to the people by which it was to be established."

V. The Second Accommodation

In drafting the Constitution in 1787 the framers, self-styled Federalists, made their first accommodation with the "genius" of the people. In campaigning for its ratification in 1788 they made their second. At the outset, the conventions in the key states—Massachusetts, New York and Virginia—either had an anti-Federalist majority or were closely divided. To swing over a small group of "antis" in each state, Federalists had to promise that they would consider amendments. This was enough to secure ratification by narrow margins in Massachusetts, 187 to 168; in New York, 30 to 27; and in Virginia, 89 to 79.

What the anti-Federalists wanted were dozens of changes in the structure of the government that would cut back national power over the states, curb the powers of the presidency as well as protect individual liberties. What they got was far less. But in the first Congress in 1789, James Madison, true to his pledge, considered all the amendments and shepherded 12 amendments through both houses. The first two of these failed in the states; one would have enlarged the House. The 10 that were ratified by December 1791 were what we have since called the Bill of Rights, protecting freedom of expression and the rights of the accused before the law. Abraham Yates considered them "trivial and unimportant." But other democrats looked on them much more favorably. In time the limited meaning of freedom of speech in the First Amendment was broadened far beyond the framers' original intent. Later popular movements thought or the Bill of Rights as an essential part of the "constitutional" and "re-publican" rights that belonged to the people.

VI. The "Losers'" Role

There is a cautionary tale here that surely goes beyond the process of framing and adopting the Constitution and Bill of Rights from 1787 to 1791. The Constitution was as democratic as it was because of the influence of popular movements that were a presence, even if not present. The losers helped shape the results. We owe the Bill of Rights to the opponents of the Constitution, as we do many other features in the Constitution put in to anticipate opposition.

In American history popular movements often shaped elites, especially in times of crisis when elites were concerned with the "system." Elites have often divided in response to such threats and according to their perception of the "genius" of the people. Some have turned in coercion, others to accommodation. We run serious risk if we ignore this distinction. Would that we had fewer Gouverneur Morrises and Alexander Hamiltons and more James Madison, and James Wilsons to respond to the "genius" of the people.

The Hope of the Framers to Recruit Citizens to Enter Public Life

JACK N. RAKOVE

It has been some time since historians have displayed conspicuous interest in the actual drafting of the Constitution or the origins of particular clauses. Modern

Jack N. Rakove, "The Structure of Politics at the Accession of George Washington," in *Beyond Confederation: Origins of the Constitution and American National Identity*, Richard Beeman, Stephen Botein, and Edward C. Carter II, eds. Copyright © 1987 by the University of North Carolina Press. Used by permission of the publisher.

political controversies have drawn renewed attention to a few provisions—notably those involving war powers and impeachment. Yet more than seventy years after Charles Beard offered *An Economic Interpretation of the Constitution,* historians still seem preoccupied with identifying the political and social alignments that favored or opposed the creation of a stronger national government. Creditors and debtors have given way to cosmopolitans and localists and, more recently, to court and country. But the thrust of inquiry has changed less than one might suppose.... Just as the framers of the Constitution tend to be submerged within the larger Federalist movement, so the specific concerns that operated within the convention often seem less important than the arguments that were made for and against ratification.

And not without reason. The concerns of framers and ratifiers *had* diverged. The struggle between large and small states that had so dominated the internal politics of the convention did not remain a pivotal issue after September 1787. Similarly, the principal result of the ratification debates was the acceptance of an idea that the framers had not taken seriously: that a bill of rights could somehow provide a valuable check against the excesses of power. Moreover, the intensity of the struggle over ratification left a body of writings and speeches whose rich detail contrasts sharply with the spare words of the Constitution and the elliptical character of the convention's debates as evidence of the fundamental divisions with the American polity. Yet for all this, the Constitution should not be viewed solely through the lens of *The Federalist* and other ratification commentaries. For, once the passions of 1788 had faded and the polemical literature they produced had fallen into an obscurity from which only modern scholarship has rescued it, the language of the Constitution retained its force. That was where contemporaries turned when constitutional disputes arose, as they did as early as June 1789, and that is where historians ought to begin as well.

Was the Constitution consciously framed to promote a filtration of talent? No doubt many Federalists supported it because they believed it would enable a better class of leaders—or simply a better class—to recover political power. But it is difficult to demonstrate that this was what either the Constitution itself mandated or the framers intended. The *formal* criteria for membership in Congress were certainly not set high: the attainment of age twenty-five and seven years of citizenship for the House, age thirty and nine years of citizenship for the Senate; and the additional requirement that a member, "when elected, be an Inhabitant of that State in [for] which he shall be chosen" are all that Article I asks. Nor did the framers seek to restrict the size of the electorate, in the way, for example, that the Whig oligarchy of early Georgian England had managed to. Members of the House of Representatives were to be elected by the same voters who had been sending "demagogues" into the state legislatures.

Moreover, when one tracks the various provisions that would regulate the process of selection through the convention, it is apparent that the course of debate led the framers *away* from the idea that the Constitution ought to erect significant barriers against entrance into public life. Perhaps the best evidence of this can be found in the fate of efforts to establish properly qualifications for appointment to office. As late as July 26, the convention had asked the Committee of

Detail to draft a provision "requiring certain qualifications of landed property and citizenship in the United States for the Executive, the Judiciary, and the Members of both branches of the Legislature." In its report of August 6, however, the committee merely proposed that the legislature should be empowered "to establish such uniform Qualifications of the Members of each House, with Regard to Property, as to the said Legislature shall seem expedient." When this provision was taken up on August 10, Charles Pinckney pointedly noted that the committee had departed from its instructions. He moved instead to insert a clause requiring legislators "to swear that they were respectively possessed of a clear unencumbered Estate." with a suitably descending scale of property for the two houses.

The ensuing debate revealed that attempts to establish property qualifications were objectionable on both practical and theoretical grounds. Two committee members explained why their report had not met Pinckney's expectations. Fix the requirement too high, John Rutledge noted, and it would anger the people; fix it too low, and the qualifications would be made "nugatory." Moreover, Oliver Ellsworth added, it was impossible to establish a scale that would work equally well for different parts of the Union or for different periods in the history of the nation. These objections were so decisive that Pinckney's motion was rejected by a simple voice vote.

But that still left open the question whether the legislature ought to possess any discretionary power to establish conditions of membership. One problem was the difficulty of employing any criterion other than property. The more telling objection lay, however, against giving the legislature any discretion. As Hugh Williamson noted, such license could allow the lawyers who might well dominate the new congress to secure "future elections … to their own body." But if qualifications could not be fixed *constitutionally,* it seemed better to do away with them entirely. Otherwise. Madison warned, the legislature would be able "by degrees [to] subvert the Constitution." The entire clause was accordingly eliminated.

If the character of national legislators could not be regulated by imposing property requirements on the elected, could the same goal be achieved by limiting the suffrage? When the Committee of Detail proposed allowing the House of Representatives to be chosen by the same voters who elected the lower houses of the state legislatures, Gouverneur Morris and John Dickinson vigorously argued in favor of restricting the franchise to landed freeholders. But this proposal was also roundly rejected. The Constitution placed no restrictions on the right of suffrage.

Nor can it be said that the framers seriously considered just how elections for the House of Representatives were to be conducted. In agreeing to vest Congress with a residual power to determine the manner of electing congressmen, they were clearly concerned with the possibility that the state legislatures would manipulate the electoral process. But what is more striking is the latitude within which the states were to be allowed to act. As Madison himself noted,

> Whether the electors should vote by ballot or vivâ voce, should assemble at this place or that place; should be divided into districts or all meet

at one place, sh[oul]d all vote for all the representatives; or all in a district vote for a number allotted to the district; these and many other points would depend on the Legislatures, and might materially affect the appointments.

Coming from one who presumably regarded the manner in which congressmen were to be elected as a critical element of the entire system—and who had once described voting by ballot as "the only radical cure for those arts of Electioneering which poison the very fountain of Liberty"—this was hardly a trivial concession. Indeed, nothing better illustrates the degree to which Madison's notion of the electoral virtues of the extended republic was simply a statement of faith. The indefinite character of his thinking on this subject was due in part to the greater priority he had been forced to place within the convention on the struggle to secure the principle of proportional representation; and it may also have reflected his disappointment that the Senate, the single branch of government on which he had originally fastened his deepest hopes, was to be elected by the state legislatures. In any event, there is no evidence that Madison had developed beyond generalities his notion of how representatives were to be elected. When in 1788 the states began adopting a variety of procedures for electing representatives—including not only district and statewide elections but also a hybrid in which electors voted statewide for members from particular districts—Madison informed Jefferson, "It is perhaps to be desired that various modes should be tried, as by that means only the best mode can be ascertained."

Decisions on other provisions also worked to remove formal barriers against election to the legislature. Instead of requiring a congressman to be "resident" in his state for a fixed period of years, the convention agreed that he need only be an "inhabitant" of the state at the time of election. When it came to deciding how legislators were to be paid, the convention did not presume that members of Congress would be independently wealthy. It authorized paying legislative salaries from the national treasury not merely to prevent the slates from retaining undue influence over their representatives, but also from an expectation that newly admitted western states might balk at supporting an adequate representation if forced to defray legislative salaries from their own limited funds.

Finally, and perhaps most revealingly, the convention relaxed the prohibition against the appointment of legislators to other offices. Of all the provisions relating to conditions of membership, this was the most sharply controverted, and it was not resolved—and then only by the narrowest margin—until September 3. The report of the Committee of Detail would have prevented legislators from accepting any federal office during the term of their election, with senators further barred from "holding any such office for one year afterwards." Supporters of these restrictions argued the conventional whiggish view that, without such restraints, the legislature would attract, as George Mason noted with typical irony, "those generous and benevolent characters who will do justice to each other's merit, by carving out offices and rewards" for their own profit. But the majority, who eventually restricted the prohibition only to offices that had been either "created" or whose "emoluments [had been] increased" during a legislator's term, were apparently swayed by equally candid arguments in favor of promoting ambition. James Wilson put the key point bluntly when he declared that "he was far from thinking the ambition which aspired to Offices of dignity and trust, an ignoble or culpable one." Thus while the narrow margin with which the diluted version of this clause was approved indicates that the framers had not reached a consensus, they would nevertheless have agreed that the revision was intended to encourage men to enter legislative service in part from forthright calculations of personal ambition. Whether the ambitions to be unleashed belonged to corruptible "office-hunters" or to "those whose talents" would "give weight to the Govern[men]t" remained to be seen.

On balance, then, the principal concern of the framers was not to limit access to national office to those who were most conspicuously qualified to occupy it, but rather to open up the process of political recruitment in the hope that better men would be moved to enter public life and prove capable of achieving electoral success. For the new government to succeed in this respect, however, it would have to rely on the actual circumstances of political life rather than the formal requirements that the Constitution itself had failed to impose. Federalist desires could be realized only if the enlarged sphere of the extended republic worked to filter talent upward or if the simple prestige and power of the new government drew qualified men away from the privacy of their law offices, plantations, and countinghouses. Neither the formal provisions of the Constitution nor the heated debates of the ratification campaign could secure such results; they depended instead on other factors—personal as well as political—that no constitution could by itself legislate.

If the adoption of the Constitution was thus meant to release new ambitions, the preservation of its intricate system of checks and balances would also depend, Madison argued in *Federalist* No. 51, on directing those ambitions toward appropriate ends. "Ambition must be made to counteract ambition," he wrote. "The interest of the man must be connected with the constitutional rights of the place." Yet despite its apparent gritty realism, this celebrated statement was no less problematic than other early predictions about the likely operation of the Constitution.

For ambition could counteract ambition only if those elected made continuation in a particular office the object of their careers. The benefits of bringing more enlightened leaders into office would be lost if they chose not to stay in positions of responsibility. But if one thing is clear about the political system that the Constitution created, it is that it long failed to promote the stability of tenure that Federalists desired and anticipated. The evidence on this point is unambiguous. Well into the next century, the new system proved embarrassingly productive in its *recruitment* of aspirants to national office, but its record on *retention* was another matter entirely. The best that can he said for Congress is that its membership was marginally more stable than that of the state legislatures. Throughout the entire first century of its history, members entered and left Congress with a frequency that stands in sharp contrast with modern standards. During this period, the median term of service in the House of Representatives fluctuated between two and four years, and the proportion of members who served more than four terms never exceeded 10 percent. From 1790 to 1870, the median age of departure from the House remained steadily fixed in the mid-forties. And although the reasons why men left the House are often hard to come by, death, old age, and electoral defeat clearly played far less of a role in attrition before the late nineteenth century than they do today....

The one group of congressmen whose ambitions can be described most easily are the ninety-odd members of the First Federal Congress of 1789–1790. Their experience in gaining and holding office marked the first test of the various predictions that had been vented while the Constitution was being adopted. The First Congress, of course, numbered fewer members than all but its immediate successor, and its ranks almost certainly included a higher proportion of prominent personalities than any later congress. To some extent, it is true, the likelihood that many of these first congressmen had taken major parts in both the Revolution and the debate over the Constitution would suggest that their motives did not accurately represent the range of ambitions that came into play once the age of the founding patriarchs gave way to the era of mass political parties. Yet even during the Revolution, decisions about the depth of political involvement—as opposed to simple allegiance—often reflected personal concerns, and by the late 1780s, recovery from the turmoil and dislocation of the war was well enough advanced to enable potential candidates to weigh the benefits and costs of office quite carefully according to the dictates of individual interest and ambition. Finally, although one cannot fault the framers of the Constitution for failing to anticipate how "change of circumstances, time, and a fuller population of our country" would affect the character of representation, the "moderate period of time" separating the drafting of the Constitution from the first elections allows us to ask how well the arguments of 1787–1788 corresponded to certain aspects of what might be called, with all due respect to Sir Lewis Namier, the structure of American politics at the accession of George Washington.

By any criterion, including those criteria that contemporaries would have applied, the victors in the first federal elections were a distinguished group. The roster of the First Congress included twenty members of the Federal Convention—among them Madison, Elbridge Gerry, Rufus King, Roger Sherman, William Samuel Johnson, Oliver Ellsworth, William Paterson, and Robert Morris—as well as a number of other men who had held prominent military or political positions during the war, such as Philip Schuyler, Elias Boudinot, Jeremiah Wadsworth, John Langdon, Richard Henry Lee, and Egbert Benson. Prestige alone offers no proof of legislative talent, but most members of the First Congress shared another trait that would have enabled contemporaries to agree that they possessed what Madison had called for in *Federalist* No. 10; "the most attractive merit, and the most diffusive and established characters." For in the milieu of the late 1780s, a notable record of involvement in the Revolution was itself the first and perhaps even sufficient test of political merit. In this respect, it is striking that fully half of the members of the First Congress were politically active before Independence, with no fewer than a third entering politics during the final crisis of 1774–1776, and an additional quarter first holding office during the remaining years of the war....

Historians generally agree that the two Federalist movements of the 1780s and 1790s were committed to the preservation or restoration of traditional principles of deference and that their leadership (at least in the northern states) tended to be drawn from an established elite whose superiority was endangered by the democratizing impulses the Revolution had released. Yet among the "dual Federalists" who sat in the First Congress, it is striking to see how many fit the image of new men who had themselves struggled to gain—and not simply inherit—prestige and influence. Recognizing that their own rise to political power and higher social status had derived from participation in the Revolution, they were no less its products for resisting what they regarded as its excesses.

By way of example, consider the uncannily parallel paths that had led Oliver Ellsworth of Connecticut and William Paterson of New Jersey to the Senate in 1789. Both were born in 1745; both were graduates of the College of New Jersey; both served terms as state legal officers; both were delegates to the Federal Convention, where they collaborated on the making of the Great Compromise; and as the capstones of their political careers, both later accepted appointments to the Supreme Court, where they served together until Ellsworth's retirement in 1800. Both came from families with solidly middle-class credentials. Ellsworth's father was a respectable farmer, selectman, and militia captain who intended his second son for the ministry but saw him turn to law instead. Paterson emigrated with his family from Ireland in 1747; by 1750 his father was established in Princeton, where he prospered as a storekeeper and helped his eldest son take advantage of all the opportunities education could bestow.

The promise of education was one thing, however; success was another matter again. When war broke out in 1775, both men were still struggling to make a respectable career at law. Ellsworth had earned all of three pounds sterling during his first three years of practice; the one promising step he had taken was to marry a Wolcott and move to Hartford, where he could profit from his in-laws' connections and status. Paterson, too, had remained a poor country lawyer. Rather than take his chances in Philadelphia or even one of the larger neighboring towns, he pursued a thankless practice in rural New Jersey; most of his work involved protecting his father's debt-troubled property.

Perhaps native ability would have brought eventual success to these two future justices had the Revolution not intervened in their lives. Certainly they did not support the Revolution because they foresaw how their careers could benefit from Independence: neither had shown any ardent interest in politics before 1775 (though Ellsworth did serve a term in the Connecticut assembly in 1773). With Paterson and Ellsworth, as with so many of their colleagues, the events of the mid-1770s can be said, not so much to have furthered ambitions previously thwarted, but rather to have created ambitions which had hardly existed. Yet while their commitment to the whig cause enabled them to acquire substantial political influence within their states, in many ways professional prominence remained their deeper object. Paterson held no office at the time of his election to the Senate; he was busy instead pursuing a hefty legal practice that had expanded enormously upon the basis of his record as wartime attorney general. For his part, Ellsworth accepted election grudgingly, informing Governor Samuel Huntington that he would have preferred to retain his seat on the Connecticut Superior Court. "Considering, however, that in the present scituation of our publick affairs, it may be a duty, for a time, to waive personal considerations, I have concluded, by the leave of Providence, to attend the Congress at its first, and perhaps two or three of its first, sessions." Ellsworth went on to serve a full six-year term before replacing John Jay as chief justice; Paterson resigned even before the First Congress expired to accept election as governor of New Jersey.

Legislation and debate appealed little to Ellsworth and Paterson, but there were other attorneys who relished these activities to a degree that irked congressmen drawn from other occupations. Few, if any, members of the First Congress commanded greater respect in these areas than the two leading Federalist representatives from Massachusetts, Theodore Sedgwick and Fisher Ames. They, too, came from moderately respectable families that had struggled to maintain an estate and improve their social standing in the cramped and jealous world of a New England town. Having lost their fathers at an early age, both were forced to rely on a college education (Sedgwick at Yale, Ames at Harvard) and the diligent pursuit of legal studies to establish their own livelihoods. Like Paterson and Ellsworth, both had experienced the pangs of disappointment and idleness that were the dues of young attorneys, and like colleagues throughout America—including William Paterson—they knew the kind of resentment, not to say enmity, that their profession attracted. They naturally equated animosity against lawyers with aversion to the rule of law itself, and they viewed Shays's Rebellion of 1786 as proof of the need to restore a due sense of obedience to the restless citizenry of Massachusetts (a lost cause if ever there was one). Having relied upon their own talents and fortitude to make their way, with some success, in the world, they found it difficult to look sympathetically on the social jealousy and resentment of class that the Shaysite uprising embodied. For Sedgwick and Ames, as for so many other attorneys to come, election to Congress provided a welcome opportunity to escape the routine bickering of court appearances while continuing to practice the professional arts of draftsmanship and oratory. To his despondent and domestically overburdened wife—"a sufferer from chronic pregnancy and loneliness," his biographer has noted—Sedgwick wrote tender letters lamenting his confinement in Congress; but his correspondence with male friends reveals his pride in the legislative art....

In certain ways, congressmen who did not feel too deeply attached to their constituencies could fit the original Madisonian ideal of representation better than those whose political loyalties never rose above their parochial roots. Yet to survey the diverse paths that brought the members of the First Congress to New York in 1789 is to realize how little relevance that ideal had to the actual recruitment and retention of national legislators. Even in 1789, when the existing political nation was still aroused over the character and fate of the Constitution and when the heady debates of the preceding months still resounded clearly, it is clear that men sought national office for various reasons, public and private, patriotic and self-interested. It is easy enough to explain why men so long committed to public life as Madison and Roger Sherman wished to attend Congress in 1789, nor is it much more difficult to gauge the balance of public and private concerns that brought Baldwin, Williamson, and the Philadelphia merchants (all members of the Federal Convention) there as well. But it is no less revealing to examine the motives of Benjamin Contee of Maryland, who may have hoped a seat in Congress would help him stave off his Philadelphia creditor, or Thomas Scott of Pennsylvania, who balked at taking his seat until he was assured that his son would inherit his position as prothonotary of Washington County. Rather than seek reelection to the Second Congress, Scott sought to retain his clerkship of the county court, but after Governor Thomas Mifflin removed him from this position, he ran successfully for the Third Congress and then, apparently, refused to run again.

In point of fact, of course, there was never a time when the political system operated solely as a filter of talent or when expedient calculations did not enter forthrightly into decisions to enter or leave Congress. Legislation was a tedious and often frustrating task that kept one away from family and business. Such appeal as it exerted in the early years of the new regime was probably felt most strongly either by those whose prior experience of the Revolution had already converted them to what John Jay called "the charms of liberty" or by those who (like Fisher Ames and William Branch Giles) were young enough to enter politics before finding themselves bound to another career. The great majority of congressmen acted on different calculations. If they sought election out of some sense of engagement with public issues, their commitment was far from permanent. And if, on the other hand, they hoped a term or two in Congress might redound to their personal advantage, the rewards they hoped to garner were more likely to come in the form of an appointment to the bench or, better yet, a customs collectorship—positions that were more secure and less demanding. Whatever the framers of 1787 may have intended, they could not alter the underlying character of political activity by constitutional fiat. At the close of the Revolution, politics remained more of an avocation than a profession. Over time, the emergence of the political party system provided a more reliable channel of recruitment than the powerful but erratic impulses of patriotism. But the persistence of high rates of turnover both in Congress and the state assemblies suggests that the dividends of legislative service were still found elsewhere, in a later appointment to a more comfortable sinecure. These were not quite the ambitions that the framers had hoped to evoke.

FURTHER READING

Akhil Reed Amar, *America's Constitution: A Biography* (2005).

Richard Beeman, *Plain, Honest Men: The Making of the American Constitution* (2009).

Richard Beeman et al., *Beyond Confederation: Origins of the Constitution and American National Identity* (1987).

George Athan Billias, *American Constitutionalism Heard Round the World, 1776–1989: A Global Perspective* (2009).

Catherine Drinker Bowen, *Miracle at Philadelphia: The Story of the Constitutional Convention* (1986).

Saul Cornell, *The Other Founders: Anti-Federalism and the Dissenting Tradition in America, 1788–1828* (1999).

Robert A. Dahl, *How Democratic is the American Constitution?* (2001).

Woody Holton, *Unruly Americans and the Origins of the Constitution* (2008).

Merrill Jensen, *The Articles of Confederation: An Interpretation of the Social-Constitutional History of the American Revolution* (1959).

Alfred Hinsey Kelly, Winfred Harbison, and Herman Belz, *The American Constitution: Its Origin and Development* (1990).

Forrest McDonald, *Novus Ordo Seclorum: The Intellectual Origins of the Constitution* (1985).

Richard B. Morris, *Witness at the Creation: Hamilton, Madison, Jay, and the Constitution* (1985).

Jack Rakove, *Original Meanings: Politics and Ideas in the Making of the Constitution* (1996).

CHAPTER 6

Competing Visions
of National Development
in the Early National Period

The first president, by unanimous vote in the electoral college, was George Washington, war hero and patriot. Washington's inauguration, which evoked among the people a feeling of pride in the nation's revolutionary past and hope for its future, ushered in a brief period of political unity. The nationalist spirit was evident in the first session of Congress, which succeeded in passing a series of key measures. The Constitution had not defined the structure of the federal judiciary, but Congress acted quickly, passing the Judiciary Act of 1789, which established judicial procedures and lower federal courts. Next, Congress imposed a tariff on imported goods to provide the federal government with revenue. Finally, as promised during the ratification debate, Congress passed the Bill of Rights, ten constitutional amendments that were sent to the states for ratification. Following ratification, Americans were guaranteed freedoms of speech and religion and given rights to bear arms and avoid "cruel and unusual punishments."

Yet the unity was short lived. Within a few years, the national government was divided into two political factions with different visions for the future of the United States. The two principal protagonists of these visions were Thomas Jefferson and Alexander Hamilton, both of whom served in Washington's cabinet. Hamilton dreamed of transforming the United States into a manufacturing giant like Britain. America, he was fond of saying, was "a Hercules in the cradle." Hamilton was also suspicious of the people—he considered the masses "turbulent and changing"—and believed the government would be strong if it won the favor of the financial elite. In contrast, Jefferson feared the growth of manufacturing because he sensed that it would decrease the citizenry's independence. His vision focused on a nation of commercial agriculture and independent farmers; virtue, he argued, was best maintained by those "who labor in the earth."

The divisions between Jefferson and Hamilton deepened when the United States was pulled into a European conflict in the 1790s. After the French Revolution unraveled into unparalleled bloodshed, France declared war on Britain, Spain, and Holland. Whereas Jefferson and his followers saw the French Revolution as heir to the American War for Independence, the people who shared Hamilton's views watched it with horror as the revolution spun out of control. Out of these differences, political groups began to coalesce. Those sympathetic to the French and fearful of Hamilton's vision formed Democratic-Republican societies. In response, another group, led by Hamilton, Washington, and John Adams, united under the Federalist banner. Acrimonious political battles and vitriolic debate became commonplace in the late 1790s. After John Adams was elected to succeed Washington, the divisions deepened as the United States became further embroiled in European conflicts and nearly went to war against France.

Adams's failures as president almost guaranteed a Democratic-Republican victory in 1800, and Jefferson heralded his election as the "revolution of 1800." Although this was undoubtedly an overstatement, his ascension to the presidency is noteworthy because the Federalists peacefully handed over their power to a hated rival. Never again would the Federalist Party control the presidency or Congress. Nonetheless, the Federalist vision endured particularly in the judiciary. The competing visions of national development, moreover, would continue to divide American society as Americans puzzled over the future of their young nation.

 QUESTIONS TO THINK ABOUT

Whose vision of America's future, Jefferson's or Hamilton's, is most appealing to you? Whose vision was most fully realized? How did the fears and hopes of those who belonged to the Federalists and to the Democratic-Republican Party differ? How did Federalists and Democratic-Republicans represent and misrepresent one another?

 DOCUMENTS

In document 1, Thomas Jefferson argues that the future of the United States is best left in the hands of the yeoman farmers, who will retain their virtue and industry. In document 2, Judith Sargent Murray calls for "the Equality of the Sexes." A friend of Abigail Adams, Murray hoped that gender equality could be a part of the new republic. Alexander Hamilton provides his vision of national development in document 3, which is in marked contrast to that of Jefferson. The next four documents illustrate the factional conflict that resulted from these very different visions of the direction of national development. In document 4, "A Peep into the Antifederal Club," a Federalist cartoonist depicts the Democratic-Republicans as unruly and pompous. Their charter reads, "The People are All/and we are the People." C. William Manning, a yeoman farmer and Jeffersonian, writes, in document 5, of his fears that the power of the few would enable them to subvert the government. Document 6 is a resolution secretly written by Jefferson for the state of Kentucky in response to a series of laws known as the Alien and Sedition Acts. In this resolution, Jefferson argues that the states have the right to say when Congress has exceeded its powers. This idea was later used by other theorists, as we see in Chapters 9 and 14. Document 7 is the ruling by Chief Justice John Marshall that states that the Constitution is paramount law. Thomas Paine returns in document 8 to eulogize Washington, who had died in 1799, as the "savior of your country... first in war, first in peace, first in the hearts of his countrymen."

1. Republican Thomas Jefferson Celebrates the Virtue of the Yeoman Farmer, 1785

In Europe the lands are either cultivated, or locked up against the cultivator. Manufacture must therefore be resorted to of necessity not of choice, to support the surplus of their people. But we have an immensity of land courting the industry of the husbandman. Is it best then that all our citizens should be employed in its improvement, or that one half should be called off from that to exercise manufactures and handicraft arts for the other? Those who labor in the earth are the chosen people of God, if ever He had a chosen people, whose breasts He has made His peculiar deposit for substantial and genuine virtue. It is the focus in which he keeps alive that sacred fire, which otherwise might escape from the face of the earth. Corruption of morals in the mass of cultivators is a phenomenon of which no age nor nation has furnished an example. It is the mark set on those, who, not looking up to heaven, to their own soil and industry, as does the husbandman, for their subsistence, depend for it on casualties and caprice of customers. Dependence begets subservience and venality, suffocates the germ of virtue, and prepares fit tools for the designs of ambition. This, the natural progress and consequence of the arts, has sometimes perhaps been retarded by accidental circumstances; but, generally speaking, the proportion which the aggregate of the other classes of citizens bears in any State to that of its husbandmen, is the proportion of its unsound to its healthy parts, and is a good enough barometer whereby to measure its degree of corruption. While we have land to labor then, let us never wish to see our citizens occupied at a workbench, or twirling a distaff. Carpenters, masons, smiths, are wanting in husbandry; but, for the general operations of manufacture, let our workshops remain in Europe. It is better to carry provisions and materials to workmen there, than bring them to the provisions and materials, and with them their manners and principles. The loss by the transportation of commodities across the Atlantic will be made up in happiness and permanence of government. The mobs of great cities add just so much to the support of pure government, as sores do to the strength of the human body.

Thomas Jefferson, *Notes on the State of Virginia* (1785), in *The Life and Selected Writings of Thomas Jefferson*, eds. Adrienne Koch and William Peden (New York: Library of America, 1984), 280.

2. Judith Sargent Murray Argues for the "Equality of the Sexes," 1790

Is it upon mature consideration we adopt the idea, that nature is thus partial in her distributions? Is it indeed a fact, that she hath yielded to one half of the human species so unquestionable a mental superiority? I know that to both sexes elevated understandings, and the reverse, are common. But, suffer me to ask, in what the minds of females are so notoriously deficient, or unequal. May not the intellectual powers be ranged under these four heads—imagination, reason, memory, and judgment. The province of imagination hath long since been surrendered to us, and we have been crowned and undoubted sovereigns of the regions of fancy. Invention is perhaps the most arduous effort of the mind; this branch of imagination hath been particularly ceded to us, and we have been time out of mind invested with that creative faculty. Observe the variety of fashions (here I bar the contemptuous smile) which distinguish and adorn the female world: how continually are they changing, insomuch that they almost render the wise man's assertion problematical, and we are ready to say, *there is something new under the sun*.... Perhaps it will be asked if I furnish these facts as instances of excellency in our sex. Certainly not; but as proofs of a creative faculty, of a lively imagination. Assuredly great activity of mind is thereby discovered, and was this activity properly directed, what beneficial effects would follow. Is the needle and kitchen sufficient to employ the operations of a soul thus organized? I should conceive not, Nay, it is a truth that those very departments leave the intelligent principle vacant, and at liberty for speculation....

Meantimes she herself is most unhappy; she feels the want of a cultivated mind. Is she single, she in vain seeks to fill up time from sexual employments or amusements. Is she united to a person whose soul nature made equal to her own, education hath set him so far above her, that in those entertainments which are productive of such rational felicity, she is not qualified to accompany him. She experiences a mortifying consciousness of inferiority, which embitters every enjoyment. Doth the person to whom her adverse fate hath consigned her, possess a mind incapable of improvement, she is equally wretched, in being so closely connected with an individual whom she cannot but despise.

Now, was she permitted the same instructors as her brother, (with an eye however to their particular departments) for the employment of a rational mind an ample field would be opened. In astronomy she might catch a glimpse of the immensity of the Deity, and thence she would form amazing conceptions of the august and supreme Intelligence. In geography she would admire Jehovah in the midst of his benevolence; thus adapting this globe to the various wants and amusements of its inhabitants. In natural philosophy she would adore the infinite majesty of heaven, clothed in condescension; and as she traversed the reptile world, she would hail the goodness of a creating God. A mind, thus filled, would have little room for the trifles with which our sex are, with too much justice,

Judith Sargent Murray, *On the Equality of the Sexes.* http://digital.library.upenn.edu/women/murray/equality/equality.html.

accused of amusing themselves, and they would thus be rendered fit companions for those, who should one day wear them as their crown....

Yes, ye lordly, ye haughty sex, our souls are by nature *equal* to yours; the same breath of God animates, enlivens, and invigorates us; and that we are not fallen lower than yourselves, let those witness who have greatly towered above the various discouragements by which they have been so heavily oppressed; and though I am unacquainted with the list of celebrated characters on either side, yet from the observations I have made in the contracted circle in which I have moved, I dare confidently believe, that from the commencement of time to the present day, there hath been as many females, as males, who, by the *mere force of natural powers*, have merited the crown of applause; who, *thus unassisted*, have seized the wreath of fame....

AND now assist me, O thou genius of my sex, while I undertake the arduous task of endeavouring to combat that vulgar, that almost universal errour.... The superiority of your sex hath, I grant, been time out of mind esteemed a truth incontrovertible; in consequence of which persuasion, every plan of education hath been calculated to establish this favourite tenet....

3. Federalist Alexander Hamilton Envisions a Developed American Economy, 1791

It is now proper to proceed a step further, and to enumerate the principal circumstances, from which it may be inferred—That manufacturing establishments not only occasion a positive augmentation of the Produce and Revenue of the Society, but that they contribute essentially to rendering them greater than they could possibly be, without such establishments. These circumstances are—

1. The division of Labour.
2. An extension of the use of Machinery.
3. Additional employment to classes of the community not ordinarily engaged in the business.
4. The promoting of emigration from foreign Countries.
5. The furnishing greater scope for the diversity of talents and dispositions which discriminate men from each other.
6. The affording a more ample and various field for enterprize.
7. The creating in some instances a new, and securing in all, a more certain and steady demand for the surplus produce of the soil.

Each of these circumstances has a considerable influence upon the total mass of industrious effort in a community. Together, they add to it a degree of energy and effect, which are not easily conceived. Some comments upon each of them, in the order in which they have been stated, may serve to explain their importance.

I. As to the Division of Labour.

It has justly been observed, that there is scarcely any thing of greater moment in the economy of a nation, than the proper division of labour. The

Alexander Hamilton, *Report on Manufactures* (1791), in *Alexander Hamilton's Papers on Public Credit, Commerce and Finance*, ed. Samuel McKee, Jr. (New York: The Liberal Arts Press, 1934), 190–192, 195–199.

separation of occupations causes each to be carried to a much greater perfection, than it could possible acquire, if they were blended. This arises principally from three circumstances.

1st—The greater skill and dexterity naturally resulting from a constant and undivided application to a single object....

2nd. The economy of time—by avoiding the loss of it, incident to a frequent transition from one operation to another of a different nature....

3rd. An extension of the use of Machinery. A man occupied on a single object will have it more in his power, and will be more naturally led to exert his imagination in devising methods to facilitate and abrige labour, than if he were perplexed by a variety of independent and dissimilar operations....

II. As to an extension of the use of Machinery a point which though partly anticipated requires to be placed in one or two additional lights.

The employment of Machinery forms an item of great importance in the general mass of national industry. 'Tis an artificial force brought in aid of the natural force of man; and, to all the purposes of labour, is an increase of hands; an accession of strength, *unincumbered too by the expence of maintaining the laborer.* May it not therefore be fairly inferred, that those occupations, which give greatest scope to the use of this auxiliary, contribute most to the general Stock of industrious effort, and, in consequence, to the general product of industry?...

If there be anything in a remark often to be met with—namely that there is, in the genius of the people of this country, a peculiar aptitude for mechanic improvements, it would operate as a forcible reason for giving opportunities to the exercise of that species of talent, by the propagation of manufactures.

VI. As to the affording a more ample and various field for enterprise.

...To cherish and stimulate the activity of the human mind, by multiplying the objects of enterprise, is not among the least considerable of the expedients, by which the wealth of a nation may be promoted. Even things in themselves not positively advantageous, sometimes become so, by their tendency to provoke exertion. Every new scene, which is opened to the busy nature of man to rouse and exert itself, is the addition of a new energy to the general stock of effort.

The spirit of enterprise, useful and prolific as it is, must necessarily be contracted or expanded in proportion to the simplicity or variety of the occupations and productions, which are to be found in a Society. It must be less in a nation of mere cultivators, than in a nation of cultivators and merchants; less in a nation of cultivators and merchants, than in a nation of cultivators, artificers and merchants.

VII. As to the creating, in some instances, a new, and securing in all a more certain and steady demand, for the surplus produce of the soil....

To secure such a market, there is no other expedient, than to promote manufacturing establishments. Manufacturers who constitute the most numerous class, after the Cultivators of land, are for that reason the principal consumers of the surplus of their labour.

This idea of an extensive domestic market for the surplus produce of the soil is of the first consequence. It is of all things, that which most effectually conduces to a flourishing state of Agriculture. If the effect of manufactories should be to detach a portion of the hands, which would otherwise be engaged in Tillage, it might possibly cause a smaller quantity of lands to be under cultivation but by their tendency to procure a more certain demand for the surplus produce of the soil, they would, at the same time, cause the lands which were in cultivation to be better improved and more productive. And while, by their influence, the condition of each individual farmer would be meliorated, the total mass of Agricultural production would probably be increased. For this must evidently depend as much, if not more, upon the degree of improvement; than upon the number of acres under culture.

It merits particular observation, that the multiplication of manufactories not only furnishes a Market for those articles, which have been accustomed to be produced in abundance, in a country; but it likewise creates a demand for such as were either unknown or produced in inconsiderable quantities. The bowels as well as the surface of the earth are ransacked for articles which were before neglected. Animals, Plants and Minerals acquire an utility and value, which were before unexplored.

The foregoing considerations seem sufficient to establish, as general propositions, That it is the interest of nations to diversify the industrious pursuits of the individuals, who compose them—That the establishment of manufactures is calculated not only to increase the general stock of useful and productive labour; but even to improve the state of Agriculture in particular; certainly to advance the interests of those who are engaged in it.

4. Federalists Represent Democratic-Republicans as Secretive, Arrogant, and Rude, 1793

ANTI-FEDERAL CARTOON, 1793. 'A Peep into the Antifederal Club': a Federalist cartoon of 1793 ridiculing the Jeffersonian anti-Federalists as an unruly mob opposed to government and in concert with the devil; Jefferson himself is shown at center right, standing on the table and orating.

5. C. William Manning, a Republican, Fears for the Future of the Nation, 1798

In the sweat of thy face shalt thou get they bread, until thou return to the ground, is the irreversible sentence of Heaven on man for his rebellion. To be sentenced to hard labor during life is very unpleasant to human nature. There is a great aversion to it perceivable in all men; yet it is absolutely necessary that a large majority of the world should labor, or we could not subsist. For labor is the sole parent of all property; the land yields nothing without it, and there is no … necessary of life but what costs labor and is generally esteemed valuable according to the labor it costs. Therefore, no person can possess property without laboring unless he gets it by force or craft, fraud or fortune, out of the earnings of others.

But from the great variety of capacities, strength, and abilities of men, there always was and always will be a very unequal distribution of property in the world. Many are so rich that they can live without labor—also the merchant, physician, lawyer, and divine, the philosopher and schoolmaster, the judicial and executive officers, and many others who could honestly get a living without bodily labors. As all these professions require a considerable expense of time and property to qualify themselves therefore, … so all these professions naturally unite in their schemes to make their callings as honorable and lucrative as possible.

Also, as ease and rest from labor are reasoned among the greatest pleasures of life, pursued by all with the greatest avidity, and when attained at once create a sense of superiority; and as pride and ostentation are natural to the human heart, these orders of men generally associate together and look down with too much contempt on those that labor.

As the interests and incomes of the few lie chiefly in money at interest, rents, salaries, and fees, that are fixed on the nominal value of money, they are interested in having money scarce and the price of labor and produce as low as possible….

But the greatest danger the many are under in these money matters is from the judicial and executive officers, especially so as their incomes for a living are almost wholly gotten from the follies and distress of the many—they being governed by the same selfish principles as other men are. They are the most interested in the distresses of the many of any in the nation; the scarcer money is and the greater the distresses of the many are, the better for them….

This is the reason why they ought to be kept entirely from the legislative body…. For in all these conceived differences of interests, it is the business and duty of the legislative body to determine what is justice, or what is right and wrong; and it is the duty of every individual in the nation to regulate his conduct according to their decisions….

The reason why a free government has always failed is from the unreasonable demands and desires of the few. They cannot bear to be on a level with their fellow creatures, or submit to the determinations of a legislature where (as they call it) the swinish multitude is fairly represented, but sicken at the idea, and are ever hankering

Scott J. Hammond, et. al., *Classics of American Political and Constitutional Thought* (2007): 767-769
C. William Manning, The Key of Libberty (1798)..

and striving after monarchy or aristocracy, where the people have nothing to do in matters of government but to support the few in luxury and idleness.

For these and many other reasons, a large majority of those that live without labor are ever opposed to the principles and operation of a free government; and though the whole of them do not amount to one-eighth part of the people, yet, by their combinations, arts, and schemes, have always made out to destroy it sooner or later.

6. Thomas Jefferson Advances the Power of the States, 1798

1. *Resolved,* That the several States composing the United States of America, are not united on the principle of unlimited submission to their general government; but that, by a compact under the style and title of a Constitution for the United States, and of amendments thereto, they constituted a general government for special purposes—delegated to that government certain definite powers, reserving, each State to itself, the residuary mass of right to their own self-government; and that whensoever the general government assumes undelegated powers, its acts are unauthoritative, void, and of no force: that to this compact each State acceded as a State, and is an integral part, its co-States forming, as to itself, the other party: that the government created by this compact was not made the exclusive or final judge of the extent of the powers delegated to itself; since that would have made its discretion, and not the Constitution, the measure of its powers; but that, as in all other cases of compact among powers having no common judge, each party has an equal right to judge for itself, as well of infractions as of the mode and measure of redress.

2. *Resolved,* That the Constitution of the United States, having delegated to Congress a power to punish treason, counterfeiting the securities and current coin of the United States, piracies, and felonies committed on the high seas, and offenses against the law of nations, and no other crimes, whatsoever; and it being true as a general principle, and one of the amendments to the Constitution having also declared, that "the powers not delegated to the United States by the Constitution, not prohibited by it to the States, are reserved to the States respectively, or to the people," therefore the act of Congress, passed on the 14th day of July, 1798, and intituled "An Act in addition to the act intituled An Act for the punishment of certain crimes against the United States," as also the act passed by them on the—day of June, 1798, intituled "An Act to punish frauds committed on the bank of the Untied States," (and all their other acts which assume to create, define, or punish crimes, other than those so enumerated in the Constitution,) are altogether void, and of no force; and that the power to create, define, and punish such other crimes is reserved, and, of right, appertains solely and exclusively to the respective States, each within its own territory.

Thomas Jefferson, *The Kentucky Resolutions of 1798.* Obtained from http://www.constitution.org/cons/kent/1798.htm Also available in *The Virginia and Kentucky Resolutions, with the Alien Sedition and Other Acts, 1798–1799* (New York: A. Lovell, 1894).

3. *Resolved,* That it is true as a general principle, and is also expressly declared by one of the amendments to the Constitution, that "the powers not delegated to the United States by the Constitution, nor prohibited by it to the States, are reserved to the States respectively, or to the people"; and that no power over the freedom of religion, freedom of speech, or freedom of the press being delegated to the United States by the Constitution, nor prohibited by it to the States, all lawful powers respecting the same did of right remain, and were reserved to the States or the people: that thus was manifested their determination to retain to themselves the right of judging how far the licentiousness of speech and of the press may be abridged without lessening their useful freedom, and how far those abuses which cannot be separated from their use should be tolerated, rather than the use be destroyed. And thus also they guarded against all abridgment by the United States of the freedom of religious opinions and exercises, and retained to themselves the right of protecting the same, as this State, by a law passed on the general demand of its citizens, had already protected them from all human restraint or interference. And that in addition to this general principle and express declaration, another and more special provision has been made by one of the amendments to the Constitution, which expressly declares, that "Congress shall make no law respecting an establishment of religion, or prohibiting the free exercise thereof, or abridging the freedom of speech or of the press": thereby guarding in the same sentence, and under the same words, the freedom of religion, of speech, and of the press: insomuch, that whatever violated either, throws down the sanctuary which covers the others, and that libels, falsehood, and defamation, equally with heresy and false religion, are withheld from the cognizance of federal tribunals. That, therefore, the act of Congress of the United States, passed on the 14th day of July, 1798, intituled "An Act in addition to the act intituled An Act for the punishment of certain crimes against the United States," which does abridge the freedom of the press, is not law, but is altogether void, and of no force.

4. *Resolved,* That alien friends are under the jurisdiction and protection of the laws of the State wherein they are: that no power over them has been delegated to the United States, nor prohibited to the individual States, distinct from their power over citizens. And it being true as a general principle, and one of the amendments to the Constitution having also declared, that "the powers not delegated to the United States by the Constitution, nor prohibited by it to the States, are reserved to the States respectively, or to the people," the act of the Congress of the United States, passed on the—day of July, 1798, intituled "An Act concerning aliens," which assumes powers over alien friends, not delegated by the Constitution, is not law, but is altogether void, and of no force.

5. *Resolved,* That in addition to the general principle, as well as the express declaration, that powers not delegated are reserved, another and more special provision, inserted in the Constitution from abundant caution, has declared that "the migration or importation of such persons as any of the States now existing shall think proper to admit, shall not be prohibited by the Congress prior to the year 1808" that this commonwealth does admit the migration of alien friends, described as the subject of the said act concerning aliens: that a provision against

prohibiting their migration, is a provision against all acts equivalent thereto, or it would be nugatory: that to remove them when migrated, is equivalent to a prohibition of their migration, and is, therefore, contrary to the said provision of the Constitution, and void.

7. Chief Justice John Marshall Argues for the Primacy of the Federal Government, 1803

The question whether an act repugnant to the constitution can become the law of the land, is a question deeply interesting to the United States.... That the people have an original right to establish for their future government such principles as, in their opinion, shall most conduce to their own happiness, is the basis on which the whole American fabric has been erected....

This original and supreme will organizes the government, and assigns to different departments their respective powers. It may either stop here or establish limits not to be transcended by those departments.

The government of the United States is of the latter description. The powers of the legislature are defined and limited; and that those limits may not be mistaken or forgotten, the constitution is written.... The distinction between a government with limited and unlimited powers is abolished if those limits do not confine the persons on whom they are imposed and if acts prohibited and acts allowed are of equal obligation. It is a proposition too plain to be contested, that the constitution controls any legislative act repugnant to it; or, that the legislature may alter the constitution by an ordinary act. Between these alternatives there is no middle ground....

Certainly all those who have framed written constitutions contemplate them as forming the fundamental and paramount law of the nation, and consequently the theory of every such government must be that an act of the legislature repugnant to the Constitution is void.

This theory is essentially attached to a written constitution, and is consequently to be considered, by this court as one of the fundamental principles of our society....

The Constitution is either a superior, paramount law, unchangeable by ordinary means, or it is on a level with ordinary legislative acts, and, like other acts, is alterable when the legislature shall please to alter it.

If the former part of the alternative be true, then a legislative act contrary to the Constitution is not law: if the latter part be true, then written Constitutions are absurd attempts, on the part of the people, to limit a power in its own nature illimitable....

It is emphatically the province and duty of the judicial department to say what the law is. Those who apply the rule to particular cases, must of necessity expound and interpret that rule. If two laws conflict with each other, the courts must decide on the operation of each....

John Marshall, Opinion in *Marbury v. Madison* (1803), in *United States Supreme Court Reporters*, V, 137.

If, then, the courts are to regard the Constitution, and the Constitution is superior to any ordinary act of the legislature, the Constitution, and not such ordinary act, must govern the case to which they both apply.

8. Thomas Paine Eulogizes George Washington, 1800

AMERICANS,

The saviour of your country has obtained his last victory. Having reached the summit of human perfection, he has quitted the region of human glory. CONQUEROR OF TIME, he has triumphed over mortality; LEGATE OF HEAVEN, he has returned with the tidings of his mission; FATHER OF HIS PEOPLE, he has ascended to advocate their cause in the bosom of his GOD. Solemn, "as it were a pause in nature," was his transit to eternity; thronged by the shades of heroes, his approach to the confines of bliss; pæaned by the song of angels, his journey beyond the stars!

The voice of a grateful and afflicted people has pronounced the eulogium of their departed hero—"*first in war, first in peace, first in the hearts of his countrymen.*" That this exalted tribute is justly due to his memory, the scar-honoured veteran, who has fought under the banners of his glory, the enraptured statesman, who has bowed to the dominion of his eloquence, the hardy cultivator, whose soil has been defended by the prodigies of his valour, the protected citizen, whose peaceful rights have been secured by the vigilance of his wisdom; yea, every fibre, that can vibrate in the heart of an American, will attest with agonized sensibility....

As the director of that important and dubious contest, which issued in the establishment, of our liberty and independence, he displayed an impressive grandeur of exertion, which marshalled into hostility the fluctuating vigour of his countrymen, and is still remembered with awe in the astonishment of nations....

Through the vicissitudes of a war, singularly fluctuating in its fortunes, and desolating in its effects, he discovered a constant principle of action, which acquired no lustre from the brilliant exploits it achieved, but derived all its glory from its own original greatness. Self-dependent, and self-elevated, it disdained the fictitious aid of circumstance; and never did it shine with more splendour and energy, than when fortune had deserted him, and his country had despaired....

The temporary structure of the old confederation, which had been planned merely for the purposes of a revolutionary government, when the passions of the people were united, was found, upon a brief experiment, to be totally incompetent to direct the affairs of an extending nation, when peace had restored the complicated occupations of life, and demanded a more uniform protection from the energies of law. The inconveniencies, resulting from its defects, had given occasion to designing demagogues, who hoped to profit by a separation of the States to foment divisions among a people, who too lightly valued the blessings they enjoyed. The union of the country was in danger; and the evil was of too baneful a nature to admit of a partial or dilatory remedy. But, how novel, how aspiring, was the hope of connecting, under one compact code of

Eulogies and Orations on the Life and Death of General George Washington (Boston, 1800) 55–66.

general jurisprudence, so many distinct sovereignties, each jealous of its independence, without impairing their respective authorities! The unbalanced bodies of the confederacy had almost overcome the attracting power, that restrained them; when the watchful guardian of his country's interests, the heart–uniting WASHINGTON appeared, the political magnet in the centre of discord, and reconciled and consolidated the clashing particles of the system in an indissoluble union of government.

ESSAYS

It is difficult for us today to understand how fragile a republic the United States was in the late eighteenth and early nineteenth centuries. Political divisions and economic weaknesses plagued the new nation, and many European powers doubted whether the United States as a nation would survive. As American leaders grappled with the weaknesses that beset their nation, they differed on its most serious flaws. The following essays illustrate the leaders' differing perceptions of the dangers that the United States faced and their prescriptions for addressing these dangers. They focus less on the debates of modern historians than on the differences between those people in the early nineteenth century who created the first political party system. Linda K. Kerber, professor of history at the University of Iowa, describes the quandaries of the Federalists, a political party whose members feared that popular democracy might spin out of control. Although they fostered economic development, they were well aware that an urban proletariat would result. As a result, they sought a stability that would temper these developments. Drew R. McCoy, a historian who teaches at Clark University, explores the dilemmas of the Jeffersonian Republicans. Focusing on the ideas of Jefferson, McCoy illustrates how the Republicans, like their Federalist antagonists, perceived challenges for the future of the United States. Fearful of creating a dependent class, Jefferson set his sights westward, where he envisioned vast tracts of land being farmed by virtuous citizens of the young republic.

The Fears of the Federalists

LINDA K. KERBER

"Little whirlwinds of dry leaves and dirt portend a hurricane," warned Fisher Ames. The Federalist saw these little whirlwinds everywhere in America: in the ineffectuality of Jeffersonian foreign policy, in the willingness to embark on projects as unpredictable as the acquisition of Louisiana, in Jeffersonian expressions of confidence in the political amateur. As the Federalist read his current events, one after another of the sources of cultural stability was being undermined by Jeffersonian enthusiasms: by the shift in the grounds and goals of scientific

From Linda K. Kerber, *Federalists in Dissent: Imagery and Ideology in Jeffersonian America*, p. 173–174, 177–179, 181–195, 199–203, 206–208, and 211–213. Copyright © 1970 Cornell University. Used by permission of the publisher, Cornell University Press.

inquiry, by the rejection of the classical curriculum, and by what was believed to be a hostility to the institutions of social order, manifested by the revision of the judiciary system and the subsequent impeachment of judges.

The Jeffersonian approach to politics struck the articulate Federalists as dangerously naive. The optimism, the ready professions of faith in popular democracy, seemed to mask a failure to comprehend the ambivalence of the American social order. To these Federalists, American society, for all its surface stability and prosperity, was torn by internal contradiction. A population which had proved its capacity for revolutionary violence would not necessarily remain tranquil in the future. Moreover, even the early stages of industrialization and urban growth were providing the ingredients of a proletariat; there already existed a volatile class of permanently poor who, it was feared, might well be available for mob action. Finally, the expectation that the republic might deteriorate into demagogery and anarchy was given intellectual support by the widely accepted contemporary definitions of what popular democracy was and the conditions necessary to its stability. "I assure you," Jonathan Jackson told John Lowell, Jr., "that I feel quite satisfied in having had to pass through one Revolution. One is full enough for mortal man." It was a common Federalist fear that the Jeffersonians were insufficiently conscious of the precariousness of revolutionary accomplishments, and that this laxity might well prove disastrous....

The expectation of violence and disintegration permeated Federalist political conversation in the opening years of the nineteenth century. "The power of the people, if uncontrolled, is ... mobbish," remarked Fisher Ames in 1802. "It is a gov't by force without discipline." When Thomas Boylston Adams undertook to follow his brother John Quincy's advice and reread Xenophon, he expected no surprises: "The Athenians doubtless afford an excellent example of the *violence* to which a Democratic government necessarily leads a people." Josiah Quincy's Slaveslap Kiddnap proclaimed his vision of "the tempestuous sea of liberty":

> now tossing its proud waves to the skies, and hurling defiance toward
> the throne of the almighty; now sinking into its native abyss, and
> opening to view its unhallowed caverns, the dark abodes of filth and
> falsehood, and rapine and wretchedness.... From the top of Monticello,
> by the side of the great Jefferson, I have watched its wild uproar, while
> we philosophised together on its sublime horrors. There, safe from the
> surge ... I have quaffed the high crowned cup to this exhilarating toast—
> TO YON TEMPESTUOUS SEA OF LIBERTY... MAY IT NEVER BE CALM.

H. L. Mencken once distinguished two varieties of democrats—those who see liberty primarily as the right of self-government, and those who see it primarily as the right to rebel against governors. American political theory usually denies the necessity to choose between the two options, but in the early years of the republic it was widely assumed that a choice had to be made. The former concept, of "positive" liberty, or the freedom to follow a "higher" pattern of behavior, has its analogues in Puritan thought, and is comparable to the elitist definition of the social order which many Americans, perhaps the majority, held in the half-century following 1770. The widespread assumption among

Federalists that their opponents espoused the alternate concept of "negative" liberty, or individual immunity from restraint, was derived in part from some of the better-known Jeffersonian aphorisms, but it was also based on the Federalists' own experience. Primarily, it reflects their sense of the precariousness of the American social order.... All around them, the Federalists of the Old Republic saw familiar social habits decaying. The most obvious sign of changing social balances was the decline of deferential behavior. After the social dislocations of the 1770's and 1780's fewer people had a pedigree of gentility and fewer still were willing to recognize such pedigrees where they existed. Surely there had always been in America egalitarians who refused to defer to their social superiors: the Quakers, for example, or the unchurched men and women who had accompanied John Winthrop to Boston and had made it so difficult for him and his associates to establish the tightly structured community of which they had dreamed. The egalitarian current of the Revolutionary era turned exceptions to the rule into harbingers of a trend; by the first decade of the nineteenth century, gentlefolk all over the nation, except perhaps in the South, were complaining that they were treated with far less respect and awe than they were accustomed to. Men who saw sullen or, at best, bland countenances where formerly they had received broad smiles and a bow, took the sullenness as a personal affront. Their insistence that America possessed the social ingredients for a "mobocracy" may have been something of a rhetorical overstatement, but it was not mere fulmination: people who would not defer to anyone seemed unpredictable and capable of "mobbishness." ...

The republic itself had been born in turbulence; that their nation had been created by rebellion and secession was never far from the Federalist mind. Eighteenth-century America had been a society in which violence was endemic; as Howard Mumford Jones has recently reminded us, mob action was common during the revolutionary era. "American mobs were amenable to cunning leadership, sometimes disguised, sometimes demagogic; they pillaged, robbed, destroyed property, defied law, interfered with the normal course of justice, legislation, and administration, occasionally inflicted physical injuries." After the Revolution, similar violence was experienced in Boston, New Haven, Philadelphia, Charleston. It may well be that Shays' Rebellion was, in contemporary context, an anomaly; as one of the few episodes in which mob violence was forcibly resisted by a state legislature, Shays' Rebellion is merely better remembered than the numerous other occasions on which legislatures were more easily intimidated. Americans were not necessarily more temperate than their French contemporaries; since they met less resistance from constituted authority, they may simply have felt less need for extreme action.

The national government, only a dozen years old when Jefferson took office, was daily insulted, at home and abroad, by men who acted as though the republic were merely a temporary expedient. The Articles of Confederation, after all, had been in force for a dozen years before they had been abandoned; there was no guarantee in 1800 that the document which replaced the Articles would have a longer life. The federal government was insulted by the British, who had refused to honor all the terms of the Peace of 1783 until required to by the Jay Treaty; by the French, whose regular seizure of American shipping resulted in a "Quasi-War," and even by the Dey of Algiers, whose Barbary pirates exacted regular tribute. It was insulted at home by men who similarly refused to regard the new government as permanently established. Critics of national policies habitually spoke as though the Union did not deserve to survive; a threat of secession was a standard response of the frustrated politician. When William Blount thought he was being permitted to wield too little power in North Carolina, he attempted to arrange for the secession of the Western Territory; when Virginia objected to the Alien and Sedition Acts, she made sure her protests would be listened to by including a veiled threat of secession. Secession was the response of a group of New England Federalists to the prediction of Jefferson's re-election in 1804, of Aaron Burr to his isolated position after the Hamilton duel. And all through the early national period, the nation was insulted by men who seemed to cherish democracy primarily as a guarantee of their right of rebellion. The best known of these insults had been the violent demonstrations headed by the "whiskey rebels" and by John Fries, but there were many other occasions of riot in the early years of the republic. These riotous demonstrations generally accomplished little, but they are not unimportant; Federalists worried about them because they provided evidence that Americans had not lost the capacity for violence which they had demonstrated during the Revolution. "If there is no country possessed of more liberty than our own," the *Palladium* remarked, "there is probably none where there are more formidable indications of the error, prejudice and turbulence that will render it insecure." The nation had malcontents enough for Gouverneur Morris to conclude: "There is a moral tendency, and in some cases even a physical disposition, among the people of this country to overturn the Government.... The habits of monarchic government are not yet worn away among our native citizens, and therefore the opposition to lawful authority is frequently considered as a generous effort of patriotic virtue." The Whiskey Boys, Fries, the men who successively raised and tore down liberty poles in New England as late as 1798, made it impossible for Federalists to relax in Arcadia. They could not assume that the New World would escape the disastrous cycle of European history; they could not assume that the pastoral landscape of the Old Republic, settled by contented yeomen, would not be replaced by the congested landscape of the Old World, occupied by malcontented *canaille*.

There was reason to fear that the capacity of the American people for mobbishness was increasing. One analysis of the American scene which Federalists found almost disarmingly appropriate had been provided, ironically enough, by Thomas Jefferson as early as 1787. The passage appears in *Notes on Virginia*, and follows Jefferson's famous remark that "Those who labour in the earth are the chosen people of God, if ever he had a chosen people." Jefferson goes on to explain the contrast he had in mind and the reasons for his preference for the husbandman:

> Dependence begets subservience and venality, suffocates the germ of
> virtue, and prepares fit tools for the designs of ambition.... The mobs of

great cities add just so much to the support of pure government, as sores do to the strength of the human body. It is the manners and spirit of a people which preserve a republic in vigour. A degeneracy in these is a canker which soon eats to the heart of its laws and constitution.

Jefferson could easily have found Federalists to agree with his statement, point by point. They would have changed the application from prediction to statement of fact, and they would not have limited their fear to "the mobs of great cities"; rather, mobbishness was a quality of which the Federalist feared all were capable. But they would have agreed that the urban poor were particularly restless, and they would have added that there seemed to be increasing numbers of poor people in America. Boston had slums by 1810; New York's seventh ward was swampy, stagnant and an unhealthy slum as early as the 1790's. Poor people were, by eighteenth-century definition, dependent on those who had jobs to offer and salaries to pay; the "manners and spirit" of the economically dependent, it was feared, could not possibly be as stalwart as those of the independent and self-sufficient yeoman. "You would never look at men and boys in workshops," said the Maryland Federalist Philip Barton Key, "for that virtue and spirit in defense [of the nation against an aggressor] that you would justly expect from the yeomanry of the country."

Now it is true enough that early America was an agricultural country; nine out of ten of her citizens still worked the land. But ... [t]he noble husbandman [writes historian Leo Marx] is a mythical image, not a description of sociological reality: "He is the good shepherd of the old pastoral dressed in American homespun." Both shepherd and yeoman are models of beings who live in a [world] from which economic pressures are absent. The self-sufficient yeoman on the family-sized farm seeks not prosperity and wealth, but stability, "a virtual stasis that is a counterpart of the desired psychic balance or peace." Only in a world like his, free of economic tension, can the omission of a class structure seem believable. The image is mythical because it ignores economic fact; it draws life from the assumption that Americans could live independent of the international marketplace. Suppose one should deny the possibility; what then becomes of the image? "Let our workshops remain in Europe," Jefferson had counseled. "It is better to carry provisions and materials to workmen there, than bring them to the provisions and materials, and with them their manners and principles. The loss by the transportation of commodities across the Atlantic will be made up in happiness and permanence of government." But America's workshops were not to remain in Europe. The men who counseled agricultural self-sufficiency, Fisher Ames sneered, were themselves "clad in English broadcloth and Irish linen, ... import their conveniences from England, and their politics from France. It is solemnly pronounced as the only wise policy for a country, where the children multiply faster than the sheep." Although the major boom in American industrialization is generally dated 1830–1865, it was rapidly becoming apparent in the early years of the nineteenth century—and to men like Tench Coxe and Alexander Hamilton and Oliver Wolcott much earlier—that the nation's destiny lay with the machine. It was inescapably obvious that with the machine would come further changes in the quality of American social life, changes in "manners and spirit."

Consciousness of the nation's industrial destiny may be said to have begun with Alexander Hamilton's great "Report on Manufactures" of 1791, the same year in which Samuel Slater began the operation of his spinning mill in Pawtucket. But American manufactures did not start with Slater; Hamilton's correspondence as he requested information for the Report reveals that manufacturing operations were already extensive. The social structure of the United States, however, seemed illsuited to the development of an industrial society; available land, prosperous commerce, the heavy demand for handcrafted items meant that few men would be content to remain day laborers. How to industrialize without workers? To this question Hamilton offered three comments: first, the increased efficiency of machinery would enable it eventually to *replace* human hands, thus cutting the need for labor to a great extent; second, new hands could be encouraged to emigrate to America; and finally, more extensive use could be made of an as yet barely tapped source of labor. In England, Hamilton explained, "all the different processes for spinning cotton, are performed by ... machines, which are put in motion by water, and attended chiefly by women and children."

Hamilton was not the progenitor of child labor in America; he was endorsing a trend, not initiating one. To get the information on which the Report was based, he had instructed Treasury agents throughout the country to report to him on the state of manufactures in their area; they, in turn, polled local businessmen and sent their letters on to the Secretary of the Treasury. The information thus collected showed that child labor was already extensive in certain segments of the economy: in yarn manufacture, in cotton and woolcarding, and in the making of nails. By 1803, Oliver Wolcott was finding it difficult to recruit boys to work in his cousin's nail factory, not because children were not working, but the contrary: "Children who have health and are not utterly depraved in their morals," he explained, "are worth money and can easily find employment." Samuel Slater's factory opened with nine workers—seven boys and two girls, none older than twelve years; the youngest was seven. When, in 1801, Josiah Quincy visited one of Slater's mills, he found that the machinery was tended by over a hundred children from four to ten years old, under a single supervisor, who were paid from 12 to 25 cents a day. "Our attendant was very eloquent," Quincy remarked in his diary, "on the usefulness of the manufacture, and the employment it supplied for so many poor children. But an eloquence was exerted on the other side of the question more commanding than his, which called us to pity these little creatures, plying in a contracted room, among flyers and cogs, at an age when nature requires for them air, space, and sports. There was a dull dejection in the countenances of all of them." The children who worked in the mills did not have air, space, and sports as an option; if they were not in the textile factories they joined the "abundance of poor children" which Noah Webster reported to be wandering about the streets, "clothed in dirty rags, illy educated in every respect." By 1809, the nation's cotton mills employed four thousand workers, of whom thirty-five hundred were women and children under age sixteen. Labor statistics, and especially statistics of child labor for the years before 1820, are very scattered, vague, and impressionistic. But they do indicate that child labor, especially in the textile regions, continued and increased. Typically whole families worked in the mills; the men were paid something less than a living wage, and families made ends meet by adding the labor of wives and children, much as Hamilton had predicted.

The prevalence of woman and child labor in early American industry is generally assessed in the context in which Hamilton had placed it. It is taken as an indication of scarcity of labor, as evidence of an expanding economy which offered most men something better to do than to work as factory operatives. Treated in this manner, child labor is seen almost as an index of American prosperity. All this may be true. But we should not ignore the other social conditions of which child labor may be an index; we should not ignore what it tells us about the men who *were* common laborers, and whose dollar a day salary, which made them the best paid common laborers in the West, did not provide for a family sufficiently so that it did not have to send its children into the mills. An American working class was being formed in the early national period, and while class lines were far more flexible, and living conditions were far better than those prevalent in Europe, they were severe enough. The number of people in the early republic who might be labeled members of a proletariat was relatively small, but the conditions of their lives were grim, for all the open-endedness and social mobility of American life. Men do not live by comparisons, but by the conditions of their own lives.

"The time is not distant when this Country will abound with mechanics & manufacturers who will receive their bread from their employers," Gouverneur Morris had predicted in the Constitutional Convention. Two decades later Morris was sounding like Montesquieu: "The strongest aristocratic Feature in our political organization is that which Democrats are more attached to, the Right of universal Suffrage." Montesquieu had suggested that universal suffrage worked to strengthen the power of the rich because the employer or landowner could command the votes of those who were economically dependent on him; Thomas Jefferson himself had warned that "Dependence begets subservience and venality." Would America be transformed when her working population became a salaried one? Would there be an American proletariat? And if there were, would it behave any differently from the European? The pastoral idea was predicated on the continued *absence* of certain things: factories, urban concentrations of population, the presence of the extremely poor. If these things were not absent, pastoral America could not exist; and wherever the northern Federalist leader looked, it seemed more and more apparent that these conditions would not be absent much longer.

The Federalist anticipated violence, in short, because his countrymen had demonstrated their capacity for it during the Revolution, and because he saw developing a class of poor and unskilled laborers who might easily be encouraged to indulge what the Federalist knew to be a general human capacity for turmoil. Over and over, Federalist spokesmen identified their greatest fear: the experimental republic would be destroyed, as the French republic had been, by the "turbulence" and "mobbishness" of which the public was capable. To curb this tendency to "mobbishness," then, was to save the republic, and an act of patriotism. "Every friend of liberty," explained one editorial writer, "would be shocked if the people were deprived of all political power.... But ... if the people will not erect any barriers against their own intemperance and giddiness, or will not respect and sustain them after they are erected, their power will be soon snatched out of their hands, and their own heads broken with it—as in France." ...

A republican democracy was assumed to be a contradiction in terms; Democratic-Republican as a party label a non sequitur. It was Federalism and Republicanism, they insisted, which went together; both defined a version of popular government characterized by the built-in, self-limiting features which popular government required if it was to endure. In categorizing Americans as "all Federalists, all Republicans" Jefferson was seen either to be making an unexpected and complete capitulation or, what was more likely, deliberately befogging the issues. The former alternative did not seem inconceivable to Federalists, who still regarded the two-party arrangement as novel. The first party to be in power had the firmly established habit of identifying itself with the government, its personnel with the national administration, and its members with the heroes of the American Revolution. Opposition to party was easily equated with a near-treasonable opposition to the government, and the development of an opposition party was often viewed as the cause, rather than the reflection, of "political rancour & malevolence."...

... Americans of both parties were aware that theirs was the only republic of the time, and that it was an extremely perilous experiment. In his examination of the causes of the War of 1812, Roger H. Brown has pointed to the American's fear that there may have been "some fatal weakness inherent in the republican form of government that accounted for its rare and fleeting occurrence." Both parties were intensely concerned for the continuation and security of their holy experiment, but their jealous protectiveness of that experiment was displayed in varying fashion. The early years of the republic were years of great accomplishment and also of tremendous frustration. It seems to have been habitual among Republicans to place the blame for that frustration on foreign nations and the conduct of foreign affairs, a way of thinking which, Brown suggests, eventually led them to justify the War of 1812. But one may also speculate that one of the sources of Federalist resistance to that war was a well-established habit of thought which tended to place blame for political failure, even in foreign affairs, on the nation's own internal weaknesses.

Repeatedly the Federalists insisted that Americans interpret the French Revolution as a cautionary tale. Democracy was never static; constant vigilance was required to keep popular government stable. And many Federalists had come to fear that Americans lacked that vigilance....

Americans of both parties were fond of the notion that the virtue of the citizen and the stability of the republic were linked. "Virtue ... is the foundation of Republics," explained a contributor to the *Gazette of the United States* who signed himself "Serranus." "In these, all Power emanating from the people, when they become corrupt, it is in vain to look for purity or disinterestedness, in the administration of their affairs. A polluted fountain must necessarily pour forth a foul and turbid stream. Hence, Morals[,] of great importance in every scheme of government, are of indispensable necessity in a free Commonwealth." Sustenance for this point of view might be found by reading Montesquieu, who taught that whereas what makes the laws effective in a despotism was fear, a republic must depend on the virtue of its citizens. "There is no great share of probity necessary to support a monarchical or despotic government; the force of the laws in one, and the Prince's arm in the other, are sufficient to direct and maintain the whole. But in a popular state one spring more is necessary, namely, virtue." The debaters in the Constitutional Convention had cited Montesquieu more often than Locke, and he continued to be quoted—and misquoted—in the popular press. During the Convention, his arguments in favor of the separation and balance of powers had proved most useful; after the form of government was settled, emphasis shifted to his insight that only a virtuous and moral citizenry could make a republic viable.

If one is willing to assume that men are naturally virtuous, then the foundations of a healthy republic were already present in American society and could be counted on to persist. But few Federalists were able to share this cheerful Jeffersonian assumption. Their attitude stemmed partly from the old Puritan awareness of man's natural depravity, but even more it stemmed from an understanding of the extreme fragility of their experiment in democracy and an awareness of the substantial demands for self-restraint and individual responsibility that republican government places on its citizens. Theirs was a style of consciousness that had been characteristic of the members of the Constitutional Convention, who had been frank in their acknowledgement—even insistence—that the sort of government they had devised depended for its continued existence on a public superior in its political sophistication to any other public, anywhere on the globe. There were to be checks and balances to restrain the corrupting influence of power, but in the last analysis it was citizens, not devices, who would have to guard the republic. The Founders were equally frank in their acknowledgement that the average American might not be able to sustain the burdens placed on him. Because the American public was better educated, more endowed with landed property than any other, the risk seemed worth taking. Americans had shown in their state governments that they were capable of self-rule, but they were also capable of riot. He had taken democracy, Gouverneur Morris said, "not only ... as a Man does his Wife for better or worse, but what few Men do with their Wives, ... knowing all its bad Qualities." ...

Only a virtuous citizenry would sustain a republic and, in a sinful world, a virtuous citizenry was made, not born. Could the Jeffersonians, who seemed so ready to ignore the issue altogether, be trusted to educate the people to virtue and enlightenment? Federalists had their doubts; for their part, the press and the pulpit seemed the most promising means of reinforcing what tendency to virtue and morality already existed. It was through the press, Thomas Green Fessenden thought, that the French had been persuaded to endorse the Revolution and the English persuaded to eschew it. "LITERATURE, well or ill-conducted ... is the great engine, by which ... all civilized States must ultimately be supported or overthrown," he asserted. Federalists treated the triumph of Thomas Jefferson, David H. Fischer has remarked, as "an object lesson in the power of the printed word," and bent their energies to establishing newspapers and increasing their circulation in an attempt to ensure that as many printed words as possible were of Federalist origin. In this they perhaps overestimated the Word, a tendency not unusual among men who believed that "'words are things," who measured the success of a republic by the excellence of its literature and oratory, and who defined their opponents as anti-intellectuals. But the effort also suggested the variant of democracy that was Federalism. Federalists insisted that they would have retained their office had the American people not been deceived. The fault lay not with republican government, but with the capacity of the opposition for deceptive techniques, and with the understandable human propensity to listen to those who spoke of happiness rather than of stern duty or of rectitude.

"I am willing you should call this the Age of Frivolity as you do; and would not object if you had named it the Age of Folly, Vice, Frenzy, Fury, Brutality, Daemons, Buonaparte, Tom Paine, or the Age of the burning Brand from the bottomless Pitt: or any thing but the Age of Reason," John Adams told a friend. In an age of unreason, something more than newspapers was required to sustain the virtue that alone could sustain the republic; something more than a liberal education was required to counteract the disorderly passions that threatened to disrupt the state. William Crafts typically warned that a nation "subject to its passions" could not possibly be virtuous; "Passion, so far as it prevails, destroys reason," counseled Tapping Reeve, "and when it gains an entire ascendancy over men, it renders them bedlamites."

In this context, Faith had a political as well as a supernatural function; the God of the Federalists often appears to behave like a fourth branch of Government. "Where is the security for property, for reputation, for life, if the sense of religious obligation desert the oaths which are the instruments of investigation in courts of justice?" George Washington had asked in the Farewell Address. "Give religion to the winds," wrote Abigail Adams, "and what tye is found strong enough to bind man to his duty, to restrain his inordinate passions? Honour is phantom. Moral principal [*sic*] feeble and unstable—nothing but a firm belief and well grounded assurance that man is an accountable being, and that he is to render that account to a Being who will not be mocked, and cannot be deceived, will prove a sufficient Barrier, or stem the torrent of unruly passions and appetites."

Religious obligation would reinforce moral obligation; moral obligation would make popular government orderly and stable. This paradoxical insistence that religious faith was a necessary ingredient in a social order which forbade the establishment of religion was both widespread and persistent....

The Jeffersonians were dangerous, Simeon Baldwin explained, because their influence was used to break down the "barrier of habitual morality... both as it respects our civil & our religious institutions ... if the restraints of Law, of education, of habit & [of what the opposition was pleased to call] superstitions and prejudice [i.e., religion] shall be entirely removed, I am confident we shall have more *positive* vice, than is even now exhibited at the South. The human propensities when released from those restraints will like the pendulum vibrate & when urged by precept & allowed by Example they will vibrate to an extreme." They were vibrating, even then, in the camp meetings of the Great Revival. Cane Ridge,

Kentucky, in the summer of 1801 set the pattern for subsequent revivals, at which salvation was demonstrated by ranting, twitching, fainting and other behavior closely resembling the cataleptic fit. The revivalists were not only saving themselves, they explained, they were redeeming the entire nation. But some people could not be comfortable in a nation so redeemed. The revival encouraged the free play of passions quite as much as militant deism did; like so many other disturbing trends in American life, it came out of a western wilderness which had voted for Jefferson and which the purchase of Louisiana had done much to enlarge. Religious liberty should mean that men were free to choose the institutional form of their faith, Federalists thought, but they feared if it were also construed to encourage the growth of deism on the one hand or of non-institutional evangelicalism on the other, then not only the churches, but the entire national establishment would be threatened.

In the years after the Revolution, the American walked a strange tightrope between optimism and pessimism. The Revolution had been both a radical break with the past and a conservative affirmation of it; that ambivalence persisted through the early years of the national experience. The Federalist characteristically searched the American social order to find the stability that would justify the Revolution; for the same purpose the Democrat searched it to find flexibility. The Jeffersonian, at least in theory, endorsed flexibility, unpredictability, open-endedness; he led the Federalist to wonder how a society so characterized could endure. The Virginia democrat lived in one of the least flexible of American social arrangements; when the Federalist found him endorsing unpredictability he logically concluded that the Virginian was a hypocrite. Men long for what they do not have; the Federalist's glorification of social stability—his castigation of the decline of deferential behavior, his objection to the annexation of the "howling wilderness" of Louisiana, his jealous maintenance of an extensive federal judiciary, his concern for the advancement of intellectuality, virtue, and traditional religious observance—may well have come out of his appreciation of the forces that were operating to increase the anxieties of American life.

The Fears of the Jeffersonian Republicans

DREW R. McCOY

Sometime during the summer or early fall of 1780, as the war for independence approached its most critical juncture and Americans faced an increasingly problematic future, the secretary of the French legation in Philadelphia, François Marbois, initiated a chain of events that would produce an intellectual and literary landmark of the Revolutionary age. As part of the French government's effort to secure useful information about its new and largely unknown ally, Marbois circulated a detailed questionnaire among influential members of the

Continental Congress. When a copy of the questionnaire found its way to Thomas Jefferson, then the besieged governor of Virginia, he seized the opportunity to organize his wide-ranging reflections on the conditions and prospects of his native country. Many revisions and several years later, when the *Notes on the State of Virginia* publicly appeared, they included what was to become Jefferson's best-known commentary on political economy. His celebration of "those who labour in the earth" as "the chosen people of God" has become a centerpiece of the republic's cultural heritage, a quintessential expression of its impassioned concern for the natural, earthbound virtue of a simple and uncorrupted people.

Jefferson's classic statement is so familiar that it might, at first glance, seem to require neither explanation nor analytical elaboration. But lurking beneath his deceptively simple paean to an agricultural way of life was a more sophisticated perception of how societies normally changed through time as well as an acute understanding of the moral and political implications of a social process that he assumed was inevitable. His memorable observations on the comparative merits of agriculture and manufactures were directly informed by a characteristically eighteenth-century conception of social change.

Jefferson was responding in the *Notes* to Marbois's inquiry about the present state of commerce and manufactures in Virginia. Making a distinction customary of the times, Jefferson reported that the Revolution had encouraged the prolific production of very coarse clothing "within our families," but for the "finer" manufactures Virginians desired, he continued, they would undoubtedly continue to rely on importations from abroad. Recognizing that such a pattern would be considered unfortunate by "the political economists of Europe," who had established the principle "that every state should endeavour to manufacture for itself," Jefferson contended that it was instead a wise and necessary response to peculiar American conditions and to the lessons of history. In Europe, where the land was either fully cultivated or "locked up against the cultivator" by the bars of aristocratic tradition, manufacturing was "resorted to of necessity not of choice." New forms of employment had to be created, in other words, for those people who could not find occupations on the land. In America, by contrast, where "an immensity of land" courted the industry of even a rapidly expanding population, an alternative form of political economy that would not force men into manufacturing was both feasible and eminently desirable. Citing the "happiness and permanence of government" in a society of independent and virtuous husbandmen, Jefferson emphasized the moral and political advantages of America's social opportunity that far outweighed narrowly economic considerations. If his countrymen foolishly and prematurely embraced manufacturing, he predicted, a consequent and inevitable corruption of morals would necessarily endanger the fabric of republican government. Once large numbers of Americans abandoned secure employment on the land to labor in workshops, they would become dependent on "the casualties and caprice of customers" for their subsistence, and such dependence had historically bred a "subservience and venality" that suffocated "the germ of virtue" and prepared "fit tools for the designs of ambition." "It is the manners and spirit of a people which preserve a republic in vigour," Jefferson cautioned his readers, since "a degeneracy in these is a canker which soon eats to the heart of its laws and constitution."

Jefferson's effusive optimism about his country's peculiar social potential could not obscure some nagging fears. He worried, on the one hand, that his contemporaries might blindly follow the maxims of European political economists, ignore his wisdom, and plunge into manufacturing. Education and a commitment to republican principles might defuse this particular danger, but a larger and less tractable problem loomed on the horizon. Jefferson recognized that the loathsome dependence, subservience, venality, and corruption that he so much dreaded— everything, in short, that he associated with European political economy—were in large part the unavoidable outgrowth of what he referred to as "the natural progress and consequence of the arts." He alluded here to a universal process that eighteenth-century social thinkers often described, a process whose repercussions might "sometimes perhaps" be "retarded by accidental circumstances," as Jefferson put it, but which inevitably had to be felt. Like most enlightened thinkers of his age, Jefferson conceived of natural laws of social and cultural development that applied to America as much as to Europe. Vast resources of land might forestall the unfavorable consequences of this "natural progress" of the arts, but he never doubted that eventually America would be swept up in an inexorable logic of social change. Jefferson's plea in the *Notes on Virginia,* a plea that he would make throughout his public life, was that his countrymen not abuse or disregard the natural advantages that could postpone, but never prevent, a familiar and politically dangerous course of social development....

Many years after his first election to the presidency, Thomas Jefferson commented that "the revolution of 1800" was "as real a revolution in the principles of our government as that of 1776 was in its form." Jefferson was undoubtedly using the term "revolution" not in the modern sense of a radical creation of a new order, but in the traditional sense of a return to first principles, of a restoration of original values and ideals that had been overturned or repudiated. For him, the election of 1800 was a revolution because it marked a turning back to the true republican spirit of 1776. Jefferson was excited by the prospect of the first implementation of the principles of America's republican revolution in the national government created by the Constitution of 1787, since in his eyes a minority faction consisting of an American Walpole and his corrupt minions had captured control of that government almost immediately after its establishment. From Jefferson's perspective, indeed, the Federalists had done more than threaten to corrupt American government by mimicking the English "court" model. Just as frightening was their apparent desire to mold the young republic's political economy along English lines, a desire reflected both in their call for the extensive development of government-subsidized manufacturing enterprises and in their attempt to stimulate a highly commercialized economy anchored to such premature and speculative ventures as an overextended carrying trade. Jefferson's fundamental goal in 1801 was to end this threatened "Anglicization" of both American government and society. In so doing he would restore the basis for the development of a truly republican political economy, one that would be patterned after Benjamin Franklin's vision of a predominantly agricultural empire that would expand across space, rather than develop through time.

Within the Jeffersonian framework of assumptions and beliefs, three essential conditions were necessary to create and sustain such a republican political economy: a national government free from any taint of corruption, an unobstructed access to an ample supply of open land, and a relatively liberal international commercial order that would offer adequate foreign markets for America's flourishing agricultural surplus. The history of the 1790s had demonstrated all too well to the Jeffersonians the predominant danger to a republican political economy of corruption emanating from the federal government. They were especially troubled by the deleterious political, social, and moral repercussions of the Federalists' financial system, which they regarded as the primary vehicle of corruption both in the political system and in the country at large. Although Jefferson concluded rather soon after his election that his administration could not safely dismantle Hamilton's entire system with a few swift strokes, he was committed to doing everything possible to control that system's effects and gradually reduce its pernicious influence. Extinguishing the national debt as rapidly as possible, reducing government expenditures (especially on the military), and repealing the Federalist battery of direct and excise taxes became primary goals of the Jeffersonians in power, who sought by such means to purge the national government of Hamiltonian fiscalism in accordance with their cherished "country" principles.

In itself, the electoral revolution of 1800 promised to remove the primary threat to a republican political economy posed by the machinations of a corrupt administration. But the Jeffersonians also had to secure the other necessary guarantors of republicanism: landed and commercial expansion. Although the pressure of population growth on the supply of land in the United States had never been a problem of the same immediate magnitude as political corruption, the social and economic dislocations of the 1780s had prompted some concern with this matter. Through the Louisiana Purchase of 1803, undoubtedly the greatest achievement of his presidency, Jefferson appeared to eliminate this problem for generations, if not for centuries, to come. But the third and thorniest problem, in the form of long-standing restrictions on American commerce, proved far more frustrating and intractable. Through an embargo and finally a war the Jeffersonians consistently tried but failed to remove this nagging impediment to the fulfillment of their republican vision.

The presidential administrations from 1801 to 1817 appear more consistent when viewed from this perspective—that is, as a sustained Jeffersonian attempt to secure the requisite conditions for a republican political economy. Securing such a political economy, as the Jeffersonians conceived of it, required more than merely capturing control of the government from a corrupt minority faction; it also required the elimination of specific dangers and the maintenance of certain conditions, and these concerns largely shaped the Jeffersonian approach to both domestic and foreign policy. There was never any question that positive, concrete measures would have to be taken to forestall the development of social conditions that were considered antithetical to republicanism. Hamilton and the Federalists had threatened to make American society old and corrupt long before its time. Now the Jeffersonians set out to reverse the direction of Federalist policy in order to maintain the country at a relatively youthful stage of development. Hoping to avoid the social evils both of barbarous simplicity and of overrefined, decadent maturity, the Jeffersonians proposed to escape the burden of an economically sophisticated society without sacrificing a necessary degree of republican civilization. Their aspiration to evade social corruption and the ravages of time was a fragile and demanding dream, and the quest to fulfill it was not without its ironies.

On the one hand, the Republican party attracted political support from scores of Americans whose outlook can properly be termed entrepreneurial. Opposition to the Federalist system was never limited to agrarian-minded ideologues who unequivocally opposed a dynamic commercial economy. Many Jeffersonians were anxious to participate in the creation of an expansive economy and to reap its many rewards. Frustrated by the failure of Federalist policies to serve their immediate needs, ambitious men-on-the-make, engaged in a variety of economic pursuits, enlisted under the banner of Jeffersonianism in a crusade to secure the advantages and opportunities they desired. Perhaps some of them saw no contradiction between their personal material ambitions and the traditional vision of a simple, bucolic republic articulated by the leader of their party. Assessing the economic psychology of many of these enterprising Jeffersonians, one scholar has suggested the complex paradox "of capitalists of all occupations denying the spirit of their occupations," adding that "it appears that many Republicans wanted what the Federalists were offering, but they wanted it faster, and they did not want to admit that they wanted it at all." Such a characterization cannot be applied, however, to Jefferson and Madison, and in their case we observe a more poignant irony. As their experience as policymakers soon demonstrated, the Jeffersonian endeavor to secure a peaceful, predominantly agricultural republic demanded a tenaciously expansive foreign policy—a foreign policy that ultimately endangered both the peace and the agricultural character of the young republic.

In developing his analysis of Britain's mercantilist political economy during the 1760s and 1770s, Benjamin Franklin had recognized that corruption could result from both natural and artificial causes. A high population density brought about by the biological pressure of population growth on a limited supply of land was one route to social decay. But as Franklin and many other eighteenth-century writers so often noted, decay also resulted from a corrupt political system that deviously induced extreme social inequality, depopulation of the countryside, urban squalor, luxury manufacturing, and the like. Both routes to corruption had devastating consequences; the difference was that while one was natural and seemingly inevitable, the other was not. During the 1780s James Madison had pondered this distinction, most notably in his correspondence with Jefferson, and had reached the rather pessimistic conclusion that even in the absence of a corrupt political system "a certain degree of misery seems inseparable from a high degree of populousness." Ultimately, he suggested, republican America would offer no exception to this rule. Although Jefferson agreed that the United States would remain virtuous only "as long as there shall be vacant lands in any part of America" and people were not "piled upon one another in large cities, as in Europe," he was confident that such a crisis would not arise "for many centuries." If social decay was to afflict the young republic, Jefferson believed that threat stemmed more from artificial than from natural causes, from a corrupt political system rather than from the inevitable pressure of population growth on the American supply of land. Nevertheless, Jefferson was not totally unconcerned with the problem of land, especially in the realm of theory and speculation. His confidence about the American future betrayed his assumption that America's western (and perhaps northern and southern) boundaries would be regularly extended, always bringing in a fresh supply of virgin land. Should that assumption be challenged, especially by a formidable foreign power, however, a theoretical problem might indeed become a more immediate and practical one.

It is interesting, in this regard, to observe Jefferson's reactions to the writings of Thomas R. Malthus, the British parson and political economist who popularized the theory of population pressure on subsistence, especially since Jefferson gave Malthus's writings particularly close attention near the end of his first presidential administration. Malthus had first presented his views on population in an anonymous pamphlet published in 1798, and his basic thesis was straightforward. Reacting against the optimistic forecasts of social improvement that were common in the late eighteenth century…, Malthus argued that given the biological facts of population and subsistence, such visions of perfectibility for the mass of mankind were chimerical. Instead, the widespread vice, misery, and poverty that so appalled these "speculative philosophers" were the inevitable lot of humanity. The problem, simply stated, was that "the power of population is indefinitely greater than the power in the earth to produce subsistence for man." The irrepressible passion between the sexes, when unchecked, resulted in a geometrical rate of population growth, whereas the supply of food and available means of nourishment could increase only arithmetically at best. This "perpetual tendency in the race of man to increase beyond the means of subsistence," Malthus explained, "is one of the general laws of animated nature, which we can have no reason to expect will change."

Malthus suggested, in short, that all societies were destined to proceed rapidly through the familiar stages of social development toward a state of overpopulation, corruption, and old age. Old age might be postponed, especially in a society with an abundance of land, but not forever. In discussing population growth in America, Malthus emphasized the point that there was no final escape from the predicament he described, for not even a vast reservoir of fertile land could repeal the natural laws of population and subsistence. "Perpetual youth" for a nation was impossible; anyone who expected the United States to remain a land with relatively little poverty and misery forever, he commented, "might as reasonably expect to prevent a wife or mistress from growing old by never exposing her to the sun and air." "It is, undoubtedly, a most disheartening reflection," he grimly concluded, "that the great obstacle in the way to any extraordinary improvement in society, is of a nature that we can never hope to overcome."

Malthus's arguments should have been especially discouraging to Americans, since he contended that the necessary social basis for republicanism was precariously ephemeral. Extreme inequality, widespread poverty, extensive landless dependency—indeed, everything Americans considered antithetical to republicanism—were, according to Malthus, biologically inevitable. American readers could take solace only in the English parson's concession that there were "many modes of treatment in the political, as well as animal body, that contribute to accelerate or retard the approaches of age."...

President Thomas Jefferson was one such reader. By early 1804 he was perusing a borrowed copy of "the new work of Malthus on population," and he pronounced it "one of the ablest I have ever seen."...

... Ironically, what Jefferson found least useful and convincing in Malthus was the population theory that the parson was best known for; the president's general praise for the essay appears to have been prompted by its restatement of laissez-faire, anti-mercantilist doctrine. Jefferson particularly chastised Malthus for failing to recognize the irrelevance of his population theory to the American experience. "From the singular circumstance of the immense extent of rich and uncultivated lands in this country, furnishing an increase of food in the same ratio with that of population," Jefferson noted, "the greater part of his book is inapplicable to us, but as a matter of speculation." Population pressure on subsistence would never be an immediate problem in America because "the resource of emigration" to virgin territory was always available. Discussing Malthus's theory with the French economist Say, Jefferson expanded this observation into a more general statement. "The differences of circumstance between this and the old countries of Europe." he wrote, "furnish differences of fact whereon to reason, in questions of political economy, and will consequently produce sometimes a difference of result." Echoing Franklin's observations of fifty years earlier, Jefferson continued: "There, for instance, the quantity of food is fixed, or increasing in a slow and only arithmetical ratio, and the proportion is limited by the same ratio. Supernumerary births consequently add only to your mortality. Here the immense extent of uncultivated and fertile lands enables every one who will labor, to marry young, and to raise a family of any size. Our food, then, may increase geometrically with our laborers, and our births, however multiplied, become effective." Jefferson went on to argue, in this regard, that America provided a further exception to the European rule of balanced economies and national self-sufficiency:

> Again, there the best distribution of labor is supposed to be that which places the manufacturing hands along side the agricultural; so that the one part shall feed both, and the other part furnish both with clothes and other comforts. Would that be best here? Egoism and first appearances say yes. Or would it be better that all our laborers should be employed in agriculture? In this case a double or treble portion of fertile lands would be brought into culture; a double or treble creation of food be produced, and its surplus go to nourish the now perishing births of Europe, who in return would manufacture and send us in exchange our

clothes and other comforts. Morality listens to this, and so invariably do the laws of nature create our duties and interests, that when they seem to be at variance, we ought to suspect some fallacy in our reasonings. In solving this question, too, we should allow its just weight to the moral and physical preference of the agricultural, over the manufacturing, man.

This statement was a striking reaffirmation of Jefferson's fundamental beliefs on the subject of political economy, a statement that differed very little from his well-known observations in the *Notes on Virginia* of twenty years earlier. Jefferson's encounter with Malthus thus served, in the end, to reconfirm his basic vision of a predominantly agricultural America that would continue to export its bountiful surpluses of food abroad. Such a republic, he believed, would best serve not only its own citizens, by permitting them to pursue a virtuous way of life, but also the European victims of a Malthusian fate, by providing them with the subsistence they desperately needed. It seems clear, above all, that Jefferson's brimming confidence during this period—expressed both in his response to Malthus and in his restatement of agrarian beliefs—must be viewed in the context of the Louisiana Purchase. With the Federalists properly and, Republicans hoped, permanently displaced from power in the national government, there was no need to worry about the dangers to a republican political economy from political corruption. With Louisiana safely added to the Union, there was also no need to worry about the danger of foreign powers choking off the American supply of land. The acquisition of Louisiana probably removed any Mathusian doubts Jefferson might have had about the long-range viability of republicanism in America. Indeed, the Louisiana question touched on so many aspects of the Jeffersonian vision of a republican political economy that it deserves much closer investigation.

The Mississippi crisis of 1801–1803, which culminated in the Louisiana Purchase, affected crucial and long-standing American concerns. Since the 1780s most Americans had regarded free navigation of the Mississippi River and the right of deposit at New Orleans as essential to the national interest. Without the access to market that these conditions permitted, westward expansion would be stalled, because settlers in the trans-Appalachian regions necessarily depended on the Mississippi and its tributaries to sustain them as active and prosperous republican farmers....

... [C]ontrol of the Mississippi permitted westerners to engage in a secure and dynamically expanding foreign commerce and, as always, Americans saw the significance of commerce in very broad social and moral terms. It was repeatedly asserted that an active commerce that provided a secure and dependable access to foreign markets was absolutely necessary to establish and maintain the republican character of western society....

By rectifying the chronic problem of an uncertain, rapidly fluctuating demand for western agricultural surpluses, the Purchase thus served an important social and moral purpose. "No ruinous fluctuations in commerce need now be apprehended," noted another western commentator, for "agriculture may depend upon those steady markets which trade shall open to industry." There could be no doubt that a "want of markets for the produce of the soil" always had disastrous consequences, for "it saps the foundations of our prosperity; subverts the end of society, and literally tends to keep us in that rude, uncultivated state, which has excited the derision and contempt of other communities." "As long as this is the state of our country," the same observer queried in familiar fashion, "what encouragement is there for the mind to throw off its native ferocity?" By permanently securing control of the Mississippi River and the promise of boundless foreign markets beyond, the Louisiana Purchase did more than pave the way for economic prosperity. By providing the incentive to industry that shaped a republican people, it laid the necessary basis for the westward expansion of republican civilization itself....

Jefferson's notion of a continuously expanding "empire of liberty" in the Western Hemisphere was a bold intellectual stroke, because it flew in the face of the traditional republican association of expansion and empire with luxury, corruption, and especially despotism. The familiar bugbear of the Roman Empire and its decline through imperial expansion was the most common source of this association. According to Jefferson and most American republicans, expansion would preserve, rather than undermine, the republican character of America. In addition to forestalling development through time and diffusing the spirit of faction, expansion was crucial to American security in its broadest sense. Removing the French from Louisiana also removed the need for a dangerous military establishment in the face of a contiguous foreign threat. It greatly reduced, too, the likelihood of American involvement in a ruinous war that would impose on the young republic the vicious Old World system of national debts, armies, navies, taxation, and the like. For a plethora of reasons, in short, peaceful expansion was sustaining the Jeffersonian republic.

But if the Louisiana Purchase removed some serious obstacles to the realization of Jefferson's republican empire, it also exposed some of the tensions and contradictions within that vision. Since the proper functioning of the empire required both westward and commercial expansion, an assertive, even aggressive, foreign policy would often be necessary to secure the republic. The Jeffersonians frequently boasted of the isolation and independence of the United States; curiously, this claim obscured the fact that American republicanism demanded both an open international commercial order and the absence of any competing presence on the North American continent. The United States could isolate itself from foreign affairs and the potential for conflict only if it was willing to resign its tenacious commitment to westward expansion and free trade. To do this, however, would be to abandon the two most important pillars of the Jeffersonian vision of a republican political economy. Indeed, given the commitment to that vision, the national independence and isolated self-sufficiency boasted of by the Jeffersonians were illusory.

FURTHER READING

Joyce Oldham Appleby, *Inheriting the Revolution: The First Generation of Americans* (2000).

Lance Banning, *The Jeffersonian Persuasion: Evolution of a Party Ideology* (1978).

Ron Chernow, *Alexander Hamilton* (2004).

Stanley Elkins and Eric McKitrick, *The Age of Federalism, 1788–1800* (1993).

Joseph J. Ellis, *American Sphinx: The Character of Thomas Jefferson* (1998).

Joanne B. Freeman, *Affairs of Honor: National Politics in the New Republic* (2002).

Linda K. Kerber, *Women of the Republic: Intellect and Ideology in Republican America* (1980).

David McCullouch, *John Adams* (2002).

James Roger Sharp, *American Politics in the Early Republic: The New Nation in Crisis* (1993).

David Waldstreicher, *In the Midst of Perpetual Fetes: The Making of American Nationalism, 1776–1820* (1997).

Philipp Ziesche, *Cosmopolitan Patriots: Americans in Paris in the Age of Revolution* (2009).

CHAPTER 7

Foreign Policy, Western Movement, and Indian Removal in the Early Nineteenth Century

American foreign policy in the early national period looked both east and west. The United States continued to maintain and develop relationships with European nations and this interaction had a profound impact on American development. For example, France sold the Louisiana territory to the United States in 1803 doubling its size with the stroke of a pen, which made the United States one of the largest nations in the world. Less advantageous for the United States was its weak standing in relation to the European powers. British and French warships harassed American ships in the early nineteenth century, and the hostile posture of the British became particularly galling for many Americans. Struggles with France and Britain caused economic problems for Americans, as they sought to protect their economy from foreign goods while still wishing to sell goods abroad. The Embargo Act of 1807, which forbade international trade to and from American ports, was largely a failure of Jefferson's administration to respond to international war and economics. By 1812, the United States, led by a group of young and aggressive legislators known as "Warhawks," declared war on Britain. After a series of battles that put the future of the United States in danger—including the British attack on Washington and Baltimore—the war turned into a stalemate. An inconclusive war finally culminated in the Treaty of Ghent in 1815. The War of 1812 had two profound consequences. First, American leaders became increasingly leery of what President Washington had called "entangling alliances" with European nations. Second, many white Americans turned their attention westward to regions peopled by members of Indian nations.

As American foreign policy became focused on relationships with Indian nations, the challenges for Indian people multiplied. Indian-white interaction had existed for centuries and native people accepted some aspects of Euro-American society and rejected others. The accelerated growth in the early nineteenth century, however, only made more urgent the Native American response. Some elements of Indian cultures fostered movements of revitalization that attempted to reclaim aspects of culture that had been lost due to Indian interaction. On occasion, these revitalization movements were powerful forces in nurturing efforts by Indians to band together and contest white society. The most notable movement began in 1805 when a Shawnee man named Lalawathika seemingly returned from death. He told of meeting the Master of Life who showed him the way to lead his people out of degradation. Known to Americans as the Prophet, he adopted the name Tenskwatawa and he began to preach a message that advocated a return to a traditional lifestyle. By 1807, he began to suggest that Indian groups unite to resist white expansion. Just prior to the War of 1812 Tenskwatawa and his brother Tecumseh had built a confederacy of Indian nations to challenge American military aims in present day Indiana. The movement ended in bloody conflict, the most notable battle being the Battle of Tippecanoe when the American army aided by frontiersmen defeated the Indian coalition.

An alternative strategy in resisting the westward migration was a selective acceptance of certain aspects of white society. In particular, people from the Creek and Cherokee nations were active in embracing aspects of white society varying from written language, farming, and even slavery. By 1827, the Cherokee drafted and ratified a constitution and began publishing their own newspaper one year later. Unfortunately for them, these innovations were dismissed by the state of Georgia. In 1828, the Cherokee constitution was annulled by the Georgia legislature. Despite—perhaps because of—legal appeals to the U.S. Supreme Court, the hostility toward the Cherokee increased. Between 1830 and 1835, Indian nations in the southeastern United States, Cherokees and Creeks included, were forced to remove to "Indian territory" in present-day Oklahoma.

QUESTIONS TO THINK ABOUT

What advantages might the United States have gained from it policies toward Europe ranging from President Washington's Farewell Address to the Monroe Doctrine? How could white-Indian interaction reflect a combination of cooperation and savagery? Which strategy used by Indians—resistance or acculturation—was more successful in grappling with the westward migration of white Americans?

DOCUMENTS

The documents in this chapter alternatively focus upon American approaches to and interactions with Europeans and Native Americans. President George Washington, in document 1, worries about entering into alliances with other nations in his Farewell Address in 1796. Document 2 moves to the frontier, where William Clark—one of the leaders Lewis and Clark journey to the Pacific Ocean—writes about his diplomatic engagements with native peoples. In a letter written in 1806 to a white man who has offered assistance in dealing with the Indians, Clark includes a speech that he delivered to the Yellowstone Indians. Document 3 is an address by Sagoyewatha, also known as Red Jacket, to a Massachusetts missionary. A member of the Seneca nation, Sagoyewatha chides the missionary for his attempt to convert the Indians to Christianity. William Cullen Bryant, who would become one of the most famous American poets, satirizes the Embargo Act in document 4 with a poem he wrote at only thirteen years old. The next two documents illustrate the conflicts between Indians and the U.S. government that developed around the time of the War of 1812. In document 5, Tecumseh, in a speech delivered to Governor William H. Harrison in 1810, recounts the misdeeds of whites and expresses his belief that the only way to stop "this evil" is for all Indians to unite. In document 6, Tecumseh's brother, Tenskwatawa, describes his vision of going to the World Above and the knowledge he gained from the journey with regard to revitalizing Indian culture. Document 7 turns our attention back to American foreign policy with Europeans. The Monroe Doctrine declares that the Western Hemisphere is closed to further European colonization. As Americans puzzled over foreign policy with Europe, the condition of Indians was deteriorating. Document 8 is an appeal by the Cherokee nation against removal from Georgia in 1830. Document 9 is President Andrew Jackson's response in 1833 where he applauds the "benevolent policy" of compelling Native Americans to move from their lands.

1. President George Washington Warns Against "Entangling Alliances," 1796

As avenues to foreign influence in innumerable ways, such attachments are particularly alarming to the truly enlightened and independent patriot. How many opportunities do they afford to tamper with domestic factions, to practice the arts of seduction, to mislead public opinion, to influence or awe the public councils! Such an attachment of a small or weak towards a great and powerful nation dooms the former to be the satellite of the latter.

Against the insidious wiles of foreign influence (I conjure you to believe me, fellow citizens) the jealousy of a free people ought to be constantly awake, since history and experience prove that foreign influence is one of the most baneful foes of republican government. But that jealousy to be useful must be impartial; else it becomes the instrument of the very influence to be avoided, instead of a defense against it. Excessive partiality for one foreign nation and excessive dislike of another cause those whom they actuate to see danger only on one side, and serve to veil and even second the arts of influence on the other. Real patriots, who may resist the intrigues of the favorite, are liable to become suspected and odious, while its tools and dupes usurp the applause and confidence of the people to surrender their interests.

The great rule of conduct for us in regard to foreign nations is, in extending our commercial relations, to have with them as little political connection as possible. So far as we have already formed engagements, let them be fulfilled with perfect good faith. Here let us stop.

Washington's Farewell Address (1796). Reprinted in *Washington's Farewell Address to the People of the United States*, Senate Publication No. 108-21 (Washington, 2004), 25–28.

Europe has a set of primary interests, which to us have none or a very remote relation. Hence she must be engaged in frequent controversies, the cause of which are essentially foreign to our concerns. Hence therefore it must be unwise in us to implicate ourselves, by artificial ties, in the ordinary vicissitudes of her politics or the ordinary combinations and collisions of her friendships or enmities.

Our detached and distant situation invites and enables us to pursue a different course. If we remain one people under an efficient government, the period is not far off when we may defy material injury from external annoyance; when we may take such an attitude as will cause the neutrality we may at any time resolve upon to be scrupulously respected; when belligerent nations, under the impossibility of making acquisitions upon us, will not lightly hazard the giving us provocation; when we may choose peace or war, as our interest guided by justice shall counsel.

Why forgo the advantages of so peculiar a situation? Why quit our own to stand upon foreign ground? Why, by interweaving our destiny with that of any part of Europe, entangle our peace and prosperity in the toils of European ambition, rivalship, interest, humor, or caprice?

It is our true policy to steer clear of permanent alliances with any portion of the foreign world—so far, I mean, as we are now at liberty to do it, for let me not be understood as capable of patronizing infidelity to existing engagements (I hold the maxim no less applicable to public than to private affairs, that honesty is always the best policy)—I repeat it therefore, let those engagements be observed in their genuine sense. But in my opinion it is unnecessary and would be unwise to extend them.

2. William Clark of the Lewis and Clark Expedition Enters into Diplomacy with Native People, 1806

Sɪʀ   In the winter of 1805, you were so obliging as to express a disposition to assist us in the execution of any measure relative to the Savages with whome you were conversant, or that you would lend your aid in furthering the friendly views of our government in relation to the Same, no object as we then informed you did at that time present itself to our view, which we conceived worthy of your attention, at present we have a commission to charge you with, which if executed, we have no doubt will tend to advance your private interest, while it will also promote those of the U. States in relation to the intercourse of her citizens with the Indian nations in the interior of North America. It is that of provailing on some of the most influensial Chiefs of those bands of Sioux who usially resort the borders of the Missouri to visit the Seat of our Government, and to accompany them there yourself with us. The Tetons of the burnt woods, Teton Ockandandas, and other bands of Tetons, Cisitons, and yanktons of the

Letter to Hugh Henney and speech prepared for Yellowstone Indians, in *The Journals of Lewis and Clark*, Meriwether Lewis and William Clark, V (1806), in *Original Journals of the Lewis and Clark Expedition, 1804–1806*, ed, Reuben Gold Thwaites (New York: Dodd, Mead, 1905), 282–283, 285–286, 299–301.

Plains are the Objects of our attention on this occasion, Particularly the Bands of Tetons; those untill some effectual measures be taken to render them pacific, will always prove a serious source of inconveniance to the free navigation of the Missouri, or at least to it's upper branches, from whence the richest portion of it's fur trade is to be derived.

The ardent wish of our government has ever been to conciliate the esteem and secure the friendship of all the Savage nations within their territory by the exercise of every consistent and pacific measure in her power, applying those of coercion only in the last resort; certain we are that her disposition towards the native inhabitants of her newly acquired Territory of Louisiana is not less friendly; but we are also positive that she will not long suffer her citizens to be deprived of the free navigation of the Missouri by a few comparatively feeble bands of Savages who may be so illy advised as to refuse her proffered friendship and continue their depridation on her citizens who may in future assend or decend that river.

We believe that the sureest guarantee of savage fidility to any nation is a thorough conviction on their minds that their government possesses the power of punishing promptly every act of aggression committed on their part against the person or property of their citizens; to produce this conviction without the use of violence, is the wish of our government; and to effect it, we cannot devise a more expedient method than that of takeing some of the best informed and most influential Chiefs with us to the U. States, where they will have an ample view of our population and resources, become convinced themselves, and on their return convince their nations of the futility of an attempt to oppose the Will of our government, particularly when they shall find, that their acquiescence will be productive of greater advantages to their nation than their most sanguine hopes could lead them to expect from oppersition.

We have before mentioned to you the intentions of our government to form tradeing establishments on the Missouri with a view to secure the attachments of the nativs and emeliorate their sufferings by furnishing them with such articles as are necessary for their comfort on the most moderate terms in exchange for their peltries and furs.... an Indian *Agent* will of course be necessary at that post, your long acquaintance and influence with those people necessary places your protentions to that appointment on the fairest Ground, and should you think proper to under take the commission now proposed, it will still further advance those pretentions....

In your communication with the *Sioux,* in addition to other considerations which may suggest themselves to your mind, you will be pleased to assure them of the friendly views of our government towards them, their power and resources, their intention of establishing trading houses in their neighborhood and the objects of those establishments, inform them that the mouth of all the rivers through [which] traders convey Merchindize to their country are now in possession of the United States, who can at pleasure cut off all communication between themselves and their accustomed traders, and consequently the interest they have in cultivateing our friendship. You may also promis them in the event of their going on with us, that they shall receive from our government a

considerable present in Merchindize, which will be conveyed at the public expence with them to their nation on their return, urge them also to go imediately,
on the ground, that their doing so will haisten the establishment of the tradeing
house in contemplation.

[Speech prepared for Yellowstone Indians]

Children   The Great Spirit has given a fair and bright day for us to meet together in his View that he may inspect us in this all we say and do.

Children   I take you all by the hand as the children of your Great father the
President of the U. States of America who is the great chief of all the white
people towards the riseing sun.

Children   This Great Chief who is Benevolent, just, wise & bountifull has
sent me and one other of his chiefs (who is at this time in the country of the
Blackfoot Indians) to all his read children on the Missourei and its waters quite
to the great lake of the West where the land ends and the [sun] sets on the face
of the great water, to know their wants and inform him of them on our return....

Children   The object of my comeing to see you is not to do you injurey but
to do you good   the Great Chief of all the white people who has more goods at
his command than could be piled up in the circle of your camp, wishing that all
his read children should be happy has sent me here to know your wants that he
may supply them.

Children   Your great father the Chief of the white people intends to build a
house and fill it with such things as you may want and exchange with you for
your skins & furs at a very low price. & has derected me [to] enquire of you, at
what place would be most convenient for to build this house. and what articles
you are in want of that he might send them imediately on my return

Children   The people in my country is like the grass in your plains noumer-
ous they are also rich and bountifull. and love their read brethren who inhabit
the waters of the Missoure

Children   I have been out from my country two winters, I am pore necked
and nothing to keep of[f] the rain.   when I set out from my country I had a
plenty but have given it all to my read children whome I have seen on my way
to the Great Lake of the West. and have now nothing....

Children   The red children of your great father who live near him and have
opened their ears to his counsels are rich and hapy have plenty of horses cows &
Hogs fowls bread &c. &c. live in good houses, and sleep sound. and all those of
his red children who inhabit the waters of the Missouri who open their ears to
what I say and follow the counsels of their great father the President of the
United States, will in a fiew years be a[s] hapy as those mentioned &c.

Children   It is the wish of your Great father the Chief of all the white people that some 2 of the principal Chiefs of this [blank space in diary.] Nation
should Visit him at his great city and receive from his own mouth. his good
counsels, and from his own hands his abundant gifts,   Those of his red children
who visit him do not return with empty hands, he [will] send them to their
nation loaded with presents

Children   If any one two or 3 of your great chiefs wishes to visit your great father and will go with me, he will send you back next Summer loaded with presents and some goods for the nation. You will then see with your own eyes and here with your own years what the white people can do for you. they do not speak with two tongues nor promis what they can't perform

Children   Consult together and give me an answer as soon as possible   your great father is anxious to here from (& see his red children who wish to visit him) I cannot stay but must proceed on & inform him &c.

3. Iroquois Chief Red Jacket Decries the Day When Whites Arrived, 1805

"Brother; Listen to what we say.

"There was a time when our forefathers owned this great island. Their seats extended from the rising to the setting sun. The Great Spirit had made it for the use of Indians. He had created the buffalo, the deer, and other animals for food. He had made the bear and the beaver. Their skins served us for clothing. He had scattered them over the country, and taught us how to take them. He had caused the earth to produce corn for bread. All this He had done for his red children, because He loved them. If we had some disputes about our hunting ground, they were generally settled without the shedding of much blood. But an evil day came upon us. Your forefathers crossed the great water, and landed on this island. Their numbers were small. They found friends and not enemies. They told us they had fled from their own country for fear of wicked men, and had come here to enjoy their religion. They asked for a small seat. We took pity on them, granted their request: and they sat down amongst us. We gave them corn and meat, they gave us poison (alluding, it is supposed, to ardent spirits) in return.

"The white people had now found our country, Tidings were carried back, and more came amongst us. Yet we did not fear them. We took them to be friends. They called us brothers. We believed them, and gave them a larger seat. At length their numbers had greatly increased. They wanted more land: they wanted our country. Our eyes were opened, and our minds became uneasy. Wars took place, Indians were hired to fight against Indians, and many of our people were destroyed. They also brought strong liquor amongst us. It was strong and powerful, and has slain thousands.

"Brother; Our seats were once large and yours were small. You have now become a great people, and we have scarcely a place left to spread our blankets. You have got our country, but are not satisfied; you want to force your religion upon us.

"Brother; Continue to listen.

Red Jacket's Reply to Reverend Cram (1805), first published in *Monthly Anthology and Boston Review* 6 (April 1809): 221–224. This document can also be found in *Red Jacket: Iroquois Diplomat and Orator*, Christopher Densmore (Syracuse, N.Y. Syracuse University Press, 1999), 135–140.

"You say that you are sent to instruct us how to worship the Great Spirit agreeably to his mind, and, if we do not take hold of the religion which you white people teach, we shall be unhappy hereafter. You say that you are right and we are lost. How do we know this to be true? We understand that your religion is written in a book. If it was intended for us as well as you, why has not the Great Spirit given to us, and not only to us, but why did he not give to our forefathers the knowledge of that book, with the means of understanding it rightly? We only know what you tell us about it. How shall we know when to believe, being so often deceived by the white people?

"Brother; You say there is but one way to worship and serve the Great Spirit. If there is but one religion; why do you white people differ so much about it? Why not all agreed, as you can all read the book?

"Brother; We do not understand these things.

"We are told that your religion was given to your forefathers, and has been handed down from father to son. We also have a religion, which was given to our forefathers, and has been handed down to us their children. We worship in that way. It teaches us to be thankful for all the favors we receive; to love each other, and to be united. We never quarrel about religion.

"Brother; The Great Spirit has made us all, but he has made a great difference between his white and red children. He has given us different complexions and different customs. To you He has given the arts. To these He has not opened our eyes. We know these things to be true. Since He has made so great a difference between us in other things; why may we not conclude that He has given us a different religion according to our understanding? The Great Spirit does right. He knows what is best for his children; we are satisfied.

"Brother; we do not wish to destroy your religion or take it from you. We only want to enjoy our own. *pathos?*

"Brother; We are told that you have been preaching to white people in this place. These people are our neighbors. We are acquainted with them. We will wait a little while, and see what effect your preaching has upon them. If we find it does them good, makes them honest, and less disposed to cheat Indians; we will then consider again of what you have said.

"Brother; you have now heard our answer to your talk, and this is all we have to say at present.

"As we are going to part, we will come and take you by the hand, and hope the Great Spirit will protect you on your journey, and return you safe to your friends."

As the Indians began to approach the missionary, he rose hastily from his seat and replied, that he could not take them by the hand; that there was no fellowship between the religion of God and the works of the devil.

This being interpreted to the Indians, they smiled, and retired in a peaceable manner.

It being afterwards suggested to the missionary that his reply to the Indians was rather indiscreet; he observed, that he supposed the ceremony of shaking hands would be received by them as a token that he assented to what was said. Being otherwise informed, he said he was very sorry for the expressions.

4. William Cullen Bryant Satirizes the Embargo Act, 1808

… WAKE Muse of Satire, in the cause of trade,
Thou scourge of miscreants who the laws evade!
Dart thy keen glances, knit thy threat'ning brows,
And hurl thine arrows at fair Commerce's foes!

MUCH injur'd Commerce! 'tis thy falling cause,
Which, from obscurity, a stripling draws;
And were his powers but equal to his zeal,
Thy dastard foes his keen reproach should feel.
Curse of our Nation, source of countless woes,
From whole dark womb unreckon'd misery flows;
Th' embargo rages like a sweeping wind,
Fear low'rs before, and famine stalks behind.
What words, oh, Muse! can paint the mournful scene,
The saddening street, the desolated green;
How hungry labourers leave their toil and sigh,
And sorrow droops in each desponding eye!

SEX the bold sailor from the ocean torn,
His element, sink friendless and forlorn!
His suffering spouse the tear of anguish shed,
His starving children cry in vain for bread!

THE farmer, since supporting trade is fled,
Leaves the rude joke, and cheerless hangs his head;
Misfortunes fall, an unremitting shower,
Debts follow debts, on taxes, taxes pour.
See in his stores his hoarded produce rot,
Or sheriff sales his profits bring to naught;
Disheartening cares in thronging myriads flow,
Till down he sinks to poverty and woe!

OH, ye bright pair, the blessing of mankind!
Whom time has sanction'd, and whom fate has join'd,
COMMERCE, that bears the trident of the main,
And AGRICULTURE, empress of the plain;
Who, hand in hand, and heav'n - directed, go

William Cullen Bryant, *The Embargo, or Sketches of the Times* (1808).

Diffusing gladness through the world below;
Whoe'er the wretch, would hurl the flaming brand,
Of dire disunion, palsied be his hand! ...

WHEN shall this land, some courteous angel say,
Throw off a weak, and erring ruler's sway ?
Rife, injur'd people, vindicate your cause!
And prove your love of Liberty and laws;
Oh wrest, sole refuge of a sinking land,
The sceptre from the slave's imbecile hand!
Oh ne'er consent, obsequious, to advance
The *willing vassal* of imperious France!
Correct that suffrage you misus'd before,
And lift your voice above a Congress' roar? ...

Go, *wretch*, resign the presidential chair,
Disclose thy secret measures foul or fair,
Go, search, with curious eye, for horned frogs,
'Mongst the wild wastes of Louisianian bogs;
Or where Ohio rolls his turbid stream,
Dig for huge bones, thy glory and thy theme; ...

5. Shawnee Chief Tecumseh Recounts the Misdeeds of Whites and Calls for Indian Unity, 1810

Brother, I wish you to give me close attention, because I think you do not clearly understand. I want to speak to you about promises that the Americans have made.

You recall the time when the Jesus Indians of the Delawares lived near the Americans, and had confidence in their promises of friendship, and thought they were secure, yet the Americans murdered all the men, women, and children, even as they prayed to Jesus?

The same promises were given to the Shawnee one time. It was at Fort Finney, where some of my people were forced to make a treaty. Flags were given to my people, and they were told they were now the children of the Americans. We were told, if any white people mean to harm you, hold up these flags and you will then be safe from all danger. We did this in good faith. But what happened? Our beloved chief Moluntha stood with the American flag in front of him and that very peace treaty in his hand, but his head was chopped by an American officer, and that American officer was never punished.

Speech to William Harrison, governor of the Indian Territory (August 11, 1810). http://injesus.com/messages/content/45035.

Brother, after such bitter events, can you blame me for placing little confidence in the promises of Americans? ...

It is you, the Americans, by such bad deeds, who push the red men to do mischief. You do not want unity among the tribes, and you destroy it. You try to make differences between them. We, their leaders, wish them to unite and consider their land the common property of all, but you try to keep them from this. You separate the tribes and deal with them that way, one by one, and advise them not to come into this union. Your states have set an example of forming a union among all the Fires, why should you censure the Indians for following that example?

But, brother, I mean to bring all the tribes together, in spite of you, and until I have finished, I will not go to visit your president. Maybe I will when I have finished, maybe. The reason I tell you this, you want, by making your distinctions of Indian tribes and allotting to each a particular tract of land, to set them against each other, and thus to weaken us....

The only way to stop this evil is for all the red men to unite in claiming an equal right in the land. That is how it was at first, and should be still, for the land never was divided, but was for the use of everyone. Any tribe could go to an empty land and make a home there. And if they left, another tribe could come there and make a home. No groups among us have a right to sell, even to one another, and surely not to outsiders who want all, and will not do with less.

Sell a country! Why not sell the air, the clouds, and the Great Sea, as well as the earth? Did not the Great Good Spirit make them all for the use of his children?

Brother, I was glad to hear what you told us. you said that if we could prove that the land was sold by people who had no right to sell it, you would restore it. I will prove that those who did sell did not own it. Did they have a deed? A title? No! You say those prove someone owns land. Those chiefs only spoke a claim, and so you pretended to believe their claim, only because you wanted the land. But the many tribes with me will not agree with those claims. They have never had a title to sell, and we agree this proves you could not buy it from them. If the land is not given back to us, you will see, when we return to our homes from here, how it will be settled. It will be like this:

We shall have a great council, at which all tribes will be present. We shall show to those who sold that they had no rights to the claim they set up, and we shall see what will be done to those chiefs who did sell the land to you. I am not alone in this determination, it is the determination of all the warriors and red people who listen to me. Brother, I now wish you to listen to me. If you do not wipe out that treaty, it will seem that you wish me to kill all the chiefs who sold the land! I tell you so because I am authorized by all tribes to do so! I am the head of them all! All my warriors will meet together with me in two or three moons from now. Then I will call for those chiefs who sold you this land, and we shall know what to do with them. If you do not restore the land, you will have had a hand in killing them!

I am Shawnee! I am a warrior! My forefathers were warriors. From them I took only my birth into this world. From my tribe I take nothing. I am the maker of my own destiny! And of that I might make the destiny of my red people, of our nation, as great as I conceive to in my mind, when I think of Weshemoneto, who rules this universe! I would not then have to come to Governor Harrison and ask him to tear up this treaty and wipe away the marks upon the land. No! I would say to him, "Sir, you may return to your own country!" The being within me hears the voice of the ages, which tells me that once, always, and until lately, there were no white men on all this island, that it then belonged to the red men, children of the same parents, placed on it by the Great Good Spirit who made them, to keep it, to traverse it, to enjoy its yield, and to people it with the same race. Once they were a happy race! Now they are made miserable by the white people, who are never contented but are always coming in! You do this always, after promising not to anyone, yet you ask us to have confidence in your promises. How can we have confidence in the white people? When Jesus Christ came upon the earth, you killed him, the son of your own God, you nailed him up! You thought he was dead, but you were mistaken. And only after you thought you killed him did you worship him, and start killing those who would not worship him. What kind of a people is this for us to trust?

Now, Brother, everything I have said to you is the truth, as Weshemoneto has inspired me to speak only truth to you. I have declared myself freely to you about my intentions. And I want to know your intentions. I want to know what you are going to do about the taking of our land. I want to hear you say that you understand now, and will wipe out that pretended treaty, so that the tribes can be at peace with each other, as you pretend you want them to be. Tell me, brother. I want to know now.

6. Tenskwatawa (the Prophet) Relates His Journey to the World Above, 1810

I died and went to the World Above, and saw it.

The punishments I saw terrify you! But listen, those punishments will be upon you unless you follow me through the door that I am opening for you!

Our Creator put us on this wide, rich land, and told us we were free to go where the game was, where the soil was good for planting. That was our state of true happiness. We did not have to beg for anything. Our Creator had taught us how to find and make everything we needed, from trees and plants and animals and stone. We lived in bark, and we wore only the skins of animals.

Thus were we created. Thus we lived for a long time, proud and happy. We had never eaten pig meat, nor tasted the poison called whiskey, nor worn wool from sheep, nor struck fire or dug earth with steel, nor cooked in iron, nor hunted and fought with loud guns, nor ever had diseases which soured our blood or rotted our organs. We were pure, so we were strong and happy.

Message of the Shawnee Prophet Tenskwatawa, "he who opens the door". Obtained from http://history.missouristate. edu/FTMiller/EarlyRepublic/tecandtensk.htm

For many years we traded furs to the English or the French, for wool blankets and guns and iron things, for steel awls and needles and axes, for mirrors, for pretty things made of beads and silver. And for liquor. This was foolish, but we did not know it. We shut our ears to the Great Good Spirit. We did not want to hear that we were being foolish.

But now those things of the white men have corrupted us, and made us weak and needful. Our men forgot how to hunt without noisy guns. Our women don't want to make fire without steel, or cook without iron, or sew without metal awls and needles, or fish without steel hooks. Some look in those mirrors all the time, and no longer teach their daughters to make leather or render bear oil. We learned to need the white men's goods, and so now a People who never had to beg for anything must beg for everything!

Some of our women married white men, and made half-breeds. Many of us now crave liquor. He whose filthy name I will not speak, he who was I before, was one of the worst of those drunkards. There are drunkards in almost every family. You know how bad this is.

And so you see what has happened to us. We were fools to take all these things that weakened us. We did not need them then, but we believe we need them now. We turned our backs on the old ways. Instead of thanking the Great Spirit for all we used to have, we turned to the white man and asked them for more. So now we depend upon the very people who destroy us! This is our weakness! Our corruption! Our Creator scolded me, "If you had lived the way I taught you, the white men could never have got you under their foot!"

And that is why Our Creator purified me and sent me down to you full of the shinning power, to make you what you were before!

No red man must ever drink liquor, or he will go and have the hot lead poured in his mouth!

No red man shall take more than one wife in the future. No red man shall run after women. If he is single, let him lake a wife, and lie only with her.

Any red woman who is living with a white man must return to her people, and must leave her children with the husband, so that all nations will be pure in their blood.

Now hear what I was told about dealing with white men! These things we must do, to cleanse ourselves of their corruption!

Do not eat any food that is raised or cooked by a white person. It is not good for us. Eat not their bread made of wheat, for Our Creator gave us corn for our bread. Eat not the meat of their filthy swine, nor of their chicken fowls, nor the beef of their cattle, which are tame and thus have no spirit in them. Their foods will seem to fill your empty belly, but this deceives you for food without spirit does not nourish you.

There are two kinds of white men. There are the Americans, and there are the others. You may give your hand in friendship to the French, or the Spaniards, or the British. But the Americans are not like those. The Americans come from the slime of the sea, with mud and weeds in their claws, and they are a kind of crayfish serpent whose claws grab in our earth and take it from us....

... Remember it is the wish of the Great Good Spirit that we have no more commerce with white men!

We may keep our guns, and if we need to defend ourselves against American white men, the guns will kill them because they are a white man's weapon. But arrows will kill American intruders, too! You must go to the grandfathers and have them teach you to make good bows and shape arrowheads, and you must recover the old hunting skills....

We will no longer do the frolic dances that excite lust. The Great Good Spirit will teach me the old dances we did before the corruption, and from these dances we will receive strength and happiness!

7. President James Monroe Declares That European Powers May Not Interfere in the Americas, 1823

... [A]s a principle in which the rights and interests of the United States are involved, that the American continents, by the free and independent condition which they have assumed and maintain, are henceforth not to be considered as subjects for future colonization by any European powers.

... Of events in that quarter of the globe, with which we have so much intercourse, and from which we derive our origin, we have always been anxious and interested spectators. The citizens of the United States cherish sentiments the most friendly, in favor of the liberty and happiness of their fellow men on that side of the Atlantic. In the wars of the European powers, in matters relating to themselves, we have never taken any part, nor does it comport with our policy so to do. It is only when our rights are invaded, or seriously menaced, that we resent injuries, or make preparation for our defense. With the movements in this hemisphere, we are, of necessity, more immediately connected, and by causes which must be obvious to all enlightened and impartial observers. The political system of the allied powers is essentially different, in this respect, from that of America. This difference proceeds from that which exists in their respective governments. And to the defence of our own, which has been achieved by the loss of so much blood and treasure, and matured by the wisdom of their most enlightened citizens, and under which we have enjoyed unexampled felicity, this whole nation is devoted. We owe it, therefore, to candor, and to the amicable relations existing between the United States and those powers, to declare, that we should consider any attempt on their part to extend their system to any portion of this hemisphere, as dangerous to our peace and safety. With the existing colonies or dependencies of any European power, we have not interfered, and shall not interfere. But, with the governments who have declared their independence and maintained it, and whose independence we have, on great consideration and on just principles, acknowledged, we could not view any interposition for the purpose of oppressing them, or controlling, in any other manner, their destiny, by any European power, in any other light than as the manifestation of

James Monroe, *The Monroe Doctrine* (1823).

an unfriendly disposition towards the United States. In the war between these new governments and Spain, we declared our neutrality at the time of their recognition, and to this we have adhered, and shall continue to adhere, provided no change shall occur, which, in the judgment of the competent authorities of this government, shall make a corresponding change, on the part of the United States, indispensable to their security.

...Our policy, in regard to Europe, which was adopted at an early stage of the wars which have so long agitated that quarter of the globe, nevertheless remains the same, which is, not to interfere in the internal concerns of any of its powers; to consider the government de facto as the legitimate government for us; to cultivate friendly relations with it, and to preserve those relations by a frank, firm, and manly policy, meeting, in all instances, the just claims of every power, submitting to injuries from none. But, in regard to those continents, circumstances are eminently and conspicuously different.

It is impossible that the allied powers should extend their political system to any portion of either continent, without endangering our peace and happiness; nor can any one believe that our Southern Brethren, if left to themselves, would adopt it of their own accord. It is equally impossible, therefore, that we should behold such interposition, in any form, with indifference. If we look to the comparative strength and resources of Spain and those new governments, and their distance from each other, it must be obvious that she can never subdue them. It is still the true policy of the United States, to leave the parties to themselves, in the hope that other powers will pursue the same course.

8. The Cherokee Nation Pleads to Remain "on the Land of Our Fathers," 1830

We are aware, that some persons suppose it will be for our advantage to remove beyond the Mississippi. We think otherwise. Our people universally think otherwise. Thinking that it would be fatal to their interests, they have almost to a man sent their memorial to congress, deprecating the necessity of a removal. This question was distinctly before their minds when they signed their memorial. Not an adult person can be found, who has not an opinion on the subject, and if the people were to understand distinctly, that they could be protected against the laws of the neighboring states, there is probably not an adult person in the nation, who would think it best to remove; though possibly a few might emigrate individually. There are doubtless many, who would flee to an unknown country, however beset with dangers, privations and sufferings, rather than be sentenced to spend six years in a Georgia prison for advising one of their neighbors not to betray his country. And there are others who could not think of living as outlaws in their native land, exposed to numberless vexations, and excluded from being parties or witnesses in a court of justice. It is incredible that Georgia should ever have enacted the oppressive laws to which reference is here made, unless she had

"Memorial of the Cherokee Nation," *Niles Weekly Register* 38 (August 21, 1830): 454–457.

supposed that something extremely terrific in its character was necessary in order to make the Cherokees willing to remove. We are not willing to remove; and if we could be brought to this extremity, it would be not by argument, not because our judgment was satisfied, not because our condition will be improved; but only because we cannot endure to be deprived of our national and individual rights and subjected to a process of intolerable oppression.

We wish to remain on the land of our fathers. We have a perfect and original right to remain without interruption or molestation. The treaties with us, and laws of the United States made in pursuance of treaties, guarantee our residence and our privileges, and secure us against intruders. Our only request is, that these treaties may be fulfilled, and these laws executed....

The removal of families to a new country, even under the most favorable auspices, and when the spirits are sustained by pleasing visions of the future, is attended with much depression of mind and sinking of heart. This is the case, when the removal is a matter of decided preference, and when the persons concerned are in early youth or vigorous manhood. Judge, then, what must be the circumstances of a removal, when a whole community, embracing persons of all classes and every description, from the infant to the man of extreme old age, the sick, the blind, the lame, the improvident, the reckless, the desperate, as well as the prudent, the considerate, the industrious, are compelled to remove by odious and intolerable vexations and persecutions, brought upon them in the forms of law, when all will agree only in this, that they have been cruelly robbed of their country, in violation of the most solemn compacts, which it is possible for communities to form with each other; and that, if they should make themselves comfortable in their new residence, they have nothing to expect hereafter but to be the victims of a future legalized robbery!

Such we deem, and are absolutely certain, will be the feelings of the whole Cherokee people, if they are forcibly compelled, by the laws of Georgia, to remove; and with these feelings, how is it possible that we should pursue our present course of improvement, or avoid sinking into utter despondency? We have been called a poor, ignorant, and degraded people. We certainly are not rich; nor have we ever boasted of our knowledge, or our moral or intellectual elevation. But there is not a man within our limits so ignorant as not to know that he has a right to live on the land of his fathers, in the possession of his immemorial privileges, and that this right has been acknowledged and guaranteed by the United States; nor is there a man so degraded as not to feel a keen sense of injury, on being deprived of this right and driven into exile.

9. President Andrew Jackson Defends Indian Removal, 1833

... It gives me pleasure to announce to Congress that the benevolent policy of the Government, steadily pursued for nearly thirty years, in relation to the removal of the Indians beyond the white settlements, is approaching to a happy consummation. Two important tribes have accepted the provision made for their

---

Andrew Jackson, *Second Inaugural Address* (1833).

removal at the last session of Congress; and it is believed that their example will induce the remaining tribes, also, to seek the same obvious advantages.

The consequences of a speedy removal will be important to the United States, to individual States, and to the Indians themselves. The pecuniary advantages which it promises to the Government are the least of its recommendations. It puts an end to all possible danger of collision between the authorities of the General and State Governments, on account of the Indians. It will place a dense and civilized population in large tracts of country now occupied by a few savage hunters. By opening the whole territory between Tennessee on the north, and Louisiana on the south, to the settlements of the whites, it will incalculably strengthen the southwestern frontier, and render the adjacent States strong enough to repel future invasion without remote aid. It will relieve the whole State of Mississippi, and the western part of Alabama, of Indian occupancy, and enable those States to advance rapidly in population, wealth, and power. It will separate the Indians from immediate contact with settlements of whites; free them from the power of the States; enable them to pursue happiness in their own way, and under their own rude institutions; will retard the progress of decay, which is lessening their numbers; and perhaps cause them gradually, under the protection of the Government, and through the influence of good counsels, to east off their savage habits, and become an interesting, civilized, and Christian community. These consequences, some of them so certain, and the rest so probable, make the complete execution of the plan sanctioned by Congress at their last session an object of much solicitude.

Towards the aborigines of the country no one can indulge a more friendly feeling than myself, or would go further in attempting to reclaim them from their wandering habits, and make them a happy, prosperous people. I have endeavored to impress upon them my own solemn convictions of the duties and powers of the General Government in relation to the State authorities. For the justice of the law, passed by the States within the scope of their reserved powers, they are not responsible to this Government. As individuals, we may entertain and express our opinions of their acts; but, as a Government, we have as little right to control them as we have to prescribe laws for other nations.

With a full understanding of the subject, the Choctaw and Chickasaw tribes have, with great unanimity, determined to avail themselves of the liberal offers presented by the act of Congress, and have agreed to remove beyond the Mississippi river. Treaties have been made with them, which, in due season, will be submitted for consideration. In negotiating these treaties, they were made to understand their true condition; and they have preferred maintaining their independence in the western forests to submitting to the laws of the States in which they now reside. These treaties being probably the last which will ever be made with them, are characterized by great liberality on the part of the Government. They give the Indians a liberal sum in consideration of their removal, and comfortable subsistence on their arrival at their new homes. If it be their real interest to maintain a separate existence, they will there be at liberty to do so without the inconveniences and vexations to which they would unavoidably have been subject in Alabama and Mississippi.

Humanity has often wept over the fate of the aborigines of this country; and philanthropy has been long busily employed in devising means to avert it. But its progress has never for a moment been arrested; and, one by one, have many powerful tribes disappeared from the earth. To follow to the tomb the last of his race, and to tread on the graves of extinct nations, excite melancholy reflections. But true philanthropy reconciles the mind to these vicissitudes, as it does to the extinction of one generation to make room for another. In the monuments and fortresses of an unknown people, spread over the extensive regions of the west, we behold the memorials of a once powerful race, which was exterminated, or has disappeared, to make room for the existing savage tribes. Nor is there any thing in this, which, upon a comprehensive view of the general interests of the human race, is to be regretted. Philanthropy could not wish to see this continent restored to the condition in which it was found by our forefathers. What good man would prefer a country covered with forests and ranged by a few thousand savages, to our extensive republic, studded with cities, towns, and prosperous farms; embellished with all the improvements which art can devise, or industry execute; occupied by more than twelve millions of happy people, and filled with all the blessings of liberty, civilization, and religion!…

ESSAYS

The westward movement of Americans had a profound and often a devastating impact on the Indians. As indigenous people faced increasing pressure in the early decades of the nineteenth century, their responses varied. Some used Christian teachings to oppose white expansion westward. Others attempted to inculcate specific aspects of American culture into their society. The following two essays illustrate two very different answers to the Indians' dilemma. Gregory Evans Dowd, a historian at the University of Michigan, focuses on attempts led by Tecumseh and his brother Tenskwatawa (also known as the Prophet) to unite Indian nations and oppose the white invasion. Note how Tenskwatawa used visions and prophecy to foster his political aims. In contrast, Theda Perdue, a member of the department of history at the University of North Carolina at Chapel Hill, analyzes the Cherokees, who embraced the "civilization" efforts of the American government as their best hope for avoiding forced removal from their homes. These struggles with civilization, Professor Perdue argues, affected Cherokee women and men in different ways.

Indians Utilizing a Strategy of Armed Resistance

GREGORY EVANS DOWD

A new order emerged in the trans-Appalachian borderlands following the defeat of pan-Indianism in the mid-1790s. Through Jay's Treaty (1794) with Britain,

From Gregory Evans Dowd. *A Spirited Resistance: The North American Indian Struggle for Unity, 1745–1815*, pp. 116–118, 128–129, 139–142, 143–144, 181, 183, 191, 193–194, 200–201. Copyright © 1993 by The Johns Hopkins University Press. Reprinted by permission of The Johns Hopkins University Press.

which like other European-American treaties ignored Indian possessions, the United States secured the military posts within its territorial claims. In the Treaty of San Lorenzo (1795), Spain recognized the American claim to lands at the core of the Creek confederacy. The influence of Britain and Spain in North America, visibly, in retreat at these treaty tables, receded still farther as truly devastating wars deranged Europe. As European power in Indian country ebbed through diplomatic channels, American power flowed aggressively to replace it. It flowed directly into Indian councils, where it found considerable Native American tolerance, if not support.

Indians believing in the need for the conscious adaptation of European ways, many of whom had been once, when armed from Europe, willing to league with nativists against the United States, now sought to come to terms with the republic. American agents, paid by the federal government, worked closely with these Indian leaders. Their combined efforts promoted a mission of "civilization." Rapidly among the Cherokees but with less success among the Creeks, Shawnees, and Delawares, the "plan of civilization," supported by the federal government and by several churches, became rooted in tribal government.

Among all the involved peoples, however, including the republic's citizens, the civilizing mission met a thicket of difficulties. The Anglo-American brambles grew not only from the opposition of citizens interested in Indian lands, but also out of an intellectual seedbed sown with incompatible crops, as many scholars have shown. An essential motivation of the mission, the assumed superiority of Anglo-American culture, entangled it from the start, for the missionaries' conviction of their religious and cultural superiority alienated the targeted peoples. This was as true of nonreligious agents as it was of the religious missionaries.

The secular employees of the mission, moreover, underestimated the obstacles that spread across their path, a failing that led them into tactical contradictions. Once they undertook the mission, they never adequately reconciled their aims with their methods. In what one scholar calls a "lapse in logic," these Americans sought to make good citizens out of the Indians, but employed coercion, cajolery, and deception to do so. The agents were under great pressure from American governments—territorial, state, and federal—to accomplish their task, with the understanding that it would increase the land available to the republic. Governments and missionaries alike claimed that if Indian men abandoned hunting and took up the plow, they could live well, and on less land. The surplus lands would then come up for grabs. In practice the process inverted. Pressured by their land-hungry countrymen, American agents among the Indians obtained land cessions from impoverished Indians even before the successful conversion of Indian men into yeomen farmers. To justify the inversion, the mission's proponents came to argue that by restricting Indian land they restricted Indian hunting and thereby compelled Indian men to farm. The American acquisition of Indian land perversely took on a philanthropic guise; taking became giving.

As early a professional historian of the era as Henry Adams noticed the moral contradictions within the civilizing mission. Adams discovered that although President Thomas Jefferson had advocated the establishment of an Indian farming class, he had sought to do so through the manipulation of Indian debt. In Adam's words, Jefferson "deliberately ordered his Indian agents to tempt the tribal chiefs into debt in order to oblige them to sell the tribal lands, which did not belong to them, but to their tribes." Jefferson, that indebted foe of debt, attempted to create an independent Indian yeomanry by driving Indian leaders into the red. This contradiction, between Federal efforts to "improve" Indian economies on the one hand, while both increasing Indian indebtedness and decreasing Indian landholding on the other, placed the civilizing mission precariously upon a badly fissured foundation. The contradiction, with the others, had to be sustained; the federal government had to meet the world opinion with a policy of benevolence while also meeting its citizens' desire for land.

The dense undergrowth of the Indians' recent history [laid] violent hazards in the way of the "plan of civilization," and the most vital and stubborn of the strands took the form of prophetic nativism. Between 1795 and 1815, individual prophets and groups of Indians claiming supernatural inspiration posed direct challenges to those leaders who advocated political and even cultural accommodation to the power of the United States. Insurgent nativists drew upon their histories of intertribal cooperation. They looked to their shared beliefs in the ritual demands of power. Turning to the spirits as well as to their intertribal comrades, they attempted to rally support against those tribal leaders who ceded land to the Americans. Prophetic parties of Shawnees, Delawares, Creeks, and many others actually broke with their accommodating countrymen to prepare an intertribal, Indian union against the expansion of the United States, an effort that eventually merged with the War of 1812....

The apocalyptic teachings of the early nineteenth-century prophets bore the two faces of doom and glory. A Delaware woman who had visions in 1806 warned that if the Big House Ceremony were not celebrated with care, a whirlwind would soon wipe out the people completely. The Trout thought the world "broken," that it "declines." The Indians to the west of the Ottawas would soon all "fall off and die," unless they sent deputies to be instructed in ritual. Handsome Lake warned of a "visitation of Sickness" if his teachings were neglected. But the fear induced by such threats was offset by the hope that came with prophetic promises. The Trout believed that, through the power of a war-club dance, the Ottawas and Chippewas would "distroy every white man in america." Tenskwatawa's first visions also contained such notions, shaped in traditional myth. He encountered a crab, a common "earth diver" in Native American creation stories, a being that brought up the muck from which the earth was made. The Great Spirit promised the Shawnee Prophet that if the Indians abided by his teachings, the crab would "turn over the land so that the white people are covered." Later Tenskwatawa indicated that Anglo-Americans were not in danger as long as they left the prophet's town at Greenville, Ohio, alone. But if the United States attempted to meet his prophecy with force, "if the white people would go to war, they would be destroyed by a day of judgement," or, according to another source, "there will be an End to the World."

On the eve of the war of 1812, prophecy in the North, despite its innovations, belonged to a developing tradition as old as the peoples' elders. Nativists had previously expressed that tradition most vigorously between 1745 and 1775, especially after 1760. They had continued to invoke it, though often in the shadow of cooperation with Great Britain, during the long wars of the 1770s through 1790s. They did so as participants in a broad movement: challenging tribal boundaries, altering Indian identity, inventing a strategy of resistance against Anglo-American expansion....

In 1809, the annuity chiefs unwittingly and negligently galvanized the nativists with another land cession. The affair began in the summer of 1809, when the secretary of war wrote Harrison that he could proceed with his desire to purchase more lands along the Wabash, but only if the governor was certain that the undertaking "will excite no disagreeable apprehension and produce no undesirable effects before It shall be made." Harrison proceeded to negotiate with the Delaware, Potowatomi, Miami, and Eel River Indians, making separate treaties with the Weas and Kickapoos later that year. The main text agreed to, the Treaty of Fort Wayne, ceded over two and one half million acres to the United States, for about two cents and acre—a high price in Indian treaties, but still a massively unequal exchange.

The Treaty of Fort Wayne has long been recognized as a milestone on the road to the battle of Tippecanoe. From this period forward in histories of the West on the eve of the War of 1812, Tenskwatawa's brother, Tecumseh, fashions and leads the pan-Indian movement....

The prophet, however, lost no power following the treaty; he still led the nativists from his headquarters at Tippecanoe. His preaching ... had always exhibited both the political overtones and material concerns that political and social historians seek to grasp and find worth grasping. Like Tecumseh, Tenskwatawa spoke out vigorously against both the Fort Wayne cession and the Indians who had agreed to it. In the spring and summer of 1810, half a year after the signing of the treaty, the Prophet informed a discovered American spy that his people were "much exasperated at the cession of Lands made last winter" and that they had "agreed that the Tract on the N. west side of the Wabash should not be surveyed." His disciples followed up this declaration by successfully opposing a surveying party in September.

Tecumseh, meanwhile, spoke out against the government chiefs long targeted by Tenskwatawa. In August 1810 Tecumseh informed Harrison that he intended "to level all distinctions to destroy the village chiefs by whom all mischief is done; it is they who sell our land to the Americans." He asked Harrison to repudiate the Fort Wayne treaty, for the annuity chiefs "had no right" to sell the claim. He did not threaten Harrison with war; rather he threatened "to kill all the chiefs who sold you this land." By retaining the American claim, Tecumseh warned, "you will have a hand in killing them." Tecumseh, like the prophet, was still less openly hostile to the United States than he was to its allies among Indian leaders....

It is on the subject of Indian unity that scholars and tale-spinners alike have most emphasized the particular wisdom of Tecumseh. Even here, although he, was an energetic ambassador and a man of martial distinction, Tecumseh, like his brother, was more participant in than progenitor of the movement we associate with his name. Tecumseh drew on both the nativist vision of his brother and the broader dreams and practical legacies of two generations of militants.

In his speech to Harrison that August, Tecumseh argued, as had Ohioan and Great Lakes Country militants for at least three decades, that "all the lands in the western country was the common property of all the tribes." No land could be sold without the consent of all. To establish the principle, he intended, as had others, to unite the tribes in a movement against American expansion. The prophet also argued that "no sale was good unless made by all the Tribes," and he welcomed Indians of all tribes to join in his spiritual revival, his rebellion against the authority of annuity chiefs, his rejection of Christianity, and his defense of Indian lands.

To support his intertribal call, the Shawnee Prophet had at his disposal a concept of Indian identity that had been developing since at least the middle of the eighteenth century, a concept embodied in the notion of the separate creation of whites and Indians. The notion did not lead directly to nativism; it was so widespread that even such federally recognized chiefs as Black Hoof and the Wyandot Tahre expressed the view at the turn of the nineteenth century. But government chiefs could never turn it to their advantage with the dexterity of the nativists, for in its logical conclusion, the doctrine meant an Indian rejection of American control.

In 1805 the Presbyterian missionary, James Hughes, found the Wyandots divided over their concept of the creation. Some believed in a single Great Spirit, others held "that there are two Gods, one the creator of the white people, and the other of the Indians, whom they call the Warrior." The Shawnee Prophet believed something akin to the latter notion, as the told C. C. Trowbridge in 1824. He recalled that at the creation "The Great Spirit then opened a door, and looking down they saw a white man seated upon the ground.... The Great Spirit told them that this white man was not made by himself but by another spirit who made & governed the whites & over whom he had no controul." The Trout, the Ottawa spokesman for the nativist movement, further defined the Americans (he distinguished, as had the Ottawa Pontiac before him, between the Anglo-Americans whose seaboard polities thrust aggressively westward and the less expansionist Canadians) as creatures of the "Evil Spirit" From "Scum of the great water."

The separate, even evil, nature of American citizens emerged also in Indian interpretations of Christianity. As in the mid-eighteenth century, some Indians turned Christianity against Christians to demonstrate the depth of the missionaries' abomination. In crucifying Jesus, these argued, Europeans had killed their own God. During the first, more militantly anti-Christian phase of Handsome Lake's mission, his half-brother Cornplanter, who "liked some ways of the white people," told the Quaker missionary Henry Simmons, "it was the white people who kill'd our Saviour." Simmons countered, "it was the Jews," and then tried to drive the point home by dragging out the already hackneyed argument that Indians were members of the lost tribes of Israel: "Indians were their descendants, for many of their habits were Similar to the Jews, in former days." We don't know what Cornplanter made of that contention—perhaps he was simply at a loss for words—but twentieth-century practitioners of the Handsome Lake Religion have made no mention of it and consider the crucifixion a deed performed by whites. They have learned that the Seneca Prophet, in his early visions, met Jesus, who described himself as "a man upon the earth who was slain by his own people." Jesus had ordered Handsome Lake to "tell your people that they will become lost when they follow the ways of the white people."

Nativistic northwesterners leaned more heavily on the argument. Responding to a Moravian missionary in 1806, one of Tenskwatawa's followers said of the crucifixion, "Granted that what you say is true, He did not die in Indian land but among the white people." In 1810 Tecumseh himself, revealing his own concerns for things spiritual, asked Harrison in the same pointed terms, "How can we have confidence in the white people[?] when Jesus Christ came upon the earth you kill'd and nail'd him on a cross." Given the Shawnee's nativistic assumptions, it was a logical question.

If, as the Shawnee Prophet said, Americans were unchangeably inimical to Indians, if "the Great Spirit did not mean that the white and red people should live near each other" because whites "poison'd the land," and if all Indians came from a common creation different from that of others, then it only made sense that Indians should unite against the American threat. In emphasizing their separation, Indians gave spiritual sanction to Native American unity.

Intertribal, Prophetic Nativism

Tecumseh has captured a more prominent place in American history than any Indian of his day, arguably of any day....

Tecumseh did *not*, however, significantly differ from his followers in culture or in vision; nor was it tribalism that blocked his success. He certainly stood out as an expert organizer, warrior, and an indefatigable traveler, although many others from the revolutionary era and the two decades that followed it could rival him even in those talents. In his hopes and in his vision, moreover, he stood with, not beyond or outside of, the militant nativists of the Eastern Woodlands. His most recent biographer, Bil Gilbert, credits Tecumseh with having "conceived of a plan for uniting the red people," but Tecumseh was not the plan's sole creator; he drew upon traditions of nativism and networks of intertribal relations that had been vibrant throughout the trans-Appalachian borderlands, reaching back into the past beyond the time of Neolin and Pontiac. With Tecumseh, also drawing from this legacy, stood the prophets.

The major northern religious leaders urged forms of intertribal unity between 1805 and 1812. Even Handsome Lake, whose Senecas were entirely surrounded by U.S. citizens, who had little direct contact with other militants, and who prudently drew back from military alliance as the War of 1812 erupted, nonetheless showed a certain solidarity with the more western Indians by demanding that his followers refuse to support the United States. Nor did Handsome Lake ignore other peoples; he sent his word to Sandusky in 1804 and visited the region in 1806. But his influence remained largely confined to the reservations east of Lake Erie.

Tenskwatawa promoted pan-Indianism not with words alone, or only with the elaboration of separation theology, but with the time-honored if paradoxical political device of secession. Like the Susquehanna Delawares and Shawnees who had fled Anglo-Iroquois authority by both removing to Ohio and settling in polyglot villages in the early eighteenth century, like the Chickamaugas who had broken with the Cherokees to settle the Tennessee with their militant Shawnee allies during the American Revolution, Tenskwatawa broke from his hosts, invited Indians of all nations to join him, and settled new towns. He did so first at Greenville (1806-8), in symbolic defiance of the Treaty of Greenville, and later at Tippecanoe (1808-12), in outright defiance of Little Turtle's claim to authority over that land. The prophet warned Little Turtle that plans for the Tippecanoe settlement had been "layed by all the Indians in America and had been sanctioned by the Great Spirit." He then informed the Miami leader that Indian unity alone would end Indian poverty and defend Indian land.

One band of Wyandots, joining the prophet in 1810, bound the movement of earlier decades by bringing with them "the Great Belt which was the Symbol of Union between the Tribes in their late war with the United States." Consciously reviving the pan-Indianism of their recent past, these Wyandots, in the prophet's words, could not "sit still and see the property of all the Indians usurped."

Drawing upon the same tradition of resistance and adhering to Tenskwatawa, the Trout also advocated Indian unity. In the spring of 1807, before Tecumseh gained notice, this Ottawa addressed Ottawas and Chippewas, requesting that each of their villages send at least two deputies to his village, L'arbre Croche, to carry out the will of the Great Spirit. And he specifically demanded, in the voice of the Great Spirit, an end to intertribal hostilities: "You are, however, never to go to War against each other. But to cultivate peace between your different Tribes, that they may become one great people." The following spring, in the turbulent wake of a large land sale by Ottawas, Chippewas, Wyandots, and Potawatomis to the United States, militants of all four tribes declared it "a crime punishable by Death for any Indian to put his name on paper for the perpose of parting with any of their lands."

The third prophet, Main Poc of the Potawatomis, stood for northern Indian solidarity, but limited his vision to what Americans would call the Old Northwest. He waged sporadic war on the trans-Mississippi Osage Indians, a war fought also by northern refugees who had already fled across that great river. Main Poc deviated in other ways: even after donning the prophetic mantle, he accepted a bribe from Wells, though it does not seem to have changed his behavior. Further, he continued to drink, advocating only temperance, while other nativists, as a rule, advocated abstinence. But Main Poc did think beyond the boundaries of his "tribe." This Potawatomi, in fact, recommended Tippecanoe to Tenskwatawa as a good site for a town. As hostilities neared in the fall of 1811, Main Poc actively sought recruits beyond his people, among the Ottawas and Chippewas....

... [T]he military and diplomatic accomplishments of the nativists who bore arms in the War of 1812 would not approach those of their militant predecessors in the revolutionary era. The odds against pan-Indian success had increased sharply since the early 1790s. By 1812 American citizens outnumbered Indians in the region between the Appalachians and the Mississippi by a margin of seven-to-one. The new states of Kentucky, Tennessee, and Ohio formed a pounding wedge that split the Indian quest for unity, already rotten with civil conflict, into two deteriorating blocs. Meanwhile Louisiana, admitted to statehood in 1812, and Missouri, established as a territory that same year, applied additional pressure from the west, disrupting Indian travel on the Mississippi River. The lower portion of the Ohio River had become similarly dominated not only by Kentucky but by the organized territories of Indiana and Illinois. The Upper Ohio, of course, had been finally lost by the independent peoples in 1795. This weighty American presence, combined with the loss of Cherokees as military allies, meant that the pan-Indian effort associated with Tecumseh would be more a severe aftershock then a seismic rift, a mere reminder of greater deeds done long ago....

The increasing regionalization was serious enough, but further weakening pan-Indianism in this period was the failure of the militant nativists to come to terms with those, among each of their own peoples, who now cooperated with the United States, those who were now—more than ever—enemies at home....

This all meant that in 1812, accommodating Indians in the North as well as in the South would stick with the United States, even to the point, for some, of firing upon their nativistic relatives. The age of Tecumseh created little room for a joint alliance of nativist and accommodationist with Britain. Not only, then, did the War of 1812 bring an end to any serious military cooperation between northern and southern Indians, it also thrust peoples of both regions into the maelstrom of civil war.

In a narrow sense, however paradoxically, these years of devastating internal conflict and pan-Indian failure saw nativism's greatest triumph, for what unity was achieved owed itself, in the largest measure, to the spread of emphatically religious nativist thought along the networks that had for years brought warriors together from across the wide trans-Appalachian borderlands. While in the late eighteenth century multiple readings of opportunities brought into the same camp Indians of various persuasions—accommodationists who saw chances for Spanish or British alliance and nativists who sought to fight the Americans at all costs—in the first decades of the nineteenth century the United States fought against groups often wholly influenced by nativism. But however much the period saw nativism's greatest success among the Indians who bordered the states, it was not pan-Indianism's greatest triumph, as it is often portrayed in studies of Tecumseh. Instead, the War of 1812 stands as pan-Indianism's most thorough failure, its crushing defeat, its disappointing anticlimax....

The nativists failed. Measured by their own goals, the failure was complete. The union of all Indians, the rescue by sacred power, and the demise of containment of the Anglo-Americans did not come about. We might expect the failure to have led to repudiation; instead the ideas continued to animate isolated groups of believers on both sides of the Mississippi. Notions of Indian unity, of separation from Americans, and of the possible rescue by the sacred powers inspired resisters of removal under Black Hawk in Illinois as well as the far more powerful

Seminoles of Florida, but the notions also lived on in the memory of people who would never again bear arms against the United States. As nativistic notions persisted, so did their Native American antitheses.

Nativism lived on in large measure because its opposition had failed just as bitterly. Within a generation of the murder of Francis and the battle death of Tecumseh, the United States had driven most of its Indian allies as well as its Indian enemies west of the Mississippi. There, and in scattered hollows throughout the East, the debates of the ages of Pontiac and Tecumseh found resonance: some continued to seek an accommodation with the United States, others argued for the irreconcilable differences separating all Indians, whatever their particular people, from the nation that stole their lands....

Tenskwatawa himself, the symbol of religious nativism in the Northwest, weathered the War of 1812 and lived out his natural life. Had nativism depended solely upon this prophet it would have had a slim chance for survival, for in his later years, richly narrated by historian R. David Edmunds, Tenskwatawa did little to honor his own memory. He gave up the armed struggle with the end of the war, and he lost most of his followers, living first as a dependent of the British and later of the Americans. But he had not lost all authority with the escape of victory. He headed a small camp of Shawnee, Kickapoo, Sauk, and Fox refugees in Ontario until about 1825, when he returned to Black Hoof's town in Ohio. There his influence increased briefly; he may even have played a leading role in a Shawnee witch scare. But in contrast to his earlier years as a defender of the northern Indians against American expansion, he collaborated in these years in American plans for removal; he turned accommodationist. He led a large Shawnee contingent on a poorly supplied, starvation-ridden, two-year migration to Kansas between 1826 and 1828. Having given up the fight, Tenskwatawa gradually lost his remaining sway among the Shawnees. He managed to display in the West some vestigial religious authority, establishing a "Prophetstown" in his new Kansan land, but with few followers to inhabit the village, it could only have stood as a humiliating reminder of his earlier triumphs and failures.

Tenskwatawa, however, had never been the single font from which all nativism had sprung. A player in a crowded field, his end was obscure and unknown to most. Among Indians throughout the era of removal, the memory of militant nativism ran a course that diverged from the downward personal trajectory of the Shawnee Prophet's career. Militant nativism survived, occasionally gaining strength, but always turning its main energies against its Indian opposition....

... In the nativists' view, their failure was not one of their prophets' misunderstandings, but of the Indians' seduction by the Anglo-Americans. The nativists could see that they had not been rescued by sacred powers, but they could also maintain that the ways of their Indian opponents has proved no more effective in preserving their lands and people. The United States, by driving its friends as well as its enemies across the Mississippi, gave force to nativistic arguments that Indians would never be welcome either in the neighborhood of whites or in the Christian heaven. It is not surprising, therefore, that Shawnees west of the Mississippi, despite the disastrous failure of their forebears' nativism, continued to speak of separate heavens for Indians and whites. It is not surprising that they spoke of an "anti-christian sage," unnamed in our record, who had just a "few years" before Josiah Gregg took his notes in the 1830s opposed the work of missionaries.

In the manner of the earlier prophets, the sage had collapsed with all the appearance of death, "and became stiff and cold, except a spot upon his breast, which still retained the heat of life." Awakening, he told his friends and family that he "had ascended to the Indian's heaven." There his grandfather gave him a warning, a warning flushed with the memory of numerous Shawnee "removals." As Anglo-America had forced them repeatedly from their homes and had failed to honor promises made even to its Indian allies, so, the grandfather warned the new prophet, would Christian promises yield no salvation, no heavenly mansion: "Beware of the religion of the white man: … every Indian who embraces it is obliged to take the road to the white man's heaven; and yet no red man is permitted to enter there, but will have to wander about forever without a resting place."

Indians Utilizing a Strategy of Accommodation

THEDA PERDUE

War and trade dominated Cherokee society in the eighteenth century, but by the end of the century, neither seemed to have much of a future. Overhunting contributed to a decline in deer, encroaching white settlements and roaming livestock destroyed the deer's habitat, and other commodities replaced deerskins in trans-Atlantic commerce. The colonial wars that had claimed thousands of lives and had destroyed orchards, fields, homes, and towns, too, seemed to be at an end. Europeans settled their differences or moved to another theater, and British colonists won their independence. The Cherokees, who had participated in European colonial expansion as allies and trading partners, found themselves with an economy geared to trade and a government shaped by warriors. The United States, invigorated by its political reorganization in 1789, had little use for such anachronistic Native societies, and it embarked on an Indian policy designed to accommodate the land needs of its expanding population and the moral imperatives of its republican ideology. The federal government took on the task of "civilizing" the Indians, that is, converting them culturally into Anglo-Americans. Although eighteenth-century changes threatened the marginalization of women politically and economically, "civilization" implied a far more dramatic transformation. Guided by an idealized view of men and women in their own society, reformers sought to turn men into industrious, republican farmers and women into chaste, orderly housewives.…

The civilization program became an official part of Cherokee relations with the federal government in 1791 when the Cherokees signed the Treaty of

From Theda Perdue, *Cherokee Women: Gender and Culture Change, 1700–1835*, University of Nebraska Press, 1998. Copyright © 1998, University of Nebraska Press. Reprinted by permission of the publisher.

Holston. The treaty provided that the federal government furnish the Cherokees with "implements of husbandry" and send residential agents to give instruction in their use. As a result of this aid, "the Cherokee nation may be led to a greater degree of civilization, and to become herdsmen and cultivators, instead of remaining in a state of hunters." In 1793 the Indian Trade and Intercourse Act committed the United States to providing agricultural implements and draft animals to all Indians and to appointing agents to instruct Native people in their use. The Cherokees, devastated by invasion and impoverished by the decline of the deerskin trade, welcomed assistance. Yet they must have been somewhat bemused by the proffered lessons in agriculture. Not only had Cherokee women been farming for centuries, but many of the crops and techniques used by Euro-Americans came from Native peoples.

In 1796 George Washington outlined the key provisions of the civilization program in a letter addressed to "Beloved Cherokees." In it, he pointed out that "you now see that the game with which your woods once abounded, are growing scarce, and you know that when you cannot find a deer or other game to kill, you must remain hungry." Washington noted that "some of you already experience the advantage of keeping cattle and hogs." He urged other Cherokees to follow their example: "Let all keep them and increase their numbers, and you will have plenty of meat. To these add sheep, and they will give you clothing as well as food." Washington also encouraged commercial agriculture: "Your lands are good and of great extent. By proper management you can raise live stock not only for your own wants, but to sell to the White people." The president recommended the use of the plow to increase production and the adoption of wheat, which he claimed "makes the best bread." To this point, the president's letter is ungendered—it appears to address all Cherokees—but then he turned to the cultivation of fiber crops: "You will easily add flax and cotton which you may dispose of to the White people; or have it made up by your own women into clothing for yourselves. Your wives and daughters can soon learn to spin and weave."

Washington's instructions did not bode well for Cherokee women. Directly addressing Cherokee men, the president implied that animal husbandry and farming were male responsibilities in a "civilized" society. Spinning, weaving, and sewing were women's work. Such expectations threatened the traditional division of labor in Cherokee society and whatever remnants of female autonomy remained. The president assumed that Cherokee men would take up the tasks and adopt the work habits common in the United States while women would become helpmates, mere auxiliaries. In order to convert men from hunters into farmers, "civilizers" had to transform Cherokee conceptions of gender.

Beyond Washington's economic message, however, was an even more ominous signal to Cherokee women: in a "civilized" society women belonged to men, who both headed households and governed the nation. The president addressed Cherokee women only through men: "*your own* women"; "*your* wives and daughters." Washington also hoped to accelerate the political centralization already under way in the Cherokee Nation. He suggested that the Cherokees send representatives to an annual meeting, the forerunner of the Cherokees'

National Council, where they could meet with United States agents and "talk together on the affairs of your nation." The president probably did not expect these representatives to include women.

The government's program to "civilize" Indians rested on an image of Indians as hunters who derived their livelihood from vast game preserves. These hunting grounds presented both an obstacle to "civilization" and a boon to those who succeeded in "civilizing" their proprietors. Native people who became farmers presumably would no longer need their excess lands and would willingly cede them for additional aid to improve their farms. Therefore, land cession supposedly benefitted both Native people and white pioneers.

Total expulsion of Native peoples from the eastern United States was an idea that dated back to the purchase of Louisiana in 1803. Thomas Jefferson suggested an exchange of lands in the East for tracts in the West, and he specifically proposed such a scheme to the Cherokees and Choctaws. Jefferson, however, did not press the issue, because he believed that Native peoples would become "civilized" live contentedly on reduced acreage, and blend into American society. Land cessions negotiated during Jefferson's administration provoked intense factionalism as well as creating population displacement, and so some Cherokees expressed interest in moving west, and the federal government encouraged individual families to migrate to what is today Arkansas. Treaties negotiated in 1817 and 1819 provided not only for land cessions but also for voluntary removal to the West. By the 1820s, two to three thousand Cherokees lived west of the Mississippi while approximately sixteen thousand remained in their homeland in the East.

Some Cherokees believed that "civilization" was their best protection against forced removal. Consequently, they spoke English, sent their children to school, and converted to Christianity. They established a Cherokees republic with written laws, a court system, and a national police force. They also tried to conform to Anglo-American notions about appropriate behavior for men and women. Trade and warfare had accentuated traditional roles for men and women, but "civilization" threatened to usher in new roles by making men farmers and women housewives.

The Cherokees who are most visible in the historical record succeeded in this transformation. They reacted to the crisis of the late eighteenth and early nineteenth centuries by trying to re-create Cherokees culture and society in ways that accommodated "civilization." As a result, Cherokees laid claim to the title of "most civilized Indian tribe" in America. Although they comprised a minority, the Cherokees who enthusiastically embraced "civilization" dominated Cherokee economic and political life as well as Cherokee history. Not surprisingly, men—particularly wealthy and powerful men—play the lead roles in this history. The documents recording their actions and beliefs usually mentioned women only incidentally. Whereas the history of these men forms a compelling narrative of Cherokee "civilization," ferreting out the experiences of women and using them to create and alternative narrative forces reconsideration of Cherokee culture change, even in a period when it seemed so dramatic.

An Indian policy developed in Washington faced an uncertain future among the people for whom it was designed. The Cherokees, like most other Native people, did not reject the civilization program, nor did they embrace it whole-heartedly. They simply adopted those aspects of the policy that seemed to address their particular set of problems. The result was not always what policy makers had intended. The Cherokees accepted many of the technological innovations offered by government agents, and Cherokee homesteads began to resemble those that dotted the rural landscape of the United States. Where gender was concerned, however, the transformation proved far less successful. Male hunters and female farmers were anathema to "civilization," and since hunting was no longer a viable enterprise, "civilizers" expected men to replace women as farm-ers. These expectations, however, failed to take into account the durability of gender conventions and the adaptability of Cherokee culture.

Benjamin Hawkins, who resided permanently with the Creeks, was also re-sponsible for implementing the civilization program among the Cherokees. When he visited the Cherokees in the fall of 1796, the men were absent, and so Hawkins spent his time primarily with women. One of his hostesses, a Mrs. Gagg, invited a group of women over to meet him: "They informed me that the men were all in the woods hunting, that they alone were at home to receive me, that they rejoiced much at what they had heard and hoped it would prove true, that they had made some cotton, and would make more and follow the instruc-tion of the agent and the advise of the President." Because "civilization" rested on agriculture and domestic manufactures, tasks women traditionally performed, the women believed that the civilization program validated what they did and promised to help them do their work more successfully on their homesteads.

Women's level of production became apparent to Hawkins when he visited women in the town of Etowah: "They informed me they performed most of the labour, the men assisted but little and that in the corn. They generally made a plenty of corn and sweet potatoes and pumpkins. They made beans, ground peas, cymblins, gourds, watermelons, collards and onions." Furthermore, these women kept live stock. One group of women told Hawkins that they raised "hogs, some cattle, and a great many poultry," and he encountered other women driving cattle to market. Women also had primary responsibility for domestic manufactures. They told Hawkins that "they made sugar, had raised some cotton, and manufactured their baskets, sifters, pots and earthen pans." Again and again they indicated to him their support for "the plan contemplated by the government for the bettering of the condition of the Red people," because they understood the concrete ways in which support for agriculture, animal husbandry, and domestic manufactures could improve their lives.

Women envisioned "civilization" bringing improvement, not profound change. The matters Hawkins discussed with them were perfectly comprehensible because farming, tending livestock, and making utilitarian items had long been part of their world. In some ways, surprisingly little had changed during the preceding century: they continued to farm as their ancestors had for centuries. Metal hoes made the job easier, but the work remained the same. Agricultural production had expanded to include a number of crops introduced by Europeans and Africans. These included watermelons, onions, collards, fruit trees, and even a little cotton. But farming remained women's work....

The prosperous farms and industrious work habits …, according to "civili-zers," represented the Cherokees' hope for the future, while hunting deer and trading skins reflected the past. Hawkins described the poverty reliance on hunt-ing had brought: "Their men hunted in their proper season and aided them with the skins in providing cloaths and blankets, such as I saw, but this was not suffi-cient to make them comfortable and the poor old men, women and children were under the necessity of sleeping as I saw them in their town house." Never-theless, many men persisted in their hunting economy. When agent Return J. Meigs arrived in 1801, he had to settle a hunting party's claim for 123 deerskins, 40 bearskins, 5 small furs, and a buffalo skin that its eight members had left in the hunting grounds the previous year when a group of whites threatened them. Like Hawkins, Meigs discovered that by November the chiefs had "gone to their hunting grounds & will not return for two or three months." Yet hunting days were numbered. By 1808 losses from hunting camps were more likely to be half a bear and some deermeat than a substantial pile of skins. Hunting, however, was one of the things that defined masculinity, and few Cherokee men were willing to forgo it. When a twenty-four-year-old man applied for admissions to the school at Brainerd, he requested permission to hunt to clothe himself: he received instead a job on the farm.

The persistence of hunting and the Cherokee's attachment to hunting grounds troubled "civilizers." Thomas Jefferson instructed Hawkins in 1803 "to promote among the Indians a sense of the superior value of a little land, well cultivated, over a great deal, unimproved." Eventually, he hoped, their hunting grounds "will be found useless, and even disadvantageous." When Cherokee men's devotion to the chase momentarily thwarted Meigs's attempt to secure a cession of the Cumber-land Mountain region in 1805, he complained: "That land is of no use to them. There is not a single family on it, & the hunting is very poor. Yet those of idle dis-positions spend much time in rambling there & often return with a stolen horse which they have afterwards to pay for. In fact it is only a nursery of savage habits and operates against civilization which is much impeded by their holding such immense tracts of wilderness." Meigs summarized the civilizer's major concerns. First of all, hunting promoted idleness rather than the industriousness on which civilization was based. Second, the common ground encouraged a disregard for private property. And finally, "wilderness" stood in direct opposition to "civilized" towns, pastures and fields. Meigs, Hawkins, Jefferson, and other "civilizers" linked the cession of hunting grounds with the civilizing process. Herdsmen and farmers presumably no longer needed vast forests, and so the United States looked forward to the acquisition of the Indians' "surplus & waste lands."

The hunting grounds were not the only target. When the United States acquired Louisiana in 1803, Jefferson suggested that the land be used to resettle Native peoples from east of the Mississippi. Meigs actively promoted the exchange of the Cherokee homeland for a new country in the west, but most Cherokees opposed the measure. In order to achieve an exchange, the United States had to alter Cherokees' conception of the land. "The Mother Earth has been divided," the Cherokee council asserted in 1801, "one part [to the] whites and the other is [to] the red people where the present have been rais[d] from their infancy to the years of manhood." For them, their country was more than a commodity to be bought and sold.

Land was not a part of the Cherokees' nascent market economy. They held land in common, and any Cherokee could use unoccupied land as long as it did not infringe on the rights of neighbors. The common ownership of realty enabled the Cherokees to invest in other forms of property, including improvements to realty such as fences and houses, which they did sell to one another. But no Cherokee sold improvements on their part of "Mother Earth" to those on the other part: they strictly curtailed property rights in realty. Ultimately, Hawkins believed "the acquirement of individual property by agricultural improvements, by raising stock, and by domestic manufactures ... will prepare them to accommodate their white neighbors with lands on reasonable terms." That is, individual ownership of other kinds of property not only "civilized" Indians, but it eventually made them more receptive to the notion that land—like deerskins, fabric, or livestock—was a commodity to be sold. The linkage between land cessions and "civilization" became increasingly apparent as Cherokees committed themselves to the program.

Most Cherokee men, long familiar with the machinations of Euro-Americans, viewed "civilization" with suspicion from the very start. One Cherokee man revealed to John Norton that upon hearing the president's plan, "many of us thought it was only some refined scheme calculated to gain an influence over us, rather than ameliorate our situation; and slighted his advice and proposals." The fact that the president of the United States, who normally sent messages about war and trade, now wanted to talk about farming was enough to make the most gullible Cherokee man suspicious. Consequently, Cherokee men at first chose to ignore the civilization program. As a result, men suffered by comparison to women. John McDonald, an intermarried white man, told Norton that "the females have however made much greater advances in industry than the males, they now manufacture a great quantity of cloth; but the latter have not made proportionate progress in Agriculture." The men's initial lack of enthusiasm and relative failure may well have derived from their assumption that because farming was women's work, "civilization" had little to do with them. For the civilization program to succeed among men, they had to adapt it to Cherokee culture....

Men found ways to contribute to agricultural productivity and compensate for the women's labor lost to spinning and weaving without actually farming themselves. In the first decade of the nineteenth century, many of them began to lease or rent land to white families on shares. The council had grave misgivings about the practice since it brought large numbers of white people into the Nation, and expelling them at the end of the year was difficult. In 1808 the council considered banning the practice, but Agent Meigs protested: "I wish you to weigh this matter well before you act because I think you will find that you will again want the help of poor [white] people to raise corn & do other work for you & in a year or two you will do it. All People that ever I know hire poor people to work for them. Some families dont want to hire because they have help enough of their own; but other families have not hands of their

own & they ought not to be deprived of having help when they can find it."
Meigs clearly saw sharecropping as a way for Cherokees to increase agricultural
productivity, but by 1811 he had changed his mind. Instead, sharecropping was a
way for Cherokee men to avoid work: "They have no need for white men as
croppers because it encourages idleness in Indians." As concern over intruders
grew, the practice of cropping declined.

Cherokees found another form of labor in African slaves. Traders had
brought their own slaves into the Cherokee country in the eighteenth century,
and Cherokee warriors had participated in a frontier slave trade. Like horse stealing, the theft of slaves presented men with an opportunity to remain warriors,
and so an illicit traffic in slaves continued well into the nineteenth century. By
the early nineteenth century, however, Cherokees also were acquiring slaves for
their own use. The transition to slave labor, like that to livestock herding, seems
to have been one in which Cherokees invested little thought. When Young
Wolf wrote his will in 1814, he explained how he managed to accumulate his
estate: "From herding my brother's cattle I recevd one calf which I took my start
from, except my own industry, & with cow & calf which I sold, I bought two
sows & thirteen piggs sometime after I was able to purchase three mares & the
increase of them since is amounted to thirty more or less & from that start I
gathered money enough to purchase a negro woman named Tabb, also a negro
man named Ceasar." By 1809 slaves in the Cherokee Nation numbered 583.
Although some of these probably belonged to whites employed by or married
to Cherokees, most belonged to Indians. According to a census taken in 1825,
the number had increased to 1,277, and by 1835 it had reached nearly 1,600.
Instead of becoming the yeoman farmers so admired by Washington and Jefferson,
most Cherokee men (like Washington and Jefferson) seemed more inclined to
adopt the aristocratic planter as a role model. Only a very few ever achieved this
goal, but those who did dominated Cherokee economic and political life.

The introduction of slave labor into the economy had a profound effect
on Cherokee women and men. Cherokees were in the process of acquiring
the racial attitudes of white southerners, and the use of this subject race in agriculture demeaned the traditional labor of women. The fact that slaves cultivated
the fields of upper-class Cherokees made all Cherokee men less likely to embrace
farming since one risked ignominy by agricultural labor. The use of slaves
in farming also challenged women's view of themselves. If growing corn contributed to the gender identity of women, what happened when black men
joined or replaced them in the fields? Gradually they saw their traditional role
as women compromised....

On the surface, the civilization program seems to have reversed the eighteenth-
century trend that concentrated economic power in the hands of men at the
expense of women. Nineteenth-century observers agreed that men lagged behind
women in adapting to the new economic order. But a market economy underlay
the civilization program as surely as it had the deerskin trade. The Cherokees were
never going to be able to create the agrarian republic of yeomen farmers envisioned,
but not practiced, by Jeffersonians. The economic expansion of the United States

drew the Cherokees into a maelstrom from which they could not have escaped even had they been so inclined. As it was, the Cherokees had long ago adapted their political and economic institutions to the demands of an international market. The vast majority of Cherokee men and women had little desire to withdraw....

... [N]ot all Cherokees shared equally in the spoils of economic expansion. In 1809 Meigs wrote to the secretary of war. "A spirit of industry does by no means pervade the general population. The greatest number are extremely poor from want of industry. The hunting life is here at an end: but a predilection for the hunter state pervades a great part of the Cherokees." These Cherokees, he believed, should move west of the Mississippi. Meigs defined "want of industry" as the refusal of "the men to labour in the Fields with their own hands." But even wealthy Cherokee men did not "labour." They merely had the capital, inherited from white fathers or acquired through trade, horse stealing, or official position, to invest in other kinds of labor. As town chiefs and members of the National Council, prominent men had the power to award themselves contracts and permits or to receive gifts, bribes, and private reservations from the federal government. These men adroitly used their capital and political positions to increase wealth and the symbol of success, individual property.

The statistical table Agent Meigs sent to the secretary of war in 1809 indicated a remarkable change in Cherokee material culture. "The Cherokees," he asserted, "[have] prospered by the pastoral life and by domestic manufactures." Livestock abounded and spinning wheels whirred throughout the Nation. In more fundamental ways, however, Cherokee lives remained remarkably untouched: the Cherokees had adapted "civilization" to their own expectations of men and women. Cherokee women used the civilization program to embellish their culture, but they did not transform it. Certainly, women added new crops, cotton in particular, and new skills such as spinning and weaving, but they continued to farm, keep house, and tend children just as they always had done. Similarly, men's culture retained the basic ethic of eighteenth-century hunting and warring. Aggression and competition, however, found expression in the rapidly expanding market economy. The deerskin trade had educated men far more than women in European economic practices and values, and the industrial and market revolutions and the civilization program made that knowledge increasingly valuable. Unlike the deerskin trade of the eighteenth century, the emerging "civilized" economy generated substantial Native wealth, considerable internal inequality, and a host of problems that the Cherokees had never before had to confront. As the first decade of the nineteenth century drew to a close, Cherokees had to resolve complex issues involving the individual ownership, state protection, legitimate enhancement, and just inheritance of property. Men and women shared many of the same concerns about both real and chattel property, but their property interests were rooted in different gender conventions: individual property reflected male culture while common ownership of realty formed the basis of women's culture. The Cherokees' attempt to reconcile the corporate ethic of farmers and the competitive ethic of entrepreneurs gave rise to the Cherokee republic.

FURTHER READING

Stephen E. Ambrose, *Undaunted Courage: Meriwether Lewis, Thomas Jefferson, and the Opening of the American West* (1997).

Stephen Aron, *How the West Was Lost: The Transformation of Kentucky from Daniel Boone to Henry Clay* (1996).

Gregory Evans Dowd, *War under Heaven: Pontiac, the Indian Nations, and the British Empire* (2002).

John Mack Faragher, *Daniel Boone: The Life and Legend of an American Pioneer* (1992).

Michael D. Green, *The Politics of Indian Removal* (1982).

Daniel G. Lang, *Foreign Policy in the Early Republic: The Law of Nations and the Balance of Power* (1985).

Matthew Mason, *Slavery and Politics in the Early American Republic* (2006).

Ernest May, *The Making of the Monroe Doctrine* (1975).

Gretchen Murphy and Donald E. Pease, *Hemispheric Imaginations: The Monroe Doctrine and Narratives of U.S. Empire* (2006).

Peter S. Onuf, *Jefferson's Empire: The Language of American Nationhood* (2000).

Greg Russell, *John Quincy Adams and the Public Virtues of Diplomacy* (1995).

J. C. A. Stagg, *Mr. Madison's War: Politics, Diplomacy and Warfare in the Early Republic* (1983).

John Sugden, *Tecumseh: A Life* (1997).

CHAPTER 8

The Transportation, Market, and Communication Revolutions of the Early Nineteenth Century

The early nineteenth century witnessed vast changes in American society that irrevocably altered the lives of most Americans. These changes were nurtured by specific efforts of leaders in government and business. In the years following the War of 1812, a group of American statesmen envisioned a national economic policy that would foster economic development. Known as the "American System," this plan called for a national bank, protective tariffs, and improved transportation and communication. The American System would not be enacted in its entirety, but beginning with the Wilderness Road in 1795, some 4,000 miles of turnpikes were constructed by 1821. Roads were complemented by the construction of canals. Most remarkable was the Erie Canal completed in 1825 that linked New York City to the American interior. In the next fifteen years, the Erie Canal was supplemented by some 3,300 miles of canals that crisscrossed the nation. When steam power was harnessed, steamboats and railroads were built to ply goods on rivers and rails. Information traveled wider and faster too. In 1780, the United States had about thirty newspapers. By 1820, that number had ballooned to more than five hundred. Then with the patenting of the electric telegraph in the 1840s, information could travel faster than ships, wagons, or horseback. In less than twenty years, telegraph lines connected not only much of the United States, but also the nation to Europe. Taken together, these changes amounted to what historians call a "transportation revolution" and a "communication revolution" wherein the costs of the transport of bulky goods fell 95 percent between 1825 and 1855, the speed of transport increased fivefold, and information could be relayed instantly and widely.

Technological changes and altered business practices proceeded apace as well. By 1850, some one thousand patents were issued by the U.S. Patent Office to inventors. And the corporation became an increasingly powerful business practice that pooled capital and distributed profits. The Supreme Court facilitated these practices when it issued a series of decisions that aided business and fostered economic development. Contracts, the Court held, were secure from the meddling of state and local officials and Congress was supreme in dealing with interstate commerce.

These changes laid the foundation for a market revolution that irreversibly altered the daily activities of people and changed the economic landscape of the nation. Before improvements in transportation and communication, people had produced much of what they ate and wore at home or in their local communities. As late as 1820, no more than one-quarter of the harvests on American farms were exported from the local community. As the market revolution progressed, people now increasingly produced commodities for sale and used the income they earned to purchase goods produced by others. Most notably, the production of cotton in the South exploded. In 1820, for example, not only had the output of cotton become over one hundred times greater than it had been thirty years before, but it now accounted from over one-half of all agricultural exports from the United States. Because regions of the nation—such as the South—possessed certain natural advantages, a national market economy developed. People in the South specialized in producing crops for export; those in the Northwest produced food to feed people in the East and the South who were specializing in export agriculture, commerce, or manufacturing.

These changes wrought opportunities and challenges alike for Americans living in the North and the South, and working in the factory and on the farm. It is true that people increasingly lived and worked in the city. In 1820, only 6 percent lived in towns of more than 2,500 people. By 1860, the figure was 20 percent. And whereas over 80 percent of Americans labored on plantations and farms in 1800, the proportion had dropped to 50 percent by 1860. Whether they toiled in the city or in rural locales, however, the cadence of their work, the use of their produce, and the structure of their families and communities were forever changed.

QUESTIONS TO THINK ABOUT

In what ways did the transportation, communication, and market revolutions change the everyday lives of Americans? Were there winners and losers in the outcome of the market revolution? On balance, was it a beneficial development? Were the South and the North on opposite ends of this development or connected? Do you think a "national market economy," in which regions of the nation specialized in certain goods for trade with other regions, would link the nation together or pull it apart?

DOCUMENTS

This set of documents illustrates efforts by Americans to facilitate a market revolution and the impact of the revolution itself on the ways in which people lived their lives. Document 1 is an early account of the forced migration of slaves from eastern states to the regions of burgeoning cotton production in the South. Document 2 is comprised of two selections from the nationalist decisions of Chief Justice John Marshall. In *McCulloch vs. Maryland* (1819), which considered whether the state of

Maryland could tax the national bank, he held both that Congress had more powers than specifically given in the Constitution and that federal laws were superior to state laws. And in *Gibbons vs. Ogden* (1824), Marshall decided that states could not grant monopolies to businesses that cross state lines. These rulings fostered economic development and national centralization. In document 3, President John Quincy Adams, in his first annual message to Congress in 1825, urged a group of internal improvement projects including exploring the West and fostering scientific research. Document 4 illustrates the struggles of a farm family in marketing their crops on the Illinois frontier. Document 5 is a memoir written by Harriet Hanson Robinson, a woman who toiled in the textile mills in Lowell, Massachusetts, in the early 1830s. Despite assurances from the mill owners that the mills were safe and respectable, Robinson focuses instead on the harsh conditions and labor unrest. In document 6, Alexis de Tocqueville in 1831 observes what he calls the "influence of democracy" on the family amid the market revolution. In document 7, Charles Dickens, the prominent English author, provides a vivid description of the frenzy of riding on a train in the early days of railroad travel. Document 8 depicts the growing significance of the mother as the center of the middle-class family, a family in which the significance of the mother in instructing her children is highlighted. Slaveholder and South Carolina Governor James Henry Hammond, in document 9, instructs his overseer how to run the cotton plantation as a thriving business.

1. Slave Charles Ball Mourns the Growth of Cotton Culture and "Sale Down the River," c. 1800

After we were all chained and handcuffed together, we sat down upon the ground; and here reflecting upon the sad reverse of fortune that had so suddenly overtaken me, I became weary of life, and bitterly execrated the day I was born. It seemed that I was destined by fate to drink the cup of sorrow to the very dregs, and that I should find no respite from misery but in the grave. I longed to die, and escape from the hands of my tormentors; but even the wretched privilege of destroying myself was denied me, for I could not shake off my chains, nor move a yard without the consent of my master....

Our master ordered a pot of mush to be made for our supper; after despatching which we all lay down on the naked floor to sleep in our handcuffs and chains. The women, my fellow-slaves, lay on one side of the room; and the men who were chained with me, occupied the other. I slept but little this night, which I passed in thinking of my wife and little children, whom I could not hope ever to see again. I also thought of my grandfather, and of the long nights I had passed with him, listening to his narratives of the scenes through which he had passed in Africa. I at length fell asleep, but we distressed by painful dreams....

Charles Ball, *Fifty Years in Chains: Or the Life of an American Slave* (New York: Dayton, and Indianapolis, Ind.: Asher and Company, 1860), 30–31, 33–35.

We left this place early in the morning, and directed our course toward the south-west; our master riding beside us, and hastening our march, sometimes by words of encouragement, and sometimes by threats of punishment. The women took their place in the rear of our line. We halted about nine o'clock for breakfast, and received as much corn-bread as we could eat, together with a plate of boiled herrings, and about three pounds of pork amongst us. Before we left this place, I was removed from near the middle of the chain, and placed at the front end of it; so that I now became the leader of the file, and held this post of honor until our irons were taken from us, near the town of Columbia in South Carolina....

We continued our course up the country westward for a few days and then turned South, crossed James river above Richmond, as I heard at the time. After more than four weeks of travel we entered South Carolina near Camden, and for the first time I saw a field of cotton in bloom.

As we approached the Yadkin river the tobacco disappeared from the fields and the cotton plant took its place as an article of general culture.

I was now a slave in South Carolina, and had no hope of ever again seeing my wife and children. I had at times serious thoughts of suicide so great was my anguish. If I could have got a rope I should have hanged myself at Lancaster. The thought of my wife and children I had been torn from in Maryland, and the dreadful undefined future which was before me, came near driving me mad.

2. Chief Justice John Marshall Advances a Broad Construction of the Constitution, 1819, 1824

McCulloch v. Maryland

The government of the Union, then (whatever may be the influence of this fact on the case), is, emphatically and truly, a government of the people. In form, and in substance, it emanates from them. Its powers are granted by them, and are to be exercised directly on them, and for their benefit....

If any one proposition could command the universal assent of mankind, we might expect it would be this—that the government of the Union, though limited in its powers, is supreme within its sphere of action. This would seem to result, necessarily from its nature. It is the government of all; its powers are delegated by all; it represents all, and acts for all. Though any one state may be willing to control its operations, no state is willing to allow others to control them. The nation, on those subjects on which it can act, must necessarily bind its component parts. But this question is not left to mere reason: the people have, in express terms, decided it ... "this constitution, and the laws of the United States, which shall be made in pursuance thereof, shall be the supreme law of the land," and by requiring that the members of the state legislatures, and the officers of the executive and judicial departments of the states, shall take the oath of fidelity to it.

John Marshall, opinion in *McCulloch v. Maryland* (1819), in *United States Supreme Court Reporters*, XVII, p. 316.

John Marshall, opinion in *Gibbons v. Ogden*, 22 U.S. I (1824).

The government of the United States, then, though limited in its powers, is supreme; and its laws, when made in pursuance of the constitution, form the supreme law of the land, "anything in the constitution or laws of any state to the contrary notwithstanding."

Gibbons v. Ogden

What do gentlemen mean by a "strict construction"? If they contend only against that enlarged construction, which would extend words beyond their natural and obvious import, we might question the application of the term, but should not controvert the principle. If they contend for that narrow construction which, in support or some theory not be found in the Constitution, would deny to the government those powers which the words of the grant, as usually understood, import, and which are consistent with the general views and objects of the instrument; for that narrow construction which would cripple the government and render it unequal to the object for which it is declared to be instituted, and to which the powers given, as fairly understood, render it competent; then we cannot perceive the propriety of this strict construction, nor adopt it as the rule by which the Constitution is to be expounded. As men whose intentions require no concealment generally employ the words which most directly and aptly express the ideas they intend to convey, the enlightened patriots who framed our Constitution, and the people who adopted it, must be understood to have employed words in their natural sense, and to have intended what they have said. If, from the imperfection of human language, there should be serious doubts respecting the extent of any given power, it is a well settled rule that the objects for which it was given, especially when those objects are expressed in the instrument itself, should have great influence in the construction. We know of no reason for excluding this rule from the present case. The grant does not convey power which might be beneficial to the grantor if retained by himself, or which can enure solely to the benefit of the grantee, but is an investment of power for the general advantage, in the hands of agents selected for that purpose, which power can never be exercised by the people themselves, but must be placed in the hands of agents or lie dormant. We know of no rule for construing the extent of such powers other than is given by the language of the instrument which confers them, taken in connexion with the purposes for which they were conferred....

What Is This Power?

It is the power to regulate, that is, to prescribe the rule by which commerce is to be governed. This power, like all others vested in Congress, is complete in itself, may be exercised to its utmost extent, and acknowledges no limitations other than are prescribed in the Constitution. These are expressed in plain terms, and do not affect the questions which arise in this case, or which have been discussed at the bar. If, as has always been understood, the sovereignty of Congress, though limited to specified objects, is plenary as to those objects, the power over commerce with foreign nations, and among the several States, is vested in Congress as absolutely as it would be in a single government, having in its Constitution the same restrictions on the exercise of the power as are found in the Constitution of the United States. The wisdom and the discretion of Congress, their identity with the people, and the influence which their constituents possess at elections are, in this, as in many other instances, as that, for example, of declaring war, the sole restraints on which they have relied, to secure them from its abuse. They are the restraints on which the people must often rely solely, in all representative governments.

The power of Congress, then, comprehends navigation, within the limits of every State in the Union, so far as that navigation may be in any manner connected with "commerce with foreign nations, or among the several States, or with the Indians tribes." It may, of consequence, pass the jurisdictional line of New York and act upon the very waters to which the prohibition now under consideration applies.

3. President John Quincy Adams Urges Internal Improvements, 1825

In assuming her station among the civilized nations of the earth it would seem that our country had contracted the engagement to contribute her share of mind, of labor, and of expense to the improvement of those and of expense to the improvement of those parts of knowledge which lie beyond the reach of individual acquisition, and particularly to geographical and astronomical science. Looking back to the history only of the half century since the declaration of our independence, and observing the generous emulation with which the Governments of France, Great Britain, and Russia have devoted the genius, the intelligence, the treasures of their respective nations to the common improvement of the species in these branches of science, is it not incumbent upon us to inquire whether we are not bound by obligations of a high and honorable character to contribute our portion of energy and exertion to the common stock? The voyages of discovery prosecuted in the course of that time at the expense of those nations have not only redounded to their glory, but to the improvement of human knowledge. We have been partakers of that improvement and owe for it a sacred debt, not only of gratitude, but of equal or proportional exertion in the same common cause....

In inviting the attention of Congress to the subject of internal improvements upon a view thus enlarged it is not my design to recommend the equipment of an expedition for circumnavigating the globe for purposes of scientific research and inquiry. We have objects of useful investigation nearer home, and to which our cares may be more beneficially applied. The interior of our own territories has been imperfectly explored. Our coasts along many degrees of latitude upon the shores of the Pacific ocean, though much frequented by our spirited commercial navigators, have been barely visited by our public ships. The River of the West,

John Quincy Adams, *Annual Message to Congress* (1825), in *The Selected Writings of John and John Quincy Adams*, ed. Adrienne Koch and William Peden (New York: Alfred A. Knopf, 1946), 361–364.

first fully discovered and navigated by a countryman of our own, still bears the name of the ship in which he ascended its waters, and claims the protection of our armed national flag at its mouth. With the establishment of a military post there or at some other point of that coast, recommended by my predecessor and already matured in the deliberations of the last Congress, I would suggest the expediency of connecting the equipment of a public ship for the exploration of the whole northwest coast of this continent.

The establishment of an uniform standard of weights and measures was one of the specific objects contemplated in the formation of our Constitution, and to fix that standard was one of the powers delegated by express terms in that instrument to Congress....

Connected with the establishment of an university, or separate from it, might be undertaken the erection of an astronomical observatory, with provision for the support of an astronomer, to be in constant attendance of observation upon the phenomena of the heavens, and for the periodical publication of his observations....

And while scarcely a year passes over our heads without bringing some new astronomical discovery to light, which we must fain receive at second hand from Europe, are we not cutting ourselves off from the means of returning light for light while we have neither observatory nor observer upon our half of the globe and the earth revolves in perpetual darkness to our unsearching eyes?

4. A Family in Illinois Struggles with Marketing Their Crops, 1831

Having thrashed and winnowed our wheat ..., our next consideration was how we were to sell it. The produce of the three acres might be about eighty bushels, one-fourth of which was but imperfectly cleared of cheat [a troublesome weed that grows in wheat], and was therefore unsaleable. We had only five sacks, ... but these even we did not require, as we subsequently learnt the store-keepers were accustomed to furnish the settlers with bags for their corn. My husband took a specimen of wheat, which as it had been sown too sparingly on the ground was a fine sample. Mr. Varley offered half a dollar per bushel in money, or a few cents more in barter. We borrowed a waggon and a yoke of oxen of one of our neighbours, and carried to the store fifty bushels. The first thing we did was to settle our meal account; we next bought two pairs of shoes for self and husband, which by this time we wanted as we did other articles of apparel, which we knew we could conveniently procure. The truth is, we had intended to have a little more clothing, but finding the prices so extravagant, we felt compelled to abandon that intention. For a yard of common printed calico, they asked half a dollar, or a bushel of wheat, and proportionate prices for other goods. We gave ten bushels of wheat for the shoes.... Our next purchase was a

Rebecca and Edward Burlend, in *A True Picture of Emigration*, ed. Milo Milton Quaife (Secaucus, N.J.: The Citadel Press, 1968), 107–109.

plough, bought in hopes that we should, at some time, have cattle to draw it, as we were tired of the hoeing system. We also bought two tin milk bowls; these and the plough cost about twenty bushels. We obtained further a few pounds of coffee, and a little meal; the coffee cost us at the rate of a dollar for four pounds; and thus we laid out the greater part of our first crop of wheat. We had only reserved about twenty bushels for seed, besides a quantity imperfectly cleared of cheat, which unfit either for sale or making bread. On balancing our account with Mr. Varley, we found we had to take about five dollars, which we received in paper money, specie being exceedingly scarce in Illinois.

5. Harriet Hanson Robinson, a "Lowell Girl," Describes Her Labor in a Textile Mill, 1831

In 1831, under the shadow of a great sorrow, which had made her four children fatherless,—the oldest but seven years of age,—my mother was left to struggle alone; and, although she tried hard to earn bread enough to fill our hungry mouths, she could not do it, even with the help of kind friends....

Shortly after this my mother's widowed sister, Mrs. Angeline Cudworth, who kept a factory boarding-house in Lowell, advised her to come to that city.

I had been to school constantly until I was about ten years of age, when my mother, feeling obliged to have help in her work besides what I could give, and also needing the money which I could earn, allowed me, at my urgent request (for I wanted to earn *money* like the other little girls), to go to work in the mill. I worked first in the spinning-room as a "doffer." The doffers were the very youngest girls, whose work was to doff, or take off, the full bobbins, and replace them with the empty ones....

... When not doffing, we were often allowed to go home, for a time, and thus we were able to help our mothers in their housework. We were paid two dollars a week; and how proud I was when my turn came to stand up on the bobbin-box, and write my name in the paymaster's book, and how indignant I was when he asked me if I could "write." "Of course I can," said I, and he smiled as he looked down on me.

The working-hours of all the girls extended from five o'clock in the morning until seven in the evening, with one-half hour for breakfast and for dinner. Even the doffers were forced to be on duty nearly fourteen hours a day, and this was the greatest hardship in the lives of these children....

I do not recall any particular hardship connected with this life, except getting up so early in the morning, and to this habit, I never was, and never shall be, reconciled, for it has taken nearly a lifetime for me to make up the sleep lost at that early age. But in every other respect it was a pleasant life. We were not hurried any more than was for our good, and no more work was required of us than we were able easily to do.

Harriet Hanson Robinson, *Loom and Spindle or Life Among the Early Mill Girls* (New York: T. Y. Crowell, 1898; reprinted, Press Pacifica, 1976), 16–22, 37–43, 51–53.

Most of us children lived at home, and we were well fed, drinking both tea and coffee, and eating substantial meals (besides luncheons) three times a day. We had very happy hours with the older girls, many of whom treated us like babies, or talked in a motherly way, and so had a good influence over us....

I cannot tell how it happened that some of us knew about the English factory children, who, it was said, were treated so badly, and were even whipped by their cruel overseers....

In contrast with this sad picture, we thought of ourselves as well off, in our cosey corner of the mill, enjoying ourselves in our own way, with our good mothers and our warm suppers awaiting us when the going-out bell should ring.

When I look back into the factory life of fifty or sixty years ago, I do not see what is called "a call" of young men and women going to and from their daily work, like so many ants that cannot be distinguished one from another; I see them as individuals, with personalities of their own. This one has about her the atmosphere of her early home. That one is impelled by a strong and noble purpose. The other,—what she is, has been an influence for good to me and to all womankind.

Yet they were a class of factory operatives, and were spoken of (as the same class is spoken of now) as a set of persons who earned their daily bread, whose condition was fixed, and who must continue to spin and to weave to the end of their natural existence. Nothing but this was expected of them, and they were not supposed to be capable of social or mental improvement....

In 1831 Lowell was little more than a factory village. Several corporations were started, and the cotton-mills belonging to them were building. Help was in great demand; and stories were told all over the country of the new factory town, and the high wages that were offered to all classes of work-people,—stories that reached the ears of mechanics' and farmers' sons, and gave new life to lonely and dependent women in distant towns and farmhouses....

But the early factory girls were not all country girls. There were others also, who had been taught that "work is no disgrace." There were some who came to Lowell solely on account of the social or literary advantages to be found there. They lived in secluded parts of New England, where books were scarce, and there was no cultivated society. They had comfortable homes, and did not perhaps need the *money* they would earn; but they longed to see this new "City of Spindles." ...

It must be remembered that at this date woman had no property rights. A widow could be left without her share of her husband's (or the family) property, a legal "incumbrance" to his estate. A father could make his will without reference to his daughter's share of the inheritance....

The law took no cognizance of woman as a money-spender. She was a ward, an appendage, a relict. Thus it happened, that if a woman did not choose to marry, or, when left a widow, to re-marry, she had no choice but to enter one of the few employments open to her, or to become a burden on the charity of some relative.

In almost every New England home could be found one or more of these women, sometimes welcome, more often unwelcome, and leading joyless, and in many instances unsatisfactory, lives. The cotton-factory was a great opening to these lonely and dependent women. From a condition approaching pauperism they were at once placed above want; they could earn money, and spend it as they pleased; and could gratify their tastes and desires without restraint, and without rendering an account to anybody....

One of the first strikes of cotton-factory operatives that ever took place in this country was that in Lowell, in October, 1836. When it was announced that the wages were to be cut down, great indignation was felt, and it was decided to strike, *en masse*....

One of the girls stood on a pump, and gave vent to the feelings of her companions in a neat speech, declaring that it was their duty to resist all attempts at cutting down the wages. This was the first time a woman had spoken in public in Lowell, and the event caused surprise and consternation among her audience.

Cutting down the wages was not their only grievance, nor the only cause of this strike. Hitherto the corporations had paid twenty-five cents a week towards the board of each operative, and now it was their purpose to have the girls pay the sum; and this, in addition to the cut in wages, would make a difference of at least one dollar a week. It was estimated that as many as twelve or fifteen hundred girls turned out, and walked in procession through the streets....

It is hardly necessary to say that so far as results were concerned this strike did no good. The dissatisfaction of the operatives subsided, or burned itself out, and though the authorities did not accede to their demands, the majority returned to their work, and the corporation went on cutting down the wages.

And after a time, as the wages became more and more reduced, the best portion of the girls left and went to their homes, or to the other employments that were fast opening to women, until there were very few of the old guard left; and thus the *status* of the factory population of New England gradually became what we know it to be to-day.

6. European Visitor Alexis de Tocqueville Considers the Influence of Democracy on the Family, 1831

I have just been considering how among democratic peoples, particularly America, equality modifies the relations between one citizen and another.

I want to carry the argument further and consider what happens within the family. I am not trying to discover new truths, but to show how known facts have a bearing on my subject.

Everyone has noticed that in our time a new relationship has evolved between the different members of a family, that the distance formerly separating father and son has diminished, and that paternal authority, if not abolished, has at least changed form.

Something analogous, but even more striking, occurs in the United States.

Pages 584–5, 587–9 from *Democracy in America* by Alexis de Tocqueville. Edited by J. P. Mayer and Max Lerner. Translated by George Lawrence. English translation copyright © 1965 by Harper & Row, Publishers, Inc. Reprinted by permission of HarperCollins Publishers.

In America the family, if one takes the word in its Roman and aristocratic sense, no longer exists. One only finds scattered traces thereof in the first years following the birth of children. The father then does, without opposition, exercise the domestic dictatorship which his sons' weakness makes necessary and which is justified by both their weakness and his unquestionable superiority.

But as soon as the young American begins to approach man's estate, the reins of filial obedience are daily slackened. Master of his thoughts, he soon becomes responsible for his own behavior. In America there is in truth no adolescence. At the close of boyhood he is a man and begins to trace out his own path.

It would be wrong to suppose that this results from some sort of domestic struggle, in which, by some kind of moral violence, the son had won the freedom which his father refused. The same habits and principles which lead the former to grasp at independence dispose the latter to consider its enjoyment as an incontestable right.

So in the former one sees none of these hateful, disorderly passions which disturb men long after they have shaken off an established yoke. The latter feels none of those bitter, angry regrets which usually accompany fallen power. The father has long anticipated the moment when his authority must come to an end, and when that time does come near, he abdicates without fuss. The son has known in advance exactly when he will be his own master and wins his liberty without haste or effort as a possession which is his due and which no one seeks to snatch from him....

When the state of society turns to democracy and men adopt the general principle that it is good and right to judge everything for oneself, taking former beliefs as providing information but not rules, paternal opinions come to have less power over the sons, just as his legal power is less too.

Perhaps the division of patrimonies which follows from democracy does more than all the rest to alter the relations between father and children.

When the father of a family has little property, his son and he live constantly in the same place and carry on the same work together. Habit and necessity bring them together and force them all the time to communicate with each other. There is bound, then, to be a sort of intimate familiarity between them which makes power less absolute and goes ill with respectful formalities.

Moreover, in democracies those who possess these small fortunes are the very class which gives ideas their force and sets the tone of mores. Both its will and its thoughts prevail everywhere, and even those who are most disposed to disobey its orders end by being carried along by its example. I have known fiery opponents of democracy who allowed their children to call them "thou."

So at the same time as aristocracy loses its power, all that was austere, conventional, and legal in parental power also disappears and a sort of equality reigns around the domestic hearth.

I am not certain, generally speaking, whether society loses by the change, but I am inclined to think that the individual gains. I think that as mores and laws become more democratic the relations between father and sons become more intimate and gentle; there is less of rule and authority, often more of confidence and affection, and it would seem that the natural bond grows tighter as the social link loosens....

Democracy too draws brothers together, but in a different way.

Under democratic laws the children are perfectly equal, and consequently independent; nothing forcibly brings them together, but also nothing drives them apart. Having a common origin, brought up under the same roof, and treated with the same care, as no peculiar privilege distinguishes or divides them, the affectionate and frank intimacy of childhood easily takes root among them....

This gentleness of democratic manners is such that even the partisans of aristocracy are attracted by it, and when they have tasted it for some time, they are not at all tempted to return to the cold and respectful formalities of the aristocratic family. They gladly keep the family habits of democracy provided they can reject its social state and laws....

I think that I may be able to sum up in one phrase the whole sense of this chapter and of several others that preceded it. Democracy loosens social ties, but it tightens natural ones. At the same time as it separates citizens, it brings kindred closer together.

7. Author Charles Dickens Describes Travel on an Early Railroad Train, 1842

Before leaving Boston, I devoted one day to an excursion to Lowell....

I made acquaintance with an American railroad, on this occasion, for the first time. As these works are pretty much alike all through the States, their general characteristics are easily described.

There are no first and second class carriages as with us; but there is a gentlemen's car and a ladies' car: the main distinction between which is that in the first, everybody smokes; and in the second, nobody does. As a black man never travels with a white one, there is also a negro car; which is a great, blundering, clumsy chest, such as Gulliver put to sea in, from the kingdom of Brobdingnag [a land where everything is huge]. There is a great deal of jolting, a great deal of noise, a great deal of wall, not much window, a locomotive engine, a shriek, and a bell.

The cars are like shabby omnibuses, but larger: holding thirty, forty, fifty, people. The seats, instead of stretching from end to end, are places crosswise. Each seat holds two persons. There is a long row of them on each side of the caravan, a narrow passage up the middle, and a door at both ends. In the centre of the carriage there is usually a stove, fed with charcoal or anthracite coal; which is for the most part red-hot. It is insufferably close; and you see the hot air fluttering between yourself and any other object you may happen to look at, like the ghost of smoke....

Except when a branch road joins the main one, there is seldom more than one track of rails; so that the road is very narrow, and the view, where there is a deep cutting, by no means extensive. When there is not, the character of the

Charles Dickens, *American Notes for General Circulation* (New York: Harper & Brothers, 1842; reprinted Harmondsworth, Eng.: Penguin, 1972), 111–113.

scenery is always the same. Mile after mile of stunted trees: some hewn down by the axe, some blown down by the wind, some half fallen and resting on their neighbours, many mere logs half hidden in the swamp, others mouldered away to spongy chips. The very soil of the earth is made up of minute fragments such as these; each pool of stagnant water has its crust of vegetable rottenness; on every side there are the boughs, and trunks, and stumps of trees, in every possible stage of decay, decomposition, and neglect. Now you emerge for a few brief minutes on an open country, glittering with some bright lake or pool, broad as many as English river, but so small here that it scarcely has a name; now catch hasty glimpses of a distant town, with its clean white houses and their cool piazzas, its prim New England church and schoolhouse; when whir-r-r-r! almost before you have seen them, comes the same dark screen: the stunted trees, the stumps, the logs, the stagnant water—all so like the last that you seem to have been transported back again by magic.

The train calls at stations in the woods, where the wild impossibility of anybody having the smallest reason to get out, is only to be equalled by the apparently desperate hopelessness of there being anybody to get in. It rushes across the turnpike road, where there is not gate, no policeman, no signal: nothing but a rough wooden arch, on which is paint "WHEN THE BELL RINGS, LOOK OUT FOR THE LOCOMOTIVE." On it whirls headlong, dives through the woods again, emerges in the light, clatters over frail arches, rumbles upon the heavy ground, shoots beneath a wooden bridge which intercepts the light for a second like a wink, suddenly awakens all the slumbering echoes in the main street of a large town, and dashes on haphazard, pell-mell, neck-or-nothing, down the middle of the road. There—with mechanics working at their trades, and people leaning from their doors and windows, and boys flying kites and playing marbles, and men smoking, and women talking, and children crawling, and pigs burrowing, and unaccustomed horses plunging and rearing, close to the very rails—there—on, on, on—tears the mad dragon of an engine with its train of cars; scattering in all directions a shower of burning sparks from its wood fire; screeching, hissing, yelling, panting; until at last the thirsty monster stops beneath a covered way to drink, the people cluster round, and you have time to breathe again.

8. A Guidebook Instructs Women on the Role of Mother, 1845

It takes a long time for the world to grow wise. Men have been busying themselves these six thousand years nearly to improve society. They have framed systems of philosophy and government, and conferred on their own sex all the advantages which power, wealth and knowledge could bestow. They have founded colleges and institutions of learning without number, and provided themselves teachers of every art and science; and, after all, the mass of mankind are very ignorant and very wicked. Wherefore is this? Because the *mother,* whom God constituted the first teacher of every human being, has been degraded by

"Maternal Instruction," *Godey's Lady's Book* (1845).

men from her high office; or, what is the same thing, been denied those privileges of education which only can enable her to discharge her duty to her children with discretion and effect. God created the woman as a *help-meet* for man in every situation; and while he, in his pride, rejects her assistance in his intellectual and moral career, he never will succeed to improve his nature and reach that perfection in knowledge, virtue and happiness, which his faculties are constituted to attain.

If half the effort and expense had been directed to enlighten and improve the minds of females which have been lavished on the other sex, we should now have a very different state of society. Wherever a woman is found excelling in judgment and knowledge, either by natural genius or from better opportunities, do we not see her children also excel? Search the records of history, and see if it can be found that a great and wise man ever descended from a weak and foolish mother. So sure and apparent is this maternal influence, that it has passed into an axiom of philosophy, it is acknowledged by the greatest and wisest of men; and yet, strange to say, the inference which ought to follow, namely, that in attempting to improve society, the first, most careful and continued efforts should be to raise the standard of female education, and qualify woman to become the educator of her children, has never yet been acted upon by any legislators, or acknowledged and tested by any philanthropists.

What is true of the maternal influence respecting sons is, perhaps, more important in the training of daughters. The fashionable schools are a poor substitute for such example and instruction as a thoroughly educated and right principled mother would bestow on her daughters. The best schools in the world will not, in and of themselves, make fine women. The tone of *family education* and of society needs to be raised. This can never be done till greater value is set on the cultivated female intellect. Young ladies must be inspired with high moral principles, noble aims, and a spirit of self-improvement to become what they ought to be. Maternal instruction is the purest and safest means of opening the fountain of knowledge to the young mind.

9. South Carolina Governor James Henry Hammond Instructs His Overseer on Running the Plantation, c. 1840s

Crop

1 A good crop means one that is good taking into consideration every thing—negroes, land, mules, stock, fences, ditches, farming utensils, &c., &c., all of which must be kept up & improved in value. The effort therefore must not be merely to make *so many* cotton bales or such an amount of other produce, but as much as can be made without interrupting the steady increase in value of the rest of the property.

"Governor Hammond's Instructions to His Overseer," in Willie Lee Rose, ed., *A Documentary History of Slavery in North America* (1976), 345–353. Copyright © 1976 by Oxford University Press, Inc.

Remarks.—There should be an increase in number, & improvement in condition & value of negroes; abundant provisions of all sorts for every thing, made on the place, carefully saved & properly housed; an improvement in the productive qualities of the land, & general condition of the plantation; mules, stock, fences & farming utensils in fine order at the close of the year; as much produce as could possibly be made under these circumstances, ready for market in good season, & of prime quality.

Overseer

... 5 The Overseer must see that all the negroes leave their houses promptly after hornblow in the morning. Once, or more a week he must visit every house after horn blow at night to see that all are in....

Remarks.—The Overseer must show no favoritism among negroes....

10 The Overseer must keep the plantation Diary regularly & carefully, note the number of hands engaged each day in various operations under proper heading, the number of sick, weather, allowances & implements given out, articles received at or sent from the plantation, births, deaths & whatever other information or remarks which may be valuable, together with an accurate summary of every thing on the plantation once a month. He must also inform the Employer, without being asked, of every thing going on that may concern or interest him.

11 The negroes must be made to obey & to work, which may be done by an Overseer, who attends regularly to his business, with very little whipping. Much whipping indicates a bad tempered, or inattentive manager, & will not be allowed. The Overseer must never on any occasion—unless in self defence—kick a negro, or strike with his hand, or a stick, or the butt-end of his whip. No unusual punishment must be resorted to without the Employer's consent....

Hours

19 The first morning horn is blown an hour before day-light. All work-hands are required to rise & prepare their cooking, &c. for the day. The second horn is blown just at good day-light, when it is the duty of the driver to visit every house & see that all have left for the field. The plow hands leave their houses for the stables, at the summons of the plow driver, 15 minutes earlier than the gang, the Overseer opening the stable doors to them. at 11½ M, the plow hands repair to the nearest weather house. At 12 M, the gang stop to eat dinner. At 1 P.M. through the greater part of the year, all hands return to work. In summer the intermission increases with the heat to the extent of 3½ hours. At 15 minutes before sun-set the plowhands, & at sun-set the rest, knock off work for the day. No work must ever be required after dark....

Town

24 Each work-hand is allowed to go to Town once a year (the women always selecting some of the men to go for them) on a Sunday, between crop gathering &

Christmas. Not more than 10 shall be allowed to go the same day. The head driver may have a cart some Saturday after Christmas that it is convenient for him to go to Town.

This rule is objectionable & must be altered.

Negro Patches

Adjoining each negro house is a piece of ground convenient for a fowl-yard & garden. No fowl-yard or garden fence shall reach nearer than 60 feet to the negro houses. Negroes may have patches in various parts of the plantation (always getting permission from the master) to cultivate crops of their own. A field of suitable size shall be planted in pindars [peanuts], & cultivated in the same manner as the general crop, the produce of which is to be divided equally among the work-hands. Negroes are not allowed to grow crops of corn or cotton for themselves, nor to have any cattle or stock of any kind of their own.

ESSAYS

The market revolution in many ways modified patterns of everyday life in the United States. In these two essays, we observe the transformation of several important aspects of life. Nancy F. Cott of Yale University focuses on the profound adjustments within the rural family—with particular reference to the modification in the roles of women—that resulted from a burgeoning market economy. Not only did patterns of labor change, but the meaning of work and the responsibilities within the home were transformed as well. Daniel Walker Howe, also of Yale University, examines the role of cotton, transportation, and communication in creating these economic changes. Although the market revolution is typically seen originating in northern cities, Howe demonstrates the critical role of slavery and southern agrarian life in transforming America. Moreover, he suggests that changes to infrastructure and communication technology were more important than changes in labor practices and business. Although both Cott and Howe find dramatic changes occurring in the United States, they disagree about the primary locations of those changes and what altered most.

The Market Revolution and the Changes in Women's Work

NANCY F. COTT

"A woman's work is never done," Martha Moore Ballard wrote in her journal one November midnight in 1795, having been busy preparing wool for spinning until that time, "and happy she whos[e] strength holds out to the end of the [sun's] rays." Ballard was sixty years old that year—a grandmother several times

Nancy F. Cott, *The Bonds of Womanhood: "Woman's Sphere" in New England, 1780–1835*, 2nd ed. (New Haven: Yale University Press, 1977, 1997). Copyright © 1977, 1997. Reprinted by permission of Yale University Press.

over—though she still had at home her youngest child of sixteen. Housekeeper and domestic manufacturer for a working farm where she baked and brewed, pickled and preserved, spun and sewed, made soap and dipped candles, she also was a trusted healer and midwife for the pioneer community of Augusta, Maine. During a quarter-century of practice continuing past her seventieth year, she delivered more than a thousand babies. The very processes of her work engaged her in community social life. In her medical work she became acquainted with her neighbors as she provided services for them, and domestic crafts, such as quilting and spinning, also involved her in both cooperative and remunerative social relationships. The pattern of her life was not atypical for the matron of a farm household, particularly in a frontier community, in the late eighteenth century....

The basic developments hastening economic productivity and rationalizing economic organization in New England between 1780 and 1835 were extension of the size of the market, increases in agriculture efficiency, reduction in transportation costs, and consequent specialization of economic function, division of labor, and concentration of industry. In late eighteenth-century towns, subsistence farming and household production for family use prevailed, supplemented by individual craftsmen (cobblers, coopers, blacksmiths, tailors, weavers, etc.) who were established or itinerant depending on density of population in their locale, and by small industrial establishments such as sawmills, gristmills, fulling mills, ironworks, and brickyards. The Revolutionary war stimulated some forms of household production (such as "homespun"), and so did the disruption of the international market during the Napoleonic wars, but more continuous lines of change moved the New England economy from its agricultural and household-production base and gave it a commercial and then industrial emphasis by 1835.

Merchant capitalism was a primary force in this transformation. Merchant capitalists took risks, supplied capital, searched out markets, and attempted to maximize profits by producing standardized goods at the least cost, thus organizing production on a larger scale than had previously been typical. Their actions commanded a shift away from home production for family use, and from local craftsmen's production of custom or "bespoke" work for known individuals, toward more standardized production for a wider market. Mercantile capitalism flourished during the enormous expansion of New England's carrying trade and re-export business that occurred from 1793 to 1807 because of the confusion of European shipping during the Napoleonic wars. This burst of shipping energy also caused subsidiary economic activities, such as shipbuilding, and complementary businesses, such as brokerage, marine insurance, warehousing, and banking, to grow. Under the brunt of the national embargo in 1807 and the subsequent war with England this blooming of the American carrying and re-export trade faded, but since much of the capital involved was transferred to manufacturing activity overall economic productivity did not diminish greatly.

The shift to market-oriented production under merchant capitalists prepared the way for the development of manufacturing and the factory system. Under the demand of the merchant capitalist for widely distributable goods, the craftsman's shop became a larger and more specialized unit, for production only rather than (as formerly) for production and retail sale. The master craftsman became the "boss" of a larger number of journeymen and apprentices. In New England another production system, limited mainly to shoes and textiles, also preceded and overlapped with industrial manufacture. This was the "putting-out" or "given-out" system, in which a merchant or master craftsman distributed materials to individuals to work on in their homes at piece-work rates, and collected and sold the finished goods. As the given-out system developed, the individuals (often women) it employed at home performed more and more specialized and fragmentary handicrafts. Indeed, the hallmarks of economic development in this period were functional specialization and division of labor. Where there had been "jacks-of-all-trades" there came specialized laborers; where there had been eclectic merchants there came importers and exporters, wholesalers and jobbers and retailers. Farmers who had produced only for subsistence trained their eyes on, and diverted some of their energies to, the market for commercial produce. New specialists appeared in fields from insurance to banking to transportation, as incorporations of businesses multiplied and turnpikes and bridges replaced wooden paths. In order to understand shifts in women's work during these years, rapid changes of this type must be kept in mind. Whether a woman lived toward the beginning or toward the end of this half-century may have informed the character of her work as much as, or more than, her geographical location, wealth, or marital status, which were other significant factors. Comparison of the kinds of work recorded in women's diaries in the earlier and later years makes that clear.

During the late eighteenth century both unmarried and married women did their primary work in households, in families. Unmarried daughters might be called upon to help their fathers in a store or shop connected to the house: Sally Ripley, a tradesman's daughter in Greenfield. Massachusetts, more than once recorded in her diary, "This morning my Father departed for Boston, & I am again entrusted with the charge of the Store." But daughters' assistance in the housewife's realm of food preparation and preservation, dairying, gardening, cleaning, laundering, soap making, candle making, knitting, and textile and clothing manufacture was the more usual case. Mothers and daughters shared these labors. The continual and time-consuming work of spinning was the most readily delegated to the younger generation, it seems. Hannah Hickok Smith of Glastonbury, Connecticut, managed to avoid spinning, because she had five daughters at home. "The girls ... have been very busy spinning this spring," she reported to their grandmother in 1800, "and have spun enough for about seventy yards besides almost enough for another carpet." Spinning must have taken precedence in the daughters' work, for when they had "no spinning to do for any consequence" then Mrs. Smith admitted that she "lived very easy, as the girls have done every thing."...

The first "manufactories" in the United States were places of business established in major cities in the 1760s to collect yarn spun and cloth woven by women in their homes by traditional hand methods. Some merchants soon put spinning wheels and looms on the premises of their manufactories, and hired women and children to work them there; but in general they employed a much larger proportion of women working in their own homes than on the manufactory premises. After Samuel Slater introduced industrial spinning machinery to New England in 1789, and other entrepreneurs established spinning mills, employing women to work the machinery, the proportions working at home and on the premises were reversed. The early mills (between 1790 and 1815) produced only yarn, which was distributed to domestic weavers like Samantha Barrett to be made into cloth. The power loom did not appear in New England until 1814. That year the Boston Manufacturing Company introduced it at Waltham, Massachusetts, uniting under one factory roof all the operations necessary to turn raw fiber into finished cloth. Factories mass-producing cotton cloth multiplied during the 1820s.

By 1830, industrial manufacture had largely superseded home spinning and weaving in New England by producing cloth more cheaply. This changed women's work more than any other single factor, and likely had more emphatic impact on unmarried women than on mothers of families. Industrialization of textiles disrupted daughters' predictable role in the household first. Mothers' lives continued to be defined by household management and child rearing. Daughters, however, often had to earn wages to replace their contribution to family sustenance. Textile mill operatives, who were almost all between the ages of fifteen and thirty, were young women who followed their traditional occupation to a new location, the factory. New England textile factories from the start employed a vastly greater proportion of women than men.

The economic and social change of the period injected uncertainty, variety, and mobility into young women's lives—into none more dramatically than the early mill operatives'. Mary Hall began industrial employment after her academy schooling and experience in schoolteaching. In November 1830 she started folding books at a shop in Exeter, New Hampshire, not happy to be removed from her family. "Yes, I shall probably be obliged to call this, to me a land of strangers, home for the present," she wrote in her dairy. "But home sweet home can never be transfer'd in the affections of Me.... How often this day amidst its cares and business have I been in imagination under the paternal roof seeing, hearing and conversing with its lov'd inhabitants." She was twenty-four years old. After seven months she returned home, because several family members were ill. In September 1831, she went to Lowell, Massachusetts, for employment as a cotton-mill operative. She worked in Lowell for the next five years, except for returns home to Concord for more than a year between 1832 and 1833, for the summer in 1834, for weeks in November and December 1834 (because of deaths in her family), and in November 1835 and June 1836. During her years in Lowell she worked for at least three different corporations.

Emily Chubbuck, whose family was probably poorer than Mary Hall's, had a more disjointed employment history. The fifth child in a New Hampshire family transplanted to upstate New York, she went to work in 1828, at the age of eleven, splicing rolls in a woolen factory. Her parents allowed her to keep her weekly wage of $1.25. When the factory closed in January 1829 she began attending a district school, to supplement the education she had received from an older sister. Two months later the factory reopened and she resumed work there.

During the next three years, as her family moved several times in attempts to make a living, she intermittently worked for a Scottish weaver twisting thread, attended an academy, washed and ironed for her family's boarders, sewed for a mantua-maker, and attended a district school. At fourteen, despite her mother's advice to apprentice herself to a milliner, she lied about her age to obtain a schoolteaching job. Her wages were only 75 cents a week plus board. She knew that she "could earn as much with the milliner, and far more at twisting thread," but she hoped for a future in literary pursuits rather than manual employment.

There was a large class of young women who would have spun at home in early decades but whose families' incomes or priorities made factory work unlikely for them. Their work too became variable and sporadic, shifting among the options of schoolteaching, needlework, domestic work, and given-out industry. None of these was really a full-time, year-round occupation. Women tended to combine them. Rachel Stearns, under pressure of necessity, became willing to intersperse sewing in another household with her schoolteaching, although earlier she had "thought it quite too degrading to go to Uncle F's and sew." Nancy Flynt, a single woman of Connecticut, wrote to her married sister around 1810, "[I am] a tugging and a toiling day and night to get a maintenance, denying myself the pleasure of calling on my nearest neighbors.... I would tell you how much work I have dispatched since I saw you, I have a great deal of sewing on hand now." The twenty-five-year-old daughter of the minister in Hawley, Massachusetts, decided she should learn to support herself "by the needle" and therefore began to learn the milliner's trade, but her health failed, preventing her from continuing. "Perhaps [I] flattered myself too much with the idea of being able to bear my own expenses," she reflected somewhat bitterly.

Given-out industry, which constituted a significant stage in the industrial development of New England, enabled women to earn money while staying at home. Two kinds of production organized this way drew heavily on women's labor: the stitching and binding of boots and shoes (concentrated in eastern Massachusetts) and the braiding, or plaiting, of straw bonnets. The latter was a handicraft designed before 1800 by New England women who used native rye straw for the material. By 1830 thousands carried it on in the employ of entrepreneurs who imported palm leaves from Cuba and distributed them to farmhouses to be made up into hats. Eliza Chaplin and her sister Caroline of Salem, Massachusetts, made and sold bonnets during the 1820s, the same years that they taught school. Julia Pierce taught school in the summer and had "plenty of work" to do in the winter, she said: "I have braided more than 100 hats and the other girls as many more." The working life of Amanda Elliot of Guilford, Connecticut, exemplifies the variety of this transitional period. Within six months in 1816–17 she devoted considerable time to splitting straw and braiding hats; noted five, new boarders; taught school; and mentioned binding shoes, in addition to usual domestic needlework, knitting, washing, and ironing. For some fortunate young women, of course, the diminution of household manufacture for the family meant greater leisure and opportunity for education. Hannah Hickok Smith's letters after 1800 revealed that spinning gradually dwindled in importance in her daughters' occupations. "As we have had much leisure time this winter," she wrote in 1816, "the girls have employed themselves chiefly in reading writing and studying French Latin and Greek."

While economic modernization changed young unmarried women's work more conspicuously than their mothers' at first, the disruption of the integral relation between the household and the business of society was bound to redefine matrons' occupations too. Wife-and-motherhood in a rural household of the eighteenth century implied responsibility for the well-being of all the family. Upon marriage a woman took on "the Cares of the world," Elizabeth Bowen admitted as she recounted her past life, at mid-century. Fond as Esther Edwards Burr was of improving her mind, she declined an opportunity to take French lessons in the 1750s with the forceful comment, "The married woman has something else to care about besides lerning [sic] French!" Sarah Snell Bryant's daily diary reported in straightforward fashion her matronly duties in an educated, respectable, but impecunious farm family in western Massachusetts. During the 1790s and early 1800s she bore and nursed six children (usually returning to household cares within a few days after childbirth), and taught them all to read the Bible before sending them to school. Generally she occupied every day in making cloth and clothing—from the "hatcheling" of flax and "breaking" of wool to the sewing of shirts, gowns, and coats—knitting gloves and stockings, baking, brewing, preserving food, churning butter, gardening, nursing the sick, making candles or soap, washing, ironing, scouring, quilting with neighbors, and even entertaining visitors. During a summer when her husband was traveling, she also taught school. Contemporaries of Sarah Snell Bryant who lived in more densely populated and commercial locations might have less labor to perform, especially if their husbands' wealth allowed their families to purchase goods and services. Martha Church Challoner, who lived in Newport, a lively Rhode Island port, in the 1760s, was able to buy various fabrics, shoes, and some basic foods. She had two black women in her house as servants (or slaves, possibly), and hired others to do washing, mending, spinning, carding, sewing, nursing. Still, she herself made candles, knit stockings, sold butter and eggs, and sewed household linens, while supervising the household....

Well into the middle decades of the nineteenth century married women's work remained centered on household management and family care, although the growing ramifications of the market economy diminished the importance of household manufacture and enlarged families' reliance on money to purchase basic commodities. Greater population density, commercial expansion, technological advances in transportation and communication, specialization in agriculture, and involvement of rural residents in given-out industry all contributed to the demise of the self-contained household economy. "There is no way of living in this town without cash," Abigail Lyman reported from Boston in 1797, and smaller towns rapidly manifested the same commercial spirit and need. Hannah Hickok Smith's account book for the years 1821–24 points out the extent to which a prosperous farm matron in an "urban"-sized commercial town— Glastonbury, Connecticut—was involved in commercial transaction. She recorded the purchase of edibles and baking supplies (spices, plums, currants, raisins, sugar, molasses, salt, wine, coffee, tea); of household items (teacups, platters, chest, jug, box, coffeepot, tinware, pins) and construction materials (pine boards, nails, steel); of writing accoutrements (paper, pen-knife, spelling book), nursing supplies (camphor, plaister) and soap, and some luxuries (snuff, tobacco, shell combs, parasol). Furthermore, she purchased at least eleven different kinds of fabric (such as dimity, brown holland, "factory cloth"), four kinds of yarn and thread, leather, and buttons; bought silk shawls, bonnets, dresses, stockings, and kid gloves, and also paid for people's services in making clothing. The farm produced the marketable commodities of grain (oats, rye, corn) and timber, animals (calves, turkeys, fowl) and animal products (eggs, hens' feathers, quills, wool, pork), and other farm produce which required more human labor, such as butter, cider, lard, and tallow....

The growing availability of goods and services for purchase might spare a married woman from considerable drudgery, if her husband's income sufficed for a comfortable living. It also heightened her role in "shoping," as Abigail Brackett Lyman spelled it (her consumer role), although that was subject to her husband's authority over financial resources. In colonial America husbands, as "providers," typically were responsible for purchasing goods—including household goods, furniture, and food staples, if they were to be bought—but in commercial towns of the late eighteenth and early nineteenth century wives more frequently became shoppers, especially for articles of dress and food. The increasing importance of monetary exchange bore hard on those who needed to replace their former economic contribution of household manufacture with income-producing employment, while meeting their domestic obligations. Taking in boarders was one alternative. Betsey Graves Johnson did that while she brought up the five children born to her between 1819 and 1830. Otherwise, married women had the same options for wage earning as single women who wished to stay at home: to take in sewing, or work in given-out industry. Schoolteaching, a slight possibility for wives, was a likelier one for widows whose children had reached school age. One widow's "cares," as described by her sister in 1841, were "enough to occupy all her lime and thoughts almost.... [She] is teaching from 16 to 20 sholars [sic] boarding a young lady, and doing the housework, taking care of her children, &c."

These constants—"doing the housework, taking care of her children"— persisted in married women's lives. Child care required their presence at home. This responsibility revealed itself as the heart of women's domestic duties when household production declined. After four years of marriage Sarah Ripley Stearns regretfully attributed her neglect of church attendance and devotional reading not to household duties but to "the Care of my Babes, which takes up so large a portion of my time of my time [sic] & attention." More than ever before in New England history, the care of children appeared to be mothers' sole work and the work of mothers alone. The expansion of nonagricultural occupations drew men and grown children away from the household, abbreviating their presence in the family and their roles in child rearing. Mothers and young children were left in the household together just when educational and religious dicta both newly emphasized the malleability of young minds. Enlightenment psychology drew tighter the connection between early influence on the child, and his or her eventual character, just as mothers' influence on young children appeared more salient....

While changes in economy and society made young women's work more social, more various and mobile, the same developments reduced the social engagement, variety, and mobility in the work of wives and mothers. Housekeeping and child care continued to require married women's presence at home, while the household diminished in population, kinds of business, and range of contacts. In an intriguing development in language usage in the early nineteenth century, "home" became synonymous with "retirement" or "retreat" from the world at large. Mary Tucker quoted approvingly in 1802 an author's assertion that "a woman's noblest station is retreat." On a cousin's approaching marriage she remarked, "Sally has passed her days in the shade of *retirement* but even there many virtues and graces have ripened to perfection, she has every quality necessary for a *good wife*." Salome Lincoln's marriage to a fellow preacher in 1835 virtually ended her extradomestic pursuits; she subsequently used her preaching talents only on occasional travels with her husband. The shifting emphasis among married women's occupations emerges clearly in the comparison of Lydia Hill Almy's occupations in 1797–99 with Mary Hurlbut's in the 1830s. The former not only kept house but let rooms, collected firewood, attended to livestock, and arranged to sell tanned skins; she considered her two children "grown out of the way" and "very little troble [*sic*]" when the younger was not yet weaned. Mary Hurlbut, in contrast, appeared solely concerned with her children's lives and prospects.

Married women's work at home distinguished itself most visibly from men's work, especially as the latter began to depart from the household/farm/craftshop to separate shops, offices, and factories. The rhythms of adult men's and women's work diverged even as did their places of work. During the eighteenth century, in agricultural towns, men and women had largely shared similar work patterns; their work, tied to the land, was seasonal and discontinuous. It was conditioned by tradition, family position, and legal obligation as well as by economic incentive. E. P. Thompson has called the dominant characteristic of work in such an agricultural/artisanal economy its "task-orientation," in contrast to the "time-discipline" required under industrial capitalism. Task-orientation implies that the worker's own sense of customary need and order dictates the performance of work. Intensification or delay occurs as a response to perceived necessity: in farming, for instance, the former occurs in harvest time, or the latter during stormy weather. Irregular work patterns typically result. "Social intercourse and labour are intermingled," Thompson also has pointed out, "the working-day lengthens or contracts according to the task—and there is no great sense of conflict between labour and 'passing the time of day.'" Persons accustomed to time-discipline, however, may consider task-oriented work patterns "wasteful and lacking in urgency." Thompson's analysis derived from his study of eighteenth-century English farmers, artisans, and laborers but can be applied to their contemporaries in New England. Even eighteenth-century colonial merchants, who, as risk-taking capitalists, might be expected to initiate disciplined work habits, structured their work lives in what Thompson would denote "preindustrial" ways, intermingling their work with recreation and with the conduct of their households. "The Founding Fathers, after all, lived in a preindustrial, not simply an 'agrarian' society," as Herbert Gutman has remarked, "and the prevalence of premodern work habits among their contemporaries was natural."

The social transformation from 1780 to 1835 signalled a transition from preindustrial to modern industrial work patterns. The replacement of family production for direct use with wage earning, the institution of time-discipline and machine regularity in place of natural rhythms, the separation of workplaces from the home, and the division of "work" from "life" were overlapping layers of the same phenomenon....

Despite the changes in its social context adult women's work, for the most part, kept the traditional mode and location which both sexes had earlier shared. Men who had to accept time-discipline and specialized occupations may have begun to observe differences between their own work and that of their wives. Perhaps they focused on the remaining "premodern" aspects of women's household work: it was reassuringly comprehensible, because it responded to immediate needs; it represented not strictly "work" but "life," a way of being; and it also looked unsystematized, inefficient, nonurgent. Increasingly men did distinguish women's work from their own, in the early nineteenth century, by calling it women's "sphere," a "separate" sphere.

Women's sphere was "separate" not only because it was at home, but also because it seemed to elude rationalization and the cash nexus, and to integrate labor with life. The home and occupations in it represented an alternative to the emerging pace and division of labor. Symbol and remnant of preindustrial work, perhaps the home commanded men's deepest loyalties, but these were loyalties that conflicted with "modern" forms of employment. To be idealized, yet rejected by men—the object of yearning, and yet of scorn—was the fate of the home-as-workplace. Women's work (indeed women's very character, viewed as essentially conditioned by the home) shared in that simultaneous glorification and devaluation.

The Changes Wrought by Cotton, Transportation, and Communication

DANIEL WALKER HOWE

On the twenty-fourth of May 1844, Professor Samuel F. B. Morse, seated amidst a hushed gathering of distinguished national leaders in the chambers of the United States Supreme Court in Washington, tapped out a message on a device of cogs and coiled wires:

From Daniel Walker Howe, *What Hath God Wrought: The Transformation of America, 1818–1848*, 1–2, 4–7, 125–126, 128–129, 131–134, 213–214, 216, 222–223, 227, 242. (New York: Oxford University Press, 2007). Reprinted by permission of Oxford University Press.

What Hath God Wrought

Forty miles away, in Baltimore, Morse's associate Alfred Vail received the electric signals and sent the message back. The invention they had demonstrated was destined to change the world. For thousands of years messages had been limited by the speed with which messengers could travel and the distance at which eyes could see signals such as flags or smoke. Neither Alexander the Great nor Benjamin Franklin (America's first postmaster general) two thousand years later knew anything faster than a galloping horse. Now, instant long-distance communication became a practical reality. The commercial application of Morse's invention followed quickly. American farmers and planters—and most Americans then earned a living through agriculture—increasingly produced food and fiber for distant markets. Their merchants and bankers welcomed the chance to get news of distant prices and credit....

The invention of electric telegraphy ... represented a climactic moment in a widespread revolution of communications. Other features of this revolution included improvements in printing and paper manufacturing; the multiplication of newspapers, magazines, and books; and the expansion of the postal system (which mostly carried newspapers and commercial business, not personal letters). Closely related to these developments occurred a simultaneous revolution in transportation: the introduction of steamboats, canals, turnpikes, and railroads, shortening travel times and dramatically lowering shipping costs.... Their consequences certainly rivaled, and probably exceeded in importance, those of the revolutionary "information highway" of our own lifetimes....

The most common name for the years ... is "Jacksonian America." I avoid the term because it suggests that Jacksonianism describes Americans as a whole, whereas in fact Andrew Jackson was a controversial figure and his political movement bitterly divided the American people....

Another term that has sometimes been applied to this period—more by historians than by the general public—is "the market revolution." I avoid this expression also. Those historians who used it have argued that a drastic change occurred during these years, from farm families raising food for their own use to producing it for distant markets. However, more and more evidence has accumulated in recent years that a market economy already existed in the eighteenth-century American colonies. To be sure, markets expanded vastly in the years after the end of the War of 1812, but their expansion partook more of the nature of a continuing evolution than a sudden revolution. Furthermore, their expansion did not occur in the face of resistance from any substantial group of people preferring subsistence farming to market participation. Most American family farmers welcomed the chance to buy and sell in larger markets. They did not have to be coerced into seizing the opportunities the market economy presented.

Accordingly, I provide an alternative interpretation of the early nineteenth century as a time of a "communications revolution." This, rather than the continued growth of the market economy, impressed contemporary Americans as a startling innovation. During the thirty-three years that began in 1815, there would be greater strides in the improvement of communication than had taken place in all previous centuries. This revolution, with its attendant political and economic consequences, would be a driving force in the history of the era....

More than any other discussion, the debate over the future of human slavery in an empire dedicated to liberty threatened to tear the country apart. The communications revolution gave a new urgency to social criticism and to the slavery controversy in particular. No longer could slave-holders afford to shrug off the commentary of outsiders. Critics of slavery seized upon the new opportunities for disseminating ideas to challenge the institution in the South itself. Alarmed, the defenders of slavery erected barricades against the intrusion of unwelcome expression. Better communication did not necessarily foster harmony....

The World That Cotton Made

The end of the War of 1812 precipitated one of the great migrations of American history. White settlers eagerly took advantage of Andrew Jackson's expropriation of 14 million acres from the Creeks. Shortly after signing the Treaty of Fort Jackson, the general sent his topographical engineer to report on the condition of the Alabama River valley. Along his route, Major Howell Tatum could observe farms with all their improvements that had been abandoned by the dispossessed natives (many of whom, ironically, had been Jackson's allies in the war). The officer concluded in his report that the land was "capable of producing, in great abundance, every article necessary to the sustenance of man or beast." Jackson encouraged white squatters to move onto the lands immediately, without waiting for survey or legal authorization. In December 1815, President Madison ordered them evicted, but his proclamation proved impossible to enforce. When the army moved people off, they came back again as soon as the soldiers had left....

Seldom in human history has so large a territory been settled so rapidly. Between 1810 and 1820, Alabama's population increased twelvefold to 128,000; Mississippi's doubled to 75,000 even though the Choctaw and Chickasaw Indian tribes still owned the northern two-thirds of the state. The population of Louisiana also doubled to 153,000, as an influx of white American southerners arrived to rival the old multicultural society of colonial New Orleans. Fittingly, when the ambitious settlers of Mississippi established a capital for their state, they called the new little settlement Jackson....

What made migration into this hazardous environment so attractive was the high price of cotton. The difficulties in processing short-staple greenseed cotton into textiles had earlier been surmounted through a series of technological innovations culminating in the development of the "saw" cotton gin ("gin" being short for "engine"). The contribution of the Connecticut Yankee Eli Whitney to this long process has been much exaggerated. But the Napoleonic Wars had inhibited international commerce and delayed the mass marketing of cotton for nearly a generation. Now, within a year of the end of hostilities in Europe and North America, the price of raw cotton doubled on the New Orleans market, reaching twenty-seven cents a pound. Wherever the soil was suitable and the farmer could count on two hundred frost-free days in the year, short-staple cotton suddenly became an economically attractive crop. The virgin earth of the New Southwest seemed ideal: While backcountry South Carolina yielded three hundred pounds of cotton per acre, the Alabama black belt could yield eight hundred or even a thousand pounds per acre. In response to an apparently insatiable world demand for textiles, U.S. cotton production soared from seventy-three thousand bales in 1800 to ten times that in 1820—the year the United States surpassed India, long the leading cotton producer. Cotton, fueling an expansion of transatlantic industrial capitalism, enormously enhanced the importance of the United States in the world economy. In 1801, 9 percent of the world's cotton came from the USA and 60 percent from Asia. Half a century later, the United States provided 68 percent of a total world production three times as large. The American South was to be the most favored place for the production of a raw material of global significance, as the Caribbean sugar islands had been in the eighteenth century or as the oil-rich Middle East would become in the twentieth.

Cotton cultivation required labor-intensive application, but chattel slavery remained legal in the states where the climate was favorable to cotton. The new marketability of short-staple cotton prompted the expansion of slave-plantation agriculture far beyond the areas that would have sustained the traditional export crops, tobacco, rice, and indigo. The spread of cotton cultivation entailed not only the westward migration of free farmers but also the massive forced migration of enslaved workers into the newly acquired lands. Not all cotton planters in the Southwest were self-made pioneers, for some already wealthy men hastened to the area and purchased large holdings, clearing the forest and draining the swamps with slave labor. Whether he owned many slaves or few, a master might bring his bondsmen with him, but sometimes he would go out and select the lands to buy first, returning (or sending agents) later to buy a workforce suited to the property. Most often, the southwestern planter bought slaves who had been transported to that region by a trader. Because the importation of slaves from overseas had been illegal since 1808, the trader's human merchandise could only come from the seaboard slave states. Contemporaries typically observed the transit of a slave coffle with disgust and shame: "a wretched cavalcade ... marching half naked women, and men loaded with chains, without being charged with any crime but that of being black, from one section of the United States to another, hundreds of miles." Such a procession could number anywhere from a dozen to over a hundred souls, who were expected to walk up to twenty-five miles a day and sleep on the ground. The long trek overland from Virginia to Mississippi or Louisiana would consume six to eight weeks and was usually undertaken in winter, when agricultural labor could best be spared. Coastal vessels, more expensive, absorbed some of the traffic when the great slave marketplace in New Orleans was the destination. Only later, after Kentucky and Tennessee acquired surpluses of slaves and began exporting them, did the phrase "sold down the river" come into common use. The slave traders favored people in the prime of life—late teens or early twenties—since they could withstand the rigors of the march and bring a good price as field hands and (in the case of the women) breeders. Small children accompanying their mothers were placed in the supply wagon. The interstate slave trade was big business; the Chesapeake Bay region alone exported 124,000 enslaved workers, mostly across the Appalachians, during the decade following 1810....

The rapid rise of "the Cotton Kingdom" wrought a momentous transformation. Cotton became a driving force in expanding and transforming the economy not only of the South but of the United States as a whole—indeed of the world. While the growing of cotton came to dominate economic life in the Lower South, the manufacture of cotton textiles was fueling the industrial revolution on both sides of the Atlantic. Most of the exported American cotton went to Britain, in particular to the port of Liverpool, convenient to the textile mills of Lancashire. During the immediate postwar years of 1816 to 1820, cotton constituted 39 percent of U.S. exports; twenty years later the proportion had increased to 59 percent, and the value of the cotton sold overseas in 1836 exceeded $71 million. By giving the United States its leading export staple, the workers in the cotton fields enabled the country not only to buy manufactured goods from Europe but also to pay interest on its foreign debt and continue to import more capital to invest in transportation and industry. Much of the Atlantic civilization in the nineteenth century was built on the back of the enslaved field hand....

The same short-staple cotton that spread plantation agriculture all over the South gave rise to textile mills. In New England, the War of 1812 climaxed a series of interruptions playing havoc with the maritime trade and fishing that had been the mainstays of the regional economy. American commerce was driven from the seas. Watching their ships rot in port, Yankee investors hit upon a solution. As southern planters solved the problem of worn-out lands and low tobacco prices by shifting their workforce to the new cotton fields, New England merchants solved their own problem by shifting capital from shipping to manufacturing. What they started to manufacture was inexpensive cloth, made from local wool and southern cotton....

Farm women had long supplemented the family income by weaving woolen yarn and cloth, using spinning wheels and hand looms at home. Now cotton from the South provided raw material much more plentiful than local sheep. So young women left home, recruited by company-owned boardinghouses in Lowell. There they put in long hours under unhealthy conditions and contracted not to leave until they had worked at least a year. But twelve to fourteen dollars a month was a good wage, and the new town had attractive shops, social activities, churches, lending libraries, and evening lectures. The "mill girls," as they called themselves, wrote and published a magazine, the *Lowell Offering*. Americans had feared industrialization, lest it create an oppressed, depraved, and turbulent proletariat. But because these women typically worked for only a few years prior to marriage, and did so in a morally protected environment, they did not seem to constitute a permanent separate working class. To observers, the community looked like an industrial utopia, more successful than the Scottish models that Francis Lowell and Nathan Appleton had toured years before. Lowell, Massachusetts, boasted the largest concentration of industry in the United States before the Civil War....

Overthrowing the Tyranny of Distance

People throughout the United States recognized the need for a better transportation system. The Great Migration had increased the number of agricultural producers wanting to get their crops from the interior to national or international markets. While some people moved westward, others were migrating to the coastal cities to work in the merchant marine and its many ancillary occupations, from shipbuilding to insurance. These city people had a need to be fed even more urgent than that of the farmers to market their crops. Pressure for improvements in transportation came at least as much from cities eager to buy as from farmers seeking to sell. Urban merchants hoped to funnel as much farm produce as possible from as large a hinterland as possible into their own market, either for consumption or transshipment elsewhere. Technology, new or newly applied, made available improvements in transportation, but constructing "internal improvements" posed problems not only physical but also economic, legal, and political....

The invention of the steamboat enhanced the comparative advantages of water transportation. In 1787, John Fitch had built the first American steamer, but he could not obtain financial backing and died in obscurity. The first commercially successful steamboat, Robert Fulton's *Clermont,* plied the Hudson River starting in 1807. Steamboats proved most valuable for trips upstream on rivers with powerful currents, of which the Mississippi was the ultimate example. In 1817, a twenty-five day steamer trip up the Mississippi from New Orleans to Louisville set a record; by 1826, the time had been cut to eight days. Pre-steamboat traffic on the Mississippi had been mostly one-way downstream; at New Orleans, boatmen broke up their barges to sell for lumber and *walked* back home to Kentucky or Tennessee along the Natchez Trace road....

For all their utility, nineteenth-century steamboats were dangerous. Between 1825 and 1830 alone, forty-two exploding boilers killed 273 people. Commenting on steamboat accidents, Philip Hone of New York City, one of the great diarists of the period, observed in 1837. "We have become the most careless, reckless, headlong people on the face of the earth. 'Go ahead' is our maxim and pass-word, and we do go ahead with a vengeance, regardless of consequences and indifferent to the value of human life." In 1838, an enormous boiler explosion in Charleston took 140 lives....

Canals further extended the advantages of water transport. Canals might connect two natural waterways or parallel a single stream so as to avoid waterfalls, rapids, or obstructions. Locks raised or lowered the water level. Horses or mules walking along a towpath moved barges through the canal; an animal that could pull a wagon weighing two tons on a paved road could pull fifty tons on the towpath of a canal. In Europe, canals had been around a long time; the Languedoc Canal connected the Mediterranean with the Bay of Biscay in 1681. In North America, canal construction had been delayed by the great distances, sparse population, and (embarrassing as it was to admit) lack of engineering and management expertise. During the years after 1815, a society eager for transportation and open to innovation finally surmounted these difficulties. Because canals cost more to construct than turnpikes, public funding proved even more important in raising the capital for them. Energy and flexibility at the state level got canal construction under way when doubts about constitutional propriety made the federal government hesitate. Many canals were built entirely by state governments, including the most famous, economically important, and financially successful of them all, the Erie Canal in New York....

As part of the celebration of the Erie Canal's completion, cannons were placed within earshot of each other the entire length of its route and down the Hudson. When Governor Clinton's boat departed from Buffalo that October morning in 1825, the first cannon of the "Grand Salute" was fired and the signal relayed from gun to gun, all the way to Sandy Hook on the Atlantic coast and back again. Three hours and twenty minutes later, the booming signal returned to Buffalo. Except for elaborately staged events such as this, communication in early nineteenth-century America usually required the transportation of a physical object from one place to another—such as a letter, a newspaper, or even a message attached to the leg of a homing pigeon. This was how it had been since time immemorial. But as transportation improved, so did communications, and improved communications set powerful cultural changes in motion....

From New York City, information dispersed around the country and appeared in local newspapers. In 1817, news could get from New York to Philadelphia in just over a day, traveling as far as New Brunswick, New Jersey, by steamer. To Boston from New York took more than two days, with the aid of steamboats in Long Island Sound. To Richmond the news took five days; to Charleston, ten. These travel times represented a great improvement over the pre-steamboat 1790s, when Boston and Richmond had each been ten days away from New York, but they would continue to improve during the coming generation. For the most important news of all, relay express riders were employed. In 1830, these riders set a record: They carried the presidential State of the Union message from Washington to New York in fifteen and a half hours.

Communications profoundly affected American business. For merchants eagerly awaiting word of crop prices and security fluctuations in European cities, the advantage of being one of the first to know such information was crucial. New Yorkers benefited because so many ships came to their port first, even though Boston and Halifax, Nova Scotia, were actually closer to Europe. The extra days of delay in receiving European news handicapped merchants based in Charleston, Savannah, or New Orleans. The availability of information affected investors of all kinds, not only commodity traders. No longer did people with money to invest feel they needed to deal only with their relatives or others they knew personally. Through the New York Stock Exchange, one could buy shares in enterprises one had never seen. Capital flowed more easily to places where it was needed. Information facilitated doing business at a distance; for example, insurance companies could better assess risks. Credit rating agencies opened to facilitate borrowing and lending; the first one, the Mercantile Agency, was established by the Tappan brothers, who also created the New York *Journal of Commerce* and bankrolled much of the abolitionist movement. In colonial times, Americans had needed messages from London to provide commercially relevant news. Now, they could get their news from New York and get it faster. Improved communications stimulated economic growth....

As early as 1822, the United States had more newspaper readers than any other country, regardless of population. This market was highly fragmented; no one paper had a circulation of over four thousand. New York City alone had 66 newspapers in 1810 and 161 by 1828, including *Freedom's Journal,* the first to be published by and for African Americans.

The expansion of newspaper publishing resulted in part from technological innovations in printing and papermaking. Only modest improvements had been made in the printing press since the time of Gutenberg until a German named Friedrich Koenig invented a cylinder press driven by a steam engine in 1811. The first American newspaper to obtain such a press was the *New York Daily Advertiser* in 1825; it could print two thousand papers in an hour. In 1816, Thomas Gilpin discovered how to produce paper on a continuous roll instead of in separate sheets that were slower to feed into the printing press. The making of paper from rags gradually became mechanized, facilitating the production of books and magazines as well as newspapers; papermaking from wood pulp did not become practical until the 1860s. Compositors still set type by hand, picking up type one letter at a time from a case and placing it into a handheld "stick." Until the 1830s, one man sometimes put out a newspaper all by himself, the editor setting his own type. The invention of stereotyping enabled an inexpensive metal copy to be made of set type; the copy could be retained, and if a second printing of the job seemed warranted (such as a second edition of a book), the type did not have to be laboriously reset. More important than innovations in the production of printed matter, however, were the improvements in transportation that facilitated the supply of paper to presses and then the distribution of what they printed. After about 1830, these improvements had reached the point where a national market for published material existed....

Late in 1833, a twenty-seven-year-old French engineer named Michel Chevalier arrived in the United States. American canals, bridges, steamboats, and railroads fascinated him. During his two-year tour of the country, he concluded that improvements in transportation had democratic implications. In former times, he remarked, with roads rough and dangerous, travel required "a long train of luggage, provisions, servants, and guards," making it rare and expensive. "The great bulk of mankind, slaves in fact and in name," had been "chained to the soil" not only by their legal and social status but also "by the difficulty of locomotion." Freedom to travel, the ability to leave home, was essential to the modern world and as democratic as universal suffrage, Chevalier explained:

> To improve the means of communication, then, is to promote a real, positive, and practical liberty; it is to extend to all the members of the human family the power of traversing and turning to account the globe, which has been given to them as their patrimony; it is to increase the rights and privileges of the greatest number, as truly and as amply as could be done by electoral laws. The effect of the most perfect system

of transportation is to reduce the distance not only between different places, but between different classes.

As Chevalier realized, improved transportation and communications facilitated not only the movement of goods and ideas but personal, individual freedom as well. Americans, a mobile and venturesome people, empowered by literacy and technological proficiency, did not hesitate to take advantage of the opportunity provided (as he put it) to turn the globe to their account.

In traditional society, the only items worth transporting long distances had been luxury goods, and information about the outside world had been one of the most precious luxuries of all. The transportation and communications revolutions made both goods and information broadly accessible. In doing so, they laid a foundation not only for widespread economic betterment and wider intellectual horizons but also for political democracy; in newspapers and magazines, in post offices, in nationwide movements to influence public opinion, and in mass political parties.

FURTHER READING

Edward J. Balleisen, *Navigating Failure: Bankruptcy and Commercial Society in Antebellum America* (2001).

Christopher Clark, *The Roots of Rural Capitalism: Western Massachusetts, 1780–1860* (1990).

Ruth S. Cowan, *A Social History of American Technology* (1997).

Daniel Walker Howe, *What Hath God Wrought: The Transformation of America, 1815–1846* (2007).

Richard R. John, *Spreading the News: The American Postal System from Franklin to Morse* (1996).

John Lauritz Larson, *Internal Improvement: National Public Works and the Promise of Popular Government in the Early United States* (2001).

Marla R. Miller, *The Needle's Eye: Women and Work in the Age of Revolution* (2006).

David Reynolds, *Waking Giant: America in the Age of Jackson* (2008).

Mary P. Ryan, *Cradle of the Middle Class: The Family in Oneida County, New York, 1790–1865* (1981).

Charles Sellers, *The Market Revolution: Jacksonian America, 1815–1846* (1991).

Michael Tadman, *Speculators and Slaves: Traders and Slaves in the Old South* (1989).

Alan Taylor, *William Cooper's Town* (1995).

George R. Taylor, *The Transportation Revolution, 1815–1860* (1951).

C. Edward White, *The Marshall Court and Cultural Change, 1815–1835* (1991).

Gavin Wright, *Slavery and American Economic Development* (2006).

CHAPTER 9

Nationalism, Sectionalism, and Expansionism in the Age of Jackson

When Frenchman Michel Chevelier witnessed a parade in New York City in 1834, he was dazzled: It was a mile-long procession lit by hundreds of torches, and it included banners, portraits of political leaders, and even a live eagle mounted on a pole (see document 7 in this chapter). "These scenes belong to history," he later wrote. "They are the episodes of a wondrous epic which will bequeath a lasting memory to posterity, that of the coming of democracy." For this visitor, the political world in the United States differed radically from that in his European home. Americans were enjoying the burgeoning of a democracy that was likely to reverberate throughout the world. Historians have found reason to substantiate these claims. In the early nineteenth century, ballot restrictions were eased so that all white men, even those who owned no property, could vote. By 1840, those Americans who could vote did so in record numbers. Politics became a pageant, filling the streets with demonstrations and parades. Andrew Jackson, elected in 1828, was heralded by his supporters as a man of the people.

However, other historians have considered these developments in a different light. Not only was universal suffrage restricted to white men, but free black men were losing their voting rights in a number of states during this period. In this purported era of democracy, Indian removal, as we saw in Chapter 7, was accelerating. The United States, many historians argue, was not a paragon of democracy, but rather "a white man's republic." Still other historians contend that the level of democracy even among white voters is overstated. Politics might have appeared as pageantry, but this was really a façade. Elections decided less than voters believed.

Whether politics represented the flowering of democracy or was a sham, political organization and behavior changed beginning in 1824. The second party system, as it is called, developed in large part in reaction to the political career of Andrew Jackson. Defeated by John Quincy Adams in 1824, Jackson vowed revenge in the next presidential election. Following his resounding victory in 1828 as leader of the Democratic Party, he set about creating a federal bureaucracy that would be loyal to him and his party. The adage "to the victor belong the spoils" was cited to defend the appointment of loyal Democrats to government jobs. A series of divisive political battles over such issues as a national bank followed. By 1834, a group of politicians who opposed Jackson's initiatives formed an alternative party, which they called the Whigs, in opposition to "King Andrew." For the next twenty years, national elections were closely contested, eligible voters participated in large numbers, and professional politicians vied for votes and rewarded their followers with patronage if they were victorious. Whereas politicians at one time had disdained campaigning for office, the second party system fostered raucous campaigns and ambitious politicians.

In this new political environment, politicians addressed issues that would continue to plague the United States in the years to come. Perhaps the most ominous was the question of states' rights and national power. In 1832, Congress passed a tariff that seemed excessive to southern political leaders. Because the southern economy continued to be based on agriculture, the South benefited less from tariffs than did the North. Senator John C. Calhoun from South Carolina responded to this "tariff of abominations" by arguing that a state had the right to "nullify" laws with which it disagreed. Jackson responded as a nationalist and declared nullification illegal. The difference even punctuated dinner conversation. On one occasion, President Jackson toasted to the "Federal Union: it must be preserved." Calhoun, the vice president at the time, responded, "The Union: next to our liberty the most dear." Ultimately a compromise was reached, but certainly there were aspects of the debate that were not settled. Historians have considered this crisis a prelude to the Civil War.

One area in which most politicians and voters could agree, however, was the urgency of expanding westward. Westward migration, so the argument went, would not only increase national power but also bring benefits to those who were conquered. By 1845, this impulse was encoded in an ideology known as "manifest destiny." According to journalist John L. O'Sullivan, it was "the fulfillment of our manifest destiny to overspread the continent." Armed with a rhetoric that knit westward expansion with national fulfillment, Americans in the 1840s pushed for annexation of western lands. The United States annexed Texas in 1845, gained Oregon in a treaty with Great Britain, and conquered regions of Mexico following the Mexican-American War, which began in 1846. As of 1848, the United States, which now comprised nearly three million square miles, had tripled in size in seventy-some years. This "white man's republic" seemingly had fulfilled its destiny. Yet storm clouds were on the horizon, as we shall see, precisely because of the territories in the West.

QUESTIONS TO THINK ABOUT

To what degree was this a period of increasing democracy? How were notions about "the people" or "the common man" used to celebrate the potential of the United States? How were these celebrations linked to expansion and "manifest destiny"? How was the issue of nullification ominous for American nationalists?

◤ DOCUMENTS

The first five documents illustrate the issues of nationalism and sectionalism during the presidency of Andrew Jackson. Document 1 records a popular song that promoted the presidential aspirations of Andrew Jackson. In document 2, Senator John C. Calhoun of South Carolina argues against the "tariff of abominations" and for an open market. In contrast, in document 3, Senator Daniel Webster of Massachusetts argues that the people have ratified a Constitution that has made the national government the supreme law of the land. President Andrew Jackson, in document 4, responds to the action of South Carolina in calling for the nullification of a federal law. Jackson agrees with Webster, arguing that no state can declare a law void because the Constitution has formed a government in which all the people are represented. Document 5 is Jackson's veto of the Bank Bill that authorized the renewal of the National Bank charter. This veto set off the Bank War that would consume American politics for some years to come. Document 6 gives us a view of the battle at the Alamo in 1836 from the point of view of a Mexican colonel. Document 7 is an observation by Michel Chevelier who marvels at a procession of Democrats in New York City in 1839. The final two documents grapple with the issue of expansion in the 1840s. Document 8 is newspaper editor John L. O'Sullivan's expectation of the march westward of Americans into California. Document 9 provides a colorful portrait by Walter Colton of the rush to the California gold fields. Note the cultural diversity of the people who are at work in the mines.

1. A Song to Put Andrew Jackson in the White House, c. 1820s

Huzza! for General Jackson.

Come all who are our country's friends,
And unto these few lines attend,
Perhaps before you reach the end
You'll find something for to mend, ...

Our opposition party say,
If Jackson should but gain the day,
There will be war without delay,
And proselytes they gain this way,
To build their fed'ral faction.

America Singing: Nineteenth-Century Song Sheets. American Memory, Library of Congress.

But all who are for liberty,
Their deepest plans can sometimes see,
But always let our motto be,
"We're determin'd to be free,"
Huzza! for Gen'ral Jackson.

We have great numbers on our side,
Old vet'rans who have been well tried,
And never yet have turn'd aside,
All opposition still outride,
Who scorn the fed'ral faction.
And when they're call'd for to defend,
Their country's rights they will attend,
And all that's in their power they'll spend,
And will sand by their old tried friend,
General Andrew Jackson. ...

If Jackson should be president,
We'll borrow guns of Government,
And you may load and I'll tend vent,
Then touch her off and let her went,
With huzza! for Andrew Jackson.
And when the people hear the gun,
The men and boys they all will run,
Expecting for to see the fun,
When they get there will all as one,
Huzza! for Andrew Jackson. ...

There's some who at our party rail,
Call us the rag-tag and bob-tail,
But we have one within our pale,
Who we are sure will never fail,
To vote for General Jackson.
The Jackson Ticket they do say,
Is blood and carnage, by the way
Of slander, yet we hope we may
Join with our southern friends and say,
Huzza! for Andrew Jackson.

2. Vice President John C. Calhoun Argues That Tariffs Disadvantage the South, 1828

The Committee do not propose to enter into an elaborate, or refined argument on the question of the Constitutionality of the Tariff System. The Gen[era]l Government is one of specifick powers, and it can rightfully exercise only the powers expressly granted, and those that may be necessary and proper to carry them into effect, all others being reserved expressly to the States, or the people. It results necessarily, that those who claim to exercise power under the Constitution, are bound to show, that it is expressly granted, or that it is necessary and proper as a means to some of the granted powers. The advocates of the Tariff have offered no such proof....

So partial are the effects of the system, that its burdens are exclusively on one side, and the benefits on the other. It imposes on the agricultural interest of the south, including the South west, with that portion of our commerce and navigation engaged in foreign trade, the burden not only of sustaining the system itself, but that also of the Government....

That the manufacturing States, even in their own opinion, bear no share of the burden of the Tariff in reality, we may infer with the greatest certainty from their conduct. The fact that they urgently demand an increase, and consider any addition as a blessing, and a failure to obtain one, a curse, is the strongest confession, that whatever burden it imposes in reality, falls, not on them but on others. Men ask not for burdens, but benefits. The tax paid by the duties on impost [*sic*] by which, with the exception of the receipts in the sale of publick land and a few incidental items, the Government is wholly supported, and which in its gross amount annually equals about $23,000,000 is then in truth no tax on them. Whatever portion of it they advance, as consumers of the articles on which it is imposed, returns to them ... with usurious interest through an artfully contrived system. That such are the facts, the Committee will proceed to demonstrate by other arguments, besides the confession of the party interested through their acts, as conclusive as that ought to be considered....

We cultivate certain great staples for the supply of the general market of the world; they manufacture almost exclusively for the home market. Their object in the Tariff is to keep down foreign competition, in order to obtain a monopoly of the domestick market. The effect on us is to compel us to purchase at a higher price, both what we purchase from them and from others, without receiving a correspondent increase in the price, of what we sell....

We are told by those who pretend to understand our interest better than we do, that the excess of production, and not the Tariff, is the evil which afflicts us, and that our true remedy is a reduction of the quantity of cotton, rice and tobacco which we raise, and not a repeal of the Tariff. They assert that low prices are the necessary consequence of excess of supply, and that the only proper correction is in diminishing the quantity.... Our market is the world,

The Papers of John C. Calhoun, ed. Clyde N. Wilson and W. Edwin Hemphill, X (Columbia: University of South Carolina Press, 1959), 444–532.

and as we cannot imitate their example by enlarging it for our products through the exclusion of others, we must decline to their advice, which instead of alleviating would increase our embarrassment. We have no monopoly in the supply of our products. One half of the globe may produce them. Should we reduce our production, others stand ready by increasing theirs to take our place, and instead of raising prices, we would only diminish our share of the supply. We are thus compelled to produce on the penalty of loosing our hold on the general market. Once lost it may be lost forever; and lose it we must, if we continue to be compelled as we now are, on the one hand by general competition of the world to sell low, and on the other by the Tariff to buy high. We cannot withstand this double action. Our ruin must follow. In fact our only permanent and safe remedy is not the rise in the price of what we sell in which we can receive but little aid from our Government, but a reduction in that which we buy which is prevented by the interference of the Government. Give us a free and open competition in our own market, and we fear not to encounter like competition in the general market of the world. If under all of our discouragement by the acts of our Government, we are still able to contend there against the world, can it be doubted, if this impediment were removed, we would force out all competitors; and thus also enlarge our market, not by the oppression of our fellow citizens of other States, but by our industry, enterprize [*sic*] and natural advantages.

3. Senator Daniel Webster Lays Out His Nationalist Vision, 1830

Sir, let me recur to pleasing recollections; let me indulge in refreshing remembrance of the past; let me remind you that, in early times, no States cherished greater harmony, both of principle and feeling, than Massachusetts and South Carolina. Would to God that harmony might again return! ...

I understand the honorable gentleman from South Carolina to maintain, that it is a right of the State legislatures to interfere, whenever, in their judgment, this government transcends its constitutional limits, and to arrest the operation of its laws.

I understand him to maintain this right, as a right existing *under* the Constitution, not as a right to overthrow it on the ground of extreme necessity, such as would justify violent revolution.

I understand him to maintain an authority, on the part of the States, thus to interfere, for the purpose of correcting the exercise of power by the general government, of checking it, and of compelling it to conform to their opinion of the extent of its powers.

I understand him to maintain, that the ultimate power of judging of the constitutional extent of its own authority is not lodged exclusively in the general government, or any branch of it: but that, on the contrary, the States may

Second reply to Hayne (January 26–27, 1830), in *Speeches and Formal Writings*, I, Daniel Webster, 285–348, as reprinted in *Daniel Webster: The Completest Man*, ed. Kenneth E. Shewmaker (Hanover, N.H.: University Press of New England, 1990), 113–120.

lawfully decide for themselves, and each State for itself, whether, in a given case, the act of the general government transcends its power.

I understand him to insist, that, if the exigency of the case, in the opinion of any State government, require it, such State government may, by its own sovereign authority, annul an act of the general government which it deems plainly and palpably unconstitutional.

This is the sum of what I understand from him to be the South Carolina doctrine, and the doctrine which he maintains. I propose to consider it, and compare it with the Constitution....

This leads us to inquire into the origin of this government and the source of its power. Whose agent is it? Is it the creature of the State legislatures, or the creature of the people? If the government of the United States be the agent of the State governments, then they may control it, provided they can agree in the manner of controlling it; if it be the agent of the people, then the people alone can control it, restrain it, modify, or reform it. It is observable enough, that the doctrine for which the honorable gentleman contends leads him to the necessity of maintaining, not only that this general government is the creature of the States, but that it is the creature of each of the States severally, so that each may assert the power for itself of determining whether it acts within the limits of its authority. It is the servant of four-and-twenty masters of different wills and different purposes and yet bound to obey all. This absurdity (for it seems no less) arises from a misconception as to the origin of this government and its true character. It is, Sir, the people's Constitution, the people's government, made for the people, made by the people, and answerable to the people. The people of the United States have declared that the Constitution shall be the supreme law. We must either admit the proposition, or dispute their authority. The States are, unquestionably, sovereign, so far as their sovereignty is not affected by this supreme law. But the State legislatures, as political bodies, however sovereign, are yet not sovereign over the people. So far as the people have given power to the general government, so far the grant is unquestionably good, and the government holds of the people, and not of the State governments. We are all agents of the same supreme power, the people. The general government and the State governments derive their authority from the same source. Neither can, in relation to the other, be called primary, though one is definite and restricted, and the other general and residuary. The national government possesses those powers which it can be shown the people have conferred on it, and no more. All the rest belongs to the State governments, or to the people themselves. So far as the people have restrained State sovereignty, by the expression of their will, in the Constitution of the United States, so far, it must be admitted, State sovereignty is effectually controlled. I do not contend that it is, or ought to be, controlled farther. The sentiment to which I have referred propounds that State sovereignty is only to be controlled by its own "feeling of justice": that is to say, it is not to be controlled at all, for one who is to follow his own feelings is under no legal control. Now, however men may think this ought to be, the fact is, that the people of the United States have chosen to impose control on State sovereignties. There are those, doubtless, who wish they had been left without restraint; but the Constitution has ordered the matter differently. To make war, for instance, is an exercise of sovereignty; but the Constitution declares that no State shall make war. To coin money is another exercise of sovereign power, but no State is at liberty to coin money. Again, the Constitution says that no sovereign State shall be so sovereign as to make a treaty. These prohibitions, it must be confessed, are a control on the State sovereignty of South Carolina, as well as of the other States, which does not arise "from her own feelings of honorable justice." The opinion referred to, therefore, is in defiance of the plainest provisions of the Constitution....

... I hold [this government] to be a popular government, erected by the people; those who administer it, responsible to the people; and itself capable of being amended and modified, just as the people may choose it should be. It is as popular, just as truly emanating from the people, as the State governments. It is created for one purpose; the State governments for another. It has its own powers; they have theirs. There is no more authority with them to arrest the operation of a law of Congress, than with Congress to arrest the operation of their laws.... The States cannot now make war; they cannot contract alliances; they cannot make, each for itself, separate regulations of commerce; they cannot lay imposts; they cannot coin money. If this Constitution, Sir, be the creature of State legislatures, it must be admitted that it has obtained a strange control over the volitions of its creators....

... Sir, the people have wisely provided, in the Constitution itself, a proper, suitable mode and tribunal for settling questions of constitutional law. There are in the Constitution grants of powers to Congress, and restrictions on these powers. There are, also, prohibitions on the States. Some authority must, therefore, necessarily exist, having the ultimate jurisdiction to fix and ascertain the interpretation of these grants, restrictions, and prohibitions. The Constitution has itself pointed out, ordained, and established that authority. How has it accomplished this great and essential end? By declaring, Sir, that *"the Constitution, and the laws of the United States made in pursuance thereof, shall be the supreme law of the land, any thing in the constitution or laws of any State to the contrary notwithstanding."*

This, Sir, was the first great step. By this the supremacy of the Constitution and laws of the United States is declared. The people so will it. No State law is to be valid which comes in conflict with the Constitution, or any law of the United States passed in pursuance of it. But who shall decide this question of interference? To whom lies the last appeal? This, Sir, the Constitution itself decides also, by declaring, *"that the judicial power shall extend to all cases arising under the Constitution and laws of the United States."* These two provisions cover the whole ground. They are, in truth, the keystone of the arch! With these it is a government; without them it is a confederation.... Congress established, at its very first session, in the judicial act, a mode for carrying them into full effect, and for bringing all questions of constitutional power to the final decision of the Supreme Court. It then, Sir, became a government. It then had the means of self-protection; and but for this, it would, in all probability, have been now among things which are past. Having constituted the government, and declared its powers, the people have further said, that, since somebody must decide on the extent of these powers, the government shall itself decide; subject, always, like other popular governments, to the responsibility to the people.

—Liberty *and* Union, now and for ever, one and inseparable!

4. President Andrew Jackson Condemns the Rights of "Nullification" and Secession, 1832

To preserve this bond of our political existence from destruction, to maintain inviolate this state of national honor and prosperity, and to justify the confidence my fellow-citizens have reposed in me, I, Andrew Jackson, President of the United States, have thought proper to issue this my proclamation, stating my views of the Constitution and laws applicable to the measures adopted by the convention of South Carolina and to the reasons they have put forth to sustain them, declaring the course which duty will require me to pursue, and, appealing to the understanding and patriotism of the people, warn them of the consequences that must inevitably result from an observance of the dictates of the convention.

The ordinance is founded, not on the indefeasible right of resisting acts which are plainly unconstitutional and too oppressive to be endured, but on the strange position that any one State may not only declare an act of Congress void, but prohibit its execution; that they may do this consistently with the Constitution; that the true construction of that instrument permits a State to retain its place in the Union and yet be bound by no other of its laws than those it may choose to consider as constitutional. It is true, they add, that to justify this abrogation of a law it must be palpably contrary to the Constitution; but it is evident that to give the right of resisting laws of that description, coupled with the uncontrolled right to decide what laws deserve that character, is to give the power of resisting all laws; for as by the theory there is no appeal, the reasons alleged by the State, good or bad, must prevail....

This right to secede is deduced from the nature of the Constitution, which, they say, is a compact between sovereign States who have preserved their whole sovereignty and therefore are subject to no superior; that because they made the compact they can break it when in their opinion it has been departed from by the other States. Fallacious as this course of reasoning is, it enlists State pride and finds advocates in the honest prejudices of those who have not studied the nature of our Government sufficiently to see the radical error on which it rests.

The people of the United States formed the Constitution, acting through the State legislatures in making the compact, to meet and discuss its provisions, and acting in separate conventions when they ratified those provisions; but the terms used in its construction show it to be a Government in which the people of all the States, collectively, are represented. We are *one people* in the choice of President and Vice-President. Here the States have no other agency than to

Andrew Jackson, "Proclamation to the People of South Carolina, December 10, 1832."

direct the mode in which the votes shall be given. The candidates having the majority of all the votes are chosen. The electors of a majority of States may have given their votes for one candidate, and yet another may be chosen. The people, then, and not the States, are represented in the executive branch.

In the House of Representatives there is this difference, that the people of one State do not, as in the case of President and Vice-President, all vote for the same officers. The people of all the States do not vote for all the members, each State electing only its own representatives. But this creates no material distinction. When chosen, they are all representatives of the United States, not representatives of the particular State from which they come. They are paid by the United States, not by the State; nor are they accountable to it for any act done in the performance of their legislative functions; and however they may in practice, as it is their duty to do, consult and prefer the interests of their particular constituents when they come in conflict with any other partial or local interest, yet it is their first and highest duty, as representatives of the United States, to promote the general good.

The Constitution of the United States … forms a *government,* not a league; and whether it be formed by compact between the States or in any other manner, its character is the same. It is a Government in which all the people are represented, which operates directly on the people individually, not upon the States; they retained all the power they did not grant. But each State, having expressly parted with so many powers as to constitute, jointly with the other States, a single nation, can not, from that period, possess any right to secede, because such secession does not break a league, but destroys the unity of a nation....

Fellow-citizens of my native State, let me not only admonish you, as the First Magistrate of our common country, not to incur the penalty of its laws, but use the influence that a father would over his children whom he saw rushing to certain ruin. In that paternal language, with that paternal feeling, let me tell you, my countrymen, that you are deluded by men who are either deceived themselves or wish to deceive you.... They are not champions of liberty, emulating the fame of our Revolutionary fathers, nor are you an oppressed people, contending, as they repeat to you, against worse than colonial vassalage. You are free members of a flourishing and happy Union. There is no settled design to oppress you.

5. President Andrew Jackson Vetoes the Bank Bill, 1832

A bank of the United States is in many respects convenient for the Government and useful to the people. Entertaining this opinion, and deeply impressed with the belief that some of the powers and privileges possessed by the existing bank are unauthorized by the Constitution, subversive of the rights of the States, and dangerous to the liberties of the people. I felt it my duty at an early period of my

James D. Richardson, ed., *A Compilation of the Messages and Papers of the Presidents, 1789–1897,* II (Authority of Congress, 1899), 576–577, 590.

Administration to call the attention of Congress to the practicability of organizing an institution combining all its advantages and obviating these objections. I sincerely regret that in the act before me I can perceive none of those modifications of the bank charter which are necessary, in my opinion, to make it compatible with justice, with sound policy, or with the Constitution of our country.

The present corporate body … enjoys an exclusive privilege of banking under the authority of the General Government, a monopoly of its favor and support, and, as a necessary consequence, almost a monopoly of the foreign and domestic exchange. The powers, privileges, and favors bestowed upon it in the original charter, by increasing the value of the stock far above its par value, operated as a gratuity of many millions to the stockholders.…

It is not our own citizens only who are to receive the bounty of our Government. More than eight millions of the stock of this bank are held by foreigners. By this act the American Republic proposes virtually to make them a present of some millions of dollars. For these gratuities to foreigners and to some of our own opulent citizens the act secures no equivalent whatever.…

But this act does not permit competition in the purchase of this monopoly. It seems to be predicated on the erroneous idea that the present stockholders have a prescriptive right not only to the favor but to the bounty of Government. It appears that more than a fourth part of the stock is held by foreigners and the residue is held by a few hundred of our own citizens, chiefly of the richest class. For their benefit does this act exclude the whole American people from competition in the purchase of this monopoly and dispose of it for many millions less than it is worth.…

It is to be regretted that the rich and powerful too often bend the acts of government to their selfish purposes. Distinctions in society will always exist under every just government. Equality of talents, of education, or of wealth can not be produced by human institutions. In the full enjoyment of the gifts of Heaven and the fruits of superior industry, economy, and virtue, every man is equally entitled to protection by law; but when the laws undertake to add to these natural and just advantages artificial distinctions, to grant titles, gratuities, and exclusive privileges, to make the rich richer and the potent more powerful, the humble members of society—the farmers, mechanics, and laborers—who have neither the time nor the means of securing like favors to themselves, have a right to complain of the injustice of their Government. There are no necessary evils in government. Its evils exist only in its abuses. If it would confine itself to equal protection, and, as Heaven does its rains, shower its favors alike on the high and the low, the rich and the poor, it would be an unqualified blessing. In the act before me there seems to be a wide and unnecessary departure from these just principles.…

Experience should teach us wisdom. Most of the difficulties our Government now encounters and most of the dangers which impend over our Union have sprung from an abandonment of the legitimate objects of Government by our national legislation, and the adoption of such principles as are embodied in this act. Many of our rich men have not been content with equal protection and equal benefits, but have besought us to make them richer by act of Congress.

By attempting to gratify their desires we have in the results of our legislation arrayed section against section, interest against interest, and man against man, in a fearful commotion which threatens to shake the foundations of our Union. It is time to pause in our career to review our principles, and if possible revive that devoted patriotism and spirit of compromise which distinguished the sages of the Revolution and the fathers of our Union.

6. Lieutenant-Colonel José Enrique de la Peña Defends Mexico's Actions Against the Texans, 1836

The insults lavished upon the nation as represented by the customs officials and commanders of military detachments, the disregard for laws, and the attitudes with which the colonists looked upon those who had given them a country were more than sufficient causes to justify war on our part. They were the aggressors and we the attacked, they the ingrates, we the benefactors. When they were in want we had given them sustenance, yet as soon as they gained strength they used it to destroy us.

The neglect, the apathy, or, even more, the criminal indifference with which all [Mexican] governments without exception have watched over the national interests; the failure to enforce the colonization laws; the lack of sympathy with which the colonists had been regarded and the loyalty that these still had for their native country; these things led us into these circumstances. Because of all this, war was inevitable, for between war and dishonor there was no doubt as to the choice....

On the 17th of February the commander in chief had proclaimed to the army: "Comrades in arms," he said, "our most sacred duties have brought us to these uninhabited lands and demand our engaging in combat against a rabble of wretched adventurers to whom our authorities have unwisely given benefits that even Mexicans did not enjoy, and who have taken possession of this vast and fertile area, convinced that our own unfortunate internal divisions have rendered us incapable of defending our soil. Wretches! Soon will they become aware of their folly! Soldiers, our comrades have been shamefully sacrificed at Anáhuac, Goliad, and Béjar, and you are those destined to punish these murderers. My friends: we will march as long as the interests of the nation that we serve demand. The claimants to the acres of Texas land will soon know to their sorrow that their reinforcements from New Orleans, Mobile, Boston, New York, and other points north, whence they should never have come, are insignificant, and that Mexicans, generous by nature, will not leave unpunished affronts resulting in injury or discredit to their country, regardless of who the aggressors may be."

This address was received enthusiastically, but the army needed no incitement; knowing that it was about to engage in the defense of the country and to avenge less fortunate comrades was enough for its ardor to become as great

José Enrique de la Peña, *With Santa Anna in Texas: A Personal Narrative of the Revolution*, trans. Carmen Perry (College Station: Texas A&M University Press, 1975), 4–5, 40–52.

as the noble and just cause it was about to defend.... For their part, the enemy leaders had addressed their own men in terms not unlike those of our commander. They said that we were a bunch of mercenaries, blind instruments of tyranny; that without any right we were about to invade their territory; that we would bring desolation and death to their peaceful homes and would seize their possessions; that we were savage men who would rape their women, decapitate their children, destroy everything, and render into ashes the fruits of their industry and their efforts. Unfortunately they did partially foresee what would happen, but they also committed atrocities that we did not commit, and in this rivalry of evil and extermination, I do not dare to venture who had the ignominious advantage, they or we! ...

When our commander in chief haughtily rejected the agreement that the enemy had proposed, [the Alamo's Commander, William B.] Travis became infuriated at the contemptible manner in which he had been treated and, expecting no honorable way of salvation, chose the path that strong souls choose in crisis, that of dying with honor, and selected the Alamo for his grave....

Our commander became more furious when he saw that the enemy resisted the idea of surrender. He believed as others did that the fame and honor of the army were compromised the longer the enemy lived.... In fact, it was necessary only to await the artillery's arrival at Béjar for these to surrender; undoubtedly they could not have resisted for many hours the destruction and imposing fire from twenty cannon....

Among the defenders there were thirty or more colonists; the rest were pirates, used to defying danger and to disdaining death, and who for that reason fought courageously; their courage, to my way of thinking, merited them the mercy for which, toward the last, some of them pleaded; others not knowing the language, were unable to do so.... The order had been given to spare no one but the women and this was carried out, but such carnage was useless and had we prevented it, we would have saved much blood on our part....

This scene of extermination went on for an hour before the curtain of death covered and ended it: shortly after six in the morning it was all finished.

7. Michel Chevelier, a French Visitor, Marvels at the Pageantry of Politics, 1839

But this entry of the hickory [that is, the entrance of Andrew Jackson] was but a bymatter compared with the procession I witnessed in New York. It was in the night after the closing of the polls, when victory had pronounced in favour of the democratic party.... The procession was nearly a mile long; the democrats marched in good order to the glare of torches; the banners were more numerous than I had ever seen them in any religious festival; all were in transparency, on account of the darkness. On some were inscribed the names of the democratic

Michel Chevelier, *Society, Manners, and Politics in the United States* (Boston: Weeks, Jordan and Company, 1839), 318–319.

societies or sections; *Democratic young men of the ninth* or *eleventh ward;* others bore imprecations against the Bank of the United States; *Nick Biddle* and *Old Nick* here figured largely, and formed the pendant of our *libera nos a malo.* Then came portraits of General Jackson afoot and on horseback; there was one in the uniform of a general, and another in the person of the Tennessee farmer, with the famous hickory cane in his hand. Those of Washington and Jefferson, surrounded with democratic mottoes, were mingled with emblems in all tastes and of all colours. Among these figured an eagle, not a painting, but a real live eagle, tied by the legs, surrounded by a wreath of leaves, and hoisted upon a pole, after the manner of the Roman standards. The imperial bird was carried by a stout sailor, more pleased than ever was a sergeant permitted to hold one of the strings of the canopy, in a catholic ceremony. From further than the eye could reach, came marching on the democrats. I was struck with the resemblance of their air to the train that escorts the *viaticum* in Mexico or Puebla. The American standard-bearers were as grave as the Mexican Indians who bore the sacred tapers. The democratic procession, also, like the Catholic procession, had its halting places; it stopped before the houses of the Jackson men to fill the air with cheers, and halted at the doors of the leaders of the Opposition, to give three, six, or nine groans. If these scenes were to find a painter, they would be admired at a distance, not less than the triumphs and sacrificial pomps, which the ancients have left us delineated in marble and brass; for they are not mere grotesques after the manner of Rembrandt, they belong to history, they partake of the grand; they are the episodes of a wondrous epic which will bequeath a lasting memory to posterity; that of the coming of democracy.

8. John L. O'Sullivan, a Democratic Newspaperman, Defines "Manifest Destiny," 1845

Texas is now ours. Already, before these words are written, her Convention has undoubtedly ratified the acceptance, by her Congress, of our proffered invitation into the Union; and made the requisite changes in her already republican form of constitution to adapt it to its future federal relations. Her star and her stripe may already be said to have taken their place in the glorious blazon of our common nationality; and the sweep of our eagle's wing already includes within its circuit the wide extent of her fair and fertile land....

Why, were other reasoning wanting, in favor of now elevating this question of the reception of Texas into the Union, out of the lower region of our past party dissensions, up to its proper level of a high and broad nationality, it surely is to be found, found abundantly, in the manner in which other nations have undertaken to intrude themselves into it, between us and the proper parties to the case, in a spirit of hostile interference against us, for the avowed object of thwarting our policy and hampering our power, limiting our greatness and

John L. O'Sullivan, editorial on Manifest Destiny and Texas Annexation, *United States Magazine and Democratic Review*, October 1837.

checking the fulfilment of our manifest destiny to overspread the continent allotted by Providence for the free development of our yearly multiplying millions. This we have seen done by England, our old rival and enemy; and by France, strangely coupled with her against us....

It is wholly untrue, and unjust to ourselves, the pretence that the Annexation has been a measure of spoliation, unrightful and unrighteous—of military conquest under forms of peace and law—of territorial aggrandizement at the expense of justice, and justice due by a double sanctity to the weak.... If Texas became peopled with an American population, it was by no contrivance of our government, but on the express invitation of that of Mexico herself; accompanied with such guaranties of State independence, and the maintenance of a federal system analogous to our own, as constituted a compact fully justifying the strongest measures of redress on the part of those afterwards deceived in this guaranty, and sought to be enslaved under the yoke imposed by its violation. She was released, rightfully and absolutely released, from all Mexican allegiance, or duty of cohesion to the Mexican political body, by the acts and fault of Mexico herself, and Mexico alone. There never was a clearer case. It was not revolution; it was resistance to revolution....

Nor is there any just foundation for the charge that Annexation is a great pro-slavery measure—calculated to increase and perpetuate that institution. Slavery had nothing to do with it. Opinions were and are greatly divided, both at the North and South, as to the influence to be exerted by it on Slavery and the Slave States....

California will, probably, next fall away from the loose adhesion which, in such a country as Mexico, holds a remote province in a slight equivocal kind of dependence on the metropolis. Imbecile and distracted, Mexico never can exert any real governmental authority over such a country.... Already the advance guard of the irresistible army of Anglo-Saxon emigration has begun to pour down upon it, armed with the plough and the rifle, and marking its trail with schools and colleges, courts and representative halls, mills and meeting-houses. A population will soon be in actual occupation of California, over which it will be idle for Mexico to dream of dominion. They will necessarily become independent. All this without agency of our government, without responsibility of our people—in the natural flow of events, the spontaneous working of principles, and the adaptation of the tendencies and wants of the human race to the elemental circumstances in the midst of which they find themselves placed.

9. Walter Colton, a Californian, Describes the Excitement of the Gold Rush, 1848

Tuesday, June 20. [1848] My messenger sent to the mines, has returned with specimens of the gold; he dismounted in a sea of upturned faces. As he drew

Walter Colton, *Three Years in California* (New York: A. S. Barnes and Co., 1850; reprinted, Stanford, Calif.: Stanford University Press, 1949), 246–249, 252–253.

forth the yellow lumps from his pockets, and passed them around among the eager crowd, the doubts, which had lingered till now, fled.... All were off for the mines, some on horses, some on carts, and some on crutches, and one went in a litter. An American woman, who had recently established a boarding-house here, pulled up stakes, and was off before her lodgers had even time to pay their bills. Debtors ran, of course. I have only a community of women left, and a gang of prisoners, with here and there a soldier, who will give his captain the slip at the first chance. I don't blame the fellow a whit; seven dollars a month, while others are making two or three hundred a day! that is too much for human nature to stand....

Tuesday, July 18. Another bag of gold from the mines, and another spasm in the community. It was brought down by a sailor from Yuba river, and contains a hundred and thirty-six ounces. It is the most beautiful gold that has appeared in the market; it looks like the yellow scales of the dolphin, passing through his rainbow hues at death. My carpenters, at work on the school-house, on seeing it, threw down their saws and planes, shouldered their picks and are off for the Yuba. Three seamen ran from the Warren, forfeiting their four years' pay; and a whole platoon of soldiers from the fort left only their colors behind. One old woman declared she would never again break an egg or kill a chicken, without examining yolk and gizzard....

Thursday, Aug. 16. Four citizens of Monterey are just in from the gold mines on Feather River, where they worked in company with three others. They employed about thirty wild Indians, who are attached to the rancho owned by one of the party. They worked precisely seven weeks and three days, and have divided seventy-six thousand eight hundred and forty-four dollars,—nearly eleven thousand dollars to each. Make a dot there, and let me introduce a man, well known to me, who has worked on the Yuba river sixty-four days, and brought back, as the result of his individual labor, five thousand three hundred and fifty-six dollars.... Make another dot there, and let me introduce a woman, of Sonoranian birth, who has worked in the dry diggings forty-six days, and brought back two thousand one hundred and twenty-five dollars. Is not this enough to make a man throw down his leger and shoulder a pick?...

Tuesday, Aug. 28. The gold mines have upset all social and domestic arrangements in Monterey; the master has become his own servant, and the servant his own lord. The millionaire is obliged to groom his own horse, and roll his wheelbarrow; and the hidalgo—in whose veins flow the blood of all the Cortes—to clean his own boots! Here is lady L——, who has lived here seventeen years, the pride and ornament of the place, with a broomstick in her jewelled hand!

ESSAYS

Historians have long wondered what the celebrations of the "common man" and "democracy," the revelry in public parades and political campaigns, and the high rates of voter turnout in elections really meant to American society and politics.

Whereas some scholars have argued that these facts illustrate a first step in the development of a civic democracy, others focus on the less appealing aspects. Historical arguments in the second group are wide-ranging, from a condemnation of politics in this period as a democracy for white men only, to a focus on the excesses of the raucous celebrations in the period. The following two essays touch on this last argument. Although Mary P. Ryan, Professor emeritus at the University of California, Berkeley, remains mindful of the inequalities of the period, she focuses on the democracy in the streets, which was as chaotic as it was colorful. But these celebrations, she contends, represent a public democracy that we rarely see today. In contrast, Glenn C. Altschuler and Stuart M. Blumin, both of whom teach at Cornell University, consider antebellum politics to be an expression of a "rude republic." Many Americans, they contend, were turned off by politics *because* of its boisterousness. Although they might honor the American republic, these historians conclude, people in the United States in this period did not honor American politics.

Antebellum Politics as Raucous Democracy

MARY P. RYAN

In April 1834 a crowd gathered at Castle Garden in New York for "a day of general rejoicing." This festival, which brought an estimated 24,000 New Yorkers to a civic landmark on the tip of Manhattan Island, was the culmination of three days of boisterous activity on the city streets. The day before, two competing parades had clogged the downtown thoroughfares. The first formed when an open meeting of 20,000 adjourned into a procession and "rigged up a beautiful little frigate in complete order and named it the *Constitution*. As this moveable political symbol passed down Wall Street it met up with a second procession and engaged in a mock naval battle with a vessel called *Veto*. A special kind of public ritual was in process. These were partisan processions staged by Whigs and Jacksonians in the course of an electoral campaign. The meetings, processions, and drama continued until about 10 P.M. on the third day of the voting, when some 15,000 souls gathered on Wall Street to learn the final tally of votes."

… Much of what is known as Jacksonian democracy was acted out on the same principles as the everyday sociability and holiday conviviality of the city. The meeting of October 1835 that launched the radical democratic politics of the Loco-Foco wing of the Jacksonian movement was recorded in the press as follows: "After the adoption of the revolutions a motion was carried that the meeting adjourn to the street in front of the Hall and form a procession with their antimonopoly Banners, Flags, etc., which was accordingly carried—and some thousands of the meeting bearing torches, candles, etc., marched up the Bowery cheering their Democratic citizens on the way." By the end of the

From Mary P. Ryan, *Civic Wars: Democracy and Public Life in the American City During the Nineteenth Century*, pp. 94–96, 108, 109–110, 112–117, 119–120, 121, 124, 129–131. Copyright © 1997. Reprinted by permission of the University of California Press.

1840s the enthusiasm had spread across the land. Whigs and Jacksonians locked horns in New Orleans as early as 1837, and in the 1849 municipal election the Democrats marched "through some of the principle [*sic*] streets with a profusion of June torches, making a splendid display. The principle feature of the procession was an artificial chicken cock of gigantic dimensions, triumphantly born aloft, and which attracted universal attention." When San Franciscans elected their first mayor in 1850, their festivities included a band stationed on the balcony above the Plaza and a parade of carts pulled by teams of horses, adorned with flags and banners, and carrying voters to the polls. And this was just a primary election. The final polling featured a dashing equestrian display in the Plaza by one Captain Bryant, who carried off the office of sheriff. The Democrats also pitched a tent in the Plaza and named it "Tammany Hall." One of the first things that the forty-niners hastily unpacked on arrival in California were these rites of representation: ward meetings, parades, partisan loyalties.

Such public displays indicate that city people defined themselves not just according to ... social groupings ... but by the political status of citizen and by a range of partisan affiliations. Political campaigns were yet another example of the immense potential for associated activity in urban public space: They were staged, like civic ceremonies, in places such as Wall Street, the Plaza, "the principle streets of the city." But there was more at stake in these partisan gatherings than in [other] aspects of civic culture.... First of all, these partisan public events were a direct exercise of political citizenship and brought into play the doctrine of popular sovereignty, a title to rights, and a token of power. With his treasured (exclusively male) franchise, the citizen became an actual participant in self-government. Second, when sovereign citizens came together for expressly political reasons, they did something more than display their cultural differences; they acknowledged and acted on their interdependency and agreed implicitly to work together to achieve some things, however circumscribed, that could not be trusted to chance, the market, or individual effort. Third, [this] political culture... put urban heterogeneity to an extreme and decisive test. A partisan election placed different opinions in open competition: It was a declaration of civic war. A participant at the founding meeting of the Loco-Focos proudly described the event as "a struggle of gladiators on the platform around the chair;—the loudest vociferations are heard, and Tammany trembles with intestine war."

The contentious urban politics of the Jacksonian era was also, as Tocqueville had divined, a major stimulant to the frenetic formation of voluntary associations during the antebellum period. "In all the countries where political associations are prohibited, civil associations are rare. It is hardly probable that this is the result of accident; but the inference should rather be, that there is a natural and perhaps a necessary connection between these two kinds of association." Political events in New York, New Orleans, and San Francisco between 1825 and 1850 lend support to Tocqueville's inference. In fact the precise distinctions between politics, government, and more general urban associations are often difficult to determine. Antebellum citizenship was most always exercised in association with one's fellows: To the pioneers of antebellum democracy, the sacred civic act was not a private exercise of conscience or the individual practice of intellect but, in the words of the Loco-Focos, "speechifying and resolutions at political meetings."…

Democratizing the Public

Public meetings were part cause and part effect of a major campaign to dissolve the bonds of deference that wove through republican institutions and to build democratic procedures. As of 1820 democracy was a relatively limited component of municipal government. The municipal charter of New York, for example, entrusted the public good to a common council that was composed of and elected by propertied citizens. Elected council members in turn rarely consulted with the citizenry, before or after they entered office. The passage from deferential republicanism to "pure democracy" was gradual but ultimately decisive. In 1821 the city of New York removed most all property restrictions on the franchise (making a pointed exception for those of African descent). The same reform was accomplished in New Orleans when a statewide constitutional convention met in 1845. City charters and state constitutions alike were rewritten to bind legislators closer to the electorate….

The purport of these reforms was to invest governmental legitimacy in representative procedures, whose advances in the 1830s and 1840s tell a familiar story: Elections became the critical act of a republican polity; the Jacksonians masterminded techniques of persuading voters; and electoral contests became a standoff between two principal party organizations. But neither the institution of representative government nor the creation of two parties was sufficient to create what the Loco-Focos would call pure democracy. That political ideal also reordered the relationships between voters and office holders, and among fellow citizens. Deference gave way to participation and converted harmony into opposition, which was the trademark of a public meeting.

Face-to-face congregations in public space were the most caustic solvents of the barrier between electors and office holders. As early as 1827, when the press had just begun addressing local issues, some public assemblages were defying the etiquette of deference. The *New York Evening Post* embraced direct democracy along with the party of Jackson in this account of a November rally: "The number who attended the late Jackson meeting in the park were so numerous and unprecedented…. Jackson is the favorite of the people." A Democratic meeting on March 28, 1834, illustrates the forward momentum of popular politics: It was called "The Great Meeting of the People—Triumphant Expression of Public Opinions." At about the same time the democratization of political institutions became a matter of debate in the Louisiana constitutional convention and moved candidates for office in New Orleans to announce themselves forthrightly as "Friendly to Popular Rights." Already in 1834 the *Bee* extolled the spirit that animated the Democratic public meetings of that era as "the power of the People when they declare their will."…

It was through the circuit of the public meetings, furthermore, that the spirit of democracy was thrust into the annals of the American political tradition.

Perhaps the most memorable public meeting of the era was that "Great Democratick Republican County Meeting" that took place in New York on October 30, 1835. Its claim to fame is the formulation of the major planks of the Democratic Party platform for well into the future—opposition to the national bank, tariffs, monopolies, and paper money. It is also justly famed for the flair of its democratic expression. This meeting made its historical mark after some party leaders, expecting a popular defeat, tried to terminate a nominating meeting by extinguishing the lights in the public hall. Then, as the story goes, "Total darkness, for a moment, prevailed; but in a twinkling of an eye hundreds of candles were pulled from the pockets of the people, which by the aid of Loco-Foco matches were immediately lighted and old Tammany, amid the cheers of the democracy blazed in her premature and resplendent glory."

The "cheers of the Democracy" that went up from the public hall in 1835 thrust the name "Loco-Foco" into the American historical record and have rightfully captured the attention of historians. Other principles, proclaimed in a more reserved manner at that meeting, also merit comment. The single largest concern of the twenty-four resolutions passed that evening in October was the rights and procedures of the public meeting. Resolution 6 put it this way: "the people have the right and duly at all times... to assemble together to consult for the common good." References to an older construction of the public, as some larger good that stood above and apart from the mixed and mundane interests of the citizenry, were overshadowed by appeals to the "people" as they "assembled together." The members of a public meeting were obliged to "Give utterances to their sentiments, give instruction to their representatives, and to apply to the legislature for redress of wrong and grievances, by address, petitions and remonstrances." Subsequent resolutions went on to spell out the procedures of popular expression, free assembly, direct elections, reduced terms in office, and majority rule. Two weeks later the *Evening Post* put this vernacular political theory forthrightly: "to carry on to the fullest extent the principles of pure democracy."...

Many antebellum politicians harbored a deep antipathy to the democracy of the public meeting. To James Brooks such political associations were hardly better than barnyard gatherings: "Men must be herded as cattle are herded. All classes, all parties, all occupations make use of societies for all purposes.... The societies of the day—not the thinking individual men who make them up—are the winds that often form the gale of public opinion." Others were still plotting to maintain suffrage as a privilege of the propertied and to install presidential authority behind the fortress of a ten-year term. But such antidemocratic sentiments were rarely spoken in a loud public voice after 1840. In the words of one historian the rivals of the Jacksonians maintained "An almost deafening silence on the entire subject of political democracy." When the political faction that opposed Andrew Jackson's attack on the Bank of the United States found its name, "The Whig Party," during the New York City municipal election of 1834, it entered the partisan fray on terms set by radical democrats. By organizing publicly in order to object to the policies of an administration sitting in Washington, they provided the final solidification of a democracy of difference: They practiced and legitimized open, institutionalized, popular opposition.

Well before the presidential election of 1840, which heralded the second party system at the national electoral level, the Whigs had gone public in New York and New Orleans. In New Orleans in 1837 they claimed "The Whig Party is actually the Democratic Party." And in New York they adopted the official title "Democratic Whigs." Soon the opposition employed the nominating procedures of the Loco-Focos, complete with ward-level public meetings and primary elections. They had installed a decisive, quite close, and cogent bipartisan political rivalry that would endure for fifteen years. As a number of historians have demonstrated, the Whigs and Jacksonians placed before the American people a clear set of ideological and programmatic choices on everything from finance to public investment, the judiciary, and the corporations. By the late 1840s the Whigs had capitulated to popular procedure and created a foundation for democratic contestation in each city. The *New Orleans Picayune* geared up for a "struggle" on election day; in San Francisco the *Alta Californian* endorsed a system of representation in which "everyone will have the opportunity to express his wishes"; and the *New York Tribune* published calls to meetings of "The Democratic Whig Party" in every ward of the city.

As the principles of democratic opposition spread from the Jacksonians to the Whigs and from the Northeast to the South and West, its physical setting became more picturesque. In New Orleans in the 1840s the haughty Whigs met at the St. Louis Hotel or the Exchange, while the more populist Democrats assembled in the open air along Canal Street. The first American-style election in San Francisco in the spring of 1850 revealed the range of spatial possibilities that had become available for electioneering purposes at midcentury. The Whigs called the faithful to deposit their ballots in a "Primary election" to take place "At the house on Clay Street, three doors below Elleard's." The Democrats chose their candidate at a primary election held in Portsmouth Square from 7 A.M. to 7 P.M. and then ratified the nomination with a mass meeting in the same central location, where they called for yet another public meeting a few days later. This announcement—"The rights of the people will Not be Sold. Independent Mass meeting to rally the nomination of the Independent Washington Club"—includes a special invitation to "mechanics, workingmen, and all who are opposed to private clichés and hackneyed politicians." Democratic procedures of nominating representatives had become habitual by 1850: They were transmitted across the continent, available to third parties, and already associated with "hackneyed politicians."

This aggressive public spirit was maintained through election day itself. The actual casting of votes ... reassembled the same people for a more prolonged, festive, and decisive public meeting. Ward meetings orchestrated this transition by appointing as many as 200 of their number to act as a "vigilance committee," pledged to stand watch over the polls for the duration of the balloting. At a time when municipalities restricted efforts to create a registry of voters as antidemocratic, the election was still a quite open convocation. The ward assemblies, nominating conventions, and elections were transfer points in a relay of authority, a direct passing of the baton of power unto another representation of the people. Meeting-place democracy shared in the public character of the civic parade: It transpired in open urban space and was diffused through segments such as wards, centered in times and spaces such as election day, and invested with a festive and contentious sociability. In scarcely two decades the sedate and constricted republican form … had been stormed and supplanted by the boisterous politics of the public meeting.…

The Political Definition of the People

The rhetoric of democracy seemed forthright: It proclaimed the rights of all the people to participate in the process of representation. But democracy as an actual political practice was something else again: It almost always came with strings attached and with specific provisos as to which people counted at any particular time and place. Of the cities of New York, New Orleans, and San Francisco between 1825 and 1850, at least this much can be said: The ranks of "the people who counted" had expanded significantly. In fact one of the major consequences of the culture of public meetings was to beg the question of who were, exactly, the people.

The Loco-Foco meeting answered this provocative question in the expansive language of "Equal Rights," ostensibly welcoming everyone into the democratic public. The first of the Loco-Foco's fabled resolutions proclaimed that "'all men are created equal'—that these United States are a nation—and that the national rights of every citizen are equal and indivisible." The third resolution elaborated, "That in a free state all distinctions but those of merit are odious and offensive and to be discouraged by a people jealous of their liberties." The principle was underscored again in resolution 4, which characterized all laws that would thwart "equal rights and privileges by the great body of the people [as] odious, unjust and unconstitutional." This notion of equal citizenship did not appear out of nowhere, however, or descend from high-minded universalistic principles of republicanism. It was championed by select social groups who had found in the public meeting a place to mobilize to claim their equal rights.

The notion of equal rights was the cutting edge (hardly the culmination) of a movement to expand access to democratic citizenship. In the early nineteenth century it was a political tool wielded most effectively by white males of the middling and lower social ranks. By the mid-1820s propertyless white men had secured the franchise, won the right to hold public office, and found a niche in the Democratic Republican Party. Soon this party of the "people" had booted the federalist "aristocracy" out of power across the nation. By the 1830s the ward-level meetings of Jacksonians styled their party the champions of the people against "the arts of the aristocracy" as practiced by the Whigs. The first mayor "ever elevated to that office by the suffrage of the people" was hailed in the *Evening Post* as a conqueror of "Besotted bank merchants" and champion of "the poor laborer who will not kneel at their footstool, who will not lay down his inestimable rights of equal political freedom, and consent to be their abject slave." By that raucous spring election of 1835 this rhetorical division of the people, between aristocrats and common men, had become a matter of electoral strategy. The Jacksonian press noted, for example, that although the fifteenth ward "is considered [in] an especial manner as the quarter of the aristocracy, yet there are enough democrats residing within it to secure the success of the democratic ticket if they will but exert themselves with spirit." In that year the Jacksonians lost the fifteenth ward, but by only a small margin....

This is not to say that the political hospitality to difference was without its clear limits as of 1850. Some barriers to being counted among the people were left intact, and others were even fortified during the age of Jackson. The political public, the whole representative circuit from the ballot box and its contiguous spaces—the parade, the nominating conventions, the rowdy congregation at the polling places—to public offices and legislative assemblies, was a pristinely white and decisively male universe. The political invisibility of both women and nonwhites coexisted with their often vivid representation in civic culture and their relatively easy access to public space. This contradiction suggests that participation in formal politics, the right to act as a citizen, was by no means an automatic translation from social and cultural publicness. This quandary requires attention.

The barrier to participation in the political public was particularly effective against women. The demand for women's suffrage raised at Seneca Falls in 1848 was seldom heard downstate, where women were seldom given even a symbolic role in partisan activities. The notice that a place for the ladies had been reserved among the Whigs gathered at New Orleans's St. Louis Hotel in 1849 was a novel appearance of women anywhere near the sites of party politics. Likewise, women seldom formed truly *public* meetings....

The status of nonwhites in the democratic public was equally anomalous and foreboding. But in this case, exclusion from citizenship was, on occasion, posed as a public and political question. In New Orleans the slave system placed the political status of all those of African American descent beyond the pale of citizenship. But once slavery was abolished in New York, democrats had to consider the meaning of citizenship for nonwhites. The constitution of 1821, the same document that removed property qualification for whites, severely restricted African American suffrage. It stipulated that only those New Yorkers of African ancestry who possessed $250 of property were entitled to vote. By this standard only 298 of almost 30,000 African Americans were granted the right. Yet this small group of enfranchised citizens pushed the democratic possibilities to their maximum. In 1837 they organized to end the property restrictions and succeeded (along with their white abolitionist allies in the Liberty Party) in placing their demands before the electorate. That referendum that demanded simply "Equal suffrage for Colored Persons" went down to a crushing defeat, by a margin of 2.6 to 1.

This mandate of the people made the hostilities to African Americans harbored by so many antebellum Americans a public matter. The Democratic Party was particularly quick to exploit these prejudices, saying, for example, that "Negroes are among but not of us" and vowing to "uphold our own race and kindred." The hostility broke out in vicious attacks on both African American neighborhoods and abolitionist conventions in New York in the 1830s....

As of 1849 the history of democratic political institutions seemed to be still advancing by precarious steps while dodging roadblocks such as race and gender. Perhaps Tocqueville's prediction of 1831 would prove right: "The further electoral rights are extended, the greater is the need of extending them: for after each concession the strength of democracy increases, and its demands increase with its strength." At the middle of the nineteenth century the progress of enfranchisement seemed to be moving onward and outward: It had leapt over distinctions of property, had beat back attempts to restrict the citizenship of the foreign born and Catholics, and had sidestepped the absolute racial standards of exclusion. Only the difference of gender seemed a categorical bar to full rights of citizenship. As of 1850 there was still a long way to go in establishing equality of citizenship, but the democratic project was set on a forward course....

The course of the democratic public through the 1830s and 1840s also ran roughshod over any refined notion of political protocol or decorum. The sheer number of what were called mobs or riots, disorderly expressions of public opinions on a panoply of issues, was higher than at any other time in American urban history. These minor civic wars were a fixture of antebellum democracy, and a goodly portion of them actually coincided with election campaigns. During the 1830s an election combined politics, ceremony, and donnybrook into one urban pageant and brought all sorts of civic differences jostling together in the streets. The processions through lower Manhattan described at the outset of this chapter and the ensuing battle between *Constitution* and *Veto* were classified as a riot in the great compendium of urban disorder collected by police chief J. T. Headley in 1873....

At the time, however, outbreaks such as this were taken more in stride, even reported in a jocular fashion. One contemporary observer of the rancorous election of 1834 reported that "A good temper prevailed" and provoked "nothing more serious as a black eye." Routine ethnic rivalries were often dismissed as "Irish shillelagh frolic" or "a furious fight ... which resulted in sundry broken heads and bloody noses." Indeed, although riots were regular occurrences in antebellum cities, they caused few fatalities. (A total of two lives were lost in scores of riots that plagued New York in the 1830s and early 1840s.) The raucous election scene in New Orleans in 1847 was reported with the same equanimity: "municipal election yesterday passed off with little disturbance ... some little squabbling" in the second municipality. Through most of the period this routine "high spirit" fell within the capacious range of civic tolerance. Not until 1845 in New York did rioting provoke a concerted attempt to establish a professional police department, and this initiative of a short-lived reform government resulted in only a minor buttressing of the old public-watch system....

In fact a riot was not so much a breakdown of democratic process as its conduct by another means. The electoral contests that were the life of a democracy were from the first washed in the rhetoric of warfare. The Loco-Focos' offensive in New York in 1835 was heralded as a "struggle of gladiators," and the whole Democratic cause was one of "Warring not against individuals but against a system of wrong and oppression." When the Whigs joined in open democratic contention, their war cries, especially in the belligerent words of James Watson Webb of the *New York Courier and Enquirer,* were even more incendiary: calls to "armour, ... fire and sword" against the "enemy." In other words the election "riots" condensed and gave a sometimes violent physical dimension to the conflict that was intrinsic to popular democracy. Any public meeting could cross over the border into a mob.... In sum, a riot was a species of political action not entirely unlike a public meeting. It was a congregation in open space to publish the collective opinion of a distinctive group. It was, like a partisan election, an act of civic warfare and an intrinsic part of what the *Evening Post* called "The great experiment we are making in popular government." Late in the 1840s this forceful expression of civic differences was still within the bonds of urban civility.

Antebellum Politics as Political Manipulation

GLENN C. ALTSCHULER AND STUART M. BLUMIN

The political procession that one day disturbed the customary quiet of the House of the Seven Gables touched a "powerful impulse" in Nathaniel Hawthorne's mysterious recluse, Clifford Pyncheon, to look out upon the "rush and roar of the human tide." The view was, however, a disappointing one, as the partisans, with their "hundreds of flaunting banners, and drums, fifes, clarions, and cymbals, reverberating between the rows of buildings," marched down too narrow a street and too close to Clifford's window. "The spectator feels it to be fool's play," Hawthorne explains, "when he can distinguish the tedious commonplace of each man's visage, with the perspiration and weary self-importance on it, and the very cut of his pantaloons, and the stiffness or laxity of his shirt-collar, and the dust on the back of his black coat." To be majestic, the procession must be seen from a more distant vantage point, "for then, by its remoteness, it melts all the petty personalities, of which it has been made up, into one broad mass of existence,—one great life,—one collected body of mankind, with a vast, homogeneous spirit animating it." Proximity might actually add to the effect on an "impressible person," but only should he, "standing alone over the brink of one of these processions,... behold it, not in its atoms, but in its aggregate,—as a mighty river of life, massive in its tide, and black with mystery, and, out of its depths, calling to the kindred depth within him."

As with the parade, so too, we would argue, with the more varied and complex processes of American electoral democracy—all can be seen from up close and from afar, by more and less "impressible" observers, absorbed in the animating spirit or attentive to the "tedious commonplace of each man's visage," beholding the "atoms" as well as the "aggregate." Historians of the United States, observing closely or from a distance, have been impressed for a very long time with the animating spirit of the nineteenth-century political spectacle, and have developed a nearly consensual view of post-Jacksonian American politics as a genuinely massive activity in which the vast majority of ordinary Americans—white, voting males, most evidently—participated with an effectiveness born of enthusiasm for and deep commitment to their political party, to specific programs and leaders, and to the idea and practice of democracy itself. "There is considerable evidence," observes Jean H. Baker, "that nineteenth-century Americans gave closer attention to politics than is the case today, thereby guaranteeing a broader, deeper under-standing of issues…. [P]arty rallies were better attended than Sunday services or even meetings of itinerant preachers," and elections "became secular holy days." This is an assessment with which more than one generation of historians would agree. Most historians would agree also that politics, and partisan commitment especially, colored many other aspects of American life. "Politics seem to enter into everything," complained a nonpartisan editor during the heat of the 1860 campaign, and William E. Gienapp has made of this the defining phrase of the penetration of politics into the lives of Clifford Pyncheon's younger and more active fellow citizens: "More than in any subsequent era," he explains, "political life formed the very essence of the pre-Civil War generation's experience." Dis-agreeing only with the temporal specificity of this claim, Michael E. McGerr restates it with a compelling metaphor, suggestive, again, of point of view. Both before and after the Civil War, he argues, the political party was not merely an institution for formulating public policy and organizing election campaigns, but "a natural lens through which to view the world."

The campaign spectacle of parades and mass rallies, and the high energy of election days in which very large proportions of eligible voters cast ballots, were only part of the process of political engagement. Prior to these events on the political calendar were the local party caucuses open to all the party's adherents, and the various nominating conventions to which these meetings of ordinary citizens sent delegates to represent them. At its grass roots, according to Robert H. Wiebe, America's parties functioned as a "lodge democracy," in which "lea-ders were made and unmade by their brothers, and all parties in the process assumed an underlying equality." More than that, the process was open to all who cared to participate: "All one needed to get into politics," Wiebe insists, "was to get into it." Fueling both the desire to join and the ongoing political battle, moreover, were partisan newspapers, maintained in cities and small towns throughout the nation, and functioning not only as local party mobilizing agen-cies and bulletin boards, but also as educators of the public, discussing political issues and providing summaries or transcripts of legislative proceedings and presi-dential and gubernatorial messages even during periods of political quiescence. "The pages of the press," McGerr asserts, "made partisanship seem essential to men's identity." Finally, the frequency of elections assured that these periods of quiescence would not last long. The election cycle varied from place to place, but everywhere in America there were annual local elections, usually in the late winter or spring, and everywhere there was some kind of partisan election—state, congressional, presidential—each year in the late summer or fall. Frequent elections meant that Americans were "perpetually acting" in a ritual of democratic reaffirmation. The political calendar, concludes Joel H. Silbey, "ensured that Americans were caught up in semipermanent and unstinting partisan warfare somewhere throughout the year every year."

This is an attractive perspective on a young and vibrant democracy, evoking the image of a political "golden age" (a phrase used from time to time to describe this era), and affirming the study of politics as a relatively unmediated manifestation of democratic American culture. The view from Clifford's window is a little more unsettling. The different expressions and postures it reveals call upon us to recognize a much more variable set of political attitudes and relations, including those less likely to affirm either the democratic responsiveness or the centrality to American life and culture of the partisan political system. Some historians have gained this view... by recognizing the direction and manipulation of nominations and campaigns by political leaders, the persisting deference by ordinary citizens to these leaders well into the era of "lodge democracy," and the essential role played by party organizers in stimulating broad participation in campaigns and elections. What is largely missing from the historical literature, however, is any sustained analysis of the nature and depth of popular political engagement, and of the possibility, even during this period of high voter turnout, spectacular campaigns, frequent elections, and a pervasive political press, of *variable* relations to political affairs on the part of those who cannot be recognized as political leaders. It is our contention that the political engagement of nineteenth-century Americans did vary significantly, over time and among ordinary citizens at any given time, and that the recognition of these variations leads to fundamental questions about Americans and their politics....

Political engagement is in many respects a behavioral phenomenon, consisting of participation of various sorts in the more and less institutionalized aspects of the political process. Men (and during the nineteenth century, only men) could be public officeholders, editors of political newspapers, officers and members of party central committees, convention delegates, and behind-the-scenes manipulators of political affairs. Or, they could attend caucuses, join campaign clubs, work at the polls, and vote; while both women and men could appear at campaign rallies, listen to speeches, read editorials in the partisan press, sign petitions, and argue politics with their friends and family. That they could also neglect to do these things—to absent themselves from a convention or rally, to read a book rather than a political newspaper, to discuss the weather rather than politics— requires us to relate political participation to the whole range of activities that constitutes a given social world, and in some fashion to measure its significance within that world.... And just as political participation can vary, so too can political attitude—from enthusiasm to indifference, from belief to skepticism, from appreciation to hostility. This, too, must be measured in some way, and related to political action as something to isolate within, but not from, American life.

The political action to which we refer was, from the 1830s through the end of the century and beyond, mostly partisan in nature. There were, to be sure, important elements of public life in American communities that the political parties often could not and did not reach: more and less official and regular "town meetings" of local citizens; local elections of certain kinds (and of all kinds in some places); religious, benevolent, and reform activities of high-minded women and men; and extralegal vigilante committees in areas where public institutions were not, or not yet, well established. Particularly in the years before the establishment of strong party institutions, there were lines of political influence and loyalty that were personal rather than partisan. But if Americans experienced for a time the pre-party "meeting-place democracy" that Mary P. Ryan has recently described, and if established local leaders continued to exercise a considerable personal influence, the reach of the institutionalized parties was clearly expanding across all of these domains. More ritualized and celebratory public events, such as Fourth of July parades and local agricultural fairs, retained their nonpartisan character through nearly all these years (though the passions of the Civil War years challenged some of them), and, as Jean Baker has convincingly argued, continued to contribute in a quite different way to the sense and meaning of civic life. But the parties, as we will discuss, quickly assumed the organization of what virtually everyone in the nineteenth century referred to when they used the term "politics." It is to this customary and popular understanding of the term that we will subscribe, relating a narrowly defined partisan politics to other forms of influence and civic life when these shared or competed for a presence on the public stage.

Several reasons for positing a more complex and conflicted relation to political affairs among Americans emerge from even a preliminary consideration of politics (understood narrowly or even broadly) as one of a number of influences, interests, and venues within the larger society and culture. Perhaps the most important of these is religion, and the fact that political democratization was paralleled in nineteenth-century America, and particularly in the antebellum era, by an increasing commitment on the part of large numbers of Americans to the beliefs and behavioral dictates of evangelical Christianity. Political historians have recognized this parallel development and have probed in considerable detail not only the ethnoreligious foundations of partisan affiliation, but also the religious roots of reform movements, such as temperance and abolition, that entered the political arena. Perhaps because of these connections, however, they have not stressed sufficiently the power of religious sensibilities to subordinate politics to what many believed were more important activities and preoccupations, and have not recognized the degree to which politics and religion could be placed by some in an adversarial relation. Richard Carwardine, for example, acknowledges that evangelicals in the 1840s railed against the new public maxim that "all is fair in politics," lamented the decline of moral standards under the rule of "maddened, wine-heated politicians," and lambasted hickory-pole and cider-barrel electioneering as a "reckless waste in useless trappings." He notes that some religious men eschewed politics entirely: "I am myself a candidate, but it is for eternal life." But these sentiments quickly fade from his narrative when Carwardine turns to the realization by evangelicals that they could not pursue their crusades against alcohol, slavery, and Catholicism by "swimming against the tide of American popular culture." Thereafter, he argues, religion and politics became parts of an "organic seamless whole."

We believe, however, that what Mark Y. Hanley has called "the Protestant quarrel with the American republic" was more enduring among a broad group of conservative Christians. Hanley describes the efforts of Ezra Stiles, Francis Wayland, Charles Hodge, Horace Bushnell, and a number of lesser-known clergy to assure that a transcendent and redemptive Christianity remain uncorrupted by the new American "liberal order." What troubled these divines was an illusory "new freedom beyond faith" that included an absorption of the mind and spirit in political affairs and an arrogant conflation of political with spiritual progress: "When did [Christ] condescend to tell us that ours is the true form of government?" asked Bushnell. "When lend himself to any such mischievous flattery as this?" Bushnell raised these questions in the context of the fervent presidential campaign of 1840, but evangelicals and other Protestants continued to insist throughout the antebellum era, and later, that politics be kept out of the pulpit and the religious press, and that men and women go beyond and beneath matters of state to examine the state of their souls. What effects did these exhortations have on the political commitment of ordinary Christians? Did some churchgoers vote in secular elections but also contain or compartmentalize their political enthusiasm? Did others withdraw from political affairs? Might not the borrowing of religious rhetoric by nineteenth-century politicians have been a device for attracting those whose deeper instincts were to protect themselves from political dangers?

A second reason for questioning the pervasiveness of political engagement is the tension, obvious in so many ways, between political activism and the pursuit of upper- and middle-class respectability. Just as evangelical Christianity and political democracy developed simultaneously in a partly conflicted relation, so too did the emergence of new forms and a heightened pursuit of social respectability coincide with the development of political practices that were widely perceived as disreputable. European visitors commented frequently on the coarseness of the new American politics—on the need to shake "one hard greasy paw" after another, on the "uncouth mosaic of expectoration and nutshells" (Mrs. Trollope's name for the characteristic American citizen was George Washington Spitchew)—and Robert Wiebe contends that some Americans eagerly translated this problem into the solution, indeed the defining virtue, of American politics in the Age of the Common Man. Without apology they created an egalitarian politics appropriate to what we call here a rude republic—a political nation just taking shape, and one that prided itself on its challenge to deference and its disdain for the formalities of polite address. This rude republic, we believe, was formed across the nineteenth century in ways that unsettled not only visiting Europeans but also many respectable Americans. Blatant office-seeking and behind-the-scenes maneuvering, the cultivation of political loyalty among newly enfranchised workers and recently arrived immigrants, the inclusion in political organizations of saloonkeepers, street toughs, and other unsavory characters, the employment of manipulative techniques of mass appeal, and the equation of these techniques with other forms of crude humbuggery, imparted an unseemliness to politics that considerably complicated the simultaneous pursuit of respectability and an active political life. William Gienapp cites one elite Philadelphian who complained of "'the mere chicanery of politics,' which made the pursuit of office 'attended by a degradation of character & sacrifice of principle startling enough to drive every man of taste & feeling into deeper shades of private life,'" and it is clear that many social elites did find it more difficult to participate in a rude republic of voting masses and saloon-based precinct captains, of torchlight parades and vulgar oratory. By no means all withdrew into "deeper shades of private life," but those elites who remained active in the party period were compelled to adjust to new and uncomfortably disreputable associations and activities.

These concerns pertain as well to those more modestly positioned individuals and families who made new claims of social respectability as part of an emerging middle class. The most complex patterns of middle-class formation were to be found in the largest cities, where politics were also perceived as being especially unseemly and corrupt. In the cities, middle-class respectability was grounded in a variety of new social environments and experiences: enlarged and refined, parlor-centered homes; similarly embellished commercial, managerial, and professional workplaces; increasingly homogeneous residential neighborhoods and business districts; a variety of new commercial and voluntary institutions providing respectable entertainment and sociability. The essence of all of these was class segregation, and in particular the insulation of middle-class individuals and families from the rough world of the native and immigrant working class. Political activities of various kinds could threaten that insulation and the sense of social well-being that went with it. Indeed, at a time when theaters, retail shopping districts, and even church congregations were increasingly segregated by class, political gatherings remained among the most socially promiscuous of the city's affairs. Was this in fact a source of political disengagement among the urban middle class? And what about the far larger number of middling folk who lived in smaller towns and in the countryside, where politics was less (or less famously) corrupt and social promiscuity less (or less obviously) problematic? Richard Bushman has demonstrated the appeal of city-bred social styles in rural and small-town America, but if rustic Americans pursued a "vernacular gentility" to confirm their middle-class status, does it follow that they faced the same complications of political engagement that we have posited for their urban counterparts? What, indeed, were the social implications of political engagement—and the effects on political engagement of upper- and middle-class social sensibilities—in both the city and the country?

In defining vernacular gentility, Bushman describes a rural middle class, "without pretensions to public office," that failed to develop the sense of public duty and privilege that had once been an important part of the aristocratic package of values and behavior. "The realm of the middling people was the family rather than town or county." This selective importation of genteel qualities is suggestive of what historians frequently have labeled "liberalism," that political theory or sensibility emphasizing individual rights over corporate responsibilities and asserting the superiority of the free market over public activity and control. Historians ordinarily discuss liberalism as a well-reasoned article of conviction, and as a mode of political action that would use politics to limit the prerogatives of the state and to enlarge individual freedoms. There is not necessarily a paradox in this, and it is surely the case that many Americans have engaged fervently in politics with just such ends in mind. But we believe it is possible to identify another kind of liberalism that did little to nurture, and much to discourage, political participation. Less theoretical or even thoughtful, more humdrum even in its description—following Bushman, we call it "vernacular liberalism"—it is no more than an unreflective absorption in the daily routines of work, family, and social life, those private and communal domains that the small governments of the era hardly touched. To be sure, there is nothing in the "realm of the family" that would have prevented its male members from an active engagement or its female members from an active interest in the larger realms of politics and the state in nineteenth-century America. But we suspect that the radical disconnectedness and "privatism" observed in America by Tocqueville and other European visitors in this period translated in many instances into a primacy of self and family that confined politics to a lower order of personal commitment than is generally recognized. Tocqueville himself argued that Americans were passionately interested in politics, but he would not have seen much or many of those people to whom we refer. Neither have many historians ferreted them out from their chimney corners and workbenches. Most Americans did vote, and for many historians that has been enough. We would look more closely at "liberalism," not merely as a political theory, but also, for some, as an apolitical way of life.

The republicanism that historians so frequently place in opposition to liberalism as a source or summation of American values was itself capable of complicating and even limiting political engagement. Most importantly, it fueled the antipartyism that historians have found during the earliest years of the second party system, and that, we believe, continued as a significant element of American political culture long after the more reluctantly partisan Whigs adopted the structures and campaign techniques pioneered by Democrats. Indeed, the feeling that parties were corrupting the political process may have strengthened as the two major parties came to resemble each other in structure and technique, and as the party system came to dominate, seemingly permanently, the republican political process. It was in this context of party hegemony and a wary public that the cult of George Washington served to express antipartyism (the Farewell Address was this movement's basic text, and was read aloud at many public gatherings), and to offer military heroism and sacrifice as a sounder basis of patriotism and republican virtue. The parties themselves understood the potentially alienating effects of this popular contrast between the politician and the military hero. They frequently offered their presidential nominations to former military commanders with otherwise minimal political credentials, and introduced military motifs into their campaigns even when no general could be found to head the ticket (rarely a problem in the post-Civil War era). Campaign biographers, as William Burlie Brown has shown, were increasingly inclined to disavow any kind of political apprenticeship for their subjects, whether or not they had been military men, and to claim that only their opponents were politicians by trade. "The conclusion is inescapable," writes Brown, "that the basic assumptions of the biographers are that their audience believes the politician is evil and party politics is evil twice compounded." And yet, inevitably, it was the party that offered military heroes and other disinterested amateurs to the voting public. No significant candidacies were mounted by such paragons of republicanism outside the party's structures and campaign machinery. Those who loathed the party and its professional politicians, therefore, had to reconcile some significantly discordant elements of the candidacy of any latter-day George Washington.

The great public-school reforms of the 1840s and beyond offer insights into this tension between party politics and a republicanism grounded in military service. School reformers developed curricula and purchased textbooks that underscored the military origins of republican virtue while making no concessions to partisan institutions. Jean Baker has argued that the experience of schooling in the antebellum era "trained young white males in their public roles of delegating power, rotating leadership, limiting power, and supporting the government." None of this entered the formal curriculum, however, and the "training" Baker alludes to consisted mainly of the manner in which restive school children resisted the tyrannies of their overbearing teachers. Against this problematic inference we would place Baker's own observation that the schools "did not introduce their students to public issues or political parties, as twentieth-century civics courses would." Remarkably, American school children of the antebellum era were given no political history of their nation. American history texts culminated in the Revolutionary War, and the message of this climactic event was the patriotic virtue of Washington and his men-at-arms. It is curricular decisions of this sort, made by men who were as convinced as Horace Bushnell was about the significance of early childhood nurturance in the shaping of enduring values, that seem to us most important in conveying the intended and actual effects of public schooling upon republican civic consciousness. Americans were taught to honor the American republic, but not American politics. For how many did this kind of republicanism remain a cultural resource for resisting engagement in the "affairs of party"?

FURTHER READING

Glenn C. Altschuler and Stuart M. Blumin, *Rude Republic: Americans and their Politics in the Nineteenth Century* (2000).

John M. Belohlavek, *"Let the Eagle Soar!": The Foreign Policy of Andrew Jackson* (1985).

William W. Freehling, *Prelude to Civil War: The Nullification Controversy in South Carolina* (1966).

Thomas R. Hietala, *Manifest Design: Anxious Aggrandizement in Late Jacksonian America* (1985).

Reginald Horsman, *Race and Manifest Destiny* (1981).

Daniel Walker Howe, *What Hath God Wrought: The Transformation of America, 1815–1846* (2007).

Richard P. McCormick, *The Second Party System: Party Formation in the Jacksonian Era* (1966).

Jon Meacham, *American Lion: Andrew Jackson in the White House* (2009).

Merrill D. Peterson, *The Great Triumvirate: Webster, Clay, and Calhoun* (1988).

Robert V. Remini, *Henry Clay: Statesman for the Union* (1991).

Mary Ryan, *Civic Wars: Democracy and Public Life in the American City during the Nineteenth Century* (1998).

Harry L. Watson, *Liberty and Power: The Politics of Jacksonian America* (1990).

Sean Wilentz, *The Rise of American Democracy: Jefferson to Lincoln* (2006).

CHAPTER 10

Reform and the Great Awakening in the Early Nineteenth Century

In his essay "Man, the Reformer," Ralph Waldo Emerson observed in 1841 that "in the history of the world the doctrine of Reform had never such scope as the present hour." Although this was perhaps an overstatement, Emerson's ideas nonetheless point to a series of reform movements aimed at the betterment of humankind. As never before in American history, movements focused on temperance, women's rights, prison reform, educational reform, compassion for retarded and handicapped people, and abolitionism coursed across the American landscape. Led by charismatic leaders such as William Lloyd Garrison, David Walker, Horace Mann, Dorothea Dix, and Lucretia Mott, these movements profoundly influenced American society. Not coincidentally, this also was an era in which new religious doctrines found adherents who formed new faiths—such as those that would become known as the Church of Latter-Day Saints and the Seventh-Day Adventists—that remain influential to the present day. This clearly was the era of "the Reformer."

We can attempt to explain the growth of reform movements in the early nineteenth century by considering four interlocking factors. First, this was a period of great societal change. Americans not only puzzled over changes in society, but questioned how old patterns of social organization might be reestablished in new forms. Religious belief and social reform were often cited as forces that might either recapture the old order or point to ways in which a new order could be created. Second, the early nineteenth century saw the growth of intellectual movements that rejected the rationalism of an earlier age. Americans were now fascinated with the gothic, with the sense of mystery, with romanticism and sentimentality. These ideas, which permeated society, are important for the purposes of this chapter because sentimentality could encourage the development of empathy for others. If Americans could "feel" the human costs of alcohol abuse or of slavery, for example, they could empathize with the victims and work to eradicate such evils. Third, many Americans continued to be imbued with a belief in progress. They continued to see the United States as a place of destiny, a nation with a mission of greatness. If conditions could improve, it followed that people should play an active role in bringing that improvement about.

Related to notions of progress and perfectibility is the fourth and perhaps the most important underlying factor: religious change. Between roughly 1795 and 1837, many Americans were roused by religious revivals that changed their views of the possibilities of the world. Known as the Second Great Awakening, this religious movement fostered the growth of Christian belief, particularly among those in denominations, such as the Methodists and the Baptists, that saw humans as having a greater role in their own salvation. If individuals could be saved, it followed that if all were delivered, the result might be a perfect society. If individuals could choose good over evil, they could eradicate sin from the world. Underlying these reform movements, then, was "millennialism," the belief that a thousand-year era of peace, harmony, and Christian brotherhood on Earth would precede the Second Coming of Christ. Given Americans' tendency to see their nation as having a role in momentous events, it was not surprising that they saw the millennium as being set in the United States.

QUESTIONS TO THINK ABOUT

In this era, some religious movements developed that underscored the possibility that everyone in society could achieve perfection and salvation. This differed from the belief in earlier eras that salvation was limited to a few people who were saved by a gracious God. How might these changing views be linked to reform movements? How did religious change focus upon the family? Did religion liberate or inhibit the lives and freedom of women? Were reformers concerned more about improving society or about controlling it? How might people in reform movements, such as abolitionism, view the government? Was it a positive or negative force?

DOCUMENTS

These documents detail the relationships among religion, reform, the family, slavery, and women's rights. In document 1, Methodist evangelist Peter Cartwright describes his conversion and the revivals that spread throughout the West. Document 2 is an appeal focusing on the evils of slavery in 1829 by David Walker, an African American. In document 3, William Lloyd Garrison, profoundly influenced by Walker, introduces his newspaper, *The Liberator,* with a call for immediate abolition. Finding some religious innovations too radical and outlandish, the author of document 4, details and denounces the "Kingdom of Matthias," a small religious community that was known for the misogynistic and anti-business tirades of its leader, Robert Matthews. In document 5, a speech and letter to the "Christian women of the South," Angelina Grimké uses religious arguments to call upon white women to act politically and rise against slavery. Dorothea Dix's letter to the Massachusetts legislature in document 6 is a chilling depiction of the treatment endured by the mentally ill in jails and almshouses. The same year as Dix's letter, 1843, was the publication of Joseph Smith's revelation regarding plural marriage for the Church of Latter-Day Saints. In document 7, Smith recounts what God spoke to him about marriage and family life. Document 8 is the Declaration of Rights and Sentiments that was adopted by the Seneca Falls Convention in 1848. Although modeled on the Declaration of Independence, notice how widely it critiques of male supremacy. Sojourner Truth, in document 9, a former member of the Kingdom of Matthias, provides a powerful expression of the relationships between women's rights and abolitionism.

1. Peter Cartwright, a Methodist Itinerant Preacher, Marvels at the Power of Religious Revivals, 1801

In 1801, when I was in my sixteenth year, my father, my eldest half brother, and myself, attended a wedding about five miles from home, where there was a great deal of drinking and dancing, which was very common at marriages in those days. I drank little or nothing; my delight was in dancing. After a late hour in the night, we mounted our horses and started for home. I was riding my race-horse.

A few minutes after we had put up the horses, and were sitting by the fire, I began to reflect on the manner in which I had spent the day and evening. I felt guilty and condemned. I rose and walked the floor. My mother was in bed. It seemed to me, all of a sudden, my blood rushed to my head, my heart palpitated, in a few minutes I turned blind; an awful impression rested on my mind that death had come and I was unprepared to die. I fell on my knees and began to ask God to have mercy on me.

My mother sprang from her bed, and was soon on her knees by my side, praying for me, and exhorting me to look to Christ for mercy, and then and there I promised the Lord that if he would spare me, I would seek and serve him; and I never fully broke that promise. My mother prayed for me a long time. At length we lay down, but there was little sleep for me. Next morning I rose, feeling wretched beyond expression. I tried to read in the Testament, and retired many times to secret prayer through the day, but found no relief. I gave up my race-horse to my father, and requested him to sell him. I went and brought my pack of cards, and gave them to mother, who threw them into the fire, and they were consumed. I fasted, watched, and prayed, and engaged in regular reading of the Testament. I was so distressed and miserable, that I was incapable of any regular business.

My father was greatly distressed on my account, thinking I must die, and he would lose his only son. He bade me retire altogether from business, and take care of myself....

There were no camp-meetings in regular form at this time, but as there was a great waking up among the Churches, from the revival that had broken out at

Peter Cartwright, *Autobiography of Peter Cartwright, the Backwoods Preacher,* ed. W. P. Strickland (New York: Phillips and Hunt, 1856), 34–35, 37–38, 45, 48–49.

Cane Ridge, before mentioned, many flocked to those sacramental meetings. The church would not hold the tenth part of the congregation. Accordingly, the officers of the Church erected a stand in a contiguous shady grove, and prepared seats for a large congregation.

The people crowded to this meeting from far and near. They came in their large wagons, with victuals mostly prepared. The women slept in the wagons, and the men under them. Many stayed on the ground night and day for a number of nights and days together. Others were provided for among the neighbors around. The power of God was wonderfully displayed; scores of sinners fell under the preaching, like men slain in mighty battle; Christians shouted aloud for joy.

To this meeting I repaired, a guilty, wretched sinner. On the Saturday evening of said meeting, I went, with weeping multitudes, and bowed before the stand, and earnestly prayed for mercy. In the midst of a solemn struggle of soul, an impression was made on my mind, as though a voice said to me, "Thy sins are all forgiven thee." Divine light flashed all round me, unspeakable joy sprung up in my soul. I rose to my feet, opened my eyes, and it really seemed as if I was in heaven; the trees, the leaves on them, and everything seemed, and I really thought were, praising God. My mother raised the shout, my Christian friends crowded around me and joined me in praising God; and though I have been since then, in many instances, unfaithful, yet I have never, for one moment, doubted that the Lord did, then and there, forgive my sins and give me religion....

[A] new exercise broke out among us, called the *jerks*, which was overwhelming in its effects upon the bodies and minds of the people. No matter whether they were saints or sinners, they would be taken under a warm song or sermon, and seized with a convulsive jerking all over, which they could not by any possibility avoid, and the more they resisted the more they jerked. If they would not strive against it and pray in good earnest, the jerking would usually abate. I have seen more than five hundred persons jerking at one time in my large congregations. Most usually persons taken with the jerks, to obtain relief, as they said, would rise up and dance. Some would run, but could not get away. Some would resist; on such the jerks were generally very severe.

To see those proud young gentlemen and young ladies, dressed in their silks, jewelry, and prunella, from top to toe, take the *jerks* would often excite my risibilities. The first jerk or so, you would see their fine bonnets, caps, and combs fly; and so sudden would be the jerking of the head that their long loose hair would crack almost as loud as a wagoners whip.

2. African American Abolitionist David Walker Castigates the United States for Its Slave System, 1829

[W]e, (coloured people of these United States of America) are the *most wretched, degraded* and *abject* set of beings that *ever lived* since the world began; and that the white Americans having reduced us to the wretched state of *slavery,* treat us in

---

David Walker, *Walker's Appeal* (1829).

that condition *more cruel* (they being an enlighted and Christian people,) than any heathen nation did any people whom it had reduced to our condition....

Are we MEN!!—I ask you, O my brethren! are we MEN? Did our Creator make us to be slaves to dust and ashes like ourselves? Are they not dying worms as well as we? Have they not to make their appearance before the tribunal of Heaven, to answer for the deeds done in the body, as well as we? Have we any other Master but Jesus Christ alone? Is he not their Master as well as ours?—What right then, have we to obey and call any other Master, but Himself? How we could be so *submissive* to a gang of men, whom we cannot tell whether they are *as good* as ourselves or not, I never could conceive. However, this is shut up with the Lord, and we cannot precisely tell—but I declare, we judge men by their works....

... Remember Americans, that we must and shall be free and enlightened as you are, will you wait until we shall, under God, obtain our liberty by the crushing arm of power? Will it not be dreadful for you? I speak Americans for your good. We must and shall be free I say, in spite of you. You may do your best to keep us in wretchedness and misery, to enrich you and your children, but God will deliver us from under you. And wo, wo, will be to you if we have to obtain our freedom by fighting. Throw away your fears and prejudices then, and enlighten us and treat us like men, and we will like you more than we do now hate you, and tell us now no more about colonization, for America is as much our country, as it is yours.—

Treat us like men, and there is no danger but we will all live in peace and happiness together. For we are not like you, hard hearted, unmerciful, and unforgiving....

If any are anxious to ascertain who I am, know the world, that I am one of the oppressed, degraded and wretched sons of Africa, rendered so by the avaricious and unmerciful, among the whites.—If any wish to plunge me into the wretched incapacity of a slave, or murder me for the truth, know ye, that I am in the hand of God, and at your disposal. I count my life not dear unto me, but I am ready to be offered at any moment. For what is the use of living, when in fact I am dead. But remember, Americans, that as miserable, wretched, degraded and abject as you have made us in preceding, and in this generation, to support you and your families, that some of you, (whites) on the continent of America, will yet curse the day that you ever were born. You want slaves, and want us for your slaves!!! My colour will yet, root some of you out of the very face of the earth!!!!!!...

See your Declaration Americans!!! Do you understand your own language? Hear your language, proclaimed to the world, July 4th, 1776—

> We hold these truths to be self evident—that ALL men are created
> EQUAL!! that they *are endowed by their creator with certain unalienable*
> *rights;* that among these are life, *liberty,* and the pursuit of happiness!!

Compare your own language above, extracted from your Declaration of Independence, with your cruelties and murders inflicted by your cruel and unmerciful fathers and yourselves on our fathers and on us—men who have never given your fathers or you the least provocation!!!!!!

3. White Abolitionist William Lloyd Garrison Calls for Immediate Abolition, 1831

To the Public

During my recent tour for the purpose of exciting the minds of the people by a series of discourses on the subject of slavery, every place that I visited gave fresh evidence of the fact, that a greater revolution in public sentiment was to be effected in the free States—*and particularly in New-England*—than at the South. I found contempt more bitter, opposition more active, detraction more relentless, prejudice more stubborn, and apathy more frozen, than among slave-owners themselves. Of course, there were individual exceptions to the contrary. This state of things afflicted, but did not dishearten me. I determined, at every hazard, to lift up the standard of emancipation in the eyes of the nation, *within sight of Bunker Hill and in the birthplace of liberty*. That standard is now unfurled; and long may it float, unhurt by the spoliations of time or the missiles of a desperate foe— yea, till every chain be broken, and every bondman set free! Let Southern oppressors tremble—let their secret abettors tremble—let their Northern apologists tremble—let all the enemies of the persecuted blacks tremble....

Assenting to the "self-evident truth" maintained in the American Declaration of Independence, "that all men are created equal, and endowed by their Creator with certain inalienable rights—among which are life, liberty and the pursuit of happiness," I shall strenuously contend for the immediate enfranchisement of our slave population. In Park-Street Church, on the Fourth of July, 1829, in an address on slavery, I unreflectingly assented to the popular but pernicious doctrine of *gradual* abolition. I seize this opportunity to make a full and unequivocal recantation, and thus publicly to ask pardon of my God, of my country, and of my brethren the poor slaves, for having uttered a sentiment so full of timidity, injustice, and absurdity. A similar recantation, from my pen, was published in the *Genius of Universal Emancipation* at Baltimore, in September, 1829. My conscience is now satisfied.

I am aware that many object to the severity of my language; but is there not cause for severity? I *will be* as harsh as truth, and as uncompromising as justice. On this subject, I do not wish to think, or speak, or write, with moderation. No! no! Tell a man whose house is on fire to give a moderate alarm; tell him to moderately rescue his wife from the hands of the ravisher; tell the mother to gradually extricate her babe from the fire into which it has fallen;—but urge me not to use moderation in a cause like the present. I am in earnest—I will not equivocate—I will not excuse—I will not retreat a single inch—AND I WILL BE HEARD....

An attempt has been made—it is still making—we regret to say, with considerable success—to inflame the minds of our working classes against the more opulent, and to persuade men that they are contemned and oppressed by

William Lloyd Garrison, Editorial, *The Liberator*, January 1, 1831.

a wealthy aristocracy. That public grievances exist, is unquestionably true; but they are not confined to any one class of society. Every profession is interested in their removal—the rich as well as the poor....

Walker's Pamphlet

The Legislature of North Carolina has lately been sitting with closed doors, in consequence of a message from the Governor relative to the above pamphlet [see Document 2, David Walker's appeal]. The south may reasonably be alarmed at the circulation of Mr Walker's Appeal; for a better promoter of insurrection was never sent forth to an oppressed people. In a future number, we propose to examine it, as also various editorial comments thereon—it being one of the most remarkable productions of the age. We have already publicly deprecated its spirit.

4. A Description of the Prophet Matthias and His Attacks on Women, 1835

ROBERT MATTHEWS—for that is the real name of the subject of this history—is a native of Washington county, in the State of New-York, and of Scotch extraction. He is about forty-five years of age, and of respectable parentage, though a mental eccentricity has characterized several members of the family. He was left an orphan at a tender age, and was brought up in the family of a respectable farmer....

At the age of about twenty years, Matthews came to the city of New-York, and worked at the business of a carpenter and house-joiner,...

Not succeeding to his wishes, however, he removed to Albany in 1827 or '28, and resumed the joiner's business as a journeyman, taking good care of his family, and attending constantly upon the public services in the sanctuary.... He very soon appeared to take an increasing interest in religious matters; attended church and social prayer meetings, and conversed frequently upon the subject.... [A] young clergyman from New-York, the Rev. Mr. Kirk, was to occupy the pulpit on a certain evening. Matthews went to hear him, and on his return home appeared to be in a state of great excitement, declaring that he had never heard any thing like preaching before, and sat up the greater part of the night repeating, expounding, and commending passages from the sermon. His enthusiasm was so great that Mrs. Matthews remarked to her daughter in the course of the night, "If your father goes to hear this man preach any more, he will go wild or crazy." He did go again to hear him a number of times—was always exceedingly pleased, and became more and more excited....

At about the same time, Matthews engaged actively in the temperance reform, in which he laboured with all his might; but he was ultra in his notions,— contending that the use of meats should be excluded, as well as of strong drinks....

William L. Stone, *Matthias and His Impostures* (1835).

In his street-preaching, consisting for the most part of more incoherent harangues than are often uttered by men in any condition of mind,...

[In one sermon, he preached] "The spirit that built the Tower of Babel is now in the world—it is the spirit of the devil. The spirit of man never goes upon the clouds—all who think so are Babylonians. 'The only heaven is on the earth. All who are ignorant of truth, are Ninevites. The Jews did not crucify Christ,—it was the Gentiles. Every Jew has his guardian angel attending him in this world. God don't speak through preachers, he speaks through me, his prophet."...

"All *real* men will be saved; all *mock* men will be damned. When a person has the Holy Ghost, then he is a man, and not till then. They who teach women are of the wicked. The communion is all nonsense: so is prayer. Eating a nip of bread and drinking a little wine won't do any good. All who admit members into their church and suffer them to hold their lands and houses—their sentence is, 'Depart yo wicked, I know you not.' All females who lecture their husbands, their sentence is the same. The sons of truth are to enjoy all the good things of this world, and must use their means to bring it about. Every thing that has the smell of woman will be destroyed. Woman is the capsheaf of the abomination of desolation—full of all deviltry. In a short time the world will take fire and dissolve—it is combustible already. All women, not obedient, had better become so as soon as possible, and let the wicked spirit depart, and become temples of truth."...

5. Angelina Grimké Appeals to Christian Women to Oppose Slavery, 1836

Now the Bible is my ultimate appeal in all matters of faith and practice, and it is to *this test* I am anxious to bring the subject at issue between us....

I have thus, I think, clearly proved to you seven propositions, viz.: First, that slavery is contrary to the declaration of our independence. Second, that it is contrary to the first charter of human rights given to Adam, and renewed to Noah. Third, that the fact of slavery having been the subject of prophecy, furnishes *no* excuse whatever to slavedealers. Fourth, that no such system existed under the patriarchal dispensation. Fifth, that *slavery never* existed under the Jewish dispensation; but so far otherwise, that every servant was placed under the *protection of law,* and care taken not only to prevent all *involuntary* servitude, but all *voluntary perpetual* bondage. Sixth, that slavery in America reduces a man to a *thing,* a "chattel personal," *robs him* of all his rights as a *human being,* fetters both his mind and body, and protects the *master* in the most unnatural and unreasonable power, whilst it *throws him out* of the protection of law. Seventh, that slavery is contrary to the example and precepts of our holy and merciful Redeemer, and *of* his apostles.

But perhaps you will be ready to query, why appeal to *women* on this subject? We do not make the laws which perpetuate slavery. No legislative power is

Angelina Grimké, "Appeal to Christian Women of the South" (1836).

vested in us; *we* can do nothing to overthrow the system, even if we wished to do so. To this I reply, I know you do not make the laws, but I also know that you *are the wives and mothers, the sisters and daughters of those who do;* and if you really suppose you can do nothing to overthrow slavery, you are greatly mistaken. You can do much in every way: four things I will name. 1st. You can read on this subject. 2d. You can pray over this subject. 3d. You can speak on this subject. 4th. You can *act* on this subject....

3. Speak on this subject. It is through the tongue, the pen, and the press, that truth is principally propagated. Speak then to your relatives, your friends, your acquaintances on the subject of slavery; be not afraid if you are conscientiously convinced it is *sinful,* to say so openly, but calmly, and to let your sentiments be known....

4. Act on this subject. Some of you own slaves yourselves. If you believe slavery is sinful, set them at liberty, "undo the heavy burdens and let the oppressed go free." If they wish to remain with you, pay them wages, if not let them leave you. Should they remain teach them, and have them taught the common branches of an English education; they have minds and those minds ought to be improved. So precious a talent as intellect, never was given to be wrapt in a napkin and buried in the earth. It is the duty of all, as far as they can, to improve their own menial faculties, because we are commanded to love God with all our minds, as well as with all our hearts, and we commit a great sin, if we forbid or prevent that cultivation of the mind in others, which would enable them to perform this duty. Teach your servants then to read &c, and encourage them to believe it is their duty to learn, if it were only that they might read the Bible....

The *women of the South can overthrow* this horrible system of oppression and cruelty, licentiousness and wrong. Such appeals to your legislatures would be irresistible, for there is something in the heart of man which *will bend under moral suasion.* There is a swift witness for truth in his bosom, which *will respond to truth* when it is uttered with calmness and dignity. If you could obtain but six signatures to such a petition in only one state, I would say, send up that petition, and be not in the least discouraged by the scoffs, and jeers of the heartless, or the resolution of the house to lay it on the table....

6. Reformer Dorothea Dix Depicts the Horrible Conditions Endured by the Mentally Ill, 1843

Gentlemen,—I respectfully ask to present this Memorial, believing that the cause, which actuates to and sanctions so unusual a movement, presents no equivocal claim to public consideration and sympathy. Surrendering to calm and deep convictions of duty my habitual views of what is womanly and becoming. I proceed briefly to explain what has conducted me before you unsolicited

Dorothea Dix, petition of the Massachusetts Legislature (1843). Also found in *Our Nation's Archive.* Erik Bruun and Jay Crosby (New York: Black Dog and Leventhal Publishers, 1999), 266–268.

and unsustained, trusting, while I do so, that the memorialist will be speedily forgotten in the memorial....

... I have seen many who, part of the year, are chained or caged. The use of cages all but universal.... [C]hains are less common; negligences frequent, wilful abuse less frequent than sufferings proceeding from ignorance, or want of consideration. I encountered during the last three months many poor creatures wandering reckless and unprotected through the country.... I have heard that responsible persons, controlling the almshouses, have not thought themselves culpable in sending away from their shelter, to cast upon the chances of remote relief, insane men and women. These, left on the highways, unfriended and incompetent to control or direct their own movements, sometimes have found refuge in the hospital, and others have not been traced. But I cannot particularize. In traversing the State, I have found hundreds of insane persons in every variety of circumstance and condition, many whose situation could not and need not be improved; a less number, but that very large, whose lives are the saddest pictures of human suffering and degradation....

DANVERS. November. Visited the almshouse. A large building, much out of repair....

Long before reaching the house, wild shouts, snatches of rude songs, imprecations and obscene language, fell upon the ear, proceeding from the occupant of a low building, rather remote from the principal building to which my course was directed. Found the mistress, and was conducted to the place which was called "the home" of the forlorn maniac, a young woman, exhibiting a condition of neglect and misery blotting out the faintest idea of comfort, and outraging every sentiment of decency. She had been, I learnt, a respectable person, industrious and worthy. Disappointments and trials shook her mind, and, finally, laid prostrate reason and self-control.... She had passed from one degree of violence to another, in swift progress. There she stood, clinging to or beating upon the bars of her caged apartment, the contracted size of which afforded space only for increasing accumulations of filth, a loud spectacle. There she stood with naked arms and dishevelled hair, the unwashed frame invested with fragments of unclean garments, the air so extremely offensive, though ventilation was afforded on all sides save one, that it was not possible to remain beyond a few moments without retreating for recovery to the outward air. Irritation of body, produced by utter filth and exposure, incited her to the horrid process of tearing off her skin by inches. Her face, neck, and person were thus disfigured to hideousness. She held up a fragment just rent off. To my exclamation of horror, the mistress replied: "Oh, we can't help it. Half the skin is off sometimes. We can do nothing with her; and it makes no difference what she eats, for she consumes her own filth as readily as the food which is brought her."...

Men of Massachusetts, I beg, I implore, I demand pity and protection for these of my suffering, outraged sex. Fathers, husbands, brothers, I would supplicate you for this boon; but what do I say.... Here you will put away the cold, calculating spirit of selfishness and self-seeking; lay off the armor of local strife and political opposition; here and now, for once, forgetful of the earthly and perishable, come up to these halls and consecrate them with one heart and one mind to works of righteousness and just judgment. Become the benefactors of your race, the just guardians of the solemn rights you hold in trust....

7. Joseph Smith Records a Revelation on Plural Marriage, 1843

1. Verify, thus saith the Lord unto you my servant Joseph, that inasmuch as you have inquired of my hand to know and understand wherein I, the Lord, justified my servants Abraham, Isaac, and Jacob, as also Moses, David and Solomon, my servants, as touching the *principle and doctrine of their having many wives* and concubines—...

4. For behold, I reveal unto you a new and an everlasting covenant; and if ye abide not that covenant, then are ye damned; for no one can reject this covenant and be permitted to enter into my glory....

37. Abraham received concubines, and they bore him children; and it was accounted unto him for righteousness,...

38. David also received many wives and concubines, and also Solomon and Moses my servants, as also many others of my servants, from the beginning of creation until this time; and in nothing did they sin save in those things which they received not of me....

61. And again, as pertaining to the law of the priesthood—if any man espouse a virgin, and desire to espouse another, and the first give her consent, and if he espouse the second, and they are virgins, and have vowed to no other man, then is he justified; he cannot commit adultery for they are given unto him; for he cannot commit adultery with that that belongeth unto him and to no one else.

62. And if he have ten virgins given unto him by this law, he cannot commit adultery, for they belong to him, and they are given unto him; therefore is he justified.

63. But if one or either of the ten virgins, after she is espoused, shall be with another man, she has committed adultery, and shall be destroyed; for they are given unto him to multiply and replenish the earth, according to my commandment, and to fulfil the promise which was given by my Father before the foundation of the world, and for their exaltation in the eternal worlds, that they may bear the souls of men; for herein is the work of my Father continued, that he may be glorified.

8. The Seneca Falls Convention Declares Women's Rights, 1848

When in the course of human events it becomes necessary for one portion of the family of man to assume among the people of the earth a position different from

---

R. Marie Griffith, ed., *American Religions: A Documentary History* (2008), 165–172.

Lydia Sigourney, "Home" (1850).

that which the laws of nature and of nature's God entitle them, a decent respect to the opinions of mankind requires that they should declare the causes that impel them to such a course.

We hold these truths to be self-evident; that all men and women are created equal; that they are endowed by their Creator with certain inalienable rights; that among these are life, liberty, and the pursuit of happiness; that to secure these rights governments are instituted, deriving their just powers from the consent of the governed. Whenever any form of government becomes destructive of these ends, it is the right of those who suffer from it to refuse allegiance to it, and to insist upon the institution of a new government, laying its foundation on such principles, and organizing its powers in such form as to them shall seem most likely to effect their safety and happiness. Prudence, indeed, will dictate that governments long established should not be changed for light and transient causes; and accordingly, all experience hath shown that mankind are more disposed to suffer, while evils are sufferable, than to right themselves by abolishing the forms to which they are accustomed. But when a long train of abuses and usurpation, pursuing invariably the same object, evinces a design to reduce them under absolute despotism, it is their duty to throw off such government, and to provide new guards for their future security. Such has been the patient sufferance of the women under this government, and such is now the necessity which constrains them to demand the equal station to which they are entitled.

The history of mankind is a history of repeated injuries and usurpation on the part of man toward woman, having in direct object the establishment of an absolute tyranny over her. To prove this, let facts be submitted to a candid world.

He has never permitted her to exercise her inalienable right to the elective franchise.

He has compelled her to submit to laws, in the formation of which she has no voice.

He has withheld from her rights which are given to the most ignorant and degraded men—both natives and foreigners.

Having deprived her of this first right of a citizen, the elective franchise, thereby leaving her without representation in the halls of legislation, he has oppressed her on all sides.

He has made her, if married, in the eye of the law, civilly dead.

He has taken from her all right in property, even to the wages she earns.

He has made her, morally, an irresponsible being, as she can commit many crimes with impunity, provided they be done in the presence of her husband. In the covenant of marriage, she is compelled to promise obedience to her husband, he becoming, to all intents and purposes, her master—the law giving him power to deprive her of liberty, and to administer chastisements.

He has so framed the laws of divorce, as to what shall be the proper causes of divorce; in case of separation, to whom the guardianship of the children shall be given; as to be wholly regardless of the happiness of women—the law, in all cases, going upon the false supposition of the supremacy of man, and giving all powers into his hands.

After depriving her of all rights as a married woman, if single and the owner of property, he has taxed her to support a government which recognizes her only when her property can be made profitable to it.

He has monopolized nearly all the profitable employments, and from those she is permitted to follow, she receives but a scanty remuneration.

He closes against her all the avenues to wealth and distinction, which he considers most honorable to himself. As a teacher of theology, medicine, or law, she is not known.

He has denied her the facilities for obtaining a thorough education, all colleges being closed against her.

He allows her in Church, as well as State, but a subordinate position, claiming Apostolic authority for her exclusion from the ministry, and, with some exceptions, from any public participation in the affairs of the Church.

He has created a false public sentiment, by giving to the world a different code of morals for men and women, by which moral delinquencies which exclude women from society, are not only tolerated but deemed of little account in man.

He has usurped the prerogative of Jehovah himself, claiming it as his right to assign for her a sphere of action, when that belongs to her conscience and her God.

He has endeavored, in every way that he could to destroy her confidence in her own powers, to lessen her self-respect, and to make her willing to lead a dependent and abject life.

Now, in view of this entire disfranchisement of one-half the people of this country, their social and religious degradation—in view of the unjust laws above mentioned, and because women do feel themselves aggrieved, oppressed, and fraudulently deprived of their most sacred rights, we insist that they have immediate admission to all the rights and privileges which belong to them as citizens of these United States.

In entering upon the great work before us, we anticipate no small amount of misconception, misrepresentation, and ridicule; but we shall use every instrumentality within our power to effect our object. We shall employ agents, circulate tracts, petition the State and national Legislatures, and endeavor to enlist the pulpit and the press in our behalf. We hope this Convention will be followed by a series of Conventions embracing every part of the country.

9. Former Slave Sojourner Truth Links Women's Rights to Antislavery, 1851

Well, children, where there is so much racket there must be something out of kilter. I think that 'twixt the negroes of the South and the women at the North, all talking about rights, the white men will be in a fix pretty soon. But what's all this here talking about?

Sojourner Truth in a speech given at a women's convention in Akron, Ohio (1851).

That man over there says that women need to be helped into carriages, and lifted over ditches, and to have the best place everywhere. Nobody ever helps me into carriages, or over mud-puddles, or gives me any best place! And ain't I a woman? Look at me! Look at my arm! I have ploughed and planted, and gathered into barns, and no man could head me! And ain't I a woman? I could work as much and eat as much as a man—when I could get it—and bear the lash as well! And ain't I a woman? I have borne thirteen children, and seen them most all sold off to slavery, and when I cried out with my mother's grief, none but Jesus heard me! And ain't I a woman?

Then they talk about this thing in the head; what's this they call it? [Intellect, someone whispers.] That's it, honey. What's that got to do with women's rights or negro's rights? If my cup won't hold but a pint, and yours holds a quart, wouldn't you be mean not to let me have my little half-measure full?

Then that little man in black there, he says women can't have as much rights as men, 'cause Christ wasn't a woman! Where did your Christ come from? Where did your Christ come from? From God and a woman! Man had nothing to do with Him.

If the first woman God ever made was strong enough to turn the world upside down all alone, these women together ought to be able to turn it back, and get it right side up again! And now they is asking to do it, the men better let them.

Obliged to you for hearing me, and now old Sojourner ain't got nothing more to say.

ESSAYS

Religious revivalism was a vital factor underlying the reform movements of the antebellum era. Religious change, moreover, was significant in and of itself. It altered the way in which people interacted with one another and with their government and society. Historians, however, disagree over what motivated Americans to embrace religious belief and what religious change meant for the larger American society. The following two essays illustrate disagreements about the place of religion and its relationship to reform. Paul E. Johnson, a historian at the University of South Carolina, focuses on the religious revivals that swept through Rochester, New York, in the 1830s. He shows how the revivals stressed not only that people were moral free agents, but also that they had a responsibility to reach out to others. The result was attempts to foster morality within society that resulted in movements of social control aimed at the working classes. In contrast, Nell Irvin Painter, of Princeton University, focuses on the life and times of Sojourner Truth, a former slave from New York. Painter shows the power of religion in Truth's life as she moves from enslavement, though the Kingdom of Matthias, and ultimately to become an outspoken critic of slavery and for women's rights. Religion in her life and relationships at times inhibited her and at other times liberated her. According to Painter, it was Truth's religious beliefs that carried her through each struggle and success.

Religious Reform as a Form of Social Control

PAUL E. JOHNSON

Charles Finney's revival enlarged every Protestant church, broke down sectarian boundaries, and mobilized a religious community that had at its disposal enormous economic power. Motives which determined the use of that power derived from the revival, and they were frankly millenarian.

As Rochester Protestants looked beyond their community in 1831, they saw something awesome. For news of Finney's revival had helped touch off a wave of religious enthusiasm throughout much of the northern United States. The revival moved west into Ohio and Michigan, east into Utica, Albany, and the market towns of inland New England. Even Philadelphia and New York City felt its power. Vermont's congregational churches grew by 29 percent in 1831. During the same twelve months the churches of Connecticut swelled by over a third. After scanning reports from western New York, the Presbyterian General Assembly announced in wonder that "the work has been so general and thorough, that the whole customs of society have changed." Never before had so many Americans experienced religion in so short a time. Lyman Beecher, who watched the excitement from Boston, declared that the revival of 1831 was the greatest revival of religion that the world had ever seen.

Rochester Protestants saw conversions multiply and heard of powerful revivals throughout Yankee Christendom, They saw divisions among themselves melt away, and they began to sense that the pre-millennial unanimity was at hand—and that they and people like them were bringing it about. They had converted their families and neighbors through prayer. Through ceaseless effort they could use the same power to convert the world. It was Finney himself who told them that "if they were united all over the world the Millennium might be brought about in three months." He did not mean that Christ was coming to Rochester. The immediate and gory millennium predicted in Revelation had no place in evangelical thinking. Utopia would be realized on earth, and it would be made by God with the active and united collaboration of His people. It was not the physical reign of Christ that Finney predicted but the reign of Christianity. The millennium would be accomplished when sober, godly men—men whose every step was guided by a living faith in Jesus—exercised power in this world. Clearly, the revival of 1831 was a turning point in the long struggle to establish that state of affairs. American Protestants knew that, and John Humphrey Noyes later recalled that "in 1831, the whole orthodox church was in a state of ebullition in regard to the Millennium." Rochester evangelicals stood at the center of that excitement.

After 1831 the goal of revivals was the christianization of the world. With that at stake, membership in a Protestant church entailed new kinds of personal commitment. Newcomers to Brick Presbyterian Church in the 1820s had agreed to obey the laws of God and of the church, to treat fellow members as brothers, and "to live as an humble Christian." Each new convert was told that "renouncing all ungodliness and every worldly lust, you give up your all, soul and body, to be the Lord's, promising to walk before him in holiness and love all the days of your life." Not easy requirements, certainly, but in essence personal and passive. With the Finney revival, the ingrown piety of the 1820s turned outward and aggressive. In 1831 Brick Church rewrote its covenant, and every member signed this evangelical manifesto:

> We [note that the singular "you" has disappeared] do now, in the presence of the Eternal God, and these witnesses, covenant to be the Lord's. *We promise to renounce all the ways of sin, and to make it the business of our life to do good and promote the declarative glory of our heavenly Father.* We promise steadily and devoutly to attend upon the institutions and ordinances of Christ as administered in this church, and to submit ourselves to its direction and discipline, until our present relation shall be regularly dissolved. We promise to be kind and affectionate to all the members of this church, to be tender of their character, and to endeavor to the utmost of our ability, to promote their growth in grace. *We promise to make it the great business of our life to glorify God and build up the Redeemer's Kingdom in this fallen world,* and constantly to endeavor to present our bodies a living sacrifice, holy and acceptable to Him.

In that final passage, the congregation affirmed that its actions—both individually and in concert—were finally meaningful only in relation to the Coming Kingdom. Everything they did tended either to bring it closer or push it farther away.

Guiding the new activism was a revolution in ideas about human ability. The Reverend William James of Brick Church had insisted in 1828 that most men were innately sinful. Christians could not change them, but only govern their excesses through *"a system of moral regulations, founded upon the natural relations between moral beings, and having for its immediate end the happiness of the community."* We have seen, however, that certain of those "natural relations" were in disarray, and that the businessmen and master workmen who were expected to govern within them were the most active participants in the revival. Evangelical theology absolved them of responsibility by teaching that virtue and order were products not of external authority but of choices made by morally responsible individuals. Nowhere, perhaps, was this put more simply than in the Sunday schools. In the 1820s children had been taught to read and then forced to memorize huge parts of the Bible. (Thirteen-year-old Jane Wilson won a prize in 1823 when she committed a numbing 1,650 verses to memory.) After 1831 Sunday-school scholars stopped memorizing the Bible. The object now was to have them study a few verses a week and to come to an understanding of them, and thus to prepare themselves for conversion and for "an active and useful Christian life." Unregenerate persons were no longer to be disciplined by immutable authority and through fixed social relationships. They were free and redeemable moral agents, accountable for their actions, capable of accepting or rejecting God's promise. It was the duty of Christian gentlemen not to govern them and accept responsibility for their actions but to educate them and change their hearts.

William Wisner, pastor at Brick Church during these years, catalogued developments that were "indispensably necessary to the bringing of millennial glory." First, of course, was more revivals. Second, and tied directly to the first, was the return of God's people to the uncompromising personal standards of the primitive Christians and Protestant martyrs. For the public and private behavior of converts advertised what God had done for them. If a Christian drank or broke the Sabbath or cheated his customers or engaged in frivolous conversation, he weakened not only his own reputation but the awesome cause he represented. While Christian women were admonished to discourage flattery and idle talk and to bring every conversation onto the great subject, troubled businessmen were actually seen returning money to families they had cheated. Isaac Lyon, half-owner of the Rochester Woolen Mills, was seen riding a canal boat on Sunday in the fall of 1833. Immediately he was before the trustees of his church. Lyon was pardoned after writing a confession into the minutes and reading it to the full congregation. He confessed that he had broken the eighth commandment. But more serious, he admitted, was that his sin was witnessed by others who knew his standing in the church and in the community, and for whom the behavior of Isaac Lyon reflected directly on the evangelical cause. He had shamed Christ in public and given His enemies cause to celebrate.

Finney's revival had, however, centered among persons whose honesty and personal morals were beyond question before they converted. Personal piety and circumspect public behavior were at bottom means toward the furtherance of revivals. At the moment of rebirth, the question came to each of them: "Lord, what wilt thou have me do?" The answer was obvious: unite with other Christians and convert the world. The world, however, contained bad habits, people, and institutions that inhibited revivals and whose removal must precede the millennium. Among church members who had lived in Rochester in the late 1820s, the right course of action was clear. With one hand they evangelized among their own unchurched poor. With the other they waged an absolutist and savage war on strong drink.

On New Year's Eve of the revival winter, Finney's co-worker Theodore Weld delivered a four-hour temperance lecture at First Presbyterian Church. Weld began by describing a huge open pit at his right hand, and thousands of the victims of drink at his left. First he isolated the most hopeless—the runaway fathers, paupers, criminals, and maniacs—and marched them into the grave. He moved higher and higher into society, until only a few well-dressed tipplers remained outside the grave. Not even these were spared. While the audience rose to its feet the most temperate drinkers, along with their wives and helpless children, were swallowed up and lost. Weld turned to the crowd and demanded that they not only abstain from drinking and encourage the reform of others but that they unite to stamp it out. They must not drink or sell liquor, rent to a grogshop, sell grain to distillers, or patronize merchants who continued to trade in ardent spirits. They must, in short, utterly disengage from the traffic in liquor and use whatever power they had to make others do the same. A packed house stood silent.

The Reverend Penney rose from his seat beside the Methodist and Baptist preachers and demanded that vendors in the audience stop selling liquor immediately. Eight or ten did so on the spot, and the wholesale grocers retired to hold a meeting of their own. The next day Elijah and Albert Smith, Baptists who owned the largest grocery and provisions warehouse in the city, rolled their stock of whiskey out onto the sidewalk. While cheering Christians and awestruck sinners looked on, they smashed the barrels and let thousands of gallons of liquid poison run out onto Exchange Street.

Within a week, Everard Peck wrote home that "the principal merchants who have traded largely in ardent spirits are about abandoning this unholy traffic & we almost hope to see this deadly poison expelled from our village." The performance of the Smith brothers was being repeated throughout Rochester. Sometimes wealthy converts walked into groceries, bought up all the liquor, and threw it away. A few grocers with a fine taste for symbolism poured their whiskey into the Canal. Even grocers who stayed outside the churches found that whiskey on their shelves was bad for business. The firm of Rossiter and Knox announced that it was discontinuing the sale of whiskey, but "not thinking it a duty to 'feed the Erie Canal' with their property, offer to sell at cost their whole stock of liquors...." Those who resisted were refused advertising space in some newspapers, and in denying the power of a united evangelical community they toyed with economic ruin. S. P. Needham held out for three years, but in 1834 he announced that he planned to liquidate his stock of groceries, provisions, and liquors and leave Rochester. "Church Dominancy," he explained, "has such influence over this community that no honest man can do his own business in his own way...."

Almost immediately, Weld's absolutist temperance pledge became a condition of conversion—the most visible symbol of individual rebirth. The teetotal pledge was only the most forceful indication of church members' willingness to use whatever power they had to coerce others into being good, or at least to deny them the means of being bad. While whiskey ran into the gutters, two other symbols of the riotous twenties disappeared. John and Joseph Christopher, both of them new Episcopalians, bought the theater next door to their hotel, closed it, and had it reopened as a livery stable. The Presbyterian Sprague brothers bought the circus building and turned it into a soap factory. Increasingly, the wicked had no place to go.

These were open and forceful attacks on the leisure activities of the new working class, something very much like class violence. But Christians waged war on sin, not workingmen. Alcohol, the circus, the theater, and other workingmen's entertainments were evil because they wasted men's time and clouded their minds and thus blocked the millennium. Evangelicals fought these evils in order to prepare society for new revivals. It was missionary work, little more. And in the winter following Finney's departure, it began to bear fruit.

With one arm evangelicals attacked the bad habits and tawdry amusements of unregenerate workingmen. With the other they offered redemption. They invited humbler men into their churches. They poured money into poor congregations, financed the establishment of new churches in working-class neighborhoods, and used their wealth and social position to help poor but deserving brethren. By the middle 1830s hundreds of workingmen were in the churches and participating in middle-class crusades.

While Finney was still in town, rich evangelicals met to organize a church for canal workers, transients, and Rochester's unchurched poor. The committee was headed by Jonothan Child, the most active Episcopal layman in Rochester, and it included rich men from every church. The new congregation was to be a "free" church which abolished pew rents in an attempt to erase class distinctions among the membership. Organized in 1832 as Free Presbyterian Church, this mission was an enormous success. The founding congregation numbered only 45 persons, most of them wealthy members from older Presbyterian churches. At the end of one year, the membership had swelled to 237. Inspired by this success, members of old churches founded Second Baptist and Bethel Presbyterian as free congregations in the mid-1830s. In these churches some of the wealthiest men in Rochester brought their families to worship in fellowship with newly pious day laborers, boatmen, and journeyman craftsmen.

At the same time Finney's converts assisted the older working-class churches in every way they could. First Methodist—made up overwhelmingly of workingmen and their families—was the largest congregation in Rochester by 1834, and much of that growth was made possible by the benevolence of wealthy evangelicals. Twice in the 1830s that unlucky congregation saw its church burn to the ground. After the fire of 1832, the Methodists obtained a loan from the bank at Hartford, recommended and countersigned by rich Presbyterians. When the church caught fire in 1834, Methodists held an open meeting in the courthouse square, attended by ministers and laymen of every denomination. They passed the hat and received enough money to build another new church. The little knot of Freewill Baptists who began meeting at the courthouse in 1836 also enjoyed revival-induced benevolence. While dividing Sundays between his congregation and the inmates of the county jail, the minister remarked, "We are treated with much kindness by all classes, and especially by all evangelical Christians." His remarks took on weight two months later, when a member of Third Presbyterian Church gave him a thousand dollars to build a meetinghouse.

Even the smallest and most despised congregations could look to Finney's converts for help. The African Methodist Church had been built in 1827 with donations from white church members, but in the 1830s that church was financially troubled. The leading trustee and the man most frequently chosen as spokesman for the Rochester black community was Austin Steward, a Main Street grocer. Steward spent his profits on the church and on the unsuccessful Wilberforce Colony in Canada. By the middle 1830s both he and his congregation were bankrupt. But Steward had been in Rochester since 1817, and he had old friends among white evangelicals. He had also been among the first of the smaller grocers to stop selling liquor. Wealthy Presbyterians organized and provided him with interest-free loans, free legal advice, and promises of exclusive patronage. And when the temperance society organized a huge non-alcoholic Fourth of

July picnic in 1837, it was Austin Steward who received the catering contract. Within a year, both Steward and the African Methodists were back on their feet.

Simultaneously, evangelicals established institutions to encourage working-men to reform themselves and to sustain those who reformed. In 1831 rich church members founded the Rochester Savings Bank to encourage working-class thrift and personal discipline, and served without pay on its board of directors. At the same time the congregations at First Presbyterian, St. Luke's Episcopal, and Free Presbyterian Churches organized schools to teach reading, writing, and proper thoughts to poor children, and to keep them away from "the highways and resorts of dissipation." The parents of these children had to contend with the wealthy women who organized the Female Charitable Society, and who went door-to-door in poor neighborhoods determining which families needed help and which deserved it. Work was scarce during the winter months, and unpredictable even during busy times. With the exceptions of the dreaded almshouse and, of course, the churches themselves, this society of Christian women was the only relief organization in Rochester.

Evangelicals encouraged working-class churches and churchmembers not out of pity or as an attempt to bribe workingmen but to build up the Kingdom of Christ in Rochester. They were enormously successful. In 1832 trustees at Second Presbyterian invited the evangelist Jedediah Burchard into their church. Burchard was a crude, half-educated man and a powerful preacher, and he drew a new kind of audience. Word moved quickly, and the revival spread again to every church. Baptist, Methodist, Presbyterian, and Episcopal ministers preached from the same pulpit, and the place of meeting shifted indiscriminately between churches. In the following year and again in 1836, Rochester ministers repeated the performance without outside help. These were powerful revivals. In many congregations—First Methodist, Second Presbyterian, and a growing number of new churches—the revivals of the middle 1830s dwarfed Finney's earlier triumph. "It begins," stated one of Finney's busy converts, "to look like the millennium...."

Enthusiasm generated in 1831 was moving into new places. For while businessmen and master craftsmen and their families continued to join churches in the 1830s, they did so in the company of large numbers of wage earners. In 1830–31 journeyman craftsmen had accounted for only 22 percent of male converts—half their proportion of the male work force. Burchard wakened the workingmen, and in subsequent years middle-class missionaries converted hundreds of wage-earning Rochesterians. A full 42 percent of the men who joined churches between 1832 and 1837 were journeyman craftsmen. The workingman's revival was in fact much larger than can be demonstrated systematically, for available evidence seriously underestimates the number of working-class converts. The records of some poor churches—First Methodist and Free Presbyterian in particular—are incomplete. And city directories excluded the most transient and thus generally the youngest and poorest men. These sources identify one in seven journeymen in 1837 as Protestant church members. Were records complete, it is likely that the figure would rise to one in four.

The revivals of 1832–36 were results of middle-class missions, and the churches that benefited from them were without exception middle-class organizations.

We are thus left with the question why hundreds of wage earners allied themselves with bourgeois evangelism in the l830s. Missionaries thought they knew the answer: revivals, they claimed, separated workingmen who were capable of discipline and self-restraint from those who were not.

They were, of course, mistaken. Many wage earners rejected strong drink and riotous amusements as vehemently as they rejected the middle class and its religion. The best bootmakers in Rochester were tramping journeymen from New York City. These independent craftsmen read widely and debated skillfully and defiantly—often on religious subjects—and they avoided excessive drinking and discouraged it in others. Among workingmen who stayed in Rochester, there is ample evidence that individual and group discipline could sustain resistance as well as pious docility. In 1833 journeyman carpenters struck for a ten-hour day, and they protected their strike by telling newcomers to come to them rather than to masters in search of jobs. They met with some success, for at one point all but two contractors agreed to their terms. The carpenters fought the same battle annually until 1836, and there were similar organizations among stonemasons, boat builders, coopers, and calkers. These were orderly, sustained, and well-planned contests with employers, and it is doubtful that they could have been conducted by a working class made up of drunkards and degenerates.

Thus the division between "rough" and "respectable" workingmen did not simply separate those who went to church from those who did not. Of nine leaders of journeymen's societies whose names are known, none belonged to a Protestant church. Indeed many workmen, drawing on traditions of republican skepticism that stretched back to the Revolution, openly opposed the churches. Celebrations of Thomas Paine's birthday were working-class festivals in the middle 1830s, and Rochester was among the few cities outside the old seaports that supported free-thought newspapers. Along with anti-evangelical diatribes and formal disproofs of the existence of God, the free-thought editors printed essays in support of strikes and suggestions that workingmen needed education and self-respect, not middle-class temperance sermons. Paine himself, we may recall, had combined irreligion with calls for education, and with active opposition to violent sports and heavy drinking. There was more than one road to self-improvement in the 1830s.

Why, then, did so many wage earners take the road pointed out by their masters? Some—perhaps most—were already tied to the business community. Many were sons and younger brothers of Finney's middle-class converts, and no doubt many others were trusty employees who followed their masters into church. Still others may have been drawn to evangelists who proclaimed a spiritual rather than a worldly aristocracy among men, and who directed some of their assaults upon the rich and powerful. But with all of this said, the most powerful source of the workingman's revival was the simple, coercive fact that wage earners worked for men who insisted on seeing them in church. In 1836 a free-thought editor announced that clerks were being forced to attend revival meetings. He quoted one of them: "I don't give a d———n. I get five dollars more in a month than before I got religion." We shall see that he was not alone.

"We hope," wrote a Baptist editor in 1834, "the time will come when men will have done employing intemperate mechanics, and when ardent spirits will cease to distract, disturb, and ruin." His hopes were based on the new willingness of Christian employers to demand not only hard work but personal piety of their employees. In the spring of 1831, William Howell completed work on one of the largest and most elegant packet boats ever put on the canal. The job employed thirty boat builders, and Howell announced with satisfaction that it was completed "without the stimulus of ardent spirits or liquid poison." Lewis Selye, a young convert who began manufacturing fire engines in 1833, advertised work for machinists, but noted that "none need apply except those of moral habits and the best of workmen." Applicants at the Rochester Woolen Mills (which hired one of the largest work forces in town) were told that they "must be of moral and temperate habits...." The iron founders Thomas Kempshall and John Bush owned another establishment that hired large numbers of men. They commented on their position for a machinist and patternmaker that "a man of steady habits will find it a pleasant situation," and added that "none but temperate men need apply."

In the 1830s Christian employers announced that only sober, God-fearing applicants need knock at their doors. The effect of that attempt to impose religious standards on the labor market can be measured partially and indirectly through analysis of population mobility. For if a workman established a fixed home in Rochester, his rootedness may have meant many things. But first of all it meant that he had found steady work. An analysis of residential stability among churchgoing and non-churchgoing wage earners between 1834 and 1838 suggests strongly that working-men who did not join churches had trouble finding jobs. Churchgoing clerks were twice as stable as non-churchgoers in the same occupation. Among journeymen and laborers, churchgoers were three-and-one-half times as likely to stay in town as were non-church members. These relationships persist, it should be noted, when they are controlled for age, property holdings, and length of prior residence. Workmen who went to church became settled residents of Rochester *because* they went to church. Their non-churchgoing workmates stayed a few months or years and then moved on to other, perhaps friendlier, towns.

Church membership played an equally powerful role in selecting those wage earners who rose to the ownership of their own stores and workshops. Opportunities for journeymen shrank during these years. In 1827, 16 percent of all men in skilled blue-collar occupations owned workshops. Within the next ten years that figure dropped to 11 percent. Simple arithmetic told journeymen that few of them could hope to become master craftsmen. Yet over half the churchgoing journeymen completed that step. Among their non-churchgoing workmates, the comparable figure was less than one in five—and this among the tiny minority who stayed in Rochester. There was a similar pattern among laborers. By 1837 one man in three possessed little or no skill and depended for his livelihood upon casual, scarce, and low-paying work. For those who wished to move up, the most sensible step was to acquire skills and thus move into better-paying and more secure employment. Two-thirds of the laborers who joined churches made that step between 1827 and 1837. Non-church members in the same occupation moved out of Rochester three times as often, and those who stayed rose at about half the rate attained by church members.

The pattern was identical among clerks. In the 1830s a position as clerk was no longer a stepping-stone to the ownership of a substantial business. More and more had to settle for a small store or for permanent wage-earning status. Few completed the step from clerk to merchant. Most of those who did belonged to Protestant churches. Of the clerks who joined churches during the revivals and who remained in Rochester in 1837, 72 percent became merchants, professionals, or shopkeepers. Most non-churchgoing clerks left Rochester. Of those who stayed, half skidded into blue-collar jobs.

While it varied between occupations, the relation between occupational advancement and membership in a church was strong throughout the wage-earning population. A full 63 percent of churchgoing wage earners who stayed in Rochester between 1827 and 1837 improved their occupational standing. Only 2 percent (one man) declined. Most of the non-church members who worked beside them in 1827 did not stay long enough to have their occupations measured twice. The few who did advanced about half as often as did church members, and they were six times as likely to decline.

The most stable and successful workmen in Rochester were those who went to church. That much can be demonstrated in a systematic way. But the reasons why church members prospered while non-church members moved away or stagnated are not so easily counted. The most obvious explanation is that membership in a church induced habits and attitudes that fit comfortably with a market economy and a disciplined work environment. It is likely that churchgoers were objectively better workers than others, that they worked hard and saved their money, and that they came to the shop sober and on time. No doubt those qualities were crucial to their success. But they were useless until other men decided to reward them. In Rochester no man made his way alone. Whether his career prospered or went sour depended on decisions made by others: decisions to hire him, to promote him, to enter into partnership with him, and to recommend him to neighbors and friends. Social mobility was a social product, and patterns of mobility cannot be explained apart from the means by which individual successes and failures were brought about. Here it will be helpful to trace the entry of individual converts into the business community in the 1830s. We shall find—and it should come as no surprise—that their mobility was directly sponsored by the churchgoing elite.

The carpenter Lauren Parsons took the simplest route. He joined his employer's church in 1831, and went into partnership with him the following year. There were others who did the same. Of the thirty-one wage-earning converts who went into business in the 1830s, sixteen did so in partnership with others. Only four joined with relatives, suggesting that, like Lauren Parsons, they were indeed recruited from outside the old business-owning families. Ten of the sixteen, however, entered business in partnership with other church members—eight of them with members of their own congregations. Here was the most direct kind of sponsorship.

But the career of Lewis Selye suggests that aid to aspiring converts went far beyond formal partnerships. In 1827 Selye was a propertyless journeyman blacksmith. Ten years later he was sole proprietor of a machine shop and fire-engine factory, and one of the richest men in Rochester. An editor described Selye's factory as "a compliment to the ingenuity and enterprise of our townsman … who has established this and other branches of business through the force of his own skill and perseverence, unaided by any stock companies or capitalists." True, Selye never formed a partnership. But he had help nonetheless. Decisions that paved the way for Lewis Selye's success were made by the town fathers themselves. He built his first fire engine in 1833 at the request of the village trustees—four months after he joined Brick Presbyterian Church. The same city officials, all of them rich church members, lent their prestigious endorsements to his advertisements.

Despite this assistance, the road was not always smooth for Lewis Selye. In 1837 a sharp decline in orders forced him to close the shop. He sold the business to Martin Briggs, a member of his church and an in-law of the powerful Scrantom family. But the transaction was never put on paper. Lewis Selye appeared as an engine builder in the directory compiled months later, and he continued throughout the 1840s as a successful manufacturer and Whig politician, and as a trustee of Brick Church. It appears that Martin Briggs had not bought him out in 1837. He had bailed him out.

Alvah Strong was another young man who reaped material as well as spiritual rewards from his association with the churches. Strong's father was a doctor and boardinghouse keeper whose clientele consisted first of laborers who dug the canal, then of Rochester workingmen. His brother owned a small candy and fruit store on Exchange Street. The Strongs were not a rich family, but their early and continuous residence in Rochester and their prominence within the Baptist Church (the father was one of the oldest members, the brother was superintendent of the Sunday school) gained them entry into the town's church-bounded community of respectability. Alvah Strong wanted to be a newspaperman. He served an apprenticeship on one Rochester weekly and worked as foreman on another in the 1820s. Then he traveled through the state working as a journeyman. In 1831 Erastus Shepard, a former employer, moved to Rochester and bought the *Anti-Masonic Enquirer*. He offered Alvah Strong a partnership, largely because Strong's "knowledge of the place, and familiarity with the people would strengthen the concern." Strong and Shepard both converted during the Finney revival. Neither had much money, and for the first few years they operated the paper on credit. "Our good name and our industry," Strong explained, "were our capital, so that we commanded credit when it was needed." Most of the money came from wealthy evangelicals who, in 1834, financed the *Enquirer*'s transition into a Whig daily.

Alvah Strong and Lewis Selye earned the friendship of rich evangelicals not only by joining their churches but by living up to Christian standards and enforcing them on others. Selye became a leading layman at Brick Church, and he demanded total abstinence of the men who worked for him. And there were no more consistent temperance editorializers than Alvah Strong and Erastus Shepard. Here, obviously, were men upon whom Christian money was well spent.

There were, of course, converts who began new lives and then slid backward. These found that the churches could dispense punishments as well as rewards. John Denio was a young printer who moved to Rochester in 1833, joined Brick Presbyterian Church, and bought the *Rochester Gem* from his fellow communicant Edwin Scrantom. During the following summer, he was seen in a hotel bar joking and drinking wine with a group of traveling salesmen. When called before the trustees of his church (yes, Lewis Selye was among them), Denio angrily denied that he had done anything wrong. He was excommunicated on the spot. Within a year, the *Gem* had been taken over by Shepard and Strong, and its ruined editor had disappeared from Rochester. Ela Burnap, an old resident of the town, experienced a similar fall from grace. In 1830 he was a master silversmith and the owner of a house on North Fitzhugh, the most uniformly wealthy block in the city. But two years later, another church member saw him drunk. He was suspended from his church. Unlike John Denio, Burnap stayed in Rochester. In 1837 the tax assessor found him working as a watchmaker and living in a rented house on the outskirts of town.

Charles Finney's revival mobilized economic power in Rochester and injected religious motives into its use. The careers of Lewis Selye, Alvah Strong, John Denio, and Ela Burnap reflect that fact. In the 1830s men seeking jobs and credit knocked at the doors of businessmen pushed by their changed souls and by enormous social pressure to prepare Rochester for the millennium. By dispensing and withholding patronage, Christian entrepreneurs regulated the membership of their own class, and to a large extent of the community as a whole. Conversion and abstinence from strong drink became crucial economic credentials. For membership in a church and participation in its crusades put a man into the community in which economic decisions were made, and at a time when religious criteria dominated those choices. By the middle 1830s there were two working classes in Rochester: a church-going minority tied closely to the sources of steady work and advancement, and a floating majority that faced insecure employment and stifled opportunities.

In the late 1820s Rochester had divided bitterly along ideological and class lines. Charles Finney's revival melted the first of those divisions, and subsequent enthusiasms transformed the second. Now society split starkly between those who loved Jesus and those who did not....

Religion as Inhibiting and Liberating: The Complicated Case of Sojourner Truth

NELL IRVIN PAINTER

SOJOURNER TRUTH, born Isabella, is one of the two most famous African-American women of the nineteenth century. The other, Harriet Tubman, the "Moses" of her people, also came out of slavery. Many people confuse the two because both lived in an era shadowed by human bondage, but Truth and Tubman were contrasting figures. New York was Truth's Egypt: Tubman's was in

From Nell Irvin Painter, *Sojourner Truth: A Life, A Symbol* (New York: W. W. Norton and Co., 1996), p. 3–4, 22–23, 25, 48, 53–56, 114–116, 157, 160–161. Copyright © 1996 by Nell Irvin Painter. Reprinted by permission of W.W. Norton & Company, Inc.

Maryland, these respective places marking each woman with a regional identity that Truth, at least, later came very much to prize. Born in about 1797, Truth was a generation older than Tubman, born in about 1821. Tubman will walk these pages from time to time, but only as a guest.

A woman of remarkable intelligence despite her illiteracy, Truth had great presence. She was tall, some 5 feet 11 inches, of spare but solid frame. Her voice was low, so low that listeners sometimes termed it masculine, and her singing voice was beautifully powerful. Whenever she spoke in public, she also sang. No one ever forgot the power and pathos of Sojourner Truth's singing, just as her wit and originality of phrasing were also of lasting remembrance.

As an abolitionist and feminist, she put her body and her mind to a unique task, that of physically representing women who had been enslaved. At a time when most Americans thought of slaves as male and women as white, Truth embodied a fact that still bears repeating: Among the blacks are women; among the women, there are blacks....

Only Truth had the ability to go on speaking, year after year for thirty years, to make herself into a force in several American reform movements. Even though the aims of her missions became increasingly secular after midcentury, Truth was first and last an itinerant preacher, stressing both itinerancy and preaching. From the late 1840s through the late 1870s, she traveled the American land, denouncing slavery and slavers, advocating freedom, women's rights, woman suffrage, and temperance.

Pentecostal that she was, Truth would have explained that the force that brought her from the soul murder of slavery into the authority of public advocacy was the power of the Holy Spirit. Her ability to call upon a supernatural power gave her a resource claimed by millions of black women and by disempowered people the world over. Without doubt, it was Truth's religious faith that transformed her from Isabella, a domestic servant, into Sojourner Truth, a hero for three centuries—at least....

ISABELLA freed herself in several steps and in three dimensions: She left slavery with the Dumonts when *she* thought the time was right; she freed herself from fear through a discovery of Jesus, love; and, empowered by her new religious faith, she broke out of the passivity of slavery by using the law toward her own ends. In so complicated a process, no one date captures her passage out of bondage. Citing the moment in July 1827 when she became legally free may conveniently date her liberation, but focusing mainly on the aspects of slavery that affected owners— the legal and the economic—obscures much of emancipation's larger significance.

There is no denying that legal and economic status counted enormously in circumscribing slaves' chances in life; but the injuries of slavery went much deeper, into the bodies and into the psyches of the people who were its victims. In their experience, slavery meant a good deal more than lack of standing before the law and endless, unpaid labor, just as there would be a good deal more to freedom than being able to make a contract or earn a shilling.

In the North, the process of emancipation was made personal by the very gradualness of the laws of most states. Slaves surely preferred to be free sooner rather than later, but their desires were hardly uppermost in the minds of state legislators. Rather, northern abolition moved incrementally, seeing to it that owners were not deprived abruptly of their accustomed labor.

In New York, discussion of abolition began in earnest in the 1780s, and in 1799 the state began the process of gradual emancipation. Slavery would end on the Fourth of July 1827. For those born before 1799, emancipation would be unconditional; but those born after 1799 might have to serve a further period of indentured servitude: until they were twenty-eight, if male, or twenty-five, if female.

This legislation would have kept Isabella and Thomas slaves until 1827. Their children owed indentured servitude for much longer: Diana until about 1840. Peter until about 1849. Elizabeth until about 1850, and Sophia until about 1851. Requirements of law and work kept the family scattered. Indentured, the children could not follow Isabella into freedom, and as a live-in domestic servant, she lacked the home she had dreamed of as she mended by firelight with her children. When Sojourner Truth became an abolitionist, some of her children were still not free....

In 1826, Isabella heard the voice of her God instructing her when to set out on her own as a free woman. Just before dawn in the late fall, she left the Dumonts' carrying only her baby, Sophia, and a supply of food and clothing so meager that it fit in a cotton handkerchief. She intended only a short journey, so as to save John Dumont trouble when he came looking for her, which she knew he was bound to do, for she was depriving him of two servants—herself and her baby—whom, according to law, he still owned. About five miles away, she called upon an old friend, Levi Rowe, who welcomed her from his deathbed and directed her to Isaac and Maria Van Wagenen of Wagondale, whom she had also known for years. Like the Dumonts, the Van Wagenens were prominent members of the Klyn Esopus Dutch Reformed Church. Unlike the Dumonts, the Van Wagenens opposed slavery. When John Dumont came to fetch Isabella, the Van Wagenens paid him $25: $20 for Isabella for a year, $5 for baby Sophia. Taking the Van Wagenens' last name (often rendered "Van Wagner" outside Ulster County), she lived a "quiet, peaceful life" with "excellent people" there for about a year....

IN MAY 1832, Isabella and the widower Elijah Pierson received a visit from a resplendently dressed figure: Robert Matthews, a Scots-American calling himself "the Prophet Matthias," whose singular manifestations of perfectionism had already created consternation upstate. Sylvester Mills, Pierson's fellow perfectionist Pearl Street merchant, vouched for him. This attractive forty-four-year-old stranger combed his hair and beard to make himself look like the chromo pictures of Jesus. When Isabella met him at the door, she knew immediately from Matthew, Chapter 16, to ask. "Art thou the Christ?" When the visitor answered, "I am," she kissed his feet and burst into tears of joy. Pierson's welcome was equally ecstatic. In the parlor, Isabella, Pierson, and Matthias exchanged their experiences of visions and voices and agreed on everything.

For a while Pierson and Matthias alternated preaching in meeting at Pierson's house, but Pierson—whom Matthias now called John the Baptist—gave up preaching after Matthias said, and his followers believed, that "God don't speak through preachers; he speaks through me, his prophet."...

Supposedly everyone belonged to the community on a footing of equality and held everything in common (as in early Christianity), and everyone worked according to physical ability. Nonetheless, a hierarchy that was very reminiscent of the world of the "Gentiles" prevailed. Matthias, called "Father," gave all the orders and sat at the head of the table. He decided when to go to work and when to practice the rituals of the kingdom, such as the communal bathing that he called baptism. No matter when he preached to his followers or how angrily and how long, they were bound to listen. Isabella no longer preached, for Matthias set preaching out of bounds for women.

Matthias had long inflicted corporal punishment on those he controlled. As Robert Matthews he had beaten his wife and children, and as the Prophet Matthias he beat Isabella for the infraction he considered abominable in women: insubordination. On an occasion when she was not feeling well—already the apparent proof that she was possessed by a "sick devil"—she had intervened when Matthias was punishing one of his young sons. Matthias lashed her with his cowhide whip, shouting, "Shall a sick devil undertake to dictate to me?" While in the kingdom he also beat his eighteen-year-old daughter so severely that she bore marks from his whip six weeks later.

Matthias's instincts were patriarchal, literally and figuratively. He did not call the kingdom "the family," but he did insist on being called "Father," and, once he had taken Ann Folger as his "match spirit" (that is, his new wife), he called her "Mother." As Mother she was still a child, for he treated everyone in the household as children, lecturing them for hours, frequently in shrill, harsh anger. Ann Folger described Matthias's power: "We consider[ed] him as God the Father possessing the Holy Ghost, and the power of bestowing it on others; the power also of executing wrath on whom he would. We regarded him as the last trumpet, answering to all the angels of wrath spoken of in the Revelation; that is the executing angels." As the last trumpet, Matthias would bend down, fill his lungs, and shout in a voice loud enough to deafen his hearers temporarily. Ann Folger admitted that "we indeed thought he did cast evil spirits out of us. We were to obey all his commands, and we showed our obedience to him.... He had the command of all things in the house."...

Though not paid as a servant would be, Isabella was still a black woman with the diminished social stature that came from having been a slave. When the formerly wealthy were about to discuss delicate or weighty matters, it was their habit to send Isabella to do work that would take her out of the room—a practice she disregarded when the kingdom was dissolving and she felt that she must have a say in crucial decisions. Even more important, in a household that included Ann Folger as a pampered lady, was Isabella's ability to work. She was a strong woman who knew how to cook, clean, and launder....

In the fall of 1844, Truth gave her first antislavery speech in Northampton. In May 1845, she spoke to the annual meeting of the American Anti-Slavery Society in New York City, identified in the National Anti-Slavery Standard only as "a colored woman who had been a slave, but more recently resident of Northampton, Mass." Truth's remarks, according to the Standard, were full of "good sense and strong feeling."

I cannot track completely Truth's antislavery and women's rights appearances, for reporters did not invariably consider her worth identifying by name, or even mentioning at all. She doubtless attended and addressed many meetings without notice between 1845 and 1850. I do know for certain that she attended and addressed a large women's rights meeting in Worcester. Massachusetts, in 1850—the first such meeting of national scope in the United States. This Worcester meeting was an immediate successor of the pioneering Seneca Falls, New York, women's convention of 1848 organized by Elizabeth Cady Stanton, Lucretia Mott, and others—including the Rochester abolitionist Amy Post, who would play so large a role in Truth's later life.

Women had been publicly vindicating their rights as women, as workers, and as blacks in the United States since the Scotswoman Frances Wright lectured in New York City in the late 1820s and the African American Maria Stewart spoke in Boston in the early 1830s. But women as speakers before mixed, or "promiscuous" audiences of women and men were rare, even when the subject was evangelical and the tradition—as in the case of women itinerant preachers—centuries older. Women lecturers like Angelina Grimké and Abby Kelley caused a sensation when they joined the anti-slavery circuit in the 1830s, since critics opposed women's right to advocate anything in public.

By 1840, the issue of women as leaders in abolitionism had split the American movement, with Garrisonians like Frederick Douglass and Abby Kelly defending women's rights, and less radical men, especially Arthur and Lewis Tappan, leaving the American Anti-slavery Society on this and other grounds. The Tappans' unwillingness to mix antislavery with other reforms, such as women's rights, is probably the main reason they do not appear in the *Narative of Sojourner Truth*. The rival society set up by the Tappans and their supporters withered, while the Garrisonian American Anti-Slavery Society flourished. After 1840, in the fashion of excommunicators, the Garrisonians pretended that the Tappans did not exist, despite their crucial early role in abolitionism.

Garrison firmly supported the 1850 women's rights meeting in Worcester and may have suggested that Douglass and Truth speak. According to a newspaper report, Truth "uttered some truths that told well," although her skin was dark and her outward appearance "uncomely." Truth spoke primarily as a preacher: "She said Woman set the world wrong by eating the forbidden fruit, and now she was going to set it right. She said Goodness never had any beginning; it was from everlasting, and could never die. But Evil had a beginning, and must have an end. She expressed great reverence for God, and faith that he will bring about his own purposes and plans."

In her concluding remarks, Lucretia Mott, a leader of the convention, mentioned Truth by name as "the poor woman who had grown up under the curse of Slavery," and repeated Truth's formulation of the finite nature of evil and the everlasting quality of good. Truth's other early reported antislavery speech in 1850, at the annual meeting of the Rhode Island Anti-Slavery Society in Providence, in November, was also vague on antislavery politics. While the men, Frederick Douglass, Charles C. Burleigh, and Charles Lenox Remond, damned the Fugitive Slave Act for hours and demanded Garrison's version of disunion—"No union with slaveholders!"—Truth was reported as brief and hesitant: "she had been a slave, and was not now entirely free. She did not know anything about politics—could not read the newspaper—but thanked God that the law was made—that the worst had come to worst; but the best must come to best."

TRUTH's first tour on the antislavery and women's rights circuit in the winter of 1851 came at Garrison's behest. He invited her to accompany him and his dear friend, the radical British Member of Parliament George Thompson, on a trip into western New York....

The Fourth of July 1854 found Truth back before white audiences, speaking at an Independence Day celebration in Framingham, Massachusetts. She spoke after a white abolitionist from Virginia described his ordeal in jail. This experience, he said, helped him appreciate the sufferings of blacks. Truth agreed. "White folks should sometimes feel the prick," she said, eliciting "laughter and cheers." Despite such merriment, her message, as recorded by the secretary of the meeting (her printer, George Brown Yerrinton), was severe and anguished:

> God would yet execute his judgments upon the white people for their oppression and cruelty. She had often asked white people why God should have more mercy on Anglo-Saxons than on Africans, but they had never given her any answer; the reason was, they [white people] hadn't got it to give. (Laughter.) Why did the white people hate the blacks? Were they [white people] not as good as they were brought up? They [black people] were a great deal better than the white people had brought them up. (Cheers.) The white people owed the colored race a big debt, and if they paid it all back, they wouldn't have anything left for seed. (Laughter.) All they could do was to repent, and have the debt forgiven them.

Abolitionists were fond of implicating orthodox Christianity in the moral economy of slavery. The regular ministry and conventional churches tolerated slavers and slavery, they said, and Truth picked up this theme. The proceeds of the sale of slave children, she says, paid for the training of ministers of the gospel....

According to [Harriet Beecher] Stowe ... Frederick Douglass once spoke emphatically at a meeting in Boston's Faneuil Hall of his lost faith that black Americans would ever gain justice from white Americans. Douglass had concluded that blacks must seize their freedom by force of arms: "It must come to blood; they must fight for themselves, and redeem themselves, or it would never be done."

Truth, sitting in the front row—so Stowe says—rejected Douglass's desperate logic:

> in the hush of deep feeling, after Douglas[s] sat down, she spoke out in her deep, peculiar voice, heard all over the house.—
> "Frederick, *is God dead?*"

Then Stowe adds a paragraph whose imagery would reappear time and again as generation after generation sought to capture Truth's essence in words:

> The effect was perfectly electrical, and thrilled through the whole house, changing as by a flash the whole feeling of the audience. Not another word she said or needed to say: it was enough....

"Frederick, *is God dead?*" made Truth an electrifying presence and a symbol of Christian faith and forbearance, a talisman of non-violent faith in God's ability to right the most heinous of wrongs. When Douglass had come to doubt, Stowe's Truth still believed in the power of God and the goodness of white people. To reinforce Truth's attachment to whites, Stowe quotes her revelation when she became a Christian: "'Dar's de white folks, that have abused you an' beat you an' abused your people.'" Jesus allows Truth to forgive them: " 'Lord, Lord, I can love *even de white folks!* "

Thanks to Stowe and the *Atlantic Monthly*, "Frederick, *is God dead?*" became the dominant symbol for Truth. For three-quarters of a century, the image of Stowe's faithful Christian delighted thousands of Americans, while the exasperated, vengeful Truth of the Book of Esther, the blood of Abel, and the taunting question, do you "wish to suck?" remained more obscure. "Sojourner Truth, the Libyan Sibyl" spread the gentleness of spiritualism over Truth's own millennial conviction that there surely would come a day of racial judgment....

FURTHER READING

Robert H. Abzug, *Cosmos Crumbling: American Reform and the Religious Imagination* (1994).

Catherine A. Brekus, *Strangers and Pilgrims: Female Preaching in America, 1740–1845* (1998).

Richard L. Bushman, *Joseph Smith: Rough Stone Rolling* (2007).

Ann Douglas, *The Feminization of American Culture* (1977).

Paul Goodman, *Of One Blood: Abolitionism and the Origins of Racial Equality* (1998).

Nathan O. Hatch, *The Democratization of American Christianity* (1991).

Peter P. Hinks, *To My Afflicted Brethren: David Walker and the Problem of Antebellum Slave Resistance* (1996).

Nancy Isenberg, *Sex and Citizenship in Antebellum America* (1998).

Paul E. Johnson and Sean Wilentz, *The Kingdom of Matthias* (1994).

Bruce Laurie, *Beyond Garrison: Antislavery and Social Reform* (2005).

Steven Mintz, *Moralists and Modernizers: America's Pre–Civil War Reformers* (1995).

Mary Ryan, *Cradle of the Middle Class: The Family in Oneida County, New York, 1790–1865* (1981).

John Wigger, *Taking Heaven By Storm: Methodism and the Rise of Popular Christianity in America* (2001).

CHAPTER 11

Commercial Development
and Immigration in the North
at Midcentury

In the thirty years before the Civil War, society in the northern states was transformed in a variety of ways. There was a huge migration westward, effectively redistributing the population of the nation. Between 1830 and 1860, the white population of the Old Northwest (the states of Ohio, Michigan, Indiana, Illinois, and Wisconsin) grew from 1.5 million to nearly 7 million. Agricultural innovations, including Cyrus McCormick's mechanical reaper and John Deere's self-polishing steel plow, enabled the fast and lucrative cultivation of the Midwest. By 1860, one-quarter of the nation's population, most of whom toiled on the land, lived in these northwestern states and they provided much of the voting power for the new Republican Party of the 1850s. As millions of people moved westward, others migrated to the cities. By 1860, there were thirty-five cities in the United States with more than 25,000 inhabitants; New York City had more than one million inhabitants. Most of these cities were located in the northern states. Many city dwellers labored for wages in factories or mills. Many of the early workers were young women who left their rural homes to labor in the factories.

Cloth manufacturing changed radically when a factory in Waltham, Massachusetts, was built that mechanized all the stages in the production of cloth and brought the whole process under one roof. The evolution of cloth factories was complemented by innovations in the use of interchangeable parts that enabled manufacturers to develop complex assembly plants that produced clocks and guns, among other products. By 1860, nearly 300,000 workers toiled in northern industries, and population densities in the city reached up to 150 people per acre. As time went on, immigrants from Europe replaced many of the young female workers in the factories and also labored on western farms. Immigration, which was a mere 150,000 in the 1820s, swelled to over 1.5 million in the 1840s and 2.2 million in the 1850s. Mainly from the German states or Ireland, these immigrants often lived in poverty in urban slums and worshipped in Roman Catholic churches. They illustrated to many Americans the dangers of urbanization, commercialization, and mechanization in the North.

These vast changes created grave challenges for northern society, especially in its growing cities. Densely settled neighborhoods became increasingly unhealthy. Workers strove to organize trade unions that would improve wages and working conditions. But wages often lagged and workers fell victim to the financial crashes in 1837 and 1857, which increased unemployment and uncertainty. Some northerners began to fear that they would become "wage slaves," people who would never be freed of their need to labor in order to stay alive. To make matters worse, the cultural differences within the cities created tensions that occasionally exploded in violence. Riots in New York, Boston, and Philadelphia, and in rural areas as well, pitted the native born against the immigrant. Immigrants often were scapegoats, and their allegiance to Roman Catholicism only made them more suspect to citizens in a largely Protestant nation.

Despite these challenges, many northerners remained optimistic that their world of commerce, farming, and manufacturing was the direction in which the United States should head. In particular, they were certain that their society was superior to the slave society in the South. As a result, they developed ideologies that explained their predicament and celebrated their society. Although some northerners feared "wage slavery," others applauded the economic mobility that workers were offered. Free laborers, so the argument went, could improve their condition through their own hard work and could ultimately become economically independent. As Abraham Lincoln observed, "The man who labored for another last year, this year labors for himself, and next year he will hire others to labor for him." The sum total of free individuals working to improve themselves created a mobile society and a growing economy. "The desire of bettering one's condition," wrote newspaper editor Horace Greeley, "is the mainspring of effort." A key element supporting the system of free labor was the availability of the vast tracts of land in the West. People could move up as they moved west. By forsaking an urban occupation, so the argument went, they relieved the pressures that built up in the city. The West was a necessary "safety valve." It is no coincidence that the Republican Party, a political organization founded in the 1850s whose membership came almost entirely from the northern states, would proclaim that it was the party of "Free Labor, Free Soil, and Free Men."

 ## QUESTIONS TO THINK ABOUT

How were economic and geographical mobility central to the experience and ideologies of northerners? Why would immigrants move to the North if they experienced oppression there? Why do you think northerners were so sensitive to terms like *wage slavery* and *white slavery?* In what ways did immigration create a more volatile northern society when it increased dramatically in the decades after 1830?

DOCUMENTS

Alexis de Tocqueville, in document 1, observes that although early-nineteenth-century Americans were among the freest and best-educated people in the world, they were unhappy. He attributes this oddity to the desire for mobility that stems from that very freeness. Document 2 was written by inventor Samuel F. B. Morse, who argues both that class division are more fluid in the United States than in Europe and that European immigration might endanger this fluidity. In document 3, Orestes Brownson offers a scathing critique of the status of workers in the North in 1840. He goes so far as to suggest that the plight of these "wage slaves" is worse than that of slaves in the South. In document 4, a Swedish immigrant reflects on life in Wisconsin in 1841 and 1842; he enjoys an independence not available in his homeland. Although he finds Americans different from his people, he does appreciate the republican form of government. Document 5 recounts the experiences of a female mill worker in Massachusetts. In document 6, George Templeton Strong describes in his diary the impact of European immigrants on New York City. No friend to immigrants, Strong compares the Irish with the Chinese. In document 7 Congressman James Bowlin recounts the opportunities in the West. He sees them as the basis for American freedom and argues that they can solve many of the ills in the urban northeast. The final document is a song from the early 1860s, "No Irish Need Apply." In it, the singer details anti-Irish sentiment in the United States and how Irish Americans should take pride in their ethnic heritage.

1. Alexis de Tocqueville Marvels at the Mobile Northern Society, 1831

In certain remote corners of the Old World you may sometimes stumble upon little places which seem to have been forgotten among the general tumult and which have stayed still while all around them moves. The inhabitants are mostly very ignorant and very poor; they take no part in affairs of government, and often governments oppress them. But yet they seem serene and often have a jovial disposition.

In America I have seen the freest and best educated of men in circumstances the happiest to be found in the world; yet it seemed to me that a cloud habitually hung on their brow, and they seemed serious and almost sad even in their pleasures.

The chief reason for this is that the former do not give a moment's thought to the ills they endure, whereas the latter never stop thinking of the good things they have not got.

It is odd to watch with what feverish ardor the Americans pursue prosperity and how they are ever tormented by the shadowy suspicion that they may not have chosen the shortest route to get it.

Alexis de Tocqueville, *Democracy in America*, Volume II (Boston: Little and J. Brown, 1841), 536–538.

Americans cleave to the things of this world as if assured that they will never die, and yet are in such a rush to snatch any that come within their reach, as if expecting to stop living before they have relished them. They clutch everything but hold nothing fast, and so lose grip as they hurry after some new delight.

An American will build a house in which to pass his old age and sell it before the roof is on; he will plant a garden and rent it just as the trees are coming into bearing; he will clear a field and leave others to reap the harvest; he will take up a profession and leave it, settle in one place and soon go off elsewhere with his changing desires. If his private business allows him a moment's relaxation, he will plunge at once into the whirlpool of politics. Then, if at the end of a year crammed with work he has a little spare leisure, his restless curiosity goes with him traveling up and down the vast territories of the United States. Thus he will travel five hundred miles in a few days as a distraction from his happiness.

Death steps in in the end and stops him before he has grown tired of this futile pursuit of that complete felicity which always escapes him.

At first sight there is something astonishing in this spectacle of so many lucky men restless in the midst of abundance. But it is a spectacle as old as the world; all that is new is to see a whole people performing in it.

The taste for physical pleasures must be regarded as the first cause of this secret restlessness betrayed by the actions of the Americans, and of the inconstancy of which they give daily examples.

A man who has set his heart on nothing but the good things of this world is always in a hurry, for he has only a limited time in which to find them, get them, and enjoy them....

When all prerogatives of birth and fortune are abolished, when all professions are open to all and a man's own energies may bring him to the top of any of them, an ambitious man may think it easy to launch on a great career and feel that he is called to no common destiny. But that is a delusion which experience quickly corrects. The same equality which allows each man to entertain vast hopes makes each man by himself weak. His power is limited on every side, though his longings may wander where they will.

Not only are men powerless by themselves, but at every step they find immense obstacles which they had not at first noticed.

They have abolished the troublesome privileges of some of their fellows, but they come up against the competition of all....

No matter how a people strives for it, all the conditions of life can never be perfectly equal. Even if, by misfortune, such an absolute dead level were attained, there would still be inequalities of intelligence which, coming directly from God, will ever escape the laws of man....

Among democratic peoples men easily obtain a certain equality, but they will never get the sort of equality they long for. That is a quality which ever retreats before them without getting quite out of sight, and as it retreats it beckons them on to pursue. Every instant they think they will catch it, and each time it slips through their fingers. They see it close enough to know its charms, but they do not get near enough to enjoy it, and they will be dead before they have fully relished its delights.

2. Inventor Samuel F. B. Morse Fears That Immigrants Will Ruin American Inequality, 1835

What is the proper effect of our democratic republican institutions upon the various classes into which human society must ever be divided? How do they affect the condition of the *rich* and the *poor,* the *educated* and the *illiterate?* Equality, the only practicable equality, is their result; not that spurious, visionary equality which would make a forced community of property, but that equality which puts no *artificial* obstacles in the way of any man's becoming the richest or most learned in the state; which allows every man without other impediment than the common obstacles of human nature and the equal rights of his neighbor impose, to strive after wealth and knowledge and happiness. True Christian republicanism, by its benevolent and ennobling principles, impels the wealthy and the educated to use their talents for the benefit of the whole community; it prompts to acts of public spirit, to self-sacrifice, and to unwearied effort to lessen the natural obstacles in the way of the poor and uneducated to competence and intellectual character, by affording them both employment and education. The kindness and benevolence thus shown to the poor beget in this class of our citizens, industry and mental effort. They feel that they are not like the proscribed of other countries, they see that the way is equally open to all to rise to the same rank of independence in mind and condition, and they consequently are without the exciting causes of envy and ill-will and bitterness of feeling towards the wealthy and educated, which exist and produce these fruits in other and arbitrary governments. Society in its two extremes is thus knit together by a mutual confidence, and a mutual interest, for causes beyond human control are ever varying the condition of men. He that is rich to-day may be poor to-morrow; and thus there is a constant interchange, a mingling of ranks, which like a healthful circulation in the natural body, begets soundness and vigor through the political body. The vicious, and voluntarily ignorant being the only portions of society naturally and justly excluded from the benefits of this system.

Let us now look at the condition of these same classes under an arbitrary government. In Austria, for example, the *poor* and *illiterate* are considered as the natural slaves of the *wealthy* and *learned.* These classes are perpetually separated by the artificial barrier of *hereditary right;* the line of separation is distinctly drawn, and in all that relates to social intercourse there is an impassable gulf. There may be condescension on the one part, but no elevation on the other. High birth, learning, wealth, and polished manners are on the one side, strengthening the hands of the arbitrary power that sustains them; on the other, low birth, ignorance, poverty, and boorishness, kept down by their intrinsic weakness, generation after generation in irretrievable subjection; the upper classes knowing that their own security is based upon the perpetuity of ignorance and superstition in the lower classes.... We have a daily increasing host of emigrants, a portion of the very class used to foreign servitude abroad. How could Austrian emissaries

Samuel F. B. Morse, *Foreign Conspiracy against the Liberties of the United States* (New York: Leavitt, Lord and Company, 1835), 159–163.

better serve their imperial master's interests, than by keeping these unenlightened men in the same mental darkness in which they existed in the countries from which they came, surrounding them here with a police of priests, and shutting out from them the light which might break in upon them in this land of light, nourishing them for riot and turbulence, at political meetings, and for bullying at the polls those of opposite political opinions? And what would be the effect of such a mode of proceedings upon that class, who have acquired by lives of honest industry and studious application, wealth, and knowledge, and political experience? Is not such a course calculated to drive them away from any participation in the politics of the country, and is not such seditious conduct intended to produce this very result? Will not men who have any self-respect, who have any sense of character, turn away and ask with feelings of indignation, where is that intelligent, sober, orderly body of *native* mechanics and artizans, who once composed the wholesome, substantial democracy of the country, and on whose independence and rough good sense the country could always rely, that well-tried body of their own fellow-citizens, accustomed to hear and read patiently, and decide discreetly? And when they see them associated with a rude set of priest-governed foreigners, strangers to the order and habits of our institutions, requiting us for their hospitable reception by conduct subversive of the very institutions which make them freemen; when they see them become the dupes of the machinations of a foreign despotic power, refusing to be undeceived, and madly rushing to their own destruction, will they not from motives of self preservation be willing to adopt any system of measures, however, arbitrary, which will secure society from violence and anarchy? When disgust at priest-guided mobs shall have alienated the minds of one class of the citizens from the other, we have then *one of the parties* nearly formed, which is necessary for the designs of despotism in accomplishing the subversion of the republic. And *the other party* is still easier formed. The alienation of feeling in the wealthier class, and their remarks of disgust, may be easily tortured into contempt for the classes below them, and then the natural envy of the poor towards the rich, will always furnish occasions to excite to violence. When hostility between these two parties has reached a proper height, the signal from the arch jugglers in Europe to their assistants here, can easily kindle the flames of civil strife. And then comes the dextrous change of systems. Frequent outrage must be quelled by military force, for the public peace must at all events be preserved, and the civil arm will have become too weak, and thus commences an *armed police*, itself but the precursor of a standing army. And which party will be the sufferer? All experience answers that *wealth* and *talent* are more than a match for mere brute force, for the plain reason that they can both *purchase* and *direct* it. The rich can pay for their protection, and soldiers belong to those who pay them.... It is the *poor* then, the *poor* and *ignorant*, not the rich and learned, that have every thing of hope and liberty to lose from the machinations of Austria. In a moral and intelligent Democracy, the rich and poor are friends and equals, in a Popish despotism the poor are in abject servitude to the rich. Let the working men, the laboring classes, well considered that their liberty is in danger, and can be preserved only by their encouragement of education and good order.

3. Essayist Orestes Brownson Condemns the Plight of "Wage Slaves," 1840

No one can observe the signs of the times with much care, without perceiving that a crisis as to the relation of wealth and labor is approaching....

In this coming contest there is a deeper question at issue than is commonly imagined, a question which is but remotely touched in your controversies about United States Banks and Sub-Treasuries, chartered Banking and free Banking, free trade and corporations, although these controversies may be paving the way for it to come up....

What we would ask is, throughout the Christian world the actual condition of the laboring classes, viewed simply and exclusively in their capacity of laborers? They constitute at least a moiety of the human race. We exclude the nobility, we exclude also the middle class, and include only actual laborers, who are laborers and not proprietors, owners of none of the funds of production, neither houses, shops, nor lands, nor implements of labor, being therefore solely dependent on their hands....

... We are not ignorant of the fact, that the merchant, who is literally the common carrier and exchange dealer, performs a useful service, and is therefore entitled to a portion of the proceeds of labor. But make all necessary deductions on his account, and then ask what portion of the remainder is retained, either in kind or in its equivalent, in the hands of the original producer, the workingman? All over the world this fact stares us in the face, the workingman is poor and depressed, while a large portion of the non-workingmen, in the sense we now use the term, are wealthy. It may be laid down as a general rule, with but few exceptions, that men are rewarded in an inverse ratio to the amount of actual service they perform....

In regard to labor two systems obtain; one that of slave labor, the other that of free labor. Of the two, the first is, in our judgement, except so far as the feelings are concerned, decidedly the least oppressive. If the slave has never been a free man, we think, as a general rule, his sufferings are less than those of the free laborer at wages. As to actual freedom one has just about as much as the other. The laborer at wages has all the disadvantages of freedom and none of its blessings, while the slave, if denied the blessings, is freed from the disadvantages. We are no advocates of slavery, we are as heartily opposed to it as any modern abolitionist can be; but we say frankly that, if there must always be a laboring population distinct from proprietors and employers, we regard the slave system as decidedly preferable to the system at wages. It is no pleasant thing to go days without food, to lie idle for weeks, seeking work and finding none, to rise in the morning with a wife and children you love, and know not where to procure them a breakfast, and to see constantly before you no brighter prospect than the almshouse. Yet these are no unfrequent incidents in the lives of our laboring population.... It is said there is no want in this country. There may be less

Orestes Brownson, "The Laboring Classes," *Boston Quarterly Review*, 1840.

than in some other countries. But death by actual starvation in this country is we apprehend no uncommon occurrence. The sufferings of a quiet, unassuming but useful class of females in our cities, in general sempstresses, too proud to beg or to apply to the almshouse, are not easily told. They are industrious; they do all they can find to do; but yet the little there is for them to do, and the miserable pittance they receive for it, is hardly sufficient to keep soul and body together....

We pass through our manufacturing villages; most of them appear neat and flourishing. The operatives are well dressed, and we are told, well paid. They are said to be healthy, contented, and happy. This is the fair side of the picture; the side exhibited to distinguished visitors. There is a dark side, moral as well as physical. Of the common operatives, few, if any, by their wages, acquire a competence. A few of what Carlyle terms not inaptly the *body-servants* are well paid, and now and then an agent or an overseer rides in his coach. But the great mass wear out their health, spirits, and morals, without becoming one whit better off than when they commenced labor.... We know no sadder sight on earth than one of our factory villages presents, when the bell at break of day, or at the hour of breakfast, or dinner, calls out its hundreds or thousands of operatives. We stand and look at these hard working men and women hurrying in all directions, and ask ourselves, where go the proceeds of their labors? The man who employs them, and for whom they are willing as so many slaves, is one of our city nabobs, revelling in luxury; or he is a member of our legislature, enacting laws to put money in his own pocket; or he is a member of Congress, contending for a high Tariff to tax the poor for the benefit of the rich; or in these times he is shedding crocodile tears over the deplorable condition of the poor laborer, while he docks his wages twenty-five per cent; building miniature log cabins, shouting Harrison and "hard cider."—And this man too would fain pass for a Christian and a republican. He shouts for liberty, stickless for equality, and is horrified at a Southern planter who keeps slaves.

One thing is certain; that of the amount actually produced by the operative, he retains a less proportion than it costs the master to feed, clothe, and lodge his slave. Wages is a cunning device of the devil, for the benefit of tender consciences, who would retain all the advantages of the slave system, without the expense, trouble, and odium of being slave-holders.

Messrs. Thome and Kimball, in their account of the emancipation of slavery in the West Indies, establish the fact that the employer may have the same amount of labor done 25 per ct. cheaper than the master. What does this fact prove, if not that wages is a more successful method of taxing labor than slavery? We really believe our Northern system of labor is more oppressive, and even more mischievous to morals, than the Southern. We, however, war against both. We have no toleration for either system. We would see a slave a man, but a free man, not a mere operative at wages. This he would not be were he now emancipated. Could the abolitionists effect all they propose, they would do the slave no service. Should emancipation work as well as they say, still it would do the slave no good. He would be a slave still, although with the title and cares of a freeman. If then we had no constitutional objections to abolitionism, we could not, for the reason here implied, be abolitionists.

The slave system, however, in name and form, is gradually disappearing from Christendom. It will not subsist much longer. But its place is taken by the system of labor at wages, and this system, we hold, is no improvement upon the one it supplants. Nevertheless the system of wages will triumph. It is the system which in name sounds honester than slavery, and in substance is more profitable to the master. It yields the wages of iniquity, without its opprobrium. It will therefore supplant slavery, and be sustained—for a time.

4. Gustof Unonius, a Swedish Immigrant, Reflects on Life in the United States, 1841–1842

Milwaukee, Wisconsin, 13 October 1841

The soil here is the most fertile and wonderful that can be found and usually consists of rich black mold. Hunting and fishing will provide some food in the beginning, but they must be pursued sparingly, otherwise time which could more profitably be spent in cultivating the soil is wasted. I beg the emigrant to consider all these factors carefully and closely calculate his assets before he starts out.... [He] will have to suffer much in the beginning, limit himself considerably, and sacrifice much of what he was accustomed to in Europe.... I caution against all exaggerated hopes and golden air castles; cold reality will otherwise lame your arm and crush your courage; both must be fresh and active.

As far as we are concerned, we do not regret our undertaking. We are living a free and independent life in one of the most beautiful valleys the world can offer; and from the experiences of others we see that in a few years we can have a better livelihood and enjoy comforts that we must now deny ourselves. If we should be overcome by a longing for the fatherland (and this seems unlikely), we could sell our farm which in eight years will certainly bring ten or twelve dollars per acre.... But I believe that I will be satisfied in America.

I am partial to a republican form of government, and I have realized my youthful dream of social equality. Others may say what they will, but there are many attractive things about it. It is no disgrace to work here. Both the gentleman and the day laborer work. No epithets of degradation are applied to men of humble toil; only those whose conduct merits it are looked down upon.... Liberty is still stronger in my affections than the bright silver dollar that bears her image....

Pine Lake, Wisconsin, 25 January 1842

... I admit that I am no friend of the big city of New York. The shopkeeper's spirit is too prevalent, but to judge the American national character from that is incorrect. I have found the Americans entirely different. We live in an industrial era and it is true that the American is a better representative of that than any other

Gustof Unonius, "Letters from a Swedish Man," in *Letters from the Promised Land: Swedes in America, 1840–1914*, ed. H. Arnold Barton (Minneapolis: University of Minnesota Press, 1975).

nationality. Despite this fact, there is something kindly in his speculation for profit and wealth, and I find more to admire in his manner than in that of the European leaders. The merchant here is withal patriotic; in calculating his own gain he usually includes a share for his country…. [T]he universities and other educational institutions, homes for the poor, and other institutions of value to society are dependent on and supported by the American merchants. Canals, railroads, etc., are all financed by companies composed of a few individuals whose collective fortunes serve the public for its common benefit and profit. One must, therefore, overlook an avariciousness which sometimes goes to extremes.

It is true that the American is a braggart…. During the struggles which rend and agitate the countries of the Old World he sees in the progress of his peaceful fatherland the results of liberty and equality which he considers impossible to obtain under any other conditions. Even though I do not wish to blame him for this, yet I do not deny that his resulting self-satisfaction expresses itself in a highly ridiculous fashion in trivial matters.

5. A Lowell Factory Girl Describes a Week in the Mill, 1845

Much has been said of the factory girl and her employment. By some she has been represented as dwelling in a sort of brick-and-mortar paradise, having little to occupy thought save the weaving of gay and romantic fancies, while the spindle or the wheel flies obediently beneath her glance. Others have deemed her a mere servile drudge, chained to her labor by almost as strong a power as that which holds a bondman in his fetters; and, indeed, some have already given her the title of "*the white slave of the North.*" Her real situation approaches neither one nor the other of these extremes. Her occupation is as laborious as that of almost any female who earns her own living, while it has also its sunny spots and its cheerful intervals, which make her hard labor seem comparatively pleasant and easy.

Look at her as she commences her weekly task. The rest of the sabbath has made her heart and her step light, and she is early at her accustomed place, awaiting the starting of the machinery. Every thing having been cleaned and neatly arranged on the Saturday night, she has less to occupy her on Monday than on other days; and you may see her leaning from the window to watch the glitter of the sunrise on the water, or looking away at the distant forests and fields, while memory wanders to her beloved country home; or, it may be that she is conversing with a sister-laborer near; returning at regular intervals to see that her work is in order.

Soon the breakfast bell rings; in a moment the whirling wheels are stopped, and she hastens to join the throng which is pouring through the open gate. At the table she mingles with a various group. Each despatches the meal hurriedly, though not often in silence; and if, as is sometimes the case, the rules of politeness are not punctiliously observed by all, the excuse of some lively country girl would be, "They don't give us time for *manners.*"

The short half-hour is soon over; the bell rings again; and now our factory girl feels that she has commenced her day's work in earnest. The time is often apt to drag heavily till the dinner hour arrives. Perhaps some part of the work becomes deranged and stops; the constant friction causes a belt of leather to burst into a flame; a stranger visits the room, and scans the features and dress of its inmates inquiringly; and there is little else to break the monotony. The afternoon passes in much the same manner. Now and then she mingles with a knot of busy talkers who have collected to discuss some new occurrence, or holds pleasant converse with some intelligent and agreeable friend, whose acquaintance she has formed since her factory life commenced; but much of the time she is left to her own thoughts. While at her work, the clattering and rumbling around her prevent any other noise from her attention, and she *must think,* or her life would be dull indeed.

Thus the day passes on, and evening comes; the time which she feels to be exclusively her own. How much is done in the three short hours from seven to ten o'clock. She has a new dress to finish; a call to make on some distant corporation; a meeting to attend; there is a lecture or a concert at some one of the public halls, and the attendance will be thin if she and her associates are not present; or, if nothing more imperative demands her time, she takes a stroll through the street or to the river with some of her mates, or sits down at home to peruse a new book. At ten o'clock all is still for the night....

6. New Yorker George Templeton Strong Berates the Immigrants in His Midst, 1838–1857

November 6 [1838]. It was enough to turn a man's stomach—to make a man adjure republicanism forever—to see the way they were naturalizing this morning at the *Hall.* Wretched, filthy, bestial-looking Italians and Irish, and creations [creatures] that looked as if they had risen from the lazarettos of Naples for this especial object; in short, the very scum and dregs of human nature filled the clerk of C[ommon] P[leas] office so completely that I was almost afraid of being poisoned by going in. A dirty Irishman is bad enough, but he's nothing comparable to a nasty French or Italian loafer....

April 28 [1848]. Orders given to commence excavating in Twenty-first Street Wednesday night.... Hibernia came to the rescue yesterday morning; twenty "sons of toil" with prehensile paws supplied them by nature with evident reference to the handling of the spade and the wielding of the pickaxe and congenital hollows on the shoulder wonderfully adapted to make the carrying of the hod a luxury instead of a labor....

Allan Nevins and Milton H. Thomas, eds., *The Dairy of George Templeton Strong* (New York: Macmillan, 1952), I:94, 318 and II:197, 348.

November 13 [1854]. Met a prodigious Know-Nothing [nativist political party] procession moving uptown, as I omnibussed down Broadway to the vestry meeting; not many banners and little parade of any kind, but a most emphatic and truculent demonstration. Solid column, eight or ten abreast, and numbering some two or three thousand, mostly young men of the butcher-boy and *prentice* type … marching in quick time, and occasionally indulging in a very earnest kind of hurrah. They looked as if they might have designs on St. Patrick's Cathedral, and I think the Celts of Prince and Mott Streets would have found them ugly customers....

July 7 [1857]. Yesterday morning I was spectator of a strange, weird, painful scene. Certain houses of John Watts DePeyster are to be erected on the northwest corner of this street and Fourth Avenue, and the deep excavations therefore are in progress. Seeing a crowd on the corner, I stopped and made my way to a front place. The earth had caved in a few minutes before and crushed the breath out of a pair of ill-starred Celtic laborers. They had just been dragged, or dug, out, and lay white and stark on the ground where they had been working, ten or twelve feet below the level of the street. Around them were a few men who had got them out, I suppose, and fifteen or twenty Irish women, wives, kinfolk or friends, who had got down there in some inexplicable way. The men were listless and inert enough, but not so the women. I suppose they were "keening"; all together were raising a wild, unearthly cry, half shriek and half song, wailing as a score of daylight Banshees, clapping their hands and gesticulating passionately. Now and then one of them would throw herself down on one of the corpses, or wipe some trace of defilement from the face of the dead man with her apron, slowly and carefully, and then resume her lament. It was an uncanny sound to hear.... Our Celtic fellow citizens are almost as remote from us in temperament and constitution as the Chinese.

7. James Bowlin, a Congressman, Marvels at the Possibilities of Western Lands, 1846

… The public lands were a trust fund in our hands for the benefit of the people—not to be held up by prohibitory, nor squandered by corrupt legislation; but to be so disposed of, as would secure to them the greatest benefits—whether that was in promoting correct principles, increasing the revenue, or in advancing the general prosperity of the country.

Land being the true basis of all individual and national prosperity, its disposition, and the tenure by which it is held, has in every age of the world, and in every civilized nation, engaged the most ardent attention of the statesman. There is no subject in the whole range of political science, that so nearly and directly interests the great body of the people, as that of the right of soil. Its disposition is not only a question of mere utility—that changes with the passing hour—but it is one involving great and important principles, upon which may hang the fate of

---

James Bowlin, speech in Congress, *The Congressional Globe*, July 6, 1846, 1059–1060.

man and governments. So intimately identified is it with the forms and systems of government, and the political rights and privileges of men, that we are frequently enabled to read the history of a nation, either for weal or for [woe], for glory or shame, in the mere regulations of her land systems. That government, no matter by what name it may be called, whose lands are scattered amongst the great body of her people, and are left unfettered by law, to pass in their natural course, from generation to generation, preserving and perpetuating an independent yeomanry, must forever enjoy a high state of political freedom. Whilst such a system is preserved, there is no focus around which to rally political power to oppress. The rays of power are scattered, and can only be concentrated over the ruins of the system itself. Upon the contrary, that government which adopts a system, and pursues a policy, tending to concentrate its soil in the hands of a few, to the detriment of the many, fettering its free passage from man to man, no matter what name it may bear, its ultimate destiny is the destruction of every vestige of equality and liberty. It is the inevitable destiny of nations to be controlled by the proprietors of the soil, and the government is free or despotic, just in proportion to the number of its rulers, or participants in political privileges. If you wish to preserve and perpetuate its democratic form, you must pursue a policy tending to disseminate the lands amongst the largest possible number of the people of the state. Hence the great principle that lies at the foundation of any system for the disposition of the public lands we may see proper to adopt....

The celebrated feudal system of more modern times was but a cunningly devised scheme to rob the great body of the people of their just and legitimate interest in the landed estate of the country, and thereby build up an aristocracy upon the ruins of popular liberty. It was but a scheme to perpetuate political power in the hands of the few to the detriment of the many; to make serfs of the people and lords of their rulers.... It is this land system that constitutes the props to uphold the monarchies of the Old World....

... [L]et us now turn our attention for a moment to the policy adopted by the European nations in colonizing this continent, and its natural and legitimate consequences; for it is a notorious fact, attested to in almost every page of American history, that they pursued a policy diametrically opposed to the system of policy adopted at home. The monarchs of England, France, and Spain, the three great colonizing nations of Europe, donated their lands to the emigrants in the newly-discovered countries—the two latter in the most liberal manner. The policy of this measure was to encourage emigration and settlement in the New World. The effect of it was to inculcate ideas of independence in the great body of the people, elevating their moral sentiments, and arousing their innate love of liberty, until it resulted in stretching a line of republics from the St. Lawrence to the Rio de la Plata. Their day-dreams of empire in the New World all dissolved at the touch of the magic wand of freedom, inculcated and nourished in the breast of the people by the fact that they were the free occupants of their own soil, and ate the bread of their own industry....

... [W]e ask no special favors to aid us in our march; we only ask that you place no obstacle in our way—that you leave our action free; and the enterprise, energy, and industry of the same people who subdue forests in their march, and make the wilderness to yield abundant harvests, will make the country prosper. The rich soil, the magnificent rivers, the mild and genial climate of the great West, all contribute to invite emigration amongst us, and that policy would be suicidal that would obstruct or retard it. The West needs population to develop its great resources; and it will be one of the blessings of this great measure that it will contribute to its increase, without impairing the best interests of other portions of the Confederacy....

But the new States have another interest at stake, which appeals strongly to the magnanimity of this Government in behalf of this measure; and that is an interest which almost as deeply concerns the whole Confederacy as the new States— and that was, their interest in bringing these lands into general occupancy and cultivation, so that they might yield a revenue in support of the Government. Under the present system the public lands are not taxed; and the States in which they lie, and from the labor of whose citizens they derive value, can exact no revenue from them. In the hands of individuals they would be taxable, and liable to be made, like other lands, tributary to the support and improvement of the State.

8. Irish Americans Sing About Their Struggles and Successes, c. 1860s

NO IRISH NEED APPLY. Written by JOHN F. POOLE, and sung, with immense success, by the great Comic-Vocalist of the age, TONY PASTOR.

I'm a dacint boy, just landed from the town of Ballyfad;
I want a situation: yis, I want it mighty bad.
I saw a place advertised. It's the thing for me, says I;
But the dirty spalpeen [rascal] ended with: No Irish need apply.
Whoo! says I; but that's an insult—though to get the place I'll try.
So, I wint to see the blaggar with: No Irish need apply.

I started off to find the house, I got it mighty soon;
There I found the ould chap saited: he was reading the TRIBUNE.
I tould him what I came for, whin he in a rage did fly:
No! says he, you are a Paddy, and no Irish need apply!
Thin I felt my dandher rising, and I'd like to black his eye—
To tell an Irish Gintleman: No Irish need apply!

I couldn't stand it longer: so, a hoult of him I took,
And I gave him such a welting as he'd get at Donnybrook.
He hollered: Millia murther! and to get away did try,

John F. Poole, "No Irish Need Apply" American Memory, Library of Congress, http://memory.loc.gov/rbc/amss/as1/as109730/001q.gif.

And swore he'd never write again: No Irish need apply.

He made a big apology; I bid him thin good-bye,

Saying: Whin next you want a bating, add: No Irish need apply!

Sure, I've heard that in America it always is the plan

That an Irishman is just as good as any other man;

A home and hospitality they never will deny

The stranger here, or ever say: No Irish need apply.

But some black sheep are in the flock: a dirty lot, say I;

A dacint man will never write: No Irish need apply!

Sure, Paddy's heart is in his hand, as all the world does know,

His praties and his whiskey he will share with friend or foe;

His door is always open to the stranger passing by;

He never thinks of saying: None but Irish may apply.

And, in Columbia's history, his name is ranking high;

Thin, the Divil take the knaves that write; No Irish need apply!

Ould Ireland on the battle-field a lasting fame has made;

We all have heard of Meagher's men, and Corcoran's brigade.

Though fools may flout and bigots rave, and fanatics may cry,

Yet when they want good fighting-men, the Irish may apply,

And when for freedom and the right they raise the battle-cry,

Then the Rebel ranks begin to think: No Irish need apply!

ESSAYS

The changing northern world created a variety of challenges for its residents in the antebellum era. Not only was migration to and within the region increasingly important, but the way people worked and where they lived was changing as well. The majority of northerners still lived on farms. However, the proportion of northern Americans that lived in cities and fed their families through work for wages was larger than that in the South, and also larger than it had been in the past. The following two essays ponder the meaning of these changes and how they were used by political parties to mobilize their voters. David R. Roediger, a historian at the University of Illinois, concentrates on the uses of the terms *white slavery* and *wage slavery* among northern Americans. He notes that these concerns were utilized in particular by leaders of the Democratic Party not only to discuss the struggles of the northern worker, but also to connect workers in the North to slaveholders in the South. In contrast, John Ashworth, who teaches history at the University of East Anglia, scrutinizes the rise of the Republican Party. This party,

Ashworth argues, was more comfortable with ideas of wage labor. Unlike earlier ideologues, who connected independence with control over property, this new group saw the possibilities of social mobility in toiling for wages. As such, these Americans were more comfortable with the new economy of wage work.

White Slaves, Wage Slaves, and Free White Labor in the North

DAVID R. ROEDIGER

In 1836, supporters of New York City's journeymen tailors papered the city with handbills featuring a coffin. The tailors had just lost a conspiracy case and with it their right to organize. The handbill encouraged protest and demanded redress in strong republican language familiar since the Revolution. It appealed to "Freemen" and to the power of "Mechanics and workingmen." But confidence that the cause of independence would prevail was at an ebb. The coffin signified that the "Liberty of the workingmen [would] be interred!" at the sentencing of the tailors. "Tyrant *masters*" had the upper hand, and the handbill's authors made a direct comparison that had been unthinkable even a decade before: "Freemen of the North are now on a level with the slaves of the South."

The "coffin handbill" shows both the new case and the continuing hesitancy with which white workers in Jacksonian America began to describe themselves as slaves. Its unqualified North–South comparison is most striking, but the document also suggests some of the ways in which white workers remained beyond comparison with slaves. The whites, if slaves, were also simultaneously "freemen." If "tyrant *masters*" had prevailed, according to one line of the handbill, another line settled for invoking the fear of "would-be masters." Nor was it clear that the "slavery" of the tailors was "wage slavery." They were cast as slaves not because they were "hirelings" but because the state had deprived them of the freedoms necessary for defending their rights. The emphasis on the "slavery" of the tailors in fact proved rather shortlived. After hearing of a more favorable court decision in another conspiracy case upstate, "the journeymen's fury abated."

Other instances of comparison between wage labor and chattel slavery between 1830 and 1860 were likewise both insistent and embarrassed. They could not have been otherwise. Labor republicanism inherited the idea that designing men perpetually sought to undermine liberty and to "enslave" the people. Chattel slavery stood as the ultimate expression of the denial of liberty. But republicanism also suggested that long acceptance of slavery betokened weakness, degradation and an unfitness for freedom. The Black population symbolized that degradation. Racism, slavery and republicanism thus combined to require comparisons of hirelings and slaves, but the combination also required white workers to distance themselves from Blacks even as the comparisons were being made.

From David R. Roediger, *The Wages of Whiteness: Race and the Making of the American Working Class* (New York: Verso, 1991), p. 65–71, 72–73, 75–77. Reprinted by permission of Verso Press.

Chattel slavery provided white workers with a touchstone against which to weigh their fears and a yardstick to measure their reassurance. An understanding of both the stunning process by which some white workers came to call themselves slaves and the tendency for metaphors concerning white slavery to collapse thus takes us to the heart of the process by which the white worker was made. It also furnishes us with an excellent vantage point from which to view the vexed relations between the labor movement and movements to abolish slavery.

The Winding Road to *White Slavery*

Use of terms like *white slavery* and *slavery of wages* in the 1830s and 1840s presents an intriguing variation on the theme of American exceptionalism. US labor historians are usually pressed to explain why American workers have historically lacked the class consciousness said to have existed elsewhere in the industrializing world. But if the antebellum US labor movement was exceptional in its rhetoric, it was exceptionally militant as it critiqued evolving capitalist social relations as a kind of slavery. France, with a revolutionary tradition that forcefully used metaphors regarding slavery to press republican attacks on political oppression, apparently saw but slight use of phrases such as *wage slavery* before the Revolution of 1848. The German states, though they produced a great popularizer of the concept of wage slavery, likewise did not witness frequent use of the term. Only Britain, where the metaphoric term *wage slavery* apparently originated in the second decade of the nineteenth century, rivalled the US in producing a discourse that regarded white hirelings as slaves. But since the spread of the metaphor in Britain was as much associated with the Tory radical politician Richard Oastler as with its use by working class Chartists, one might regard the antebellum US labor movement as exceptional in being the world leader in militant criticisms of wage work as slavery.

Of course, concern over "slavery" was very much in the air in Jacksonian America, whose citizens worried variously that Catholics, Mormons, Masons, monopolists, fashion, alcohol and the national bank were about to enslave the republic. Nonetheless, the use of the white slave metaphor for wage workers ought not be dismissed as merely another example of the "paranoid" style of antebellum politics. It might instead be profitable to view the paranoid style itself as a republican tradition much enlivened by the horrific example of chattel slavery and fears engendered by the growing failure of the American republic to produce a society of independent farmers and mechanics among whites.

By the Age of Jackson, several changes had created the setting in which white workers would begin to make and press, as well as deny and repress, comparisons between themselves and slaves. The rise, after 1829, of a highly visible movement to abolish slavery evoked reexamination of the line between slavery and freedom. Since free Blacks and slave rebels played so central a role in the Black freedom movement, the tendency to equate blackness and servility was likewise called into question. If abolitionism did not recruit more than a minority of white workers, it did make clear that equations between race and fitness for liberty were not eternal truths but objects of political debate.

Meanwhile, the experiences of the white artisans themselves encouraged the consideration of white slavery as a possible social category. In a nation agonizing over the fate of the Republic as the last of its revolutionary generation passed from the scene, urban craftsmen fought monumental struggles, concentrated between 1825 and 1835, for a ten-hour working day. Linking these struggles to time for self-education and full citizenship, the growing labor movement advocated the ten-hour system as the key to workers' independence and to the nation's. Seeking the immediate freedom of being less bossed by increasingly profit-driven masters—and ultimately to be free from having a boss—artisans who undertook concerted actions contrasted the fetters they felt and the liberty they longed for at every possible turn. The workers who gained the ten-hour day in the great 1835 Philadelphia general strike, for example, massed in Independence Square, marched to fife and drum and carried ten-hour banners alongside others proclaiming "LIBERTY, EQUALITY AND THE RIGHTS OF MAN."

The responses of employers tended to sharpen the artisans' sense that a great contest between freedom and its opposite was unfolding and encouraged them to raise the issue in terms of white slavery. In some cases, employers made the initial comparison of free US labor with British "slaves" and with Black slaves. They insisted that the ten-hour system could not function in the United States because the nation had to compete with Britain. The response of the *Working Man's Advocate* to this argument in 1832 reflected labor's view of the British system as utterly degrading. "Are we to slave thirteen or fourteen hours a day," the *Advocate* asked, "because the Manchester spinner or the Birmingham blacksmith so slaves?" As ten-hour struggles continued, US workers learned more about British resistance to long hours and answered employers' objections that British competition must be met in new ways that challenged the idea that only British workplaces encouraged servility. The *New England Artisan* wondered in 1834, "If the poor and oppressed but gallant working men of Great Britain have the daring hardihood to declare that they will work but eight hours ..., how should the comparatively free ... American working citizen feel?" In the midst of the shorter hours campaigns of the 1830s, some immigrant US workers also came to maintain that work in America was harder than it had been in Britain. When it was later argued that the ten-hour system could not prevail in Northern states because workplaces on that schedule could not match the production of Southern slave labor, the extent of the republican freedom of the white worker was still more sharply called into question.

Opposed to these substantial reasons for white workers to at least entertain comparisons of themselves and slaves was the continuing desire *not* to be considered anything like an African-American. Not only was the verb *slave* used, as we have seen, to indicate the performance of work in ways unbecoming to whites, but new and negative phrases such as *white nigger* (that is, "drudge") and *work like a nigger* (that is, "to do hard drudging work") came into American English in the 1830s, at roughly the same time that the term *white slavery* became prominent. Richard Henry Dana's searing indictment of the oppression of antebellum sailors in *Two Years before the Mast* took care to quote an irate captain screaming at his crew: "You've got a driver over you! Yes, a *slave-driver,—a nigger driver!* I'll see who'll tell me he isn't a NIGGER slave!"

Such usages, which should give considerable pause to those who believe race and class are easily disentangled, remind us that comparing oneself to a slave or to any Black American could not be lightly undertaken in the antebellum United States. Moreover, it should be obvious that for all but a handful of committed abolitionists/labor reformers, use of a term like *white slavery* was not an act of solidarity with the slave but rather a call to arms to end the inappropriate oppression of whites. Critiques of white slavery took form, after all, alongside race riots, racially exclusive trade unions, continuing use of terms like *boss* and *help* to deny comparison with slaves, the rise of minstrel shows, and popular campaigns to attack further the meager civil rights of free Blacks.

In such a situation, it is not surprising that labor activists rather cautiously backed into making comparisons between white workers and slaves. Many of the earliest comparisons emphasized not that whites were enslaved but rather that they were threatened with slavery. In Dover, New Hampshire in 1828, leaders of four hundred striking women textile workers both connected and disconnected themselves to chattel slavery by asking who among them could "ever bear the shocking fate of slaves to share?" In 1833, male and female members of the Manayunk (Pennsylvania) Working People's Committee refused a wage cut because it would, as they put it, "rivet our chains still closer" and, over time, "terminate, if not resisted, in slavery." In 1834 Lowell's female strikers permitted themselves considerable ambiguity. In a single paragraph they cast themselves as virtually in "bondage," as threatened with *future* slavery by the "oppressing hand of avarice" and as the "daughters of freemen" still. Two years later protesting Lowell women sang:

> Oh! I cannot be a slave;
> I will not he a slave.
> For I'm so fond of liberty
> That I cannot be a slave.

For male artisans, who led the first labor movement, the rise of a small sector of full-fledged factory production both symbolized threats to independence and offered the possibility to experiment with application of the slavery metaphor to white (often child and female) factory workers without necessarily applying it to *themselves*. The factory system tended to confine and discipline workers to an unprecedented extent, at least by the 1840s. Moreover, it was identified with the degrading, antirepublican labor said to be required in Europe, a comparison that gave force to labor leaders' branding of it as a "gaol" or a "Bastille."

That US textile factories employing large workforces of single women (and smaller ones employing whole families) justified their management practices as paternalistic ones only sharpened suspicions of them. Blacklists and the whipping of workers in some small mills likewise provoked outrage. In the 1834 textile strike in Dover, one complaint of the women workers was the management called them "their *slaves.*" Perhaps the managers meant to refer to their own paternal responsibilities in adopting this usage, or perhaps to their dictatorial powers. In any case, they hit just the wrong note. Quitting and other forms of informal protest far outdistanced strikes among early mill workers, but for male artisans contemplating the new industrial system the issue of permanent "factory slavery" was a fearsome one....

Once made, comparisons to slaves could of course be extended, and artisans sometimes did come to be included in them. By 1835, for example, [Seth] Luther [author of *Address to the Workingmen of New England*] was helping to write the "Ten-Hour Circular," which bitterly castigated "slavery among [white] mechanics." Stephen Simpson, intellectual leader and first Congressional candidate of the Philadelphia Working Men's party, began his 1831 *Working Man's Manual* by arguing that factory slavery had taken root in Britain where a "serf class" worked in manufacturing but that it could never grow in the US, which had disconnected the age-old links among "slavery, labor [and] degradation" and had made work the province of a "community of FREEMEN." Simpson then proceeded to take virtually all other possible positions. He noted the presence of huge numbers of slaves in the South, where he admitted that "labour shares in ... disgrace, because it is a part of the slave," Within a few lines the US was characterized as a society sustained by a "mixture of slavery and labor." White women and children suffered special exploitation because "custom ... classed them with slaves and servants." And, for that matter, Simpson argued, all Northern workers faced a situation in which "capital [was] the Master" and in which employers calculated wages in a manner like that of the "lords of the South [who oppress] sable herds of brutalized humanity."

Some workers, usually in factories, did describe themselves and their peers as already and fully enslaved. As early as 1831, Vermont operatives protested that they were "slaves in every sense of the word," while Lynn shoemakers of the 1840s saw themselves as having "masters—aye, masters" and as being "slaves in the strictest sense of the word." Lowell textile women echoed the Vermont mill-hands, describing themselves as slaves to long hours, as slaves to the "powers that be" and as "slaves in every sense of the word."

However, radical artisans remained more comfortable discussing the "slavery" of others than that of themselves. George Henry Evans, the printer, labor leader and land reformer who probably did more than anyone else to popularize the terms *white slavery* and *slavery of wages*, could be direct and sweeping in describing even male artisans as, if landless, then unequivocally enslaved. "Stealing the man away from his land, or his land away from the man," he argued, "alike produces slavery." Even Evans's individual writings did not tend to discuss the "slavery" of artisans but instead to concentrate on that of tenant farmers, the unskilled, women workers and child laborers. Though eloquent and expressive of the real fears of white workers, comparisons with slaves did not automatically lead to sustained self-examination among those groups of "hirelings" who were most active in organized labor in the antebellum years....

Slavery of wages came to be used alongside *white slavery* by land reformers and utopian socialists in the last half of the 1840s, often in dialogue with abolitionists. Its wording raised the old issue of whether hireling labor and republican independence could coexist. But its very precision and directness raised problems. Many of those being described as slaves were not wage-earners. Thus, tenant farmers and those imprisoned for debt were frequently discussed, but the problem of the latter was precisely that they could not enter the wage labor market. Most early labor activists remained tied to one of the major political parties, usually the Democrats, and sought unity among the "producing classes," including small employers. To refer to such employers as "masters, aye masters," made sense in terms of fleshing out the metaphor of slavery of wages, but it did not make political sense. Moreover, many masters were simply self-employed workers or men who sporadically employed others while depending mainly on their own labor. Many failed and again became wage-earners. Some evidence suggests that small employers paid better than manufacturers with larger workshops, and clearly merchant capitalists often pressured masters to maintain tough labor policies. Journeymen *aspired* to run a small shop of their own. "Men must be masters," Whitman wrote, "under themselves."

Metaphors regarding the slavery of wages thus confronted the problem that, if the worker could be called a *slave*, the wage-paying master could not, except in the heat of labor conflict, really be regarded as a *slavemaster*. One stopgap solution was to hold that the master himself was a "slave." Boston's "Ten-Hour Circular" thus argued:

> We would not be too severe on our employers [for] they are slaves to the Capitalists, as we are to them.... But we cannot bear to be the servant of servants and slaves to oppression, let the source be where it may.

Evans, in keeping with his emphasis on land and rent, similarly maintained that small manufacturers in Lynn were mastered by landlords who owned their shops, while the New York *Mechanic* complained of the "capitalists ... bossing all the mechanical trades."

The advantages of the phrase *white slavery* over *wage slavery* or *slavery of wages* lay in the former term's vagueness and in its whiteness, in its invocation of *herrenvolk* republicanism. *White slavery* was particularly favored by radical Democratic politicians for a time because it could unite various elements of their coalition—wage workers, debtors, small employers and even slaveholders—without necessarily raising the issue of whether the spread of wage labor was always and everywhere antirepublican. Abolitionists, free Blacks, bankers, factory owners and prison labor could, in sundry combinations, be cast as villains in a loose plot to enslave white workers. Moreover, *white slavery* did not necessarily require a structure solution—arrest of the spread of hireling labor. Although some who employed the term did go on to argue that all long-term wage dependency was bondage, *white slavery* itself admitted solutions short of an attack on the wage system. White workers could be *treated* better—reforms could occur, as they did in the "coffin handbill" case—and the comparison with slavery could be exorcised.

White slavery also served well because it did not call into question chattel slavery itself, an issue that sharply divided the labor movement, the Jacksonians and the nation....

… One of the slave South's most eloquent defenders during the 1830s congressional debates over whether to accept petitions from abolitionists was Ely Moore, the nation's first labor Congressman, first president of the National Trades' Union and editor of the *National Trades' Union* newspaper. Moore denounced abolition not only as a "blind, reckless, feverish fanaticism" but also as a plot to rob whites of their independence. These charges found substantial echoes, though also some opposition, in the early labor press. The ex-Chartist Philadelphia typesetter, bookseller and labor reformer John Campbell followed his 1848 book, *A Theory of Equality*, three years later with *Negromania*, a cranky and vicious early attempt to popularize racist pseudo-science. Both the books were pleas for white unity inside the Democratic party. *America's Own and Fireman's Journal*, a labor paper of the 1850s, approvingly republished Las Casas's "A Plea for Slavery."

In the New York City labor movement, despite George Henry Evans's tempering influence, the tendency to indict white slavery and to support Black slavery was especially strong…. Walsh's wild popularity from the early forties to the early fifties stemmed from the resonance of his freewheeling attacks on what he called "white wages slavery" with the accent on both of the adjectives. "You are slaves," he thundered to his followers, "and none are better aware of the fact than the heathenish dogs who call you freemen," while outspokenly supporting Southern slavery and even its extension into Kansas and Nebraska. Walsh's bitterest factional opponent within New York City's artisan Democracy, the lockmaker Levi Slamm, echoed this combination of proslavery and attacks on "black-hearted tyrants" who held "white slaves." Slamm, editor of *The Plebeian*, organized the "coffin handbill" protest whose dramatic characterization of white workers as slaves begins this [essay]. John Commerford, the New York chairmakers' leader who … may have been the most popular Jacksonian labor leader, joined a number of trade unionists and radical Democrats who excoriated white slavery and gave political support to the South's premier proslavery politician, John C. Calhoun.

The proslavery affinities of those who denounced white slavery have attracted some passing notice from historians, who have offered various explanations. The fear of job competition with emancipated Blacks has received emphasis—perhaps even overemphasis, in that only a minority of proslavery indictments of white slavery raised the issue of job competition and that it was then usually raised in combination with broader fears of amalgamation. Labor's animosity to "middle class" and moralistic abolitionist leaders has also been mentioned. So have the necessity to guard the Republic from potentially fatal divisions over slavery and the need to preserve the Democracy as the party of reform, even at the cost of conciliating slaveholders. John Ashworth's work offers the most forceful recent restatement of the old, much debated view of the Jacksonian Democrats as (among whites) a party of the political egalitarianism and social leveling. Surely the Democrats' positions on such issues as free trade, banking, imprisonment for debt, prison labor and, to an extent, land reform, gave some substance to their populism. Ashworth adds an inventive twist that makes the radical labor/proslavery position seem less anomalous, arguing that because Jacksonians could imagine no citizenship but full, equal citizenship they were less able to imagine emancipation of Blacks than more elitist parties. Other historians have even held that Yankee labor radicals were engaged in a sophisticated attempt to exploit splits within the ruling class by allying for a time with proslavery Southerners. This last position probably credits the labor radicals with more acumen than they in fact had, but it may describe what a particularly cerebral radical like Orestes Brownson thought he was doing for a time.

However great the value of existing explanations for the considerable coming together of radical labor and proslavery, these explanations deserve to be supplemented by a simpler one: the very structure of the argument against white slavery typically carried proslavery implications. As Eric Foner has recently observed, radical labor's comparisons of "white" and Black slavery often found the latter less oppressive than the former. Radicals argued, on shreds of evidence, that Southern masters worked their Black slaves far fewer hours per day—perhaps only half the number required by Northern employers. They computed rates of exploitation that putatively showed that a much greater proportion of the value produced by a Black slave was returned to him or her than was returned to the white slave in the North. Even writers who argued that white and Black slavery were roughly equal nonetheless showed a sharp tendency to cite only comparisons favorable to this latter. For example, a comparison of the two labor systems in the *Mechanics' Free Press* in 1830— probably the first such direct and significant one made by organized labor—set out to show that the two differed only "in name." But it then compared the life of a free laborer, full of the threat of starvation, over-exertion, deprived children and uncomforted sickness, with that of the slave with a "master interested in prolonging his life." Even Evans, who strove for balance, found that the "slave to the Land-Lord and capitalist class is in a worse, aye a *worse* condition than the slave who has a master of his own" and reprinted arguments that emancipation without land reform would worsen Black slaves' positions tenfold.

Artisan radical and early historian John Finch cited the "well-known fact that the blacks of the South enjoy more leisure time and liberty and fare quite as well as the operatives in the northern or eastern manufacturing districts." He added that the same comparison more or less applied to whites in "other mechanical pursuits." Orestes Brownson, who at times found white workers closer to freedom than Blacks, could at other junctures argue that slave labor is "except so far as feelings are concerned ... decidedly the least oppressive.... The laborer at wages has all the disadvantages of freedom and none of its blessings, while the slave, if denied the blessings, is freed from the disadvantages."

The most common comparison, repeated by Walsh and several others, was that the "poor negro" was a "farm horse" with one master who would protect him when he could "toil no more," while the "poor white man" was a "horse in a livery stable" hired to many masters and therefore overworked by all and without protection when infirmed. Chattel slavery was, in this view, better than white slavery, a point fraught with proslavery paternalist implications and not lost on the Southern editors who reprinted articles carrying such opinions.

Free Labor and Wage Labor in the North

JOHN ASHWORTH

... We cannot understand the political universe in which the Republicans flourished without first considering some of the opinions of the patron saint of American democracy, Thomas Jefferson. Jefferson defined the American democratic creed and the values of republicanism in his struggle with the Federalists in the 1790s. Although the Republican party of the 1850s constantly harked back to Jefferson and indeed claimed inspiration from such Jeffersonian triumphs as the Northwest Ordinance of 1787, the Republican victory of 1860 in fact marked the overthrow of the Jeffersonian system. Under the impact of the economic changes associated with the market revolution, the Republicans redefined the American democratic tradition and, in their triumph over the South in the Civil War, destroyed the regime established in 1776 and reconstituted by the Jeffersonian triumph of 1800.

Jefferson's agrarianism, his belief in states' rights, his commitment to limited government—indeed all the major tenets of the Jeffersonian political faith—are all too well known to require any rehearsal here. Nevertheless, it is worth recalling his view of agriculture. This received its most eloquent expression in the *Notes on Virginia*, where Jefferson explained that the farmers' independence and moral purity made them "the chosen people of God, if ever He had a chosen people." In the 1820s the Jeffersonian mantle was picked up by those who rallied to Andrew Jackson. And as the principles of Jacksonian Democracy were defined in the course of Jackson's two administrations, especially under the impact of the struggle with the Bank of the United States, they came increasingly to resemble those of John Taylor of Caroline, high priest of Jeffersonian Democracy. Once again, praise was heaped on agriculture and on the landed interest. Thus, in 1839 the *Democratic Review*, semiofficial magazine of the party, did precisely as Jefferson had done a half-century earlier and compared city and country. The conclusion was a quintessentially Jeffersonian one:

> The farmer is naturally a Democrat—the citizen may be so, but it is in spite of many obstacles. In the country a more healthy moral atmosphere may be said to exist, untainted by the corruptions and contagions of the crowded city, analogous to its purer breezes which the diseased and exhausted denizen of the latter is from time to time compelled to seek for the renovation of his jaded faculties of mind and body. In the city men move in masses.... In the country, on the other hand, man enjoys an existence of a healthier and truer happiness, a nobler mental freedom, a higher native dignity—for which a poor equivalent is found in that superficial polish produced by the incessant mutual attrition, and that more intense life, if we may so speak, excited by the perpetual surrounding stimulus that belong to cities. He is thrown more on

John Ashworth, "Free Labor, Wage Labor, and Slave Power: Republicanism and the Republican Party in the 1850s," in Melvyn Stokes and Stephen Conway, eds., *The Market Revolution in America: Social, Political, and Religious Expressions, 1800–1880*, University Press of Virginia, 1996. Reprinted by permission of the University Press of Virginia.

himself. Most of his labors are comparatively solitary, and of such kind as to leave his mind meanwhile free for reflection. Every thing around him is large, open, free, unartificial, and his mind insensibly, to a greater or less extent, takes a corresponding tone from the general character of the objects and associations in the midst of which he lives and moves and has his being. He is less dependent on the hourly aid of others, in the regular routine of his life, as likewise on their opinions, their example, their influence. The inequalities of social distinctions, the operation of which is attended with equal moral injury to the higher and the lower, affect less his more simple and independent course of life. He is forced more constantly to think and act for himself, with reference to those broad principles of natural right, of which all men alike, when unperverted by artificial circumstances, carry with them a common general understanding. And to live he must labor: all the various modes by which, in great congregations of men, certain classes are ingeniously able to appropriate to themselves the fruits of the general toil of the rest, being to him alike unknown and impracticable. Hence does he better appreciate the true worth and dignity of labor, and knows how to respect, with a more manly and Christian sympathy of universal brotherhood, those oppressed masses of the laboring poor, whose vast bulk constitutes the basis on which alone rests the proud apex of the social pyramid. In a word, he is a more natural, a more healthy, a more independent, a more genuine *man,*—and hence, as we have said above, the farmer is naturally a democrat; the citizen may be so, but it is in spite of many obstacles. We have here briefly, in passing, alluded to the reasons for our preference of the political support of the country over that of the city; and to the causes of the fact that, as a general rule, the former has always been found to be the true home of American democracy; while in the latter, and in their circumradiated influence, has usually been found the main strength of that party by which, under one form and name or another, the progress of the democratic principle has, from the outset, been so bitterly and unremittingly opposed.

For Jefferson and the Jacksonians alike, the farmer who was most estimable was not the tenant, but the freeholder. He it was who enjoyed the independence that was so necessary to participation in a democratic government.

One can argue that Jeffersonian and Jacksonian Democracy provided a considerable measure of covert support for slaveholders, whose plantations were, in Democratic rhetoric, smoothly assimilated into the farm. But what this tradition could not easily accommodate was the wage laborer. This is less surprising than might be thought. It is too easily forgotten that for most of human history the status of the wage laborer has been a humble one indeed. Americans were heirs to a long and venerable tradition of hostility to wage labor. From Aristotle to the English revolution and beyond, one prominent political thinker after another stressed that the wage worker was akin to a slave. As Aristotle put it, "No man can practise virtue who is living the life of a mechanic or labourer."

These attitudes survived in Europe for hundreds of years…. And they re-emerged in the United States to inform both Jeffersonian and Jacksonian views of wage labor. Not surprisingly, a party that was unhappy with the dependence entailed by tenant farming was unenthusiastic about the relationship between employer and worker. In fact, those who were most implacable in their hostility to the banking system—the key political issue of the 1830s—tended also to be the most distrustful of wage labor. At the furthest reaches of the Democratic party was Orestes Brownson, who, as is well known, in 1840 proposed that the party prohibit the inheritance of property. Less well known, however, is the view of wages that he expressed at the same time, Brownson's goal was to "combine labor and capital in the same individual," and he argued that it was agriculture, more than any other pursuit, that could achieve this. But even in the agricultural sector the situation was deteriorating, since "the distance between the owner of the farm, and the men who cultivate it" was "becoming every day greater and greater." Yet this problem shrank into insignificance when compared with the scene in the towns and manufacturing villages, where "the distinction between the capitalist and the proletary" was "as strongly marked as it is in the old world." For Brownson the ultimate threat to individual autonomy was the wages system. Wages were "the cunning device of the devil," and the wage system had to be eliminated, "or else one half of the human race must forever be the virtual slaves of the other."

Brownson was an unusual Democrat and an erratic partisan. More measured in his utterances was New York Senator Silas Wright, who was known to speak for the Van Burenites, in the late 1830s and early 1840s the dominant group within the party. Wright focused attention on manufacturing and complained of "the great power which the manufacturing capitalist must hold over the employee, and, by necessary consequence, over the living, the comfort, and the independence of the laborer." Similarly, Amos Kendall, one of Andrew Jackson's closest collaborators, urged the sons of farmers to remain on the farm rather than to seek employment in factories.

For Kendall the worthy citizen was either a farmer or an "independent mechanic." Here he perhaps left the way open for a modest amount of wage labor. What did he mean by *independent?* Unfortunately, it is difficult to answer this question. An independent mechanic, according to Kendall, was one who could refuse "to sell his services to any man on other conditions than those of perfect equality—both as citizens and men." Kendall may have meant here the self-employed craftsman, who sold his services not to an employer, but instead to the consumer. Or he may have meant a wage worker, whose terms of employment were not such as to produce large inequalities of wealth, power, and esteem. How were such terms to be attained? Kendall did not specify.

Other Democrats had trouble with wage labor. Like Kendall they believed that independence was essential, and like him they were unsure whether it was compatible with employment for wages. The Washington *Globe* referred approvingly to, in effect, two kinds of mechanic or artisan and had no difficulty in defining the first. He was none other than the self-employed craftsman. But a string of subordinate clauses was necessary to offer even an approximate definition of the second. The newspaper spoke of "the healthy mechanic or artisan, who works for himself at his own shop, or if he goes abroad, returns home to his meals every day, and sleeps under his own roof every night; whose earnings are regulated by the wants of the community at large, not by the discretion of a pernicious master; whose hours of labor depend on universal custom; who, when the sun goes down, is a freeman until he rises again, who can eat his meals in comfort, and sleep as long as nature requires." The problem was that the *Globe*, like Kendall and like other Democrats, did not explain how the conditions necessary for acceptable forms of wage labor were to be obtained.

In these circumstances, it was not surprising that the northern Democrats in the 1850s did not extol the wage labor system of the North. Although they were quite certain that free labor was superior to slave labor, they did not glorify wage labor. From the mid-1840s onward, of course, the nation's economy revived, and the resulting prosperity weakened Democratic radicalism. Some of it, nevertheless, persisted into the 1850s. Thus Theophilus Fisk claimed that free-soilism and abolition distracted northern workers from "their own grievous wrongs and intolerable oppressions." More significant, Fernando Wood, campaigning for Breckinridge in 1860, insisted that "until we have provided and cared for the oppressed laboring man in our own midst, we should not extend our sympathy to the laboring men of other states." As mayor of New York city in 1857, Wood set out a view of the condition of northern labor that both revived Democratic radicalism of previous decades and revealed a jaundiced view of the condition of northern wage workers: "In the days of general prosperity they [the working classes] labor for a mere subsistence whilst other classes accumulate wealth, and in the days of general depression they are the first to feel the change, without the means to avoid or endure reverses. Truly it may be said that in New York those who produce everything get nothing, and those who produce nothing get everything. They labor without income, whilst surrounded by thousands living in affluence and splendor who have income without labor."

These views were distinctly uncommon within the Democratic party in the 1850s. They were more common, however, than the celebrations of wage labor in which Republicans (as we shall see) frequently indulged. A prevalent view was simply to record the condition of the wage worker and to argue that he had no cause for complaint. Unlike that of the Republicans, Democratic rhetoric in no way privileged the role of the wage laborer or the relationship between employer and worker. Such had not been Democratic practice in the past; such was not Democratic practice in the 1850s.

In fact, most Democrats abstained from a close analysis of the northern labor system. Republicans, however, did not. While it is true that their rhetoric emphasized free labor, it is equally true that all who listened knew that Republicans had not merely reconciled themselves to wage labor, but had instead come to view it as a key element in the social order, the cement of the northern social system. Freedom, equality, the Union, American democracy itself—all depended, in Republicans' eyes, on the existence of wage labor. This view distinguished them sharply from northern Democrats; it was this, above all, that separated the two parties in the 1850s.

The importance of wage labor in the thinking of Republicans is implicit or explicit in some of the speeches of Charles Sumner. Prior to the election of 1860, Sumner began to adopt a shorthand phrase to refer to southern slavery. He began to call it "labor without wages," confident, it would seem, that this phrase would convey to his listeners the injustice inherent in the master–slave relation. In June 1860, all the evil effects of slavery were traced to its "single object of compelling men to work without wages." This, he repeated a month later, was its "single motive," its "single object." For the greater part of human history labor has been done without wages, and for much of that time, as we have seen, it would have been grounds for complaint if a system had compelled men to work *with* wages. On the same occasion, Sumner employed a familiar argument against slavery when he claimed that it was contrary to God's intentions for mankind. Less familiar, however, was his assumption about wages. "When God created man in his own image," he declared, "and saw that his work was good, he did not destine his fellow creature for endless ages to labor without wages, compelled by the lash." The rhythm of this sentence seems to require that a heavy emphasis be placed upon "without wages," perhaps as heavy as "compelled by the lash." The implication is surely that God approves of wage labor.

Sumner's attitude was made even more explicit in a rhetorical question that he put to the Senate in 1860. Speaking of "the slaveholder," he asked, "How can he show sensibility for the common rights of fellow citizens who sacrifice daily the most sacred right of others merely to secure *labor without wages?* With him a false standard is necessarily established, bringing with it a blunted moral sense and clouded perceptions, so that, when he does something intrinsically barbarous or mean, he does not blush at the recital." Here, then, is the reason Sumner believed that to refer to slavery as "labor without wages" could convey the enormity of the evil. He seems to have viewed wage labor, properly rewarded, as an anchor of morality. The passage makes no sense unless it is assumed that the wage laborer is worthy of respect or esteem. Gone is the old hostility.

Sumner, of course, was a spokesman for Radical Republicanism and represented Massachusetts, the state with the most developed economy in the Union. By contrast, Lincoln was a moderate and came from a far more agricultural state, albeit one whose economy was advancing rapidly in the 1850s. Although his social thought has often been analyzed, the significance and novelty of his view of wage labor have not been fully appreciated. In one respect, however, his views were entirely traditional: he remained somewhat critical of the worker who remained, for the duration of his working life, a wage earner. As he told a Milwaukee audience in 1859, "If any continue through life in the condition of the hired laborer," it was "because of either a dependent nature which prefers it, or improvidence, folly or singular misfortune." In the same vein, Lincoln tended to repel southern charges of wage slavery not by defending the status of the wage earner as a wage earner, but instead by pointing to his opportunities to cease to work for wages. Thus in 1856 he noted that many southerners were claiming that their slaves were "far better off than northern freemen." Lincoln did not take the modern view and reject the comparison by denying the dependence of the wage earner. Instead he charged southerners with an egregious error: "What a mistaken view do these men have of northern laborers! They think that men are always to remain laborers here—but there is no such class. The man who labored for another last year, this year labors for himself, and next year he will hire others to labor for him." Thus mobility legitimated wage labor. Lincoln also took pleasure in recording how small a proportion of the labor of the North was done for wages. At Cincinnati in 1859, he remarked that the wage system entailed "a relation of which I make no complaint." But, he added, "I do insist that the relation does not embrace more than one-eighth of the labor of the country." Though this estimate was almost certainly far wide of the mark, it may be more important to note Lincoln's defensive tone here. Clearly he was glad that wage earners did not constitute a larger proportion of the northern workforce.

At the same time, however, Lincoln glorified the wage labor—and not merely the free labor—system of the North. We can perhaps best understand this by looking at his view of mobility. More than any previous president, Lincoln emphasized social mobility. As early as 1856, he was attributing American greatness to the fact that in the United States "every man can make himself." For Jefferson and Jackson, freedom and equality had necessitated an agrarian society in which the freeholding farmer would, whether or not he went to the West, remain a freeholding farmer for his entire life, gradually acquiring a "competence" for his old age. Such a society would be characterized by an equality of conditions rather than merely an equality of opportunity. Indeed, inequalities of outcome, while inevitable, would present a danger; they would in no sense be necessary to the functioning of the economy. For Lincoln, however, the citizens of the United States, or at least those of the northern states, were engaged in "a race of life." Unequal outcomes are implicit in—indeed the very purpose of—a race. In 1864 he told an Ohio regiment that they were fighting "to secure such an inestimable jewel" as "equal privileges in the race of life." Lincoln's other favorite metaphor was also one that conveyed the idea of mobility and, more specifically, upward mobility. This involved the image of weights being lifted from shoulders. In February 1861, he told a Philadelphia audience that the unity of the nation had hitherto been maintained by "something in that Declaration [of Independence] giving liberty not alone to the people of this country, but hope to the world for all future time." This was the promise "that in due time the weights should be lifted from the shoulders of all men, and that all should have an equal chance." In his special session message of July 4, 1861 he again used both this image and the race-of-life metaphor to explain the purpose of the struggle. The Union itself was now explicable in terms of social mobility.

Mobility had also subtly narrowed the Jacksonian view of equality and liberty so that both were now understood in terms of equality of opportunity. Addressing another Ohio regiment in 1864, the President declared that "nowhere in the world is presented a government of so much liberty and equality." As if to define his terms, he immediately added, "To the humblest and poorest among us are held out the highest privileges and positions." If opportunities were equal and plentiful, then Americans were free and equal. Little wonder, then, that Lincoln invited Americans to internalize the goal social mobility, as he himself had done. "I hold [that] the value of life," he once said, is "to improve one's condition."

How was mobility to be secured? Lincoln held that "when one starts poor, as most do in the race of life, free society is such that he knows he can better his condition; he knows that there is no such fixed condition of labor, for his whole life." It was this that distinguished free labor, "which has the inspiration of hope," from slave labor, "which has no hope." For "the power of hope upon human exertion, and happiness, is wonderful." Yet, just as free labor was essential for social mobility, so, for Lincoln, were wages essential to free labor. And just as mobility legitimated wage labor, so was wage labor essential for mobility. In all Lincoln's descriptions of mobility the need for wage labor was either explicit or implicit. On one occasion free labor was actually defined in terms of the individual's progress from the rank of wage laborer to that of employer. Thus at Milwaukee in 1859 he spoke of "the prudent, penniless beginner in the world," who "labors for wages awhile, saves a surplus with which to buy tools or land for himself, then labors on his own account another while, and at length hires another new beginner to help him." The conclusion was significant: "This say its advocates, is *free* labor [emphasis added]—the just and generous and prosperous system, which opens the way for all—gives hope to all, and energy, and progress, and improvement of condition to all." Finally, and even more explicitly, at Cincinnati the same year he announced that the very purpose of American democracy was to facilitate the progress of the wage laborer: "This progress, by which the poor, honest, industrious, and resolute man raises himself, that he may work on his own account, and hire somebody else, is that progress that human nature is entitled to, is that improvement in condition that is intended to be secured by those institutions under which we live, is the great principle for which this government was really formed." Thus, for Lincoln democracy, the Union, freedom, equality, even the Declaration of Independence could not be understood except in terms of mobility, free labor, and wages.

Lincoln was not alone in these opinions. In New York City the *Times*, an exponent of conservative Republican thought, while the economy was in recession in 1857, replied to southern critics of northern society. "Our best answer," it claimed, "is that the majority of those who suffer from a panic here are by the time the next one comes around in a position not to fear it," For "the Northern artisans of 1837 ... are the merchants, traders, farmers and statesmen of 1856 and 1857." This was thanks to "free labor," which was "our glory and our safeguard." Thus, for the *Times,* the stability of the northern social system depended on free labor and social mobility. And free labor clearly required wage labor.

There was thus a marked difference between Republican and northern Democratic perceptions of the northern social order. While both groups did not doubt that, so far as the North was concerned, free labor was superior to slavery, the Republicans enthused about the relationship between employer and wage earner, while the Democrats did not. In 1859, the *Chicago Times* neatly illustrated this difference when it chided Lincoln after one of his speeches and claimed that he had misrepresented the condition of northern workers, only 10 percent of whom could become employers. The Republicans and the Democrats saw free labor and the contrast with slavery differently. Essentially Republicans saw slavery and free labor (with its foundation in the wages system) as the bases for divergent social systems; northern Democrats perceived them rather as distinct interests.

What does it mean to say that certain values formed the core of a party's beliefs? One possible answer might be that these values were those that the party's spokesmen most often articulated. In this eventuality, it would be possible to determine which were the key Republican values by counting the references made to the slave power, to free labor, and to wage labor. In this contest it is entirely possible that the slave power would emerge the winner, wage labor a poor third. But such an analysis would be profoundly unsatisfactory.

It is frequently the case that the various components of an ideology or a world-view are interdependent, with each reinforcing, and reinforced by, many of the others. It is also, however, frequently the case that such interdependence is asymmetrical; some components give rise to others, but are less dependent upon them. So it was with wage labor and the slave power in Republican thought. Republicans saw a slave power where Democrats did not, because their faith in the northern social system was so great that they could explain the success of slavery in the South and even (to some extent) in the West only by claiming that normal democratic processes had been subverted or overturned. Since the free labor and wage labor system of the North was deemed "natural," it followed that a slave power was required to explain its failure to take hold in the South and the attempts to spread an alternative system into the West and even the North. Hence the Republicans' preference for a wage labor system can explain their references to the slave power. But this interdependence was asymmetrical: in no sense did a belief in the slave power give rise to Republican perceptions of wage labor.

There is, moreover, additional cause to emphasize the importance of wage labor. For such an emphasis immediately opens up a connection with the dominant economic processes of the mid-nineteenth century. In 1800 only about 10 percent of the American workforce was employed for wages; by 1860 the figure was about 40 percent, heavily concentrated, of course, in the North. The Democratic party, with its strength increasingly concentrated in the South, could not develop a wage labor or even a free labor ideology; indeed, it was all northerners could do to prevent their southern colleagues from placing a proslavery plank in the party platform. Finally, of course, the party split in 1860 over precisely this issue. But for some years before this Democrats in the North had experienced great difficulty in engaging with the dominant economic processes of their time. Perhaps if the panic of 1857 had lasted, a revival of the antibank and anticommercial sentiment of the 1830s and early 1840s might have solved this problem. But it did not. In these circumstances, northern Democrats were impelled to fall back on an appeal to the ethnocultural values that they had always espoused, but now without the economic and social underpinning they had previously had. In this sense, therefore, theirs was an increasingly dislocated ideology.

Here is an additional reason why the Silbey interpretation of Republicanism is unsatisfactory. Not only were the Republicans profoundly divided on all the ethnocultural questions that did not involve slavery; they knew, as most southerners knew, that the slavery question transcended issues like rum and Romanism.

It raised too many vital questions about the nation's political economy to be treated in the way that the parties had treated the ethnocultural issues. A society's labor system—the question whether it should be based upon slavery or wages—is simply more important than the decision whether to introduce laws on temperance. Most partisans and observers in the 1850s knew that this was so. Of course the northern Democrats would have liked nothing more than to have subsumed slavery under the heading of "cultural politics," since they would then have had a more potent appeal to the electorate. But the history of the 1850s is, in a sense, the history of the frustration of these hopes.

In the longer view, the Republican achievement was momentous. The election of Lincoln and the victory of the North in the Civil War meant that a fundamental—indeed revolutionary—change in American politics had occurred. The American democratic tradition, forged by Jefferson and by Jackson, had given covert support to the slaveholder by assimilating the slaveholding plantation into the farm. The American democratic tradition as reconstituted in the political upheavals of the 1850s and 1860s would instead rest American democracy upon the relationship between employer and employee, between capitalist and worker, a relationship now hailed as a quintessential characteristic of a "free" society. There it remains to this day.

FURTHER READING

Stuart W. Bruchey, *Enterprise: The Dynamic Economy of a Free People* (1990).

John Mack Farragher, *Sugar Creek: Life on the Illinois Prairie* (1986).

Jon Gjerde, *The Minds of the West: Ethnocultural Evolution in the Rural Middle West, 1830–1917* (1997).

James O. Horton and Lois E. Horton, *In Hope of Liberty: Culture, Community and Protest Among Northern Free Blacks, 1700–1860* (1996).

David Hounshell, *From the American System to Mass Production, 1800–1932* (1985).

Joan M. Jensen, *Loosening the Bonds: Mid-Atlantic Farm Women, 1750–1850* (1986).

John F. Kasson, *Civilizing the Machine: Technology and Republican Values in America, 1776–1900* (1976).

Bruce Laurie, *Artisans into Workers: Labor in Nineteenth-Century America* (1997).

Kerby A. Miller, *Emigrants and Exiles: Ireland and the Irish Exodus to North America* (1985).

William Moran, *The Belles of New England: The Women of the Textile Mills and the Families Whose Wealth They Wove* (2004).

Christine Stansell, *City of Women: Sex and Class in New York City, 1789–1860* (1986).

Stephan Thernstrom, *Poverty and Progress: Social Mobility in a Nineteenth Century City* (1964).

Peter Way, *Common Labour: Workers and the Digging of North American Canals 1780–1860* (1993).

Sean Wilentz, *Chants Democratic: New York City and the Rise of the American Working Class, 1788–1850* (1984).

CHAPTER 12

Agriculture and Slavery in the South at Midcentury

The cotton gin (short for "cotton engine") was a very simple device that had revolutionary implications. Patented by Eli Whitney in 1794, it was able to remove the seeds from short-staple cotton without damaging the fibers. Because short-staple cotton, unlike its long-staple counterpart, did not require wet, semitropical climates, it could be grown throughout much of the antebellum South. The cotton gin, then, played a central role in reinvigorating the southern economy and solidifying the slave system. Already by 1800, cotton and slavery together were spreading westward. Between 1815 and 1840, cotton output jumped from 200,000 to 1.35 million bales, each of which weighed four hundred pounds. Another cotton boom began in 1849, when output reached 2.85 million bales, and lasted until 1860, when 4.8 million bales were produced. Southern planters confidently proclaimed that "cotton was king."

By 1860, almost four million people lived and worked as slaves on a belt of land stretching from Virginia into Texas. Slavery and race, moreover, influenced almost every aspect of southern society. Although most white people considered slave owning a source of economic mobility and social status and gave political deference to the wealthy planters, more than two-thirds of white families in the region owned no slaves. These non-slaveowning whites often found themselves pushed off the better land by affluent cotton, sugar, or rice entrepreneurs. Thus slavery also had its costs for many white people. Although not all black people in the South were enslaved, the "free people of color," some quarter of a million people, found their position in southern society increasingly circumscribed. As the nineteenth century wore on and the status of slave increasingly came to be equated with African ancestry, "free people of color" faced growing legal disadvantages. The rise of the cotton South, in sum, created a curious combination of opulence and misery.

Southerners justified, condemned, and accommodated themselves to the slave system in a variety of ways. Many white southerners became increasingly aware that slavery was being criticized as a system of labor whose time had passed. As Americans in the North and Europeans worked to abolish the system, the white South both developed ideologies that justified slavery and increased its vigilance over enslaved people. The master class advanced a myth of paternalism like that discussed in Chapter 2. They presented themselves as custodians of the welfare of a grateful and harmonious slave society. Some went so far as to argue that slavery was "a positive good" rather than simply a necessary evil. All societies contained a working class, they argued, and enslaved people were better off than the "wage slaves" of the North because the slaveowner truly cared for his people. As apologists for slavery made these arguments, however, the South also developed increasingly harsh "slave codes" that reflected a growing fear of slave revolts incited by abolitionists. The North Carolina law prohibiting slaves to read and write, for example, contended that literacy "has a tendency to excite dissatisfaction in their minds."

In fact, laws against literacy were one among many factors that excited dissatisfaction among slaves. After toiling from sunrise to sundown, slaves were nonetheless vulnerable to complaints—supplemented by physical punishment—that they had not worked well enough. If white women could object to slavery because of illicit relationships between their men and their slaves, slave women were obviously at even greater risk. Perhaps most disheartening was the fact that an imperious master might separate slaves from their loved ones through sale.

Slaves were not powerless, of course. They used the paternalist ideology to illustrate the inherent contradictions between the ideal of a benevolent master and the reality of cruelty in slave life. Slaves also developed strategies within their own community to temper the cruelties of enslavement. The family and local neighborhoods served as arenas in which children were socialized. Christian belief likewise was a powerful resource that simultaneously allowed slaves to look to a better life after death and criticize the system of slavery in which they were set. How one might be both a slaveowner and a Christian was a telling question that few could adequately answer.

QUESTIONS TO THINK ABOUT

How might southern apologists for slavery have used the northern "wage slave" discussed in the last chapter to justify slavery? To what extent do you agree with this argument? How did slaves use religious belief and kinship to temper their plight? Did this strategy play into the hands of slaveholders? Did white women benefit from slavery or suffer because of it? How were non–slaveholding whites and "free people of color" affected by the institution of slavery?

DOCUMENTS

These documents illustrate the deep imprint that slavery and plantation agriculture made on southern society. Document 1 is a North Carolina law that prohibits teaching slaves to read or write. Slave revolts and knowledge of the growing abolitionist movement in the North, many white southerners feared, would be furthered through literacy. Document 2 is a bizarre account by a physician that describes certain diseases that are peculiar to African Americans, such as running away. If some whites deemed slavery a necessary evil, others began to see it as a "positive good," as document 3 illustrates. In this selection, George Fitzhugh praises the peace and quiet of the South in comparison with the North. Slaves had a different view from that of Fitzhugh. Josiah Henson, in document 4, describes the punishments that slaves encountered and, worse yet, the divisions of family and friends that occurred when slaves were sold. Document 5 is a celebration of the white yeoman farmer by a white southerner who argues that non-slaveholding whites nonetheless support slavery. In document 6, Harriet Jacobs describes her trials as a young woman living in slavery. Jacobs argues that female slaves were in particular jeopardy because of the actions of powerful male slave-owners. Whereas Jacobs scolds white mistresses who did not protect female slaves, Mary Boykin Chestnut's diary in document 7 provides us with the perspective of a slave mistress who comes close to blaming women slaves for making the plantation similar to a harem. In document 8, Frederick Law Olmsted concludes that the slave economy as a whole is not profitable. Document 9 contains the lyrics of several songs sung by slaves. The songs voice their fears, frustrations, and faiths.

1. A North Carolina Law Prohibits Teaching Slaves to Read or Write, 1831

Whereas the teaching of slaves to read and write, has a tendency to excite dissatisfaction in their minds, and to produce insurrection and rebellion, to the manifest injury of the citizens of this State: Therefore, *Be it enacted by the General Assembly of the State of North Carolina, and it is hereby enacted by the authority of the same,* That any free person, who shall hereafter teach, or attempt to teach, any slave within the State to read or write, the use of figures excepted, or shall give or sell to such slave or slaves any books or pamphlets shall be liable to indictment in any court of record in this State having jurisdiction thereof, and upon conviction, shall, at the discretion of the court, if a white man or woman, be fined not less than one hundred dollars, nor more than two hundred dollars, or imprisoned; and if a free person of color, shall be fined, imprisoned, or whipped, at the discretion of the court, not exceeding thirty nine lashes, nor less than twenty lashes.

Be it further enacted, That if any slave shall hereafter teach, or attempt to teach, any other slave to read or write, the use of figures excepted, he or she may be carried before any justice of the peace and on conviction thereof, shall be sentenced to receive thirty nine lashes on his or her bare back.

2. Samuel Cartwright, a Southern Doctor, Theorizes About the Peculiar Diseases of Slaves, 1851

1.—DISEASES AND PECULIARITIES OF THE NEGRO RACE.
By Dr. Cartwright of New-Orleans—(Concluded.)
DRAPETOMANIA, OR THE DISEASE CAUSING NEGROES TO RUN AWAY.

Drapetomania is from δραπέτης, a runaway slave, and μανια, *mad or crazy*. It is unknown to our medical authorities, although its diagnostic symptom, the

"A North Carolina Law Forbidding the Teaching of Slaves to Read and Write" (1831), as reprinted in *A History of the U.S.: Sourcebook and Index,* Joy Hakim (New York: Oxford University Press, 1999), 108.

Dr. Cartwright, "Diseases and Peculiarities of the Negro Race," *De Bow's Review,* 2 (September 1851): 331–332, 334–336.

absconding from service, is … well known to our planters and overseers…. The cause, in the most of cases, that induces the negro to run away from service, is as much a disease of the mind as any other species of mental alienation, and much more curable, as a general rule. With the advantages of proper medical advice, strictly followed, this troublesome practice that many negroes have of running away, can be almost entirely prevented, although the slaves be located on the borders of a free state, within a stone's throw of the abolitionists….

To ascertain the true method of governing negroes, so as to cure and prevent the disease under consideration, we must go back to the Pentateuch, and learn the true meaning of the untranslated term that represents the negro race. In the name there given to that race, is locked up the true art of governing negroes in such a manner that they cannot run away. The correct translation of that term declares the Creator's will in regard to the negro; it declares him to be the submissive kneebender. In the anatomical conformation of his knees we see "*genu flexit*" written in his physical structure, being more flexed or bent, than any other kind of man. If the white man attempts to oppose the Deity's will, by trying to make the negro anything else than "*the submissive knee-bender,*" (which the Almighty declared he should be,) by trying to raise him to a level with himself, or by putting himself on an equality with the negro; or if he abuses the power which God has given him over his fellow-man, by being cruel to him, or punishing him in anger, or by neglecting to protect him from wanton abuses of his fellow-servants and all others, or by denying him the usual comforts and necessaries of life, the negro will run away; but if he keeps him in the position that we learn from the Scriptures he was intended to occupy, that is, the position of submission; and if his master or overseer be kind and gracious in his bearing towards him, without condescension, and at the same time ministers to his physical wants, and protects him from abuses, the negro is spell-bound, and cannot run away….

When left to himself, the negro indulges in his natural disposition to idleness and sloth, and does not take exercise enough to expand his lungs and to vitalize his blood, but dozes out a miserable existence in the midst of filth and uncleanliness, being too indolent, and having too little energy of mind to provide for himself proper food and comfortable lodging and clothing. The consequence is, that the blood becomes so highly carbonized and deprived of oxygen, that it not only becomes unfit to stimulate the brain to energy, but unfit to stimulate the nerves of sensation distributed to the body. A torpor and insensibility pervades the system; the sentient nerves distributed to the skin lose their feeling in so great a degree, that he often burns his skin by the fire he hovers over without knowing it, and frequently has large holes in his clothes, and the shoes on his feet burnt to a crisp, without having been conscious of when it was done. This is the disease called dysæsthesia….

The complaint is easily curable, if treated on sound physiological principles…. Any kind of labor will do that will cause full and free respiration in its performance, as lifting or carrying heavy weights, or brisk walking; the object being to expand the lungs by full and deep inspiration and expirations, thereby to vitalize the impure circulating blood by introducing oxygen and expelling carbon....

According to unaltered physiological laws, negroes, as a general rule to which there are but few exceptions, can only have their intellectual faculties awakened in a sufficient degree to receive moral culture and to profit by religious or other instructions, when under the compulsatory authority of the white man; because, as a general rule to which there are but few exceptions, they will not take sufficient exercise, when removed from the white man's authority, to vitalize and decarbonize their blood by the process of full and free respiration, that active exercise of some kind alone can effect....

... The dysæsthesia æthiopica adds another to the many ten thousand evidences of the fallacy of the dogma that abolitionism is built on; for here, in a country where two races of men dwell together, both born on the same soil, breathing the same air, and surrounded by the same external agents—liberty, which is elevating the one race of people above all other nations, sinks the other into beastly sloth and torpidity; and the slavery, which the one would prefer death rather than endure, improves the other in body, mind and morals; thus proving the dogma false, and establishing the truth that there is a radical, internal or physical difference between the two races, so great in kind, as to make what is wholesome and beneficial for the white man, as liberty, republican or free institutions, etc., not only unsuitable to the negro race, but actually poisonous to its happiness.

3. Virginian George Fitzhugh Argues That Slavery Is a Positive Good That Improves Society, 1854

At the slaveholding South all is peace, quiet, plenty and contentment. We have no mobs, no trade unions, no strikes for higher wages, no armed resistance to the law, but little jealousy of the rich by the poor. We have but few in our jails, and fewer in our poor houses. We produce enough of the comforts and necessaries of life for a population three or four times as numerous as ours. We are wholly exempt from the torrent of pauperism, crime, agrarianism, and infidelity which Europe is pouring from her jails and alms houses on the already crowded North. Population increases slowly, wealth rapidly. In the tide water region of Eastern Virginia, as far as our experience extends, the crops have doubled in fifteen years, whilst the population has been almost stationary. In the same period the lands, owing to improvements of the soil and the many fine houses erected in the country, have nearly doubled in value. This ratio of improvement has been approximated or exceeded wherever in the South slaves are numerous. We have enough for the present, and no Malthusian★ spectres frightening us for the

---

George Fitzhugh, *Sociology for the South, or the Failure of Free Society* (Richmond, Va.: A. Morris, 1854), Appendix, 253–255.

★Reverend Thomas Malthus was a British economic philosopher who, in 1798, argued that there was a tendency in nature for populations to exceed their means of subsistence and resources, resulting in disease, famine, and other suffering.

future. Wealth is more equally distributed than at the North, where a few millionaires own most of the property of the country. (These millionaires are men of cold hearts and weak minds; they know how to make money, but not how to use it, either for the benefit of themselves or of others.) High intellectual and moral attainments, refinement of head and heart, give standing to a man in the South, however poor he may be. Money is, with few exceptions, the only thing that ennobles at the North. We have poor among us. But none who are overworked and under-fed. We do not crowd cities because lands are abundant and their owners kind, merciful and hospitable. The poor are as hospitable as the rich, the negro as the white man. Nobody dreams of turning a friend, a relative, or a stranger from his door. The very negro who deems it no crime to steal, would scorn to sell his hospitality. We have no loafers, because the poor relative or friend who borrows our horse, or spends a week under our roof, is a welcome guest. The loose economy, the wasteful mode of living at the South, is a blessing when rightly considered; it keeps want, scarcity and famine at a distance, because it leaves room for retrenchment. The nice, accurate economy of France, England and New England, keeps society always on the verge of famine, because it leaves no room to retrench, that is to live on a part only of what they now consume. Our society exhibits no appearance of precocity, no symptoms of decay. A long course of continuing improvement is in prospect before us, with no limits which human foresight can descry. Actual liberty and equality with our white population has been approached much nearer than in the free States. Few of our whites ever work as day laborers, none as cooks, scullions, ostlers, body servants, or in other menial capacities. One free citizen does not lord it over another; hence that feeling of independence and equality that distinguishes us; hence that pride of character, that self-respect, that give us ascendancy when we come in contact with Northerners. It is a distinction to be a Southerner, as it was once to be a Roman Citizen.

4. African American Josiah Henson Portrays the Violence and Fears in Slave Life, 1858

I was born June 15th, 1789, in Charles County, Maryland.... My mother was a slave of Dr. Josiah McPherson, but hired to the Mr. Newman to whom my father belonged. The only incident I can remember which occurred while my mother continued on Mr. Newman's farm, was the appearance one day of my father with his head bloody and his back lacerated. He was beside himself with mingled rage and suffering. The explanation I picked up from the conversation of others only partially explained the matter to my mind; but as I grew older I understood it all. It seemed the overseer had sent my mother away from the other field hands to a retired place, and after trying persuasion in vain, had resorted to force to accomplish a brutal purpose. Her screams aroused my father at his distant work, and running up, he found his wife struggling with the man.

Josiah Henson, *Uncle Tom's Story of His Life: An Autobiography of the Rev. Josiah Henson* (London: 1877).

Furious at the sight, he sprung upon him like a tiger. In a moment the overseer was down, and, mastered by rage, my father would have killed him but for the entreaties of my mother, and the overseer's own promise that nothing should be said of the matter. The promise was kept—like most promises of the cowardly and debased—as long as the danger lasted....

... The authorities were soon in pursuit of my father. The fact of the sacrilegious act of lifting a hand against the sacred temple of a white man's body ... this was all it was necessary to establish. And the penalty followed: one hundred lashes on the bare back, and to have the right ear nailed to the whipping-post, and then severed from the body....

The day for the execution of the penalty was appointed. The Negroes from the neighboring plantations were summoned, for their moral improvement, to witness the scene. A powerful blacksmith named Hewes laid on the stripes. Fifty were given, during which the cries of my father might be heard a mile, and then a pause ensued. True, he had struck a white man, but as valuable property he must not be damaged. Judicious men felt his pulse. Oh! he could stand the whole. Again and again the thong fell on his lacerated back. His cries grew fainter and fainter, till a feeble groan was the only response to his final blows. His head was then thrust against the post, and his right ear fastened to it with a tack; a swift pass of a knife, and the bleeding member was left sticking to the place. Then came a hurrah from the degraded crowd, and the exclamation, "That's what he's got for striking a white man." A few said, "it's a damned shame"; but the majority regarded it as but a proper tribute to their offended majesty....

... [F]rom this hour he became utterly changed. Sullen, morose, and dogged, nothing could be done with him. The milk of human kindness in his heart was turned to gall.... No fear or threats of being sold to the far south—the greatest of all terrors to the Maryland slave—would render him tractable. So off he was sent to Alabama. What was his fate neither my mother nor I have ever learned....

Our term of happy union as one family was now, alas! at an end. Mournful as was [Dr. McPherson's] death to his friends it was a far greater calamity to us. The estate and the slaves must be sold and the proceeds divided among the heirs. We were but property—not a mother, and the children God had given her.

Common as are slave-auctions in the southern states, and naturally as a slave may look forward to the time when he will be put upon the block, still the full misery of the event—of the scenes which precede and succeed it—is never understood till the actual experience comes. The first sad announcement that the sale is to be; the knowledge that all ties of the past are to be sundered; the frantic terror at the idea of being "sent south"; the almost certainty that one member of a family will be torn from another; the anxious scanning of purchasers' faces; the agony at parting, often forever, with husband, wife, child—these must be seen and felt to be fully understood. Young as I was then, the iron entered into my soul. The remembrance of breaking up of McPherson's estate is photographed in its minutest features in my mind. The crowd collected around the stand, the huddling group of Negroes, the examination of muscle, teeth, the exhibition of agility, the look of the auctioneer, the agony of my mother—I can shut my eyes and see them all.

My brothers and sisters were bid off first, and one by one, while my mother, paralyzed by grief, held me by the hand. Her turn came, and she was bought by Isaac Riley of Montgomery County. Then I was offered to the assembled purchasers. My mother, half distracted by the thought of parting forever from all her children, pushed through the crowd, while the bidding for me was going on, to the spot where Riley was standing. She fell at his feet and clung to his knees, entreating him in tones that a mother only could command, to buy her baby as well as herself, and spare to her one, at least of her little ones. Will it, can it be believed that this man, thus appealed to, was capable not merely of turning a deaf ear to her supplication, but of disengaging himself from her with such violent blows and kicks, as to reduce her to the necessity of creeping out of his reach, and mingling the groan of bodily suffering with the sob of a breaking heart? As she crawled away from the brutal man I heard her sob out, "Oh, Lord Jesus, how long, how long shall I suffer this way!" I must have been then between five and six years old. I seem to see and hear my poor weeping mother now. This was one of my earliest observations of men; an experience which I only shared with thousands of my race.

5. Southern Author Daniel Hundley Robinson Depicts the White Yeoman Farmer, 1860

And of all the hardy sons of toil, in all free lands the Yeomen are most deserving of our esteem. With hearts of oak and thews of steel, crouching to no man and fearing no danger, these are equally bold to handle a musket on the field of battle or to swing their reapers in times of peace among the waving stalks of yellow grain....

Know, then, that the Poor Whites of the South constitute a separate class to themselves; the Southern Yeomen are as distinct from them as the Southern Gentleman is from the Cotton Snob. Certainly the Southern Yeoman are nearly always poor, at least so for as this world's goods are to be taken into the account. As a general thing they own no slaves; and even in case they do, the wealthiest of them rarely possess more than from ten to fifteen. But even when they are slaveholders, they seem to exercise but few of the rights of ownership over their human chattels, making so little distinction between master and man, that their negroes invariably become spoiled, like so many rude children who have been unwisely spared the rod by the foolish guardians....

Again, should you go among the hardy yeomanry of Tennessee, Kentucky, or Missouri, whenever or wherever they own slaves (which in these States is not often the case) you will invariably see the negroes and their masters ploughing side by side in the fields; or bared to the waist, and with old-fashioned scythe [vying] with one another who can cut down the broadest swath of yellow

---

D. R. Hundley, Esq., *Social Relations in Our Southern States* (New York: Henry B. Price, 1860), 192–193, 197, 219.

wheat, or of the waving timothy; or bearing the tall stalks of maize and packing them into the stout-built barn, with ear and fodder on, ready for the winter's husking. And when the long winter evenings have come, you will see blacks and whites sing, and shout, and husk in company, to the music of Ole Virginny reels played on a greasy fiddle by some aged Uncle Edward....

[T]he Southern Yeomanry are almost unanimously pro-slavery in sentiment. Nor do we see how any honest, thoughtful person can reasonably find fault with them on this account. Only consider their circumstances, negrophilist of the North, and answer truthfully; were you so situated would you dare to advocate emancipation? Were you situated as the Southern Yeoman are—humble in worldly position, patient delvers in the soil, daily earning your bread by the toil-some sweat of your own brows—would you be pleased to see four millions of inferior blacks suddenly raised from a position of vassalage, and placed upon an equality with yourselves? made the sharers of your toil, the equals and associates of your wives and children? You know you would not. Despite your maudlin affectation of sympathy in behalf of the Negro, you are yet inwardly conscious that you heartily despise the sotty African, and that you deny to even the few living in your own midst an equality of rights and immunities with yourselves.

6. Harriet Jacobs Deplores Her Risks in Being a Female Slave, 1861

During the first years of my service in Dr. Flint's family, I was accustomed to share some indulgences with the children of my mistress. Though this seemed to me no more than right, I was grateful for it, and tried to merit the kindness by the faithful discharge of my duties. But I now entered on my fifteenth year— a sad epoch in the life of a slave girl. My master began to whisper foul words in my ear. Young as I was, I could not remain ignorant of their import. I tried to treat them with indifference or contempt. The master's age, my extreme youth, and the fear that his conduct would be reported to my grandmother, made him bear this treatment for many months. He was a crafty man, and resorted to many means to accomplish his purposes. Sometimes he had stormy, terrific ways, that made his victims tremble; sometimes he assumed a gentleness that he thought must surely subdue.... He peopled my young mind with unclean images, such as only a vile monster could think of. I turned from him with disgust and hatred. But he was my master. I was compelled to live under the same roof with him— where I saw a man forty years my senior daily violating the most sacred com-mandments of nature. He told me I was his property; that I must be subject to his will in all things.... No matter whether the slave girl be as black as ebony or as fair as her mistress. In either case, there is no shadow of law to protect her from insult, from violence, or even from death.... The mistress, who ought to protect the helpless victim, has no other feelings towards her but those of

Harriet Jacobs, *The Trials of Girlhood* (1861), as reprinted in *Our Nation's Archive*, ed. Erik Brunn and Jay Crosby (New York: Black Dog and Leventhal Publishers, 1999). 291–293.

jealousy and rage. The degradation, the wrongs, the vices that grow out of slavery, are more than I can describe. They are greater than you would willingly believe. Surely, if you credited one half the truths that are told you concerning the helpless millions suffering in this cruel bondage, you at the north would not help to tighten the yoke. You surely would refuse to do for the master, on your own soil, the mean and cruel work which trained bloodhounds and the lowest class of whites do for him at the south....

I once saw two beautiful children playing together. One was a fair white child; the other was her slave, and also her sister. When I saw them embracing each other, and heard their joyous laughter, I turned sadly away from the lovely sight. I foresaw the inevitable blight that would fall on the little slave's heart. I knew how soon her laughter would be changed to sighs. The fair child grew up to be a still fairer woman. From childhood to womanhood her pathway was blooming with flowers, and overarched by a sunny sky. Scarcely one day of her life had been clouded when the sun rose on her happy bridal morning.

How had those years dealt with her slave sister, the little playmate of her childhood? She, also, was very beautiful; but the flowers and sunshine of love were not for her. She drank the cup of sin, and shame, and misery, whereof her persecuted race are compelled to drink.

In view of these things, why are ye silent, ye free men and women of the north? Why do your tongues falter in maintenance of the right? Would that I had more ability! But my heart is so full, and my pen is so weak! There are noble men and women who plead for us, striving to help those who cannot help themselves. God bless them! God give them strength and courage to go on! God bless those, every where, who are laboring to advance the cause of humanity!

7. Southerner Mary Chestnut Describes Her Hatred of Slavery from a White Woman's View, 1861

I wonder if it be a sin to think slavery a curse to any land. Men and women are punished when their masters and mistresses are brutes, not when they do wrong. Under slavery, we live surrounded by prostitutes, yet an abandoned woman is sent out of any decent house. Who thinks any worse of a Negro or mulatto woman for being a thing we can't name? God forgive us, but ours is a monstrous system, a wrong and an iniquity! Like the patriarchs of old, our men live all in one house with their wives and their concubines; and the mulattoes one sees in every family partly resemble the white children. Any lady is ready to tell you who is the father of all the mulatto children in everybody's household but her own. Those, she seems to think, drop from the clouds. My disgust sometimes is boiling over. Thank God for my country women, but alas for the men! They are probably no worse than men everywhere, but the lower their mistresses, the more degraded they must be....

Mary Boykin Chestnut, *A Diary from Dixie* (1861), ed. Ben Ames Williams (Boston: Houghton Mifflin, 1949), 21–22, 122–123, 162.

I hate slavery. You say there are no more fallen women on a plantation than in London, in proportion to numbers; but what do you say to this? A magnate who runs a hideous black harem with its consequences under the same roof with his lovely white wife, and his beautiful and accomplished daughters? He holds his head as high and poses as the model of all human virtues to these poor women whom God and the laws have given him. From the height of his awful majesty, he scolds and thunders at them, as if he never did wrong in his life. Fancy such a man finding his daughter reading "Don Juan." "You with that immoral book!" And he orders her out of his sight. You see, Mrs. Stowe did not hit the sorest spot. She makes Legree a bachelor.

Someone said: "Oh, I know half a Legree [villain in *Uncle Tom's Cabin*], a man said to be as cruel as Legree. But the other half of him did not correspond. He was a man of polished manners, and the best husband and father and church member in the world." "Can that be so?" "Yes, I know it. And I knew the dissolute half of Legree. He was high and mighty, but the kindest creature to his slaves; and the unfortunate results of his bad ways were not sold. They had not to jump over ice blocks. They were kept in full view, and were provided for, handsomely, in his will. His wife and daughters, in their purity and innocence, are supposed never to dream of what is as plain before their eyes as the sunlight. And they play their parts of unsuspecting angels to the letter. They profess to adore their father as the model of all earthly goodness."

"Well, yes. If he is rich, he is the fountain from whence all [blessings] flow."

"The one I have in my eye, my half of Legree, the dissolute half, was so furious in his temper, and so thundered his wrath at the poor women that they were glad to let him do as he pleased if they could only escape his everlasting fault-finding and noisy bluster.".…

"… The make-believe angels were of the last century.… Women were brought up not to judge their fathers or their husbands. They took them as the Lord provided, and were thankful.".…

"You wander from the question I asked. Are Southern men worse because of the slave system, and the facile black women?"

"Not a bit! They see too much of them. The barroom people don't drink, the confectionary people loathe candy. Our men are sick of the black sight of them!" …

Martha Adamson is a beautiful mulattress, as good looking as they ever are to me. I have never seen a mule as handsome as a horse, and I know I never will; no matter how I lament and sympathize with its undeserved mule condition. She is a trained sempstress, and "hired her own time, as they call it; that is, the owner pays doctor's bills, finds food and clothing, and the slave pays his master five dollars a month, more or less, and makes a dollar a day if he pleases. Martha, to the amazement of everybody, married a coal-black Negro, the son of Dick the Barber, who was set free fifty years ago for faithful services rendered Mr. Chestnut's grandfather. She was asked: How could she? She is so nearly white. How could she marry that horrid Negro? It is positively shocking! She answered that she inherits the taste of her white father, that her mother was black.

8. Northerner Frederick Law Olmsted Depicts the Economic Costs of Slavery, 1861

One of the grand errors out of which this rebellion has grown came from supposing that whatever nourishes wealth and gives power to an ordinary civilized community must command as much for a slaveholding community. The truth has been overlooked that the accumulation of wealth and the power of a nation are contingent not merely upon the primary value of the surplus of productions of which it has to dispose, but very largely also upon the way in which the income from its surplus is distributed and reinvested. Let a man be absent from almost any part of the North twenty years, and he is struck, on his return, by what we call the "improvements" which have been made: better buildings, churches, schoolhouses, mills, railroads, etc. In New York city alone, for instance, at least two hundred millions of dollars have been reinvested merely in an improved housing of the people; in labour-saving machinery, waterworks, gasworks, etc., and much more. It is not difficult to see where the profits of our manufacturers and merchants are. Again, go into the country, and there is no end of substantial proof of twenty years of agricultural prosperity, not alone in roads, canals, bridges, dwellings, barns and fences, but in books and furniture, and gardens, and pictures, and in the better dress and evidently higher education of the people. But where will the returning traveller see the accumulated cotton profits of twenty years in Mississippi? Ask the cotton-planter for them, and he will point in reply, not to dwellings, libraries, churches, schoolhouses, mills, railroads, or anything of the kind; he will point to his negroes—to almost nothing else. Negroes such as stood for five hundred dollars once, now represent a thousand dollars. We must look then in Virginia and those Northern Slave States which have the monopoly of supplying negroes for the real wealth which the sale of cotton has brought to the South. But where is the evidence of it? where anything to compare with the evidence of accumulated profits to be seen in any Free State? If certain portions of Virginia have been a little improving, others unquestionably have been deteriorating, growing shabbier, more comfortless, less convenient. The total increase in wealth of the population during the last twenty years shows for almost nothing. One year's improvements of a Free State exceed it all.

It is obvious that to the community at large, even in Virginia, the profits of supplying negroes to meet the wants occasioned by the cotton demand have not compensated for the bar which the high cost of all sorts of human service, which the cotton demand has also occasioned, has placed upon all other means of accumulating wealth; and this disadvantage of the cotton monopoly is fully experienced by the negro-breeders themselves, in respect to everything else they have to produce or obtain.

Frederick Law Olmsted, *The Cotton Kingdom: A Traveler's Observations on Cotton and Slavery in the American Slave States,* I (New York: Mason Brothers, 1861), 24–26.

9. Three Slave Songs Recorded by Whites, 1867

"GIVE UP THE WORLD."

De sun give a light in de heaven all round,
De sun give a light in de heaven all round,
De sun give a light in de heaven all round,
Why don't you give up de world?
My brud-der don't you give up de world?
My brud - der, don't you give up de world?
My brud - der, don't you give up de world?
We must leave de world be - hind.

"MANY THOUSAND GO."

"No more peck o' corn for me,

No more, no more,-

No more peck o' corn for me,

Many tousand go.

"No more driver's lash for me, (*Twice.*)

No more, &c.

"No more pint o' salt for me, (*Twice.*)

No more, &c.

"No more hundred lash for me, (*Twice.*)

No more, &c.

"No more mistress' call for me,

No more, No more,-

No more mistress' call for me,

Many tousand go."

"I WANT TO GO HOME."

"Dere's no rain to wet you,

O, yes, I want to go home.

Dere's no sun to burn you,

O, yes, I want to go home;

O, push along, believers,

O, yes, &c.

Dere's no hard trials,

O, yes, &c.

Slave Songs of the United States (1867).

Dere's no whips a-crackin',

O, yes, &c.

My brudder on de wayside,

O, yes, &c.

O, push along, my brudder,

O, yes, &c.

Where dere's no stormy weather,

O, yes, &c.

Dere's no tribulation,

O, yes, &c."

 # ESSAYS

The contradictions of a world of slaves and slaveholders in a nation that prided itself on individual freedom and rights have long occupied historians. Scholars have considered how white slaveholders reconciled their commitments to liberty with their commitments to slavery. Moreover, scholars have examined how slaves used these contradictions to carve out greater power in what by all accounts was a brutal institution. The two essays in this chapter illustrate how historians have stressed the incongruities of freedom and slavery. Walter Johnson, a historian at Harvard University, focuses on the slave trade, which laid bare the horrors of slavery. If slaveholders could argue that life as a slave was eased by a master-slave paternalism, they found it much more difficult to explain away the commodification of people that were bought and sold. In the slave trade, slavery was clearly a business of buying and selling goods. Anthony Kaye, who teaches history at Penn State University, focuses not on the mobility of slaves as emblematic of the Old South, but on the neighborhoods and families created and imagined by African Americans. Kaye shows how slaves created space in their worlds in terms of neighborhoods, intimate relationships, and struggle. Whereas Johnson finds mobility and capitalism at the core of southern slaveholding, Kaye finds neighborhoods and family life at the core of slaves' lives.

Slaves and the "Commerce" of the Slave Trade

WALTER JOHNSON

The history of the antebellum South was made (and occasionally unmade) in the slaves pens. There, through the black arts of the trade, people were turned into products and sold at a price; there, human bodies were stripped, examined, and

Reprinted by permission at the publisher from *Soul by Soul: Life Inside the Antebellum Slave Market* by Walter Johnson, pp. 214–220, Cambridge, Mass.: Harvard University Press, Copyright © 1999 by the President and Fellows of Harvard College.

assigned meaning according to the brutal anatomy lessons of slaveholding ideology; there, slaveholders daily gambled their own fantasies of freedom on the behavior of the people whom they could never fully commodify; there, enslaved people fashioned communities and identities that enabled them to survive one of the most brutal forcible dislocations of human history; and there, sometimes, slaves were able to shape a sale to suit themselves. In the slave market, slaveholders and slaves were fused into an unstable mutuality which made it hard to tell where one's history ended and the others began. Every slave had a price, and slaves' communities, their families, and their own bodies were suffused with the threat of sale, whether they were in the pens or not. And every slaveholder lived through the stolen body of a slave.

In the half century before the Civil War, the back-and-forth bargaining of slaveholder and slave was repeated two million times in a pattern that traced the outline of southern history. Central to this history was the role played by the interstate trade in the transformation of the South from a declining tobacco economy stretched along the eastern seaboard to a thriving cotton economy that reached westward as far as Texas. Right behind the soldiers and squatters who, during the first quarter of the nineteenth century, began to drive the Indian inhabitants of the lower South into the arid plains of the West came the slave traders and the coffles of people who, through their labor and reproduction, transformed those rich and emptied lands into "The Cotton Kingdom" in the century's second quarter. Of the million or so slaves who moved southwest and transformed the depopulated forests of the deep South into the richest staple-producing region of the world, two thirds were carried there by slave traders.

The transformation of the slaveholders' economy brought with it a transformation of the lives of the slaves upon whom it depended. Most important were the separations. The trade decimated the slave communities of the upper South through waves of exportation determined by slaveholders' shifting demand—first men, then women, and finally children became featured categories of trade. As they were driven south and west by the people they called "soul drivers," those slaves carried with them the cultural forms—the songs, the stories, the family names, and the religion—out of which they forged the commonalities that supported their daily struggle against slavery. By the time of the Civil War, southern slaves had a common culture that stretched from Maryland to Texas, a spirited mirror-image of the pattern traced by the trade in their bodies. Indeed, as war broke out, settled communities and rebuilt families were beginning to emerge at the trade's southern outlet.

Even as it transformed the geography of both white and black life in the South, the criss-crossed pattern of the slave trade knit the political economy of slavery into a cohesive whole. Long after intensive tobacco farming had eroded the fertility and profitability of the slave-cultivated fields of the Chesapeake, the slave trade enabled Virginia and Maryland planters to retain their ties to the political economy of slavery. As much as anything else in the years leading up to the Civil War, the planters of the Chesapeake were slave farmers who held onto their wealth and status by supplying the cotton boom with the offspring of slaves idled by the decline of tobacco. Even as the political economy of slavery moved south and west, the slave trade bound the diverging fortunes of the emerging regions of the South into mutual benefit. Indeed, in the 1850s, when for a time it seemed that the upper South was being overtaken by a renewed tobacco boom, the trade began to flow northward as well as southward.

As important as the trade was in the spatial expansion of slavery, the slave trade also played a crucial role in the reproduction of the slaveholding regime over time. Even when the prosperous slaveholders of the antebellum South did not produce their legacies through the direct purchase of slaves for their heirs, they relied upon that market to provide the standard of comparison (the dollar values) according to which they divided their estates. The everyday role of the slave market in the reproduction of the southern social order, however, was far less abstract than that: it was in the slave market that the rising men of the ante-bellum South built the stakes that had been provided them by their forebears into legacies of their own. And it was in the slave market that the political economy of slavery daily deepened the roots of its own support among southern whites as nonslaveholders were turned into slaveholders. Indeed, as they faced the sectional conflict that threatened to end history as they knew it, southern politicians consid-ered radical measures to insure that non-slaveholders would support the regime of slavery into the future. In the same series of conventions that led to secession and in the same journals and newspapers that carried news of the rising political conflict to the white citizens of the South, slaveholding politicians considered reopening the African slave trade in order to lower the price of slaves and increase the pro-portion of slaveholders within the population. "That minute you put it out of the power of common farmers to purchase a Negro man or woman to help him in his farm or his wife in the house," wrote one Louisiana editor in support of reopening the African trade, "you make him an abolitionist at once." The future of slavery, the editor argued, could be bought in the slave market.

That future, it became increasingly apparent, would come to pass (or not) in the West. Over the course of the antebellum period, the incendiary value of cotton, the wayward dreams of migrating slaveholders, and the ruthless efficiency of the slave trade had pushed slavery to the outer limits of "the South." First in Missouri, then in Texas, and finally in Kansas and Nebraska, political conflict over slavery was increasingly defined by the question of how far west it would be allowed to spread. With every slave sold from the declining eastern seaboard to slavery's expanding western frontier, the South pushed the nation a step closer to its ultimate showdown over slavery. And, once again, it was perhaps less an irony of history than an axiom of historical process that the sharpest critics of "the Slave Power," the abolitionist critics of slavery who would provide their own push toward Civil War, armed themselves with arguments that had been pro-duced along the leading edge of slavery's expansion.

For all of the smoothing over and covering up that characterized their daily activities, the slave pens provided a remarkably clear exposition of the nature of slavery—a person with a price. There were of course, other available definitions, other answers to the question "What is slavery?" answers that emphasized pro-duction or paternalism or politics or violence, And there were other places to go to see slavery: plantations where the slave mode of production was visible in the fields; white churches and universities across the South where the spiritual and moral benefits of slavery were floridly proclaimed; northern and European cotton-finishing factories where the full reach of "the slave economy" was daily evident; the halls of Congress where the influence of the "Slave Power" was tallied in a series of compromises between "North" and "South" which outlined the political history of the antebellum period. Increasingly, however, and with revolutionary effect, opponents of slavery argued that slavery was best seen in the slave market.

It had not always been so. The central document of early abolitionism, Theodore Dwight Weld's *American Slavery As It Is* (1839), had very little to say about the slave market. It was, instead, a catalog of bodily tortures. Drawing upon southern newspapers and runaway advertisements which sought to identify escaped slaves by their mortifying injuries, Weld was able to draw back the veil that protected "the peculiar institution" from critical eyes. Slavery for Weld was a system of unchecked brutality, made grotesquely visible on the suffering bodies of the slaves. Even today, in an age inured to violence by movie-made brutality, *American Slavery As It Is* is hard to read. And yet nineteenth-century slaveholders were quick to develop an answer to this critique of slavery's inhumane brutality. The maimings and the rapes were isolated episodes, they argued, and they set about publicizing the "paternalist" reforms that would restore to the system of slavery its good name. They broke the system of slavery into hundreds of thousands of isolated sets of human relations between individual masters and individual slaves and argued that the violence of slavery was a matter of generally benevolent human relations gone awry, of the personal failings of particular owners, of bad masters who gave slavery a bad name, not an inevitable feature of the system itself.

Thinking about the slave trade, however, made possible an entirely different account of the relation between master and slave J. W. C. Pennington described his motivation for writing his narrative of slavery this way: "My feelings are always outraged when I hear them speak of 'kind masters,' 'Christian masters,' 'the mildest form of slavery,' 'well fed and well clothed slaves' as extenuations of slavery." Pennington did not deny that such things existed, hut he thought that they were misleading forms taken by a more fundamental relation: "The being of slavery, its soul and its body, lives and moves in the chattel principle, the property principle, the bill of sale principle; the cart-whip, starvation, and nakedness, are its inevitable consequences," he wrote. Sale from a good master to a bad one, from the "mildest form of slavery" to the "worst of which the system is possible," from the "favorable circumstances" of slavery in Maryland, Virginia, and Kentucky to the killing fields of Alabama, Mississippi, and Louisiana was, in Pennington's formulation, "the legitimate working of the great chattel principle." "It is no accidental result," he continued, "it is the fruit of the tree. You cannot constitute slavery without the chattel principle—and with the chattel principle you cannot save it from these results. Talk not about kind and Christian masters. They are not masters of the system. The system is master of them." Through an outline of the philosophy and practice of the slave trade, Pennington was able to convey the complicity of all slaveholders (no matter their individual merits) in the most brutal results of the system of slavery.

Through his exegesis of "the chattel principle" Pennington placed the slave trade at the center of the abolitionist critique of slavery; other former slaves accomplished the same thing through telling the stories of their own experiences in the trade. Charles Ball, William Wells Brown, Solomon Northup, and John Brown all included lengthy discussion of the slave trade in their published narratives. Lewis Clarke (along with William Wells Brown) lectured extensively about the trade. Henry Bibb concluded his narrative with a list of his owners and the prices they had paid for him: "In 1836 'Bro.' Albert Sibley of Bedford, Kentucky, sold me for $850 to 'Bro.' John Sibley, and in the same year he sold me to 'Bro.' William Gatewood of Bedford, for $850. In 1839 'Bro.' Gatewood sold me to Madison Garrison, a slave trader of Louisville, Kentucky, with my wife and child—at a depreciated price because I was a run away. In the same year he sold me with my family to 'Bro.' Whitfield, in the city of New Orleans, for $120. In 1841 'Bro.' Whitfield sold me from my family to Thomas Wilson and Co., black-legs. In the same year they sold me to a 'Bro.' in the Indian Territory. I think he was a member of the Presbyterian Church." Like Henry Bibb, who outlined his own history of slavery with a series of sales sealed between supposedly Christian slaveholders, these survivors put the slave trade at the center of their account of what slavery was and what was wrong with it.

Join to their efforts those of white abolitionists like William Lloyd Garrison, who emblazoned the masthead of *The Liberator* with an engraving of an auction stand labeled with the sign "Slaves, Horses, and other Cattle to be sold at 12 O' Clock," of traveling observers like Fredrika Bremer, Charles Weld, and Frederick Law Olmsted, who went to the slave market rather than the cotton field or legislative chamber when they wanted to see "slavery," and, finally of Harriet Beecher Stowe, who, taking a page from Pennington, articulated the connection between the kindly but ineffectual Kentucky slaveholder Mr. Shelby—"a man of humanity" she called him—and Louisiana's brutal Simon Legree by putting the family-separating trade plied by the heartless "slave driver" Haley at the center of *Uncle Tom's Cabin*. Carried north by the escapees, the indigenous antislavery of the enslaved South—the ideology of "the chattel principle" as it was represented in slaves' stories and songs about the trade—was reworked into a central element of the northern abolitionist critique of slavery.

The crude spectacle that was daily on view in the slave pen—human body publicly stripped, examined, priced, and sold—thus became an image that stood for the whole of slavery. The daily process of the trade provided a template through which opponents of slavery could establish the connections between the upper South and the Lower, between kind masters and brutal ones, between slaveholders' loose talk about their affection for their slaves and the unmistakable material reality of a person with a price. By thinking their way through the slave trade, critics of slavery like Pennington could articulate the links that joined individual slaveholders to the broader system and argue that the essence of slavery lay in the worst of its abuses rather than the rosiest of its promises. The daily process of the slave pens created a type of knowledge about the nature of slavery that was indispensable to its critics—the information necessary to dismantle the proslavery argument was produced along the leading edge of slavery's history.

That history ended in 1865. The slave pens themselves were boarded up and closed for a time—all signboards advertising slaves for sale in Union-held New Orleans were taken down on January 1 of 1864—and the pens were later sold. They became boarding houses and cotton brokerages; on the site of one of the largest there is now a bank. Through those gates had passed the people who made the history of the antebellum South—the traders who had outlined that history with their market time and speculative maps, the buyers who had filled in the traders' outline with the fantasies through which slaveholders made sense of the world, and the slaves themselves, in whose fallible bodies and resistant wills the history of the antebellum South had finally been made material.

And when slavery was over and the slave market was closed, former slaves and slaveholders alike found themselves marooned on a shoal of history. The longings of slaveholders to hold onto the past as it receded from their grasp are well-documented: their reactionary paternalism, their lost-cause, politics of nostalgia, and the coercive labor discipline they began to enforce through the state. Well-known, too, is the disbelief they experienced, the sense of betrayal they talked about, when their slaves left them behind. For many former slaves, it was likewise too late to go back—not to slavery or the slave market hut to the places and families they had been forced to leave behind. They faced a future that was at first defined only by what it was not: in the words of the freedom song "Many Thousands Gone," "No more auction block for me, no more driver's lash for me, no more peck of corn for me, no more mistress call for me." Some placed newspaper advertisements for lost family members and took to the roads in an effort to travel backwards in time to the families, friends, and places they had known before the trade. Others stayed where they were, seizing the first chance that many of them had ever had to make their marriages legal and to make up their own minds about the relationship of their households to the wider markets for labor and goods. Still others pushed on in search of a brighter future—first toward southern cities and later westward and northward in search of freedom. In 1865, their history began again.

The Neighborhoods and Intimate Lives of Slaves

ANTHONY E. KAYE

John Wade, a slave on the Terry plantation in Jefferson County, Mississippi, could claim many friends in his vicinity. Wade knew Aaron Barefield and his people on Poplar Hill well enough to take note when Barefield's son went to Natchez during the Civil War in the wake of a Union raid into the hinterland. And Barefield the younger knew his father's friend well enough to brighten at the mention of Wade's name years later: "I knew John Wade during the war and know him yet, too; in fact I knew him before the war; we lived on joining places." Wade also had other contacts on Polar Hill. "I have known Harriet Pierce all my life," he recalled; "we lived in the same neighborhood."

From Anthony E. Kaye, *Joining Places: Slave Neighborhoods in the Old South* (University of North Carolina Press, 2007), p. 2–6, 51–53, 77, 79, 81–82. Copyright © 2007 by the University of North Carolina Press. Reprinted by permission of the publisher.

"Neighborhood," this seemingly prosaic term, opens a window with a panoramic view of antebellum slave society.

Slave neighborhoods cut across Jefferson County, up and down the Natchez District in Mississippi, and throughout the South. They prevailed from the Chesapeake to the trans-Mississippi West and virtually everywhere in between in the Upper South and the Old Southwest. This is where Frederick Douglass grew up, Nat Turner launched his inspired revolt, men and women struggled in obscurity all their days. In some locales, neighborhoods marked the field of discipline or the terrain of marriage and family life, the dominion where a coterie of old folks held sway. In others, this was the circuit worked by slave preachers, where seekers repaired to their praying grounds and convened for religious meetings. In some precincts, neighborhoods were the quarters of every kind of fraternizing. The geography of kinship, work, sociability, and struggle overlapped with neighborhoods in different ways in different regions. Neighborhoods might encompass some of these social relations or all of them and more. Everywhere neighborhoods covered different geographic areas. In short, they were pervasive but not uniform. Neighborhoods in the Natchez District, then, were similar but not identical to those migrants had left in the Upper South....

Planters began turning this fertile soil during the eighteenth century, when the region was still a modest prize traded in diplomatic settlements among the French, English, and Spanish, who named it the Natchez District. Southwest Mississippi was an anchor in the Jeffersonian vision of a commercial farming republic during the 1790s. The Louisiana Purchase finally guaranteed American sovereignty over the length of the Mississippi and an outlet for exports from the cotton frontier. By then, Congress had already decided the slaves in the district would be mostly American born. The act organizing the Mississippi Territory in 1798 prohibited importing slaves from Africa or anywhere else abroad and authorized slaveholders to bring their chattels from anywhere in the United States. Many of those slaves had come from Africa by the trans-Atlantic trade before undertaking their second middle passage to Mississippi. Even after the United States dropped out of the international slave trade, Americans smuggled an untold number of Africans into the Deep South, Mississippi included.

Slaves were essential to local planters' hopes for the region. One coterie declared in a petition to Congress that without slavery, their farms would be merely "waste land." From their vantage point, the district still extended beyond the territory to include lands along the west bank of the Mississippi. The district also persisted as a regional identity among the planters, many of whom presided over plantations in Louisiana or Mississippi from a town seat in Natchez. By the time Mississippi joined the Union in 1817, settlers had already organized the district into five counties: Wilkinson, Adams, Jefferson, Claiborne, and Warren.

Here slaves carved out neighborhoods in one of the most princely domains in the Cotton Kingdom. Many arrived from the Upper South in a forced march accompanying owners, and most had been acquired via the slave trade. Throughout the antebellum period, most slaves were only a generation or two removed from the Upper South. Slaves outnumbered the rest of the population by a ratio of two to one in 1830 and three to one at the end of the antebellum period. By 1840, the Natchez District also included the three Mississippi counties that produced the most cotton in the state, which was now ensconsed among the first rank of the United States producing the staple. Wear and tear from all these strivings was already starting to show on the land, most dramatically where the soil collapsed into deep ravines. The district was home to only two of the state's five most productive counties in 1849, none ten years later. Yet these planters still had few peers for riches. Wilkinson, Jefferson, and Claiborne numbered among the dozen wealthiest counties in the country in 1860. The size of slave-holdings in the district though smaller than those in the Louisiana sugar country and the rice kingdom in the low country, were three times those of the South as a whole, on a par with the South Carolina Sea Islands.

In the Natchez District, slaves defined neighborhoods precisely, as adjoining plantations, because this was the domain of all the bonds that constituted their daily routine. Slaves worked and went visiting on adjoining plantations and attended dances, Christmas celebrations, and other big times there—weddings, religious services, and prayer meetings, too. Slaves courted, married, and formed families across plantation lines. Here slaves told their stories, conversed, gossiped, conspired, and collected intelligence about intimate relations, parties, and other affairs; about the staple, the livestock, and other goods; about newcomers to the neighborhood, drivers, overseers, and brutal owners; about harsh words, whippings, and other run-ins. Adjoining plantations were also where slaves lay out, purloined food, and otherwise contended with the powers that be. Neighborhoods encompassed the bonds of kinship, the practice of Christianity, the geography of sociability, the field of labor and discipline, the grounds of solidarity, the terrain of struggle. For slaves, neighborhoods served as the locus of all the bonds that shaped the contours of their society.

Neighborhoods were dynamic places. To endure, they could not be otherwise. Making places is always a process. Making places under the exactions of slavery and slave trading, which enabled owners to unmake neighborhood ties as readily as slaves make them, was a perpetual struggle. Slaves were continually sent out of the Natchez District after their forced migration from the Upper South. They were sold as punishment, mortgaged for debt, bequeathed to heirs, and pressed into caravans by owners migrating to distant parts along the rolling southern frontier. The planters' exchanges of human property reproduced the plantation household across generations, further into the Deep South, and created a steady traffic in and out of slave neighborhoods in the district. Slaves were forever giving up their neighbors and incorporating folks new to the place. This is not to say that individual people could be replaced exactly; rather, the social relations they had forged, broken by their departure, had to carry on. Men and women still had to keep up all the ties—intimate relations, work, trade, struggles, links to adjoining plantations—that bound neighborhoods together. Slave neighborhoods were in a constant state of making, remaking, and becoming....

Slaveholders were inextricable figures in slave neighborhoods. The planters had their own neighborhoods, too, bigger than those of the slaves. From the slaves' standpoint, their neighborhood was enclosed within the slaveholders' neighborhood and surrounded by it. Slaves in the Natchez District and/elsewhere in the

South mounted fewer revolts than their peers elsewhere in the Americas not because they loved master more but because they knew where power was located.

What is most remarkable about neighborhoods is not how little slaves achieved in struggle on these grounds but how much. They used the neighborhood to monitor intimate relations and gain recognition for permanent unions between men and women unrecognized by law. The slaves established the neighborhood as a field where runaways could find respite from increasingly exacting regimes of labor and discipline. The slaves' critical achievement, though, was the neighborhood itself. Despite planters' attempts to control mobility–by the whip, the law, the slave patrol, and the pass system–slaves forged enduring bonds to adjoining plantations. Men and women multiplied the possibilities of courtship, worship, amusement, struggle, and collective identity, of love, faith, pleasure, and solidarity; extended networks of kinfolk, friends, collaborators, and Christians; gave permanence to their neighborhoods by creating and recreating the bonds that held them together, even as slaveholders constantly sold people in and out of the place. By pressing social ties across plantation lines, in short, slaves attenuated the power relations of slavery and cleared some ground for themselves to stand on....

Mary Ann Helam was a reluctant bride, perhaps because she had endured a great many separations in her day. There were her parents and her daughter away off in Kentucky, and she had already lost two husbands. She buried one and was sold away from Robert Helam but kept his name anyhow. Now in 1845, her owner, Latham Brown, was asking her to marry William Madison. She refused, but Brown would not take no for an answer. "I was told to marry this man by my master," Helam recalled. "I got 50 lashes on my back to make me marry him," And so a pledge exacted at the whipping post was taken as a vow at Belle Grove Church, "a colored peoples church."

At the wedding, the bride, the groom, and their neighbors somehow made a start at consecrating the marriage, despite its unlovely beginnings. Among the slaves in attendance were two from the Brown place. The rest, she noted, were slaves "in the neighborhood." Over twenty years, Helam and Madison turned a forced concubinage into an enduring marriage, even if she maintained a certain distance and marked it by keeping the surname Helam. Her old friend, Rose Ballard, married at Belle Grove that day, too, and Helam and Madison named their first child a year later after Ballard's husband, Sidney. The boy died at just one month, but their two other children, Eli and his younger sister, Elizabeth, survived to adulthood. The baths Helam gave Madison were less a romantic interlude than a wifely service. "I done it to Keep him clean when he would come in from the field tired hot and dusty," she explained. Yet there was a touching intimacy to this chore as well, and she "washed him all *over many* times." When he enlisted in the Union army in 1863, he bought her some lumber, and she built a house in Natchez, where his regiment camped for a time. Madison returned to her from Vicksburg in May 1866, his face "hollow and sunken," with a feeling that told him he was "sick in his heart." He was only skin and bones: "He asked me to wash him. I washed him all over, and the next day he died."

Intimate relations were fraught with tension for slaves because the weight of mastery bore heavily on even the most personal bonds. In the absence of legal recognition for spouses, forever subject to separation and vulnerable to the sexual predations of owners and their agents, men and women sought order for their attachments by contriving a structure of intimate relations. Comprising that structure was a set of understandings about different types of conjugal relationships—how they were created, what a couple could expect of each other, and how these unions related to one another.

In the Natchez District, slaves made fine distinctions between "sweethearting," "taking up," "living together," and marriage. Sweethearting—neither permanent, nor monogamous, nor subject to the neighborhood's sanction—was an open-ended relationship for the young. Taking up was temporary, too, but was for mature couples prepared to submit to neighbors' informal recognition. Living together, by contrast, was a permanent bond, perhaps the most familiar to modern eyes, and entitled men and women to share a surname as well as a cabin. Marriage was permanent as well, yet distinguished from cohabitation by the formal recognition of weddings. The boundary between living together and marriage, slaves believed, was essential to the integrity of the bond between husband and wife. Rights and duties did not set unions apart. Sweethearting and taking up overlapped from that standpoint. So did living together and marriage. What distinguished them was how slaves and owners sanctioned these unions. The endless task of creating and re-creating this structure, of articulating its rules and enforcing them as norms, was a neighborhood undertaking. As neighbors fastened bonds between men and women, they clinched the most binding ties in the neighborhood....

Slaves fashioned the structure of intimate relations as they came to terms with the conflicting desires of men and women as well as the capricious interventions of owners. Planters as well as their drivers and overseers forced themselves sexually on bondwomen. Slaves knew all too well that no couple was master of their own fate when owners had the power to sell, bequeath, or hire out either party as an exercise in discipline, as a bequest to children upon marriage, to settle a debt, or to divide an estate among heirs. Some measure of the toll these transactions exacted can be reckoned from Union army registers of marriages performed in 1864 and 1865 at Natchez, Vicksburg, and Davis Bend. Among 3,846 men and women reporting previous spouses, nearly one of every six aged twenty or over reported a forced separation by an owner. The likelihood of separation increased over time. More than a third of all couples with one partner at least years old had come through at least one broken union— one in five women thirty years old and over, one in four men....

Indeed, no tie bound the neighborhoods of southwestern Mississippi more tightly than marriage. After the wedding, often a neighborhood event, the husband became a fixture over at his wife's quarters. The proximity of adjoining plantations facilitated more frequent visiting than was possible in an "abroad marriage," which typically permitted couples to spend weekends together. In the Natchez District, some married men had a standing pass to spend one night during the week, usually Wednesdays, as well as Saturdays and Sundays with their families. Edward Hicks beat the path every day between his cabin on Oak Ridge and his wife's, only three-quarters of a mile off on the adjoining Grant place. The relationship between spouses naturally created other bonds of kinship that crossed plantation lines. Henry Hunt, who was sold from Virginia to Warren County in his early teens during the mid-1830s, got around as a teamster but married a woman in his neighborhood in 1848. She already had a son, Jefferson, who was nine years old by then. Marriage thus made Hunt both a stepfather and a husband. As husbands and wives became mothers and fathers, they begat new connections in the neighborhood—among generations, among families, among kin of all kinds.

Men shouldered many burdens to bring together spouses and neighborhoods. The mandatory negotiations with owners, for example, were conducted by the groom. When it came time to request permission to live together or marry, he was obliged to do the asking. If a couple belonged to different owners, he talked to her white people as well. This diplomacy was no easy task. Couples had a lot riding on his words, and testy slaveholders could get unpleasant even about the best intentions. Henry Lewis's owners cast aspersions on his request to marry Tishne Price, although they eventually agreed. When "my husband asked my old master for me," she recalled, Lewis was dismissed as a neophyte. "You have only been here four years, and you want to marry your mistress' body servant." Lewis, who had nerve but not the cheek his owner implied, stood his ground. "Well, she loves me and I love her," he responded. Price was not spared the abuse, but it seemed to take her by surprise, particularly when master asked whether Lewis was the best she could do. "I might do worser," she ventured....

No one confounded the order slaves tried to impose on conjugal unions more than planter men. The ravages of the planters were too numerous to catalog. They turned a blind eye on drivers and overseers who had their way with slave women. They raped their people, seduced them, and imposed on them with a combination of force and cajolery that defies latter-day distinctions between consensual sex and sexual coercion. Some slaveholders were deterred by a husband's presence. Mary Ann Holmes had a husband belonging to another owner at the time she bore her daughter, Eliza, by Austin Williams. But neither the bond between spouses nor the proximity of husbands accorded much protection to women belonging to planters of Gabriel Shield's ilk. He gave his consent for two house servants, Eveline and James Perano, to live together but had her sleep in the big house. For Shields, the arrangement conveniently kept his nurse close by his children and preserved his own easy access to her for nearly a decade. Eveline Perano bore one child by Shields while she had two with her husband. Then in the late 1850s, Shields sent him to another plantation in Louisiana and broke up the Peranos' tenuous union for good....

Slaves made their structure of intimate relations prevail in many ways, all of which constituted victories, moral and practical, of a high order. This structure hissed and sputtered with contradictions, to be sure, and breaches opened up in the quarters. Drivers placed themselves outside it, and some unions were not incorporated into it. Nowhere in the Americas did slaves entirely protect conjugal life from the trespasses of owners and their agents, and the Natchez District was no exception. Slaves did not even have a tenable means of calling owners to account for the worst outrages. That slaves managed to give any structure at all to unions between men and women, considering the powers that bore down on them, was no mean feat. That they imposed this order, imperfect as it was, on their owners was an ingenious work of social engineering. That they obtained owners' cooperation was the most difficult maneuver of all, tactic slaves used to good effect in other struggles as well. Slaves achieved all of these ends by making the most personal bonds profoundly social. A wedding only gave formal, full-blown expression to the regulating of intimate relations that took place in every neighborhood. Sweethearting, taking up, living together, and marriage dispersed affinities throughout the neighborhood and grounded them there.

FURTHER READING

Ira Berlin, *Slaves Without Masters: The Free Negro in the Antebellum South* (1974).

Erskine Clarke, *Dwelling Place: A Plantation Epic* (2005).

Catherine Clinton, *The Plantation Mistress: Woman's World in the Old South* (1982).

Richard Follett, *The Sugar Masters: Planter's and Slaves in Louisiana's Cane World, 1820–1860* (2007).

Elizabeth Fox-Genovese, *Within the Plantation Household: Black and White Women of the Old South* (1988).

Elizabeth Fox-Genovese and Eugene Genovese, *The Mind of the Master Class* (2005).

Michael A. Gomez, *Exchanging our Country Marks: The Transformation of African Identities in the Colonial and Antebellum South* (1998).

Herbert G. Gutman, *The Black Family in Slavery and Freedom, 1750–1925* (1976).

James Oliver Horton and Lois E. Horton, *Slavery and the Making of America* (2004).

Charles F. Irons, *The Origins of Proslavery Christianity: White and Black Evangelicals in Colonial and Antebellum Virginia* (2008).

Suzanne Lebsock, *The Free Women of Petersburg: Status and Culture in a Southern Town, 1784–1810* (1984).

Stephanie McCurry, *Masters of Small Worlds: Yeoman Households, Gender Relations, and the Political Culture of the Antebellum South Carolina Low Country* (1995).

Michael O'Brien, *Conjectures of Order: intellectual Life and the American South* (2003).

Albert J. Raboteau, *Slave Religion: The "Invisible Institution" in the Antebellum South* (2004).

Brenda E. Stevenson, *Life in Black and White: Family and Community in the Slave South* (1997).

Gavin Wright, *The Political Economy of the Cotton South* (1978).

CHAPTER 13

Careening Toward Civil War

For many Americans, the signing of the Treaty of Guadalupe Hidalgo on February 2, 1848, was a moment of fulfillment and a cause for jubilation. The United States had just won a war against Mexico and had gained title to some 500,000 square miles of land. Although in retrospect we may see the Mexican-American War as a war of aggression by the United States, many Americans at the time saw it as the realization of manifest destiny. The nation now encompassed nearly three million square miles; in some seventy years, the United States had become a transcontinental colossus. Ironically, this national victory planted the seeds for civil war. As Americans celebrated, they had to determine politically the ways in which the newly acquired lands would be developed. For nearly thirty years, American politicians had attempted to create a balance between slave and free states. Now the issue of how or if slavery would be extended westward became the question of the day. As politicians endeavored to deal with the question, Americans of various stripes became actively engaged in the debate and increasingly illustrated the fact that perhaps this was not an issue that had a political solution. Americans became increasingly violent in their political and economic opinions.

Both before the 1840s and afterward, politicians typically attempted to arrive at compromise. Because there were two strong national political parties vying for power, it was in their interests to maintain a spirit of compromise between the North and South. Accordingly, after bitter debate, Congress passed the Compromise of 1850, which purportedly solved the problem. One part of the compromise admitted California as a free state, thus forever creating an imbalance between free and slave states. Another component of the compromise was the Fugitive Slave Act, which empowered slaveowners to go to court to recapture people who had escaped northward. Alleged fugitives were denied the right of trial by jury, and white people in the North were required to abet efforts to recapture fugitive slaves. As Americans soon found out, however, this time compromise did not solve the problem; in fact, it may have worsened it.

Distrust among Americans multiplied in the 1850s, in part because of the failure of the attempts at compromise. The abolitionist movement grew in the North, in part because of the publication of Uncle Tom's Cabin, *a novel by Harriet Beecher Stowe that powerfully indicted slavery and the Fugitive Slave Act. Many northerners contended that their region, with its growing population, flourishing industry, and "free labor," was* the best model for America's future. They worried about a "slave power conspiracy" that seemingly controlled the national government and was intent on spreading slavery westward, to the detriment of white farmers who also wanted to farm the available western lands. With increased reliance on the economy of the slave trade, southern whites seemed to need more and more land. At the same time, white people in the South became increasingly distrustful of northerners. In the southern view, northerners were promoting abolitionism and thus endangering the system of plantation slavery, which from their perspective was what created an ordered and stable society.

As these divisions grew, the strains on the political party systems became so great that a political crisis developed in the 1850s. First the Whig Party, then the newly formed American Party, and finally the Democratic Party were unable to address the concerns of their constituents. These failures were compounded by further attempts to address the question of slavery. The Kansas-Nebraska Act in 1854 resulted in de facto civil war in Kansas Territory shortly after its passage; the Dred Scott decision in 1857 convinced many northerners that the Supreme Court was proslavery; and John Brown's raid in 1859 persuaded many white southerners that northern abolitionists were intent on fomenting slave rebellion. In 1860, when Abraham Lincoln became the first candidate of the Republican Party to be elected president, he received only 39 percent of the popular vote and only a little over 1 percent of the vote in slave states. Many white southerners considered Lincoln to represent not just the North, but the incendiary abolitionist elements of northern society. Within five weeks of Lincoln's election, seven legislatures of the Lower South had called for elections to consider secession. By February 22, they had formed a new nation, written a constitution, and inaugurated their new president, Jefferson Davis. Ten days remained before Lincoln would take office. The United States was on the brink of its bloodiest war.

QUESTIONS TO THINK ABOUT

Was the Civil War inevitable? Can you think of ways in which compromises might have forestalled the division between the North and the South? Were economic or political issues at the base of the conflict? Of the documents you have read in this chapter, which is most conciliatory toward the other side? Which is most antagonistic?

DOCUMENTS

During the debate that ended in the Compromise of 1850, Senator John C. Calhoun in document 1 warns about the divisions that have grown between the sections. He argues that these divisions will increase as the disequilibrium between North and South in the national government grows. In document 2, Frederick Douglass powerfully depicts the hypocrisy of celebrating American freedom on the Fourth of July as long as slavery exists. The reactions to *Uncle Tom's Cabin* varied, as the two reviews included as document 3 illustrate. Whereas a literary journal in the South considers Stowe's depiction of slavery to be too harsh, an abolitionist paper objects to the nonviolence of Uncle Tom. In document 4, a series of letters written in "bleeding Kansas" in 1856, a southerner recounts the violence between southerners and "Yankees" that existed in the territory following the Kansas-Nebraska Act. The violence in Kansas ultimately was duplicated on the floors of Congress. Senator Charles Sumner's speech, delivered in May of 1856, about the "crime against Kansas," document 5, was viewed by many white southerners as excessive. Sumner was attacked some days later by a relative of Senator Butler, who is vilified in the speech. Document 6 is Chief Justice Roger Taney's decision in *Dred Scott v. Sanford,* which was hailed by proslavery southerners and condemned by antislavery northerners. Among other things, Taney held that neither slaves nor free black people could sue in court because they were not citizens and that no law could be passed to prohibit slavery in the territories. In document 7, Abraham Lincoln and Stephen Douglas debate the future of slavery and the legality of slavery in the territories. Although Lincoln and Douglas were running for a U.S. Senate seat from Illinois, they replayed the debate two years later when they ran for president. In document 8, Senator William Seward celebrates the system of free labor and argues that conflict between societies based on free and slave labor is irrepressible. After John Brown led a raid into the South in hopes of fostering a slave revolt, he became a hero to many northerners, and his calm speech (document 9) in the face of execution, denying any intentions of violence, only served to increase his popularity. Finally, in document 10, just eight months before Lincoln's election, the *Charleston Mercury* argues that slavery must be protected in the territories because the spread of the American nation westward and southward is all but inevitable.

1. Senator John C. Calhoun
Proposes Ways to Preserve the Union, 1850

I have, Senators, believed from the first that the agitation of the subject of slavery would, if not prevented by some timely and effective measure, end in disunion.... [T]he Union is in danger. You have thus had forced upon you the greatest and the gravest question that can ever come under your consideration: How can the Union be preserved?...

The first question, then,... is: What is it that has endangered the Union?

To this question there can be but one answer: That the immediate cause is the almost universal discontent which pervades all the States composing the southern section of the Union....

... What is the cause of this discontent? It will be found in the belief of the people of the southern States, as prevalent as the discontent itself, that they cannot remain, as things now are, consistently with honor and safety, in the Union. The next question to be considered is: What has caused this belief?

John C. Calhoun, "Proposal to Preserve the Union," speech on the Compromise of 1850.

One of the causes is, undoubtedly, to be traced to the long-continued agitation of the slave question on the part of the North, and the many aggressions which they have made on the rights of the South during the time....

There is another, lying back of it, with which this is intimately connected, that may be regarded as the great and primary cause. That is to be found in the fact that the equilibrium between the two Sections in the Government, as it stood when the Constitution was ratified and the Government put in action has been destroyed.... [A]s it now stands, one section has the exclusive power of controlling the Government, which leaves the other without any adequate means of protecting itself against its encroachment and oppression....

[The] great increase of Senators, added to the great increase of the House of Representatives and the electoral college on the part of the North, which must take place under the next decade, will effectually and irretrievably destroy the equilibrium which existed when the Government commenced....

As ... the North has the absolute control over the Government, it is manifest that on all questions between it and the South, where there is a diversity of interests, the interests of the latter will be sacrificed to the former, however oppressive the effects may be....

If the agitation goes on, the same force, acting with increased intensity, as has been shown, will finally snap every cord, when nothing will be left to bind the States together except force....

How can the Union be saved? To this I answer, there is but one way by which it can be, and that is by adopting such measures as will satisfy the States belonging to the southern section that they can remain in the Union consistently with their honor and their safety.

2. Frederick Douglass Asks How a Slave Can Celebrate the Fourth of July, 1852

Fellow-citizens, pardon me, allow me to ask, why am I called upon to speak here to-day? What have I, or those I represent, to do with your national independence? Are the great principles of political freedom and of natural justice, embodied in that Declaration of Independence, extended to us? and am I, therefore, called upon to bring our humble offering to the national altar, and to confess the benefits and express devout gratitude for the blessings resulting from your independence to us?

Would to God, both for your sakes and ours, that an affirmative answer could be truthfully returned to these questions! Then would my task be light, and my burden easy and delightful. For who is there so cold, that a nation's sympathy could not warm him? Who so obdurate and dead to the claims of gratitude, that would not thankfully acknowledge such priceless benefits? Who so stolid and selfish, that would not give his voice to swell the hallelujahs of a

Frederick Douglass, Fourth of July Oration (1852), in *The Life and Writings of Frederick Douglass*, Vol. II, *Pre-Civil War Decade, 1850–1860,* ed. Philip S. Foner (New York: International Publishers Co., Inc. 1950). Obtained from http://www.pbs.org/wgbh/aia/part4/4h2927t.html.

nation's jubilee, when the chains of servitude had been torn from his limbs? I am not that man. In a case like that, the dumb might eloquently speak, and the "lame man leap as an hart."

But such is not the state of the case. I say it with a sad sense of the disparity between us. I am not included within the pale of glorious anniversary! Your high independence only reveals the immeasurable distance between us. The blessings in which you, this day, rejoice, are not enjoyed in common. The rich inheritance of justice, liberty, prosperity and independence, bequeathed by your fathers, is shared by you, not by me. The sunlight that brought light and healing to you, has brought stripes and death to me. This Fourth July is yours, not mine....

What, to the American slave, is your 4th of July? I answer; a day that reveals to him, more than all other days in the year, the gross injustice and cruelty to which he is the constant victim. To him, your celebration is a sham; your boasted liberty, an unholy license; your national greatness, swelling vanity; your sounds of rejoicing are empty and heartless; your denunciation of tyrants, brass fronted impudence; your shouts of liberty and equality, hollow mockery; your prayers and hymns, your sermons and thanksgivings, with all your religious parade and solemnity, are, to Him, mere bombast, fraud, deception, impiety, and hypocrisy—a thin veil to cover up crimes which would disgrace a nation of savages. There is not a nation on the earth guilty of practices more shocking and bloody than are the people of the United States, at this very hour.

Go where you may, search where you will, roam through all the monarchies and despotisms of the Old World, travel through South America, search out every abuse, and when you have found the last, lay your facts by the side of the everyday practices of this nation, and you will say with me, that, for revolting barbarity and shameless hypocrisy, America reigns without a rival.

3. Reviewers Offer Differing Opinions About *Uncle Tom's Cabin*, 1852

I.

In the execution of her very difficult task, Mrs. Stowe has displayed rare descriptive powers, a familiar acquaintance with slavery under its best and its worst phases, uncommon moral and philosophical acumen, great facility of thought and expression, feelings and emotions of the strongest character....

The appalling liabilities which constantly impend over such slaves as have "kind and indulgent masters" are thrillingly illustrated in various personal narratives; especially in that of "Uncle Tom," over whose fate every reader will drop the scalding tear, and for whose character the highest reverence will be felt. No insult, no outrage, no suffering, could ruffle the Christ-like meekness of his spirit, or shake the steadfastness of his faith. Towards his merciless oppressors, he cherished no animosity, and breathed nothing of retaliation. Like his Lord and

---

(I) William Lloyd Garrison, Review in *The Liberator*, March 26, 1852, 50.

Master, he was willing to be "led as a lamb to the slaughter," returning blessing for cursing, and anxious only for the salvation of his enemies. His character is sketched with great power and rare religious perception. It triumphantly exemplifies the nature, tendency and results of CHRISTIAN NON-RESISTANCE. We are curious to know whether Mrs. Stowe is a believer in the duty of non-resistance for the white man, under all possible outrage and peril, as well as for the black man.... That all the slaves at the South ought, "if smitten on the one cheek, to turn the other also"—to repudiate all carnal weapons, shed no blood, "be obedient to their masters," wait for a peaceful deliverance, and abstain from all insurrectionary movements—is every where taken for granted, because the VICTIMS ARE BLACK. *They* cannot be animated by a Christian spirit, and yet return blow for blow, or conspire for the destruction of their oppressors. *They* are required by the Bible to put away all wrath, to submit to every conceivable outrage without resistance, to suffer with Christ if they would reign with him.... Is there one law of submission and non-resistance for the black man, and another law of rebellion and conflict for the white man? When it is the whites who are trodden in the dust, does Christ justify them in taking up arms to vindicate their rights? And when it is the blacks who are thus treated, does Christ require them to be patient, harmless, long-suffering, and forgiving? And are there two Christs?

II.

We have devoted a much larger space to the plot of "Uncle Tom's Cabin" than we designed...; it only remains for us to consider briefly those points upon which the authoress rests her abuse of the Southern States, in the book as a whole. These may be reduced to three—the cruel treatment of the slaves, their lack of religious instruction, and a wanton disregard of the sacred ties of consanguinity in selling members of the same family apart from each other.

... [M]any of the allegations of cruelty towards the slaves, brought forward by Mrs. Stowe, are absolutely and unqualifiedly false. As for the comfort of their daily lives and the almost parental care taken of them on well-regulated plantations, we may say that the picture of the Shelby estate, drawn by Mrs. Stowe herself, is no bad representation. The world may safely be challenged to produce a laboring class, whose regular toil is rewarded with more of the substantial conflicts of life than the negroes of the South. The "property interest" at which the authoress sneers so frequently in "Uncle Tom's Cabin," is quite sufficient to ensure for the negro a kindness and attention, which the day-laborer in New England might in vain endeavor to win from his employer....

The lack of religious instruction for slaves is a charge against the South, in great favor with Northern fanatics, many of whom are deplorably in want of "religious instruction" themselves, and vastly beneath the pious slave in that love for their neighbour which is the keystone of the Christian arch. Yet never was there a charge more extravagant. We can tell these worthies that throughout the Southern States a portion of every house of worship is set apart for the

---

(II) Unsigned (probably John R. Thompson), Review in *Southern Literary Messenger*, October 1852, 637–638.

accommodation of slaves; that upon very many plantations, may be seen rude but comfortable buildings, dedicated to God, where stated preaching of His Holy Word is ordained; that Sabbath schools for negroes are established in several of the Southern cities; and that in every Southern family, almost without an exception, where morning and evening prayers are held, the domestics of the household are called together to unite in them.... Writers like Mrs. Stowe, in treating of this subject, assume that there can be no acquaintance with gospel truth among a class who are not permitted to learn to read. But how many of the early Christians were ignorant and illiterate persons? The fishermen of Galilee were men without instruction when they first followed the fortunes of the lowly Nazarene. As for Mrs. Stowe, she is answered upon this point in her own pages. Uncle Tom was no scholar, and after many years of diligent application could at last read his bible with difficulty. Yet where shall we find a nobler and purer exemplification of the "beauty of holiness" than in him? It is, indeed, a triumphant vindication of the institution of slavery against Mrs. Stowe's assaults, that in a slaveholding community, a character so perfect as "Uncle Tom" could be produced....

The sundering of family ties among the negroes is undoubtedly a dreadful thing as represented by Abolition pamphleteers. Nor have we any desire to close our eyes to the fact that occasionally there do occur instances of compulsory separation involving peculiar hardship. But ... in the very State which Mrs. Stowe has chosen for her most painful incident of this character, there are statutory regulations mitigating very much the severity of this condition of affairs, and we may add that every where the salutary influence of an enlightened public opinion enforces the sale of near relatives in such manner as that they may be kept as much as possible together. We are of opinion too that heart-rending separations are much less frequent under the institution of slavery than in countries where poverty rules the working classes with despotic sway. But admit the hardship to its full extent, and what does it prove? Evils are inseparable from all forms of society and this giant evil (if you will call it so) is more than counterbalanced by the advantages the negro enjoys.

4. Axalla John Hoole, a Southerner, Depicts "Bleeding Kansas," 1856

Kansas City, Missouri, Apl. 3d., 1856

My Dear Brother ...

The Missourians (all of whom I have conversed with, with the exception of one who, by the way, I found out to be an Abolitionist) are very sanguine about Kansas being a slave state & I have heard some of them say it *shall* be. I have met with warm reception from two or three, but generally speaking, I have not met

William Stanley Hoole, ed., "A Southerner's Viewpoint of the Kansas Situation" (1856–1857), *Kansas Historical Quarterly*, Vol. 3 (1934).

with the reception which I expected. Everyone seems bent on the Almighty Dollar, and as a general thing that seems to be their only thought....

... Give my love to [the immediate family] and all the Negroes....

Your ever affectionate brother, Axalla.

Lecompton, K. T., Sept. 12, 1856

My dear Mother ...

You perceive from the heading of this that I am now in Lecompton, almost all of the Proslavery party between this place and Lawrence are here. We brought our families here, as we thought that we would be better able to defend ourselves when altogether than if we scattered over the country.

Lane came against us last Friday (a week ago to-day). As it happened we had almost 400 men with two cannon—we marched out to meet him, though we were under the impression at the time that we had 1,000 men. We came in gunshot of each other, but the regular soldiers came and interferred, but not before our party had shot some dozen guns, by which it is reported that five of the Abolitionists were killed or wounded. We had strict orders from our commanding officer (Gen'l Marshall) not to fire until they made the attack, but some of our boys would not be restrained. I was a rifleman and one of the skirmishers, but did all that I could to restrain our men though I itched all over to shoot....

... I am more uneasy about making money than I am about being killed by the Yankees...

Your Affectionate Son.

Douglas, K. T., July the 5th., 1857

Dear Sister

I fear, Sister, that coming here will do no good at last, as I begin to think that this will be made a Free State at last. 'Tis true we have elected Proslavery men to draft a state constitution, but I feel pretty certain, if it is put to the vote of the people, it will be rejected, as I feel pretty confident they have a majority here at this time. The South has ceased all efforts, while the North is redoubling her exertions....

One of our most staunch Proslavery men was killed in Leavensworth a few days ago. It is hard to ascertain the facts in relation to the murder correctly, but as far as I can learn, there was an election for something. The man who was killed (Jas. Lyle) went up to the polls and asked for a ticket. An Abolitionist handed him one which he, Lyle, tore in two. The other asked him why he did that; he replied he did all such tickets that way. The Abolitionist told him he had better not do so again, when Lyle told him if he would give him another he would. It was given him, and he tore it also, at which the Abolitionist drew a bowie knife and stabbed Lyle to the heart, then ran a few paces, drew a revolver, and commenced firing at the dying man. The fellow was taken prisoner and eighty men were sent from Lawrence that night, by Jim Lane, to keep Lyle's friends from hanging him. Gov. Walker put out for Leavensworth on Friday to have the prisoner carried to the fort, in order to keep the Abolitionists from rescuing him, or prevent Lyle's friends from hanging him by mob law....

You must give my love to all.... Tell all the Negroes a hundred Howdies for us....

Your Affectionate Brother, Axalla.

5. Senator Charles Sumner Addresses the "Crime Against Kansas," 1856

MR. PRESIDENT:

You are now called to redress a great transgression. Seldom in the history of nations has such a question been presented....

Take down your map, sir, and you will find that the Territory of Kansas, more than any other region, occupies the middle spot of North America.... A few short months only have passed since this spacious and mediterranean country was open only to the savage who ran wild in its woods and prairies; and now it has already drawn to its bosom a population of freemen larger than Athens....

Against this Territory, thus fortunate in position and population, a crime has been committed, which is without example in the records of the past....

... It is the rape of a virgin Territory, compelling it to the hateful embrace of Slavery; and it may be clearly traced to a depraved longing for a new slave State, the hideous offspring of such a crime, in the hope of adding to the power of slavery in the National Government....

... The strife is no longer local, but national. Even now, while I speak, portents hang on all the arches of the horizon threatening to darken the broad land, which already yawns with the mutterings of civil war. The fury of the propagandists of Slavery, and the calm determination of their opponents, are now diffused from the distant Territory over widespread communities, and the whole country....

... [A] madness for Slavery which would disregard the Constitution, the laws, and all the great examples of our history; also a consciousness of power such as comes from the habit of power; a combination of energies found only in a hundred arms directed by a hundred eyes; a control of public opinion through venal pens and a prostituted press; an ability to subsidize crowds in every vocation of life—the politician with his local importance, the lawyer with his subtle tongue, and even the authority of the judge on the bench; and a familiar use of men in places high and low, so that none, from the President to the lowest border postmaster, should decline to be its tool; all these things and more were needed, and they were found in the slave power of our Republic. There, sir, stands the criminal, all unmasked before you—heartless, grasping, and tyrannical....

Senator Charles Sumner, speech in the U.S. Senate on the "Crime Against Kansas," delivered May 19–20, 1856; reprinted in *Evening Journal* (Albany, N.Y.), May 22–23, 1856.

... I must say something of a general character, particularly in response to what has fallen from Senators who have raised themselves to eminence on this floor in championship of human wrongs. I mean the Senator from South Carolina (Mr. Butler), and the Senator from Illinois (Mr. Douglas).... The Senator from South Carolina has read many books of chivalry, and believes himself a chivalrous knight, with sentiments of honor and courage. Of course he has chosen a mistress to whom he has made his vows, and who, though ugly to others, is always lovely to him: though polluted in the sight of the world; is chaste in his sight. I mean the harlot, Slavery. For her, his tongue is always profuse in words. Let her be impeached in character, or any proposition made to shut her out from the extension of her wantonness, and no extravagance of manner or hardihood of assertion is then too great for this Senator. The frenzy of Don Quixote, in behalf of his wench, Dulcinea del Toboso, is all surpassed. The asserted rights of Slavery, which shock equality of all kinds, are cloaked by a fantastic claim of equality. If the slave States cannot enjoy what, in mockery of the great fathers of the Republic, he misnames equality under the Constitution in other words, the full power in the National Territories to compel fellowmen to unpaid toil, to separate husband and wife, and to sell little children at the auction block then, sir, the chivalric Senator will conduct the State of South Carolina out of the Union! Heroic knight! Exalted Senator! A second Moses come for a second exodus!

... [T]he Senator in the unrestrained chivalry of his nature, has undertaken to apply opprobrious words to those who differ from him on this floor. He calls them "sectional and fanatical"; and opposition to the usurpation in Kansas he denounces as "an uncalculating fanaticism."... He is the uncompromising, unblushing representative on this floor of a flagrant sectionalism, which now domineers over the Republic, and yet with a ludicrous ignorance of his own position unable to see himself as others see him..., he applies to those here who resist his sectionalism the very epithet which designates himself....

... [T]he Senator from Illinois (Mr. Douglas) is the Squire of Slavery, its very Sancho Panza, ready to do all its humiliating offices.... Standing on this floor, the Senator issued his rescript, requiring submission to the Usurped Power of Kansas; and this was accompanied by a manner—all his own—such as befits the tyrannical threat. Very well. Let the Senator try. I tell him now that he cannot enforce any such submission. The Senator, with the slave power at his back, is strong; but he is not strong enough for this purpose....

The Senator dreams that he can subdue the North. He disclaims the open threat, but his conduct still implies it. How little that Senator knows himself or the strength of the cause which he persecutes! He is but a mortal man; against him is an immortal principle. With finite power he wrestles with the infinite, and he must fall. Against him are stronger battalions than any marshalled by mortal arm[,] the inborn, ineradicable, invincible sentiments of the human heart[;] against him is nature in all her subtle forces; against him is God. Let him try to subdue these.

6. Chief Justice Roger Taney
Determines the Legal Status of Slaves, 1857

The question is simply this: Can a negro, whose ancestors were imported into this country, and sold as slaves, become a member of the political community formed and brought into existence by the Constitution of the United States, and as such become entitled to all the rights, and privileges, and immunities, guarantied by [the Constitution] to the citizen? One of which rights is the privilege of suing in a court of the United States in the cases specified in the Constitution....

... We think they [negroes] are not, and that they are not included, and were not intended to be included, under the word "citizens" in the Constitution, and can therefore claim none of the rights and privileges which [it] ... secures to the citizens of the United States. On the contrary, they were at the time considered as a subordinate and inferior class of beings, who had been subjugated by the dominant race, and, whether emancipated or not, yet remained subject to their authority, and had no rights or privileges but such as those who held the power and the Government might choose to grant them....

In discussing this question, we must not confound the rights of citizenship which a State may confer within its own limits, and the rights of citizenship as a member of the Union. It does not by any means follow, because he has all the rights and privileges of a citizen of a State, that he must be a citizen of the United States....

The question then arises, whether the provisions of the Constitution, in relation to the personal rights and privileges to which the citizen of a State should be entitled, embraced the negro African race, at that time in this country, or who might afterwards be imported, who had then or should afterwards be made free in any State; and to put it in the power of a single State to make him a citizen of the United States....

The court think the affirmative of these propositions cannot be maintained. And if it cannot, the plaintiff in error could not be a citizen of the State of Missouri ... and consequently, was not entitled to sue in its courts....

It is difficult at this day to realize the state of public opinion in relation to that unfortunate race, which prevailed in the civilized and enlightened portions of the world at the time of the Declaration of Independence, and when the Constitution of the United States was framed and adopted. But the public history of every European nation displays it in a manner too plain to be mistaken.

They had for more than a century been regarded as beings of an inferior order, and altogether unfit to associate with the white race, either in social or political relations; and so far inferior, that they had no rights which the white man was bound to respect; and that the negro might justly and lawfully be reduced to slavery for his benefit....

And in no nation was this opinion more firmly fixed or more uniformly acted upon than by the English Government and English people....

Roger Taney, opinion in *Dred Scott v. Sanford* (1857).

The opinion thus entertained and acted upon in England was naturally impressed upon the colonies they founded on this side of the Atlantic. And accordingly, a negro of the African race was regarded by them as an article of property, and held, and bought and sold ... in every one of the thirteen colonies....

[Laws passed in the thirteen colonies] show that a perpetual and impassable barrier was intended to be erected between the white race and the one which they had reduced to slavery, and governed as subjects with absolute and despotic power....

[T]here are two clauses of the Constitution which point directly to the negro race as a separate class of persons, and show clearly that they were not regarded as a portion of the people or citizens of the Government then formed.

One of these clauses reserves to each of the thirteen States the right to import slaves until the year 1808.... And by the other provision the States pledge themselves to each other to maintain the right of property of the master, by delivering up to him any slave who may have escaped from his service, and be found within their respective territories....

The only two provisions [of the Constitution] which point to [slaves] and include them, treat them as property, and make it the duty of the Government to protect it; no other power, in relation to this race, is to be found in the Constitution....

[T]he court is of the opinion, that, upon the facts stated in the plea of abatement, Dred Scot was not a citizen of Missouri within the meaning of the Constitution of the United States, and not entitled as such to sue in its courts.

7. Senate Candidates Abraham Lincoln and Stephen Douglas Debate Their Positions on Slavery, 1858

Mr. Douglas' Opening Speech

At half past two, Mr. Douglas took the front of the platform....

MR. DOUGLAS said—Ladies and gentlemen. I appear before you to-day for the purpose of discussing the leading political topics which now agitate the public mind....

... Mr. Lincoln here says that our government cannot endure permanently in the same condition in which it was made by its framers. It was made divided into free States and slave States. Mr. Lincoln says it has existed for near eighty years thus divided; but he tells you that it cannot endure permanently on the same principles and in the same conditions relatively in which your fathers made it. ["Neither can it."—*Times*] Why can't it endure divided into free and slave States? Washington, as the President of the Convention, Franklin, and

Abraham Lincoln and Stephen Douglas, *The Lincoln-Douglas Debates of 1858* (New York: Oxford University Press, 1965), 45, 53–56, 59, 61–63, 77.

Madison, and Hamilton, and Jay, and the patriots of that day, made this government divided into free States and slave States, leaving each State perfectly free to do as it pleased on that subject of slavery. ["Right, right."—*Times*] Why can't it exist upon the same principles upon which our fathers made it. ["It can."—*Times*] Our fathers knew when they made this government that in a country as wide and broad as this with such a variety of climate, of interests, of productions, as this that the people necessarily required different local laws and local institutions in certain localities from those in other localities. They knew that the laws and regulations that would suit the granite hills of New Hampshire would be unsuited to the rice plantations of South Carolina. ["right, right,"—*Times*] Hence, they provided that each State should retain its own Legislature and its own sovereignty, with the full and complete power to do as it pleased within its own limits in all that was local and not national. [Applause.—*Times*] One of the reserved rights of the States was that of regulating the relation between master and slave, or the slavery question.... I therefore say that uniformity in the local laws and local legislations of the different States was neither possible nor desirable. If any uniformity had been adopted, it must inevitably have been the uniformity of slavery everywhere, or the uniformity of negro citizenship and negro equality everywhere.

   ... Now, I ask you, are you in favor of conferring upon the negro the rights and privileges of citizenship? ["No, no." —*Times*] Do you desire to strike out of our State Constitution that clause which keeps slaves and free negroes out of the State, and allow the free negro to flow in ["never,"—*Times*] and cover our prairies with his settlements. Do you desire to turn this beautiful State into a free negro colony?... I believe that this government was made on the white basis. ["Good," *Times*] I believe it was made by white men for the benefit of white men and their posterity forever, and I am in favor of confining the citizenship to white men—men of European birth and European descent, instead of conferring it upon Negroes and Indians, and other inferior races....

   ... I do not believe the Almighty ever intended the negro to be the equal of the white man. ["Never, never."—*Times*] If he did he has been a long time demonstrating the fact. [Laughter.—*Tribune;* Cheers.—*Times*] For six thousand years the negro has been a race upon the earth, and during that whole six thousand years—in all latitudes and climates wherever the negro has been—he has been inferior to whatever race adjoined him. The fact is he belongs to an inferior race and must occupy an inferior position....

   ... What shall be done for the free negro?... [W]e must leave each and every other State to decide for itself beyond our limits....

Mr. Lincoln's Reply

... Mr. Lincoln then came forward and was greeted with loud and protracted cheers from fully two-thirds of the audience....

   ... [L]et me say I think I have no prejudice against the Southern people. They are just what we would be in their situation. If slavery did not now exist amongst them, they would not introduce it. If it did now exist amongst us, we should not instantly give it up....

When southern people tell us they are no more responsible for the origin of slavery, than we; I acknowledge the fact. When it is said that the institution exists, and that it is very difficult to get rid of it, in any satisfactory way, I can understand and appreciate the saying. I surely will not blame them for not doing what I should not know how to do myself. If all earthly power were given me, I should not know what to do, as to the existing institution. My first impulse would be to free all the slaves, and send them to Liberia,—to their own native land. But a moment's reflection would convince me, that whatever of high hope (as I think there is) there may be in this, in the long run, its sudden execution is impossible. If they were all landed there in a day, they would all perish in the next ten days; and there are not surplus shipping and surplus money enough in the world to carry them there in many times ten days. What then? Free them all, and keep them among us as underlings? Is it quite certain that this betters their condition?... What next? Free them, and make them politically and socially, our equals? My own feelings will not admit of this; and if mine would, we well know that those of the great mass of white people will not.... We can not, then, make them equals. It does seem to me that systems of gradual emancipation might be adopted; but for their tardiness in this, I will not undertake to judge our brethren of the south.

When they remind us of their constitutional rights, I acknowledge them, not grudgingly, but fully, and fairly; and I would give them any legislation for the reclaiming of their fugitives, which should not, in its stringency, be more likely to carry a free man into slavery, than our ordinary criminal laws are to hang an innocent one.

But all this; to my judgment, furnishes no more excuse for permitting slavery to go into our own free territory, than it would for reviving the African slave trade by law. The law which forbids the bringing of slaves *from* Africa; and that which has so long forbid the taking them *to* Nebraska, can hardly be distinguished on any moral principle; and the repeal of the former can find quite as plausible excuses as that of the latter....

... I have no purpose directly or indirectly, to interfere with the institution of slavery in the states where it exists. I believe I have no lawful right to do so, and I have no inclination to do so. I have no disposition to introduce political and social equality between the white and the black races. There is a physical difference between the two, which in my judgment will probably forever forbid their living together on terms of respect, social and political equality, and ... I ... am in favor of the race to which I belong having the superior position; but I hold that because of all this there is no reason at all furnished why the negro after all is not entitled to all that the declaration of independence holds out, which is, "life, liberty, and the pursuit of happiness."...

... When he [Douglas] is saying that the negro has no share in the Declaration of Independence, he is going back to the year of our revolution, and, to the extent of his ability, he is muzzling the cannon that thunders its annual joyous return. When he is saying, as he often does, that if any people want slavery they have a right to have it, he is blowing out the moral lights around us. When he says that he don't care whether slavery is voted up or down, then, to my

thinking, he is, so far as he is able to do so, perverting the human soul and erad-
icating the light of reason and the love of liberty on the American continent.

8. Republican William Seward Warns of an Irrepressible Conflict, 1858

Our country is a theatre, which exhibits, in full operation, two radically different
political systems; the one resting on the basis of servile or slave labor, the other
on the basis of voluntary labor of freemen.

The laborers who are enslaved are all negroes, or persons more or less purely
of African derivation. But this is only accidental. The principle of the system is,
that labor in every society, by whomsoever performed, is necessarily unintellec-
tual, groveling and base; and that the laborer, equally for his own good and for
the welfare of the state, ought to be enslaved. The white laboring man, whether
native or foreigner, is not enslaved, only because he cannot, as yet, be reduced to
bondage....

... One of the chief elements of the value of human life is freedom in the
pursuit of happiness. The slave system is not only intolerable, unjust, and inhu-
man, towards the laborer, whom, only because he is a laborer, it loads down
with chains and converts into merchandise, but is scarcely less severe upon the
freeman, to whom, only because he is a laborer from necessity, it denies facilities
for employment, and whom it expels from the community because it cannot
enslave and convert him into merchandise also.... The free-labor system con-
forms to the divine law of equality, which is written in the hearts and consciences of man, and therefore is always and everywhere beneficent.

The slave system is one of constant danger, distrust, suspicion, and watchful-
ness. It debases those whose toil alone can produce wealth and resources for defense, to the lowest degree of which human nature is capable....

The free-labor system educates all alike, and by opening all the fields of industrial employment, and all the departments of authority, to the unchecked and
equal rivalry of all classes of men, at once secures universal contentment, and
brings into the highest possible activity all the physical, moral and social energies
of the whole state....

Hitherto, the two systems have existed in different states, but side by side
within the American Union. This has happened because the Union is a confederation of states. But in another aspect the United States constitute only one nation. Increase of population, which is filling the states out to their very borders,
together with a new and extended net-work of railroads and other avenues, and
an internal commerce which daily becomes more intimate, is rapidly bringing
the states into a higher and more perfect social unity or consolidation. Thus,
these antagonistic systems are continually coming into closer contact, and
collision results....

William Seward, "The Irrepressible Conflict," speech given at Rochester, N.Y. (October 25, 1858), in *The Works of William H. Seward*, IV (new edition), ed. George Baker (Boston: Houghton, Mifflin, and Company, 1884), 289–302.

Shall I tell you what this collision means?... It is an irrepressible conflict between opposing and enduring forces, and it means that the United States must and will, sooner or later, become either entirely a slaveholding nation, or entirely a freelabor nation....

... In the field of federal politics, slavery, deriving unlooked-for advantages from commercial changes, and energies unforeseen from the facilities of combination between members of the slaveholding class and between that class and other property classes, early rallied, and has at length made a stand, not merely to retain its original defensive position, but to extend its sway throughout the whole Union.... The plan of operation is this: By continued appliances of patronage and threats of disunion, they will keep a majority favorable to these designs in the senate, where each state has an equal representation. Through that majority they will defeat, as they best can, the admission of free states and secure the admission of slave states. Under the protection of the judiciary, they will, on the principle of the Dred Scott case, carry slavery into all the territories of the United States now existing and hereafter to be organized. By the action of the president and the senate, using the treaty-making power, they will annex foreign slaveholding states. In a favorable conjecture they will induce congress to repeal the act of 1808, which prohibits the foreign slave trade, and so they will import from Africa, at the cost of only twenty dollars a head, slaves enough to fill up the interior of the continent.... When the free states shall be sufficiently demoralized to tolerate these designs, they reasonably conclude that slavery will be accepted by those states themselves....

I think, fellow citizens, that I have shown you that it is high time for the friends of freedom to rush to the rescue of the constitution, and that their very first duty is to dismiss the democratic party from the administration of the government.

9. Abolitionist John Brown Makes His Last Statement to the Court Before Execution, 1859

I have, may it please the Court, a few words to say. In the first place, I deny everything but what I have all along admitted: of a design on my part to free slaves. I intended certainly to have made a clean thing of that matter, as I did last winter, when I went into Missouri and there took slaves without the snapping of a gun on either side, moving them through the country, and finally leaving them in Canada. I designed to have done the same thing again on a larger scale. That was all I intended. I never did intend murder, or treason, or the destruction of property, or to exercise or incite slaves to rebellion, or to make insurrection.

... Had I interfered in the manner which I admit, and which I admit has been fairly proved—for I admire the truthfulness and candor of the greater portion of the witnesses who have testified in this case—Had I so interfered in

John Brown, Last Statement to the Virginia Court (1859).

behalf of the rich, the powerful, the intelligent, the so-called great, or in behalf of any of their friends, either father, mother, brother, sister, wife or children, or any of that class, and suffered and sacrificed what I have in this interference, it would have been all right. Every man in this Court would have deemed it an act worthy of reward rather than punishment.

This Court acknowledges, too, as I suppose, the validity of the law of God. I see a book kissed, which I suppose to be the Bible, or at least the New Testament, which teaches me that all things whatsoever I would that men should do to me, I should do even so to them. It teaches me, further, to remember them that are in bonds as bound with them. I endeavored to act up to that instruction. I say I am yet too young to understand that God is any respecter of persons. I believe that to have interfered as I have done, as I have always freely admitted I have done, in behalf of His despised poor, I did no wrong, but right. Now, if it is deemed necessary that I should forfeit my life for the furtherance of the ends of justice, and mingle my blood further with the blood of my children and with the blood of millions in this slave country whose rights are disregarded by wicked, cruel, and unjust enactments, I say, let it be done.

Let me say one word further. I feel entirely satisfied with the treatment I have received on my trial. Considering all the circumstances, it has been more generous than I expected. But I feel no consciousness of guilt. I have stated from the first what was my intention, and what was not. I never had any design against the liberty of any person, nor any disposition to commit treason or incite slaves to rebel or make any general insurrection. I never encouraged any man to do so, but always discouraged any idea of that kind.

10. The *Charleston Mercury* Argues That Slavery Must Be Protected, 1860

The right to have [slave] property protected in the territory is not a mere abstraction without application or practical value. In the past there are instances where the people of the Southern States might have colonized and brought new slave States into the Union had the principle been recognized, and the Government, the trustee of the Southern States, exercised its appropriate powers to make good for the slaveholder the guarantees of the Constitution.... When the gold mines of California were discovered, slaveholders at the South saw that, with their command of labor, it would be easy at a moderate outlay to make fortunes digging gold. The inducements to go there were great, and there was no lack of inclination on their part. But, to make the emigration profitable, it was necessary that the [slave] property of Southern settlers should be safe, otherwise it was plainly a hazardous enterprise, neither wise nor feasible. Few were reckless enough to stake property, the accumulation of years, in a struggle with active prejudices amongst a mixed population, where for them the law was a dead letter through the hostile indifference of the General Government, whose duty it was,

"Prospects of Slavery Expansion," *Charleston Mercury*, February 28, 1860.

by the fundamental law of its existence, to afford adequate protection—executive, legislative, and judicial—to the property of every man, of whatever sort, without discrimination. Had the people of the Southern States been satisfied they would have received fair play and equal protection at the hands of the Government, they would have gone to California with their slaves.... California would now have been a Slave State in the Union....

What has been the policy pursued in Kansas? Has the territory had a fair chance of becoming a Slave State? Has the principle of equal protection to slave property been carried out by the Government there in any of its departments? On the contrary, has not every appliance been used to thwart the South and expel or prohibit her sons from colonizing there?... In our opinion, had the principle of equal protection to Southern men and Southern property been rigorously observed by the General Government, both California and Kansas would undoubtedly have come into the Union as Slave States. The South lost those States for the lack of proper assertion of this great principle....

New Mexico, it is asserted, is too barren and arid for Southern occupation and settlement.... Now, New Mexico ... teems with mineral resources.... There is no vocation in the world in which slavery can be more useful and profitable than in mining.... [Is] it wise, in our present condition of ignorance of the resources of New Mexico, to jump to the conclusion that the South can have no interest in its territories, and therefore shall waive or abandon her right of colonizing them?...

We frequently talk of the future glories of our republican destiny on the continent, and of the spread of our civilization and free institutions over Mexico and the Tropics. Already we have absorbed two of her States, Texas and California. Is it expected that our onward march is to stop here? Is it not more probable and more philosophic to suppose that, as in the past, so in the future, the Anglo-Saxon race will, in the course of years, occupy and absorb the whole of that splendid [but] illpeopled country, and to remove by gradual process, before them, the worthless mongrel races that now inhabit and curse the land? And in the accomplishment of this destiny is there a Southern man so bold as to say, the people of the South with their slave property are to consent to total exclusion...? Our people will never sit still and see themselves excluded from all expansion, to please the North.

ESSAYS

Historians have long debated the causes of the Civil War. Some scholars have argued that the war could have been avoided, that a generation of blundering politicians had ineptly maneuvered the nation into war. Other historians have agreed with William Seward, a statesman from New York who served in President Lincoln's cabinet, that the war was an "irrepressible conflict." Some focus on political differences between the North and South, whereas others show greater attention to economic distinctions between "free" and "slave" labor.

The following two essays reflect historical debates over the causes of the war. Michael F. Holt, professor of history at the University of Virginia, concentrates on the political causes of the Civil War. The divisions between the North and South had existed for decades, Professor Holt argues, but it was only when the political process broke down that Americans were led down the road to the Civil War. In contrast, Bruce Levine, the J. G. Randall Professor of History at the University of Illinois, Urbana-Champaign, focuses upon the differing economic systems of the North and the South and claims that the political debates make sense in light of the economic backgrounds. Although both northern and southern whites were dedicated to increasing their wealth, the different economies created by slavery and by free labor framed the conflict between the South and the North. Levine concludes that to understand why so many northerners and southerners were willing to fight in the Civil War, historians must take the socioeconomic circumstances seriously.

The Political Divisions That Contributed to Civil War

MICHAEL F. HOLT

The Civil War represented an utter and unique breakdown of the normal democratic political process. When one section of the country refused to accept the decision of a presidential election, secession and the ensuing war became the great exception to the American political tradition of compromise. The rending of the nation was the one time that conflict seemed too irrepressible, too fundamental, to be contained within common consensual boundaries. Because the war was such an anomaly, both participants and later historians have been fascinated with its causes since the shooting started.

The literature on the causation of the Civil War is vast and requires no detailed review here. Basically historians have been divided into two camps, although there have been a number of variations in each. Because the war pitted one section against another, many insist that a fundamental and intensifying conflict between the North and South brought it on. Members of this group have differed about the sources of sectional division, but most have argued that irreconcilable differences over Negro slavery inexorably ruptured one national institution after another between 1830 and 1860 until those differences produced war in 1861. In reply revisionist historians have minimized the internal solidarity of both the North and the South and the seriousness of the disputes between them. They have blamed the war instead on the mistakes of political leaders and the efforts of agitators such as the abolitionists and Southern fire-eaters. Despite the variations of the debate, the central issue has always been the role of slavery in causing the war, and recently the fundamentalists have won the larger audience. Historians like Eugene Genovese and Eric Foner have established beyond cavil the reality and gravity of ideological, economic, and political conflict

Michael F. Holt, *The Political Crisis of the 1850s* (New York: W. W. Norton & Company, 1983), 1–6, 12–16. Reprinted by permission of the author.

between the free labor society of the North and the slave-based plantation society of the South. Slavery and irreconcilable views about the desirability of slavery's expansion lay at the base of that sectional clash, they argue, and the unwillingness of either section to tolerate the triumph of the other's values produced the war. Thus we have returned to an older view that sectional conflict over Negro slavery caused the Civil War.

Without disputing the reality of sectional conflict between North and South, one can still point out that the sectional conflict interpretation leaves certain crucial questions about the breakup of the nation unanswered, For one thing, to delineate the factors that divided North from South does not by itself explain why the slave states behaved so differently from each other during the secession crisis. When secession first occurred and the Confederacy was formed, only seven states in the Deep South withdrew, yet eight other slave states chose to remain in the union. True, four more states joined the Confederacy once Abraham Lincoln called up troops after the firing on Fort Sumter, but resistance to overt federal coercion was far different from secession in anticipation of a Republican administration. If a desire to protect or extend black slavery caused Southerners to break up the nation, why didn't all the slave states react the same way in the initial crisis?

More important, the argument that an escalating sectional conflict between North and South before April 1861 produced war between them after that date does not really explain why a conflict of long duration produced war then and not at some other time. The problem is how a basic conflict between sectional interests and values that had long been carried on in peaceful channels such as politics abruptly became a shooting war after smoldering for decades, and why it did so at one time instead of at another. What produced the sectional hostility, in other words, was not necessarily what caused armed conflict in 1861. Ideological differences, after all, do not always produce wars.... [T]here most certainly was sectional conflict between North and South over slavery-related matters, yet that conflict, or cold war, had existed at least since the Constitutional Convention of 1787. Can a conflict that lasted almost three-fourths of a century explain why war broke out in 1861 and not earlier? If slavery or even the slavery extension issue caused the war, for example, why not in 1820 or 1832 or 1846 or 1850 or 1854? The basic problem concerning the war, in short, has less to do with the sources of sectional conflict than with the war's timing. The important question is not what divided North from South, but how the nation could contain or control that division for so long and then allow it suddenly to erupt into war.

This [essay] argues that the answers to these questions about varying Southern behavior and the timing of the Civil War lie in the political crisis of the 1850s. The key to Civil War causation is to be found in the reasons why the American political system could no longer contain the sectional conflict, not in the conflict itself. The [essay] differs from those of the fundamentalists by focusing less on the intensifying conflict than on the capacity of politicians and political structures to confine it to normal political channels. It argues that the change in that capacity had less to do with the explosiveness of the slavery issue *per se* than with a whole range of political developments, some of which created and others of which were responses to a crisis of confidence in the normal political process. Moreover, while I agree with revisionists that the individual decisions of politicians were important in exacerbating the situation, my emphasis is less on their ineptitude or the fanaticism of agitators than it is on the mechanics or dynamics of the political system itself.

The political crisis of the 1850s had two interrelated dimensions. The first was a fundamental reshaping of the nature of party competition. A national two-party system of Whigs and Democrats, which had functioned superbly for twenty years in all parts of the country and had helped contain the sectional conflict, collapsed. A realignment of voters followed between 1853 and 1856 in which a Democratic majority was replaced by an anti-Democratic majority in the North, even as the Democrats assumed an unassailable position in the South. Finally, new parties were organized, and out of the turmoil of the late 1850s the anti-Southern Republican party emerged triumphant. Because Southern secession was a direct response to the victory of the Republican party in the presidential election of 1860, there was a direct causal link between those political developments and the outbreak of war. One cannot account for Southern secession without accounting for the political events in the North that drove the South out of the Union. The political reorganization and realignment that replaced the national competition between Whigs and Democrats with a sectional competition between the Northern Republican party and a predominantly Southern Democracy was a major factor in the disruption of the Union.

More was involved in the collapse of the old two-party system, however, than merely the disappearance of national parties with affiliations across sectional lines. An equally crucial development took place at the state and local level. There, in the political arenas closest to the people, older frameworks of competition also dissolved. Voters with local needs and grievances that were every bit as important, if not more important, to them than national issues no longer had familiar party alternatives through which to seek political action. In this vacuum they tried to form new parties to meet their immediate needs, and much of the story of the political reorganization of the 1850s that led to civil war is to be found in those efforts. Local and state politics were just as crucial as national developments in shaping the political crisis of the 1850s.

The second aspect of the political crisis of the 1850s has received far less notice from historians, but it was just as critical as the first. This [essay] will attempt to demonstrate that the collapse of the old framework of two-party rivalry aggravated and in part reflected a loss of popular faith in the normal party political process to meet the needs of voters, to redress personal, group, and sectional grievances. Malignant distrust of politicians as self-centered and corrupt wirepullers out of touch with the people spread like an epidemic during the 1850s. So, too, did dissatisfaction with political parties as unresponsive and beyond popular control. Americans grew impatient with the inefficacy of traditional political methods and institutions. Widespread disgust with politics as usual engendered cries for reform that helped to destroy the old parties, propel voters to new affiliations, and shape new parties as ways were sought to return power to the people.

Underlying and intensifying the sense of crisis in the 1850s was a deep-seated republican ideology that had suffused American politics since the time of the Revolution. To Americans of the antebellum period, republicanism meant a number of things, and different Americans emphasized different parts of the creed. But to most white Americans who perceived political developments through the framework of republicanism, it meant, in Lincoln's words, government by and for the people, a government whose power over the people was restrained by law, and whose basic function was to protect the equality and liberty of individuals from aristocratic privilege and concentrations of arbitrary or tyrannical power. When Americans differed with each other politically, it was not so much over the desirability of republican government as over their perceptions of what most threatened its survival....

Most Americans, North and South, therefore, were concerned with the same thing in the 1850s: the need to reform the political process in order to preserve republicanism and return political power to the people. Where they differed was in the way they defined the antirepublican plot and in the steps they took to combat it. Some saw the political pretensions of the hierarchical Catholic Church, directed by the Pope, as the major subverter of the American republic, and they formed a new political organization that promised to restore government to the people and to purify the corrupt political process by insisting that native-born Protestant Americans rule America. Others claimed with justice that this new anti-Catholic organization was itself a menace to republicanism. Yet the somewhat paradoxical result was that those on opposing sides regained confidence that they could do battle for republicanism within the party political process.

The common fear for the republic also fed the fire of sectional antagonism. Northerners and Southerners both identified powerful and hostile groups in the other section who would destroy their liberty and reduce them to an unequal status. This was made politically possible, even likely, because the collapse of the old two-party system in the early 1850s had been accompanied by a resurgence and exacerbation of naked sectional conflict between North and South. One of the reasons that conflict became so emotional, in turn, was that each section began to view the other as the subverter of republicanism, as a lawless and usurping tyrant bent on perverting the traditional basis of society and government. Hence the secessionist impulse in the Deep South was another manifestation of the national sense of crisis, of disgust with politicians and the old political process, and of the search for reform to save republicanism. Whatever else secession represented, it was a rejection of the normal political process that other Americans by 1860 were still content to work through, a refusal not only to tolerate the election of Lincoln hut also to believe that the system could neutralize whatever threats he represented.

Like other Americans in the 1850s, Southerners had lost faith in politics as usual. Unlike Americans elsewhere, however, men from the Deep South never regained their faith in the efficacy of party politics. Thus they proved more receptive to the message that secession itself was necessary to restore republicanism. I will argue, in other words, that sectional extremism flourished in the Deep

South precisely because no new framework of two-party competition had appeared there—as it had in the North and upper South—to help restore public confidence that republicanism could once again be secured by normal political methods....

Politicians had long recognized that group conflict was endemic to American society and that the vitality of individual parties depended on the intensity of their competition with opposing parties. Thomas Jefferson had perceived in 1798 that "in every free and deliberating society, there must, from the nature of man, be opposite parties, and violent dissensions and discords." "Seeing that we must have somebody to quarrel with," he wrote John Taylor, "I had rather keep our New England associates for that purpose, than to see our bickerings transferred to others." Even more explicit in their recognition of what made parties work were the founders of New York's Albany Regency in the 1820s. They deplored the lack of internal discipline and cohesion in the Jeffersonian Republican party once the Federalists disappeared, and they moved quickly to remedy it. Although any party might suffer defeats, they realized, "it is certain to acquire additional strength ... by the attacks of adverse parties." A political party, indeed, was "most in jeopardy when an opposition is not sufficiently defined." During "the contest between the great rival parties [Federalists and Jeffersonians] each found in the strength of the other a powerful motive of union and vigor" Significantly, those like Daniel Webster who deplored the emergence of mass parties in the 1820s and 1830s also recognized that strife was necessary to perpetuate party organization and that the best way to break it down was to cease opposition and work for consensus. Politicians in the 1840s and 1850s continued to believe that interparty conflict was needed to unify their own party and maintain their voting support. Thus an Alabama Democrat confessed that his party pushed a certain measure at the beginning of the 1840 legislative session explicitly as "the best means for drawing the party lines as soon as possible" while by 1852, when opposition to the state's Democracy appeared to disintegrate, another warned perceptively, "I think the only danger to the Democratic party is that it will become too much an omnibus in this State. We have nothing to fear from either the Union, or Whig party or both combined. From their friendship and adherence much." Many of the important decisions in the 1840s and 1850s reflected the search by political leaders for issues that would sharply define the lines between parties and thus reinvigorate the loyalty of party voters.

If conflict sustained the old two-party system, what destroyed it was the loss of the ability to provide interparty competition on *any* important issue at *any* level of the federal system. Because the political system's vitality and legitimacy with the voters depended on the clarity of the definition of the parties as opponents, the blurring of that definition undid the system. What destroyed the Second Party System was consensus, not conflict. The growing congruence between the parties on almost all issues by the early 1850s dulled the sense of party difference and thereby eroded voters' loyalty to the old parties. Once competing groups in society decided that the party system no longer provided them viable alternatives in which they could carry on conflict with each other, they repudiated the old system by dropping out, seeking third parties that would meet their needs, or turning to nonpartisan or extrapolitical action to achieve their goals. Because the collapse of the Second Party System was such a vital link in the war's causation, therefore, one arrives at a paradox. While the Civil War is normally viewed as the one time when conflict prevailed over consensus in American politics, the prevalence of consensus over conflict in crucial parts of the political system contributed in a very real way to the outbreak of war in the first place.

One of the reasons the Second Party System functioned for so long despite the presence of sectional antagonism was the federal system. Historians of the politics of the 1840s and 1850s, indeed, of most periods, have not adequately assessed the impact of the federal system on parties. They have assumed that forces operating at one level of political activity caused developments at all levels. Historians of the prewar period have especially been obsessed with national events. If slavery ruptured the national parties in Congress, if the speeches and correspondence of national leaders were filled with remarks about slavery, slavery must have destroyed the old parties and shaped political developments. As the new voting studies show, however, this assumption may be unwarranted.

Yet even grass-roots voting studies frequently neglect the most crucial arena of political activity in the nineteenth century—the states. Most of the legislation that affected the everyday lives of people was enacted at state capitals and not at Washington. State parties formed the core of the political system, not the flimsy national organizations that came together once every four years to contest the presidency. To voters and politicians, therefore, control of a state's government was often more important than electing men to Congress; consequently, within an individual state, the competitiveness of a party in gubernatorial and legislative elections was often more influential in determining its longevity than national affairs. Attention has been inordinately focused on Washington, but the real story of the political reorganization of the 1850s is to be found in individual states with their varying conditions. In accounting for the demise of the Second Party System, for example, one must be careful to distinguish between the sectional divisions within national parties and the death of state parties within each section. The old Whig party disintegrated, the Democratic party was reshaped, and voters realigned not in presidential elections where national party cohesion mattered, but in state and local elections where parties in each section could go their own way. Similarly, the pace at which the new Republican party arose, the nature of its coalition, and the emergence of a new two-party framework in the South varied from state to state according to conditions within them. Only by recognizing the complexity caused by the division of powers within the federal system can one arrive at a more accurate portrayal of the political antecedents of war.

For a long while the federal system was a key to the health of the Second Party System. Because both parties functioned at different levels, politicians had the luxury of saying different things in different parts of the country. They could define for home audiences lines of interparty conflict that did not necessarily apply to the country as a whole. Many voters, probably the vast majority, learned of national and even state issues only what their local politicians and newspapers told them. In this situation politicians could make issues that hurt their parties at one level help them at another. Issues involving slavery that disrupted the parties along sectional lines in Congress, for example, were often debated along party lines in the states. New York Whigs and Georgia Whigs could have diametrically opposed views on a matter involving slavery, but at home they could use their divergent positions to strengthen themselves against the common Democratic foe. Before a home audience what mattered most was not that the Whigs disagreed with each other in Congress, but that they differed from the Democrats in their state. The ability of the old system to provide party alternatives on slavery-related matters at the state level, indeed, was the major reason why the Second Party System managed the sectional conflict for so long, even when national parties were divided by it.

The advantages of the federal system went beyond even this important mechanism. State parties battled over more than national issues. There was a whole range of state issues over which they could conflict, issues they could use to reinforce the image of party difference or often to divert attention from disrupting national matters. At the local level, moreover, parties could add parochial concerns to the list of state and national questions over which they contended. Although national and state parties might eschew clear party positions on temperance or religion, for example, local party newspapers could adopt opposing stands to attract voters interested in one side or the other of those issues. At some level or other of the multitiered federal government structure, almost every issue that entered the political arena could be fought on party lines. Multilevel party competition thus normally reinforced the voters' faith in existing parties as vehicles for competing ethnic, economic, religious, and regional groups in the society at large. Only when the image of party difference disappeared at all levels and when, as a result, faith in the parties waned, did the political conditions develop in the North and South that led to the breakup of the nation.

The Economic Divisions That Contributed to Civil War

BRUCE LEVINE

The American Civil War was, by general agreement, the most important event in the history of the United States. It altered the internal structure of American society more profoundly than had the Revolution. With the exception of the Haitian revolution, it was the most thoroughgoing and far-reaching assault on bound labor to occur in the Western Hemisphere. It not only dethroned the once dominant planter elite politically but eliminated it as a slaveholding class by emancipating 4 million human chattels....

Many traditional accounts of the Civil War's origins concentrate upon the thoughts and actions of the elite (and their impact on legislation and party systems) to the exclusion of other influences. But a mere glance at the massive popular mobilization that made the war possible indicates the need for a wider

From Bruce Levine, *Half Slave and Half Free: The Roots of Civil War* (Hill and Wang, 1992), p. 3–4, 17–18, 26–27, 36–37, 44–45, 56–58, 69–70. Reprinted by permission of Farrar, Straus, and Giroux.

perspective. Almost 3 million men donned Union blue or Confederate gray between 1861 and 1865. And though both officer corps were top-heavy with graduates of elite military institutions, planters, merchants, and professionals, the rank and file of each army was overwhelmingly composed of farmers, skilled workers, and urban and rural laborers. Of the Union forces, moreover, about half a million had been born abroad, and another 185,000 were African-Americans, nearly three-quarters of them freedmen recruited in the slave states. Although both sides eventually adopted conscription, the size and power of the Union and Confederate armies—and especially at the outset—owed far more to the voluntary service of their citizen-soldiers. Before the war had ended, one out of every five would give up his life; untold others would be maimed. No other war in the nation's history has taken so heavy a toll.

Any satisfactory analysis of the war's origins must account for this unequaled degree of popular mobilization and sacrifice. What impelled so many—rich, middling, and poor; white and black; native-born and immigrant—to risk and sacrifice so much? What brough them, their families, and the nation as a whole to that point? To answer such questions,... antebellum political history [must be examined] in the light of the broader economic,... developments that shaped the lives of the American people....

The Southern Slave Economy

In the first month of the Civil War, Confederate President Jefferson Davis reminded the Confederate Congress that in the American South slave labor had

> convert[ed] hundreds of thousands of square miles of wilderness into cultivated lands covered with a prosperous people; towns and cities had sprung into existence, and had rapidly increased in wealth and population under the social system of the South;... and the productions in the South of cotton, rice, sugar and tobacco, for the full development and continuance of which the labor of African slaves was and is indispensable, had swollen to an amount which formed nearly three-quarters of the exports of the whole United States and had become absolutely necessary to the wants of civilized man. With interests of such overwhelming magnitude imperiled, the people of the Southern States were driven by the conduct of the North to the adoption of some course of action to avert the danger with which they were openly menaced.

A substantial body of literature accumulated in the antebellum South in which slave owners shared experiences with their labor system and advice on how best to manage it. In one such essay, North Carolina planter Dr. John F. Tompkins spelled out the premise of this discussion more explicitly than most bothered—or preferred—to do. "In the first place," he asked in the *Farmers' Journal* in 1853, "for what purpose does the master hold the servant? Is it not that by his labor he, the master, may accumulate wealth?"

The question was rhetorical; general agreement was assumed, as well it could be. New World slavery harnessed the ancient status of bound labor to decidedly modern purpose—the large-scale, profit-oriented production of commodities for a capitalist world market.

Only by grasping this two-sided, hybrid character can the South's slave system—and its effect on all it touched—be understood. On the one hand, the demands and rhythms of the world market created this system and dictated much about the way it functioned. Those who produced these commodities, on the other hand, were themselves commodities owned by others. This decisive fact distinguished the inner workings of the slave economy from those based on independent petty proprietorship, free wage labor, or both. Members of an Alabama agricultural society stressed this simple but profoundly important point in 1846:

> Our condition is quite different from that of the non-slaveholding section of the United States. With them their only property consists of lands, cattle and planting implements. Their laborers are merely hirelings, while with us our laborers are our property....

Slavery was first and foremost a way of obtaining and controlling the workers whose efforts produced such wealth. But the social mobility celebrated in the passage above could operate in both directions. The slave-owning farmer or planter who ignored the requirements of profit making and labor control at the least risked substantial debts and pressures to sell some land or slaves to pay them off. At worst he flirted with the complete loss of his estate.

Despite the generally high price of cotton, most slave owners were quite mindful of such dangers in the antebellum South. Out of forty sons of Augusta-area slaveholders sampled in the 1850 census, twelve (or 30 percent) were nonslaveholders a decade later. The "proper management [of slaves] constitutes the chief success of the planter," a Carolina overseer cautioned in 1836. "If he has not a proper control of them, he had much better give up planting; for as sure as he continues they will ruin him." A Virginia planter warned in 1852 against displaying excessive leniency in setting slave work loads. "The result [of doing that] is, in many cases, the master breaks, the white family is left in poverty, and the poor negroes sold." Cotton planter Thomas B. Chaplin of South Carolina found himself in just such circumstances early in life. In the face of sharp fluctuations in cotton prices during the 1840s, Chaplin's attempt to play the country gentleman drove him deeply into debt. He confided to his diary in the spring of 1845:

> Trouble gathers thicker and thicker around me. I will be compelled to send about ten prime negroes to Town on next Monday, to be sold. I do this rather than have them seized in Beaufort, by the Sheriff ... I never thought that I would be driven to this very unpleasant extremity ... to separate families[,] Mothers and daughters—Brothers and sisters—all to pay for your own extravagances....

During the antebellum decades, as we have seen, the absolute number of slaveholders grew substantially. But the white population of the South increased even faster. The escalating price of salves kept a growing share of southern whites outside slaveholder ranks. As a result, a shrinking proportion of southern whites owned slaves: 36 percent in 1830, 31 percent in 1850, and only 26 percent by 1860.

In terms of raw wealth, the chasm separating the average slaveholder and the average farm-operating nonslaveholder in the cotton kingdom was huge. The former (with assets valued at nearly $25,000) was approximately fourteen times richer than the latter (about $1,800) in 1860. But like those whites who owned slaves, the majority who did not composed a very heterogeneous population....

Given the choice, therefore, most white wage earners (and about 90 percent of all immigrants) preferred to take their chances in the free states and territories. White workers who remained in the South repeatedly complained about having to compete with slaves as well as poorly paid free blacks. A convention of 400 to 500 white mechanics in Atlanta thus resolved in 1851 that "the instruction of negroes in the Mechanic Arts is a source of great dissatisfaction to the mechanical interest, prejudicial to Southern youths engaging in industrial pursuits." On the very eve of secession, a group of white mechanics in Texas wrote the state legislature to "solemnly object to being put in competition with Negro Mechanics." Such resentments frequently boiled over into assaults upon the hapless slaves themselves. A gang of angry white workers thus beat and ejected the slave caulker Frederick Douglass from a Baltimore shipyard in 1836.

Attempts by free workers to restrict the slave owners' freedom to employ human property as they wished were irritating enough. A far more ominous danger loomed, however. As urban commercial and industrial life expanded in the slave states, the planter elite grew increasingly worried that this budding resistance to the slave owners' prerogatives would flower into more generalized antislavery sentiment. Once again, Frederick Douglass's experience suggests the substance behind such fears. On the Baltimore docks one day, a youthful Douglass helped two Irishmen unloading a scow. Afterward, one of them "expressed the deepest sympathy with me, and the most decided hatred of slavery." The two men then advised Douglass "that I ought to run away and go to the North, that I should find friends there, and that I should then be free as anybody." At the time, the wary young slave feigned disinterest. But "I nevertheless remembered their words and their advice and looked forward to an escape to the North." And in 1838, as Douglass did make his bid for freedom as a fugitive slave, he encountered a German blacksmith he knew riding the same northbound train. The man stared at him intently, and Douglass was certain he'd been recognized. The blacksmith, however, "had no heart to betray me. At any rate, he saw me escaping and held his peace."

As the Civil War approached, slave owners saw such dangerous attitudes spreading. Vigilantes expelled the Irish bricklayer Tom Burch from Edgefield, South Carolina, in 1859 for using "seditious language" potentially creating "very great injury among our negroes." A Charleston daily denounced such foreign-born free workers as a "curse rather than a blessing to our peculiar institution." James Henry Hammond's ambition to attempt to "reconcile industry with ... slave labour, agricultural advancement, and Southern tone" was evidently bearing some bitter fruit.

The Northern Economy of "Free" Labor

Between 1790 and 1840, the northern population as a whole multiplied five times. But in the same years, residents of nonsalve areas west of the Alleghenies multiplied in number fully forty-two times. Ohio achieved statehood in 1803. Indiana in 1816, and Illinois two years later in 1818. Michigan entered the Union in 1837, Iowa in 1846, Wisconsin in 1848, and California in 1850. Maine, a frontier region within the Northeast, became a state in 1820....

Together, the transportation revolution, commercialization of agriculture, and the growth of the West—and, for that matter, of the cotton South—created a tremendous domestic market for manufactured goods. Enterprising individuals (Some of them merchants, others artisans, and still others commercial farmers) eyed these opportunities with growing interest. During the first half of the nineteenth century, they set out to claim a share of the potential profits by expanding and reorganizing northern industry. Production of thread, yarn, and then most textiles moved from home to factory. In the artisanal crafts (notably shoemaking, tailoring, and furniture production), employment and output increased and the nature of the work process changed. Grain-milling and meat-packing establishments grew into major enterprises. These sectors and others then developed expanded needs of their own. Growing firms turned out spinning, weaving, and sewing machines, farm equipment, machine tools, steam engines, locomotives, and track. Coal and iron mines and foundries expanded to meet the insistent demand for their products.

One result was a leap in the productivity of human labor. In mining and manufacturing, output per worker increased by half in real terms in just the twenty years prior to the Civil War. Frederick Douglass, having reached New England in his flight from slavery in 1838, marveled at the "striking and gratifying contrast" he observed between the productive efficiency of the North and that of the South. "Main strength—human muscle," he wrote, "unassisted by intelligent skill, was slavery's method of labor." In New Bedford, Massachusetts, Douglass discovered a greater disposition to find substitutes for (or, better, supplements to) paid labor. "In a southern port," he wrote, "twenty or thirty hands would be employed to do what five or six men with the help of one ox would do at the wharf in New Bedford." Even the maidservant's labor in New Bedford was rendered more efficient with the help of "sinks, drains, self-shutting gates, pounding-barrels, washing-machines, wringing machines, and a hundred other contrivances for saving time and money."

The development of northern industry, commerce, and labor productivity translated into a truly staggering increase in total wealth. Between 1840 and 1860, the value added in agriculture nationwide rose by 90 percent (in fixed dollars). Over the same years, value added in manufacturing increased 350 percent—and this advance was concentrated overwhelmingly in the free states, chiefly in the Northeast. The urbanization of the North was also startling. In 1790, fewer than one in ten Northeasterners had lived in towns or cities. By 1860, the proportion had surpassed one in three in New England and in the middle Atlantic states as well. New York City boasted more than a million residents by 1860 (if one includes Brooklyn, then still formally independent), and Philadelphia was the home of half a million. These became the dominant manufacturing cities in the nation. Increasingly industrial and urban, the Northeast replaced the South as the western farmers' chief customer.

The expansion of domestic commerce and manufacturing reshaped society in the free states. The northern rich grew far wealthier. In 1860, southern planters still dominated the ranks of the United States' economic elite, comprising three-fifths of the richest 1 percent of the country's population. But concentration of wealth in the North had advanced too. The richest 5 percent of northern adults held more than half the region's total property in 1860. And this concentration was even more marked in the cities. In 1800, for example, half the taxable property in Philadelphia had belonged to the richest 10 percent of its residents. By 1850, an even larger proportion of the wealth had gravitated into the hands of the richest 1 percent. In 1820, only hundred New Yorkers claimed personal property worth more than $20,000. By 1845, nearly a thousand individuals boasted personal assets in excess of $100,000. Twenty, in the meantime, had become "millionaires," a word that had just entered the popular vocabulary. Boston was soon claiming eighteen millionaires, and Philadelphia another twenty-five....

Between the American Revolution and the Civil War, society in the free states had undergone momentous transformation. As early as the 1830s, one immigrant likened it to "one gigantic workshop, over the entrance to which there is the blazing inscription, 'No admission here, except on business.'" Tocqueville observed admiringly that "no people in the world have made such rapid progress in trade and manufacturing." In 1847, Daniel Webster—by then a Massachusetts senator and champion of the state's business interests—had long since forgotten early misgivings about industrial development. "It is an extraordinary era in which we live," he enthused that year in a speech celebrating extension of the Northern Railroad. "Remarkable for scientific research into the heavens, the earth, and what is beneath the earth," the times were "more remarkable for still for the application of this scientific research to the pursuits of life." By 1860 at the latest, the North's manufacturing sector was second only to Britain's in output and actually surpassed Britain's in degree of mechanization. A team of British investigators, reading the handwriting on the wall, concluded in the 1850s that the United States would shortly "rear up a fabric of commercial greatness, such as the world has hitherto been a stranger to" and so "enabling her soon to rival ourselves as, hitherto, the chief manufacturers of the world."

There was, however, a grimmer aspect to this impressive economic progress. One of the most visible and worrisome products of commercial development and industrialization in the North was a growing dependent population—free of slavery yes, but free of much property as well. In this respect, the evolution of "free labor" society reminded more and more observers of the bleaker results of England's earlier industrialization. "Our good city of New York." Philip Hone noted despairingly in 1847, "has already arrived at the state of society to be found in the large cities of Europe; overburdened with population, and where the two extremes of costly luxury and living, expensive establishments, and improvident waste are presented in daily and hourly contrast with squalid misery and hopeless destitution."

FURTHER READING

Tyler G. Anbinder, *Nativism and Slavery* (1994).

Robert Dykstra, *Bright Radical Star: Black Freedom and White Supremacy on the Hawkeye Frontier* (1993).

Eric Foner, *Free Soil, Free Labor, Free Men: The Ideology of the Republican Party Before the Civil War* (1970).

Lacy K. Ford, Jr., *Origins of Southern Radicalism: The South Carolina Upcountry, 1800–1860* (1988).

William W. Freeling, *The Road to Disunion: Secessionists at Bay, 1776–1854* (1990).

William W. Freeling, *The Road to Disunion: Secessionists Triumphant, 1854–1861* (2007).

William E. Gienapp, *The Origins of the Republican Party, 1852–1856* (1986).

James L. Huston, *Calculating the Value of the Union: Slavery, Property Rights, and the Economic Origins of the Civil War* (2003).

Bruce Levine, *Half Slave and Half Free: The Roots of the Civil War* (1992).

Manisha Sinha, *The Counterrevolution of Slavery: Politics and Ideology in Antebellum South Carolina* (2000).

Kenneth M. Stampp, *America in 1857: A Nation on the Brink* (1991).

Mark W. Summers, *The Plundering Generation: Corruption and the Crisis of the Union, 1849–1861* (1987).

Elizabeth R. Varon, *Disunion: The Coming of the American Civil War* (2008).

CHAPTER 14

The Civil War

Events moved quickly after Abraham Lincoln assumed the presidency on March 4, 1861. When Lincoln attempted to resupply Fort Sumter, an outpost in the harbor of Charleston, South Carolina, that was still controlled by Union forces, the Confederate army shelled the fort; the federal troops surrendered on April 13, 1861. This brief bombardment began a long civil war from which a second revolution would be forged.

When the war began, few expected that it would last four horrifying years. Confederate leaders believed that the world's need for cotton would lead other nations to support their cause. They realized that the Union armies would have to conquer the Confederacy, and they expected that most northerners would tire of war before this could be achieved. Strategists for the Union advocated the "anaconda plan," which coupled a blockade of southern port cities with a military thrust down the Mississippi River valley to divide the Confederacy. In theory, this plan would squeeze the economic life out of the Confederacy, causing its citizenry to sue for peace.

The war went badly for the Union in the early campaigns, particularly in the eastern theater. Indecisive Union generals failed to take advantage of their superior military strength, while able Confederate military leaders, such as Robert E. Lee and "Stonewall" Jackson, befuddled the Union armies. The tide turned in mid-1863 when the Union won two battles in rapid succession, at Vicksburg in the western theater and at Gettysburg in the east. Under the leadership of Ulysses S. Grant and William Tecumseh Sherman, the Union forces took advantage of their numerical strength. These two formerly obscure generals utilized an idea of "total war," which meant that they were willing to wage war against the civilian population as well as against the army and government of their enemy. Shortly after Lincoln's reelection in 1864, Sherman began his "march to the sea," which devastated Georgia. By December 21, 1864, his army had reached the sea at Savannah. Within four months, General Lee surrendered.

The war was revolutionary on many levels. In some ways it might be called the world's first modern war. For the first time, armies engaged in trench warfare. Using rifles that could fire up to five hundred yards, soldiers killed people they could not see. Railroads were used to transfer armies; ironclad ships faced one another in naval combat. As a result, the loss of life suffered by the armies was frightening. In all, 620,000 men died as a result of battle and disease. One out of every six white males in the southern states aged thirteen to forty-three in 1860 was dead five years later. An additional half million men were maimed during the war, and yet another half million spent some time in overcrowded and unsanitary prison camps. People throughout the world observed the war with wonderment and horror. This was what future wars would be like.

In part because of these horrors, American society was transformed. Northern society was not unified behind the war effort, and dissent grew when the government suspended the right of habeus corpus and introduced a draft. The result was riots in northern cities and a heightened distrust of Lincoln's leadership. Basic questions of rights during war thus plagued society. Women's roles expanded as well, in part because men were at war, but also because women actively sought ways, such as participation in the Sanitary Commission, to support the war effort. In the Confederacy, the exigencies of war forced its leader to consider measures that had been unthinkable prior to the war. A confederacy formed on the rights of states found that it needed to centralize its government during war. A culture based on the splendor of a rural world had to foster industrialization in order to fight a war. And a society based on slavery ultimately considered arming slaves to fight in the Confederate army. As the war destroyed southern society, all Americans had to ponder how that society would be reconstructed following the war's conclusion. One monumental change became clear by 1863: the Emancipation Proclamation signaled the end of slavery in the South. African Americans throughout the United States mobilized to end slavery. Whether fighting for the Union army or fleeing their plantation homes to provide aid to invading forces, black people were instrumental in turning the war into a conflict to end slavery. By 1864, Lincoln had come to agree. In his Second Inaugural Address, he imagined that the war would continue "until every drop of blood drawn from the lash shall be paid by another drawn from the sword." Americans nevertheless would continue to ponder how much this national cleansing would alter the trajectory of the nation.

QUESTIONS TO THINK ABOUT

What advantages did the Confederacy have at the outset of the Civil War? What were the Union's advantages? Why did the Union ultimately win the war? How did war strain and change the societies in both the North and South? What freedoms would former slaves most anticipate and desire? Which questions about the future of the United States were answered by the Civil War? Which questions were not?

DOCUMENTS

The first two documents illustrate the varied opinions during the early years of the Civil War. In document 1, Senator Robert Toombs, in a speech given just days after Lincoln was elected, describes how he is an outlaw in the North and how secession resembles the Declaration of Independence in 1776. In contrast, Frederick Douglass, in document 2, looks to the future and demands the emancipation of the slaves. Freed slaves, he assures his readers, will conduct themselves well in a "natural order of human relations." The next four documents depict the lives of people who lived through the war. Document 3 contains excerpts from the diary of a southern white woman where she discusses her fears and deprivations. Document 4 is a letter to President Lincoln from James Henry Gooding, a black soldier. Gooding pleads to be treated—and paid—like a real soldier rather than a mere laborer. Document 5, Tally Simpson, a Confederate soldier, in a letter home, describes the battle of Gettysburg and the devastation of the Confederate troops as a result. Mary A. Livermore recounts in document 6 her work in the Sanitary Commission, an organization staffed mainly by women that cared for sick and wounded soldiers. The final four documents consider the later years of the war. The final three documents deal with the second half of the war. Document 7 contains two political cartoons representing emancipation. The first, by a pro-southern author, suggests that demonic forces led Lincoln when writing the Emancipation Proclamation and that it would unleash chaos. The second, by northern artist Thomas Nast, portrays how African Americans experienced the shift from slavery to freedom. In document 8, Congressman Clement Vallandigham of Ohio focuses on the questions of civil liberty in the North and as such disagrees with Lincoln's characterizations of the war. Vallandigham, a Democrat who opposed the war, condemns actions by Lincoln such as the suspension of the right of habeas corpus as a "reign of terror." Document 9 is Lincoln's Second Inaugural Address in 1865. In it, he expresses a desire to "bind up the nation's wounds," but also refers in almost apocalyptic terms to the war as an atonement for the sin of slavery.

1. Senator Robert Toombs Compares Secession with the American Revolution, 1860

... But we are told that secession would destroy the fairest fabric of liberty the world ever saw, and that we are the most prosperous people in the world under it. The arguments of tyranny as well as its acts, always reenact themselves. The arguments I now hear in favor of this Northern connection are identical in substance, and almost in the same words as those which were used in 1775 and 1776 to sustain the British connection. We won liberty, sovereignty, and independence by the American Revolution—we endeavored to secure and perpetuate these blessings by means of our Constitution. The very men who use these arguments admit that this Constitution, this compact, is violated, broken and trampled underfoot by the abolition party. Shall we surrender the jewels because their robbers and incendiaries have broken the casket? Is this the way to preserve liberty? I would as lief surrender it back to the British crown as to the abolitionists. I will defend it from both. Our purpose is to defend those liberties. What baser fate could befall us or this great experiment of free government than to

Robert Toombs, speech (November 1860), in *The Rebellion Record, 1862–1863,* Supplement to I, ed. Frank Moore (GP Putnam, 1864), 367–368. Also found in *Secession Debated: Georgia's Showdown in 1860,* eds. William W. Freehling and Craig M. Simpson (New York: Oxford University Press, 1992), 48–49.

have written upon its tomb: "Fell by the hands of abolitionists and the cowardice of its natural defenders." If we quail now, this will be its epitaph.

We are said to be a happy and prosperous people. We have been, because we have hitherto maintained our ancient rights and liberties—we will be until we surrender them. They are in danger; come, freemen, to the rescue. If we are prosperous, it is due to God, ourselves, and the wisdom of our State government. We have an executive, legislative, and judicial department at home, possessing and entitled to the confidence of the people. I have already vainly asked for the law of the Federal Government that promotes our prosperity. I have shown you many that retard that prosperity—many that drain our coffers for the benefit of our bitterest foes. I say bitterest foes—show me the nation in the world that hates, despises, villifies, or plunders us like our abolition "brethren" in the North. There is none. I can go to England or France, or any other country in Europe with my slave, without molestation or violating any law. I can go anywhere except in my own country, whilom [i.e., at one time] called "the glorious Union"; here alone am I stigmatized as a felon; here alone am I an outlaw; here alone am I under the ban of the empire; here alone I have neither security nor tranquillity; here alone are organized governments ready to protect the incendiary, the assassin who burns my dwelling or takes my life or those of my wife and children; here alone are hired emissaries paid by brethren to glide through the domestic circle and intrigue insurrection with all of its nameless horrors. My countrymen, "if you have nature in you, bear it not." Withdraw yourselves from such a confederacy; it is your right to do so—your duty to do so. I know not why the abolitionists should object to it, unless they want to torture and plunder you. If they resist this great sovereign right, make another war of independence, for that then will be the question; fight its battles over again—reconquer liberty and independence. As for me, I will take any place in the great conflict for rights which you may assign. I will take none in the Federal Government during Mr. Lincoln's administration.

If you desire a Senator after the fourth of March, you must elect one in my place. I have served you in the State and national councils for nearly a quarter of a century without once losing your confidence. I am yet ready for the public service, when honor and duty call. I will serve you anywhere where it will not degrade and dishonor my country. Make my name infamous forever, if you will, but save Georgia.

2. Frederick Douglass Calls for the Abolition of Slavery, 1862

... If I were asked to describe the most painful and mortifying feature presented in the prosecution and management of the present war on the part of the United States Government, against the slaveholding rebels now marshalled against it,

Frederick Douglass, "The Future of the Negro People of the Slave States," *Douglass' Monthly*, March 1862.

I should not point to Ball's Bluff, Big Bethel, Bull Run, or any of the many blunders and disasters on flood or field; but I should point to the vacillation, doubt, uncertainty and hesitation, which have thus far distinguished our government in regard to the true method of dealing with the vital cause of the rebellion. We are without any declared and settled policy—and our policy seems to be, to have no policy....

But why, O why should we not abolish slavery now? All admit that it must be abolished at some time. What better time than now can be assigned for that great work—Why should it longer live? What good thing has it done that it should be given further lease of life? What evil thing has it left undone? Behold its dreadful history! Saying nothing of the rivers of tears and streams of blood poured out by its 4,000,000 victims—saying nothing of the leprous poison it has diffused through the life blood of our morals and our religion —saying nothing of the many humiliating concessions already made to it— saying nothing of the deep and scandalous reproach it has brought upon our national good name—saying nothing of all this, and more the simple fact that this monster Slavery has eaten up and devoured the patriotism of the whole South, kindled the lurid flames of a bloody rebellion in our midst, invited the armies of hostile nations to desolate our soil, and break down our Government, is good and all-sufficient cause of smiting it as with a bolt from heaven....

But to return. What shall be done with the four million slaves, if emancipated? I answer, deal justly with them; pay them honest wages for honest work; dispense with the biting lash, and pay them the ready cash; awaken a new class of motives in them; remove those old motives of shriveling fear of punishment which benumb and degrade the soul, and supplant them by the higher and better motives of hope, of self-respect, of honor, and of personal responsibility. Reverse the whole current of feeling in regard to them. They have been compelled hitherto to regard the white man as a cruel, selfish, and remorseless tyrant, thirsting for wealth, greedy of gain, and caring nothing as to the means by which he obtains it. Now, let him see that the white man has a nobler and better side to his character, and he will love, honor, esteem the white man.

But it is said that the black man is naturally indolent, and that he will not work without a master. I know that this is a part of his bad reputation; but I also know that he is indebted for this bad reputation to the most indolent and lazy of all the American people, the slaveholders—men who live in absolute idleness, and eat their daily bread in the briny sweat of other men's faces. That the black man in Slavery shirks labor—aims to do as little as he can, and to do that little in the most slovenly manner—only proves that he is a man....

Again, it is affirmed that the Negro, if emancipated, could not take care of himself. My answer to this is, let him have a fair chance to try it. For 200 years he has taken care of himself and his master in the bargain. I see no reason to believe that he could not take care, and very excellent care, of himself when having only himself to support....

It is one of the strangest and most humiliating triumphs of human selfishness and prejudice over human reason, that it leads men to look upon emancipation as an experiment, instead of being, as it is, the natural order of human relations. Slavery, and not Freedom, is the experiment; and to witness its horrible failure we have to open our eyes, not merely upon the blasted soil of Virginia and other Slave States, but upon a whole land brought to the verge of ruin.

We are asked if we would turn the slaves all loose. I answer, Yes. Why not? They are not wolves nor tigers, but men. They are endowed with reason—can decide upon questions of right and wrong, good and evil, benefits and injuries—and are therefore subjects of government precisely as other men are.

3. Margaret Junkin Preston Describes Southern Suffering in Her Diary, 1862

April 3d, 1862: ...

Darkness seems gathering over the Southern land; disaster follows disaster; where is it all to end? My very soul is sick of carnage. I loathe the word—*War*. It is destroying and paralyzing all before it. Our Schools are closed—all the able-bodied men gone—stores shut up, or only here and there one open; goods not to be bought, or so exorbitant that we are obliged to do without. I actually dressed my baby all winter in calico dresses made out of the lining of an old dressing-gown; and G. in clothes concocted out of old castaways. As to myself, I rigidly abstained from getting a single article of dress in the entire past year, except shoes and stockings. Calico is not to be had; a few pieces had been offered at 40 cents per yard. Coarse, unbleached cottons are very occasionally to be met with, and are caught up eagerly at 40 cents per yard. Such material as we used to give ninepence for (common blue twill) is a bargain now at 40 cents, and then of a very inferior quality. Soda, if to be had at all, is 75 cents per lb. Coffee is not to be bought. We have some on hand, and for eight month have drunk a poor mixture, half wheat, half coffee. Many persons have nothing but wheat or rye.

These are some of the *very trifling* effects of this horrid and senseless war. Just now I am bound down under the apprehension of having my husband again enter the service; and if he goes, he says he will not return until the war closes, if indeed he come back alive. May God's providence interpose to prevent his going! His presence is surely needed at home; his hands are taken away by the militia draught, and he has almost despaired of having his farms cultivated this year. His overseer is draughted, and will have to go, unless the plea of sickness will avail to release him, as he has been seriously unwell. The [Virginia Military] Institute is full, two hundred and fifty cadets being in it; but they may disperse at any time, so uncertain is the tenure of everything now. The College [Washington College] has five students; boys too young to enter the army....

Major Problems in the History of the American South, Volume I (1990): 498–500.

August 2d: ... What straits war reduces us to! I carried a lb. or so of sugar and coffee to Sister Agnes lest she should not have any, and she gave me a great treasure—a *pound of soda!* When it can be had, it is $1.25 per lb....

Sept. 3d: ... Yesterday asked the price of a calico dress; "Fifteen dollars and sixty cents!" Tea is $20, per lb. A merchant told me he gave $50. for a pound of sewing silk! The other day our sister, Mrs. Cocke, purchased 5 gallons of whiskey, for which, by way of favor, she only paid $50.! It is selling for $15. per gallon. Very coarse unbleached cotton (ten cent cotton) I was asked 75 cts. for yesterday. Eight dollars, a pair for servants' coarse shoes. Mr. P. paid $11. for a pair for Willy. These prices will do to wonder over after a while.

10 o'clock P.M. Little did I think, when I wrote the above, that such sorrow would overtake this family so soon! News came this afternoon of the late fearful fight on Manassas Plains, and of Willy Preston *being mortally wounded*—in the opinion of the surgeons! His Father was not at home, and did not hear the news for some time. Oh! the anguish of the father-heart! This evening he has gone to Staunton; will travel all night in order to take the cars tomorrow morning. I am afraid to go to bed, lest I be roused by some messenger of evil tidings, or (terrible to dread) the possible arrival of the dear boy—dead! Father in Heaven! Be merciful to us, and spare us this bitterness!

Sept. 4th: The worst has happened—our fearful suspense is over: Willy, the gentle, tender-hearted, brave boy, lies in a soldier's grave on the Plains of Manassas! This has been a day of weeping and of woe to this household. I did not know how I loved the dear boy. My heart is wrung with grief to think that his sweet face, his genial smile, his sympathetic heart are gone. My eyes ache with weeping. But what is the loss to me, compared to the loss to his Father, his sisters, his brothers! Oh! his precious stricken Father! God support him to bear the blow! The carriage has returned, bringing me a note from Mr. P. saying he had heard there was faint hope. Alas! the beloved son has been five days in his grave. My poor husband! Oh! if he were only here, to groan out his anguish on my bosom. I can't write more.

4. James Henry Gooding, an African American Soldier, Pleads for Equal Treatment, 1863

MORRIS ISLAND, S.C.

SEPTEMBER 28, 1863

YOUR EXCELLENCY, ABRAHAM LINCOLN:

Your Excellency will pardon the presumption of an humble individual like myself, in addressing you, but the earnest solicitation of my comrades in arms besides the genuine interest felt by myself in the matter is my excuse, for placing before the Executive head of the Nation our Common Grievance.

James Henry Gooding to Abraham Lincoln, in *A Documentary History of the Negro People in the U.S.*, ed. Herbert Aptheker (New York: Citadel Press, 1951), 482–484.

On the 6th of the last Month, the Paymaster of the Department informed us, that if we would decide to receive the sum of $10 (ten dollars) per month, he would come and pay us that sum, but that, on the sitting of Congress, the Regt. [regiment] would, in his opinion, be allowed the other 3 (three). He did not give us any guarantee that this would be, as he hoped; certainly he had no authority for making any such guarantee, and we cannot suppose him acting in any way interested.

Now the main question is, are we Soldiers, or are we Laborers? We are fully armed, and equipped, have done all the various duties pertaining to a Soldier's life, have conducted ourselves to the complete satisfaction of General Officers, who were, if anything, prejudiced against us, but who now accord us all the encouragement and honors due us; have shared the perils and labor of reducing the first strong-hold that flaunted a Traitor Flag; and more, Mr. President, to-day the Anglo-Saxon Mother, Wife, or Sister are not alone in tears for departed Sons, Husbands and Brothers. The patient, trusting descendant of Afric's Clime have dyed the ground with blood, in defence of the Union, and Democracy. Men, too, your Excellency, who know in a measure the cruelties of the iron heel of oppression, which in years gone by, the very power their blood is now being spilled to maintain, ever ground them in the dust.

But when the war trumpet sounded o'er the land, when men knew not the Friend from the Traitor, the Black man laid his life at the altar of the Nation— and he was refused. When the arms of the Union were beaten, in the first year of the war, and the Executive called for more food for its ravenous maw, again the black man begged the privilege of aiding his country in her need, to be again refused.

And now he is in the War, and how has he conducted himself? ... Obedient and patient and solid as a wall are they. All we lack is a paler hue and a better acquaintance with the alphabet.

Now your Excellency, we have done a Soldier's duty. Why can't we have a Soldier's pay? You caution the Rebel chieftain, that the United States knows no distinction in her soldiers. She insists on having all her soldiers of whatever creed or color, to be treated according to the usages of War. Now if the United States exacts uniformity of treatment of her soldiers from the insurgents, would it not be well and consistent to set the example herself by paying all her soldiers alike?

We of this Regt. were not enlisted under any "contraband" act. But we do not wish to be understood as rating our service of more value to the Government than the service of the ex-slave. Their service is undoubtedly worth much to the Nation, but Congress made express provision touching their case, as slaves freed by military necessity, and assuming the Government to be their temporary Guardian. Not so with us. Freemen by birth and consequently having the advantage of thinking and acting for ourselves so far as the Laws would allow us, we do not consider ourselves fit subjects for the Contraband act.

We appeal to you, Sir, as the Executive of the Nation, to have us justly dealt with. The Regt. do pray that they be assured their service will be fairly appreciated by paying them as American Soldiers, not as menial hirelings. Black men, you may well know, are poor; three dollars per month, for a year, will supply their needy wives and little ones with fuel. If you, as Chief Magistrate of the Nation, will assure us of our whole pay, we are content. Our Patriotism, our enthusiasm will have a new impetus, to exert our energy more and more to aid our Country. Not that our hearts ever flagged in devotion, spite the evident apathy displayed in our behalf, but we feel as though our Country spurned us, now we are sworn to serve her. Please give this a moment's attention.

5. Tally Simpson, a Confederate Soldier, Recounts the Battle of Gettysburg, 1863

Bunker's Hill Va
Saturday, July 18th /63

My dear Carrie

It had been a very long time since I received a letter from you when your last arrived, and I'll assure you it afforded me much pleasure.

Ere this reaches its destination you will have heard of the terrible battle of Gettysburg and the fate of a portion of our noble Army. I am a good deal of Pa's nature—extremely hopeful. But I must confess that this is a gloomy period for the Confederacy. One month ago our prospects were as bright as could well be conceived. Gallant Vicksburg, the Gibraltar of the West and the pride of the South, has fallen the victim to a merciless foe. Port Hudson has surrendered unconditionally, and it is now reduced to a fact that cannot be disputed that the Mississippi is already or must very soon be in the possession of the Yankees from its source to its mouth. And what good will the Trans Mississippi be to the Confederacy thus cut off?

A few weeks ago Genl Lee had the finest Army that ever was raised in ancient or modern times—and commanded by as patriotic and heroic officers as ever drew a sword in defence of liberty. But in an unfortunate hour and under disadvantageous circumstances, he attacked the enemy, and tho he gained the advantage and held possession of the battlefield and even destroyed more of the foe than he lost himself, still the Army of the Potomac lost heavily and is now in a poor condition for offensive operations. I venture to assert that one third of the men are barefooted or almost destitute of necessary clothing. There is one company in this regt which has fifteen men entirely without shoes and consequently unfit for duty. This is at least half of the company alluded to. The night we recrossed the river into Virginia, Harry's shoes gave out, and he suffered a great deal marching over rough turnpikes. But when he reached Martinsburg, he purchased a pair of old ones and did very well afterwards.

Guy R. Everson and Edward H. Simpson, Jr., eds., *"Far, Far from Home": The Wartime Letters of Dick and Tally Simpson, Third South Carolina Volunteers* (New York: Oxford University Press, 1994), 256–259.

'Tis estimated by some that this Army has been reduced to at least one fifth its original strength. Charleston is closely beset, and I think must surely fall sooner or later. The fall of Vicksburg has caused me to lose confidence in something or somebody, I can't say exactly which. And now that gunboats from the Mississippi can be transferred to Charleston and that a portion of Morris Island been taken and can be used to advantage by the enemy, I fear greatly the result of the attack. I trust however, if it does fall, its gallant defenders will raze it to the ground that the enemy cannot find a single spot to pitch a tent upon the site where so magnificent a city once raised, so excitingly, its towering head. Savannah will follow, and then Mobile, and finally Richmond.

These cities will be a loss to the Confederacy. But their fall is no reason why we should despair. It is certainly calculated to cast a gloom over our entire land. But we profess to be a Christian people, and we should put our trust in God. He holds the destiny of our nation, as it were, in the palm of his hand. He it is that directs the counsel of our leaders, both civil and military, and if we place implicit confidence in Him and go to work in good earnest, never for a moment losing sight of Heaven's goodness and protection, it is my firm belief that we shall be victorious in the end. Let the South lose what it may at present, God's hand is certainly in this contest, and He is working for the accomplishment of some grand result, and so soon as it is accomplished, He will roll the sun of peace up the skies and cause its rays to shine over our whole land. We were a wicked, proud, ambitious nation, and God has brought upon us this war to crush and humble our pride and make us a better people generally. And the sooner this happens the better for us....

Your ever affec cousin

T. N. Simpson

James is quite well and stands these marches finely. He sends his love to his family and to all the negros generally. He likewise wishes to be remembered to his master and all the white family.

6. Mary A. Livermore, a Northern Woman, Recalls Her Role in the Sanitary Commission, 1863

Organizations of women for the relief of sick and wounded soldiers, and for the care of soldiers' families, were formed with great spontaneity at the very beginning of the war. There were a dozen or more of them in Chicago, in less than a month after Cairo was occupied by Northern troops. They raised money, prepared and forwarded supplies of whatever was demanded, every

Mary A. Livermore, *My Story of the War: A Woman's Narrative of Four Years Personal Experience* (Hartford, Conn.: A. D. Worthington and Company, 1889), 135–137.

shipment being accompanied by some one who was held responsible for the proper disbursement of the stores. Sometimes these local societies affiliated with, or became parts of, more comprehensive organizations. Most of them worked independently during the first year of the war, the Sanitary Commission of Chicago being only one of the relief agencies. But the Commission gradually grew in public confidence, and gained in scope and power; and all the local societies were eventually merged in it, or became auxiliary to it. As in Chicago, so throughout the country. The Sanitary Commission became the great channel, through which the patriotic beneficence of the nation flowed to the army....

Here, day after day, the drayman left boxes of supplies sent from aid societies in Iowa, Minnesota, Wisconsin, Michigan, Illinois, and Indiana. Every box contained an assortment of articles, a list of which was tacked on the inside of the lid....

One day I went into the packing-room to learn the secrets of these boxes,— everyone an argosy of love,—and took notes during the unpacking. A capacious box, filled with beautifully made shirts, drawers, towels, socks, and handkerchiefs, with "comfort-bags" containing combs, pins, needles, court-plaster, and black sewing-cotton, and with a quantity of carefully dried berries and peaches, contained the following unsealed note, lying on top:—

> DEAR SOLDIERS,—The little girls of—send this box to you. They hear that thirteen thousand of you are sick, and have been wounded in battle. They are very sorry, and want to do something for you. They cannot do much, for they are all small; but they have bought with their own money, and made what is in here. They hope it will do some good, and that you will all get well and come home. We all pray to God for you night and morning....

Another mammoth packing-case was opened, and here were folded in blessings and messages of love with almost every garment. On a pillow was pinned the following note, unsealed, for sealed notes were never broken:—

> MY DEAR FRIEND,—You are not *my* husband nor son; but you are the husband or son of some woman who undoubtedly loves you as I love mine. I have made these garments for you with a heart that aches for your sufferings, and with a longing to come to you to assist in taking care of you. It is a great comfort to me that God loves and pities you, pining and lonely in a far-off hospital: and if you believe in God, it will also be a comfort to *you*. Are you near death, and soon to cross the dark river? Oh, then, may God soothe your last hours, and lead you up "the shining shore," where there is no war, no sickness, no death. Call on Him, for He is an ever-present helper.

7. Two Artistic Representation of Emancipation, 1863, 1864

LINCOLN SIGNING THE EMANCIPATION PROCLAMATION.—FROM A SOUTHERN WAR ETCHING.

EMANCIPATION CARTOON. Abraham Lincoln signing the Emancipation Proclamation—a Southern point of view. Reproduction of an etching from Adalbert J. Volck's *Confederate War Etchings*.

This *Harper's Weekly* cartoon by Thomas Nast celebrates the Emancipation Proclamation by President Abraham Lincoln on January 1, 1863.

8. Congressman Clement Vallandigham
Denounces the Union War Effort, 1863

The men who are in power at Washington, extending their agencies out through the cities and states of the Union and threatening to reinaugurate a reign of terror, may as well know that we comprehend precisely their purpose. I beg leave to assure you that it cannot and will not be permitted to succeed. The people of this country endorsed it once because they were told that it was essential to "the speedy suppression or crushing out of the rebellion" and the restoration of the Union; and they so loved the Union of these states that they would consent, even for a little while, under the false and now broken promises of the men in power, to surrender those liberties in order that the great object might, as was promised, be accomplished speedily.

They have been deceived; instead of crushing out the rebellion, the effort has been to crush out the spirit of liberty. The conspiracy of those in power is not so much for a vigorous prosecution of the war against rebels in the South as against the democracy in peace at home....

... Now, if in possession of the purse and the sword absolutely and unqualifiedly, for two years, there be anything else wanting which describes a dictatorship, I beg to know what it is....

I will not consent to put the entire purse of the country and the sword of the country into the hands of the executive, giving him despotic and dictatorial power to carry out an object which I avow before my countrymen is the destruction of their liberties and the overthrow of the Union of these states....

The charge has been made against us—all who are opposed to the policy of this administration and opposed to this war—that we are for "peace on any terms." It is false. I am not, but I am for an immediate stopping of the war and for honorable peace. I am for peace for the sake of the Union of these states....

[A]nd I, unlike some of my own party, and unlike thousands of the Abolition Party, believe still, before God, that the Union can be reconstructed and will be. That is my faith, and I mean to cling to it as the wrecked mariner clings to the last plank amid the shipwreck.

9. Abraham Lincoln Calls for Peace and Justice
in His Second Inaugural Address, 1865

On the occasion corresponding to this four years ago, all thoughts were anxiously directed to an impending civil-war. All dreaded it—all sought to avert it. While the inaugural address was being delivered from this place, devoted altogether to *saving* the Union without war, insurgent agents were in the city seeking to *destroy* it without war—seeking to dissolve the Union, and divide effects,

Clement Vallandigham's Copperhead Dissent (1863), in *Speeches, Arguments, Addresses, and Letters of Clement L. Vallandigham,* Clement L. Vallandigham (New York: J. Walter and Co., 1864), 479–502.

Abraham Lincoln, Second Inaugural Address, 1865.

by negotiation. Both parties deprecated war; but one of them would *make* war rather than let the nation survive; and the other would *accept* war rather than let it perish. And the war came.

One eighth of the whole population were colored slaves, not distributed generally over the Union, but localized in the Southern part of it. These slaves constituted a peculiar and powerful interest. All knew that this interest was, somehow, the cause of the war. To strengthen, perpetuate, and extend this interest was the object for which the insurgents would rend the Union, even by war; while the government claimed no right to do more than to restrict the territorial enlargement of it. Neither party expected for the war, the magnitude, or the duration, which it has already attained. Neither anticipated that the *cause* of the conflict might cease with, or even before, the conflict itself should cease. Each looked for an easier triumph, and a result less fundamental and astounding. Both read the same Bible, and pray to the same God; and each invokes His aid against the other.... If we shall suppose that American Slavery is one of those offences which, in the providence of God, must needs come, but which, having continued through His appointed time, He now wills to remove, and that He gives to both North and South, this terrible war, as the woe due to those by whom the offence came, shall we discern therein any departure form those divine attributes which the believers in a Living God always ascribe to Him? Fondly do we hope—fervently do we pray—that this mightly scourge of war may speedily pass away. Yet, if God wills that it continue, until all the wealth piled by the bond-man's two hundred and fifty years of unrequited toil shall be sunk, and until every drop of blood drawn with the lash, shall be paid by another drawn with the sword, as was said three thousand years ago, so still it must be said "the judgments of the Lord, are true and righteous altogether".

With malice toward none; with charity for all; with firmness in the right, as God gives us to see the right, let us strive on to finish the work we are in; to bind up the nation's wounds; to care for him who shall have borne the battle, and for his widow, and his orphan—to do all which may achieve and cherish a just, and a lasting peace, among ourselves, and with all nations.

☆ ESSAYS

The Civil War ended slavery, but historians have debated who was most responsible for the Emancipation Proclamation. James M. McPherson, professor emeritus of history at Princeton University, stresses the political genius of Abraham Lincoln, arguing that Lincoln played a crucial role in engineering three revolutions during the Civil War, one of which was the abolition of slavery. Professor McPherson emphasizes the political difficulties that Lincoln faced in bringing about abolition. Although Lincoln moved cautiously during the early years of war, his proclamation of emancipation completely changed the meaning of the war because it proclaimed a revolutionary new aim of the war. A group of scholars led by Ira Berlin, a member of the department of history at the University of

Maryland, argues in contrast that the responsibility for the Emancipation Proclamation lies with the slaves themselves. President Lincoln, he contends, entered the Civil War only to save the Union, and Confederate leaders were convinced that slavery would endure. It was the actions of slaves, he argues, that forced Lincoln to come to terms with emancipation. By moving to the Union army, they not only aided the war effort, but ultimately forced the issue. If he began as a president intent only on saving the Union, Lincoln ultimately became known as the Great Emancipator. But his legacy would not have occurred, Professor Berlin and his colleagues believe, had it not been for African Americans' forcing the issue.

The Role of Abraham Lincoln in the Abolition of Slavery

JAMES M. MCPHERSON

The foremost Lincoln scholar of a generation ago, James G. Randall, considered the sixteenth president to be a conservative on the great issues facing the country, Union and slavery. If conservatism, wrote Randall, meant "caution, prudent adherence to tested values, avoidance of rashness, and reliance upon unhurried, peaceable evolution, [then] Lincoln was a conservative." His preferred solution of the slavery problem, Randall pointed out, was a program of gradual, compensated emancipation with the consent of the owners, stretching over a generation or more, with provision for the colonization abroad of emancipated slaves to minimize the potential for racial conflict and social disorder. In his own words, Lincoln said that he wanted to "stand on middle ground," avoid "dangerous extremes," and achieve his goals through "the spirit of compromise ... [and] of mutual concession." In essence, concluded Randall, Lincoln believed in evolution rather than revolution, in "planting, cultivating, and harvesting, not in uprooting and destroying." Many historians have agreed with this interpretation. To cite just two of them: T. Harry Williams maintained that "Lincoln was on the slavery question, as he was on most matters, a conservative"; and Norman Graebner wrote an essay entitled "Abraham Lincoln: Conservative Statesman," based on the premise that Lincoln was a conservative because "he accepted the need of dealing with things as they were, not as he would have wished them to be."

Yet as president of the United States, Lincoln presided over a profound, wrenching experience which, in Mark Twain's words, "uprooted institutions that were centuries old, changed the politics of a people, transformed the social life of half the country, and wrought so profoundly upon the entire national character that the influence cannot be measured short of two or three generations." Benjamin Disraeli, viewing this experience from across the Atlantic in 1863, characterized "the struggle in America" as "a great revolution.... [We] will see, when the waters have subsided, a different America." The *Springfield*

(Mass.) *Republican*, an influential wartime newspaper, predicted that Lincoln's Emancipation Proclamation would accomplish "the greatest social and political revolution of the age." The historian Otto Olsen has labeled Lincoln a revolutionary because he led the nation in its achievement of this result.

As for Lincoln himself, he said repeatedly that the right of revolution, the "right of any people" to "throw off, to revolutionize, their existing form of government, and to establish such other in its stead as they may choose" was "a sacred right—a right, which we may hope and believe, is to liberate the world." The Declaration of Independence, he insisted often, was the great "charter of freedom" and in the example of the American Revolution "the world has found ... the germ ... to grow and expand into the universal liberty of mankind." Lincoln championed the leaders of the European revolutions of 1848; in turn, a man who knew something about those revolutions—Karl Marx—praised Lincoln in 1865 as "the single-minded son of the working class" who had led his "country through the matchless struggle for the rescue of an enchained race and the reconstruction of a social world."

What are we to make of these contrasting portraits of Lincoln the conservative and Lincoln the revolutionary? Are they just another example of how Lincoln's words can he manipulated to support any position, even diametrically opposed ones? No. It is a matter of interpretation and emphasis within the context of a fluid and rapidly changing crisis situation. The Civil War started out as one kind of conflict and ended as something quite different. These apparently contradictory positions about Lincoln the conservative versus Lincoln the revolutionary can be reconciled by focusing on this process. The attempt to reconcile them can tell us a great deal about the nature of the American Civil War.

That war has been viewed as a revolution—as the second American Revolution—in three different senses. Lincoln played a crucial role in defining the outcome of the revolution in each of three respects.

The first way in which some contemporaries regarded the events of 1861 as a revolution was the frequent invocation of the right of revolution by southern leaders to justify their secession—their declaration of independence—from the United States. The Mississippi convention that voted to secede in 1861 listed the state's grievances against the North, and proclaimed: "For far less cause than this, our fathers separated from the Crown of England."...

For Lincoln it was the *Union*, not the Confederacy, that was the true heir of the Revolution of 1776. That revolution had established a republic, a democratic government of the people by the people. This republic was a fragile experiment in a world of kings, emperors, tyrants, and theories of aristocracy. If secession were allowed to succeed, it would destroy that experiment. It would set a fatal precedent by which the minority could secede whenever it did not like what the majority stood for until the United States fragmented into a dozen pitiful, squabbling countries, the laughing stock of the world. The successful establishment of a slaveholding Confederacy would also enshrine the idea of inequality, a contradiction of the ideal of equal natural rights on which the United States was founded. "This issue embraces more than the fate of these United States," said Lincoln on another occasion. "It presents to the whole family of man, the question, whether a constitutional republic, or a democracy ... can, or cannot, maintain its territorial integrity." Nor is the struggle "altogether for today; it is for a vast future.... On the side of the Union it is a struggle for maintaining in the world that form and substance of government whose leading object is to elevate the condition of men ... to afford all an unfettered start, and a fair chance in the race of life."

To *preserve* the Union and *maintain* the republic: these verbs denote a conservative purpose. If the Confederacy's war of independence was indeed a revolution, Lincoln was most certainly a conservative. But if secession was an act of counter-revolution to forestall a revolutionary threat to slavery posed by the government Lincoln headed, these verbs take on a different meaning and Lincoln's intent to conserve the Union becomes something other than conservatism. But precisely what it would become was not yet clear in 1861.

The second respect in which the Civil War is viewed as a revolution was in its abolition of slavery. This was indeed a revolutionary achievement—not only an expropriation of the principal form of property in half the country, but a destruction of the institution that was basic to the southern social order, the political structure, the culture, the way of life in this region. But in 1861 this revolutionary achievement was not part of Lincoln's war aims.

From the beginning of the war, though, abolitionists and some Republicans urged the Lincoln administration to turn the military conflict into a revolutionary crusade to abolish slavery and create a new order in the South. As one abolitionist put it in 1861, although the Confederates "justify themselves under the right of revolution," their cause "is not a revolution but a rebellion against the noblest of revolution." The North must meet this southern counterrevolution by converting the war for the Union into a revolution for freedom. "WE ARE THE REVOLUTIONISTS," he proclaimed. The principal defect of the first American Revolution, in the eyes of abolitionists, had been that while it freed white Americans from British rule it failed to free black Americans from slavery. Now was the time to remedy that defect by proclaiming emancipation and inviting the slaves "to a share in the *glorious second American Revolution*." And Thaddeus Stevens, the grim-visaged old gladiator who led the radical Republicans in the House of Representatives, pulled no punches in this regard. "We must treat this [war] as a radical revolution," he declared, and "free every slave—slay every traitor—burn every rebel mansion, if these things be necessary to preserve" the nation.

Such words grated harshly on Lincoln's ears during the first year of the war. In his message to Congress in December 1861 the president deplored the possibility that the war might "degenerate into a violent and remorseless revolutionary struggle." It was not that Lincoln *wanted* to preserve slavery. On the contrary, he said many times: "I am naturally anti-slavery. If slavery is not wrong, nothing is wrong." But as president he could not act officially on his private "judgment [concerning] the moral question of slavery." He was bound by the Constitution, which protected the institution of slavery in the states. In the first year of the war the North fought to preserve this Constitution and restore the Union as it had existed before 1861. Lincoln's theory of the war held that since secession was illegal, the Confederate states were still legally in the Union although temporarily under the control of insurrectionists. The government's purpose was to suppress this insurrection and restore loyal Unionists to control of the southern states. The conflict was therefore a limited war with the limited goal of restoring the status quo ante bellum, not an unlimited war to destroy an enemy nation and reshape its society. And since, in theory, the southern states were still in the Union, they continued to enjoy all their constitutional rights, including slavery.

There were also several political reasons for Lincoln to take this conservative position in 1861. For one thing, the four border slave states of Missouri, Kentucky, Maryland, and Delaware had remained in the Union; Lincoln desperately wanted to keep them there. He would like to have God on his side, Lincoln supposedly said, but he *must* have Kentucky. In all of these four states except Delaware a strong pro-Confederate faction existed. Any rash action by the northern government against slavery, therefore, might push three more states into the Confederacy. Moreover, in the North itself nearly half of the voters were Democrats, who supported a war for the Union but might oppose a war against slavery. For these reasons, Lincoln held at bay the Republicans and abolitionists who were calling for an antislavery war and revoked actions by two of his generals who had proclaimed emancipation by martial law in areas under their command.

Antislavery Republicans challenged the theory underlying Lincoln's concept of a limited war. They pointed out that by 1862 the conflict had become in theory as well as in fact a full-fledged war between nations, not just a police action to suppress an uprising. By imposing a blockade on Confederate ports and treating captured Confederate soldiers as prisoners of war rather than as criminals or pirates, the Lincoln administration had in effect recognized that this was a war rather than a mere domestic insurrection. Under international law, belligerent powers had the right to seize or destroy enemy resources used to wage war—munitions, ships, military equipment, even food for the armies and crops sold to obtain cash to buy armaments. As the war escalated in scale and fury and as Union armies invaded the South in 1861, they did destroy or capture such resources. Willy-nilly the war *was* becoming a remorseless revolutionary conflict, a total war rather than a limited one.

A major Confederate resource for waging war was the slave population, which constituted a majority of the southern labor force. Slaves raised food for the army, worked in war industries, built fortifications, dug trenches, drove army supply wagons, and so on. As enemy property, these slaves were subject to confiscation under the laws of war. The Union Congress passed limited confiscation laws in August 1861 and July 1862 that authorized the seizure of this human property. But pressure mounted during 1862 to go further than this—to proclaim emancipation as a *means* of winning the war by converting the slaves from a vital war resource for the South to allies of the North, and beyond that to make the abolition of slavery a *goal* of the war, in order to destroy the institution that had caused the war in the first place and would continue to plague the nation in the future if it was allowed to survive. By the summer of 1861, most

Republicans wanted to turn this limited war to restore the old Union into a revolutionary war to create a new nation purged of slavery.

For a time Lincoln tried to outflank this pressure by persuading the border slave states remaining in the Union to undertake voluntary, gradual emancipation, with the owners to he compensated by the federal government. With rather dubious reasoning, Lincoln predicted that such action would shorten the war by depriving the Confederacy of its hope for the allegiance of these states and thereby induce the South to give up the fight. And though the compensation of slaveholders would be expensive, it would cost much less than continuing the war. If the border states adopted some plan of gradual emancipation such as northern states had done after the Revolution of 1776, said Lincoln, the process would not radically disrupt the social order.

Three times in the spring and summer of 1862 Lincoln appealed to congressmen from the border states to endorse a plan for gradual emancipation. If they did not, he warned in March, "it is impossible to foresee all the incidents which may attend and all the ruin which may follow." In May he declared that the changes produced by his gradual plan "would come gently as the dews of heaven, not rending or wrecking anything. Will you not embrace it?… You can not, if you would, be blind to the signs of the times." But most of the border-state representatives remained blind to the signs. They questioned the constitutionality of Lincoln's proposal, objected to its cost, bristled at its veiled threat of federal coercion, and deplored the potential race problem they feared would come with a large free black population. In July, Lincoln once more called border-state congressmen to the White House. He admonished them bluntly that "the unprecedentedly stern facts of the case" called for immediate action. The limited war was becoming a total war; pressure to turn it into a war of abolition was growing. The slaves were emancipating themselves by running away from home and coming into Union lines. If the border states did not make "a decision at once to emancipate *gradually* … the institution in your states will be extinguished by mere friction and abrasion—by the mere incidents of the war." In other words, if they did not accept an evolutionary plan for the abolition of slavery, it would he wiped out by the revolution that was coming. But again they refused, rejecting Lincoln's proposal by a vote of twenty to nine. Angry and disillusioned, the president decided to embrace the revolution. That very evening he made up his mind to issue an emancipation proclamation. After a delay to wait for a Union victory, he sent forth the preliminary proclamation on September 22—after the battle of Antietam—and the final proclamation on New Year's Day 1863.

The old cliché, that the proclamation did not free a single slave because it applied only to the Confederate states where Lincoln had no power, completely misses the point. The proclamation announced a revolutionary new war aim— the overthrow of slavery by force of arms if and when Union armies conquered the South. Of course, emancipation could not be irrevocably accomplished without a constitutional amendment, so Lincoln threw his weight behind the Thirteenth Amendment, which the House passed in January 1865. In the meantime two of the border states, Maryland and Missouri, which had refused to consider gradual, compensated emancipation in 1862, came under control of emancipationists who pushed through state constitutional amendments that abolished slavery without compensation and went into effect immediately—a fate experienced by the other border states, Kentucky and Delaware, along with the rest of the South when the Thirteenth Amendment was ratified in December 1865.

But from the time the Emancipation Proclamation went into effect at the beginning of 1863, the North fought for the revolutionary goal of a new Union without slavery. Despite grumbling and dissent by some soldiers who said they had enlisted to fight for the Union rather than for the "nigger," most soldiers understood and accepted the new policy. A colonel from Indiana put it this way: whatever their opinion of slavery and blacks, his men "desire to destroy everything that gives the rebels strength." Therefore "this army will sustain the emancipation proclamation and enforce it with the bayonet." Soon after the proclamation came out, General-in Chief Henry W. Halleck wrote to General Ulysses S. Grant near Vicksburg that "the character of the war has very much changed within the last year. There is now no possible hope of reconciliation with the rebels.... We must conquer the rebels or be conquered by them.... Every slave withdrawn from the enemy is the equivalent of a white man put *hors de combat*." One of Grant's field commanders explained that "the policy is to be terrible on the enemy. I am using negroes all the time for my work as teamsters, and have 1,000 employed."

Lincoln endorsed this policy of being "terrible on the enemy." And the policy soon went beyond using freed slaves as teamsters' and laborers. By early 1863 the Lincoln administration committed itself to enlisting black men in the army. Arms in the hands of slaves constituted the South's ultimate nightmare. The enlistment of black soldiers to fight and kill their former masters was by far the most revolutionary dimension of the emancipation policy. And, after overcoming his initial hesitation, Lincoln became an enthusiastic advocate of this policy. In March 1863 he wrote to Andrew Johnson, military governor of occupied Tennessee: "The bare sight of fifty thousand armed, and drilled black soldiers on the banks of the Mississippi, would end the rebellion at once. And who doubts that we can present that sight, if we but take hold in earnest?" By August 1863, when the Union army had organized 50,000 black soldiers and was on the way to enlistment of 180,000 before the war was over, Lincoln declared in a public letter that "the emancipation policy, and the use of colored troops, constitute the heaviest blow yet dealt to the rebellion."

When conservatives complained of the revolutionary nature of these heavy blows, Lincoln responded that the nation could no longer pursue "a temporizing and forbearing" policy toward rebels. "Decisive and extensive measures must be adopted." Conservatives who did not like it should blame the slaveholders and fire-eaters who started the war. They "must understand," said Lincoln in an angry tone, "that they cannot experiment for ten years trying to destroy the government, and if they fail still come back into the Union unhurt." In a metaphor that he used several times, Lincoln said that "broken eggs cannot be mended." The egg of slavery was already broken by 1862; if the South continued fighting it must expect more eggs to be broken, so the sooner it gave up "the smaller [would] be the amount of that which will be beyond mending." Lincoln's fondness for this metaphor is interesting, for modern revolutionaries sometimes use a similar one to justify the use of violence to bring about social change: you cannot make an omelet, they say, without breaking eggs—that is, you cannot make a new society without destroying the old one.

Another way of illustrating how Lincoln came to believe in this revolutionary concept is to quote from his second inaugural address, delivered at a time when the war had gone on for almost four terrible years. On the one hand were the famous words of the second inaugural calling for the binding up of the nation's wounds, with malice toward none and charity for all. With these words Lincoln invoked the New Testament lesson of forgiveness; he urged a soft peace once the war was over. But although he believed in a soft peace, it could be won only by a hard war. This was an Old Testament concept, and for Lincoln's Old Testament vision of a hard war, examine *this* passage from the second inaugural: "American Slavery is one of those offences which, in the providence of God.... He now wills to remove [through] this terrible war, as the woe due to those by whom the offence came.... Fondly do we hope—fervently do we pray—that this mighty scourge of war may speedily pass away. Yet if God wills that it continue, until all the wealth piled by the bondman's two hundred and fifty years of unrequited toil shall be sunk, and until every drop of blood drawn with the lash, shall be paid by another drawn with the sword, as was said three thousand years ago, so still it must be said 'the judgments of the Lord, are true and righteous altogether.'"

This was the language not only of the Old Testament, but also of revolution. In the second respect in which the Civil War has been viewed as a revolution—its achievement of the abolition of slavery—Lincoln fits the pattern of a revolutionary leader. He was a reluctant one at first, to be sure, but in the end he was more radical than Washington or Jefferson or any of the leaders of the first revolution. They led a successful struggle for independence from Britain but did not accomplish a fundamental change in the society they led. Lincoln did preside over such a change. Indeed, as he put it himself, also in the second inaugural, neither side had anticipated such "fundamental and astounding" changes when the war began.

These words introduce the third respect in which the Civil War can be viewed as a revolution: it destroyed not only slavery but also the social structure of the old South that had been founded on slavery, and it radically altered the power balance between the North and the South. It changed the direction of American development. This was what Mark Twain meant when he wrote that the war had "uprooted institutions that were centuries old ... transformed the social life of half the country, and wrought so profoundly upon the entire national character." It was what Charles A. Beard meant when he wrote ... that the Civil War was a "social cataclysm ... making vast changes in the arrangement of classes, in the distribution of wealth, in the course of industrial development."

The war ended seventy years of southern domination of the national government and transferred it to Yankee Republicans who controlled the polity and economy of the United States for most of the next seventy years. It increased northern wealth and capital by 50 percent during the 1860s while destroying 60 percent of southern wealth. The output of southern industry in proportion to that of the North was cut in half by the war; the value of southern agricultural land in relation to that of the North was cut by three-fourths.

These changes occurred because when the Civil War became a total war, the invading army intentionally destroyed the economic capacity of the South to wage war. Union armies ripped up thousands of miles of southern railroads and blew up hundreds of bridges; Confederate cavalry raids and guerrilla operations behind Union lines in the South added to the destruction. More than half of the South's farm machinery was wrecked by the war, two-fifths of its livestock was killed, and one-quarter of its white males of military age—also the prime age for economic production—were killed, a higher proportion than suffered by any European power in World War I, that holocaust which ravaged a continent and spread revolution through many of its countries....

Although Abraham Lincoln was a compassionate man who deplored this destruction and suffering, he nevertheless assented to it as the only way to win the war. After all, he had warned southerners two years earlier that the longer they fought, the more eggs would be broken. Now, in 1864, he officially conveyed to Sheridan the "thanks of the nation, and my own personal admiration and gratitude, for [your] operations the Shenandoah Valley"; he sent Sherman and his army "grateful acknowledgments" for their march through Georgia....

What conclusions can we draw, then, that make sense of those contrasting pictures of Lincoln the conservative and Lincoln the revolutionary quoted at the beginning of this essay? Although it may seem like an oxymoron, Lincoln can best be described as a conservative revolutionary. That is, he wanted to conserve the Union as the revolutionary heritage of the founding fathers. Preserving this heritage was the *purpose* of the war; all else became a means to achieve this end. As Lincoln phrased it in his famous public letter to Horace Greeley in August 1862, "My paramount object in this struggle *is* to save the Union, and is *not* either to save or to destroy slavery.... What I do about slavery and the colored race, I do because I believe it helps to save the Union." By the time he wrote these words, Lincoln had made up his mind that to save the Union he must destroy slavery. The means always remained subordinated to the end, but the means did become as essential to the northern war effort as the end itself. In that sense perhaps we could describe Lincoln as a pragmatic revolutionary, for as a pragmatist he adapted the means to the end. Thus we can agree with the historian Norman Graebner who was quoted earlier as stating that Lincoln "accepted the need of dealing with things as they were, not as he would have wished them to be." But instead of concluding, as Graebner did, that this made Lincoln a conservative, we must conclude that it made him a revolutionary. Not an ideological revolutionary, to be sure—Lincoln was no Robespierre or Lenin with a blueprint for a new order—but he was a pragmatic revolutionary who found it necessary to destroy slavery and create a new birth of freedom in order to preserve the Union.

"The dogmas of the quiet past," Lincoln told Congress in December 1862, "are inadequate to the stormy present. As our case is new, we must think anew, and act anew." It was *the war itself*, not the ideological blueprints of Lincoln or any other leader, that generated the radical momentum that made it a second American revolution. Like most wars that become total wars, the Civil War snowballed into huge and unanticipated dimensions and took on a life and purpose of its own far beyond the causes that had started it. As Lincoln said in his second inaugural address, neither side "expected for the war the magnitude or the duration which it has already attained." Or as he put it on another occasion, "I claim not to have controlled events, but confess plainly that events have controlled me." But in conceding that the war rather than he had shaped the thrust and direction of the revolution, Lincoln was perhaps too modest. For it was his own superb leadership, strategy, and sense of timing as president, commander in chief, and head of the Republican party that determined the pace of the revolution and ensured its success. With a less able man as president, the North might have lost the war or ended it under the leadership of Democrats who would have given its outcome a very different shape. Thus in accepting "the need of dealing with things as they were," Lincoln was not a conservative statesman but a revolutionary statesman.

The Role of African Americans in the Abolition of Slavery

IRA BERLIN, BARBARA J. FIELDS, STEVEN F. MILLER, JOSEPH P. REIDY, AND LESLIE S. ROWLAND

The beginning of the Civil War marked the beginning of the end of slavery in the American South. At first, most white Americans denied what would eventually seem self-evident. With President Abraham Lincoln in the fore, federal authorities insisted that the nascent conflict must be a war to restore the natural union, and nothing more. Confederate leaders displayed a fuller comprehension of the importance of slavery, which Vice-President Alexander Stephens called the cornerstone of the Southern nation. But if Stephens and others grasped slavery's significance, they assumed that the Confederate struggle for independence would require no change in the nature of the institution. A Southern victory would transform the political status, not the social life, of the slave states; black people would remain in their familiar place. Despite a vigorous dissent from Northern abolitionists, most white people—North and South—saw no reason to involve slaves in their civil war.

Excerpt from *Slaves No More: Three Essays on Emancipation and the Civil War* by Ira Berlin. Barbara J. Fields, Steven F. Miller, Joseph P. Reidy, and Leslie S. Rowland. Reprinted with the permission of Cambridge University Press.

Slaves had a different understanding of the sectional struggle. Unmoved by the public pronouncements and official policies of the federal government, they recognized their centrality to the dispute and knew that their future depended upon its outcome. With divisions among white Americans erupting into open warfare, slaves watched and waited, alert for ways to turn the military conflict to their own advantage, stubbornly refusing to leave its outcome to the two belligerents. Lacking political standing or public voice, forbidden access to the weapons of war, slaves nonetheless acted resolutely to place their freedom—and that of their posterity—on the wartime agenda. Steadily, as opportunities arose, they demonstrated their readiness to take risks for freedom and to put their loyalty, their labor, and their lives in the service of the federal government. In so doing, they gradually rendered untenable every Union policy short of universal emancipation and forced the Confederate government to adopt measures that severely compromised the sovereignty of the master. On both sides of the line of battle, Americans came to know that a war for the Union must be a war for freedom.

The change did not come easily or at once. At first, Northern political and military leaders freed slaves only hesitantly, under the pressure of military necessity. But, as the war dragged on, their reluctance gave way to an increased willingness and eventually to a firm determination to extirpate chattel bondage. The Emancipation Proclamation of January 1, 1863, and the enlistment of black soldiers into Union ranks in the following months signaled the adoption of emancipation as a fundamental Northern war aim, although that commitment availed little until, vindicated by military victory. Even after the surrender of the Confederacy, slavery survived in two border states until the Thirteenth Amendment became part of the United States Constitution in December 1865.

Whereas Union policy shifted in favor of emancipation, Confederate leaders remained determined to perpetuate slavery. But the cornerstone of Southern nationality proved to be its weakest point. Slaves resisted attempts to mobilize them on behalf of the slaveholders' republic. Their sullen and sometimes violent opposition to the Confederate regime magnified divisions within Southern society, gnawing at the Confederacy from within. In trying to sustain slavery while fending off the Union army, Confederate leaders unwittingly compromised their own national aspirations and undermined the institution upon which Southern nationality was founded. In the end, the victors celebrated slavery's demise and claimed the title of emancipator. The vanquished understood full well how slavery had helped to seal their doom.

The war provided the occasion for slaves to seize freedom, but three interrelated circumstances determined what opportunities lay open to them and influenced the form that the struggle for liberty assumed: first, the character of slave society; second, the course of the war itself; and third, the policies of the Union and Confederacy governments. Although none of these operated independently of the others, each had its own dynamic. All three were shaped by the particularities of Southern geography and the chronology of the war. Together, they made the destruction of slavery a varying, uneven, and frequently tenuous process, whose complex history has been obscured by the apparent certitude and finality of the great documents that announced the end of chattel bondage. Once the evolution of emancipation replaces the absolutism of the Emancipation Proclamation and the Thirteenth Amendment as the focus of study, the story of slavery's demise shifts from the presidential mansion and the halls of Congress to the farms and plantations that became wartime battlefields. And slaves—whose persistence forced federal soldiers, Union and Confederate policy makers, and even their own masters onto terrain they never intended to occupy—become the prime movers in securing their own liberty....

In April 1861, within days of Lincoln's call for volunteers to protect the nation's capital and put down the rebellion, the first Northern soldiers arrived in Washington. During the succeeding months, their numbers increased manyfold. As they took up positions around Washington and in the border states, they encountered slaves set in motion by the new disciplinary measures, by the attempts to conscript them into Confederate labor gangs or to refugee them to the interior, and—most importantly—by the desire to be free.

Before long, fugitive slaves began to test their owners' assertions about Yankee abolitionism. Those who ventured into Union army lines early in the war were mostly young men. Camps composed of hundreds of soldiers could be forbidding and dangerous places for women and children, and keeping up with an army on the march was nearly impossible for all but young and healthy adults. Fugitive-slave men also outnumbered women and children because men generally had greater opportunities to leave the home farm or plantation. Slave artisans, wagoners, and boatmen often had permission to move about in the course of their work, and sometimes to seek employment on their own; nearly all of them were men. Moreover, where slave hiring was common—as it was throughout the Upper South—seasonal agricultural labor kept hired men on the move between owner and employer....

Confrontations between slaveholders and soldiers multiplied as the number of Union troops in the slave states increased. In late May 1861, when Virginia voters ratified secession, federal forces crossed the Potomac into the northern part of the state, and disputes between masters and military officers became endemic. The conflicts soon made their way into the press, rousing the ire of abolitionists who were outraged by the use of federal soldiers as slave catchers. In July, antislavery congressmen pushed a resolution through the House of Representatives declaring it "no part of the duty of the soldiers of the United States to capture and return fugitive slaves." Although the resolution had no binding effect, it bolstered antislavery sentiment within the Northern army.

The rumblings of congressional radicals were only one indication of the Lincoln administration's difficulty in sustaining a consistent policy regarding slavery. Orders to return fugitive slaves to their owners—designed to preserve the loyalty of the border states and encourage unionism in the Confederacy— lost their rationale once Northern soldiers encountered slaves whose owners were patently disloyal....

... Now their [black laborers'] numbers increased rapidly as federal commanders discovered what Confederate officers had known all along: Slaves and free-black people were the most readily available—sometimes the only—source of military labor. Nearly every army post, supply depot, and wood yard acquired a contingent of black men to clear camps, build roads, construct fortifications, chop wood, and transport supplies. Few naval vessels lacked a handful of black men who handled the dirty and difficult business of coaling. Union commanders also found that black men, free and slave, possessed a variety of skills and were knowledgeable wagoners, scouts, and pilots. White workers—Northern and Southern—disdained certain kinds of labor as "nigger work," but black men and women stood able and often willing to take up the task—particularly if it would assure their liberty. The generally accepted notion that white people could not labor in tropical climates further increased reliance on black workers as the Union army marched south....

Former slaves who labored for the Union army or took refuge in the contra-band camps did not remain satisfied with their own escape from slavery. Almost as soon as they reached the safety of federal lines, they began plotting to return home and liberate families and friends. Some traveled hundreds of miles into the Con-federate interior, threading their way through enemy lines, eluding Confederate pickets, avoiding former masters, and outrunning the slave catchers hired to track them down. Not all succeeded, but when they did, their courage helped hundreds escape bondage and informed still others of the possibility of freedom. Occasion-ally, these brave men and women received assistance from sympathetic Union sol-diers and commanders, who accompanied former slaves back to the old estates or provided material assistance to those intent upon returning to free others. The bar-gain seemed mutually beneficial—the Union army gained additional laborers, and the former slaves secured the liberty of their loved ones.

The growing importance of black labor increased support for emancipation in the North. Abolitionists publicized the role of black laborers, arguing that their service to the Union made them worthy of freedom and citizenship. Other Northerners, indifferent or even hostile to the extension of civil rights to black people, also saw value in the exchange of labor for freedom. Expropriation of the slaveholders' property seemed condign punishment for treason. And they noted that by doing the army's dirty work, black laborers freed white soldiers for the real business of war. Samuel J. Kirkwood, governor of Iowa, was ap-palled to learn that one of his state's regiments had "*sixty men on extra duty* as teamsters &c. whose places could just as well be filled with *niggers*." He urged the military authorities to employ additional black laborers to do such "*negro work*." Indicating the drift of Northern opinion, Governor Kirkwood added a few words on the subject of enlisting black men as soldiers: "When this war is over & we have summed up the entire loss of life it has imposed on the country I shall not have any regrets if it is found that a part of the dead are *niggers* and that *all* are not white men."

Cynical though they were, such sentiments strengthened the hand of aboli-tionists, white and black, who urged the arming of black men with muskets as well as shovels. They had long maintained that enlisting black soldiers would enhance the military might of the Union, while also securing emancipation and pushing the nation toward racial equality. Their earlier efforts to introduce black men into military service had been peremptorily dismissed, sometimes with sharp rebuke. But as public opinion turned against slavery, the proponents of black enlistment met with increasing success. In the summer and fall of 1862, the first black soldiers entered Union ranks in the Sea Islands of South Carolina, in southern Louisiana, and in Kansas....

On New Year's Day, 1863, ... the Emancipation Proclamation fulfilled his [Lincoln's] pledge to free all slaves in the states still in rebellion. Differences between the preliminary proclamation of September and the final pronouncement of January suggest the distance Lincoln and other Northerners had traveled in those few months. Gone were references to compensation for loyal slaveholders and colonization of former slaves. In their place stood the determination to incorporate black men into the federal army and navy. As expected, the proclamation applied only to the seceded states, leaving slavery in the loyal border states untouched, and it exempted Tennessee and the Union-occupied parts of Louisiana and Virginia. Nonetheless, its simple, straightforward declaration—"that all persons held as slaves" within the rebellious states "are, and henceforward shall be, free"—had enormous force.

As Lincoln understood, the message of freedom required no embellishment. However deficient in majesty or grandeur, the President's words echoed across the land. Abolitionists, black and white, marked the occasion with solemn thanksgiving that the nation had recognized its moral responsibility, that the war against slavery had at last been joined, and that human bondage was on the road to extinction. But none could match the slaves' elation. With unrestrained—indeed, unrestrainable—joy, slaves celebrated the Day of Jubilee. Throughout the South—even in areas exempt from the proclamation—black people welcomed the dawn of a new era.

In announcing plans to accept black men into the army and navy, the Emancipation Proclamation specified their assignment "to garrison forts, positions, stations, and other places, and to man vessels"—evidently proposing no active combat role and, in fact, advancing little beyond the already established employment of black men in a variety of quasi-military positions. Nonetheless, black people and their abolitionist allies—who viewed military service as a lever for racial equality, as well as a weapon against slavery—seized upon the President's words and urged large-scale enlistment. Despite continued opposition from the advocates of a white man's war, the grim reality of mounting casualties convinced many Northerners of the wisdom of flexing the sable arm. Moreover, once the Emancipation Proclamation had made the destruction of slavery a Union war aim, increasing numbers of white Northerners thought it only fitting that black men share the burden of defeating the Confederacy....

As black soldiers joined white soldiers in expanding freedom's domain, the Union army became an army of liberation. Although the Emancipation Proclamation implied an auxiliary role, black soldiers would not permit themselves to be reduced to military menials. They longed to confront their former masters on the field of battle, and they soon had their chance. The earliest black regiments acquitted themselves with honor at the battles of Port Hudson, Milliken's Bend, and Fort Wagner in the spring and summer of 1863, and black soldiers thereafter marched against the Confederacy on many fronts. Meanwhile, scores of black regiments served behind the lines—protecting railroads, bridges, and telegraph lines; manning forts; and fending off guerrillas and rearguard rebel attacks. Their services became essential to the Union war effort as Northern armies advanced deep into Confederate territory, lengthening the lines of communication and supply. The subversive effect of black soldiers on slavery, first demonstrated on the South Atlantic coast and in southern Louisiana, increased with the number of black men in federal ranks. By war's end, nearly 179,000—the overwhelming majority slaves—had entered the Union army, and another 10,000 had served in the navy.

Military service provided black men with legal freedom and more. In undeniable ways, it countered the degrading effects of Southern slavery and Northern discrimination. Soldiering gave black men, free as well as slave, a broader knowledge of the world, an acquaintance with the workings of the law, access to some rudimentary formal education, and a chance to demonstrate their commitment to freedom for themselves and their people. Battlefield confrontations with the slaveholding enemy exhilarated black soldiers by proving in the most elemental manner the essential equality of men, In their own eyes, in the eyes of the black community, and, however reluctantly, in the eyes of the nation, black men gained new standing by donning the Union blue.

Large-scale enlistment of black soldiers deepened the federal government's commitment to all former slaves. Although black men contributed to the Northern cause both as laborers and as soldiers, it seemed more difficult to deny support to the families of those who shouldered muskets than to the families of those who wielded shovels. When the army mustered black soldiers from the Confederate states, it implicitly—and sometimes explicitly—agreed to protect and provide for their families and friends. Adjutant General Thomas understood the relationship between recruiting soldiers and caring for their families as fully as any federal officer. When he began recruiting black regiments in the Mississippi Valley, he organized contraband camps as he established recruitment stations; often the two were the same. Commanders in other parts of the Union-occupied Confederacy followed a similar course, though their efforts never kept pace with the number of black refugees....

The deterioration of slavery in the Union-occupied Confederacy had no immediate effect on the institution in the Union's own slave states. Having stood by the old flag when the other slave states seceded, Delaware, Maryland, Kentucky, and Missouri were not included in the Emancipation Proclamation. Insistent upon slavery's full legal standing under the federal constitution, slaveholders in the border states rejected Lincoln's repeated urgings that they adopt some plan of gradual, compensated emancipation. Indeed, their minority position as slaveholders in the Union seemed only to stiffen their resolve. Rather than bend to the winds of change, they deployed old defenses of their right to human property and fashioned new ones. Border-state legislatures bolstered antebellum slave codes, which were rigorously enforced by local officials. State courts not only upheld these laws and sustained the rights of slaveholders, but also entertained suits against anyone who interfered with slavery, including officers of the United States army.

The legality of slavery narrowed the avenues to freedom in the border states, but slaves hazarded them nonetheless. From the earliest months of the war, many of them had found refuge with Northern regiments, and some gained employment as military laborers. In Missouri, especially along the Kansas border, a virtual civil war within the Civil War provided slaves with opportunities to leave their owners, and in Maryland, proximity to the District of Columbia afforded fugitive slaves a safe haven. The slaves' persistence and the receptivity of federal troops and army quartermasters forced border-state slaveholders into rearguard actions that undermined their unionist credentials. By the end of 1863, exasperated army officers and federal officials had tired of feuding with masters who appeared to care more for their property than for the Union. As Lincoln had predicted, the "friction and abrasion" of war were eroding slavery in the border states....

Still, slavery did not give way in the border states until black men began entering the Union army in large numbers. In the summer of 1863, with the enlistment of black men already proceeding in the North and in the Union-occupied Confederacy, federal authorities inaugurated black recruitment in Maryland and Missouri. Reluctant to offend slaveholding unionists, President Lincoln and the War Department at first authorized the enlistment only of free blacks and of slaves whose owners were disloyal. But black men—including the slaves of loyal owners—volunteered so enthusiastically that it proved nearly impossible to restrict enlistment. This was particularly true once nonslaveholding white men recognized that black recruits reduced conscription quotas that they would otherwise have to fill. Nonslaveholders demanded that slaves be enlisted as well as—and sometimes instead of—free blacks. In Maryland, where nonslaveholding farmers feared that the enlistment of free-black men would diminish their work force while leaving that of the slaveholders intact, this demand reached its highest pitch. In all the border States, antislavery partisans united in urging the elimination of distinctions between slaves of the loyal and those of the disloyal. With the ready compliance of black volunteers, recruiters stepped up enlistment, circumventing regulations regarding the status of the recruits or the politics of their owners....

With slavery in shambles and Northern victory increasingly sure, unionists in much of the occupied South concluded the business of emancipation. Federal officials and army commanders turned on their slaveholding allies and made it clear that the liquidation of slavery was prerequisite for readmission to the Union. Antislavery unionists, previously stymied by slaveholding loyalists, took control of the unionist coalitions and pressed for immediate abolition. Early in 1864, Arkansas loyalists enacted constitutional changes ending slavery. Unionists in states partly or wholly exempt from the Emancipation Proclamation followed suit, in Louisiana late in 1864 and in Tennessee early in 1865. As Lincoln had hoped, these new state constitutions placed emancipation upon firmer ground, beyond the reach of judicial challenge to the confiscation acts or the Emancipation Proclamation.

Union military success also strengthened the North's own commitment to freedom. Sherman's triumph at Atlanta helped Lincoln beat back a challenge for the presidency by George B. McClellan, the former general-in-chief. The previous spring, with reelection in doubt, congressional support for emancipation had faltered. The Senate had approved a constitutional amendment abolishing slavery, but when it came before the House, the Democratic opposition had denied it the two-thirds majority required for passage. In January 1865, with Lincoln reelected and the Republicans securely in power, the House approved the amendment and forwarded it to the states for ratification. As the state legislatures opened their debates, the President and the Congress turned in earnest to the task of postwar reconstruction. In early March, Lincoln signed legislation creating the Bureau of Refugees, Freedmen, and Abandoned Lands (or Freedmen's Bureau, as it became known) to supervise the transition from slavery to freedom. A joint resolution adopted the same day liberated the wives and children of black soldiers, regardless of their owner's loyalty, and thereby provided a claim to freedom for tens of thousands of border-state slaves whose bondage had been impervious to law or presidential edict....

After the war, freedpeople and their allies—some newly minted, some of long standing—gathered periodically to celebrate the abolition of slavery. They spoke of great deeds, great words, and great men, praising the Emancipation Proclamation and the Thirteenth Amendment and venerating their authors. A moment so great needed its icons. But in quieter times, black people told of their own liberation. Then there were as many tales as tellers. Depending upon the circumstances of their enslavement, the events of the war, and the evolution of Union and Confederate policy, some recounted solitary escape; others, mass defections initiated by themselves or the Yankees. Many depicted their former owners in headlong flight, and themselves left behind to shape a future under Union occupation. Others told of forced removals from home and family to strange neighborhoods and enslavement made more miserable by food shortages, heightened discipline, and bands of straggling soldiers. Still others limned a struggle against slaveholders whose unionist credentials sustained their power. More than a few black people shared the bitter memory of escaping slavery only to be reenslaved when the Northern army retreated or they ventured into one of the Union's own slave states. Some recalled hearing the news of freedom from an exasperated master who reluctantly acknowledged the end of the old order; others, from returning black veterans, bedecked in blue uniforms with brass buttons. Those who had escaped slavery during the war often had additional stories to relate. They told of serving the Union cause as cooks, nurses, and laundresses: as teamsters and laborers; as spies, scouts, and pilots; and as sailors and soldiers. Even those who had remained under the dominion of their owners until the defeat of the Confederacy and had been forced to labor in its behalf knew that their very presence, and often their actions, had played a part in destroying slavery.

These diverse experiences disclosed the uneven, halting, and often tenuous process by which slaves gained their liberty, and the centrality of their own role in the evolution of emancipation. The Emancipation Proclamation and the Thirteenth Amendment marked, respectively, a turning point and the successful conclusion of a hard-fought struggle. But the milestones of that struggle were not the struggle itself. Neither its origins nor its mainspring could be found in the seats of executive and legislative authority from which the great documents issued. Instead, they resided in the humble quarters of slaves, who were convinced in April 1861 of what would not be fully affirmed until December 1865, and whose actions consistently undermined every settlement short of universal abolition.

Over the course of the war, the slaves' insistence that their own enslavement was the root of the conflict—and that a war for the Union must necessarily be a war for freedom—strengthened their friends and weakened their enemies. Their willingness to offer their loyalty, their labor, and even their lives pushed Northerners, from common soldiers to leaders of the first rank, to do what had previously seemed unthinkable: to make property into persons, to make slaves into soldiers, and, in time, to make all black people into citizens, the equal of any in the Republic. White Southerners could never respond in kind. But they too came to understand the link between national union and universal liberty. And when the deed was done, a new truth prevailed where slavery had reigned: that men and women could never again be owned and that citizenship was the right of all. The destruction of slavery transformed American life forever.

FURTHER READING

David Herbert Donald, *Lincoln* (1998).

Drew Gilpin Faust, *Mothers of Invention: Women of the Slaveholding South in the American Civil War* (1996).

Drew Gilpin Faust, *This Republic of Suffering: Death and the American Civil War* (2009).

Shelby Foote, *The Civil War: A Narrative*, three vols. (1958–1974).

William Gienapp, *Abraham Lincoln and Civil War America* (2002).

Joseph T. Glatthaar, *Forged in Battle: The Civil War Alliance of Black Soldiers and White Officers* (1989).

Allan C. Guelzo, *Lincoln's Emancipation Proclamation: The End of Slavery in America* (2006).

Harold Holzer, Edna Greene Medford, and Frank Williams, *The Emancipation Proclamation: Three Views* (2006).

Bruce Levine, *Confederate Emancipation* (2007).

Chandra Manning, *What this Cruel War Was Over: Soldiers, Slavery, and the Civil War* (2008).

James M. McPherson, *Battle Cry of Freedom: The Civil War Era* (1988).

Mark E. Neely, Jr., *The Fate of Liberty: Abraham Lincoln and Civil Liberties* (1992).

Phillip S. Paludan, *"A People's Contest": The Union and the Civil War, 1861–1865* (1989).

George C. Rable, *The Confederate Republic: A Revolt Against Politics* (1994).

Charles Royster, *The Destructive War: William Tecumseh Sherman, Stonewall Jackson, and the Americans* (1991).

Nina Silber, *Daughters of the Union* (2005).

Michael Vorenberg, *Final Freedom: The Civil War, the Abolition of Slavery, and the Thirteenth Amendment* (2001).

CHAPTER 15

Reconstruction

Even before the Civil War was over, President Lincoln and congressional leaders began to puzzle over how best to reintegrate the people of the South into the Union. Before he was assassinated, President Lincoln proposed the "10 percent plan," which would have allowed a state government to reestablish itself once one-tenth of those who had voted in 1860 took an oath of loyalty to the United States. Radicals in Congress were appalled by the seemingly lenient plan and pushed through their own bill, which increased the proportion to one-half of the voters who were required to swear that they had never supported secession. Lincoln's assassination cut short this increasingly scathing debate and drastically altered the mood of Reconstruction. According to poet Herman Melville, the assassination shifted the northern mood. "They have killed him, The Forgiver," Melville versed, "The Avenger takes his place." What really took Lincoln's place was conflict and chaos for nearly fifteen years. Political disagreements over Reconstruction policy were vast, and the strategies advocated were so varied that Reconstruction took a crooked road. As approaches to rebuilding the South shifted, the hopes among some to transform southern society grew and then were dashed. Ultimately, despite important legal precedents that were made in the era, many of the social, political, and economic conventions that had characterized antebellum society endured after Reconstruction ended. Eventually, the racial system of segregation came to replace the system of slavery.

Although people differed on what was the best policy for Reconstruction, everyone agreed that the Confederate states were in dire straits and the primary goal of Reconstruction was to reincorporate those states politically and socially into the Union. The war had devastated the South: entire cities lay in ruins; two-thirds of southern railroads had been destroyed; and at least one-third of its livestock had disappeared. Likewise, the abolition of slavery unalterably transformed southern society at the same time that it gave hope to people freed from their bondage (known as freedmen). Following Lincoln's death, many believed that Andrew Johnson, who succeeded Lincoln as president, would advocate a severe Reconstruction of the South. Instead, Johnson engineered a plan that seemed to many Northerners as much too charitable. Ironically, Johnson's course of action, combined with the intransigence of unrepentant Southern leaders, was a major force in bringing about the era of Radical Reconstruction beginning in 1866. Because he was so impolitic, Johnson strengthened the resolve of Congress to enact a more radical policy. After the Republican

Party won a resounding victory in the elections of 1866, Congress reconvened in 1867 and set out to punish rebellious southern whites while offering more rights and freedoms to African Americans.

If Reconstruction was engineered in Washington, new social conventions were forged in the South that would be extremely important in the future. The lives of former slaves were dramatically changed and freedmen expressed their understanding of freedom in a variety of ways. Significantly, many African Americans played important roles in the new Republican Party of the South, and by 1868 black men were seated for the first time in southern state legislatures. These political gains, however, were short-lived. In spite of the electoral successes of African Americans, the Democratic Party enjoyed increasing political success in the South as former Confederates eventually had their political rights restored. Changes in the electorate in conjunction with intimidation shifted the trajectory of Reconstruction once again as radical transformation was replaced with a movement toward the white South's term for reclaiming the world they had known before the Civil War.

The end of Reconstruction was hastened by events in the North as well as the South. Ulysses S. Grant, elected president in 1868, was a better general than politician and his administration was already mired in scandal shortly after he took office. By 1873, the nation was rocked by a financial panic that led Americans into a depression lasting six years. Scandal and depression weakened the Republican Party. Meanwhile Congress and the Supreme Court were weakening in their resolve to continue a strict policy of Reconstruction. The death knell of Reconstruction was the national election of 1876, when it became clear that the North was no longer willing to pursue its earlier goals. The election of the Democratic candidate for president was avoided only by a compromise in 1877 wherein Rutherford B. Hayes would be declared president if he promised to withdraw federal troops from those states in the South where they still remained. The deal was made. Reconstruction was over—northern and southern whites agreed that national reunion was more important than the defense of civil rights for black men and women.

QUESTIONS TO THINK ABOUT

What were the failures of Reconstruction and what were its successes? Why did it collapse, to the extent that it did? How successful was the Union in reincorporating the southern states and people? Did Reconstruction come to an end primarily because the North abandoned it or because it was opposed by the South? How did African Americans feel about the possibilities and the terrors of Reconstruction?

DOCUMENTS

The first three documents represent the diversity of feelings at the end of the war regarding the federal government and rights for African Americans. Document 1 is an oration given by William Howard Day, an African American minister, in 1865. Notice how—unlike African Americans before the Civil War—he now celebrated the federal government. Day proclaimed the Fourth of July as "our day," the United States as "our nation," and Washington, D.C., as "our capital." In the South, though, many whites opposed the federal government and wanted to keep former slaves as second-class citizens. Document 2 is a song from the South where the white vocalist proclaims his hatred for the federal government. In law, many southern states enacted "black codes" immediately after the war, one of which is given in document 3. This example from Louisiana in 1865 illustrates the many ways in which the rights of "freedom" were abridged. The next two documents showcase conflict within the federal government over Reconstruction. In document 4, President Andrew Johnson argues against black suffrage. In contrast, Thaddeus Stevens, a Radical representative in Congress, argues for passage of the Reconstruction Act of 1867 in document 5 because he believes that only an unfaltering federal presence will prevent "traitors" from ruling the South. The bitterness that ensued resulted in the impeachment of President Andrew Johnson. Document 6, the opening argument in the impeachment trial, enumerates the accusations against President Johnson. The next two documents show frustrations with the civil rights agendas of Reconstruction. In document 7, Elizabeth Cady Stanton—one of the authors of the Declaration of Sentiments in Chapter 10—argues that the very radicals who are pushing for increased rights for freed slaves are deferring the issue of women's suffrage. Document 8 is the testimony of a freed woman about the violence of the Ku Klux Klan. The final two documents detail sectional feelings at the end of Reconstruction. Document 9 is a poem from Father Abram Ryan, a Catholic priest of the South. It illustrates the enduring notion of a "lost cause" and love for the Confederate States of America that was maintained by many white southerners well after reconstruction. "The Blue and The Gray," another Reconstruction poem, is document 10. It expresses the hopes for North-South reconciliation in the form of mutual love and respect for white Union and Confederate soldiers.

1. William Howard Day, an African American Minister, Salutes the Nation and a Monument to Abraham Lincoln, 1865

… We meet under new and ominous circumstances to-day. We come to the National Capital—our Capital—with new hopes, new prospects, new joys, in view of the future and past of the people; and yet with that joy fringed, tinged, permeated by a sorrow unlike any, nationally, we have ever known. A few weeks since all that was mortal of Abraham Lincoln was laid away to rest. And to-day, after the funeral cortege has passed, weeping thoughts march through our hearts—when the muffled drum has ceased to beat in a procession five hundred, aye, two thousand miles long, the chambers of your souls are still echoing the murmur—and though the coffin has been lowered into its place, "dust to dust," there ever falls across our way the coffin's shadow, and, standing in it, we come to-day to rear a monument to his blessed memory, and again to

Celebration by the Colored People's Educational Monument Association (1865).

pledge our untiring resistance to the tyranny by which he fell, whether it be in the iron manacles of the slave, or in the unjust written manacles for the free....

Up to now our nation,... [t]he shout of the freeman and the wail of the bondman have, I repeat, always been heard together, making "harsh discords." Hitherto a damning crime has run riot over the whole land. North and South alike were inoculated with its virus. It has lain like a gangrene upon the national life, until the nation, mortified, broke in twain. The hand of slavery ever moulded the Christianity of the nation, and wrote the national songs. What hand wrote the laws of the nation and marked this National District all over with scars? What hand went into the Capitol and half murdered Charles Sumner, nature's nobleman?...

All the heroes of all the ages, bond and free, have labored to secure for us the right we rejoice in to-day. To the white and colored soldiers of this war, led on as they were by our noble President and other officers, in the presence of some of whom I rejoice to-day, are we indebted, in the providence of God, for our present position. For want of time, I pass by any more detailed mention of the noble men and their noble deeds. Together they nobly labored—together they threw themselves into the breach which rebellion had made across the land, and thus closed up that breach forever. And now, in their presence, living and dead, as over the prostrate form of our leader, Abraham Lincoln—by the edge of blood-red waves, still surging, we pledge our resistance to tyranny, (I repeat,) whether in the iron manacles of the slave, or in the unjust written manacles of the free....

It is related in the diary of one of the writers of old that when the slave trade was at its height, a certain vessel loaded with its human freight started under the frown of God and came over the billows of the ocean. Defying God and man alike, in the open daylight, the slave was brought up from the hold and chained to the foot of the mast. The eye of the Omnipotent saw it, and bye and bye the thunders muttered and the lightnings played over the devoted vessel. At length the lightning leaped upon the mast and shivered it, and, as it did this, also melted the fetter which fastened the black slave to it; and he arising unhurt, for the first time walked the deck a free man.

Our ship of state, the Union, has for eighty years gone careering over the billows; our slave has been chained to our mast in the open daylight, and in the focal blaze of the eighteen centuries gone by, and we have hurried on in our crime regardless alike of the muttering of the thunder and the flashes of the lightning, until in one devoted hour the thunderbolt was sped from the hand of God. The mast was shivered; the ship was saved; but, thank God, the slave was free....

2. A Southern Song Opposes Reconstruction, c. 1860s

O, I'm a good old Rebel,

Now that's just what I am,

"O, I'm a Good Old Rebel," c. 1860s.

For this "Fair Land of Freedom"
I do not care at all;

I'm glad I fit against it—
I only wish we'd won,
And I don't want no pardon
For anything I done.

I hates the Constitution,
This Great Republic too,
I hates the Freedman's Buro,
In uniforms of blue;

I hates the nasty eagle,
With all his brags and fuss,
The lyin', thievin' Yankees,
I hates 'em wuss and wuss.

I hates the Yankee nation
And everything they do,
I hates the Declaration
Of Independence too;

I hates the glorious Union –
'Tis dripping with our blood –
I hates their striped banner,
I fit it all I could....

Three hundred thousand Yankees
Is stiff in Southern dust;
We got three hundred thousand
Before they conquered us;

They died of Southern fever
And Southern steel and shot,

I wish they was three million
Instead of what we got.

I can't take up my musket
And fight 'em now no more,
But I ain't going to love 'em,
Now that is sarten sure;

And I don't want no pardon
For what I was and am,
I won't be reconstructed
And I don't care a damn.

3. Louisiana Black Codes Reinstate Provisions of the Slave Era, 1865

Section 1. *Be it therefore ordained by the board of police of the town of Opelousas*. That no negro or freedman shall be allowed to come within the limits of the town of Opelousas without special permission from his employers, specifying the object of his visit and the time necessary for the accomplishment of the same....

Section 2. *Be it further ordained,* That every negro freedman who shall be found on the streets of Opelousas after 10 o'clock at night without a written pass or permit from his employer shall be imprisoned and compelled to work five days on the public streets, or pay a fine of five dollars.

Section 3. No negro or freedman shall be permitted to rent or keep a house within the limits of the town under any circumstances, and any one thus offending shall be ejected and compelled to find an employer or leave the town within twenty-four hours....

Section 4. No negro or freedman shall reside within the limits of the town of Opelousas who is not in the regular service of some white person or former owner, who shall be held responsible for the conduct of said freedman....

Section 5. No public meetings or congregations of negroes or freedmen shall be allowed within the limits of the town of Opelousas under any circumstances or for any purpose without the permission of the mayor or president of the board....

Section 6. No negro or freedman shall be permitted to preach, exhort, or otherwise declaim to congregations of colored people without a special permission from the mayor or president of the board of police....

Condition of the South, Senate Executive Document No. 2, 39 Cong., 1 Sess., pp. 92–93.

Section 7. No freedman who is not in the military service shall be allowed to carry firearms, or any kind of weapons, within the limits of the town of Opelousas without the special permission of his employer, in writing, and approved by the mayor or president of the board of police....

Section 8. No freedman shall sell, barter, or exchange any articles of merchandise or traffic within the limits of Opelousas without permission in writing from his employer or the mayor or president of the board....

Section 9. Any freedman found drunk within the limits of the town shall be imprisoned and made to labor five days on the public streets, or pay five dollars in lieu of said labor.

Section 10. Any freedman not residing in Opelousas who shall be found within the corporate limits after the hour of 3 p.m. on Sunday without a special permission from his employer or the mayor shall be arrested and imprisoned and made to work....

Section 11. All the foregoing provisions apply to freedmen and freedwomen....

E. D. ESTILLETTE,
President of the Board of Police.
JOS. D. RICHARDS, *Clerk.*

Official copy:

J. LOVELL,
Captain and Assistant Adjutant General.

4. President Andrew Johnson Denounces Changes in His Program of Reconstruction, 1867

It is manifestly and avowedly the object of these laws to confer upon negroes the privilege of voting and to disfranchise such a number of white citizens as will give the former a clear majority at all elections in the Southern States. This, to the minds of some persons, is so important that a violation of the Constitution is justified as a means of bringing it about. The morality is always false which excuses a wrong because it proposes to accomplish a desirable end. We are not permitted to do evil that good may come. But in this case the end itself is evil, as well as the means. The subjugation of the States to negro domination would be worse than the military despotism under which they are now suffering. It was believed beforehand that the people would endure any amount of military oppression for any length of time rather than degrade themselves by subjection to the negro race. Therefore they have been left without a choice. Negro suffrage was established by act of Congress, and the military officers were commanded to

Andrew Johnson, "Third Annual Message" (December 3, 1867), in *A Compilation of Messages and Papers of the Presidents, 1789–1897,* VI, ed. James D. Richardson (Washington, D.C.: Bureau of National Literature and Art, 1899), 564–565.

superintend the process of clothing the negro race with the political privileges torn from white men.

The blacks in the South are entitled to be well and humanely governed, and to have the protection of just laws for all their rights of person and property. If it were practicable at his time to give them a Government exclusively their own, under which they might manage their own affairs in their own way, it would become a grave question whether we ought to do so, or whether common humanity would not require us to save them from themselves. But under the circumstances this is only a speculative point. It is not proposed merely that they shall govern themselves, but that they shall rule the white race, make and administer State laws, elect Presidents and members of Congress, and shape to a greater or less extent the future destiny of the whole country. Would such a trust and power be safe in such hands?

The peculiar qualities which should characterize any people who are fit to decide upon the management of public affairs for a great state have seldom been combined. It is the glory of white men to know that they have had these qualities in sufficient measures to build upon this continent a great political fabric and to preserve its stability for more than ninety years, while in every other part of the world all similar experiments have failed. But if anything can be proved by known facts, if all reasoning upon evidence is not abandoned, it must be acknowledged that in the progress of nations negroes have shown less capacity for government than any other race of people. No independent government of any form has ever been successful in their hands. On the contrary, wherever they have been left to their own devices they have shown a constant tendency to relapse into barbarism. In the Southern States, however, Congress has undertaken to confer upon them the privilege of the ballot. Just released from slavery, it may be doubted whether as a class they know more than their ancestors how to organize and regulate civil society.

5. Congressman Thaddeus Stevens Demands a Radical Reconstruction, 1867

.... It is to be regretted that inconsiderate and incautious Republicans should ever have supposed that the slight amendments [embodied in the pending Fourteenth Amendment] already proposed to the Constitution, even when incorporated into that instrument, would satisfy the reforms necessary for the security of the Government. Unless the rebel States, before admission, should be made republican in spirit, and placed under the guardianship of loyal men, all our blood and treasure will have been spent in vain. I waive now the question of punishment which, if we are wise, will still be inflicted by moderate confiscations, both as a reproof and example. Having these States, as we all agree, entirely within the power of Congress, it is our duty to take care that no injustice shall remain in

Thaddeus Stevens, speech in the House (January 3, 1867), *Congressional Globe,* 39 Cong., 2 Sess., Vol. 37, pt. 1, pp. 251–253. This document can also be found in *Radical Republicans and Reconstruction,* ed. Harold M. Hyman (Indianapolis, Ind., and New York: Bobbs-Merrill, 1967), 373–375.

their organic laws. Holding them "like clay in the hands of the potter," we must see that no vessel is made for destruction. Having now no governments, they must have enabling acts. The law of last session with regard to Territories settled the principles of such acts. Impartial suffrage, both in electing the delegates and ratifying their proceedings, is now the fixed rule. There is more reason why colored voters should be admitted in the rebel States than in the Territories. In the States they form the great mass of the loyal men. Possibly with their aid loyal governments may be established in most of those States. Without it all are sure to be ruled by traitors; and loyal men, black and white, will be oppressed, exiled, or murdered. There are several good reasons for the passage of this bill. In the first place, it is just. I am now confining my argument to negro suffrage in the rebel States. Have not loyal blacks quite as good a right to choose rulers and make laws as rebel whites? In the second place, it is a necessity in order to protect the loyal white men in the seceded States. The white Union men are in a great minority in each of those States. With them the blacks would act in a body; and it is believed that in each of said States, except one, the two united would form a majority, control the States, and protect themselves. Now they are the victims of daily murder. They must suffer constant persecution or be exiled. The convention of southern loyalists, lately held in Philadelphia, almost unanimously agreed to such a bill as an absolute necessity.

Another good reason is, it would insure the ascendancy of the Union party. Do you avow the party purpose? exclaims some horror-stricken demagogue. I do. For I believe, on my conscience, that on the continued ascendancy of that party depends the safety of this great nation. If impartial suffrage is excluded in rebel States then every one of them is sure to send a solid rebel representative delegation to Congress, and cast a solid rebel electoral vote. They, with their kindred Copperheads of the North, would always elect the President and control Congress. While slavery sat upon her defiant throne, and insulted and intimidated the trembling North, the South frequently divided on questions of policy between Whigs and Democrats, and gave victory alternately to the sections. Now, you must divide them between loyalists, without regard to color, and disloyalists, or you will be the perpetual vassals of the free-trade, irritated, revengeful South. For these, among other reasons, I am for negro suffrage in every rebel State. If it be just, it should not be denied; if it be necessary, it should be adopted; if it be a punishment to traitors, they deserve it.

But it will be said, as it has been said, "This is negro equality!" What is negro equality, about which so much is said by knaves, and some of which is believed by men who are not fools? It means, as understood by honest Republicans, just this much, and no more: every man, no matter what his race or color; every earthly being who has an immortal soul, has an equal right to justice, honesty, and fair play with every other man; and the law should secure him those rights. The same law which condemns or acquits an African should condemn or acquit a white man. The same law which gives a verdict in a white man's favor should give a verdict in a black man's favor on the same state of facts. Such is the law of God and such ought to be the law of man. This doctrine does not mean that a negro shall sit on the same seat or eat at the same table with a white man. That is a matter of taste which every man must decide for himself. The law has nothing to do with it.

6. Representative Benjamin Butler Argues That President Andrew Johnson Be Impeached, 1868

This, then, is the plain and inevitable issue before the Senate and the American people:

Has the President, under the Constitution, the more than kingly prerogative at will to remove from office and suspend from office indefinitely, all executive officers of the United States, either civil, military, or naval, at any and all times, and fill the vacancies with creatures of his own appointment, for his own purposes, without any restraint whatever, or possibility of restraint by the Senate or by Congress through laws duly enacted?

The House of Representatives, in behalf of the people, join this issue by affirming that the exercise of such powers is a high misdemeanor in office....

Who does not know that Andrew Johnson initiated, of his own will, a course of reconstruction of the rebel States, which at the time be claimed was provisional only, and until the meeting of Congress and its action thereon? Who does not know that when Congress met and undertook to legislate upon the very subject of reconstruction, of which he had advised them in his message, which they alone had the constitutional power to do, Andrew Johnson last aforesaid again changed his course, and declared that Congress had no power to legislate upon that subject; that the two houses had only the power *separately* to judge of the qualifications of the members who might be sent to each by rebellious constituencies, acting under State organization which Andrew Johnson had called into existence by his late *fiat*, the electors of which were voting by his permission and under his limitations? Who does not know that when Congress, assuming its rightful power to propose amendments to the Constitution, had passed such an amendment, and had submitted it to the States as a measure of pacification, Andrew Johnson advised and counselled the legislatures of the States lately in rebellion, as well as others, to reject the amendment, so that it might not operate as a law, and thus establish equality of suffrage in all the States, and equality of right in the members of the electoral college, and in the number of the representatives to the Congress of the United States?...

Who does not know that from the hour he began these, his usurpations of power, he everywhere denounced Congress, the legality and constitutionality of its action, and defied its legitimate powers, and, for that purpose, announced his intentions and carried out his purpose, as far as he was able, of removing every true man from office who sustained the Congress of the United States? And it is to carry out this plan of action that he claims the unlimited power of removal, for

Trial of Andrew Johnson, President of the United States, on Impeachment by the House of Representatives for High Crimes and Misdemeanors (Washington, D.C.: Government Printing Office, 1868), 96, 121–123.

the illegal exercise of which he stands before you this day. Who does not know that, in pursuance of the same plan, he used his veto power indiscriminately to prevent the passage of wholesome laws, enacted for the pacification of the country and, when laws were passed by the constitutional majority over his vetoes, he made the most determined opposition, both open and convert, to them, and, for the purpose of making that opposition effectual, he endeavored to array and did array all the people lately in rebellion to set themselves against Congress and against the true and loyal men, their neighbors, so that murders, assassinations, and massacres were rife all over the southern States, which he encouraged by his refusal to consent that a single murderer be punished, though thousands of good men have been slain; and further, that he attempted by military orders to prevent the execution of acts of Congress by the military commanders who were charged therewith. These and his concurrent acts show conclusively that his attempt to get the control of the military force of the government, by the seizing of the Department of War, was done in pursuance of his general design, if it were possible, to overthrow the Congress of the United States; and he now claims by his answer the right to control at his own will, for the execution of this very design, every officer of the army, navy, civil, and diplomatic service of the United States. He asks you here, Senators, by your solemn adjudication to confirm him in that right, to invest him with that power, to be used with the intents and for the purposes which he has already shown.

The responsibility is with you; that safeguards of the Constitution against usurpation are in your hands; the interests and hopes of free institutions wait upon your verdict. The House of Representatives has done its duty. We have presented the facts in the constitutional manner; we have brought the criminal to your bar, and demand judgment at your hands for his so great crimes.

Never again, if Andrew Johnson go quit and free this day, can the people of this or any other country by constitutional checks or guards stay the usurpations of executive power.

I speak, therefore, not the language of exaggeration, but the words of truth and soberness, that the future political welfare and liberties of all men hang trembling on the decision of the hour.

7. Elizabeth Cady Stanton Questions Abolitionist Support for Female Enfranchisement, 1868

To what a depth of degradation must the women of this nation have fallen to be willing to stand aside, silent and indifferent spectators in the reconstruction of the nation, while all the lower stratas of manhood are to legislate in their interests, political, religious, educational, social and sanitary, moulding to their untutored will the institutions of a mighty continent....

Elizabeth Cady Stanton, "Who Are Our Friends?" *The Revolution*, 15 (January 1868).

While leading Democrats have been thus favorably disposed, what have our best friends said when, for the first time since the agitation of the question [the enfranchisement of women], they have had an opportunity to frame their ideas into statutes to amend the constitutions of two States in the Union.

Charles Sumner, Horace Greeley, Gerrit Smith and Wendell Phillips, with one consent, bid the women of the nation stand aside and behold the salvation of the negro. Wendell Phillips says, "one idea for a generation," to come up in the order of their importance. First negro suffrage, then temperance, then the eight hour movement, then woman's suffrage. In 1958, three generations hence, thirty years to a generation, Phillips and Providence permitting, woman's suffrage will be in order. What an insult to the women who have labored thirty years for the emancipation of the slave, now when he is their political equal, to propose to lift him above their heads. Gerrit Smith, forgetting that our great American idea is "individual rights," in which abolitionists have ever based their strongest arguments for emancipation, says, this is the time to settle the rights of races; unless we do justice to the negro we shall bring down on ourselves another bloody revolution, another four years' war, but we have nothing to fear from woman, she will not revenge herself!...

Horace Greeley has advocated this cause for the last twenty years, but to-day it is too new, revolutionary for practical consideration. The enfranchisement of woman, revolutionizing, as it will, our political, religious and social condition, is not a measure too radical and all-pervading to meet the moral necessities of this day and generation.

Why fear new things; all old things were once new.... We live to do new things! When Abraham Lincoln issued the proclamation of emancipation, it was a new thing. When the Republican party gave the ballot to the negro, it was a new thing, startling too, to the people of the South, very revolutionary to their institutions, but Mr. Greeley did not object to all this because it was new....

And now, while men like these have used all their influence for the last four years, to paralyze every effort we have put forth to rouse the women of the nation, to demand their true position in the reconstruction, they triumphantly turn to us, and say the greatest barrier in the way of your demand is that "the women themselves do not wish to vote." What a libel on the intelligence of the women of the nineteenth century. What means the 12,000 petitions presented by John Stuart Mill in the British Parliament from the first women in England, demanding household suffrage? What means the late action in Kansas, 10,000 women petitioned there for the right of suffrage, and 9,000 votes at the last election was the answer. What means the agitation in every State in the Union? In the very hour when Horace Greeley brought in his adverse report in the Constitutional Convention of New York, at least twenty members rose in their places and presented petitions from every part of the State, demanding woman's suffrage. What means that eloquent speech of George W. Curtis in the Convention, but to show that the ablest minds in the State are ready for this onward step?

8. Lucy McMillan, a Former Slave in South Carolina, Testifies About White Violence, 1871

SPARTANBURGH, SOUTH CAROLINA, July 10, 1871.

LUCY McMILLAN (colored) sworn and examined.

By the CHAIRMAN:

QUESTION. Where do you live?

ANSWER. Up in the country. I live on McMillan's place, right at the foot of the road.

QUESTION. How far is it?

ANSWER. Twelve miles.

QUESTION. Are you married?

ANSWER. I am not married. I am single now. I was married. My husband was taken away from me and carried off twelve years ago....

QUESTION. How old are you now?

ANSWER. I am called forty-six. I am forty-five or six.

QUESTION. Did the Ku-Klux come where you live at any time?

ANSWER. They came there once before they burned my house down. The way it was was this: John Hunter's wife came to my house on Saturday morning, and told they were going to whip me. I was afraid of them; there was so much talk of Ku-Klux drowning people, and whipping people, and killing them. My house was only a little piece from the river, so I laid out at night in the woods. The Sunday evening after Isham McCrary was whipped I went up, and a white man, John McMillan, came along and says to me, "Lucy, you had better stay at home, for they will whip you anyhow." I said if they have to, they might whip me in the woods, for I am afraid to stay there. Monday night they came in and burned my house down; I dodged out alongside of the road not far off, and saw them. I was sitting right not far off, and as they came along the river I know some of them. I know John McMillan, and Kennedy McMillan, and Billy Bush, and John Hunter. They were all together. I was not far off, and I saw them. They went right on to my house. When they passed me I run further up on the hill to get out of the way of them. They went there and knocked down and beat my house a right smart while. And then they all got still, and directly I saw the fire rise.

Testimony Taken by the Joint Select Committee to Inquire Into the Condition of Affairs in the Late Insurrectionary States: South Carolina, Volume 4 (1872).

QUESTION. How many of these men were there?

ANSWER. A good many; I couldn't tell how many, but these I knew. The others I didn't.

QUESTION. Were these on foot or on horseback?

ANSWER. These were walking that I could call the names of, but the others were riding. I work with these boys everyday. One of them I raised from a child, and I knew them. I have lived with them twelve years.

QUESTION. How were they dressed?

ANSWER. They had just such cloth as this white cotton frock made into old gowns; and some had black faces, and some red, and some had horns on their heads before, and they came a-talking by me and I knew their voices.

QUESTION. How far were you from where they were?

ANSWER. Not very far. I was in the woods, squatted down, and staid still until they passed; but then I run further up the hill.

QUESTION. Have you any family with you there?

ANSWER. I had one little daughter with me. I had one grown daughter, but my grown daughter had been up the country to my mother's staying, and my little girl was staying there with me.

QUESTION. Had you your little girl out with you?

ANSWER. Yes, sir; I could not leave her there.

QUESTION. What was the reason given for burning your house?

ANSWER. There was speaking down there last year and I came to it. They all kept at me to go. I went home and they quizzed me to hear what was said, and I told them as far as my senses allowed me.

QUESTION. Where was the speaking?

ANSWER. Here in this town. I went on and told them, and then they all said I was making laws; or going to have the land, and the Ku-Klux were going to beat me for bragging that I would have land. John Hunter told them on me, I suppose, that I said I was going to have land....

9. Father Abram Ryan Proclaims Undying Love for the Confederate States of America, 1879

C. S. A.

Do we weep for the heroes who died for us?

Who living were true and tried for us,

And dying sleep side by side for us;—

Father Ryan's Poems (Mobile: John L. Rapier and Company Publishers, 1879).

The Martyr-band

That hallowed our land

With the blood they shed in a tide for us.

Ah! fearless on many a day for us

They stood in the front of the fray for us,

And held the foeman at bay for us,

And tears should fall

Fore'er o'er all

Who fell while wearing the gray for us.

How many a glorious name for us,

How many a story of fame for us,

They left,—would it not be a blame for us,

If their memories part

From our land and heart,

And a wrong to them, and shame for us?

No—no—no—they were brave for us,

And bright were the lives they gave for us,—

The land they struggled to save for us

Will not forget

Its warriors yet

Who sleep in so many a grave for us.

On many and many a plain for us

Their blood poured down all in vain for us,

Red, rich and pure,—like a rain for us;

They bleed,—we weep,

We live,—they sleep—

"All Lost"—the only refrain for us,

But their memories e'er shall remain for us,

And their names, bright names, without stain for us,—

The glory they won shall not wane for us,

In legend and lay

Our heroes in gray

Shall forever live over again for us.

10. Francis Miles Finch Mourns and Celebrates Civil War Soldiers from the South and North, 1867

The Blue and the Gray

By the flow of the inland river,

Whence the fleets of iron have fled,

Where the blades of the grave-grass quiver,

Asleep are the ranks of the dead:

Under the sod and the dew,

Waiting the judgment-day;

Under the one, the Blue,

Under the other, the Gray....

From the silence of sorrowful hours

The desolate mourners go,

Lovingly laden with flowers

Alike for the friend and the foe;

Under the sod and the dew,

Waiting the judgment-day;

Under the roses, the Blue,

Under the lilies, the Gray.

So with an equal splendor,

The morning sun-rays fall,

With a touch impartially tender,

On the blossoms blooming for all:

Frances M. Finch, "The Blue and the Gray: And Other Verses" (New York: Henry Holt and Company, 1909), 1–3.

Under the sod and the dew,
Waiting the judgment-day;
Broidered with gold, the Blue,
Mellowed with gold, the Gray.

So, when the summer calleth,
On forest and field of grain,
With an equal murmur falleth
The cooling drip of the rain:
Under the sod and the dew,
Waiting the judgment-day,
Wet with the rain, the Blue
Wet with the rain, the Gray.

Sadly, but not with upbraiding,
The generous deed was done,
In the storm of the years that are fading
No braver battle was won:
Under the sod and the dew,
Waiting the judgment-day;
Under the blossoms, the Blue,
Under the garlands, the Gray

No more shall the war cry sever,
Or the winding rivers be red;
They banish our anger forever
When they laurel the graves of our dead!
Under the sod and the dew,
Waiting the judgment-day,
Love and tears for the Blue,
Tears and love for the Gray.

ESSAYS

The collapse of Reconstruction had enormous costs for the African-American population of the South. Arguably, its failure also postponed the economic and social recovery of the entire region until well into the twentieth century. Historians have long debated the meaning of Reconstruction and particularly the reasons for its abandonment. In the first essay, Steven Hahn of the University of Pennsylvania shows that former slaves and Confederates were both prepared to mount an armed defense of their goals, reflecting a long tradition of Southern violence that had previously undergirded slavery. He argues that Reconstruction came to an end when freedmen lost the military support of the North, which had tired of the sixteen-year conflict (1861–1877). Essentially, the freedmen were outgunned. David W. Blight of Yale University takes a somewhat different tack. He depicts Reconstruction as a process in which two important but incompatible goals vied for attention: reconciliation and emancipation. The nation needed to heal the sectional divide in order to function as one country, yet it had also fought the war, at least in part, to bring justice to the former slaves. As it turned out, Southern resistance narrowed the terms on which reconciliation was possible. The emancipationist promise of the war was stunted as a result, and eventually forgotten in the attempt to minimize the differences between "the Blue and the Gray." Reconstruction became a contest over the memory and meaning of the war. Black southerners lost.

Continuing the War: White and Black Violence During Reconstruction

STEVEN HAHN

In March 1867, nearly two years after the Confederate armies had begun to surrender and more than a year after Congress had refused to seat representatives from the former Confederate states, the mark of Radicalism was indelibly inscribed into the cornerstone of the reconstructed American republic. It did not herald the draconian policies—imprisonments and executions, massive disfranchisement, or confiscation of landed estates—that some Republicans had advocated and many Rebels had initially feared. And it required a combination of white southern arrogance and vindictiveness, presidential intransigence, and mounting African American agitation before it could be set. But with the Military Reconstruction Acts, Congress gave the federal government unprecedented power to reorganize the ex-Confederate South politically, imposed political disabilities on leaders of the rebellion, and, most stunning of all, extended the elective franchise to southern black males, the great majority of whom had been slaves. Never

Reprinted by permission of the publisher from *A Nation Under Our Feet: Black Political Struggles in the Rural South* by Steven Hahn, pp. 165, 177, 178–181, 183, 184, 186, 189, 190, 219, 224–226, 265–269, 280, 281, 286, 288–292, 307, 308, 310–312, Cambridge, Mass.: The Belknap Press of Harvard University Press, Copyright © 2003 by the President and Fellows of Harvard College.

before in history, and nowhere during the Age of Revolution, had so large a group of legally dependent people been enfranchised....

By the summer of 1867, complaints of "armed organizations among the freedmen," of late-hour drilling, and of threatening "assemblages" had grown both in volume and geographical scope. The entire plantation South appeared to pulse with militant and quasi-military activity. But now, in the months after the passage of the Reconstruction Acts, investigation revealed a more formal process of politicization, and one tied directly to the extension of the elective franchise and the organizational initiatives of the Republican party. From Virginia to Georgia, from the Carolinas to the Mississippi Valley and Texas, the freed people showed "a remarkable interest in all political information," were "fast becoming thoroughly informed upon their civil and political rights," and, most consequentially, were avidly "organizing clubs and leagues throughout the counties." Of these, none was more important to the former slaves or more emblematic of the developing character of local politics in the postemancipation South than the often vilified and widely misunderstood body known as the Union League.

Emerging out of a network of organizations formed in the northern states in 1862 and 1863 to rally public support for the Lincoln administration and the war effort, the Union League embraced early the practices of both popular and patrician politics. Bound by secrecy, requiring oaths and rituals much in the manner of the Masons, and winning a mass base through local councils across the Midwest and Northeast, the league also took hold among loyalist elites meeting in stately clubs and townhomes in Philadelphia, New York, and Boston. In May 1863, a national convention defined goals, drew up a constitution, and elected officers, and councils were soon being established in Union-occupied areas of the Confederate South to advance the cause. Once the war ended, the league continued its educational and agitational projects and spread most rapidly among white Unionists in southern hill and mountain districts, where membership could climb into the thousands. But committed as the league was "to protect, strengthen, and defend all loyal men without regard to sect, condition, or race," it began as well to sponsor political events and open a few councils for the still unfranchised African Americans—chiefly in larger cities like Richmond, Norfolk, Petersburg, Wilmington, Raleigh, Savannah, Tallahassee, Macon, and Nashville.

With the provision for a black franchise and voter registration encoded in the Reconstruction Acts, league organizers quickly fanned out from these urban areas into the smaller towns and surrounding countryside, and particularly into the plantation belt....

It was arduous and extremely dangerous work, for as organizers trekked out to where the mass of freedpeople resided, they fell vulnerable to swift and deadly retaliation at the hands of white landowners and vigilantes. Having organized the Mount Olive Union League Council in Nottoway County, Virginia, in July of 1867, the Reverend John Givens reported that a "colored speaker was killed three weeks ago" in neighboring Lunenberg County. But Givens determined to "go there and speak where they have cowed the black man," hoping "by the help of God" to "give them a dose of my radical Republican pills and neutralize the corrosive acidity of their negro hate.."...

The formation of a Union League council officially required the presence of at least nine loyal men, each twenty-one years of age or older, who were, upon initiation, to elect a president and other officers from among those regarded as "prudent, vigilant, energetic, and loyal," and as "possess[ing] the confidence of their fellow citizens." They were expected to hold meetings weekly, to follow the ceremony, and to "enlist all loyal talent in their neighborhood.."...

The experience and operations of local councils depended to some extent on the training and ability of the organizer, but perhaps even more on the social and political conditions in the specific counties and precincts. In hilly Rutherford County, North Carolina, where only one in five inhabitants was black and where the Whig party had been dominant before the Civil War, the Union League seemed to function—at least initially—in an unusually open and relaxed manner. One Saturday a month at noon, the courthouse bell in the village of Rutherfordton would be rung to announce a meeting and summon "every citizen who wished to come." Membership in the league was not concealed and some men who had served in the Confederate army belonged....

Yet where blacks made up between one-third and two-thirds of the population—and where, not incidentally, the great majority of Union League councils was to be found—the situation was rather different. Here, most league members were black and they encountered a substantial and largely antagonistic population of whites. Whether they met weekly, biweekly, or monthly (and there was considerable variation), they relied on word of mouth rather than bells, horns, or posters; they usually assembled at night; and they generally favored sites that would attract as little adverse attention as possible, often posting armed sentinels outside. Some league councils either organized their own drilling companies or linked with companies that already existed. One observer in the South Carolina piedmont district of Abbeville fretfully reported that local leagues with "their Captains, and other Officers," were meeting "with their Guns ... in secret places, but do not meet twice in the same place." Recognizing the dangers, the freedman Caleb, who worked for a particularly hostile landowner in Maury County, Tennessee, where blacks formed just under half of the population, chose another course: he went to his employe in April 1867 "and whol[l]y den[i]ed having any thing to do with the Un[i]on League," insisting that he "has not joined it nor never will.."...

The Union League sprang to life through the plantation districts because its goal of mobilizing black support for the national government and the Republican party fed on and nourished the sensibilities and customs that organizers found in many African American communities. League councils served as crucial political schools, educating newly enfranchised blacks in the ways of the official political culture. New members not only were instructed in the league's history, in the "duties of American citizenship," and in the role of th[e] Republican party in advancing their freedom, but also learned about "parliamentary law and debating," about courts, juries, and militia service, about the conduct of elections and of various political offices, and about important events near and far. With meetings often devoted, in part, to the reading aloud of newspapers, pamphlets, and government decrees, freedmen gained a growing political literacy even if most could neither read nor write....

Indeed, league councils quickly constituted themselves as vehicles not only of Republican electoral mobilization, but also of community development, defense, and self-determination. In Harnett County, North Carolina, they formed a procession "with fife and drum and flag and banner" and demanded the return of "any colored children in the county bound to white men." In Oktibbeha County, Mississippi, they organized a cooperative store, accepting "corn and other products ... in lieu of money," and, when a local black man suffered arrest, "the whole League" armed and marched to the county seat. In Randolph County, Alabama, and San Jacinto County, Texas, they worked to establish local schools so that, as one activist put it, "every colored man [now] beleaves in the Leage."...

Among the diverse activities that Union League councils across the former Confederate South pursued in 1867, few commanded more immediate attention than those required to implement the provisions and goals of the Reconstruction Acts. Within months, the Republican party had to be organized in the states and counties, delegates had to be nominated and elected to serve in state constitutional conventions, new state constitutions enfranchising black men and investing state governments with new structures and responsibilities had to be written and ratified, and the general congressional expectations for readmission to the Union had to be fulfilled. First and foremost, the outlines of a new body politic had to be drawn and legitimated through a process of voter registration....

During Reconstruction, black men held political office in every state of the former Confederacy. More than one hundred won election or appointment to posts having jurisdiction over entire states, ranging from superintendent of education, assistant commissioner of agriculture, superintendent of the deaf and dumb asylum, and member of the state land commission to treasurer, secretary of state, state supreme court justice, and lieutenant governor. One African American even sat briefly as the governor of Louisiana. A great many more—almost eight hundred—served in the state legislatures. But by far the largest number of black officeholders were to be found at the local level: in counties, cities, smaller municipalities, and militia districts. Although a precise figure is almost impossible to obtain, blacks clearly filled over 1,100 elective or appointive local offices, and they may well have filled as many as 1,400 or 1,500, about 80 percent of which were in rural and small-town settings....

Union League and Republican party activists therefore had to prepare carefully for election day lest their other efforts be nullified. They had to petition military commanders and Republican governors to appoint favorable (and dismiss hostile) election officials and to designate suitable polling sites, particularly if Democrats still controlled county governing boards. They had to get their voters to the polls, at times over a distance of many miles, and make sure that those voters received the correct tickets. They had to minimize the opportunities for bribery, manipulation, and intimidation. And they had to oversee the counting of ballots. Voting required, in essence, a military operation. Activists often called a meeting of fellow leaguers or club members the night before an election to provide instructions and materials. The chairman of the Tunica County, Mississippi, Republican executive committee had men come to the town of Hernando from all over the county on the day before the election and distribute tickets to those political clubs meeting that night. At times groups of black voters might spend the night before an election on a safe plantation or in the woods, perhaps sending a small party ahead to check for possible traps or ambushes, and then move out at first light to arrive at the polls well before their opponents or "rebel spies" could gather. Henry Frazer, who organized for the Republican party in Barbour County, Alabama, claimed that he went out with as many as "450 men and camped at the side of the road" before going into the town of Eufaula at eight in the morning where they would "stand in a body until they got a chance to vote."…

Protecting black Republican voters from white intimidation was only the most obvious goal of such martial organization and display, however. There was also the need to prod the timid and punish the apathetic or disloyal within their own communities. Activists learned early that elections could only be carried by securing overwhelming allegiance to the Republican party and then by ensuring that the eligible voters overcame fear or inertia to cast ballots. Political parades and torchlight processions during election campaigns and on the eve of polling—often with black men dressed in their club uniforms, beating drums, "hallooing, hooping," and, on occasion, riding full gallop through the streets—thereby served several purposes: to inspire enthusiasm, advertise numbers and resolve, and coax the participation of those who might otherwise abstain. Where coaxing proved insufficient, more coercive tactics could be deployed. Union League members in a North Carolina county, upon learning of three or four black men who "didn't mean to vote," threatened to "whip them" and "made them go." In another county, "some few colored men who declined voting" were, in the words of a white conservative, "bitterly persecute[ed]." One suffered insults, the destruction of his fences and crops, and "other outrages."

Especially harsh reprisals could be brought against blacks who aligned with conservatives and Democrats, for they were generally regarded not merely as opponents but as "traitors." As black Mississippian Robert Gleed put it, "[W]e don't believe they have a right to acquiesce with a party who refuse to recognize their right to participate in public affairs." In the rural hinterlands of Portsmouth, Virginia, black Republicans attacked "colored conservatives" at a prayer meeting and beat two of them badly. In southside Virginia's Campbell County, a black man who betrayed the Union League was tied up by his heels and suspended from a tree for several hours until he agreed to take an oath of loyalty.…

When the U.S. Congress conducted an investigation of the Ku Klux Klan in the early 1870s, more than a few of the reputed leaders testified that the organization was a necessary response to the alarming activities and tactics of the Union League. They complained of secret oaths, clandestine meetings, accumulations of arms, nocturnal drilling, threatening mobilizations, and a general flaunting of civilities among former slaves across the plantation South. In so doing, they helped construct a discourse, later embraced by apologists for slavery and white supremacy, that not only justified vigilantism but also demonized Radical Reconstruction for its political illegitimacies. The enfranchisement of ignorant and dependent freedmen by vengeful outsiders, the Klansmen insisted, marked a basic corruption of the body politic and a challenge to order as it was widely understood....

Ku Klux Klan leaders and sympathizers who blamed the Union League for their resort to vigilantism were at least right about the chronology. Union League mobilizations generally preceded the appearance of the Klan. But the character and activities of the league itself reflected a well-established climate of paramilitarism that assumed both official and unofficial forms. Already during the summer and fall of 1865, despite the presence of a Union army of occupation, bands of white "regulators," "scouts," and cavalrymen rode the countryside disciplining and disarming freedpeople who looked to harvest their crops, make new labor and family arrangements, and perhaps await a federally sponsored land redistribution....

From the first, the Klan proved particularly attractive to young, white men who had served in the Confederate army. All of the founders in Pulaski, Tennessee, were youthful Confederate veterans, and most everywhere former Confederate officers, cavalrymen, and privates sparked organization and composed the bulk of membership. Klan dens and other vigilante outfits often became magnets for returning soldiers and, at times, they virtually mirrored the remainders of specific Confederate companies. Powell Clayton, the Republican governor of Arkansas who effectively combated the Klan, complained in retrospect about the Confederates being paroled or allowed to desert without surrendering their arms, ammunition, and horses. To this extent, the Klan not only came to embody the anger and displacement of a defeated soldiery and to capitalize on the intensely shared experiences of battlefields and prison camps; it also may be regarded as a guerilla movement bent on continuing the struggle or avenging the consequences of the official surrender.

But the very associations between the Klan and the Confederate army suggest a deeper historical and political context, for Confederate mobilization itself was enabled by longstanding and locally based paramilitary institutions. Militias were perhaps most important because state governments required the enrollment of all able-bodied white men while leaving much of the organizational initiative to counties and neighborhoods, where volunteer companies could elect their own officers, make their own by-laws, and then secure recognition by the legislature. The militias, in turn, were closely connected with slave patrols—for a time through formal control, and more generally by way of personnel and jurisdiction—which policed the African American population, instructed all white men in their responsibilities as citizens in a slave society, and could be enlisted as something of a posse by the state in the event of emergency. A martial spirit and military presence thus suffused the community life of the antebellum South....

The geography of Klan activity was, in essence, a map of political struggle in the Reconstruction South. Klan-style vigilantism surfaced at some point almost anywhere that a substantial Republican constituency—and especially a black

Republican constituency—was to be found: from Virginia to Florida, South Carolina to Texas, Arkansas to Kentucky. Reports of "outrages" and "depredations" emanated from areas that were heavily black (eastern North Carolina, west-central Alabama), heavily white (east Tennessee, northwest Georgia), and racially mixed (eastern Mississippi, northwest South Carolina, east-central Texas). But whether the eruptions were brief or prolonged and whether they achieved their objectives depended on the nature and effectiveness of black resistance and, by extension, the readiness of the state Republican governments to respond with necessary force....

Union Leagues and Republican party clubs had, in some places, already begun to mount a response to Klan violence, at times bringing pressure against suspected Klan leaders. Black members of a Pickens County, Alabama, Union League boycotted a white landowner thought to be "head of the Ku Klux." They were so effective that, in his words, he "could not hire a darkey at any price." In a number of locales scattered across the plantation districts, they appear to have taken even more direct and destructive action by torching the mills, barns, and houses of former slaveholders. But the leagues and clubs more likely moved to put themselves on a paramilitary footing, if they had not embraced rituals of armed self-defense from the outset. Black Union Leaguers in Darlington County, South Carolina, fearing Klan violence, gathered weapons, took control of a town, and threatened to burn it down in the event of attack. Near Macon, Mississippi, the combination of local outrages and the very bloody Meridian riot led blacks to organize "secretly" and ready themselves to "meet the mob." "There will be no more 'Meridians' in Mississippi," a white ally of theirs declared. "Next time an effort of this kind is made there will be killing on both sides." The tenor of conflict and mobilization in Granville County, North Carolina, in the fall of 1868 was such that a prominent Democrat offered Union League members a bargain: "If we would stop the leagues he would stop the Ku Klux."...

Like Tennessee, neighboring Arkansas had a white population majority, a solid base of Unionist sentiment in the mountains of the northwest, and a Republican party that looked to punish former Confederates. But Arkansas had been remanded to military rule by the Reconstruction Acts of 1867, and in the spring of 1868 eligible voters put Republicans in command of the general assembly and the carpetbagger Powell Clayton in the governor's chair. A native of Pennsylvania and a civil engineer by training, Clayton had been out in Kansas during the 1850s and commanded a Union cavalry regiment in Arkansas during the war, where he saw a good deal of action against Confederate guerrillas. After the surrender, he settled in Arkansas and bought a plantation, but run-ins with ex-Confederate neighbors led him into politics; he first helped to organize the state Republican party and then accepted the party's nomination for governor. By the time of Clayton's inauguration in July, Klan activity was sufficiently pronounced in the southern and eastern sections of the state that he wasted no time in responding: with the approval of the legislature, he began mobilizing a state militia and, as intimidation of Republican voters and local officials intensified and a Republican congressman fell victim to a Klan ambush, he declared marital law in ten counties. Armed skirmishes between militiamen and Klansmen, together with arrests, trials, and a few executions, followed. By early 1869, the Klan had pretty well "ceased to exist" in Arkansas....

The accession of Republican Ulysses S. Grant to the presidency in March of 1869 offered some welcome possibilities to those governors who stood ready to deploy state militia units. Previously, the Johnson administration had refused requests for arms, and governors were left scrambling to equip their troops. Arkansas's Powell Clayton first tried to borrow guns from various northern states and then, when this failed, sent an emissary to New York to purchase rifles and ammunition. Unfortunately, a contingent of well-prepared Klansmen intercepted the shipment between Memphis and Little Rock. Florida's carpetbag governor Harrison Reed chose to go personally to New York to procure arms soon after the legislature passed a militia law in August 1868, but the result was even more embarrassing. Under the nose of a federal detachment, Klansmen boarded the train carrying the armaments to Tallahassee and destroyed them. Grant, on the other hand, proved more receptive than Johnson and made substantial supplies of weapons available to Governors Holden and Scott in the Carolinas....

The Klan's effectiveness depended on a wider political climate that gave latitude to local vigilantes and allowed for explosions of very public violence. Louisiana and Georgia, which alone among the reconstructed states supported Democrat Horatio Seymour for the presidency in 1868, had at least seven bloody riots together with Klan raiding that summer and fall. The term "riot," which came into wide use at this time, quite accurately captures the course and ferocity of these eruptions, claiming as they did numerous lives, often over several days, in an expanding perimeter of activity. But "riot" suggests, as well, a disturbance that falls outside the ordinary course of political conduct, and so by invoking or embracing it we may miss what such disturbances can reveal about the changing dynamics and choreography of what was indeed ordinary politics in the postemancipation South....

Consider the Camilla riot in southwest Georgia, which captured the greatest attention but shared many features of the others. In late August 1868, Republicans in the state's Second Congressional District, most of whom were black, met in the town of Albany and nominated William P. Pierce, a former Union army officer, failed planter, and Freedmen's Bureau agent, for Congress. It would not be an easy campaign.... A "speaking" in the town of Americus on September 15 brought menacing harassment from local whites and Pierce barely escaped violence. But he did not interrupt plans for a similar event in Camilla on Saturday, September 19.

News of the rally—which would feature Pierce, several other white Republicans, and Philip Joiner, a former slave, local Loyal League president, and recently expelled state legislator—circulated through the neighboring counties. So, too, did rumors of a possible attack by armed whites who, it was said, proclaimed that "this is our country and we intend to protect it or die." Freedpeople did have ample cause for alarm. Camilla, the seat of relatively poor, white-majority Mitchell County in an otherwise black majority section of the state, crackled with tension. Gunfire had broken out there during the April 1868 elections, and many of the blacks had resolved that they would "not dare … go to town entirely unarmed as they did at that time." The white Republican leaders tried to quell these fears when the Dougherty County contingent gathered on their plantations on Friday night the 18th; and as the group moved out on Saturday morning for the twenty-odd mile trek to Camilla, most heeded the advice to leave their weapons behind and avoid a provocation.…

But to the whites of Camilla, such a procession could only constitute a "mob," with no civil or political standing, and mean "war, revolution, insurrection, or riot of some sort." Once spotted on Saturday morning, it thereby sparked another round of rumors, these warning of an "armed body of negroes" heading toward the town. Although evidence suggests that local Democrats had been busy for at least two days accumulating weapons and preparing to respond with force, the rumors clearly sped the mobilization of the town's "citizens," who appointed a committee to ride out with the sheriff and "meet the approaching crowd." A tense exchange followed, with the Republican leaders explaining that they only wished "to go peaceably into Camilla and hold a political meeting," and the sheriff warning them not to enter the town with arms.…

Suddenly, a local drunkard, waving a double-barreled shotgun, ran out to the wagon and, significantly, demanded that the drumming (associated both with a citizens' militia and slave communication) cease. A moment later he fired, and the "squads" of white townsmen immediately joined in. Freedmen who had guns briefly returned the volleys and then, with the others, commenced a desperate flight for safety. The sheriff and his "deputies" followed them into the woods and swamps with deadly purpose, some looking for "that d——d Phil Joiner." Joiner escaped, but eleven days later he reported that "the mobbing crowd is still going through Baker County and every Colored man that is farming to his self or supporting the nominee of Grant and Colfax he either have to leave his home or be killed."

Prospects for black retaliation briefly ran very high. As word of the shooting spread through Dougherty County that Saturday evening, agitated freedmen in Albany sought out the local Freedmen's Bureau agent. Some talked of going immediately to Camilla to rescue and protect those who remained at risk. A few hours later, African Methodist minister Robert Crumley heatedly reminded his congregants that he had advised those bound for Camilla the night before not to go with fewer than 150 well-armed men, and then suggested traveling there en masse the next day to "burn the earthy about the place." The Freedmen's Bureau agent managed to discourage such a course by promising a full investigation and urging his superiors in Atlanta to send federal troops. The investigation showed Camilla to be a massacre that had left at least nine African Americans dead and many more wounded. But all that came out of Atlanta was a proclamation by Republican governor Rufus Bullock urging civil authorities to keep the peace and safeguard the rights of the people. Election day proved to be remarkably quiet in southwest Georgia because the contest was over well before. Only two Republicans bothered to cast ballots in Camilla, and the turnout was so low elsewhere in the district that the Democrats, despite being greatly outnumbered among eligible voters, registered an official victory. There would be resurgences of local black power in the future, but this was the beginning of the end for Republican rule in Georgia.…

And yet we must not underestimate the extent and tenacity of black resistance. White toughs did, to their misfortune, in the village of Cainhoy, a short distance from Charleston. Attempting to intimidate a Republican speaker at a "joint discussion" in mid-October, they found themselves outgunned as well as outnumbered by a black crowd that included several militia companies. When the smoke cleared, five whites lay dead and as many as fifty had been wounded. Most in evidence among the coast, such militance was nonetheless to be found at various points in the interior. As rifle club activity intensified in Barnwell County, a "company of negroes," acting on their own authority, appropriated arms issued during Governor Scott's administration and threaten[ed] to destroy the town" of Blackville. In Darlington County, a "negro militia company consisting," according to a local Democrat, "of the worst elements in this section," continued to drill and cause "a great deal of trouble," coming in one instance to the aid of a favored trial justice. Sporadically, there were acts of arson and sabotage, ambushes and assaults....

The paramilitary politics of the Reconstruction South had previously produced dual state governments in Louisiana (1872), Texas (1873), and Arkansas (1874), but in 1876–1877 they also provoked a national crisis of governance. Not only were the state returns contested in both South Carolina and Louisiana, but there, as well as in Florida, the electoral college returns were contested too, leaving the outcome of the Presidential race—and control of the executive branch—in doubt. As Republicans and Democrats struggled to reach an accord before Grant's term expired in early March, tensions and threats that harked back to the winter of 1860–1861 seemed to abound. Yet through all of this, what appeared to be taking shape was less a "compromise" than a shared political sensibility in northern ruling circles that questioned the legitimacies of popular democracy. That sensibility had always been in evidence among conservatives and had spread during the 1850s, only to be pressed to the margins by the revolutionary mobilizations of the 1860s. It now expressed itself as weariness with the issues of Reconstruction, as skepticism about the capabilities of freedpeople, as concerns about the expansion of federal powers, as revulsion over political corruption, and, especially, as exasperation with the "annual autumnal outbreaks" in the Deep South and the consequent use of federal troops to maintain Republican regimes there.

It required elaborate fictions and willful ignorance for critics to argue, as some did, that the military had no business rejecting the popular will in the South. For if detachments of federal troops at the statehouses in Columbia, South Carolina, and New Orleans, Louisiana, alone enabled Republicans to hand onto the last threads of power, their Democratic rivals made no effort to conceal their own dependence on superior force of arms. In Louisiana, Democratic gubernatorial claimant and former Confederate brigadier general Francis T. Nicholls quickly demonstrated his understanding of political necessities. He designated local White League units as the legal state militia, commandeered the state arsenal, and took control of the New Orleans police. In South Carolina, Wade Hampton's allies succeeded in garrisoning the state capitol with as many as six thousand Red Shirts, while rifle clubs drove out Republican officeholders in upcountry counties....

The withdrawal of federal troops from the statehouses of South Carolina and Louisiana in April of 1877 did not therefore mark the end of their role in protecting the rights and property of American citizens; it only marked the end of their role, at least for nearly another century, in protecting the rights and property of African Americans and other working people....

Ending the War: The Push for National Reconciliation

DAVID W. BLIGHT

Americans faced an overwhelming task after the Civil War and emancipation: how to understand the tangled relationship between two profound ideas—*healing* and *justice*. On some level, both had to occur; but given the potency of racial assumptions and power in nineteenth-century America, these two aims never developed in historical balance. One might conclude that this imbalance between outcomes of sectional healing and racial justice was simply America's inevitable historical condition, and celebrate the remarkable swiftness of the reunion, as Paul Buck did in his influential book, *The Road to Reunion* (1937). But theories of inevitability—of irrepressible conflicts or irrepressible reconciliations—and rarely satisfying. Human reconciliations—when tragically divided people unify again around aspirations, ideas, and the positive bonds of nationalism—are to be cherished. But sometimes reconciliations have terrible costs, both intentional and unseen. The sectional reunion after so horrible a civil war was a political triumph by the late nineteenth century, but it could not have been achieved without the resubjugation of many of those people whom the war had freed from centuries of bondage. This is the tragedy lingering on the margins and infesting the heart of American history from Appomattox to World War I....

Reconstruction was one long referendum on the meaning and memory of the verdict at Appomattox. The great challenge of Reconstruction was to determine how a national blood feud could be reconciled at the same time a new nation emerged out of war and social revolution. The survivors on both sides, winners and losers in the fullest sense, would still inhabit the same land and eventually the same government. The task was harrowing: how to make the logic of sectional reconciliation compatible with the logic of emancipation, how to square black freedom and the stirrings of racial equality with a cause (the South's) that had lost almost everything except its unbroken belief in white supremacy. Such an effort required both remembering and forgetting. During Reconstruction, many Americans increasingly realized that remembering the war, even the hatreds and deaths on a hundred battlefields—facing all those graves on Memorial Day—became, with time, easier than struggling over the enduring ideas for which those battles had been fought....

Reprinted by permission of the publisher from *Race and Reunion: The Civil War in American Memory* by David W. Blight, pp. 3, 31, 44–47, 51, 64, 65, 69–71, 77–81, 83, 86, 87, 89, 91, 92, 97, Cambridge, Mass.: The Belknap Press of Harvard University Press, Copyright © 2001 by the President and Fellows of Harvard College.

In the immediate aftermath of the war, defeated and prostrate, it appeared to many that white Southerners would accept virtually any conditions or terms laid upon them. This was the initial conclusion of the northern journalist Whitelaw Reid, who believed that even black suffrage would be "promptly accepted"— that is, until he observed white Southern defiance revived by President Johnson's conciliatory Reconstruction measures. After his Southern tour, Reid left a mixed warning to policymakers about the disposition of white Southerners in 1866. "The simple truth is," Reid concluded, "they stand ready to claim everything, if permitted, and to accept anything, if required." Other Northern journalists observing the South reached similar conclusions. The initial war-bludgeoned compliance on the part of white Southerners gave way within a year to what Trowbridge called a "loyalty ... of a negative sort: it is simply disloyalty subdued." A correspondent for the *New York Tribune* reported from Raleigh, North Carolina, that "the spirit of the Rebellion is not broken though its power is demolished." And a Northerner who had just returned from six months in South Carolina and Georgia informed Thaddeus Stevens in February 1866 that "the spirit which actuated the traitors ... during the late rebellion is only subdued and *allows* itself to be *nourished* by *leniency*."

Against this backdrop, Andrew Johnson offered to the South his rapid Reconstruction policy. In late May 1865, Johnson announced his plan for the readmission of Southern states. It included a broad provision for amnesty and pardon for those participants in the rebellion who would take a loyalty oath to the Union. High-ranking ex-Confederate government officials were excluded from pardons for the time being, as were all Southerners who owned $20,000 or more worth of property. The latter group had to apply personally to the President for a pardon. Johnson's plan further required each former Confederate state to call a convention to revise its antebellum constitution, renounce secession, and accept the Thirteenth Amendment abolishing slavery; they would then be promptly restored to the Union.

Johnson's plan put enormous authority back in the hands of white Southerners, but without any provisions for black civil or political rights. Indeed, Johnson himself was a thoroughgoing white supremacist and a doctrinaire state rightist. He openly encouraged the South to draft its notorious Black Codes, laws enacted across the South by the fall of 1865 that denied the freedmen political liberty and restricted their economic options and physical mobility. Designed as labor controls and a means for plantation discipline, such laws were part of the new constitutions produced by these "Johnson governments," and they expressed clearly white Southerners' refusal to face the deeper meanings of emancipation. Presidential Reconstruction, as it evolved in 1865, allowed Southerners to recreate governments of and for white men. Moreover, Johnson was openly hostile to the Freedmen's Bureau, the agency created by Congress in the last months of the war to provide food, medical care, schools, and labor contract adjudication for the freedpeople. The President overruled military and Freedmen's Bureau efforts to redistribute some land from masters to ex-slaves. By the fall of 1865, pardoned ex-Confederates were reclaiming their lands, and with such presidential encouragement, reclaiming political power....

Profoundly different memories and expectations collided in 1865-67, as presidential Reconstruction collapsed and the Republicans in Congress wrested control of the process away from Johnson. "These people [white Southerners] are not loyal; they are only conquered," wrote Union Brigadier General James S. Brisbin to Thaddeus Stevens in December 1865. "I tell you there is not as much loyalty in the South today as there was the day Lee surrendered to Grant. The moment they lost their cause in the field they set about to gain by politics what they had failed to obtain by force of arms." Brisbin thought the Black Codes would "reduce the blacks to a slavery worse than that from which they just escaped." Johnson's leniency seemed only to restore an old order and risk losing the very triumph that the Union forces had just won with so much sacrifice....

The radical Republicans had a genuine plan for Reconstruction. Their ideology was grounded in the notion of an activist federal government, a redefinition of American citizenship that guaranteed equal political rights for black men, and faith in free labor in a competitive capitalist system. The radicals greatly expanded federal authority, fixing their vision, as Sumner put it, on "the general principles" of "a national security and a national faith." Their cardinal principle was *equality before the law,* which in 1866 they enshrined in the Fourteen Amendment, expanding citizenship to all those born in the United States without regard to race. The same year Congress renewed the Freedmen's Bureau over Johnson's veto and passed the first civil rights act in American history.

Such legislation became reality because most Northerners were not ready to forget the results, and especially the sacrifices, of the war. The Southern states' rejection of the Fourteenth Amendment and Johnson's repeated vetoes of Reconstruction measures (as well as his repudiation at the polls in the Congressional elections of 1866) gave the radicals increased control over federal policy. In 1867 Congress divided the ex-Confederate states into five military districts and made black suffrage a condition of readmission to the Union. By 1870 all ex-Confederate states had rejoined the Union, and in most, the Republican Party—built as a coalition of "carpetbaggers" (Northerners who moved South), "scalawags" (native Southerners who gave allegiance to the new order), and thousands of black voters—held the reins of state government. Indeed black voters were the core constituency of Southern Republicanism and the means of power in 1867–68....

As Congress engaged in the fateful debates over national policy in 1866–67, the floors of the House and Senate became arenas of warring memories. Many Republicans were clearly driven by a combination of retribution against the South, a desire to remake the Constitution based on black equality, and a quest for long-term political hegemony. Stevens left no doubt of his personal attitude toward ex-slaveholders and ex-Confederates. "The murderers must answer to the suffering race," he said on May 8, 1866. "A load of misery must sit heavily upon their souls." The public debate in Congress was often sanguinary; it challenged everyone's ability to convert primal memory into public policy. "I know that there is a morbid sensibility, sometimes called mercy," declared Stevens, "which affects a few of all classes, from the priest to the clown, which has more sympathy for the murderer on the gallows than for his victim." Yankee retribution never had a more vehement voice than Stevens, and no one ever waved the "bloody shirt" with greater zeal. "I am willing they shall come in when they are ready," Stevens pronounced. "Do not, I pray you, admit those who have slaughtered half a million of our countrymen until their clothes are dried, and until they are reclad. I do not wish to sit side by side with men whose garments smell of the blood of my kindred."

"Bloody shirt" rhetoric lasted a long time in American politics; it was more than a slogan, and in these early years, it had many uses and diverse practitioners. As both raw personal memory and partisan raw material, the "bloody shirt" was a means to establish war guilt and a method through which to express war-induced hatreds....

Death and mourning were everywhere in America in 1865; hardly a family had escaped its pall. In the North, 6 percent of white males aged 13–43 had died in the war; in the South, 18 percent were dead. Of the 180,000 African Americans who served in the Union army and navy, 20 percent perished. Diseases such as typhoid, dysentery, and pneumonia claimed more than twice as many soldiers as did battle. The most immediate legacy of the war was its slaughter and how to remember it.

Death on such a scale demanded meaning. During the war, soldiers in countless remote arbors, or on awful battlefield landscapes, had gathered to mourn and bury their comrades, even while thousands remained unburied, their skeletons lying about on the killing fields of Virginia, Tennessee, or Georgia. Women had begun rituals of burial and remembrance in informal ways well before the war ended, both in towns on the homefront and sometimes at the battlefront. Americans carried flowers to graves or to makeshift monuments representing their dead, and so was born the ritual of "Decoration Day," known eventually also as Memorial Day.

In most places, the ritual was initially a spiritual practice. But very soon, remembering the dead and what they died for developed partisan fault lines. The evolution of Memorial Day during its first twenty years or so became a contest between three divergent, and sometimes overlapping, groups: blacks and their white former abolitionist allies, white Northerners, and white Southerners With time, in the North, the war's two great results—black freedom and the preservation of the Union—were rarely accorded equal space. In the South, a uniquely Confederate version of the war's meaning, rooted in resistance to Reconstruction, coalesced around Memorial Day practice. Decoration Day, and the ways in which it was observed, shaped Civil War memory as much as any other cultural ritual. The story of the origins of this important American day of remembrance is central to understanding how reconciliationist practices overtook the emancipationist legacies of the Civil War....

The "First Decoration Day," as this event came to be recognized in some circles in the North, involved an estimated ten thousand people, most of them black former slaves. During April, twenty-eight black men from one of the local churches built a suitable enclosure for the burial ground at the Race Course. In some ten days, they constructed a fence ten feet high, enclosing the burial ground, and landscaped the graves into neat rows. The wooden fence was whitewashed and an archway was built over the gate to the enclosure. On the arch, painted in black letters, the workmen inscribed "Martyrs of the Race Course." At nine o'clock in the morning on May 1, the procession to this special cemetery began as three thousand black schoolchildren (newly enrolled in freemen's schools) marched around the Race Course, each with an armload of roses and singing "John Brown's Body." The children were followed by three hundred black women representing the Patriotic Association, a group organized to distribute clothing and other goods among the freedpeople. The women carried baskets of flowers, wreaths, and crosses to the burial ground. The Mutual Aid Society, a benevolent association of black men, next marched in cadence around the track and into the cemetery, followed by large crowds of white and black citizens....

According to a reminiscence written long after the fact, "several slight disturbances" occurred during the ceremonies on the first Decoration Day, as well as "much harsh talk about the event locally afterward." But a measure of how white Charlestonians suppressed from memory this founding in favor of their own creation of the practice a year later came fifty-one years afterward, when the president of the Ladies Memorial Association of Charleston received an inquiry for information about the May 1, 1865, parade. A United Daughters of the Confederacy official wanted to know if it was true that blacks and their white abolitionist friends had engaged in such a burial rite. Mrs. S. C. Beckwith responded tersely: "I regret that I was unable to gather any official information in answer to this." In Southern and national memory, the first Decoration Day was nearly lost in a grand evasion.

As a Northern ritual of commemoration, Memorial Day officially took hold in May 1868 and 1869, when General John A. Logan, commander-in-chief of the Grand Army of the Republic (GAR), called on all Union veterans to conduct ceremonies and decorate the graves of their dead comrades. In general orders issued each of the two springs, Logan called for a national commemoration unlike anything in American experience save possibly the Fourth of July. In "almost every city, village, and hamlet church-yard in the land," charged Logan's circular, those who died to "suppress the late rebellion" were to be honored annually "while a survivor of the war remains." On May 30, 1868, when flowers were plentiful, funeral ceremonies were attended by thousands of people in 183 cemeteries in twenty-seven states. The following year, some 336 cities and towns in thirty-one states (including the South) arranged Decoration Day parades and orations. The observance grew manifold with time. In 1873, the New York legislature designated May 30 a legal holiday, and by 1890 every other Northern state had followed its lead....

For white Southerners, Memorial Day was born amidst the despair of defeat and the need for collective expressions of grief. By 1866, local memorial associations had formed in many Southern communities, organized largely by women. Some new cemeteries were founded near battlefields, while existing ones in towns and cities were expanded enormously to accommodate the dead. In both sections, but especially in the South, the first monuments erected tended to be placed in cemeteries—the obvious sites of bereavement. By the 1890s, hardly a city square, town green, or even some one-horse crossroads lacked a Civil War memorial of some kind. But through most of the Reconstruction years, the cemetery remained the public site of memorialization; obelisks and stone pyramids appeared as markers of the recent past that so haunted every community. Often directed by social elites who could fund monuments, the Southern "memorial movement ... helped the South assimilate the fact of defeat," as Gaines Foster writes, "without repudiating the defeated."...

By the early 1870s, a group of ex-Confederate officers in Virginia had forged a coalition of memorial groups that quickly took over the creation of the Lost Cause tradition. They did so through print as much as through ritual commemorations. In 1866, former Confederate general Daniel H. Hill founded the magazine *The Land We Love*, a periodical devoted to demonstrating the skill and prowess of Confederate armies against all odds. By 1869, Hill's journal had become *Southern Magazine*, and most importantly, the Southern Historical Society (SHS) was founded as the vehicle for presenting the Confederate version of the war to the world. By 1876, the SHS began publishing its regular *Southern Historical Society Papers*, a series that ran for fourteen years under the editorship of a former Confederate chaplain, John William Jones. The driving ideological and emotional force behind the SHS was the former Confederate general Jubal Early. Early had fled to Mexico at the end of the war and vowed never to return to his native Virginia under the federal flag. Despite such bluster, and because of threatening poverty, Early returned to his hometown of Lynchburg in 1869. He made himself, as Gaines Foster observes, into the "prototypical unreconstructed Rebel." His principle aim was not only to vindicate Southern secession and glorify the Confederate soldier, but also to launch a propaganda assault on popular history and memory....

In the South, monument unveiling days took on a significance equal to, if not greater than, Memorial Day. In Richmond, Virginia, on October 26, 1875, Confederate veterans by the thousands staged their first major coming-out as a collective force. At the unveiling of the first significant monument to a Confederate hero, a standing statue of Stonewall Jackson sculpted by the British artist T. H. Foley, nearly fifty thousand people gathered for an unprecedented parade and a ceremony....

At major intersections on the parade route, veterans, ladies memorial associations, and "the indefatigable K.K.K." (Ku Klux Klan) had assembled artisans to construct arches and towers with elaborate decorations honoring Jackson. The largest arch, at Grace and Eighth Streets, included huge letters that read: "Warrior, Christian, Patriot." Above the inscription was a painting representing a stone wall, "upon which was resting a bare saber, a Bible, and a Confederate cap."...

One dispute among the planners of the Jackson statue unveiling nearly derailed the event. Governor Kemper was the grand marshal of the ceremonies and had carefully planned the parade to the Capitol Square in Richmond. Kemper was nervous that "nothing shall appear on the 26th to hurt the party" (Democrats). He feared that the "least excess" in the Confederate celebration would give yet another "bloody shirt" to Northern Republicans, and he asked the leaders of the Confederate veterans to restrain their displays of battle flags. Only days before the big event, Jubal Early wrote to Kemper complaining of rumors that black militia companies and civilians were to be "allowed in the procession." "I am inexpressibly shocked at the idea," said Early. He considered the involvement of blacks "an indignity to the memory of Jackson and an insult to the Confederates." Black Richmonders, the total of which Early judged to be between twenty thousand and thirty thousand, would swarm into the square, he believed, and whites would be forced to "struggle for place with buck negroes … anxious to show their consequence." Believing that blacks would wave "pictures of Lincoln and Fifteenth Amendment banners," Early threatened not to attend, and to take other veterans with him, if Kemper executed the plan.

In ferocious responses, Kemper told Early to mind his own business and begged him to "stay at home." Black militia officers and ministers in Richmond had petitioned Kemper to take part in the procession. For racial "peace" in the city, the governor accepted the petitioners' request. The small contingent of blacks were placed at the extreme rear of a parade several miles long, numbering many thousands of white marchers…. The position of blacks in this bitter argument between the ultimate irreconcilable [Jubal Early] and a redeemer-reconciliationist governor remained utterly subordinate. One would eliminate them altogether from Confederate memory; the other would declare them loyal and dispatch them to the rear of parades. In the long history of Lost Cause tradition, both got their wish.

As the immense crowd assembled at the state capital grounds where the Jackson monument was to be unveiled, Kemper welcomed them as the Democrat-redeemer governor of Virginia. He announced that Jackson was a national hero, not merely a Southern saint, whose memory was to be a "common heritage of glory" for both sections. The massive ceremony served as the South's reminder to the North of its insistence on "respect." The unveiling declared, in effect, that Reconstruction, as Northern Republicans had imagined it, was over….

In 1874–75, Union and Confederate veterans began to participate in Memorial Day exercises together in both North and South. In the wake of Memorial Day, 1875, in North Carolina, a black citizen in Raleigh, Osborne Hunter, anxiously observed in a letter to a newspaper "a noticeable spirit of reconciliation pervading the political atmosphere of both the Republican and Democratic parties of this state." In August 1874, the Democrats had regained power in North Carolina, and the highly racialized election had hinged, in part, on Southern resistance to federal enforcement of black civil rights. Until May 1875, blacks in Raleigh had always played a major role in Decoration Day ceremonies in that city. That year they were discouraged from participating, as the occasion was declared to be only a "soldier's turn-out." At the mark of a "decade in the history of freedom," concluded Hunter, Decoration Day seemed to be only an occasion for "ignoring the colored citizen and the colored voter."…

The disputed election of 1876 and the electoral crisis that culminated in the Compromise of 1877 brought the Republican Rutherford B. Hayes to the presidency, as well as the final three remaining Southern states not under Democratic control into that party's fold. Reconciliation seemed to sweep over the country's political spirit, as the Union survived another potential severing by sectional and partisan strife. Although it was hardly the first time that commentators in both sections had declared the final conclusion to the issues of the war, the political settlement of 1877 easily took its place as the traditional "end" of Reconstruction (a label it has carried ever since).

On Memorial Day, May 30, 1877, New York City experienced an array of parades and ceremonies unprecedented since the formal inception of the holiday nine years earlier. Virtually every orator and editorial writer declared the day one of forgetting, forgiveness, and equality of the Blue and the Gray veterans....

Decoration Day, 1877 in New York culminated with a special indoor event at the Brooklyn Academy of Music. The planning committee, dominated by democrats, had invited the prominent ex-Confederate general, lawyer, and then Brooklyn resident Roger A. Pryor to be orator of the evening. A committee member, Joseph Neilson, opened the proceedings with an explicit appeal for reconciliation. Neilson declared all the "causes" of the "late domestic contention" forgotten. As the voice of "healing," Pryor took the podium before an audience of nearly one thousand to deliver his extraordinary address, "The Soldier, the Friend of Peace and Union."...

Unlike many Memorial Day orators, Pryor did not hide the issue of race behind a rhetoric of reunion. The war had nothing directly to do with slavery, he proclaimed, in what became an article of faith to Southern vindicationists and their Northern allies. Southerners were comfortably reconciled to the destruction of slavery because it had only been the "occasion not the cause of secession." Slavery was an impersonal force in history, a natural phenomenon subject only to divine control and beyond all human responsibility. It was good while it lasted, good once it was gone; no Southerner fought in its defense, and no Northerner died to end it. It just went away, like a change in the weather....

Following Pryor, former Union general Isaac S. Catlin delivered the final address of the evening. In full sympathy with the former Confederate's speech, Catlin spoke of military pathos and glory, of the victimhood and heroism of all soldiers on both sides. "I love the memory of a soldier," said Catlin. "I love the very dust that covers his mouldering body." Catlin called on all to be "exultant" that slavery was dead. "Is this not enough?" he asked. "Is it not enough that we are all American citizens, that our country is saved, that our country is one?" In this doctrine of "enough," the emancipationist legacy of the war had become bad taste among gentlemen soldiers. The "divine doctrine of forgiveness and conciliation" was the order of the day.

Dissent from this Blue-Gray reconciliationist version of the war's memory, while now on the margins, was by no means silenced in the larger culture or in New York. One year later, as though they had decided to invite a direct response to Pryor and his ilk, the integrated Abraham Lincoln Post of the GAR asked Frederick Douglass to address them in Madison Square on Decoration Day. As he did on so many occasions during the last quarter of his life, Douglass rose to the challenge with fire and indignation, offering an alternative, emancipationist memory of the war. "There was a right side and a wrong side in the late war," insisted Douglass "that no sentiment ought to cause us to forget."...

The reconciliationists were using memory to send the nation down the wrong road to reunion, he believed. Douglass had no patience for endless tales of Southern woes. "The South has suffered to be sure," he said, "but she has been the author of her own suffering."...

The story of Civil War memory and the ritual of Decoration Days continued well beyond 1885 with the emancipationist legacy fighting endless rearguard actions against a Blue-Gray reconciliation that was to sweep through American culture. Those who remembered the war as the rebirth of the republic in the name of racial equality would continue to do battle with the growing number who would remember it as the nation's test of manhood and the South's struggle to sustain white supremacy.

FURTHER READING

Eric Anderson and Alfred Moss, eds., *The Facts of Reconstruction* (1991).

Michael Les Benedict, *A Compromise of Principle: Congressional Republicans and Reconstruction* (1974).

Edward J. Blum, *Reforging the White Republic: Race, Religion, and American Nationalism, 1865–1898* (2005).

Laura Edwards, *Gendered Strife and Confusion: The Political Culture of Reconstruction* (1997).

Eric Foner, *A Short History of Reconstruction, 1863–1877* (1990).

Tera Hunter, *To 'Joy My Freedom: Southern Black Women's Lives and Labors After the Civil War* (1997).

Charles Lane, *The Day Freedom Died: The Colfax Massacre, the Supreme Court, and the Betrayal of Reconstruction* (2008).

Leon Litwack, *Been in the Storm So Long: The Aftermath of Slavery* (1979).

Moon Ho-Jung, *Coolies and Cane: Race, Labor, and Sugar in the Age of Emancipation* (2008).

Michael Perman, *The Road to Redemption* (1984).

Heather Cox Richardson, *The Death of Reconstruction: Race, Labor, and Politics in the Post-Civil War North* (2001).

Heather Cox Richardson, *West from Appomattox: The Reconstruction of America after the Civil War* (2008).

Jonathan Wiener, *Social Origins of the New South* (1978).